A Bridge of Longing

For Shana

פּאַפּיר איז דאָך װײַס און װײַס איז טינט איז דאָך שװאַרץ,

צו דיר, מײַן זיס לעבן, ציט דאָך מײַן האַרץ!

A BRIDGE OF LONGING

The Lost Art of Yiddish Storytelling

✦

DAVID G. ROSKIES

HARVARD UNIVERSITY PRESS

Cambridge, Massachusetts

London, England

Third printing, 1996

Publication of this book was assisted by a grant
from the Lucius N. Littauer Foundation.

First Harvard University Press paperback edition, 1996

Library of Congress Cataloging-in-Publication Data

Roskies, David G., 1948–
A bridge of longing : the lost art of Yiddish storytelling /
David G. Roskies.
p.   cm.
Includes index.
ISBN 0-674-08139-0 (cloth)
ISBN 0-674-08140-4 (pbk.)
1. Yiddish literature—History and criticism.
2. Storytelling.
I. Title.
PJ5124.R67   1995
839'.0933—dc20   94-45963
CIP

Designed by Gwen Frankfeldt

Preface

This book about the loss and partial recovery of oral traditions was itself shaped by oral lore. Four moments stand out in my mind. The first occurred midway into a course I was teaching almost by rote, in the 1970s. A student named Lynn Gottlieb raised her hand and suggested that our proper subject might not be modern Hebrew and Yiddish literature at all, much less "Critical Methodologies in Jewish Literature," but rather the lost art of storytelling. Lost because Walter Benjamin had said it was lost, back in 1936, and because Lynn Gottlieb, along with her friends in experimental theater, was trying to relearn it. The second was a conversation with Dan Miron at Jackson Hole, a restaurant on Madison Avenue, where a handful of comments led me to Der Nister's symbolist tales; and the third was with my sister, Ruth Wisse, as we sat in her Montreal home on the day of I. B. Singer's funeral and talked about Singer's demonic strategies. Finally, there was a long discussion walking down Amsterdam Avenue with Hillel Schwartz, as we bandied about the idea of creative betrayal. Here is his retelling of it, taken from a longer poem:

> The issue, says David, oblivious, is betrayal,
> how the lie of the tale is also its sweep, like this
> avenue lit by dayglow monikers and the long fuses of Camels
> or the coral fires of reefer madness. Farther down
> toward the Big House of preternatural history, Nachman of Bratslav
> in leather and moccasins dances over the bones of the dead
> with marchingbund banners and rip-winkling megillahs,

> filled scalp to sole with the joys of loving and conceiving,
> David is saying, the folk, whoever they were meant to be,
> salt or soda of the earth, blood or bicarbonate.

Which means that whoever warms to this subject becomes the object of an irreverent tale.

When my own story began to take shape—in word and image—Arthur Green, Avraham Holtz, Abe Igelfeld, Raymond Scheindlin, Dvora Shurman, Michael Stern, and Sara Zfatman gave to individual chapters of their time and acumen, as did Abraham Novershtern and Hillel Schwartz, who critically read the whole manuscript. Yosl Birstein helped me to negotiate the Itzik Manger Archive at the Jewish National and University Library in Jerusalem and gave generously of his private files as well. Abraham Sutzkever invited me to rework chapters of the book into Yiddish, and the response they elicited from the Yiddish-reading audience was gratifying. In the final stages, I had valuable help from my nephew, Jacob Wisse. Together we discovered the gritty and zany side of stylized Jewish folk art.

Unlike the subjects of my book, however, who hid their modernity behind a folksy facade, I can hardly pretend that this book, with its pages of notes, grew solely out of intimate conversations with this one and that. Were it not for my training in Yiddish studies, which began at the Hebrew University of Jerusalem in 1967–68, I would never have been able to tell the story behind the story. Although Khone Shmeruk will doubtless frown at the more fanciful parts of my narrative, it is to his teaching and scholarship that I owe the greatest debt. His name reappears in the notes like a mantra. He also supplied me with his own bibliography of I. B. Singer's published stories, which was essential to my own chapter on Singer.

Beyond acknowledging a profound debt of thanks to my teachers and friends, many of whom (it seems) are named Abraham, I am beholden to the generosity of two institutions that know me only as a name. It is my pleasure to thank the John Simon Guggenheim Memorial Foundation for granting me a fellowship at the start of this project and the American Council of Learned Societies for supporting me during a subsequent sabbatical leave. The friendly voice and firm editorial hand of Margaretta Fulton at Harvard University Press were just what I needed to guide the book through to the finish. Still and all, it is one's family that takes on the greatest burden. All of my son's life coincides with the writing of this book. Aryeh is now planning to make "our next book" a storybook for children.

I dedicate *A Bridge of Longing* to my wife, Shana, for turning mourning into gladness.

Contents

Illustrations

Zuni Maud (1891–1956), in Herman Gold, *Mayselekh* (Tales). New York: Farlag yidish lebn, 1928. *p. 34*

Arthur Kolnik (1890–1971), "Kaddish," in *A gilgl fun a nign* (The Transmigration of a Melody), 20 woodcuts on a hasidic tale by I. L. Peretz. Paris, 1948. *p. 43*

Anonymous (c. 1880), "Joseph Serving His Brothers," in *Die Josefslegende in aquarellieren Zeichenungen eines unbekannten russischen Juden der Biedermeierzeit*. Berlin: Schocken Verlag, 1937. Photo by Bruce Schwarz. *p. 48*

Yosl Kotler (1896–1935), cover for Herman Gold, *Mayselekh*. *p. 59*

Anonymous, "Joseph Riding Out to Meet His Father," *Die Josefslegende in aquarellieren Zeichenungen*. Photo by Bruce Schwarz. *p. 71*

El Lissitzky (1890–1941), in Leyb Kvitko, *Vaysrusishe folkmayses, fun vaysrusish* (White Russian Folktales). Moscow: Jewish Section in the Commisariat for Public Education, 1923, printed in Berlin. YIVO Library, New York. *p. 82*

El Lissitzky, in Leyb Kvitko, *Vaysrusishe folkmayses*. *p. 89*

El Lissitzky, in Leyb Kvitko, *Vaysrusishe folkmayses*. *p. 92*

Ben-Zion Zukerman (1890–1944), in I. L. Peretz, *Zibn gute yor* (Seven Good Years). Vilna: Kletskin, c. 1916. YIVO Library, New York. *p. 101*

Jakob Steinhardt (1887–1968), "In the Times of the Messiah," in Jizchok-Leib Peretz, *Gleichnisse*. Berlin: Fritz Gurlitt Verlag, 1920. Library of the Jewish Theological Seminary of America, New York. Photo by Suzanne Kaufman. *p. 107*

Yosl Bergner, (b. 1920), "It's No Good," no. 29 in *59 Illustrations to All the Folk Tales*

Who will dream You?
Who will remember?
Who will deny You?
Who will yearn after You, then?
Who will flee You, over a bridge of longing,
Only to return again?

—Jacob Glatstein, 1946

1

The People of the Lost Book

> When the king heard the contents of the Scroll of
> the Teaching, he rent his clothes.
>
> —2 Kings 22:11

When our story truly begins, in the first decade of the nineteenth century, the Jews of central and eastern Europe are a people of storytellers. Men went off to pray three times daily; between afternoon and evening prayers, they swapped a tale or two. On the Sabbath and holidays they returned to the study house or synagogue to hear a *maggid*, an itinerant preacher, weave stories into lengthy singsong sermons. Little boys across the Yiddish-speaking world encountered the same classical curriculum: the Story of Stories, that is, the Bible with Rashi's eleventh-century commentary. Their *rebbe* or teacher translated the holy texts into *khumesh-taytsh*, a Yiddish reserved for this purpose alone, and explained obscure points with stories drawn from the *aggadah*, ancient rabbinic lore. "His tales were truly boundless," a young man recalled about his otherwise strict and taciturn rebbe:

> Stories of dead souls who came every night to the cold synagogue to pray; stories of reincarnated souls or wandering spirits, straying about in search of eternal rest because of the lies they had told their mothers. . . . He had stories about demons and devils who watched for opportunities to snatch a sinner and devour his soul; stories about Samael and Lilith, who would take control of the spirits of the wicked after their death, and the like. He described to us all the torments of Hell as if he were an eyewitness. Our hair stood on end, we shuddered, our mouths fell open and we craved more.

When the boys graduated to the more solemn study of Talmud, they uncovered a trove of legends about the great rabbinic sages. At home or in the marketplace, women drew their own repertory of stories from life and from moral tracts. There were Yiddish storybooks too, though they were frowned upon by men and by *maskilim,* the purveyors of Enlightenment. And just when it seemed that the winds of change blowing in from the west were about to turn these folk into philosophers, bankers, and mistresses of salons, a countermovement called Hasidism swept in from the east and breathed new life into sacred songs and tales. Out of the hasidic movement came the first great Yiddish storyteller, Rabbi Nahman of Bratslav.[1]

But when our story provisionally ends, in the last decade of the twentieth century, what remains of this folk culture are Yiddish theater melodies without their lyrics, a few vulgarisms in the mother tongue, a religion stripped of its stories and superstitions, and a reinvented folklore that tries to pass for the real thing. In the Rabbinical School where I teach (and where this book was first conceived), students are drilled in the art of homiletics. They are taught to deliver a conceptual sermon (modeled on a Protestant tradition) that is designed to break with the anecdotal style used by Old World preachers. It seems hardly worth the effort, since these third- and fourth-generation American Jews have no memory of songs, or stories, or of much else passed on by word of mouth from immigrant forebears.

To be sure, the impassioned embrace of modernity from one century's end to the next was also accompanied by an outright rejection. In hasidic pockets of the world—from Antwerp to Brooklyn to the Meah Shearim quarter in Jerusalem—children once again study Torah in Yiddish, fathers delight in a good maggidic sermon, and brides are regaled by a wedding jester, the *badkhn.* This spirited revival of folk religion is calculated to turn back the clock, and allowing for a few hundred years of solitude, the offspring of these east European Jewish pietists might even succeed.[2]

These are not the rites and ceremonies that my story is about. Instead I invite the reader to the wedding of some friends of mine, a Jewish couple in their early thirties who are more traditional than their American-born parents. My friends have revived certain wedding customs that their parents have never known, except for scenes remembered from the Yiddish stage: the *badekns* ceremony in which the groom covers the bride's hair with a veil; the prenuptial *tish* (table) where the groom's learned discourse on the Torah is constantly interrupted by song. Even program notes were distributed beforehand so that the guests would understand what's going on. And a good thing, too, because from an orthodox point of view, not everything traditional at this wedding will be strictly kosher.

For one thing, the bride holds forth at a separate women's table—an innovation possible only in America where women with Judaic training have joined the fight for equal rights. For another, two rings instead of one are exchanged under the wedding canopy, and the Hebrew formula recited by the groom and bride is as egalitarian as the Talmud (after lengthy search) allows.

Less artfully self-conscious is the feast that follows. Here a youthful all-male band plays dozens of wedding songs set to biblical lyrics. Young and old dance variations on the hora, approximations of a *sher* (scissors dance), and a thoroughly hilarious *keytsad merakdim* ("How Does One Dance [Before the Bride]"). Though men and women dance together—in violation of traditional orthodox practice—only the women seem to know the Israeli folk-dance steps.

Off to one side stands Alina, a woman dressed in workaday clothes. She is not the abandoned wife of the charlatan groom, as would doubtless be the case in a Yiddish melodrama. Stranger than fiction, she is a Polish Catholic anthropologist who specializes in east European Jewish ethnography. Based on her extensive knowledge of Jewish wedding customs—gleaned in part from interviews with elderly Poles who remember prewar hasidic weddings—Alina is struck by the novelty of this one. She recognizes that the rabbi's personal address to the bride and groom as they stand beneath the wedding canopy is a Protestant touch; in Roman Catholic and orthodox Jewish practice, the central rituals are never tampered with. Furthermore, she notes, the restorative impulse of bride and groom has not extended to the hiring of a badkhn, the bard whose job it is to regale the guests and move them to tears—all in doggerel rhyme. This is because the badkhn's art is inseparable from *dos yidishe vort*, the Jewish vernacular, and no one in these circles speaks Yiddish.

Alina asks me where the songs come from. I have to admit that most of them were composed during the past quarter century—by Shlomo Carlebach, by Ben Zion Shenker, and by the many contestants at Israel's song festivals. In an age when every adolescent owns a CD player or tape recorder, Hebrew songs travel as fast as any other product of the counterculture. Nor have the dances been passed down from parents to children, simply because the previous generation of American Jews, even the orthodox among them, danced nothing but waltzes, foxtrots, tangos, and the jitterbug. Wedding musicians in those days included little more than "Hava Nagilla" in their Jewish repertory. The conduits for Jewish dances these days are American Zionist summer camps or Israeli kibbutzim.

Thinking back, I realize that for all their eclecticism, their conscientious use of program notes, and their desire to innovate while remaining firmly within traditional bounds, my friends had orchestrated a Jewish wedding that was real. It was existentially compelling. What's more, they were tapping layers of creativity with generative powers of their own: the kibbutz culture of the 1920s and 1930s begat the Hebrew summer camp culture of the 1940s and 1950s, which begat the neohasidic revival of the 1960s and 1970s. How, then, could one draw a line between invention and authenticity?

Alina's use of prewar Poland to measure the distance traveled by American Jews was less than foolproof. Why should Polish Hasidism, which by the 1930s had become as thoroughly politicized as the rest of Polish Jewry, be any measure of authenticity? Why should a Jewish past reconstructed out of ethnographic memoirs and the imperfect recollections of Polish Catholic peasants be any more believable than the stylized wedding scenes in Yiddish movies?

Perhaps the difference lies in the stature of past traditions. Alina thought she had found the archeological remains of the Polish-Jewish past. The hasidim of Brooklyn, New Square, and Monsey who miraculously survived the Holocaust doubtless believe that they have resurrected the living past, but to hedge their bets they have created ultraorthodox clones of the consumer society, from McDovids to Shlock Rock. Occupying a middle ground were my newly married friends for whom the Tradition could be preserved only by making it serve their modern sensibilities.

The Jews who occupy that middle ground, seeking to synthesize old and new, form the subject of my book. Their attempt to address contemporary concerns in the language(s) of tradition I will call "creative betrayal." To use the word "betrayal" in describing a modern orthodox wedding may strike some readers as harsh. They might even find it a term of opprobrium, which it is not. David Lowenthal's "creative anachronism" might be more felicitous, except that my friends were not "reading back" into the past what they thought was already there.[3] They knew full well that to create an egalitarian wedding ceremony within a legal system built on strict distinctions of gender was to engage in an act of subversion, however noble. The knowledge that we live "after the tradition" is the sine qua non of creative betrayal.[4]

At the heart of their old-fashioned Jewish wedding lay the artful fashioning of a new tradition. In this respect, my friends stood in a long and illustrious line of Jewish reinventors, from Nahman of Bratslav to Yosl Birstein. These are the focus of my book: writers, artists, and intellectuals who choose to reinvent the past because, like my friends, they are far removed from the folk, its stories and songs. After long search, they uncovered from among the traditional forms of Jewish self-expression the ones that were most open to radical reinterpretation.

My book is all about loss and reinvention. Its protagonists are modern Jewish revolutionaries, rebels, and immigrants who tried to salvage for a nontraditional audience forms of the culture assumed to be traditional. Where the folk originals were no longer extant, accessible, or relevant, their stylized Yiddish folktales, monologues, ballads, lovesongs, lullabies, and Purim plays were the next best thing. Indeed, so artful was the camouflage that wherever there are people who look to Yiddish as an authentic expression of *yidishkayt*, it is to these artifacts that they first turn.

Every act of re-creation is essentially subversive, and every successful re-creation is always parasitic. That is what the French sociologist of literature Robert Escarpit means when he defines all literary creativity as an act of "creative treason."[5] Put less stridently, he is stating the obvious: every work of art feeds off the art that came before it. No artist can create ex nihilo, most certainly not the Johnny-come-latelies of Jewish eastern Europe who didn't even have their own Hebrew word for "literature" until the 1860s.[6] As for Yiddish, the lowly vernacular, it was a kind of Third World culture that had at least 150 years of European art and literature to catch up with—which it did, with a vengeance. By 1910, I. L. Peretz complained that modern Yiddish literature could already boast of "a shrewd, sickly sideglance . . . à la Chekhov; a garbled Maupassant, via Russian translation; a caricature of the talentless Sanin [by Artsibashev]."[7] What it lacked, according to Peretz, was tradition. When Peretz and the other Yiddish writers finally found what they were looking for in the past, they might have been guilty of betraying their traditional sources, but they could never be accused of deadly treason.

The Hebrew for "betrayal" is *begidah,* from the root *b-g-d,* which can also mean to dress or to cloak. Both meanings should be kept in mind throughout this book: there were those whose creative reappropriation of Jewish folk sources was a willful and aggressive act of betrayal, and there were those who took a more conservative approach that recloaked the discarded materials of the past.

My first guide through the hidden byways of internal Jewish renewal is the linguist and cultural historian Max Weinreich. In his magnum opus, *History of the Yiddish Language,* Weinreich introduced the concept of "vertical legitimation."[8] The genius of Ashkenazic Jewry (the Yiddish-speaking Jews of eastern and central Europe), according to Weinreich, was its ability to read all creativity back into the past. In the cultural as in the legal realm, every innovation was legitimated on the grounds that it had been there to begin with. Renewal was wrought vertically, through time, rather than horizontally, through geography. Instead of urging Jews to learn from the surrounding culture and its accomplishments, Ashkenazic thinkers and jurists pushed for change in the name of Moses, Akiba, and Judah the Pietist. The hallowed past was an inexhaustible source of the new.

With the Enlightenment there came a program for radical change. For the first time, an ideology inimical to Jewish corporate behavior and aimed at flattening civilization down to a set of universally held principles, became the westernized blueprint of Jewish renewal. A vocal group of intellectuals found that the Jews of the Yiddish-speaking hinterland fell short on every score: in their forms of self-government, their means of livelihood, their manner of dress, their modes of expression. To rally their benighted brethren, the first generation of east European Jewish innovators became wolves in shepherds' clothing. Theirs was a treasonous art if there ever was one. They learned to imitate the sacred tale, the sermon, the spoken anecdote, so as to laugh them off the stage of history, once and for all. They were predators feeding off the seemingly unusable past.

When, however, the dream of instant Enlightenment collapsed, and a new movement for Jewish self-determination took its place, the strategy of vertical legitimation got a new lease on life. Suddenly, with national groups everywhere touting their own folklore, the Yiddish language and arcane folk customs were reclaimed as "national" treasures. The inevitable result of launching a rescue operation in the name of so militantly secular a program was that traditional folk art—or aggadah—was torn from the warp and woof of Jewish religion and turned into a modern icon. And just as inevitably, the Yiddish and hasidic folklore produced by the Jewish neo-romantics of eastern Europe was mostly fake. "Creative betrayal" yielded a species of "fakelore," carefully selected and ideologically reshaped by secular writers for a secular audience.[9]

None of this rescue work came easily, for the modern writers intent upon resurrecting the past were amnesiacs themselves. "Afn pripetshik," the perennial Yiddish favorite, a song about the Hebrew schoolteacher inducting his young charges into the secrets and sorrows of the alphabet, was the work of a lawyer from Kiev named Mark Warshawski. As Sholem Aleichem's protégé, he performed his invented folksongs wearing top hat and tails at Zionist fundraisers. The Jewish alphabet loomed so large in Warshawski's folk imagination because he himself had forgotten how to use it.[10]

"Der rebe Elimeylekh," meanwhile, with its hasidic fiddles, timbrels, and drums, was a clever Yiddishization of "Ol' King Cole Was a Merry Old Soul" by Moyshe Nadir, the enfant terrible of New York's Lower East Side. Bridging the gap between Old World and New was the often used rhyme of *freylekh* (happy, joyous) with *Elimeylekh* and its further link to a famous hasidic master from Nadir's native Galicia, Elimelech of Lizhensk (d. 1786). The song was all the rage in Poland when stage stars of Second Avenue fame brought it over from New York in the early 1920s.[11]

What's more, there was subversion at work beneath the pious facade of not a few Yiddish classics. I. L. Peretz's "Kabbalists," as we shall see, were a pair of starving, self-deluded, communal freeloaders, while his "Bontshe the Silent" turned the Jewish sacred legend of the hidden saint on its head. Even Sholem Aleichem created in Tevye the Dairyman a decidedly atypical Jew, who felt closest to God when out of doors and was endowed with far more wisdom and humanity than any rabbi or hasid in the rest of Sholem Aleichem's fiction.

Sholem Aleichem, Peretz, Nadir, and the rest were, it should be made clear at the outset, secular writers who had long since slammed the gates of the "ghetto" behind them—on the synagogue and study house, on the shtetl and its whole mythic landscape. They had traveled very far from home, using Yiddish, modern Hebrew, Russian, Polish, and German, so that they and the "folk" no longer spoke the same language. Before they could retell a traditional tale and modernize a folk motif, these writers, musicians, and graphic artists had many formal obstacles to overcome.

They also had to contend with their own alienation from the sources of tradition.[12]

Surprisingly, the key that had unlocked the ghetto gates from within and allowed them to flee to the great seats of European culture was also the key to readmittance. They returned not as penitents, in sackcloth and ashes, but well groomed, in starched collar and tie, as champions of a cultural renaissance. What they had learned from reading Gogol, Heine, and Oscar Wilde was how to salvage a past. Rimsky-Korsakov urged his Jewish students at the St. Petersburg conservatory to incorporate Jewish folk motifs into their compositions, just as the Five (himself, Cui, Balakirev, Borodin, and Moussorgsky) were doing. So the students rushed home to become fieldworkers in their native towns and were amazed at what they heard. Sometimes Jewish art students traveled as far afield as the Bezalel Academy in Jerusalem in order to learn such specialized crafts as coppersmithery and carpetweaving. But whether their medium was words, music, thread, or metal, modern Jewish artists would never have sought inspiration from the folk were it not for the goading and guidance of these worldly instructors.[13]

Cosmopolitan writers began to reimagine themselves as members of the folk—through characters in their own stories, as when Peretz rewrote the hasidic wondertales of Nahman of Bratslav, and through the folksy pen names many of them adopted. Samuel Clemens had first to become Mark Twain before he could produce his folk humor. So, too, with the aspiring young novelist named Solomon Rabinovitsh from the big city of Kiev, who turned himself into "Sholem Aleichem" before fully realizing what it would mean to become "Mr. How-Do-You-Do." Only as the great comedian of Jewish dissolution would a satirist and serious writer be welcomed as the favorite guest in Yiddish-speaking households everywhere. Shloyme-Zanvl Rappoport thought that by assuming the underground identity of Semyon Akimovich—miner and agitator—he, too, would succor the world, since the only world that mattered was the long-suffering Russian folk. Only after a dramatic return to the scene of his youthful rebellion—to the godforsaken locales of his own "folk"—did the name S. Ansky become synonymous with *The Dybbuk*, that perfect Jewish folk play. And so it goes, for Pinkhes Kahanovitsh, alias Der Nister (The Hidden One); and Isidore Helfand, reborn as the homey Itzik Manger; and Yitskhok Singer-Warshawski—translator, proofreader, journalist, writer of naturalist fiction—who turned himself into Isaac Bashevis Singer, fabulist for children of all ages.[14]

When self-conscious modernists turned into latter-day folk artists, the result was an oxymoron, a creative betrayal. I am by no means the first to discover this paradox. "Both Bialik and Berdyczewski were, as creative artists, close to the type of the conservative revolutionary or the revolutionary conservative." So writes Dan Miron in his study of the Hebrew fin de siècle.[15] "Both were people who, on the strength of their attachment to [literary] traditions, engaged in an ever fiercer struggle with these very traditions. These they subjected to the most ruthless scrutiny precisely because they valued them so and treated them with utmost seriousness." In less bellicose language, Gershon Shaked makes the identical claim about the great Hebrew prose writer, *Shmuel Yosef Agnon: A Revolutionary Traditionalist*.[16] The plotline of rebellion–loss–return that runs through the lives of so many born-again storytellers also invites a psychoanalytic approach. This is what Roger Sale has done in his masterful *Fairy Tales and After: From Snow White to E. B. White*[17] and what Dan Miron has done for Hayyim Nahman Bialik, the Hebrew poet laureate who made *aggadah* a household word in the salons of Jewish eastern Europe.[18] Their books are an important complement to my own, which seeks to understand the interplay in modern Jewish culture of Aleph (aggadah-as-art), Beth (biography), and Gimel *(Gemeinschaft)*. My biographical concerns, however, are primarily cultural. I want to document the anger and alienation that accompanied a young Jew's birth as an artist in order to demonstrate how the mature artist came to produce a folk persona through whom to speak.

The *Gemeinschaft,* the small community, the people for whom the stories, songs, and theatrical spectacles were originally intended, is a necessary key to the past significance of stylized Jewish folk art, just as the fragmented, assimilated *Gesellschaft* of today is a key to its meaning in the wake of the Holocaust. What I hope to restore is a dynamic sense of how each generation of modern Jews—and audience alike—stumbled on the same cultural treasures all over again. Each time the trove is discovered anew, it prompts some kind of negotiated return, a reconciliation between the present and the forgotten past, the self and the folk.

To be sure, the makeup of that "folk" is reconfigured in the process. A central tenet of the Jewish cultural revolution was to enfranchise those who for centuries had occupied the margins of Jewish patriarchal society: the women and children, the vagabonds and jesters. No sooner did serious fieldwork begin than seasoned women storytellers were found, in city, village, and collective farm, each with her own repertory and style: Sonye nicknamed *di khakhome,* the Wisewoman, in the Mohilev province; Khinye Lifshits in Kremenchug; Peshe-Rive Sher in Kozlovitsh; Khave Rubin in Smorgon; Brokhe the Stocking Maker from Roslov; and Judah Leib Cahan's own Aunt Rokhl, in Vilna.[19] Thanks to this democratic impulse, the radical menfolk gave artistic voice to the oral traditions of their neglected sisters and stepmothers: Peretz, through the rewritten laments and lovesongs he collected for a ruble apiece among the Jewish seamstresses of the Warsaw slums; Sholem Aleichem, through his stepmother's curses, rearranged in alphabetical order, then through the folkspeech of Sheyne-Sheyndl from Kasrilevke, still later through the rambling monologue of Yente the Dairy Vender; Itzik Manger, through his modern ballads about love and loss, and through his "revised folk version" of the Bible starring Mother Sarah, Hagar, Rachel, Ruth, and Queen Esther; even I. B. Singer, often accused of misogyny (and worse), brought the *bobe-mayse,* the old wives' tale, back to life through the figures of Matl and Aunt Yentl. Yet emancipated Jewish women, who had also read their Goethe and the Brothers Grimm, Pushkin and Gogol, Nietszche and Freud, did not succumb, like their brothers-in-arms, to the romance of storytelling. When Jewish women found a secular Yiddish voice, it was far removed from the home and hearth where mothers still sat, telling stories. They might compose naive and playful children's verse, or acknowledge their pious grandmothers through a narrative veil, but they themselves seldom wrote *as if* they were salt of the earth, simple balladeers, artists of the folk. When Jewish women won the right to vote, they voted the radical ticket all the way.[20]

So near, and yet so far. Just how much of the folk culture was deemed salvageable would depend on how much modernity could be repackaged as an authentic expression of the folk, which in turn would depend on the nature of the folk idiom itself. Though pride of place in my story will be given to stories in prose and stories in verse, it is worth revisiting the Yiddish folksong revival at the moment when all of Yiddishdom was about to pull up stakes and scatter to the four corners of the earth.

The same Zionist weekly, *Der yid* (The Jew), which in its first year of publication (1899) featured the memoirs of Mendele the Bookseller, two new installments of the Tevye monologues, more shtetl tales by I. L. Peretz, poems about the Psalmster and the Prophet, and a score of satiric feuilletons, topped off this revivalist menu with Warshawski's alphabet "folk-song." This last, published a few weeks before the first release in Yiddish of two authentic "folktales," was proof that the ideologues of cultural renewal were finally, at this late date, willing to allow the value of the folk and its lore. It also showed how much more they invested in the reinvention of Jewish folklore than in preserving the "real thing." The provenance of Warshawski's alphabet song, after all, was a Kiev salon, not some dingy schoolroom in Shnipeshok or Mazl-Bozhets. Like Sholem Aleichem, like Bialik, those vying for the soul of the Jewish masses defined folklore not as some artifact *of* the folk, but as something created *for* the folk. As always, they were moved to do so not by the folk itself but by literary trends in Russian, Polish, and German high culture.[21]

Everyone agreed that a national movement required its own songs. Naftali Herz Imber's "Hatikvah" (The Hope, 1878) was already for Zionists what Ansky's "Di shvue" (The Oath, 1901) was soon to become for the Jewish Labor Bund: a new hymn whose diction and western melodic line made the Jewish claim to the brave new world of tomorrow. At issue were the songs of tradition. Was there room in the folksong revival for the melancholy and mysticism of the synagogue and study house, or was the authentic core of the folk repertory plebeian and, above all, secular?[22]

And who even knew what the "authentic core" was? When, in 1898, two young Russian-Jewish historians, Saul Ginzburg and Peysakh Marek, appealed in Russian and Hebrew to members of the urban intelligentsia to collect Yiddish folksongs, they offered no guidelines whatsoever.[23] The stamp of the songs' authenticity, as far as the collectors were concerned, was the Jewish historical experience they reflected: the status of women in traditional society, the establishment of the first agricultural colonies in the south of Russia, the forced induction of minors into paramilitary cantonist battalions during the reign of Nicholas I, and the abortive attempt to modernize elementary Jewish education. Many of these songs, the open letter claimed, were being forgotten, pushed out by more recent songs and by the more dramatic events of the past decade. What little had been collected was published in scholarly journals in the West, while here, in the Pale of Jewish settlement, in far-flung market towns where the old songs were still being sung, nothing had yet been done.

The open letter produced eastern Europe's first cadre of amateur *zamlers,* or collectors, who in fact could not distinguish between a real or an invented folksong. One of them, a young recruit named Avrom Reisen, was doing his service to the tsar by playing in a military band. Reisen and four of his comrades from Lithuania contributed over 80 percent of the 300-odd songs in the Ginzburg and Marek edition of *Yiddish Folksongs in Russia* (1901).[24] To compensate for the amateur quality of the submissions, the editors eliminated all songs of literary origin, as well as those written by wedding jesters. Operating with a prior concept of naive folk poetry, Ginzburg and Marek excluded texts deemed too sophisticated. This is where all the trouble began. Apparently word had not yet reached Moscow and St. Petersburg that, for quite some time, modern Yiddish writers had been fashioning folklike songs that the "folk," in turn, adapted to its own ends. Despite all precautions, several such recycled songs stole their way into the Ginzburg-Marek anthology.

Because they prized Yiddish folksongs as a Jewish memory bank, Ginzburg and Marek favored the songs that seemed to preserve the oldest stratum of that memory. Though Religious, National, and Holiday Songs accounted for merely 41 songs, the editors put them first. Thus they threw down the Zionist gauntlet as well, privileging those songs that followed their prescription for the future. A sense of the past, as embodied by the Historical Songs that came next, was their personal agenda as historians. The largest rubric by far, Lovesongs, they sandwiched into fifth place. Small wonder that when Peretz's chief informant, Judah Leib Cahan, reached America and was able to publish his own collection, 130 lovesongs appeared up front, as "the most beautiful and most important of our folksong repertory," as the Yiddish lyric par excellence. The aesthetic revolution in Yiddish poetry that began on New York's Lower East Side now had the folksong to fall back on in lieu of Jews, God, and History.[25]

For all their competing political aims, Ginzburg, Marek, and Cahan agreed that songs composed by the professional *badkhonim* were inauthentic. "A hired rhymster" was Ginzburg and Marek's way of dismissing the venerable institution of the wedding jester. They viewed him as a mere clown and mood manipulator, who deserved the low status accorded to him in society and his grotesque portrayal in literature (32). The jester's arcane humor, according to Cahan, contributed to the "dry atmosphere" that characterized petit-bourgeois Jewish life (27). A badkhn's songs remained his alone, never penetrating the folk. Why then the animus, if the poor badkhn was a thing of the past? Because the real folksong had to be—

according to romantic notions—an unmediated expression of the folk, and the folk—according to progressive Jewish politics—were women, children, workers, and soldiers. Instead of doctoring the evidence, as modern Yiddish storytellers were learning to do, the collectors of Yiddish folksongs simply redefined the cultural norm. At the center of Jewish lore they placed what used to have no status at all: lullabies, children's rhymes, soldiers' songs, ballads, songs of work and play.

Sholem Aleichem had done as much in his own way to recenter Jewish culture on the marvels of everyday life. His personal folksong favorites were amusing panegyrics to the *baleboste* (hostess, landlady).[26] But as the great reinventor of Yiddish folklore, Sholem Aleichem could hardly accept the romantic and narrowly academic notion of anonymous authorship. And so it was that he launched the publication of Mark Warshawski's *Yiddish Folk Songs* in 1900, with an ecstatic endorsement, and thereby provoked the first serious debate between the purists and the pragmatists.

Sholem Aleichem saw "all of Jewish life, with all its joys and sorrows," reflected in Warshawski's songs.[27] He lavished special praise on the song of a pious Jew who proclaimed God's justice even as he spit up blood ("By the Synagogue"), and on Warshawski's drinking song ("Queenie Dear") that ended with a toast to enemies. Sholem Aleichem credited Warshawski with turning Jewish sorrows into a source of hope by means of cheerful melodies and unadorned Yiddish.

This was altogether too much for the music critic Joel Engel, fresh from his epoch-making lecture on Jewish folk music in November 1900 at the Moscow polytechnic museum. There Engel demonstrated that authentic Jewish folk music was "oriental," its truest expression preserved in hasidic and liturgical melodies. Engel now poured out his wrath on Warshawski for having the nerve to label his lyrics "folksongs," since they were neither old nor sufficiently widespread to be sung by the folk at large. Worse, the tunes were mostly lifted—from the dance hall. "Listening to Warshawski's songs," Engel protested, "one would think that Jews don't sing anything but polkas, mazurkas, quadrilles."[28]

Rushing to the defense of his protégé, Sholem Aleichem argued that folksongs were "all songs written in the simple Jewish folk language . . . put out for the sake of the folk."[29] As proof that the function of a text was more important than its origins, Sholem Aleichem pointed to his own song on the mass immigration to America, "Shlof mayn kind" (Sleep, My Child).

Published in 1892, it was already widely sung and appeared as a traditional lullaby in the Ginzburg-Marek anthology. Not altogether happy with what the simple Jewish folk had done to his song, however, Sholem Aleichem corrected the Ginzburg-Marek version in his copy of the book. When writing the song, he had used a common form of parallelism to underscore that "America is for everyone, / They say, the greatest piece of luck, / For the Jews, it's Paradise, / A rare and precious place." To do this, he merely set off *far yedn* (for everyone) from *far yidn* (for the Jews) by means of a single vowel. This was either too subtle or too parochial for the folksinger, who sang in both lines of America's blessings "for everyone," thus incurring the author's ire.[30]

Sholem Aleichem was clearly advancing his own view that popular culture was religious ritual, legend, and myth adapted to earthly needs, just as Engel's orientalism was of a piece with that of Martin Buber and the Bezalel school of art in Jerusalem.[31] For Sholem Aleichem, the upbeat tempos of polkas, mazurkas, and quadrilles were precisely the point. Whoever warmed to the sound of hasidic music in a soulful minor key had no business studying the dynamic, essentially secular life of the folk. Like the editor of *Der yid* who thought that Yiddish folktales were those told against the backdrop of shtetl poverty, Sholem Aleichem fashioned the legendary town of Kasrilevke with its happy-go-lucky paupers to entertain the readers of the same paper.[32] Folklore was life, and Jewish life would not stand still for the benefit of Moscow and Petersburg cognoscenti.

What especially confused the self-styled guardians of folk purity were the macaronic songs they collected. Where did they come from, these songs that mixed Hebrew, Yiddish, and Slavic, and what did they reveal about Jewish life in eastern Europe? Ginzburg and Marek believed that only linguistic hybrids could have produced this refrain:

> *Mar goluseynu*—perebudyem
> *Le'artseynu* fort poydëm!
>
> (*How bitter our exile*—[but] we'll make it through,
> So *to our homeland* let's be off! (no. 17)

The italicized words are Hebrew, the rest Russian and Yiddish. Did it mean that the Jews of Lithuania were once fluent in Russian? Or were these songs the work of *Nikolayever soldatn*, children who were inducted into the cantonist brigades of the tsar, then served their twenty-five-year army stint, and ultimately settled among the Slavic population?

That these songs might have originated not on the periphery but at the very center of Jewish religious life is something the Petersburg secularists could never imagine. Yet this is precisely what the amateur folklorist and passionate Yiddishist Noyakh Prylucki put forth in a slim volume, *Yiddish Folksongs* (Warsaw, 1910), dedicated exclusively to religious and holiday themes.[33] Radicalizing Engel's position, he argued that the key to Jewish folk culture and to "folk psychology" lay in these macaronic and quasi-liturgical songs. As Yiddish was the culture of *yidishkayt,* the innermost reaches of the Jewish religious soul were expressed through hasidic song. When hasidim reached a peak of religious ecstasy, all linguistic boundaries collapsed. The fixed liturgy could no longer express the intensity of their experience.

Thanks to the kabbalistic doctrine of *tikkun,* of which more in the next chapter, the hasidim had license not only to interpolate other languages into their prayers but also to interpret other languages in the light of Scripture. Thus "I went to the nut grove / To see the budding of the vale" (Song of Songs 6:11) contained the mysterious word *egoz,* which reminded the hasidim of a Polish song about a mother instructing her son to pick nuts from a tree. The Polish lyrics had to be a parable, an allegorical cloak for the hidden, mystical meaning—just as the Song of Songs was itself an allegory about God and Israel. Though the Polish lyrics spoke of *chłopczyki,* little boys who were too short to reach the nuts, the parallel Yiddish lyrics spoke of *yidelekh,* "little Jews" whose spiritual merit fell short of the mark. *Zay kenen nisht dergraykhn, / Zay kenen nisht dergraykhn* (they cannot reach, they cannot reach; no. 34). And so the layering of languages was not a result of linguistic assimilation somewhere in the Slavic outback, but a product of a Jewish mystical curriculum that reached its fullest expression in the tales of Reb Nahman. According to Prylucki, Polish hasidim reserved this song especially for Passover.[34]

So the concept of the "folk" had been turned on its head in only one decade of song collecting. The academic debate over origin and function (Engel versus Sholem Aleichem) had given way to the more basic question of whether authentic Yiddish folksongs were religious or secular; whether their *Sitz im Leben* was the dance hall (Cahan) or the house of prayer (Prylucki). When the full picture of the Jewish nineteenth century came into view, this is what emerged: the great Jewish movements, Hasidism and the Haskalah, had each generated its own impressive repertory of songs; and while anonymous songs were indeed the norm in the workplace, at home, and in school, the badkhn functioned as folk bard at weddings and the *Purim-shpiler* as folk dramatist in the one-day-a-year theater season sanctioned by tradition. Then at the end of the century, with the mass immigration to America, the migration in Europe from the shtetl to the city, and the rise of secular ideologies, all these songs—the hasidic and maskilic, the anonymous and the authored, those sung at weddings and those performed on Purim—became part of a new, urban folk culture that survives to this day in the memory of first- and second-generation immigrants, and on cassette tapes.[35]

Songs are useful markers at a particularly hazardous turn in the road— the mass embarkation of east European Jewry. Useful, because the folklore revival began with the collecting of folksongs (and proverbs); because songs were easily emancipated from the shtetl's "theocratic order" and therefore traveled much better than more complex folklore genres (stories or Purim plays); because in no other medium did highbrow writers reap such quick rewards for stooping to conquer in the plebeian forms of Jewish self-expression. The poet, dramatist, and critic Aaron Zeitlin is hardly a household name, for all that he was once aligned with I. B. Singer, but Zeitlin's song, "Dona, Dona," one of two he wrote expressly for the American Yiddish stage, is known throughout the world. And no one among the rival groups of Yiddish literati, seated at separate tables at the Café Royale on New York's Second Avenue, could ever imagine that the sole survivor of their cultural renaissance would be a matinee idol, Aaron Lebedeff, then performing his vaudeville routines just down the block; that Lebedeff would become for the New World what Sholem Aleichem was for the Old.[36]

Whether as professional songwriters, composers, and performers or as highbrow artists, poets, and storytellers, these first-generation rebels and immigrants wanted to salvage only a few recyclable parts (the aesthetic or parodic, the romantic or didactic) of the old folk culture. Yet what little was salvaged proved remarkably resilient in the face of historical and demographic upheavals.

These new storytellers and songsters represent more than a holding pattern. Each in his own way created copies that were better than the original: better aesthetically and better able to withstand the onslaught of history.

Seduced by America, Jewish immigrants abandoned Yiddish, leaving only its songs. Yet when all seemed lost, a late arrival named Yitskhok Bashevis revived the "demonic" and thereby crossed the boundaries between two worlds, English and Yiddish. A decade before that, in interwar Poland, there appeared a troubadour, Itzik Manger, who almost singlehandedly revived the parodic and dramatic folk arts. And a decade before that, in the Soviet totalitarian republics, one Yiddish storyteller, Der Nister, came back into the cold to produce the boldest of fantasies. Together, their creative efforts established the pattern of rebellion–loss–retrieval that I have labeled "creative betrayal."

Writ large, creative betrayal runs through modern Jewish culture as a whole. Writ small, it informs the work of a particular group of Jewish storytellers, graphic artists, and musicians from eastern Europe. To read the modern Yiddish stories crafted to sound like pious or playful folktales, to view the naive illustrations that accompany the texts, and to hear the invented folksongs that reproduce the old rhymes and rhythms is to discover a surrogate world of perfect wholeness.

Yet the postwar generations, hungry for roots, seem incapable of understanding the hard-nosed modernity of the writers they revere. By demonstrating how the Yiddish writers in particular challenged the traditional values of the very traditions they were reclaiming, I hope to show that there was no going back for them except as moderns. The art of creative betrayal, I propose, is that which can be rescued most productively from a Jewish traditional culture that tried so hard to be modern.

It happened in the time of King Josiah that a lost scroll of the Covenant—probably the core section of Deuteronomy—was discovered during repair work on the Temple. So mired in idolatry had the people of Judah become that their true religion was all but forgotten. "When the king heard the contents of the Scroll of the Teaching, he rent his clothes." Immediately he sent for his ministers: "Go, inquire of the Lord on my behalf, and on behalf of the people, and on behalf of all Judah, concerning the words of this scroll that has been found. For great indeed must be the wrath of the Lord that has been kindled against us, because our fathers did not obey the words of this scroll to do all that has been prescribed for us" (2 Kings 22:11–13). One book—and the Covenant was renewed. One scroll discovered and read aloud—and a whole society was turned from its forgetfulness.

The Jews of modernity are the People of the Lost Book. Yet when modern Jews try to reclaim something of value from the lost books of their culture, they are painfully self-conscious about it. They bring their relativism and their critical and aesthetic sensibilities to bear upon the hallowed texts and melodies of the past.

Not one Book—but many. The past is no longer a finished scroll: we choose it from among various books and competing tales. Jews of European extraction have staked their claim on the place they know least about: the east European shtetl, the medieval Jewish market town of Russia, Poland, and Galicia. Here, presumably, Jews danced and prayed all day until the cossacks came and burned the place down.[37] The rich legacy of German Jewry, in contrast, with its salons, philosophers, and dueling societies, is too refined, too close to home, to allow for nostalgia. Especially after the Holocaust, as Jack Wertheimer notes, the popular image of German Jews is of people "obsessed with assimilation and eager to dissociate themselves from the rest of world Jewry." As the folk wisdom has it, the German Jews were then brutally punished by the Nazis for trying to escape their Judaism. This "cautionary tale," Wertheimer ruefully muses, might have been invented by the *Ostjuden* to get back at their snobbish cousins.[38]

What the European descendants of Judea hear is not the word of a living God but something quaint, primitive, and quite passé. At Havurat Shalom, a religious commune and house of study in the late 1960s, my friends and I fancied ourselves to be followers of Nahman of Bratslav, but except for one visit by a true Bratslav hasid, we drew our vision of the Rabbi from books both sacred and secular. Another visitor, the radical theologian Richard L. Rubenstein, startled us with the revelation that the hasidim have always been strictly observant Jews. This did not sit well with our egalitarian services and other experiments in religious syncretism. Like the neoromantics before us, we preferred the hasidim as aborigines, not as men, women, and children who survived and made their own uncomfortable accommodations with the present.[39]

All in all, the Jews of modernity are very different from the Judean subjects of King Josiah. Modern Jews are self-conscious and equivocal. They choose from among a multiplicity of available pasts, giving preference to the dying past over the living past. They turn cultural renewal into political action or inaction. Yet in one respect they are alike: the reading of their lost scroll takes place in public.

Betrayal is creative only if it draws from the life of the collective and feeds back into it. The shtetl is preferable to the salon because "life is with people," to quote the most influential of all shtetl fantasies.[40] Hasidism is preferable to other forms of Jewish orthodoxy because hasidim invented new male bonding rituals, and they danced and sang and clapped their hands during prayer. Storytelling is preferable to solitary study because stories include both men and women, young and old, the learned and the simple.

Jews mourn the death of a relative for seven days. During this period, the bereaved are never alone. They are required to pray three times a day in a *minyan*, quorum of ten. Each day it is customary for someone knowledgeable to teach a chapter of the Mishnah in memory of the deceased. Then, after public prayer and study, everyone sits down to recall the deceased—in story after story.

2

The Master of Prayer
NAHMAN OF BRATSLAV

The rabbi traveled to the zaddik and he cried: "*Gevald,*
gevald! Help me, oh help me! Alas for those who are
lost and are no longer found!"
—Nahman of Bratslav, 1807

Stories, it was once believed, offer a temporary reprieve from death. So
Scheherazade stayed her execution at the hands of the Sultan with fantasy, suspense, and eroticism enough to last a thousand and one years. So
too the seven noble women and three amorous men who fled the plague-
ridden city of Florence in 1348. While they did nothing to alleviate the
collective horror, they managed to stave off their own fear of death in a
ten-day-long contest of bawdy and irreverent tales. But six centuries after
Boccaccio, when the poet Itzik Manger assembled a minyan of ten Holocaust survivors in an imaginary bunker, each Jew hailing from a different
part of Europe, he could finish no more than two stories of this modern
Decameron. The muse simply failed in the face of such catastrophe.[1]

How much redemptive weight can stories bear? For Walter Benjamin,
storytelling was the answer to modern angst. Storytelling conjured up a
world of communal listening, of young and old alike sharing and shaping
the collective memory of the folk; a world where each individual storyteller,
according to Benjamin, was a master of local traditions, rooted in the soil,
or a mercurial figure just returned from his travels. Whether a master of
local or exotic tales, Benjamin's storyteller inhabited a moral universe of
experience rather than an alienated world of facts. The storyteller used
"transparent layers" of personal and collective experience, of wisdom and
practical knowledge gained over centuries, in much the same way as a
craftsman used the tools and techniques passed down from master to apprentice. By choosing the Russian storyteller Nikolai Leskov (1831–1895)

to occupy the center of this idyllic, preindustrial landscape, Benjamin implicitly repudiated the Nazi image of the past, with its Teutonic knights and pagan bloodlust, and the Nazi vision of a racially purged Europe. As Benjamin tells it, the Slavic-born storytellers inherit the earth.[2]

Stories, however ephemeral and insubstantial, can stay the executioner's hand or offer a humane countervision in a world gone mad. But stories have never enjoyed autonomy within the Jewish tradition. Live audiences of today, whether they sign up for "The Oral Tradition: Jewish Stories for Adults" at the 92nd Street Y in New York City or whether they attend the Annual Storytelling Festival in Jonesborough, Tennessee, have little in common with the orthodox practice of Jewish men studying sacred texts out loud. These men are not only heir to a learned tradition that devalued stories and storytelling, but also are at work within a closed circle in which the meaning of the tales is governed by strict rules of interpretation. The reason one needs to learn the art of Jewish storytelling today at community centers, conferences, and workshops is that stories were preserved—that is to say, recorded and revered—within the folio pages of a *seyfer,* a sacred tome in Hebrew-Aramaic, or not at all.[3]

The Torah was the book of life, the source of law *and* lore. So thoroughly did the rabbis accomplish their task of binding one to the other that the study of Halachah, the Jewish law, was inconceivable without recourse to the lore of Aggadah, and vice versa. Some legal interpreters and commentators made frequent use of their favorite aggadic tales while others made do with a cryptic reference to folk traditions current in their own day.

The Mishnah (codified around 250 C.E.) teaches that a man may not be alone with two women but a woman can be alone with two men. The Gemara (codified in 450 C.E.) has a *beraita* (a source contemporary with the Mishnah) that contradicts the mishnaic ruling. Abba Saul taught that when a child dies within thirty days of birth, there is no need of a coffin. The dead child may be carried out in one's bosom. But how many people should accompany the corpse? Abba Saul said: "Even by one man and two women!" The real argument, then, centers on human behavior in extremis. Abba Saul believes that in a period of intense mourning, man's lustful passion is inactive, and the rabbis of the Mishnah believe precisely the opposite. To prove their point they stenographically cite the following evidence: "Even as the story of [or 'the case concerning'] a certain woman: it once happened that she took him out" (Babylonian Talmud, Kiddushin 80b).

Schooled in rabbinic shorthand, every Talmud student immediately turns to Rashi, the eleventh-century commentator, for elucidation. Rashi fills in the plot as follows: "A woman carried out a live child, pretending that it was dead, so that she might satisfy her lust unsuspected." His curiosity roused, the student turns next to the Tosafot, Rashi's disciples, whose commentary appears on the opposite side of the folio page. Here the plot is finally laid out in graphic detail, by Hananel ben Hushi'el, a North African rabbi of the eleventh century. Once there was a widow who grieved terribly at her husband's grave. There happened to be a soldier nearby guarding a crucified corpse. After seducing the widow, he discovered that the corpse had been stolen from the cross. The widow, now fully reconciled to her grief, urged him to replace the corpse with that of her husband. And so "she took him out" and hung him up instead. "This proves," concludes the commentator, "that even in a state of intense mourning, her passions got the better of her."

The rabbis did their job well, weaning the excitable Jewish mind away from too much fancy but providing just enough narrative for the story to function as a brainteaser. The Talmud student could care less that Hananel probably heard the story in the garrison town of Kairouan, which then stood at the crossroads of world folklore, or that ten centuries earlier the story was popularized by the Roman satirist Petronius as "The Matron of Ephesus."[4] The important thing was to decide whether the story supported or disputed the privileged mishnaic opinion.[5]

Stories that did legal duty in rabbinic texts were marked by a specific label, ma'aseh (from which the Yiddish mayse would later derive). Exactly like the Latin gesta, ma'aseh could mean either a factual occurrence or the account thereof. Thus the Hebrew phrase ma'aseh be, usually rendered "a tale is told of," more plausibly means "a case concerning."[6] In order to rebut their opponent, Abba Saul, the rabbis cited case law, not folktale.

The ma'asim, or deeds, recounted by the rabbis in their synagogue sermons and study-house debates, were never meant to stand alone, however dramatic they seem to us, however widely they may have circulated among the "folk." The wondrous death of the deadly lizard who dared to bite the praying Hanina ben Dosa, a first-century "man of deed," as the Mishnah called him, was turned by the rabbis into an exemplary tale of how all Jews should pray with total concentration.[7] The personal trials and achievements of even the greatest rabbinic personalities, such as Eliezer ben Hyrcanus, who sacrificed all for the sake of Torah, only to be excommunicated at the end of his career; or Rabbi Akiva, whose grasp of Torah was the envy of Moses himself, but who died at the hands of the Romans, some say, as a martyr—these and other extraordinary events were consistently played down. The stuff of epic, romance, farce, and fantasy, they were lost in the sea of the Oral Tradition. They were buried within complex legal debates called *sugyot* or scattered among the wordgames, creative philology, parables, and fables used by the rabbis to read each of their contemporary concerns out of or into the Torah.[8]

As long as invention meant the discovery of something already in Scripture, the story could never be fully "emancipated" from the Book of Books. The very concept of emancipation—the concern for individual autonomy, hence for tales that chart the self's journey through time, hence for narrative flow—is one of many modern constructs totally at odds with the self-understanding of rabbinic Judaism. If anything, the Jewish (re)turn to storytelling during the Middle Ages was made in the name of de-emancipation: it was a way of legitimating legendary motifs borrowed far and wide or a newer repertory of tales by invoking the authority of the hallowed texts.[9]

The permanence of medieval Jewish culture was vouchsafed by the existence of the *seyfer,* the weighty tome, the canonical text, sanctified by virtue of its language (Hebrew-Aramaic), its subject matter (halachic, aggadic), its point of origin (Sinai, Yavneh, the talmudic academy), and its intended readers (men). The medium of the Yiddish *mayse-bikhl* (the modest story or chapbook that made its first appearance in sixteenth-century Italy) was its contrasting message: it was anonymous and cheap, contained a single narrative unit that could be read at a single sitting, and was written (and printed) in the vernacular. Jewish compilers seized upon the chapbook as a way of cutting the Hebrew giant down to saleable size. They raided the classical collections for juicy items; removed these dramatic plots from their learned context; and published each unit separately, including just enough Hebrew-Aramaic "markers" to render the work kosher.[10] It was singularly in Yiddish that the ephemerality of storybooks became their chief virtue.

As the seyfer was seamless, timeless, and permanent, the flimsy maysebikhl was but a brief distraction. Ideally, those Yiddish chapbooks translated from the Talmud, the Midrash, and the Apocrypha could be attached to a specific holiday: the apocryphal book of Macabees and Tobith to be read on Hannukah; the story of Rabbi Meir and the Ten Lost Tribes on

Shavuoth; the destruction of the temple on Tisha b'Av.[11] It did not take long, however, for some enterprising editor to seek the more lucrative market of sanctioned reading for the Sabbath, those fifty-two days in the year when Jews could reasonably be expected to look into a nonsacred book. Out of this desire came the famous *Mayse-bukh* (Basle, 1602), a huge anthology of over 250 tales.

Here was a book for all seasons that tried to pass itself off as a seyfer. Why study Talmud and the legal commentaries, the Lithuanian-born book-peddler Jacob ben Avrom went so far as to claim, when his *Mayse-bukh* could answer all rabbinic queries? "The rabbi and rabbi's wife and every man, all except someone really schooled in Talmud," could win friends and influence people simply on the strength of the midrashim and sacred tales that he, the faithful compiler, had assembled.[12] Even practical halachic issues, he had the gall to claim, could be settled by reference to his storybook. Still occupying the moral high ground, Jacob ben Avrom went on to excoriate such "licentious" secular reading material as the *Ku-bukh, Dietrich von Berne,* and *Meister Hilderbrant,* "which merely send you into a fever." It was a sin to have such books in one's possession, let alone to read them on the Sabbath.

Read skeptically, as every sales pitch should be, the printer's preface to the *Mayse-bukh* might lead us to conclude that the Renaissance had finally created a cultural climate in which the story no longer needed to function as the foundation of faith; it could live simply as narrative. Why, otherwise, did the printer protest so much? Unless he was hedging his bets, why did same printer go on to publish a Yiddish adaptation of a German bestseller, *The Seven Sages of Rome?* As for the *Mayse-bukh* itself, little more than half the tales actually derived from the Talmud, via the popular *Ein Ya'akov,* the original layperson's guide to the Talmud. A third were thinly disguised legends and novellas of international provenance, and under a separate heading Jacob Ben Avrom introduced a cycle of early medieval tales about the life of the founding fathers of Ashkenaz, Rabbi Shmuel Hasid (Samuel the Pious) and his son Rabbi Judah. If this did not signal the emancipation of Yiddish storytelling, then what did?[13]

The *Mayse-bukh* indeed became the Yiddish "folk book" par excellence, spawning many other story collections in its wake; and it gave future editors license to publish accounts, an amalgam of folklore and chronicle, which preserved the memory of local events, heroes, and heroines. And many a tale recorded in the *Mayse-bukh* made its way back to the Yiddish-speaking folk, which stripped it clean of all didacticism. But the medium of the *Mayse-bukh* in its own time and place heralded the integration of Yiddish into the Torah-centered world of Ashkenazic Jewry, a place where the *seyfer* was the source of all knowledge. What the Yiddish story lost in revolutionary potential it gained in restorative power.[14]

"They say that stories put you to sleep," he told his disciples, "but I say that through stories you can awaken people from their sleep." Rabbi (Reb) Nahman ben Simhah of Bratslav (1772–1810) was the first Jewish religious figure to place storytelling at the center of his creative life. These were neither occasional tales, as retold intact by his great-grandfather, Israel Ba'al Shem Tov (the Besht), to illustrate the hidden workings of the Shekhinah, the Divine Presence, nor tales recounted in praise of the Besht, but tales of Nahman's own invention. Devoid of the standard heroes, settings, and props of Jewish storytelling—no Elijah the Prophet working behind the scenes, no mythical Sambatyon River, no Sabbath or holiday—these stories were informed by Nahman's personal mythology, by his reading of Psalms and the Zohar, by his messianic striving.[15]

Born in a moment of despair, his tales have a tragic urgency. The hoped-for act of restoration, which is the goal of every seeker in every tale, is deadlocked, deferred, and only sometimes fully realized. These are stories of a world in crisis, of faith under siege. The present evil is ubiquitous, whether it comes from the geopolitical upheaval brought on by the Napoleonic wars or from the primal sin of Sabbatianism, the false messianic movement of the late seventeenth century and the root cause of the crisis of faith; whether the evildoers are close at hand, in the person of his arch-rival, the Shpoler Zeyde, who hounds his every move, or in the *khokhem*, the freethinker, who denies the existence of God.

Reb Nahman turned to storytelling when all else failed, when he could not reveal his messianic program outright, because the frontal approach had forced the hand of Satan. In the summer of 1806 Reb Nahman announced to his hasidim: "Ikh vel shoyn onheybn mayses dertseyln," (the time has come for me to begin telling stories), since all his other efforts had failed.[16] Thus modern Yiddish storytelling was born. And it was no easy birth, for a member of the Jewish elite did not simply stand up before his followers one summer's day and start telling fairy tales when everything in the system of traditional Judaism militated against it. There had to be a radical will and a hidden way.[17]

The events leading up to the summer of 1806 formed a three-act drama. The first was a period of frenetic activity, as Reb Nahman threw himself into the cause of universal redemption. His messianic calendar, from Rosh Hashanah 1804 onward, was cluttered with extraordinary efforts on all fronts: instituting rites of purification; collecting, editing, and disseminating his teachings; the birth of his son Shloyme Ephraim, upon whom great messianic hope was now placed; Nahman's mysterious journey to Shargorod; and finally the instruction to his disciples to don white garments.[18]

In the second act, the revolution failed. The mission of the disciples to proclaim the messianic era received no support; Shloyme Ephraim lay dead of a childhood disease; the hasidic establishment openly attacked Reb Nahman for heresy; and the inner ranks of his disciples began to thin. It was to rouse those remaining followers from their spiritual slumber, to reconsecrate them to the arduous task of redemption in a world alive with evil and tragedy, that Nahman began telling stories.

What was needed in the third act was a return to something elemental. Reb Nahman's discovery of a new symbolic language came after he had mastered all the traditional forms of Jewish self-expression: the languages of prayer and song; of biblical, rabbinic and kabbalistic exegesis; of ethical exhortation. Were it not for the present crisis that forced Reb Nahman to rechannel his redemptive faith into a more potent—albeit more hidden—medium, he would never have gone back to so primitive a form. But neither would he be content merely to retell what others had told before him. To serve as a proper vehicle for spiritual revolution, the fund of available stories had to be transformed.

"In the tales which other people tell," he counseled his disciples in the summer of 1806,

> there are many secrets and lofty matters, but the tales have been ruined in that they are lacking much. They are confused and not told in the proper sequence: what belongs at the beginning they tell at the end and vice versa. Nevertheless, there are in these tales which other people tell lofty and hidden matters. And the Besht (may his holy memory be a blessing) could "unite unities" by means of tales. When he saw that the upper conduits were ruined and he could not repair them through prayer, he would repair and join them by means of a tale. (Y 7, E 32–33)[19]

Hasidism, to be sure, was a more fertile ground for the tales that other people tell than rabbinic Judaism ever was. The idea of God's immanence in everything, no matter how lowly or trivial, was a central tenet of Hasidism, beginning with the Besht, the founder of Hasidism. Quoting Isaiah (6:3), Reb Nahman elaborated upon the same teaching: "*His presence fills all the earth!* God's glory is proclaimed even from tales told by the gentiles; as it is written [1 Chron. 16:24], *Tell of His glory among the nations.*"[20] The songs of shepherds, by the same token, or marching tunes could also be a conduit to God, and Hasidism ushered in a musical revival among the Jews of eastern Europe. But just as it took Rabbi Akiva to unlock the allegorical meaning of Solomon's Song of Songs, only a great *zaddik*, someone schooled in the hieroglyphics of the holy, could discover the divine emanations in the stories told by lowly peasants.

In Bratslav the operative category was not immanence but *tikkun*, the myth of cosmic mending that went back to Isaac Luria (1534–1572). Reb Nahman was the first to suggest that the *shevirah*, the primal act of breakage that scattered sparks of holiness throughout the profane universe, had affected even the tales that other people tell. Their internal order was destroyed, along with whatever secret and lofty matters they might contain. To merely retell them with proper *kavvanah* (absorption) was not enough. The tikkun could only work if the tales themselves were redeemed from their profane outer shell. Only then could the zaddik use the mended tale to reunite the sefirot and to awaken his disciples from their slumber.

This was the blueprint for creative renewal. Reb Nahman was a kind of romantic philologist, like the Brothers Grimm, just then beginning their work some 1500 kilometers to the west.[21] Whereas they looked to the German folk for a simplicity that would embody wholeness, Reb Nahman's restorative program was more cosmic and dialectical. He did not want to create a seamless narrative out of disparate traditions—he ripped out all the seams and started over. To effect the perfect camouflage would be to defeat his purpose, which was to signal the real meaning of the tale. That meaning was coded into the story's deviation from the norm. The more difficult the tale—in its details, its plotting, its bizarre symbolism—the more redemptive weight it carried. The more aberrant the tale, the more obvious the fact that it did have a hidden meaning.[22]

Reb Nahman made his task more difficult still by choosing precisely the type of story that the Germans call *Märchen* and that in English is usually rendered "fairy tale" or "wondertale." The more obvious choice would have been the legends, those wondrous deeds and histories recorded in the Talmud, the midrashim, and the *Mayse-bukh,* which bore witness to the contact of holy persons with God and the supernatural. Some were sacred tales of long ago; others were local legends set in Regensburg, Prague, and even as close to home as Okup, birthplace of the Besht. The *vunder-mayse,* in contrast, told of magic potions that changed a person's face; of young men who turned into birds; of travelers who crossed the Sambatyon River to the Jewish Neverland wherein resided the Ten Lost Tribes; of seduction and abduction; of marriages made in heaven that were frustrated on earth. Miracles were commonplace, as was repetition, for the isolated episodes of the fairy tale made up a plot of action. They were generally regarded as fiction.[23]

How romantic to imagine Reb Nahman, scion of two hasidic dynasties, roaming through the forests and soaking in the oral lore of Orthodox pilgrims and Ukrainian serfs! How else could he have come by "the tales which other people tell"? But Nahman did not draw his inspiration directly from the folk, Jewish or gentile; he turned to storybooks in Hebrew and Yiddish. Of magic potions he might have read at some length in *A Beautiful Story [Ayn sheyne historye] That Goes by the Name Bove Mayse,* a prose reworking of the Yiddish Renaissance classic by Elia Levita, *Bovo d'Antona* (Isny, 1541). Nahman's elaborate tale "The King and the Emperor," about a bride and her three suitors, might easily have come from *Mordecai and Esther, a Beautiful and Wondrous Story about a Groom and a Bride,* the most popular Yiddish romance of the nineteenth century.[24] To cover his tracks, as it were, he eliminated the Jewish names, places, and temporal settings. Instead of the Prophet Elijah helping Boruch, the son of Rabbi Fridman, as in the story of the bride and groom, Nahman's fairy-tale heroes were unnamed; their actions transcended natural laws and took place somewhere no more specific than a town, a palace, or a desert. Within their new archetypal settings and intricate plots, these characters were meant to bear new mystical meanings. By reinventing these tales so that they might yield their messianic and kabbalistic secrets, Nahman was restoring them to a pristine form they had never known within Jewish recorded time. No one less than the greatest zaddik of his generation could counteract the combined forces of Satan and the shevirah.

Thus Reb Nahman's return to fairy tales was only his point of departure, just as the Grimms were inspired by the study of modern German folklore to reassemble the scattered sparks of teutonic mythology into primal myths that were still potent. In the light of what they discovered in the distant past, they concluded that German fairy tales, even their own collection of *Household Tales,* were nothing more than "broken-down myths," narratives of belief that were crushed by European Christianity.[25] Nahman took a different approach to closing the chasm between myth and mere story. He set out to *remythologize* many of these same fairy tales by reaching back to ancient times.

Adapting terms from the Zohar, the holiest mystical book of the Kabbalah, Reb Nahman distinguished between tales "in the midst of days," which told of past but incomplete redemption, and the Ur-tale "of the years of antiquity." The former told of God's beneficence in the past, such as stories of the patriarchs or the Exodus, or even more recently, in the days of the Besht. The Ur-tale represented "the most archaic memories, hidden fears, and unspoken fantasies of the self, as well as those of the universe."[26] More concretely, these tales of the primal years predicted the great act of final redemption that for Nahman still lay in the future. Since that final redemption had not yet taken place and the Messiah had not yet come, the stories were usually left unfinished.[27] In mending the disorder of Jewish and European fairy tales, Nahman discovered the language of pure myth.

Reb Nahman enacted the three-act drama from radicalism to crisis to creative retrieval in just under two years. In the four years left him to live, Nahman mastered the neglected art of storytelling. As Nathan of Nemirov tells it, the master threw himself into it body and soul. Words could not express the profundity of these tales; even the most exact transcription could not do justice to the drama of their first live telling. "For by means of body movement—rocking his head back and forth, winking his eyes and hands gesticulating—it was by these means in particular that the learned [listener] was enlightened to understand just a little; he was amazed at what he beheld, and his eyes perceived from afar the wonders of the Lord and the greatness of his [Nahman's] holy Torah" (6).

As always in Judaism, when the oral Torah was finally written down it assumed canonical status. In this case, Reb Nahman left instructions to Nathan of Nemirov to issue the tales with an exact Hebrew translation printed above the Yiddish original. When modern Yiddish storytelling made its public debut, therefore, it did so as a bilingual *seyfer,* not as a

Yiddish mayse-bikhl. Nathan appended a Hebrew preface, a short biography of the author, and other teachings of the master that threw some light on the hidden meanings of the tales.[28] And like every seyfer, this one too grew exponentially as each generation added its own commentaries and super-commentaries from Nathan of Nemirov's detailed explication of selected tales, first published after Nathan's death in 1845, to the beautiful *Seyfer sipurey mayses* (Jerusalem, 1979) that I hold in my hands right now, updated to include a commentary from the beginning of the twentieth century.[29]

These commentaries bear out once again that context is nine-tenths of the meaning in the art of storytelling. Because they appreciated Reb Nahman's genius for deriving cosmic significance from incidental detail, his hasidim paid careful attention to the structure and the seeming redundancy of the tales. Because they studied his texts in exactly the same way as other sacred texts, they understood his tales as multivalent, as militating against a single and narrowly allegorical meaning. Because they were *di toyte khsidim,* the dead Hasidim, who accepted no other teacher after Nahman, they knew him to be the hidden hero of his tales.

Among the many traditions that Bratslav Hasidism exploited to its advantage was the standard division of labor between Hebrew and Yiddish. Bilingual texts were always aimed at a differentiated Jewish audience. Because Hebrew remained the language of the learned Jewish male, the Hebrew record of Nahman's stories, parables, and dreams was more complete and reliable than the Yiddish original.[30] The Yiddish was for *proste mentshn,* the simple folk, especially women. They were far less likely to be alive to the multiple levels of Scripture, Talmud, and Zohar operating beneath the narrative surface. They could be satisfied with a delightful story and a straightforward moral.[31] So far, business as usual. But since, for the first time, the scribe felt mandated to preserve the *spokenness* of Nahman's original, not deviating to the right or to the left; and since Hebrew had been used solely as a high literary language, Nathan had to invent a hybrid Hebrew style that would capture Nahman's spoken Yiddish. Unlike the editor of the Hebrew *Shivḥei haBesht* (In Praise of the Ba'al Shem Tov), Nathan did not try to compensate for the loss of vitality by making his Hebrew version resonate with scriptural and other learned echoes.[32] Instead, it was Yiddish syntax and vocabulary that echoed throughout, often deviating from the grammar of rabbinic Hebrew—and from the elevated style of rabbinic speech.[33] How could a thinker and teacher of Nahman's calibre allow this to happen? Surely this quasi-colloquial style implied a learned author who, for mysterious reasons, had begun to tell stories that only an ideal (male) reader and disciple of the Rebbe could understand.

The element of surprise in the Yiddish text, printed below the Hebrew, cut in the same direction. The *Tales* of Nahman of Bratslav dispensed entirely with the archaic style that Yiddish editors and printers almost universally employed, and reproduced instead the Yiddish as actually spoken in eastern Europe.[34] Here, for the first time, the oral quality of the text was the measure of its authenticity. Whatever learned Hebrew phrases echoed in Reb Nahman's telling were presumably put there by Nahman himself, not by a scribe who was trying to raise the spoken narrative to a literary standard. The transparently idiomatic quality of the Yiddish implied a storyteller talking to a live audience.

Stories as told to several intended audiences necessarily carried a plurality of meanings. As the work of an artist who was using Jewish tradition in a wholly personal way,[35] the tales demanded the kind of pluralistic interpretation that was normally reserved for Scripture. In mystical circles, the mnemonic for the fourfold reading of Scripture was PaRDeS, which stood for *peshat, remez, derash[ah]*, and *sod*.[36] The PaRDeS model was never actually applied to the *Tales*, but it could have been. The fourfold reading model goes a long way toward an understanding of both the traditional hasidic commentaries and the critical research that came later.

The moment one takes Nahman's poetic manifesto seriously, that there is a universal fund of motifs and plots that were scattered in the primal act of *shevirah*, then there is much to be learned from studying the structure and patterning of the tales in their mended, Bratslavian form. The *peshat*, or contextual, approach would take the tales that other people tell as its point of departure. The key to meaning is the deviant structure of the story, the discrepancy the reader feels between this tale and all the others from the past. If the order of events within the body of the tale should be thus-and-so and that order is skewed in Nahman's retelling; or if the rule that all things in a folktale repeat three times is violated; or if the standard motif of the sleeping beauty is turned on its head, then the secret of the story's *tikkun* surely lies there.

The *derash*, or homiletic, approach looks for one-to-one correspondences. When the stories are read as allegories, each element in the plot is explained in terms of another meaning rooted in traditional sources and concepts. In this scheme, the literal meaning falls away. The merchant is no longer a merchant, but Satan in disguise. The king is read as God and the Kingdom of Lies as the world of human affairs. Sometimes Reb Nahman throws such allegorical clues into the stories themselves. More frequently, they appear at the end, in a highly abbreviated scriptural shorthand and in smaller print, presumably put there by the scribe Nathan. Some have argued that this is no more than a smokescreen, a conscious attempt to neutralize the highest level of reading, or sod.

Read as sod, kabbalistically, the *Tales* do double duty. For every cruel reversal on earth, for every arduous quest, there is a corresponding drama enacted simultaneously in the upper realms, and the two are mutually dependent. The tales are about worlds in collision and the forces of good and evil fighting it out. Each individual motif is the derivative of the divine configuration of sefirot, while the sum of the plot recapitulates—in whole or in part—the Lurianic myth of tsimtsum, shevirah, and tikkun. This is a reading reserved for adult male initiates.

None of these structural, homiletic, and kabbalistic methods, however, directly addresses the existential drama of the storyteller himself and, through him, of every person listening to the tale. So one more approach to the *Tales* is needed, which does not depend on preexisting plot structures, scriptural and rabbinic sources, or kabbalistic symbols. The subtext is Reb Nahman's own life and complex personality. This is the most difficult method of all because the text is conditioned by Nahman's unfolding life, rather than *being* his life.

While Reb Nahman was alive, the personal experience he brought to each subsequent tale kept changing. There was a year-and-a-half break between the telling of the eighth and the ninth tale, when Nahman traveled to the city of Lemberg to be treated for tuberculosis. When he picked up his storytelling again in the winter of 1809, he was not the same person. The stories reflected that change in their length and extraordinary complexity. After his death, of tuberculosis, the drama of discovery now centered on the written clues to his internal life scattered among his other writings. As the reader learns more about Nahman, the sum of the story's existential meanings changes too.

Informed by that biographical knowledge, the reader-listener discovers that Reb Nahman is both the Wise Man *and* the Simpleton; both the zaddik whose prayers are efficacious and the leprous prince he finally heals. Most spectacularly, Nahman is revealed as all the Seven Beggars at once, and then some. Just as the purpose of the bilingual transcript is to conjure up the living presence of the Master in the very act of storytelling, so the existential-biographical reading tries to make contact with the living author for whom the written text is but an intermediary. When the audience discovers its own existential drama being played out in the storyteller's multiple personae, only then does the final barrier fall.

"On the way I told a tale [of such power] that whoever heard it had thoughts of repentance. This is it." Thus Reb Nahman recreates the precise moment for the telling of his first tale, which he now repeats for the benefit of his chief disciple. Nathan will later title this tale "The Loss of the Princess" and add titles to the other twelve as well. Perhaps because it is the first, it still reads much like other tales. A princess is taken into captivity; a hero volunteers to set her free and undergoes severe tests until he does. Yet there is much happening on the peshat level of reading that does not fit the mold. Nahman gives the happy ending away at the very outset—but when the story does conclude, the climax is missing: "(And how he freed her he [Reb Nahman] did not tell.) And finally he [the viceroy] did free her." The viceroy-hero, moreover, fights no dragons and kills no witches. Instead he undergoes three prolonged tests that involve fasting, crying, and perseverance. There is no erotic element. After the viceroy fails the second time around, the princess awakens him from his sleep—the sleeping-beauty motif in reverse—and when all is said and done, there is no hint that the triple ordeal will end in marriage.[37]

An allegorical reading makes sense of some, but by no means all, of these discrepancies. The king, as usual, is God, and the princess is the Shekhinah, the female aspect of God in His nearness to the world. Since the destruction of the temple, she accompanies Israel in exile. That leaves the viceroy as a stand-in for the people of Israel. With all three main characters accounted for, each of the viceroy's three trials translates into another phase of Israel's sacred history: like Adam, the viceroy tastes the forbidden apple; like Noah, he drinks of the forbidden wine; and his seventy-year sleep corresponds to the Babylonian exile. If Israel repents of its evil ways, then the Shekhinah will someday be restored to her proper place in God's Temple.

The story also offers an ethical lesson for each individual. For instance,

אזוי און אזוי, הערט אלע אוים !
איצטער איז די מעשה אוים !

Zuni Maud, in Herman Gold, *Mayselekh* (Tales; 1928)

the viceroy at first has no trouble entering the palace where the princess is held captive, for this is the devil's habitat—"dos ort vos iz nit gut," in the words of the story. Anyone can enter, but getting out is another matter. In contrast, the place of her last captivity, a pearly castle on a golden mountain, is difficult to breach. In a place where "everything is very expensive," you need to bribe your way in, and only the pure of heart can manage to save themselves from its corruption. That escape route is never mapped.

The precise redemptive calendar falls into place only on the next level of reading, for the king is none other than Keter, the Crown, and his six sons are the lower sefirot: Power and Mercy, Majesty and Endurance, Beauty and Foundation.[38] The reason the king favors his only daughter over them is that she is Sovereignty, the queen, the bride, whose reunion with the Godhead is the ultimate goal of cosmic tikkun. Once the reader is alerted to the messianic urgency of this tale, then the opposite, demonic forces come alive as well. It begins with an act of tsimtsum, of the king retracting his love for his daughter with the harsh words "*der nit guter zol dikh aveknemen,* may the Devil take you away!" Her sudden disappearance is the act of shevirah that follows. The viceroy's quest to return her to her proper place necessarily leads him into the world of evil and seduction. Only by purging the root of evil in one's soul can the redemptive process be completed.

Not everyone, of course, can hope to achieve this. That is why the viceroy is none other than Nahman, the zaddik hador, the champion of redemption. That is why the storyteller lavishes so much attention on the viceroy's tears and prayers, which call attention to the hero's effort to overcome his physical passions, his theological doubts, and his yearning for material wealth.[39] In this existential reading, the viceroy's debate with the three giants in the desert no longer seems like a stalling tactic, mere repetition, but as the only way the hero's struggle can be resolved. Here as elsewhere in the *Tales,* the desert is a place of both seduction and purification.[40] Henceforth the desert is the favored setting of radical self-confrontation in Reb Nahman's symbolic landscape.

Then there are the demons, who wear so many guises. They have been around in Jewish narrative at least since Job. There, at least, Satan worked behind the scenes and chose his victim with utmost care, but if to judge from the Talmud and midrashim, his emissaries were an everyday presence in all rabbinic households. The extreme asceticism of the thirteenth-century German pietists restored something of Satan's elite proclivities: overcoming his temptations is what separated the true pietists from mere sinners. Finally given free rein by the spread of kabbalistic teachings, a multitude of demons populated the sermons and ethical tracts of the Jewish Middle Ages.[41] Now, as Nahman's generation approaches the eleventh hour before the final redemption, the demons pull out all the stops. They work alone or in groups, in person or by proxy. The evil may be set in motion by the demonic behavior of kings, princesses, and their maidservants (tales

4 and 11) or when the ruling elite has recourse to sorcerers who then carry out its nefarious plans (tale 5). Sometimes there are whole kingdoms where evil and foolishness reign supreme (tales 6, 12); sometimes the demons in their separate habitations can be provoked to self-destruct (tale 3). Satan himself may waylay the unsuspecting victims (tale 8). On rarer occasions he can be the rod of God's wrath (tale 9).

Were the hero or heroine to combat the evil alone, he or she would have little hope of success. Mortals may draw upon the powers of prayer and introspection, but there are also forces in the universe that come to the aid of humans. There are giants who know every aspect of the world; one tree that, if watered, would destroy all the demons; an iron staff that grows at the place where the 365 courses of the sun meet; a poem that can only be sung by one person correctly; a magical instrument that can be exchanged for the knowledge of how to deduce one thing from another; a hand with a map of all the worlds and all occurrences past, present, and future; a blind beggar who can see through reality; the True Man of Kindness who enables time to exist. As the demons are the agents of shevirah, the mystical unities are the agents of tikkun.

Walking the tightrope between these dialectical forces, the hero can fall and be destroyed; he can reach his desired goal; or, as in the case of "The Lost Princess," he can be left hanging in mid-air. These are heroes possessed of divine madness, of exemplary beauty and ugliness, of utter selflessness and gratuitous cruelty. The lyrical and passive princess of the first tale becomes the relentless egoist of the second, a princess who gets her suitors drunk before disposing of them, and who kills an innocent prince when she sights him scrambling up a mast half-naked.[42] No other form of self-expression—not prayer or commentary or ethical exhortation—could dramatize Reb Nahman's sense of life in extremis as effectively as these fantastically elaborated tales of anonymous kings, queens, courtiers, and wandering beggars. To give them names would delimit the scope of universal crisis—not Ivan the Prince or Ivan the Fool; not Elijah the Prophet or the star-crossed lovers Mordecai and Esther; not the Besht and his famous disciples—but an unnamed aristocracy scheming, wandering, suffering anywhere and everywhere. Instead of named cities, towns, and villages, a symbolic landscape of two thousand mountains, seven waters, singing forests, and enormous deserts. Instead of Sabbaths and festivals, endless time punctuated by sudden disaster and joyous weddings.

What makes the crisis real within this rarefied world of symbolic and anonymous action is Nahman's talent for historical realism, psychological insight, and social satire. The Napoleonic wars once caught Reb Nahman off the coast of the land of Israel; back home in the Ukraine, he followed Napoleon's progress through Europe with keen interest.[43] These dramatic events must have quickened in Reb Nahman a sense of déjà vu: had not the Jews of Spain and Portugal also succumbed to a King Ferdinand and Queen Isabella who had wanted to conquer the world? Had not Solomon Ibn Verga described the tragic consequences of the expulsion in his six-teenth-century chronicle, *The Sceptre of Judah*?[44] Did not the repetition of conquest and apostasy augur ill for the Jews of Europe?

"Once there was a king who decreed for his country exile or conversion. Whoever wanted to stay in the country would have to convert, and if not, he would be exiled from the country." Some of the king's subjects abandon their wealth, but others choose to remain and live the life of Marranos. "Secretly they practiced the Jewish religion, but in public they were not allowed to do so." When the king dies his son rules more cruelly still, and the ministers plot to kill him. One among them is a secret Jew who reveals the plot to the king and as a reward is allowed to practice his religion freely, "to put on prayershawl and phylacteries in public." Then the son dies too and is followed by a grandson who rules with kindness. As a precaution against meeting his father's fate, he consults with astrologers, who predict "that his seed would be destroyed unless he took heed of the ox and the lamb." Thus it is recorded and then he dies.

The great-grandson who assumes the throne returns to the path of evil and orders all oxen and sheep banished from his kingdom. In his drive to conquer the world, he fashions a man out of metal that consists of all the seven kinds of metal in the world, for each of the seven planets.

> And he placed him on a high mountain. All the seven planets shone on that man. When a person needed some advice, whether to make a certain deal or not, he would stand opposite the limb made from the kind of metal that corresponded to the part of the world where he came from, and would think whether or not to do it. If he was supposed to do it, that limb would light up and shine, and if not, the limb would darken. The king did all this, and thus, he conquered the entire world and collected much money. (Y 39, E 101)

For the man of metal to function properly, however, the king has to "humble the proud and exalt the humble," so the king, slavishly literal in all things, does just that throughout his kingdom. The old Jewish minister suddenly finds himself reduced once more to living the life of a Marrano.

One reversal works another. The king dreams that the constellations of Taurus (the ox) and Aries (the lamb) are laughing at him—confirmation of the terrible omen contained in the Book of Records. When the dream interpreters cannot allay the king's fears, there appears a wise man whose father taught him about an iron staff that grows at the crossroads of the sun's 365 courses. "When whosoever was fearful came to this place, he was saved from his fear." Led by the wise man, the king sets out with his wife and family until, at the crossroads, they meet a destructive angel who maps out the obstacles ahead. Finally they come upon a fire. And the king sees that "kings and Jews, wrapped in prayershawl and *tefilin,* were walking through the fire." The wise man, armed with his father's warnings, will not proceed further, but the king, seeing other kings walking safely through the flames, forges ahead with his wife and sons and all his seed, and they are consumed in the flames.

Back in the palace, the Marrano minister explains this dramatic turn of events to the other ministers. "The astrologers saw," he now openly mocks, "and did not know what they saw." The omen has nothing to do either with real oxen and sheep or with their celestial counterparts. "From the skin of the ox one makes *tefilin,* and from the wool of the lamb one makes fringes for the prayershawl, and through them he and his seed were destroyed. Those kings in whose country Jews lived dressed in *tallith* and *tefilin* walked through the fire, and were not harmed at all" (Y 42, E 103).

As historical legend, "The King Who Decreed Conversion" is familiar enough. Ever since Joseph became viceroy over Egypt and Mordecai bested Haman in King Ahasuerus' court, God has rescued His people through His chosen ministers. Reinforcing the surface plot of palace intrigue—and a folktale chronology of three kings plus one—is a more subtle narrative strand about illusion and reality. In this kingdom Jews have to pretend to be non-Jews and traitors pretend to be loyal servants. Each king after the first is labeled "wise," regardless of his actual deeds. The great-grandson in turn becomes so wise that "he fell upon a clever plan" to fashion a kind of metal golem. Reb Nahman undermines that pretense to wisdom by using the word *khokhme* for "clever plan," from the same root as *khokhem,* "wise man." The attribution of wisdom to each of the earthly rulers builds up contrapuntally to the appearance of a true wise man. His knowledge, he repeatedly stresses, comes down to him from his father. And so the kingdom founded on lies, brute force, and false wisdom is finally destroyed by the combined force of traditional wisdom, simple piety, and sublime knowledge.

The allegorical reading confirms that the story is structured on the dichotomy between the worlds of truth and falsehood. According to Nathan's cryptic comments at story's end, all the astonishing symbols, including the wise man's mysterious itinerary, are rooted in Torah, the Book of Truth. To be precise, the story can be read as a running commentary, verse by verse, on the second chapter of Psalms, the book that Reb Nahman committed to memory early in life.[45] The nations that raged and the peoples that plotted against the Lord and against His anointed (verse 1) exclaimed: "Let us break the cords of their yoke,/ shake off their ropes from us!" (verse 2). The Talmud in Avodah Zarah already identified the cords in this passage with the leather straps of tefilin and the ropes with the fringes of the prayershawl. The Lord's response was to laugh at the blasphemers from His heavenly throne (verse 4), just as the constellations laugh at the last of the wicked kings. Then God spoke to them in anger, terrifying them in His rage (verse 5), like the destructive angel at the crossroads. In demonic opposition to the king whom God enthroned on Zion, His holy mountain (verse 6), the evil king has installed a composite metal statue of all the earthly rulers whose advice was sought by everyone—instead of God's (verse 8). "You shall break them with an iron rod," said the Lord (verse 9)—and so it is.

For those who view Nahman as the precursor of Jewish modernism, such a homiletic reading is anathema. It turns the most exciting and mysterious passages in his tales into pablum for the pious. If everything is rooted in Scripture, and in the Psalter at that, then the Jewish story is clearly not "emancipated." But for those who wish to plumb the wellsprings of Reb Nahman's imagination, and to understand why his voice alone broke through the stodgy conventions of tradition, such spadework is indispensable. For who else could unpack the tight rhetoric of Psalms into a metahistorical plot linking Joseph to Mordecai to the Inquisition to the Napoleonic conquest? Is this any less creative than the Rabbi's messianic agenda, which in any event had to be cloaked in unobjectionable terms?

Perhaps Nathan's commentary should have allowed that the grotesque description of the Man of Seven Metals owes more to Adam Kadmon, the

Primordial Man of the Zohar, than to Psalms 2:6. The secret world of the Godhead was manifested in Primordial Man, who drew together the seven sefirot.[46] In demonic contrast, the Man of Metal embodies all that is base and corrupt in the world of illusion. Certainly the metal man stands in counterpoint to the destructive angel who guards the iron rod at the crossroads of the sun's courses. For just as the second act of shevirah in the story—the point at which the Jewish minister has to go into hiding again—is ushered in by the fashioning of the all-knowing idol, the presence of the angel at the crossroads heralds the final fiery act of tikkun.

The most active agent of tikkun, it turns out, is not the wise man with his father's traditions but the minister, who takes credit for the king's downfall and has the last triumphant word. And a fitting end it is for a man who was born into a kingdom of lies, after the exile of the faithful had already occurred. At great personal risk, he gambles and wins his freedom to pray as a Jew, only to have it snatched away at the whim of a mad king who considers himself a sage. The minister is forced to live most of his life in disguise, and even when he is granted "freedom of religion" he can never pray with a requisite quorum of other Jews. He stands alone wearing prayershawl and tefilin, surrounded by enmity, while they, in their simple piety, are off somewhere else protected by a wall of fire.

Could this be Reb Nahman, the zaddik as Marrano, a character with true visionary and introspective powers? Once, during that fateful voyage to Israel, at a moment when everything seemed lost, Nahman resolved that, should he be sold as a slave and prevented from living the ritual life of a Jew, he would still be able to observe the commandments in spirit.[47] That formative experience, now reimagined as a story, is resolved through a hero who can thwart the powers of darkness *only* by living in disguise. In the real world of idolatry, war, and falsehood, the way to achieve his goal is to cut himself off from his people, from prayer, from public observance. The seeker's soul is born into a world of falsehood, and that is where the redemptive struggle must be waged.

The hero as tightrope walker, as master dissimulator, as Marrano. These are versions of existential loneliness more terrifying than the typical isolation of the fairy-tale hero who, as hated stepchild or lone adventurer, invariably establishes a new and more lasting affiliation.[48] What happens to the viceroy after he returns the princess to her father? And what of the minister who can practice freely as a Jew once more but has left his coreligionists far behind? All the more terrifying, then, when the ending of the story is not deferred until a messianic tomorrow, but is unequivocally tragic.

This brings us to "The Rabbi and his Only Son," the most overtly autobiographical of Reb Nahman's thirteen tales. The story harks back to his earliest years gathering disciples in Medvedevke. Akin to such real-life figures as Dov of Cheryn, the rabbi's son must overcome many obstacles in order to find proper spiritual counsel. The fictional son who "felt that there was some imperfection in himself, but he did not know what it was, so he felt no delight in his study and prayer," corresponds to Dov, who fell into a state of inner turmoil and depression on the eve of his trip to see Reb Nahman.[49] In lieu of the stern rabbinic father who does everything he can to thwart his son's desire, Dov's own teacher had warned against having any contact with the young rabbi. Reb Nahman adds an overlay of generational conflict between the young, who are drawn to Hasidism, and the older rabbinic elite, who remain adamantly opposed.

Since the days of Isaac Luria, such tales of *hitkarvut* (discipleship) carry obvious propaganda value. They celebrate and propagate the powers of the mystical hero to *draw close* the souls of those who have strayed.[50] Failed encounters, in this scheme, are also fraught with messianic meaning. Such is the famous tale about the Besht seeking his Sephardic counterpart, Rabbi Hayyim ibn Atar, so that the two of them together might bring the Messiah. Perhaps in allusion to this tale, Reb Nahman uses the kabbalistic code words *ma'or katan*, the small light (or the moon, sovereignty), to describe the rabbi's son. So hardly has the story begun than it reverberates with autobiographical, historical, and messianic echoes.[51]

It also reads like a conventional folktale in which everything is tripled. The story is divided into three main parts. The middle section describes three aborted attempts by the father and son to reach the zaddik. After the third attempt, when the son dies, he appears to his father three times in a dream. The son is angry and instructs his father to visit the zaddik in order to discover why. Now the bereaved father sets out alone and, stopping at the same inn as before, he recognizes the merchant who convinced them to turn back. Here the story takes a surprising turn, even as it wraps all the loose ends together.

> And the merchant opened his mouth and told him: "Why, I can swallow you if you want me to."
>
> He [the father] said to him: "What are you talking about?"
>
> And he replied: "Do you remember? When you traveled with your son, first

the horse fell on the bridge, and you returned. Then the axles broke. Then you met me and I told you the zaddik was frivolous. And now that I've done away with your son you're free to travel on. For your son was in the aspect of 'the small light,' and that zaddik . . . is in the aspect of 'the great light,' and if they had united, the Messiah would have come. But now that I have done away with him, you're allowed to travel."

   In the middle of his words he disappeared, and the rabbi had no one to talk to. The rabbi traveled to the zaddik and he cried: "Gevald, gevald! Help me! Oh help me! *Ḥaval ʿal deʾavdin velo mishtakḥin!* Alas for those who are lost and are no longer found!" (Y 61, E 137–138)

Lest there be any doubt as to the merchant's true identity, Nathan explains that he is Samael, the devil. "For this is how the Evil One behaves. First he incites the person, and if the latter obeys, God forbid, he [the devil] himself taunts the person and wreaks personal vengeance upon him for obeying. May the Lord blessed be He rescue us from his hands and return us to the real truth. Amen."

The classical story repertory had its sublime and tragic moments—the excommunication of Eliezer ben Hyrcanus; the martyrdom of Rabbi Akiva; the deathbed scene of Isaac Luria; Joseph della Reina's last-minute failure to capture Satan; the Besht's failed intercession for the martyrs of Pavlysh— but that moment was always somehow mitigated and neutralized. Even when the story was not embedded within a larger discussion (why a man may not be alone with two women but a woman can be alone with two men), God and His judgment remained inviolate. Human error, hubris, and heroism all confirmed the ultimate authority of God. If there were choices to be made, the wrong choice always proved illusory; biblical monotheism did not allow for two equally valid choices. Reb Nahman, while adhering to the compositional rules of telling a saint's tale and remaining within a believable historical setting, produces a story that is dead-ended.[52]

To begin with, there is the zaddik, falsely accused of being a *kal,* light-headed and frivolous, and of having openly transgressed. There is veiled reference here to the bitter feud with the Shpoler Zeyde, who stopped at nothing to link Reb Nahman's name with the Sabbatian heresy. In the story, the devil comes cloaked as a traveling merchant. In real life he can live dangerously close to home.[53]

Then there is the son, who struggles on three fronts: with the authority of his father who disparages the zaddik's learning and seeks every excuse

Arthur Kolnik, "Kaddish," woodcut on a hasidic tale by Peretz (1948)

to return home; with the demonic obstacles laid in his path; and with his inner obstacles to faith. He of the exalted soul, whose personal salvation might have brought the redemption of the world, is finally destroyed by the combination of the three.

Most tragic of all is the father who is neither devil nor saint. Nathan's homespun moral tacked on to the end tries to alleviate the pain, but the anguished cry—in Aramaic and Yiddish—is Reb Nahman's very last word. *Ḥaval 'al de'avdin velo mishtakḥin* is what is said to honor the memory of the dead. *Gevald, gevald* (which appears only in the Yiddish) is an outburst of unrequited grief. This is the voice of the storyteller himself, whose only surviving son died the year before. Though still an infant, Shloyme Ephraim loomed very large in his father's messianic plans. Yes, the devil was to blame, but no less than the father: guilty of overbearing pride, of driving the unities of Beauty and Sovereignty apart, of killing his partner in redemption. Once, on Mount Moriah, a father's only son was spared by the intercession of an angel. There too, the Midrash tells us, Satan was sent to frustrate the resolve of man.[54] Here, in contrast, a father succumbed and sacrificed his only son on the altar of his own self-interest.

Increasingly, Reb Nahman invented plots that center on a complex and dramatic contest between those who live in a world of illusion and those who break through to the truth of existence.[55] There were sound biographical reasons for such inventions. In the summer of 1807 Reb Nahman detected in himself the first signs of tuberculosis, the disease that had just killed his wife Sosia. That fall he left for Lemberg, a center of commerce and enlightenment, to seek medical treatment. Upon his return some eight months later, he came to view himself as a new kind of survivor, having entered the kingdom of falsehood and seen the modern heresy in all its scope. Rousing himself and his disciples to fight the great battle that lay ahead, he resumed his storytelling in the winter of 1809. All the longer tales (nos. 9–13) date from the intensely creative year that followed.[56]

Most memorable is the contest waged between "The Wise Man and the Simpleton," the khokhem and the tam. We already know from his earlier tales that *khokhme* can cut both ways, used for evil as well as for good. In traditional sources, however, the epithet *tam* always carried positive associations. There was Jacob, "a quiet man *(ish tam)*, dwelling in tents" (Gen. 25:27); Job, who "was wholehearted *(tam)* and upright and one that feared God and shunned evil" (Job 1:1); and the third of the four sons in the Passover Haggadah. Like his namesake, the tam of Reb Nahman's story decides to stay put when his wealthy father loses everything but the parental house. Being of "a plain and common mind," the simpleton takes up shoemaking and settles down to an austere life, while his good friend and former classmate responds to his own father's impoverishment by setting out to seek adventure and knowledge. Because of his restless nature and hatred of physical labor, this wise man wanders from place to place and from one profession to another. In all, he masters seven wisdoms: goldsmithery, gem cutting, medicine, Latin, writing, philosophy, and science, but with this vast fund of knowledge "the world began to seem like nothing in his eyes" (Y 65, E 145). So he decides to return home where he can at least show off what he has learned. "And he suffered greatly on the road, since he had no one to talk to because of his wisdom."

The simpleton, meanwhile, never fully masters the one craft of being a cobbler. Rather than pursue external goals and material gains, he is happy in his minimal existence. Though the object of ridicule, he always responds:

> "Nor on leytsones, Only no mockery!" And as soon as they answered him without mockery, he listened to them and began talking with them. He did not want to be overly shrewd (ibertrakhtn khokhmes) since it too was a mockery of sorts and he was a simple man. And when he saw that their intention was to mock, he used to say: "So what if you are more clever than I? You will still be fools!" (Y 68, E 148)

Though simple, he knows the difference between simplicity and folly, which is ultimately the difference between good and evil.[57]

The reunion of the two sons and neighbors concludes the first part of the story and draws a sharp contrast between them. Though he ridicules his friend's behavior as that of a madman, it is the wise man's home that lies in ruins and the simpleton's house that provides refuge. More acute still is his suffering for wanting to achieve perfection. He suffers because his mastery is questioned by local philistines and because he alone knows that the lauded work is flawed. Later, when the two friends debate the matter of foolishness, the simpleton not only holds his ground but goes so far as to predict, "With the Lord, blessed be He, everything is possible. And it is possible that in an instant I should attain your cleverness" (Y 71, E 150).

This sets the stage for the reversal of their fortunes. It happens that their epithets (Wise Man and Simpleton) become known to the king, who calls them for an audience. The simpleton's response is joyous and spontaneous. "No joke?" he asks, and when at each stage he is assured that the request is serious, he does what is required and rises at last to become a minister. The wise man's response is to deny the king's existence and to convince the king's messenger of the same. The two of them then set out together and soon become beggars. In this sorry state they eventually arrive in the domain of the new minister, where there lives a famous faith healer known as a ba'al shem. Naturally, the wise man (himself a doctor) ridicules the ba'al shem's powers and is soundly beaten for such heresy. Seeking redress, he goes through the ranks of the bureacracy until he comes before the simpleton minister himself. Thus they have come full circle, the wise man reduced to rags and the simpleton possessing wealth and practical wisdom.

Were this a folktale about Little Ivan and Big Ivan, it would end here, but Reb Nahman goes further. Only their external circumstances have changed, after all. The simpleton has merely been raised to a ministerial position while the wise man, though pauperized, is unrepentant. A true miracle is needed to alter the status quo. So, in the third and final episode, it is the devil who sets out to test them, not the king. Each acts exactly on cue: the simpleton rushes to the ba'al shem for a protective amulet while the wise man sets out for the encounter with military protection. The simpleton is saved, and the wise man and his traveling companion are thrown into a muddy torture pit. "And they suffered excruciating torments for several years."

Then, accompanied by the ba'al shem, the simpleton minister discovers the wise man in the mire. "My brother," exclaims the wise man on seeing his old friend. Despite the years of torture, the man still denies the devil his due. "See how they beat and torment me, those hooligans, for no reason!" he protests. Astounded by such stubborn denial, the simpleton minister asks the ba'al shem to perform a miracle, "and show them that this is the Devil and not men." Only when the mire disappears and the devil turns to dust does the wise man (and presumably his companion too) admit that there was a king, and a true ba'al shem.

Unlike the other stories, this one is stark, polemical, and gritty. Its dialogue and characterization are true to life, as are the specific issues of faith and denial. A Yiddish guide to popular medicine had recently appeared in the Ukraine, unremitting in its criticism of faith healers and old wives' remedies.[58] This was something Reb Nahman could not let pass, not because he had to protect his great-grandfather's reputation, but because once you placed your trust in science instead of God, the door to apostasy was thrown open. In their responses to the ba'al shem, the two major figures of the story act out their opposing world views. The rationalist believes only what the eye can see and has delved so deeply into philosophical matters that he denies the existence both of the king and the devil. The simpleton's path of joy and simple faith leads him to trust implicitly in the ba'al shem's powers. The true path of faith is through serving the king and not through scientific inquiry. It is a faith that can alter the course of nature.

As charming and precise as is Reb Nahman's portrayal of religious simplicity, his counter-portrait is surprisingly accurate.[59] It is clear that Reb Nahman has visited the seat of reason himself. Elsewhere he taught that only the zaddik can risk studying the seven wisdoms, for a lesser mortal would surely stumble and fall.[60] In keeping those seven wisdoms from his disciples, he did not differentiate between works of medieval Jewish philosophy and the new heretical tracts. But where did that leave him? The zaddik too must "suffer greatly on the road, since he has no one to talk to because of his wisdom." Alone in his ivory tower of perfection, tortured by knowledge and wisdom that he cannot share with anyone, constantly plagued by the fear of pollution, he desperately needs to be redeemed by the simple and the pure. "Only no mockery," says the simpleton, whose innocence saves him from doing evil. The wise man must first acknowledge that the devil is real before he can admit the error of his ways. As the one who has glimpsed, even for a moment, a universe devoid of the king—of God—he must live with that terror for the rest of his life.

What is happening in Nahman's tales—the happy resolution of "The Wise Man and the Simpleton" notwithstanding—is that the contest between alternatives has become more extreme. He pits a life of utter denial against a life of boundless joy. There is no middle path. The stories are getting longer now, becoming apocalyptic staging grounds for the final cosmic battle. Yet there is a concomitant burst of lyrical, fantastical, and ecumenical energy. Instead of sisters scheming against brothers, husbands against wives, ministers against their king; instead of a father bereft of a son and a wise man bested by a simpleton, Reb Nahman releases his characters from their terrible isolation, enabling them to orchestrate the final redemption. In the final two tales, which account for two-fifths of the volume, the cast of characters is infinitely more complex. Only a master storyteller can keep them all together; only an audience schooled in memorization can recall the half of it in proper sequence.

Far from human habitation there lives a Master of Prayer, who establishes an order of holy hermits. Elsewhere there exists another "voluntary society" that is also sealed off from the outside, but for opposite ends: it is a pagan hierarchy predicated solely on the acquisition of wealth.

To this first set of oppositions, Nahman adds another. Once there was a royal court with a king and a queen, a princess and a child, an orator and a wise man, a keeper of the king's treasure and a faithful friend, a warrior and a master of prayer, one more wondrous than the next. But one day

Anonymous, "Joseph Serving His Brothers" (c. 1880)

"there arose a great tempest in the world. And the tempest upset and confused the entire world. It turned desert into settlement and turned ocean into dry land" (Y 160, E 229). In this act of shevirah the royal court was dispersed, and each court member lost contact with the others. There arose many sects, each devoted to some form of idolatry: one worshipped only honor, another celebrated destruction and murder, a third practiced sexual orgies, and so on. A modern commentator has mapped it out in the accompanying table.[61]

In the vast orchestration of tikkun that follows, each member of the royal entourage is acclaimed by another idolatrous sect, which then submits to purification. The "debased virtue" is turned back into its "higher virtue." The Master of Prayer is acclaimed king over a band of zaddikim who had engaged only in prayer, "but now the Master of Prayer opened their eyes until they became venerable *zaddikim*" (Y 174, E 238). Though the Master of Prayer remains distinct from the others, he no longer operates alone. He has his own group of zaddikim, receives tactical guidance from the warrior,

Member of Court	Exemplar	Debased Virtue	Higher Virtue
King	God	Honor	Glory
Queen	–	Murder, destruction	
Princess	Shekhinah	Orgiastic fecundity	Divine abundance
Warrior	Precursor of messiah	Physical prowess	Spiritual prowess
Faithful Friend	Abraham	Drunkenness	Unlimited love
Wise Man	Moses	Cleverness	Torah, wisdom
Treasurer	Aaron, high priest	Wealth	Blessing
Orator	King David, Levites	Verbosity	Praise of God
Infant	Messiah	Health, care of body	Perfection
Master of Prayer	Elijah, zaddik of generation	–	Prayer

and succeeds in reuniting all the lost members of the royal court, now called *der heyliker kibuts,* the Holy Community.

Yet the combined force of cosmic tikkun fails to crack the hardest nut of all—the Land of Wealth. When the Master's disciples go off on their own to convert that land, having overheard the Master sigh despondently, "Who knows how far they can go astray this way?" (Y 144, E 217), they try to replicate the way the Master originally proselytized sinners. The disciples begin, as he did, with the "lowly people" and work their way up the social ladder. They use the identical argument, "saying that money was not the purpose of life, but that the chief purpose of life was worship of the Lord" (Y 144, E 218). Their pleas fall on deaf ears. These people actually perform human sacrifice in order to ensure greater wealth, and they have an elaborate system of checks and balances to ensure that only the truly wealthy are honored. When the disciples bring back a report that the inhabitants have established idols of the most wealthy, the Master decides to take action himself.

But he fails to win over even the lowliest of those who guard the perimeter of the fortified city; when he gains easy entry, he finds the inhabitants obsessed with the impending attack of the warrior. The warrior wants only their submission, not their wealth, but precisely because he disdains what they worship, to capitulate would be tantamount to conversion. Out of fear they begin sacrificing the least wealthy people (whom they call *khayelekh*, little beasts) to the gods. They take out their wrath on the Master of Prayer as well, for disparaging the latest rescue plan to seek aid from a neighboring and supremely wealthy kingdom. Nothing so far in this world of mammon violates the laws of human folly. Only at this point, a third of the way through, does the storyteller introduce a dimension beyond time and space (as the Master hints at some hidden knowledge about the warrior). "At the palace of the King with whom I stayed," says the Master of Prayer, "was a hand, that is, there was a picture of a hand with five fingers and with all the lines which are on a hand. And this hand was a map of all the worlds. And everything which has been from the creation of the heavens and the earth until the end of time, and will be afterwards was drawn on that hand" (Y 155, E 225). It was by means of that hand, he goes on to explain, that he gained entry into the fortified city and could foretell the downfall of the neighboring wealthy kingdom. Convinced of the hand's prophetic powers, the inhabitants press the Master for more details, and he launches into the tale of the royal court and its tragic dispersion.

When the story of the Land of Wealth picks up again many pages later, the Master has already joined forces with the warrior, whom he recognizes as a lost member of the royal court. The warrior explains that the only cure to the passion for money is through the drastic measure of his magic sword. The wealthy, meanwhile, have returned to their folly with a vengeance, sacrifices and all, and despite everything they've heard they send messengers to the neighboring kingdom to rescue them from the warrior. On the way the messengers meet a man carrying a cane studded with diamonds. Awestruck by such wealth, they kneel before him. The man says that this is nothing compared to the king's treasure, which, when displayed before them, inspires even greater awe.

> However, they made no sacrifices (according to their opinion, this man was a God and they would surely have sacrificed themselves to him) because the emissaries were ordered not to make sacrifices along the way, for they feared that if they wanted to make sacrifices along the way, not one of them would remain. For if one might find a treasure along the way, or if one of them went to the outhouse and found a treasure there, he would begin to sacrifice himself and no one would remain among them. (Y 175, E 239–240)

It is an exquisite parody of religious fanaticism. Brainwashed into worshipping everything that glitters, these people have to protect themselves from their own religious fervor, lest they martyr themselves to the cause. The grotesque spectacle of dying for wealth inside a foul outhouse is no incidental detail. It is all explained in the marvelous scatalogical climax. Here the warrior uses a kind of behaviorist treatment to cure the emissaries of their passion for wealth. He leads them through a controlled experiment in which one wind makes them hungry while a countervailing wind carries a stench. Several repetitions later the warrior says, "Can't you see that there is nothing here that should stink? It must be you yourselves who stink." When they finally get the desired food, it brings on a veritable orgy of self-repugnance:

> No sooner had they eaten from the foods than they threw away their money. Each one dug a pit and buried himself in it out of great shame, because they felt that their money stank exactly like excrement, for they had tasted of the food. They tore at their faces and buried themselves and could not lift up their heads at all. Each was ashamed of the other. (Y 190, E 249)

Purged of their lust for money, they are ready as a group to be cleansed by prayers of penitence. "And the King became ruler of the whole world, and the whole world returned to God and all engaged only in Torah, prayer, repentance, and good deeds. Amen. May it be His will."

Scatology as eschatology, one might say. As Reb Nahman lets out all the stops, perhaps feeling that time is running out, he chooses new down-to-earth settings in which to enact the final messianic drama. Just as the members of the royal court— symbolic standins for the sefirot— must get their hands dirty in the gross idolatries of pride, murder, sex, drunkenness, and the like, so must the zaddik resort to extreme forms of shock treatment in order to break down the human passion for money. The viceroy's task in liberating the kidnapped princess was simple when compared to this vast mobilization of cosmic and earthly forces.

Everything has become more complex, dense, and demanding in these tales: the plot, the characters, and the figure of the storyteller. For as the first of the Yiddish storytellers, Reb Nahman is also the first to invent a persona, a fictional role that justifies how and why he came to tell stories in the first place. That persona is the Master of Prayer, and the key to his complexity lies in the name itself.

In Yiddish he is merely a *baal-tfile*, a Jewish everyman who leads the congregation in prayer. He need not be learned or rich, but his piety must be beyond reproach. Indeed, he must humble himself before the Lord in order to make his prayers efficacious. As it happens, the English equivalents, "prayer leader" and "master of prayer," are quite misleading, since they suggest precisely the opposite: someone who stands above and beyond the pious flock.[62] Such figures have appeared in earlier tales—the Prince of Jewels, the unreachable zaddik (the Great Light), the Marrano minister—but as a Jewish folk type the baal-tfile is a cousin to the *tam,* the cobbler of simple faith and few demands. The baal-tfile empowers others by virtue of his own self-negation.

Yet as the story unfolds we discover the Master's membership in the elect Holy Community, who hold the restoration of the cosmos in their hands. Like the other nine figures, he has been forced to descend into the cesspools of human depravity in order to effect healing. Unlike the others, he is seized with a sense of apocalyptic urgency. He forms a fellowship of disciples, who learn his ways but still cannot do what he can do. They fail to move the idolatrous Land of Wealth, thus forcing him to leave the utopian community and to stand before kings and to debate even with the palace guards. Out there in the world of power and greed, his message of piety and purgation meeting with universal scorn, he must prove his mastery, reveal his hidden knowledge, reunite the cosmic forces that have been torn apart.

All this proseletyzing, agitating, and organizing has, of course, served a clearly defined goal: a baal-tfile cannot pray alone. He needs a quorum. Without the others, without the profane, his prayers are nothing. Without them, even his intense piety will not bring the words on the page alive before God. He is much like the storyteller, then, who carries the divine spark but who operates here on earth with standard phrases, fixed plots, and cannot be effective unless there are at least nine other people present to answer Amen. As with the divinely inspired storyteller, his powerful words can rouse a whole world to penitence, even as they move a small group of disciples to the building of utopia.

If there is catharsis in hearing a difficult story through to its finale, there is perhaps even greater pathos in a complex tale that never ends. The "Tale of the Seven Beggars" is Reb Nahman's unfinished symphony, a grand replay of his major themes. Here too there is a hero (a prince) who falls into heresy through a misguided quest for wisdom; here too there is a primal disaster that confounds the world; here too there are contests between those who seem gifted and and those whose deformity is a mask of the sublime; here too the setting for tikkun—the joyful wedding of the lost children—is a pit; and here too it takes the combined efforts of seven wondrous beggars to restore the prince to his throne. So much has been written about this tale, and so often has it been stylized, that it would take another book to do it justice.[63] Yet the part of this story that has most excited the Jewish imagination deserves mention, for it marks both the culmination of Reb Nahman's art and the beginning of the storytelling renaissance to come.

It is the third day of the wedding feast in the pit, and in reponse to the cries and longing of the newlyweds, a stuttering beggar appears with a gift. Like the blind and deaf beggars who preceded him, his deformity is but a mask. He stutters only when he mouths words that do not praise the Holy One and are imperfect. Otherwise he "can recite riddles and poems and songs so marvelous that there is no creature in the universe who would not wish to hear them. And in these songs lies all wisdom." There is a True Man of Kindness who can vouch for his miraculous powers, but therein lies a story.

This story takes the same narrative form as with the two beggars before, that of a boasting contest. This time wise men are boasting of their scientific and metallurgical inventions. Then comes one man who claims to be as wise as the day, to which the stutterer counters, "Like which day are you wise?" With that question the stutterer is proclaimed the wisest of them all. Why? Therein lies another story.

This last story has to do with the creation of time. Time is created through the deeds of kindness that the stutterer collects and brings to the True Man of Kindness (der emeser ish khesed).

> Now there is a mountain. On the mountain stands a rock. From the rock flows a spring. And everything has a heart. The world taken as a whole has a heart. And the world's heart is of full stature, with a face, hands, and feet. Now the toenail of that heart is more heart-like than anyone else's heart. The mountain with the rock and spring are at one end of the world, and the world's heart stands at the other end. The world's heart stands opposite the spring and yearns and always longs to reach the spring. The yearning and longing of the heart for the spring is extraordinary. It cries out to reach the spring. The spring also yearns and longs for the heart. (Y 211, E 268)

The heart suffers from both without and within: without because it is being scalded by the sun, within because of its yearning. When the first becomes too much to bear, a large bird flies overhead and shields it from the sun with its wings. But even during that brief respite, the heart continues to long for the spring. There is no resolution for this yearning because, if the heart approaches the hill, it can no longer see the peak or look at the spring. Not to see the spring even for an instant would destroy the heart entirely. "And how could the world exist without its heart?"

As for the spring, it does not exist in consecutive time. "The only time the spring has is that one day which the heart grants it as a gift. The moment the day is finished, the spring, too, will be without time and it will disappear," destroying the heart as well. To mark the day's passing, the heart and the spring begin to express their longing by singing riddles and poems and songs. This is the moment the True Man of Kindness is waiting for. Just as the day is about to end, he grants the gift of a new day to the heart, who then gives it over to the spring. And so another day is secured.

Now each new day arrives with its own distinct poems and music, depending on what day it is. The time that the True Man of Kindness has to grant derives from the stutterer himself, who travels about collecting the good deeds. So the stutterer is the wisest of all because he alone initiates the process of time through his actions, and knows the riddles and songs appropriate to each new day.

Again one can point to a chapter of Psalms that may have inspired some of Reb Nahman's imagery:

> Hear my cry, O God,
>   heed my prayer.
> From the end of the earth I call to You;
>   when my heart is faint,
>   You lead me to a rock that is high above me.
> For you have been my refuge,
>   a tower of strength against the enemy.
> O that I might dwell in Your tent forever,
>   take refuge under Your protecting wings. (Ps. 61:2–5)

But this would only reveal the degree to which the storyteller has transformed the biblical text and context. The parable itself is not a prayer or a psalm. Rather, it recasts the *experience* of prayer, the awesome and unbridgeable gap between the worshipper and God, into a language at once personal and poignant. It is no surprise that Reb Nahman composed many songs of his own—tunes without words and haunting melodies set to

Hebrew and Yiddish lyrics—which would take on a life of their own, wherever Jews were in despair.[64]

Once again there are kabbalistic substitutes for the symbols Nahman employs—the heart is the Shekhinah is the true zaddik longing for God—but the sense of wounded passion in this tale-within-a-tale-within-a-tale is wholly new. The yearning for an impossible intimacy. The paradox of a dialectical faith that calls for God's distance rather than His presence, for without distance there is no longing, and without longing there is no faith. The cosmic struggle not to bring back the unities but to comingle moments of particularized time and the primal source of Time, which exists outside time. All this is unique to Reb Nahman's theology and artistic vision.[65] It is the true match between the existential struggle of the storyteller and the materials of his story.

Reb Nahman was the first modern Jewish classicist, the sum of everything that came before and the harbinger of the revival to come. He changed the way his immediate audience listened to a Yiddish story, the way future generations of Jewish writers were to view the art of storytelling, the way we, in retrospect, read Jewish tales and the way we write about them. Were it not for Reb Nahman, this book on modern Yiddish storytelling would begin with Isaac Meir Dik in the 1850s or with I. L. Peretz in the 1890s. Instead, it must begin with the closing of the biblical canon, and even before that, with the primal catastrophe that brought the world into being.

The cultural significance of the *Tales* cannot be exaggerated. They are the great watershed, from which the many streams of Jewish creativity—scriptural, liturgical, rabbinic, kabbalistic—are drawn all at once. By reaching back to the "primal years" both of his own psyche and of his people, Reb Nahman made the fairy tale speak—both to the tragic finality of death and to the joy of communal and cosmic healing. By bridging Hebrew and Yiddish, the scholars and the folk, mythic past and historic present, Reb Nahman invented a new form of Jewish self-expression. Bringing his passion and learning to bear on the act of storytelling, he made the evanescent tale into the stuff of a seyfer. The learned storyteller turned his craft into a source of prayer, into a numinous text to be recited by the faithful. There had been stories that sages told about the patriarchs, prophets, and priests; there had been stories that disciples spread about their saints. Not until Nahman ben Simha of Bratslav was there a rabbi-poet who made himself the mythic hero of tales of such power that they might awaken the world.

3

The Master of Lore
ISAAC MEIR DIK

Den in undzere tsaytn endert zikh in yor vi far tsaytn
in a gantsn dor. (For in our times, a year works changes
as great as a generation in times of yore.)

—I. M. Dik, 1864

What about the women? They didn't trade with Leipzig, Koenigsberg or Vienna. They had no access to the study of Talmud. They could read the Yiddish *In Praise of the Ba'al Shem Tov* or the bilingual *Tales* of Reb Nahman, but stayed at home when their husbands made a pilgrimage to the rebbe. Women had to make do, for the most part, with recycled goods from generations past. They were a captive audience for new reading matter in Yiddish.

If Sholem Yankev Abramovitsh's historical memory can be trusted, learned women in Lithuania in the 1840s sustained themselves on a strict diet of Yiddish Bible stories and homilies. The *Tsene-rene* (Come Out and See, 1622) had become so popular a homiletic commentary on the Bible that women chanted it aloud on Friday nights, and no Jewish home was complete without a copy. On more serious occasions they read an ethical tract called *The Shining Candelabrum* (1701). On Saturday nights the whole family gathered to read aloud from the famous *Book Jashar,* and whatever that left out of the life and adventures of the biblical Joseph was more than made up for in the newer *Greatness of Joseph.* Jewish women, it seems, were well served by Hebrew sacred classics rendered in a learned Yiddish style.[1]

So where was there room for change if the entire literate population of east European Jews could still have their intellectual and aesthetic needs met by works that were centuries old? The closed system of Jewish culture was certainly the greatest obstacle for those, like the young Abramovitsh

(b. 1836), who were impatient for change. When, in the 1860s, he decided that what Jews needed most was socially responsible fiction in a language they could all understand, Abramovitsh donned the disguise of Mendele the Bookseller. This is how he announced his wares to his male and female readers: "*Ruml* is what I deal in, that is to say, in Bibles, festival and daily prayerbooks, penitential prayerbooks, Yiddish prayers for women (*tkhines*) and other religious tomes (*sforim*) of that sort. You can also find all kinds of stories (*mayses*) and a few of the new-fangled booklets (*bikhlekh*)."[2] If there was any room to maneuver, it had to be found somewhere on this list.

Occupying the center of the Jewish cultural inheritance were the *ruml-sforim,* works that were indispensable for the day-to-day and season-to-season life of an observant Jew. *Ruml* was a trade name, an acronym for *sifrei Rabbanim UMeLamdim,* canonical texts in Hebrew and Aramaic written by (and often for) rabbis and teachers.[3] Though Mendele limited his list to prayerbooks for men and women, a more specialized seyfer could be anything from a Talmud to the *Tales* of Reb Nahman. Yiddish, too, had come a long way since the advent of printing, so that Yiddish works like the *Tsene-rene* could aspire to the canonical status of sforim by virtue of their religious subject matter and their dependence on a Hebrew-Aramaic source—even if no direct source existed. Still, to issue a new seyfer when so many of the old ones were in service was to tread on sacred ground.

Tolerated but enjoying no official status whatsoever were the *mayses* that Mendele threw in next to last. To be sure, the rabbinic elite issued a constant stream of stern formulaic warnings against the deleterious effect of reading fiction—especially on the holy Sabbath—and by the beginning of the nineteenth century, the actual number of secular chapbooks available in Yiddish was very small indeed.[4] When maskilim like Isaac Meir Dik lashed out against the secular Yiddish romance, they were hard pressed to come up with more than three titles: *The Thousand and One Nights, Tsenture Venture,* and the *Bove-mayse. Tsenture Venture* was nothing more than the "Adventures of Sinbad the Sailor," itself an excerpt from *The Thousand and One Nights,* while the *Bove-mayse* was a prose reworking of Elia Levita's *Bovo d'Antona* of Yiddish Renaissance fame.[5] These venerable tales came complete with a redeeming moral message or two, at least on the title page, and were presumably not read in the more learned homes in Lithuania.

Perhaps because they posed no serious threat, the innocent-looking chapbooks might someday become the vehicle of maskilic propaganda. In the meantime, chapbooks sold for two to five kopecks, and itinerant book-peddlers lent them out for the duration of the Sabbath for *a kopike nitsgelt,* a mere penny.[6] Who besides women and ignorant men ever read them to begin with? The rabbinic and hasidic leadership reserved the fires of excommunication instead for the "new-fangled booklets" that crafty old Mendele threw in almost as an afterthought.[7] Trying to pass as a traditional bookpeddler, Mendele would not openly flaunt the sale of books anathematized in most circles as *treyf-poslen,* especially because his own works were just that.

Now *treyf* means impure and so does *posl,* the one pertaining to the realm of food and the other to ritual. Together they mean untouchable, a secular book that a Jew is forbidden to read. The only group for whom the *treyf-poslen* were not *treyf* were the maskilim, who viewed these works of philosophy, history, natural science, poetry, fiction, and drama as exemplars of a countercultural classicism. Written for the most part in pseudo-biblical Hebrew and imitating the norms of the European (mostly German) Enlightenment, these books bespoke the new secular authority that the maskilim hoped would permeate Jewish life and letters.[8]

Their external appearance also embodied the new, western aesthetic. Maskilic works cultivated a highly untraditional look. They used the square Hebrew typeface, not the cursive so-called Rashi script. The layout was expansive (wide margins, white space). Punctuation (colons, semicolons, question and exclamation marks) was modern. They were small in size, as opposed to the heavy talmudic tomes. Many of the new-fangled texts were printed with "one line sticking out and the other in," thus openly flaunting the east European Jewish aversion to verse, other than in bibles and prayerbooks.[9] If that wasn't bad enough, these heretical works were often published in such impious cities as Vienna and carried long lists of subscribers, called *prenumerantn,* among whom there were even Christians.[10]

It happened in the heyday of the cultural wars between Hasidism and the Haskalah that a treyf-posl tried to pass itself off as a seyfer. Twice before Joseph Perl (1773–1839) had tried to combat the spread of the hasidic movement in Galicia, once through a German monograph *Über das Wesen der Sekte Chassidim,* and once through an outrageous bilingual parody of Reb Nahman's "Tale of the Lost Princess." But these remained in manuscript while *Sefer megalleh temirin* (The Revealer of Secrets) finally saw the light

Yosl Kotler, cover for Herman Gold, *Mayselekh* (1928)

of day in 1819.[11] It was an unusual seyfer, to say the least—the work of a mysterious editor named Ovadia ben Petahia, who miraculously procured the authentic correspondence of two Galician hasidim along with the letters of some minor characters embroiled in the plot. The plot, in turn, involved the desperate and ultimately disastrous attempt of the hasidim to steal a copy of an antihasidic German book that bore a striking resemblance to the very monograph authored by Perl. Flawlessly parodying various Hebrew styles, Perl was equally attentive to matters of traditional typography: he used only the most rudimentary punctuation; supplied long and learned commentaries in Rashi script; crowded the title page with a hasidic genealogy and a faked hasidic endorsement. The only giveaway was the place of publication, Vienna, and the printer's name, Anton Strauss. How a Christian printer in a city barred to most Jews would publish a hasidic seyfer was something that required a separate booklet to explain.[12] The elaborate hoax apparently backfired, for after a brief period of credulity, the hasidim bought up and destroyed all available copies. Wise to these new maneuvers on the part of Galician maskilim, the hasidim dispatched a Yiddish treyf-posl called *The Duped World* with great alacrity.[13]

Whereas the audience for a Hebrew seyfer had to be vigilant against forgery and heresy, the Yiddish-reading public was lucky to see any new titles at all. Many factors conspired to preserve the piety and propriety of everything done in Yiddish, from a weighty bilingual seyfer to a 32-page mayse-bikhl. Until the 1830s, Yiddish was still printed in the special typeface called *vaybertaytsh* (literally, women's Yiddish). That alone made it safe—and more difficult to read. Compounding the problem was a literary language that preserved the archaic spelling, syntax, and vocabulary of a Yiddish no longer spoken in the east. Gradually things began to change, especially in the Ukraine, the heartland of Hasidism, and in works of unquestionable piety. When reissuing the classics, Ukrainian printer-publishers began to adopt modern phonetic spelling, more colloquial diction, and the square typeface. The new square look for Yiddish (with vocalization marks) was dubbed *ivre-taytsh,* and was not only easier to read but had the added advantage of emancipating *taytsh* from the exclusive domain of women.[14]

Once Yiddish began to look more accessible and to read more colloquially on the printed page, the chapbook market became attractive to the purveyors of popular culture. It was also the perfect vehicle for subversion. Ironically, the first thing subverted was the Enlightenment itself. So great was the hunger for new narratives and so conservative were the tastes of the Yiddish reader, that printers, editors, and translators were encouraged to take the most innovative works of the Hebrew Haskalah and repackage them as pious Yiddish *mayse-bikhlekh.* Thus the anonymous *David's Greatness and the Kingdom of Saul* (1801) offered "many stories . . . of how King Saul held arguments with King David and also about the love of David and

Jonathan. . . . Many parables are also brought with much ethical teaching about faith in the Creator, blessed be He, and everyone can learn a moral from this."[15] Could anyone object to a storybook about King David, progenitor of the Messiah, especially one that ended with his proclaiming faith in the world to come? How shocked the pious and unsophisticated male and female readers of this chapbook would have been to discover that a mere seven years before (in 1794) the Hebrew original had been published "mit Amsterdamer schriften" by the famous Christian printer and patron of the Haskalah, Anton von Schmidt of Vienna; that its author was Yosef Ha'efrati miTropplowitz, whose praises were sung by three eminent maskilim; that the whole text had been written in unrhymed syllabic verse and concluded with a free rendition of a poem by Swiss poet Albrecht von Haller. And the beautifully printed treyf-posl had come complete with a list of subscribers.[16]

The Yiddish translator, one Naftoli Hirsh bar Dovid, did his job well.[17] He changed the focus from *The Kingdom of Saul (Melukhat Sha'ul)* to the greatness of David and turned a stormy tragedy into a pious parable. He knew enough to render poetry as prose and to replace the German poem with a concluding speech on the world to come, plus an epilogue that mitigated Saul's tragic death by suicide: "And he [David] shall be King forever, as it is written in the Torah: 'David King of Israel lives and exists forever.' "

Biblical dramas successfully repackaged as homiletic narratives met with instant success. How pitiful were the few dozen paid subscribers for a neoclassical Hebrew closet drama when compared to a mass audience that might even adapt the play for its yearly Purim-shpil, a form of folk theater that was very much alive throughout eastern Europe. The all-time favorite of the Purim-shpil repertory was *The Selling of Joseph,* for like the Purim story itself, it was set in a royal court, with an erotic subplot and a dramatic recognition scene. Thus there was already an audience for a new biblical drama about Joseph, by Hayyim Avraham Katz, called *Milhama beshalom* (War into Peace, 1797), especially since the *Milhama* came armed with a bona-fide rabbinic endorsement. No Enlightenment work this, it dramatized the Joseph story by interpolating polemical dialogues culled from the medieval Jewish philosophers.[18] Reissued in 1801 as the anonymous *Gdules Yoysef* (The Greatness of Joseph), the Yiddish chapbook appeared without explanatory footnotes, and the text was redivided to follow the lectionary cycle of the synagogue. Other than its adaptability for Purim, *The Greatness of Joseph* gained new relevance in the 1820s when Tsar Nicholas began drafting Jewish minors into the army. Many a tear was shed for the fate of young Josephs sold into slavery.[19] Abramovitsh's mother in the Lithuanian shtetl of Kapulie presumably cried as well.

With a pious title page and epilogue and constant reminders of a Hebrew (preferably biblical) source, Yiddish readers felt themselves quite at home. The intimate, reiterative, and didactic style of Jewish ethical writing could also compensate for a story that was not so familiar, such as the adventures of Robinson Crusoe or *The Discovery of America* by Columbus, Cortés, and Pizarro. In *Robinson, the Story of Alter Leb,* our man Friday was turned into our man Shabes (Sabbath) and the narrator affected a pious Jewish demeanor, quoting proverbs and the Bible. Adapted by yet another Galician maskil not from Defoe but from a German writer for children, Robinson's adventures were recast in the voice of a successful merchant from Lemberg who sometimes interrupted the story to castigate the hero and to address his audience directly: "People who have no faith and are afraid of spirits, demons, elfs, magic and other such nonsense, as soon as the slightest thing happens to them, they immediately have a fit, they're seized with it on the spot and they lose their reason; they tremble like fish in the water."[20] Thus Robinson, alias Alter Leb, should have known better than to panic when discovering footprints on the island. Yiddish popular literature was clearly made for "telling" and not for "showing."

Several, then, were the ways in which the Yiddish mayse-bikhl made its medium the message. By adhering to an established format of anonymous authorship and pious title, the Yiddish chapbook preserved the place of storytelling within the religious canon. When the source was new, chapbook writers found a precedent: in the Bible, in the postbiblical Jewish past, or in an authorial voice that spoke in the name of Jewish tradition. The general message was reducible to a matter of ethical conduct or religious belief, be it faith in the world to come or (more controversially) faith in the rational faculties of man. The moral of the story, in turn, linked the Yiddish mayse-bikhl firmly with the cumulative and unbroken tradition of *mussar,* or ethical literature, which remained the dominant form of Jewish self-expression from the tenth to the nineteenth century.[21]

But who would write for women if one could write exclusively for men? Who would "degrade the honor of their pen" by writing in Yiddish if they could affect a pure biblical Hebrew? Who would turn to pious narrative if Schiller was their model of perfection? The first generation of east European maskilim would—because they weren't quite so modern as we make them out to be; because they needed a way of infiltrating the enemy camp; and because they were faced with otherwise insurmountable odds.

First among the odds was the inscrutable Tsar Nicholas I (1825–1855). After five years of petitions and litigation on the part of maskilim, rival printers, and other malcontents in the empire, Nicholas issued an "Ukase Concerning the Censorship of Jewish Books and Concerning the Jewish Presses." As of January 1837 and for the next ten years, the only Jewish press allowed to operate in the entire Russian part of the empire was the Vilna press of Rom and Tipograf. When the maskilim realized how unresponsive Rom was to publishing their enlightened works, they appealed to Count Uvarov, the minister of education, who then issued a second license to the Shapira brothers of Zhitomir. But neither the Vilna nor the Zhitomir press, together enjoying an absolute monopoly on the Jewish printed word from 1847 until July 1862, saw any need to cater to the maskilim. The Shapiras in any event were hasidim, and the Rom press had no desire to antagonize its orthodox clientele.[22] The maskilim who started out with such high hopes were left high and dry. "Just as in ancient times," wrote the Vilna maskil Dik in 1861, "the Israelites went down to the Philistines to set a spur and to forge a ploughshare, so too did every writer who was concerned for the welfare of his people go down to Koenigsberg to publish his work at great cost."[23] Meanwhile, the censorship clauses of the ukase were being vigorously enforced by the government-appointed Jewish censors, who removed anything objectionable from the classic works of popular fiction, ethical literature, and moral philosophy.[24]

Under Tsar Nicholas the battle waged by maskilic informers, censors, and official government advisers achieved mixed results. They could infiltrate the sacred texts or openly antagonize the Jewish masses by banning certain books outright, but on the ground the "enlighteners" were an embattled minority—one from a town and two from a clan (Jer. 3:14). They needed an institutional base if they were to establish a credible alternative. This the enlightened despots provided them in the form of crown schools (first in Galicia, in Russia as of 1844) and rabbinical seminaries (1847). It was as teachers and preachers in Israel that the maskilim learned how to close the gap between utopian theory and effective propaganda.[25]

Products of a traditional heder and yeshiva education (Joseph Perl was even a hasid in his youth), the first generation of east European maskilim were not freethinkers. They wanted Judaism purged of its mystical accretions, freed of its regional customs, and returned to a more pristine, decorous, and rational form. The role of religion was to inculcate faith in God, not fear of the devil. Demons and angels, heaven and hell, had no place in the appreciation of God's natural wonders or in the building of moral character. The maskilim drew a sharp line between arcane "custom" and the essential core of Jewish observance.[26] Perl fired a teacher in his German-Jewish elementary school in Tarnopol for smoking on the Sabbath. Dik was a trustee in the first "reformed" congregation in Vilna, the Tohoras Hakoydesh, but resigned when it began attracting ignorant parvenus instead of true maskilim. Even the radical maskil Abramovitsh produced singable Yiddish translations of the Sabbath hymns and labored for years on a rhymed translation of Psalms.[27]

With a base of operations and a steady income from teaching either in the crown schools or in one of the two rabbinical seminaries, the enlighteners still had far to go. Most Jews would never set foot in a reformed congregation, would never send their children to anything but a traditional heder, and would not be caught dead reading an epic poem on King Saul. But Jewish merchants did need an almanac, prospective grooms could certainly use a new letter-writing manual, and Jews of all ages hungered for moral guidance and Bible translations in a language they could understand. Thus an almanac that listed the Jewish hall of fame could also include a few religious reformers; a letter to one's future inlaws could underline the value of foreign languages; a tale about the sages could exemplify loyalty to the state; and a passage from Proverbs could teach one to beware a phony hasid.[28]

In addition to making the camouflage fit the crime, the maskilim began to look for a permanent stand-in, a double, "an authorial voice that spoke in the name of Jewish tradition" and in their own name as well. So they hit upon the maggid as the alter ego of choice: the lay Jewish preacher who was also a teacher and social reformer. In their uphill struggle to wrest authority away from the communal oligarchy and the archconservative rabbinate, they could do no better than cast themselves in a role at once traditional and maverick. The maggid, whether salaried or itinerant, functioned in all the roles the maskilim wished for themselves: moral guide, interpreter of tradition, and chief entertainer of ordinary Jews. Not only did the early maskilim easily identify with the maggid's social and religious concerns, but the maggid's traditional voice was very close to their own. He too loved parable and allegory; he too delighted in showing off a new interpretation of Scripture, Talmud, or Midrash; he too was better able to tell, to deliver his didactic message, than to show.

Politically, the choice of a maggidic role was also astute, in that the maskilim hoped to forge an alliance with the non- and antihasidic orthodoxy, the misnagdim, whose rationalism and greater tolerance dovetailed with the maskilic program for reform. In the White Russian stronghold of rationalist orthodoxy, the area Jews called "Lite" (Lithuania), maskilic hopes for such an alliance ran particularly high. With Nicholas I dead and the Crimean War ended, a rabbi and former kosher slaughterer from White Russia, Eliezer Lipmann Silbermann, established *Hamaggid,* Russia's first Jewish weekly newspaper. Since the old ukase was still in effect, the paper had to be printed on the Prussian side of the Lithuanian border, but in name, didactic tone, and mildly reformist program, *Hamaggid* represented the marriage of enlightenment and tradition that the Lithuanian Haskalah was famous for.[29]

The marriage worked well for some, poorly for others. Once Alexander II inaugurated the reforms of 1855–1874, new and more radical publications in Hebrew, Yiddish, Russian, and Polish began to proliferate, and the need for pious camouflage was no longer felt in some maskilic quarters. Newly licensed to teach in a government school, twenty-four-year-old Sholem Yankev Abramovitsh fought on all literary fronts: as Hebrew literary critic (1860), translator from the German of a natural-science textbook (1862), writer of realistic prose fiction in Hebrew (1862) and in Yiddish (1864). Making his Yiddish debut in a newspaper, the Odessa-based *Kol mevaser,* Abramovitsh retained only those aspects of medieval Yiddish culture that he considered worth parodying. He retrieved the figure of the *pakn-treger,* the itinerant bookseller whose inventory was beyond reproach. As a Jewish everyman who plied his trade through a fictional shtetl landscape, Mendele could take on everything his benighted Jews considered sacred. And he especially delighted in the mock-maggidic preface.[30]

Mendele was a demonic double. If he could afford to be somewhat lax in his religious observance, to parody the maggidic sermon and the pious mayse-bikhl, and to do some "publishing" on the side, it is because Abramovitsh, his creator, belonged to a new cadre of maskilim whose literary careers were shaped by the cosmopolitan world of the press, with its appeal to public opinion, to men and women of all classes and all regions.[31] Abramovitsh's works grew exponentially larger from one version to the next as his Mendele persona grew ever bolder. While Abramovitsh became the measure of modernity in Hebrew and Yiddish letters, "Mendele" became a folk hero in his own right. The Yiddish treyf-posl had finally come into its own.

Yet the mayse-bikhl was by no means dead. Though White Russia was the center of opposition to everything Hasidism stood for, and though the whole maskilic agenda militated against storytelling, with its appeal to folklore, superstition, and the irrational, it was a maskil from Vilna who brought the art of Yiddish storytelling into the age of mass communication. Abramovitsh's landsman Isaac Meir Dik (1814–1893) achieved phenomenal success in the stodgy medium of the mayse-bikhl and in the voice of a born-again maggid.

He called himself "the youngest among the writers" (after Judges 6:15), by which he meant the first generation of Vilna maskilim, Hebraists and scholars all. In every respect, he fit in. As a newlywed away from parental control, he brawled and boozed with the other imported bridegrooms in the Lithuanian town of Zupran and studied German grammar with the local priest. When his first wife died, he married into a well-to-do hasidic family in Nesvizh, where he continued to study secular works on the sly. Somehow he learned to read Polish and Russian as well. He later lamented his lack of education and regretted that his father, a wheat dealer by vocation and a cantor by avocation, had never trained him to be anything but a teacher of traditional texts. But at least he didn't starve, for after returning to Vilna with his second wife, he tutored Hebrew in wealthy homes and for thirteen years (1851–1864) had a well-paying job (at 225 rubles a year) as a teacher in a crown school for children.[32]

Dik was a front-line maskil only in his thirties—the one period of his life that left a paper trail in the official annals of enlightenment. It was then that he was briefly arrested after being denounced by the Vilna orthodoxy. It was then that he organized a clandestine fellowship of maskilim, which then turned into a break-away "reformed congregation."[33] In July 1843 he and his cronies secretly petitioned the deputy minister of education to abolish the traditional clothes that Jews wore—and the ban went into effect a year later.[34] In 1846, on the occasion of Sir Moses Montefiore's visit to Vilna, they submitted a devastating report on "The State of the City of Vilna in These Times," which blamed repressive government policy for the plight of the Jews.[35]

Dik's lasting claim to maskilic fame, however, was his pride and joy—a clever talmudic parody. *The Tractate on Poverty* first appeared in a maskilic miscellany (Berlin, 1848), but two years later his *Tractate No Money . . . with Commentaries, Tosaphot and Maharsha* completed the farce with a perfect imitation of talmudic layout and typography. He signed it "One of the Students of the [Secret] Fellowship" and it earned him a place in the pantheon of learned parodists.[36]

Then something happened to Dik, prompted in part by the exigencies of Jewish publishing in tsarist Russia. Hebrew authors, he complained in 1861, had to peddle their wares from house to wealthy house. They were at the mercy of both the ignorant masses and the harsh critics who praised a writer only after he died.

> Seeing this, I feared to publish all that my pen had brought forth in the Hebrew language and I degraded the honor of my pen to recount an abundance of divers stories in *yidish-taytsh,* the vernacular now spoken, to our shame and sorrow, among our people dwelling in the land (Lithuania, Poland, Byelorussia). I wrote them for the benefit of the daughters of our people who have eyes only for the Yiddish [translation of the] Pentateuch, which is writ in a stumbling tongue and wherein unseemly passages can be found that should never be uttered by the mouths of pious women and maidens.[37]

He took up the despised vernacular, something no Vilna maskil did more than once in a lifetime, and he settled for a female readership, as long as he could wean women away from their archaic Yiddish Bible, their romances, and their hasidic wondertales. By writing hundreds of stories "in a fine style, full of ethical teaching, free of any words of eroticism and blemish," he tried to "instruct the women to walk in the paths of righteousness and to turn away from all evil." To assure that these uplifting stories "not be obstructed in their journey and that they make their way directly to the customers' hands," he bound them "in old-fashioned coverings in the manner pleasing to our people." Finally, so as not to reveal the maskilic identity of the author, he "did not indicate [his] name on their title pages." For consciously exploiting the medium of the anonymous chapbook and the voice of the traditional maggid, Dik was instantly rewarded. His little books "were grabbed up in a hundred thousand copies and the booksellers receive new requests each day."

Thus preaching carried some earthly rewards as well. When Dik lost his job at the crown school (1864), he made a virtue of necessity and signed the first contract ever to supply the prestigious firm of Rom with three folios a week of Yiddish popular literature at two or three rubles apiece.[38] This made Dik the first professional Yiddish writer—except that the lucrative contract (for 300 rubles a year) was never renewed, and publication of many titles was delayed by a feud between the widow Rom and her sons. It took seven years for the initial consignment to be published, in dribs and drabs. With no royalties allowed, no additional fee for subsequent editions, the unemployed teacher had to rely on his wife's pawnbrokerage (run out of their apartment) to make ends meet. As much as he despised money-lending, he also did some of that on the side.[39]

Forced to compromise, Dik found compensatory rewards in churning out anonymous and pseudonymous Yiddish chapbooks. To remain a maskil and assure a modicum of glory, he published a few satiric memoirs in Hebrew and paid for them out of his own pocket.[40] But for the next thirty years it was Yiddish storytelling—sometimes sentimental, sometimes satiric, but always full of ethical teaching, free of any blemished or erotic words—that gave him a creative outlet and guaranteed an audience. Once the telltale initials AMaD, for Ayzik Meyer Dik, appeared on a 44-page chapbook published by Rom in 1868, they became an instant trademark throughout the Yiddish-speaking Pale. The learned gentleman from Vilna who hid behind these initials then began to address his female readers more directly, and in his private life moved ever closer to the figure he cut in his own stories.

Despite his earlier petition to ban traditional Jewish clothing, Dik himself did not shave off his beard. He wore a mid-length gaberdine coat until his dying day. (The gaberdine was supposed to be the first article to go.) Visitors found him wearing a skullcap and bent over a volume of the Midrash Tanhuma.[41] By this time, too, he kept a very low profile at the reformed Tohoras Hakoydesh, and his letters expressed a growing disillusionment with his fellow maskilim.[42] These biographical facts—that Dik never abandoned his own traditional appearance, that he loved nothing better than to study Midrash, and that he distanced himself from the radical reformers—made his particular choice of avocation all the more compelling. No messianic or midlife crisis prompted his turn to a career as a Yiddish storyteller. A man had to make a living, and he knew he could never make it in Hebrew. Yet there was no maskil better suited for the job than he.

The role, rhetoric, and language of the maggid were just what Dik needed to succeed as an enlightened storyteller. This maggid not only preached in the vernacular, he also published his story-sermons in the spoken language—perhaps for the first time in history.[43] Through Yiddish a modern Jew in Vilna could tell stories in his own voice, could draw directly from his own experience, and could share with an avid readership what really mattered. Through constant reference to Scripture and rabbinic commentary, Dik could close the gap between piety and religious reform, sacred text and secular experience, himself and his female readers. Always poised for a good joke, Dik could maintain an indelicate balance between the pulpit and the local pub. Once he let go of radical reform causes and began to fancy himself a sedentary preacher, a middle-aged, semiretired municipal maggid, Dik was ready to become the great teller of contemporary Jewish lore.

The scope of his writing was encyclopedic. He adapted Hebrew classics both sacred and secular, wrote moralistic tracts in prose and verse, prayers for women, sacred lives, popular histories, travel accounts, jestbooks, collections of fables, proverbs, and riddles, rogues' tales, domestic romances, adventure stories, realistic satires, biographies of self-taught men, and sensational novelettes.[44] As a jack-of-all-trades, Dik switched tactics from one medium to another, but gradually learned how to domesticate the materials he translated, borrowed, or plagiarized. Whatever his medium, whether fantasy or satire, history or travelogue, he eventually came round to Vilna and environs, to the here-and-almost-now of the world he and his readers knew best. There he discovered his strength.

"Where there is no vision (*ḥazzon*) the people perish (Prov. 29:18)," Dik once explained to fellow maskil Reuven Brainin.[45] In maskilic parlance, *ḥazzon* was the mandate to harness the imagination for ethical ends as the prophets had done in biblical times. Prophecy, the maskilim insisted, was dead, but the Bible—as a source of language, sublime poetry, names of flora and fauna, sacred landscapes, models of heroism and selfless love—

most assuredly was not. For five kopecks or less, Dik supplied his female readers with a comparable "vision": the land of Israel as a place of true miracles, from ancient times even unto the present; wondrous events set in biblical and Arab lands whose rational cause was ultimately revealed for—as everyone knows—the Arabs are a superstitious lot; and a rich gallery of passionate heroes and villains. With Isaiah prophesying in the background, the aristocratic lovers of Abraham Mapu's *The Love of Zion* (1853) pursued their hearts' desire in pure biblical Hebrew to the delight of adult male readers in Lithuania and beyond.[46] Adapting, for example, a tale about the Patriarch Abraham from Persian poet Sa'adi through the probable mediation of the Jewish philosopher Nahman Krochmal, Dik produced *Di geduld* (Patience, 1855), which could be read both as a universal parable of tolerance and as a cautionary legend meant specifically for Jews. The Jews, "who have lived dispersed throughout the world these 1800 years," were exiled from their land, it said, because of Abraham's impatience with a heathen hunter.[47]

Yet the God who exiled Israel to drive home a lesson in tolerance had also wrought miracles for Israel. Miracles were the big sticking point for storytellers who doubled as enlightened preachers. The very miracles that Dik recounted as true in his various tales and travelogues of the Holy Land, he ridiculed in stories set closer to home. "Our women have no ear and no feeling for pure ethics," he complained in 1877. "They only want to hear about miracles and wonders, whether they be true or false. For them a real buy is the story of Joseph della Reina, of how he led the devil on a chain or, for lack of anything better, the nonsense about Elijah appearing in the guise of an old man to be the tenth in a quorum at a Yom Kippur service in some village or other."[48] To be sure, David and Elijah regularly did intervene on behalf of those in need, as attested to in *Stories of the Holy Land* (1863), proving that miracles had not disappeared from the Land, and whosoever discounted these miracles as mere natural phenomena was on a slippery halachic slope. Today the tainted maskil made light of the splitting of the Red Sea, and tomorrow he would be eating pork fried in butter.[49] Dik instructed his readers that loving the Holy Land and mourning its destruction were religious obligations for every Jew.[50]

Guardian of enlightened faith, Dik had a harder time of it than Sir Walter Scott, who simply drew a line between two kinds of romance narrative: "that which, being in itself possible, may be a matter of belief at any period;

Anonymous, "Joseph Riding Out to Meet His Father" (c. 1880)

and that which, though held impossible by more enlightened ages, was yet
consonant with the faith of earlier times."[51] Where and when did enlightenment begin if everywhere Jews were still fanatically pious, much more
so since the rise of Hasidism, and Jewish women were still buying the oldest
bobe-mayses on the market? And where did "the faith of earlier times" end,
if the Bible's authority lived on through the Talmud, Midrash, Zohar, and
the medieval commentaries?

The joy of being a moderate maskil was that you could exploit the faith
of earlier times as folklore and thoughtful entertainment. Properly edited,
prefaced, and annotated, even a book of practical Kabbalah like *Palmistry*
(1869) was grist for the maskilic mill.[52] The maskil took pains, like good
Sir Walter, to maintain a strict separation between then and now, them and
us. In the preface Dik assured the *tayere lezerin,* his dear female reader,
that the book was of no practical use whatever. Rather, she should view its
contents like the medicines and potions prescribed by the Talmud that great

sages have forbidden us to use in our day and age when human nature, not to mention human beliefs, has been fundamentally altered.[53] The preface was important because many Jews, as Dik well knew, still practiced the art of palmreading, and many more believed in its divinational powers.

The joy of being a maggid was that all the boundaries were blurred through constant reference to the sacred texts. The maggid's storytelling manner allowed for endless digressions. The maggid's desire to view present behavior in the light of classical texts allowed him to reduce the most complex plot to a set of universal truths. A learned male from Vilna, who labored only for the benefit of his people, sermonically harmonized sex, crime, and piety; folklore, fantasy, and history.

On the list of the world's evils, fantasy was so dangerous that it had to be combatted with a three-pronged attack. To supplant the titillating and fantastical romances with morality and logic required (1) fighting fantasy with fantasy; (2) fighting fantasy with fact; and (3) enlisting maggidic strategies to make fantasy appear both Jewish and normative. Sacred legends of the Holy Land, sometimes under the banner of a seyfer, could spearhead the campaign for "good fantasy."

A more subversive approach was to enter the enemy camp in the guise of fantasy and then to reveal the enemy as a fake.[54] To this end Dik invented and adapted a number of pseudo-biblical, "oriental," and medieval tales in which divine providence worked not through miracle but through coincidence. Nothing supernatural happens in such oriental thrillers as *A Terrible Story from Turkey* and *The Bell in Baghdad* (both 1855) or *Eternal Life* (1857); in the biblical mini-romances *Pious Tirzah, The Banished Son,* or *The Test* (all 1856); or in such medieval exempla as *The Fainter or the Man Who Appeared to Be Dead* and *The Impoverished Man* (both 1855) or *Terror in the Night: The Fears of the Night of Hoshana Rabba* (1856). Heroes learned the useless pursuit of immortality, to honor their father and mother, that women could not be trusted, and were warned against premature burial in narratives "which may be a matter of belief at any period," but worked best in an exotic, historically removed setting.

Jewish law called for burying the dead within twenty-four hours. The maskilim raised a cry against this practice because it conflicted with advances in medicine. What better way to address the issue than to have the hero left for dead in the Frankfurt Jewish cemetery in the year 1025 and have him nursed back to health—by a righteous gentile, no less—with special herbs? As for the superstitions that surrounded the night of Hoshana Rabba (a subject he would return to with greater effect a decade later), the operative message was to fear the Lord every day of the year.[55]

If credible tales set in the times of King Solomon, Pasha Abdullah, and the hoary Middle Ages yielded such practical results, how much more so tales set closer to home. *The Impoverished Man* (1855) was a modest 24-page affair "copied and collected by Y. Shapiro" (the name of an actual bookseller).[56] Its rhymed title page announced "A wondrous story that happened to one R. Zaddok Pikante of Nikolsburg."

> Es iz fun der mayse aroptsunemen a muser-haskl az der mentsh zol nit ton keyn falsh un in der grester noyt zol men zikh hitn fun betlbroyt. Un oyf eybik iz yener farflukht, der vos hot nor eyn mol farzukht. Veykuyom bonu "al tevieynu loy liydey matnas bosor vodom."

> From this tale one can learn the moral that a person should do no wrong and even when in greatest need should beware of beggar's bread. He who tastes therefrom but once is cursed forevermore. May the prayer be fulfilled: "*Do not cause us [O Lord] to be in need of human gifts.*"

The camouflage could not have been better. Paragraphs would begin in Hebrew, to suggest the sacred source from which "Y. Shapiro" had copied it. The hero's piety, generosity, and aristocracy are established in the second paragraph. The reversal of fate, which propels every folktale plot forward, occurs in paragraph three: Reb Zaddok and his financially astute (but nameless) wife have lost their thriving linen business in a fire. After various failed attempts at restitution, the community elders draft an affidavit that Reb Zaddok is to circulate for financial aid. Only it happens that the rabbi of Nikolsburg is none other than the famous Reb Shmelke (1726–1778) "revered by Jews and Christians alike," who has never endorsed a rabbinic seyfer, let alone an affidavit for a destitute merchant. Finally Reb Shmelke relents, moved by Reb Zaddok's and his wife's personal appeal, but not before issuing this stern warning:

> Listen, Reb Zaddok. I am doing you no favor. It is surely true that you will amass a fortune but I have never yet seen a person taste the bread of beggary who could later tear himself away from it. I have read that when you wish to rid your house of mice you should catch a few, lock them up in an iron cage and starve them for so long until they begin eating each other up. When you let the last one out it will not eat anything else but mice. So too the man who

has tasted the bread of beggary only once; he will no longer look for another source of livelihood. No other business in the world will be to his taste save for begging. (9–10)

It is surely convenient that a crusader for Jewish "productivity" should emerge in the mid-eighteenth century. And since the argument he adduces is so pithy and persuasive, the reader is morally prepared for the dire prediction to come true.

To counteract Reb Shmelke's unerring sense of social morality, there appears a *bal-darsher,* an itinerant preacher "who was much more clever than pious." The preacher convinces Reb Zaddok, already on the way home with 4000 thalers in contributions, to sell him the affidavit for another 400 thalers. Then, passing himself off as "Reb Zaddok, the Exhorter of Nikolsburg," the preacher amasses a greater fortune still, only to die suddenly in a small French town. With that inheritance, Reb Zaddok's wife rebuilds the family business and remarries Levi Hurvitz, another linen merchant in town. The real Reb Zaddok, meanwhile, has been robbed of his money and, with no affidavit in hand, becomes a beggar plying his miserable trade as far away from home as possible.

When the ravaged victim finally does return home, it is just in time for the circumcision of his wife's newborn son. The recognition scene between husband and wife has fatal repercussions: Mrs. Hurvitz dies of shock, Reb Zaddok is banished from Nikolsburg, and Reb Shmelke punishes those notables who talked him into signing the affidavit.

If *The Impoverished Man* was the very model of conventional piety—in its style, format, and plotting—then how did Dik turn a sacred legend into a gruesome lesson in self-help? For one thing, he stripped the rabbi of miraculous powers. Not so the anonymous storyteller, who attributed the same tale to the great Ezekiel Landau of Prague (1713–1793), crediting him with having resurrected the dead woman at story's end. "Then the Rabbi addressed both of her husbands and instructed each of them to issue her a writ of divorce, and they did as he commanded."[57] For another, Dik made sure to punish the couple with a bastard son. Had the hero, for example, returned home to the circumcision of his own son (the wife having conceived before he left), her second marriage would have been null and void. This indeed is how yet another anonymous folk version resolved the bastard dilemma.[58] Dik, who needed the rabbi as a mouthpiece for enlightenment, knew that a miracle would only weaken the story's call for rational reform. And if the best way to drive the message home was through multiple tragedy, then the messy status of the innocent child was a small price to pay.[59]

Children paying for the sins of their fathers have come up before—in Reb Nahman's "The Rabbi and His Only Son," none less than Satan was at work behind the scenes before appearing in person at story's end. Satan's triumph signaled the close of a cosmic drama that would never play itself out, because only *that* son, born to *that* father, yearning for *that* particular zaddik, was destined to usher in the messianic era. The players in *The Impoverished Man,* in contrast, could be any merchant down on his luck, any set of notables, any smooth-talking crook, who together conspired against the rational distribution of wealth. Had the clear-headed and thoroughly unsentimental Reb Shmelke been heeded, tragedy would have been averted. Mitigating the tragedy was the lesson for next time—there would always be a next time—that if each man should learn his proper place, God's hand would continue to guide His flock along the path of enlightened self-interest.

One storyteller had his sights on the heavens, the other on his hopes for the earth. One was convinced that miracles were the touchstone of reality, the other that reality was its own reward. Both used the past to buttress their authority: Reb Nahman, rooting every quest in the language of myth; Dik, drawing analogies from Scripture and the classics. Two types of Yiddish storytellers were inaugurated: the romantic-messianic storytellers, who mined the fund of otherwordly plots to achieve a revolution of the spirit, and the tellers of grotesque-sentimental tales, who exploited ancient and local lore to restore the Jewish body politic.

For the next thirty years, Dik used every conceivable forum to hammer away at the same bourgeois enlightenment themes: a well-rounded education for one's children; removing women from the marketplace and returning them to hearth and home; never using marriage as a source of undeserved wealth and status. The old Yiddish romances had also employed some far-flung and far-fetched plots, but they invariably celebrated marriages that were made in heaven. Dik's exotic romances confirmed—through happy or sad endings—the rise of the bourgeois male suitor. As a teller of exotic places, Dik displayed his versatility by letting his predictable cast of evil stepmothers, runaway daughters, and banished sons run loose anywhere from Jerusalem to Capetown, from a plantation in Guadeloupe to Vermont (which he thought was a town in Canada).

As a teller of local traditions, Dik was home free. Here he could exploit his inside knowledge of Jewish character and custom, language and humor. Here, moreover, he could invent his own gallery of heroes and rogues drawn directly from life, not from earlier or translated fiction. (Nor would he have far to look for comic material, since Motke Khabad, the famous prankster, was his downstairs neighbor.[60]) If, as some have argued, the emergence of a local aristocracy was the measure of emancipation in the art of Jewish storytelling, then no one contributed more to that process in the nineteenth century than Isaac Meir Dik.[61]

Reb Shmelke's cameo appearance in *The Impoverished Man* of 1855 was only the beginning of a conscious effort to supplant the zaddik and miracle worker with a rationalist, nonhasidic rabbi as hero. Himself a descendant of Rabbi Yom Tov Lipmann Heller (1579–1654), Dik translated and supplemented his forebear's autobiography in *Stories of the Gaon, Author of "Tosaphot Yom Tov"* (1864) and a year later tried to make a culture hero of Abraham Danzig (1748–1820) in *Seyfer beys Avrom*. "He came to Vilna on account of business," wrote Dik in his gushing preface to the latter work,

> and earned his living strictly from trade, though study always remained of paramount importance . . . his pronunciation was pure German. He dressed entirely [in traditional] Jewish [garb], though very clean and proper. He lived well and expansively and in a highly dignified manner for he was a worldly man and it was a joy to speak to him. . . . As an able Leipzig merchant he always knew what merchandise to order for he was never idle even for a moment. (7)

The rabbinic ideal was a man who combined Torah with business acumen. In the ethical will that followed, Danzig instructed his sons on what prayer to recite for success in business, how to lend money on interest, and how to leave a will of their own.

Though greatly idealized, Dik's fictional rabbis were portrayed in scrupulously human terms. Theirs was a faith in God, a faith that had no truck with the devil. Indeed, his rabbinic heroes were not above exploiting other people's superstitions so that justice and morality might prevail. This is what happens in *The Ceremony of the Torah Completion* (1868), Dik's superb historical romance set in seventeenth-century Poland.[62] It is the story of Reb Yosl the Parvenu, who gains wealth and power by making use of the anarchy in Poland following the cossack revolt, but also seeks legitimation for his crimes by ordering a Torah scroll written in his name. The

man who unmasks him is the brilliant halachist Rabbi David Halevi (1586–
1667), author of the *Tur zahav,* who is seen here as a henpecked husband
and underpaid rabbi of the town of Olyk.

We first meet the rabbi as one of three people in town who does *not*
attend the bacchanal that passes for a Torah celebration. He responds to
his wife's persistent arguments in favor of attending with a list of Reb Yosl's
misdemeanors (he doesn't know of his crimes) that disqualify a man from
undertaking so exalted a task. No less a historical personage than Count
Potocki suddenly arrives to validate that decision. It appears that Reb Yosl
committed the most heinous crime yet on the way to town for the ceremony: he failed to rescue a Jewish messenger from freezing to death in the
snow and stole his money instead. Fortunately the messenger was resus-
citated by the Count. To pressure Reb Yosl into confessing his crime, the
rabbi devises a plan to exploit his superstitious fears. "I know that those
who do not fear God," says the rabbi to the Count, "fear the Devil instead,
or fear the dead" (27). Together, the two men stage an elaborate hoax
involving dreams and the hand of the dead man coming alive to seize the
perpetrator.[63] The criminal confesses all, his wealth is donated to charity,
and he himself is driven from town. The rabbi delivers an uplifting sermon
on never swearing falsely, on never cheating Jews or gentiles, and on always
displaying the proper piety toward the writing of a Torah scroll. So im-
pressed is the Count by the Polish translation thereof that he awards the
rabbi the entire 10,000 gulden leasor's fee for the town, thus repaying the
rabbi a thousandfold for whatever he lost by not attending the ill-begotten
ceremony.

Was this fighting fiction with fiction or fiction with fact? The title page,
the use of historical characters and Polish towns, and constant recourse to
Hebrew headings from a putative town chronicle (would a Hebrew source
ever lie?) attested to its facticity. The superb plotting and dialogue revealed
the hand of a seasoned storyteller. For the teller of local traditions, the
prize was a new rabbinic hero acting to expose all crime and superstition
and speaking out on behalf of a universal standard of morality.

In the chapbook, the moderate maskil could have it all. He could invent
an authentic Hebrew source for an invented Yiddish story that extolled the
life and deeds of the great European rabbis. He could follow the normal
practice of learned Jewish storytellers, mixing fact and fiction for the sake
of a good moral and rereading the past in the light of the present. By laying

claim to the lineage of an illustrious forebear, Dik was less concerned with perpetuating the traditional Jewish view of history—may the accumulated merit of the ancestors redound to the later generations—than with portraying the sages in an enlightened image. Dik assembled a portrait gallery of distinguished rabbis, from Heller and David Halevi to Reb Shmelke of Nikolsburg, all the way to Abraham Danzig of his own Vilna childhood, in order to unveil a proto-maskilic hall of fame.

Yet a storyteller who saw the drama of exile and redemption played out on the stage of secular history, by human actors alone, could not use memory for the sake of moral improvement in quite the same way as traditional hagiographers had. And a storyteller whose audience had become more fragmented than ever—men and women, pietists and enlighteners, east and west—could no longer assume that one kind of story would appeal to all. A storyteller for whom change was both inevitable and desirable, who felt that the old way of life was about to disappear (would that it happen a little sooner!) had to engage in a form of triage in order to save what he deemed worthy of saving.

So he divided the past, once timeless and covenantal, into a local and farcical realm, and drew the sharpest possible line between "earlier times" and "more enlightened ages." He used the history of past events and personalities to underscore the progress Jews had made since the dawn of emancipation. The privations suffered by Rabbi Heller could only have happened then; nowadays, under the benign rule of Alexander II, Russian Jews enjoyed equal rights, engaged freely in trade, and their educated children could achieve high rank in the empire.[64] Russian Jews, in particular, could count their blessings now that the Polish republic had been replaced by the tsarist empire. "*Khelem a shtot un Poyln a medine,* Poland is as much a state as [the proverbial fools' town of] Chelm is a city," Dik was fond of saying.[65] The one Polish nobleman worthy of praise was the aforementioned Count Potocki, not only because of his friendship with Rabbi Halevi, but also because one of the Potockis, Count Valentine, converted to Judaism and died a martyr. Dik rewrote the legend of the Ger Tsedek (the righteous convert), as he was called, to kindle the one bright light in Poland's counterreformation.[66]

No one was better positioned to shape Jewish collective memory in eastern Europe than the maskil who posed as a storyteller. For the maskil had access to Hebrew, German, Polish, and Russian historical sources; to secular as well as sacred texts; to what the Christians had to say about Jews as well as what Jews said about themselves. Hebrew was the source of internal history—of the massacres (1648–1649) and false messiahs (Shabbetai Zvi and Jacob Frank).[67] Polish was the source of local legends, about a count who died as a Jew and a magic stone that lay outside the city walls.[68] Russian provided access to more current events, such as the clothing decree of 1844.[69] But it was from German above all, and especially from German-Jewish sources, that Dik could piece together a normative history of Jewish life in Germanic lands prior to the emancipation. Ever since Wolf Pascheles began publishing his *Gallerie der Sipurim* (1847–1864), Prague had become the source and favored setting of Jewish *Sagen, Märchen und Geschichten*.[70] Thus it was the rabbi of Prague, in Dik's *The Savior* (1866), who intervened with the pope to annul an expulsion decree. And why merely fight with the pope if a rabbi's son could become one himself, as in *Reb Simon Barbun the Rabbi of Mayence, or The Triple Dream* (1874)? Lest Jews forget the most lasting miracle of their European exile, Dik celebrated the rise of the house of Rothschild in *The Greatness of Rothschild* (1865).[71]

According to the teller of local traditions, west European Jews had attained a marriage of piety and worldliness long before their backward brethren to the east. As far back as Metz in the year 1500, enlightened young Jews named Abigail and Joshua ben Joseph could fall in love thanks to the benevolent custom of *The Sabbath Meal Ticket* (1872). Centuries later, that happy marriage continued to thrive in the small towns of Prussia closest to the Polish border, as in *Vögele der Maggid*, Aaron Bernstein's romance of 1858, which Dik translated and embellished with ethnographic detail drawn from his own amazing knowledge of Ashkenazic folkways.[72]

Western Europe was not the problem. Any Jewry, after all, whose piety remained unpolluted by Hasidism and that had the good sense to abandon Yiddish for German, had much to commend it to future generations. But what of eastern Jews, who still bore these dual marks of Cain? Alone among the maskilim of his generation, Dik discovered local heroes, other than the rabbis, whose deeds were worthy of recall and whose exploits were worth exploiting. Besides Prague and Mayence and Metz, where acts of spiritual greatness had been commonplace, he turned the area in and around Vilna into a Yiddish-speaking version of the wild east, where men and and even women displayed their physical prowess. If once there was a Judith "who murdered the great Holophernes who was Nebuchadnezzar's commander-in-chief," there was also *Judith the Second* (1875) of Vilna, who helped capture a whole band of notorious robbers. Similarly, the rough-and-tumble eighteenth century produced men of mythical strength like the legendary *Sholem the Peddler* (1877), who bested the evil Count Demsky and fought a bear bare-handed. Less laudable but equally thrilling was *The Life History of Notte the Thief* (1887). On native ground, where Dik knew the inns, roads, villages, and local lore, his earthy characters were marked much less by their piety than by their passions.[73]

Everything was possible before the partitions of Poland (the first in 1772, the second in 1793, and the third in 1795). That is when people still believed in haunted houses, ghosts, werewolves, and Lilith; when a ba'al-shem was merely an expert in amulets; when dreams were sources of divination because people were closer to God.[74] Though Dik never said as much, the cut-off point for traditional Jews to perform miracles, heroic exploits, and acts of exemplary piety was the last partition of 1795. Thus, when Dik assembled a gallery of rabbinic heroes and their wives in *Moralistic Tales* (1875), the closest in time and place were Isaiah Zhukhovitser (who lived in Lithuania "eighty years ago") and Rabbi Raphael Hakohen, a contemporary of Elijah ben Solomon Zalman, the Gaon of Vilna (1720–1797). To remind his female readers, however jarringly, that rabbis no longer cornered the spiritual market, Dik concluded with tales about Jewish merchants in Paris and Amsterdam. Because they worked no miracles, they exemplified morality.[75]

Through chronicles and romances, adventure stories and exempla, the Yiddish storyteller fashioned a normative past out of motley rabbis, merchants, tavern girls, and peddlers. In the west, he enshrined the learned and monied class that combined Torah and a knowledge of languages, faith and practicality. That would teach his female readers what dossier to look for when falling in love. In the east, he celebrated the spunk and fearlessness of the frontier—Judith, like Rabbi Halevi before her, laughed off the fear of ghosts and demons—even as he preached the advantages of a Russian imperial state.

But in the east, where the past was not yet a foreign country, there was so pervasive a legacy of blight that the popular chronicler felt duty-bound to expose it. To do so, however, required more stringent means. All the old ethical tracts put together could not demolish the rotting edifice of the past as effectively as a biting exposé of individual and communal folly. To reveal the farcical side of Jewish life in the past that was really the present, the teller of local traditions threw off the constraints of pure piety and entered the fray as a full-fledged satirist.

Turning a satiric eye on the last hundred years of Jewish life in Poland and Russia, Dik found—with the few exceptions already noted—a tale of unmitigated error. Reassembled in sequential order, his books form a chronicle of local folly something like this. Following the awesome *Night of the 15th of Kislev,* a hospital for the poor was established in Vilna in 1771, providing a permanent site of Jewish squalor and communal exploitation. Half a century later, around the year 1819, *The Jewish Ambassador* paid a visit to St. Petersburg and then to Vilna, thus making Lithuania fertile ground for all kinds of quacks and tricksters. The benevolent tsars then tried to whip the recalcitrant Jews into civilized shape, but the various reforms were met with hysterical resistance: *The First Recruitment* of 1827; *The Panic* of 1835, and *The Change in Jewish Clothing That Occurred in 1844.* Jewish history was an upside-down world, where an apparition could found an institution and a criminal could pass as a savior. Jews responded to the noble intentions of the tsar as they would to cosmic punishment. Local customs were an invitation to schnorr, carouse, and otherwise violate the norms of civilized behavior.

Take the annual midwinter feast of the burial society, for instance.[76] As in biblical times, when the natural cycle worked in harmony with the religious cult, so too among "our little Jews of Ayalon [an anagram of Vilna]" a mere ninety years ago, the seasonal clock ticked in perfect time with every Jewish feast and festival. Thus, on the fifteenth day of the month of Kislev, every upstanding Jewish male was getting ready to fast in preparation for the all-night bacchanal thrown by the powerful Khevre Kadishe (burial society). (The poor needn't have bothered, for they fasted all year long and were neither inducted nor honorary members in any event.)

On this particular night, the only one making his rounds on the deserted streets of Ayalon is the *bal-dover,* the Angel of Death, put out to find no one at home and no one from whom to inquire. All the more so when he comes upon a brightly lit hall packed with 300 men, celebrating by cursing his name, enacting mock eulogies and otherwise blaspheming against death. Unable to enter, because not one of the guests appears on his death roster for that night ("and he agonized over it like someone whose lottery ticket was only one number off from the winning number," 20), Death has

El Lissitzky, in Leyb Kvitko, *Vaysrusishe folkmayses* (White Russian Folktales; 1923)

to wait for Elinke Bulke, the very drunk sexton of the society, to come outside and relieve his bladder. Provoked by the stranger's impertinent questions, the sexton throws up the sumptuous meal before deigning to respond.

"Listen to him! Local customs he says!" exclaimed the sexton. "Show me one place in the whole world where the fifteenth of Kislev is not a holiday. Why even if you travel to the ends of the earth, to the other side of the Sambatyon [River], the fifteenth of Kislev will be celebrated. And you're playing dumb!" (23)

When this drunken bravura does nothing to enlighten the angelic expert on Jewish affairs, who always carries a Hebrew Bible under his wing, the society's *zoger* or preacher-teacher is called outside for a learned debate. Why, the Angel is particularly anxious to know, do the men keep screaming *"billo hamoves lanetsokh,* he will destroy death forever," if they neither know where the words came from (chap. 25 of Isaiah) nor wish to be robbed of a livelihood were the words to come true. "This is no curse," replies the zoger. "This is our Hurrah, for the meaning is that death causes something to perish for ever and always. That's how we know for sure that the dead will never return to ask for their burial fees back!" (33).

Torn between laughter and rage, Death resolves to abolish death so as to punish the society members for their abysmal ignorance and their ruthless exploitation of the dead. He flies to heaven to tender his resignation, but the heavenly tribunal offers a compromise: that a hospital be established for the poor and thereby eliminate his exhausting search for victims in the outlying cellars and slums. With all the paupers dying under its aegis, the burial society will be pauperized as well.

Through a mock myth of origins, Dik cuts everything down to size: Death with his thousand eyes and his sword dripping with three different poisons; the communal institutions that rob the poor to give to the rich; the arcane beliefs and practices that enshrine ignorance and license drunken revelry. The crux of the joke is the contrast between Death—sober, analytic, governed by rules and regulations—and his emissaries on earth—boozing and guzzling, pissing and puking, perverting and blaspheming. The fantasy and feasting of night is vanquished by the reason of day, the polluted past by the hygienic future. Ayalon now has a bona-fide hospital.

Yet even in the enlightened nineteenth century, when educated people read newspapers in German, unscrupulous men could take advantage of false hopes and false pride. It was enough for someone to appear in Vilna dressed "half Jewish, half Christian, in a long satin gaberdine without a sash, in satin socks and in a kind of shoes called *chizmes* with emerald tips" for everyone to be taken in—from His Eminence Abraham Danzig all the way down to Reb Chaim Bass, trainer of choir boys.[77] And if Vilna was easy prey to fashionable tricksters with false political credentials, how much more so the isolated small towns where news of the Jewish "ambassador" from Morocco could still be exploited long after he had already been exposed?

The economic disorder that prevailed in pre-tsarist Poland was to blame for effectively isolating the Jews. Everything essayed later by the tsar to "normalize" Jewish life was met with fanatic, if ineffectual, resistance. Instead of happily exercising the obligations of equal citizens, the Jews viewed *The First Recruitment* of 1827 as an evil decree. "On the morrow our rabbinic leaders opened up our old arsenal and armed our community with the old weapons of our old King David, that is, they began to recite his Psalms."[78] Dik's humor failed him here, for who wouldn't choose the "old weapons" over the new, if it meant twenty-five years in uniform over and above the years spent as a babe-in-arms? Back then, in 1827, the impending draft was no laughing matter for the Jews of Vilna, and even viewed in retrospect, when these cantonist battalions were a thing of the past, the people's folly was no match for the tsar's. Fortunately, the decree of 1835 banning juvenile marriages was more benignly inspired and more comically circumvented.

Dik, recently remarried himself, had witnessed the shock effects of the decree in the Lithuanian town of Nesvizh. Rather than recall the event as an autobiographical memoir, he chose a satiric venue.[79] For starters, he renamed the town Heres, from Isaiah's prophecy (19:18), "One shall be called the City of Destruction." This gave the name a double stigma, for the commentators had punned *heres*/destruction with *ḥeres*/clay. The shtetl, then, was both a place of economic ruin and a city of clay idols. As a center of hasidim—his own inlaws among them—Heres combined the inbred foolishness of every small town with the particular brand of Jewish idolatry imported from the Ukraine.

To properly launch his mock-mythic tale, Dik has the news arrive on the Ninth of Av as the Jews are all assembled in the house of study lamenting the destruction of the temple.[80] A messenger brings a letter to the rabbi who, already primed for national mourning, bursts into tears, rents his robe, and tears at his hair. This sends the congregation into a panic. Somehow they manage to get through the recitation of the dirges, then rush off to the rabbi's home where he announces a decree far more evil than pharaoh's: no daughter in Israel can marry before the age of sixteen and no son before the age of eighteen. He advises them to marry off their children in greatest secrecy on this very day of fasting.

From then on, all shtetl clerics become soldiers in the war against Satan. The rabbi who doubles as a hasidic rebbe begins at once matching and marrying the children from the poorer hasidic homes (and also sells a good many prayershawls needed by every groom). The land-shadkhn or regional matchmaker is so busy that he can negotiate with the town Croesus only out of doors. The cantor, who doubles as the ritual slaughterer and triples as the town scribe, manages to slaughter chickens in the breathing space between writing out marriage contracts and conducting ceremonies. His wife, meanwhile, sells wedding bands, tassels, and glasses needed for ceremonial breaking. The wedding jester only has time to perform directly under the canopy before another couple comes forward. Half the town's musicians remain parked at the communal canopy while the other half accompanies the bride and groom. The narrator, too, has not a moment to spare, since he is in constant demand as a tenth man at each wedding, and his all-purpose hat is pressed into service for poor grooms. His wife is up all night every night accompanying prospective brides to the ritual bath, even prepubescent girls who go beyond the call of duty "so that the law of ritual immersion not be forgotten in Israel."[81]

How effectively the poverty-stricken and backwoods shtetl can mobilize for the sake of heaven! The only holdouts are the few wealthy merchants, born in big cities, who spend little time in town. They are neither hasidim nor misnagdim and are thus immune to shtetl foolishness. Yet after two weeks' time they and especially their wives succumb to the universal panic as well. Even casual visitors are swept up in the marriage mill. As all normal activity in the shtetl ceases—no learning and no trade—and all normal matches have long since been made, doddering widowers are married off to strapping young women; nine-year-old boys to eighteen-year-old girls; hunchbacks to the healthy; rich to the poor. The youngest brides and grooms have to be carried to the canopy by their parents. Rising to new heights of resourcefulness in the face of this unprecedented challenge, the rabbi rules that since there aren't enough prayershawls to go around and since the Talmud states "the corpse should be brought before the bride," then the dead can be buried without a prayershawl and prayershawl priority given to the grooms.

By the time the decree is actually made public, the town has already awoken to the disaster of its own making. Most of the hastily made matches have ended in divorce or abandonment. Commerce and crafts have come to a complete standstill. The only surplus is in wet nurses, as in Egypt, when pharaoh decreed that all male children be cast into the waters of the Nile.

All that is left of Jewish myth is its perversion; all that remains of historical memory is carnival, farce, and failure. If a letter arrives from the outside world, instant pandemonium ensues. As soon as the entire shtetl population and that of the surrounding villages are drawn into the act, all boundaries break down—between fasting and feasting, the rich and the poor, the young and the old, the living and the dead. Never have nature and morality been more askew than when the little Jews of Ayalon and Heres practice their fantastical rites and mobilize their communal folly.

Once again the comparison with Reb Nahman underscores how differently a hasid and a maskil turned history back into story. For the hasidic narrator, earthly rulers, who forced their will on their subjects and decreed conversion on their Jews, were living in a world of illusion. Earthly rulers, like everyone else, obeyed the cosmic logic of the Torah. It took someone versed in the Torah's symbolism—in the language of Psalms, for example— to decipher the signs in heaven as on earth. For the enlightened storyteller, the earthly ruler could do no wrong. The tsar alone had the power to mandate that the folk change its blind and backward ways. The error of the folk was rooted in ossified traditions that perverted the spirit of the Torah, whereas the Torah's true meaning was revealed in the unfolding of secular history. History, for Isaac Meir Dik, would purge the people of its collective folly. For Nahman of Bratslav, history was but a stage of personal and collective purgatory, to be followed by the final abolition of time itself.

Until history ran its course, there was plenty for the enlightened storyteller to write about, especially someone who personally recalled almost the entire nineteenth century and who reached back vicariously to the one before. And so Dik developed a series of mnemonics to help his readers along. Comical names, arcane occupations, a belt, a hat, a movable screen—these were Dik's ways of cutting the undifferentiated past down to laughable size.

The bad characters could be recognized by their names. The barbaric east resonated from the Slavic diminutives Boruske, Yoshke, Dobke, Khaytsikl, or from names that sounded altogether vulgar, such as Tshortke. Dik's anger at the "disrespect of our Lithuanian Jews for debasing and distorting our sacred Hebrew names" was particularly acute in the case of Yoshke, since Joseph was the favored name of his bourgeois lovers.[82] Worse yet was for men to be named after their wives, for only under a feudal order did a man's identity, if not his very livelihood, derive from a woman. No wonder that Tsipe Yente's Reb Traytl, the small-town Rothschild, was finally exposed by Chaim Itsik Brodzovski, the only man in town with a surname.[83] In one case, that of Reb Shmaye Aliter, the name was the essence of the personality as well. "Among us in Linove [another anagram of Vilna]," Dik announced on the title page of *Reb Shmaye the Holiday Well-Wisher* (1860), "we say of someone who is very busy that he is *farshmayet*," so presumably all this running around wishing people Happy Holiday entered the language as well.[84]

The boors and rogues in Dik's stories could also be recognized by their occupation. Though they went by many names, schnorring off the feudal economy and the ossified medieval customs was what they all had in common. Class A schnorrers were *baley-darsher, moykhikhim, zoger un safdonim* (expounders, hell-fire sermonizers, preachers, and eulogizers). Those in Class B were too ignorant to teach the Torah and so they resorted merely to "telling stories about great men, miracles of the saints." There was a greater variety of schnorrers in Class C: wonderworkers (*baleysheymes*), proofreaders, booksellers, matchmakers, grass widows or fathers-in-law looking for runaway sons; young women collecting charity to buy their way out of a levirate marriage. Class D was made up of wandering beggars pure and simple. (Some parasitic professions, such as disreputable cantors, also broke down into several subgroups.[85])

Once identified by name and occupation, each of these living exemplars of the thankfully-soon-to-be-forgotten past was almost ready to appear as the antihero of a separate tale. The only thing missing was an essential character flaw, all the more memorable when attached to a particular object or setting. Yekele Goldshleger, for instance, could always be identified by his yellow *paravanshtshik* (movable screen).[86] The screen was not only a device for the narrator to plot the rogue's progress and to overhear his love talk, but also a symbol of Yekele's character: he could set up shop with any woman anytime, anywhere. The yellow screen did not hide his exploits, but proclaimed them.

To plot the schnorrer's progress in *Reb Shmaye the Holiday Well-Wisher,* Dik combines sacred clothing and sacred time. After taking up two whole chapters with a detailed description of Reb Shamye's five caps, two hats, and marvelous frock, Dik finally introduces the climactic night of Hoshana Rabba when all this ritual clothing is called into action.

> *Mehavley shav asher he'eminu doroys avru.* Among the many follies in which past generations believed there was a silly belief in what in German is called *ein Doppelgänger,* i.e., they believed that certain people appear as doubles in two separate places at once. The very same thing was said in Linove of our holiday greeter on the night of Hoshana Rabba. For he was seen in several places at once and in each place he wore another hat. One person, for instance, reported seeing him at ten minutes to ten going to the bath wearing his hat with the flaps. Someone else reported seeing him at the very same moment wearing his *khoti-shabesl* [half-Sabbath hat] and drinking a glass of March beer in Dobke's Tavern. Also, a peasant woman saw him at the same time standing at the ballot box in the Gravedigger's Synagogue and he was wearing a round cap. Then again, someone swore that he saw him just then wearing a *shtrayml* at the banquet of the Talmud Study Society, but other people arrived to report that he was last seen at the synagogue of the Shive Kruim Society. (47–48)

Each stop on Reb Shmaye's nocturnal passage is as carefully chosen as the specific headgear. For the hats are designed to keep everyone guessing. Is he bathing in preparation for his sacred task or taking a few stiff drinks? Is he hanging out with the corrupt and corpulent members of the burial society, who were getting ready for their annual election, or sponging off the elite members of the Talmud study society just then completing another tractate? Perhaps he is proving his piety by reciting psalms. If it is posssible for one man to exploit the whole of Jewish society in one fell swoop, the night of Hoshana Rabba is surely the time to do it, for

> Children were in fear of him on this night. Pregnant women avoided looking at him, for he had a frightening appearance. He looked just like Reb Moyshe

El Lissitzky, in Leyb Kvitko, *Vaysrusishe folkmayses* (1923)

Groynim. At around midnight he took up position in the middle of the street and was surrounded by a large crowd of people. He told each person whether or not he [or she] would survive the year, for [Shmaye] was able to read the shadow. He wouldn't even accept payment, but a year's supply of beer was already put aside on his behalf. On this night he would often be seen at the cemetery in the *rabonim-shtibl* with a Yom Kippur candle in his hand and he would perform ablutions before and after in the large river that runs next to the burial ground. (48–49)

As already intimated in the Hebrew heading to this chapter and the fancy Doppelgänger label, Reb Shmaye the clairvoyant is nothing but a fake. He is finally exposed at a feast as a miser and glutton, like another of his number, Reb Traytl, the small-town Rothschild of later fame. By analogy, Yekele Goldshleger's class of con men are routinely caught red-handed posing as faith healers and miracle workers. Justice and bourgeois civility prevail as the old folkways and the class of "professionals" who sponge off them are swept into the dustbin of history.[87]

Jewish folk life, so dense and so public, with its vulgar names and oriental clothes, its arcane rites and dizzying array of ritual objects, its drinking and its schnorring, would all vanish with the dawning of the New Day. Meanwhile, the most visible sign of Jewish "orientalism" was clothing—the ritual belts, hats, and gaberdines; the different ways women knotted their kerchiefs and the men wore their sidelocks. Dik's particular forte in this area perhaps had something to do with his signing that petition to ban distinctive Jewish clothing. True son of the Lithuanian Haskalah, Dik used Yiddish to combat Yiddish, fantasy to fight fantasy, folklore to get rid of folklore. By dividing the past into romance and farce, heroism and skulduggery, he ensured that his *tayere lezerin* would remember why bourgeois society was the light at the end of the tunnel:

And now, my dear female reader, in this little book put your trust, for I have rendered olden times in a manner that is just. . . . Such tales make the very best meals for every nation that wants a notion of its distant days which people think were better than today. Yet our ancient Sage teaches [Eccl. 7:10]: "Do not say: 'How has it happened that former times were better than these?' For you are saying this out of unwisdom." To wit, because you haven't read my verse you don't know that things were once a lot worse.[88]

What kind of maggid was it who preached the inexorable progress of civilization? Who eliminated heaven and hell and most halachic guidelines?

Who used the power of his wit to persuade those who rarely heard a real maggid in the flesh—the women? How was it that instead of concluding with the standard formula "and a redeemer will come to Zion," Dik's stories were replete with false messiahs, tricksters in pious garb? Lithuania was famous for its *shtot-maggidim,* its resident preachers who belonged to the learned aristocracy, and Dik must have fancied himself one of their number. But his preaching was hardly the stuff of a weekly sermon. The only holi-days that fired his imagination were those he could laugh at: the Khevre Kadishe feast, the night of Hoshana Rabba, the Purim bacchanal, Reb Kalmen Sheleykesker's farcical seder.

When Isaac Meir the maggid was in really good form, he concentrated on the folk observance of Jewish holidays. It made for a dozen laughs a minute. Such a rich source of humor was Reb Kalmen from Sheleykesok, *The Country Bumpkin* (1867).[89] Reb Kalmen was the fool who took every-thing at face value, including colloquial expressions; who exploited every opportunity to get drunk ("whether from the fermented booze or the Pass-over booze"); who butchered the prayers like nobody's business. His me-morial prayers and Passover seders were a thing to behold. His seders lasted until sunrise, first, because Kalmen's Hebrew left something to be desired, and second, because he recited the Haggadah from a siddur printed in Dyhernfürth, the text of which was followed by dirges for Tisha b'Av, which the devout Reb Kalmen dutifully added. Every now and again Kalmen would look into a small mirror, relying on the passage, "A person ought to *view himself* as if he personally left Egypt." When it came time to sing "Eḥad mi yodeya" (Who Knows One?), Kalmen would cover his eyes, exactly as he did three times a day when reciting "Hear, O Israel, the Lord our God, the Lord is *One!*" At seder's end, Reb Kalmen would grind up the remaining afikoman to use as mouse repellent, for "nothing more may be eaten fol-lowing the afikoman." And when once it happened that their cat ate the shank bone on the seder plate, Kalmen's pock-marked daughter Dobruske promptly mated her with a tomcat, following the adage, "a girl who eats the shank bone is soon to be betrothed." Who needed hell-fire sermons if one could regale the crowd with the folklore of holidays observed in the breach?

Equally odd for a stand-in maggid was the language he used. The mag-gidic style was elevated, a *heykher gang,* as Lithuanian Jews would put it. Since the maggid alternated between colloquial and learned phrases, Dik

El Lissitzky, in Leyb Kvitko, *Vaysrusishe folkmayses* (1923)

peppered his stories with Hebrew quotations, some real, some invented. But since Dik disparaged the use of Yiddish—and his local variant was a touch archaic to begin with—he began introducing an ever higher quota of High German and later Russian phrases in an effort to "improve" his women's vulgar speech and vocabulary. Neither the female reader nor Dik's publisher was particularly thrilled with the results.[90]

Dik patronized his female audience, who in his view were more in need of instruction than the men. Women's tastes were crude (witness their predilection for miracle tales). Naturally vain and frivolous, their innate shortcomings were given free rein by Polish rulers who for centuries had encouraged the women to go against nature and take over the Jewish economy. Most susceptible to sin was the the woman innkeeper for (as Rashi explained), Rahav, who sheltered Joshua and his men, was not a prostitute, a *zonah*, but someone who supplied her customers with food, *mazzon*.[91] While the men needed to spend less time in the synagogue study house to assume a more vigorous entrepreneurial role, the women needed to model themselves on the biblical woman of valor (Prov. 31:10–31), becoming good housewives and devoted mothers.[92]

And so it went: for every point, a biblical counterpoint; for every lesson, a rabbinic bon mot. And though the effect could sometimes be cloying, and often intrusive, it was second nature to Dik. What Psalms, the Zohar, and the Lurianic Kabbalah had been for Nahman of Bratslav, midrash was to Isaac Meir Dik. It was the ground upon which his Jewish—and religious— imagination flourished. In lieu of attending storytelling workshops in Tennessee as students do today, Dik studied the way the rabbis brought Scripture to bear on everyday life. Where they digressed, he digressed. Where they sacrificed narrativity for the sake of yet another twist on a biblical word or phrase, so did he, especially in his learned and cumbersome footnotes to the tales.

For the maskil from Vilna, the rabbinic Bible was the touchstone of reality. And sometimes the two worlds merged into one, the Bible and Vilna taking the surest measure of Jewish behavior. "Not one of them ventured so much as a mile out of town," wrote Dik of the Jews in the fictional shtetl of Lapets, "and their notion about the wide world was like that of Lot's daughters who thought that Sodom was the world and that once it was destroyed there were no men left for them to take except their own father; or a better example, like our Vilna *melamdim* (Hebrew schoolteachers) who were born in the synagogue courtyard, spend their whole life there and still consider themselves to be worldly, because they know its geography inside out."[93]

As biblical analogies cut Jewish reality down to parodic size, they elevated Jewish romance to the level of myth. The sanctity of Abigail's home in sixteeenth-century Metz is immediately apparent to the poor yeshiva student who was her father's guest for the Sabbath, because "the challah was covered with an expensive gold-embroidered cloth that glittered like the drops of dew that once covered the manna."[94] Joshua ben Joseph expresses his profound gratitude with these biblical analogies:

> Dear Abigail, the Shunammite woman did not take such pains for Elisha as you did for me this Sabbath . . . what's more, the Shunammite showed favor to a man who had no need of her favors while you troubled yourself for someone who was in need. (29)

> And the head of the carp which you placed on my plate on Friday night is the same to me as the trough of water which Rebecca poured for Eliezer. (31)

Making good on his debt of gratitude, Joshua promises to take Abigail's hand in marriage upon his return. Meanwhile she keeps pressing the hankerchief he left behind to her heart "as Potiphar's wife once did with Joseph's garment which he left lying next to her" (35, footnote).

Joseph is the paradigm of male beauty, sexual abstinence, suffering rewarded. Virtually all the recognition scenes in Dik's romances are compared to that in pharaoh's court. Whole stories are cut from the cloth of the Joseph saga, though sometimes, for variation, the garment is remade to fit a girl.[95] The measure of Dik's own filial loyalty is the degree to which his romantic heroes and heroines abide by the midrashic norms of love, sex, and matrimony.

Midrash defined the cultural norm; the maggid delivered the normative message. But instead of doing so in front of the men of a Sabbath morning in the main synagogue or on a Sabbath afternoon in the study house, the maggid now performed exclusively for the women, who could read his tales and parables in their own homes, either to themselves or aloud to others. And in these ethical tales the villain was often an ignorant or itinerant preacher himself, who convinced a fallen merchant from Nikolsburg to sell his cherished affidavit or who ranked first in a long list of schnorrers. The hero was a distinguished rabbi who knew how to preach, like David Halevi in his famous ecumenical sermon, or Abraham Danzig in his celebrated

ethical will. And when once Isaac Meir the maggid manqué found a true-
life preacher to bear his message, the result was a story-within-a-story-
within-a-story better than anything found before in a mayse-bikhl.

Easily half of Dik's works, whether low comic or high romantic, preach
the same hackneyed message: "*es iz ambestn dos yeder mentsh zol ton nur
mit zaynem glaykhn,* it is best that each person should be matched only
with his equal."[96] At the root of Jewish moral corruption, it would seem,
was the false pride of parents who wanted to marry their children into a
higher class. Such a match, if consummated, led inevitably to the downfall
of parents and children alike. In *Boruske the Watchman* (1871), Dik let
someone else preach this message for a change, none other than the most
famous maggid who ever lived—Jacob Kranz, the Dubner Maggid (1741–
1804). His ideological credentials were impeccable: close to the Gaon of
Vilna, Kranz had been an outspoken opponent of the hasidim. As a folk
hero he was second to none, because his life inspired legends and his parables circulated orally in his native Lithuania and beyond.[97]

Not implausibly, Dik claims to have privileged information ("nowhere
before published") both on the life and work of his illustrious landsman.
Apparently the subject of bad matches was very close to the Maggid's heart
because rabbinic ancestry had blinded his parents to the blatant flaws and
deformities of the prospective bride and thus brought about their son's
matrimonial martyrdom. (Was it any coincidence that so many of Dik's
rabbinic stand-ins were tormented by their wives?[98])

One day, our henpecked Maggid is approached by a man of high standing
who is ready to marry beneath his class for the sake of the bride's money.
This reminds the Maggid of the incident between Abraham and his servant
Eliezer. "What if the woman does not consent to follow me to this land?"
Eliezer replied when Abraham sent him on a mission to find a wife for Isaac
(Gen. 24:5). The rabbis understood this as a ploy to advance his own
daughter as a candidate for Isaac. But Abraham rebuffed Eliezer and said,
"You are cursed and my son is blessed." That is to say, Eliezer descended
from the Canaanites whom Noah had cursed while Abraham came from
Shem whom Noah had blessed.[99] Why, asks the Dubner Maggid, did the
midrash not say the reverse, that one who was blessed should not join with
the one who was cursed, since the better party was logically the one to
hold back? The true story of Boruske the Watchman that happened in his
home town of Dubno will explain what the rabbis had in mind.[100]

This once, the story is narrated live within a dramatized setting, without the mediation of a bookish author armed with long explanatory footnotes. The chapbook medium was becoming an artistic liability for Dik. So sometimes he pretended to be lifting the work at hand from an old *pinkes* or community ledger (as in *The Cantor, 1874*). That allowed for rhymed prose and other bookish delights. Sometimes he built the story around conversations that he, Isaac Meir of Vilna, happened to overhear, whether next to the municipal well (*Seven Servant Girls at the Pump with Seven Jugs Taking Water for Tea*, 1873) or en route in *The Kovno Coach* (1874). Never before *Boruske the Watchman*, however, did he actually exploit the preaching situation as such. None of his stories was set inside the synagogue or study house. The closest Dik ever got to live rabbinic storytelling was on the day the Dubner Maggid was asked for matrimonial advice.

The Maggid's speech is of course learned, but not inaccessible. He bunches most of his scriptural references into the story's preamble and allows the small cast of characters to do most of their own talking. There is, to begin with, Reb Ephraim "Tshortl's," pillar of the community:

> Er var a yid a mufleg, a meyukhes, a datn fun groysn kharakter, a bal-tsdoke, un a groyser meshupe beparnose, un dertsu nokh an oysek betsorkhey tsibur beemune; un var azoy a groyser khoshev in shtot dos men flegt nit ton on im vos a hor iz vert. Levad dem var er a groyser bal-neemones dos men flegt ayntsoln bay im ale shlishis-geltn, kolishe geltn. Un vayl er var a groyser khokhem var er bay yeder asife der rosh hamedabrim. (10)

> He was an outstanding person [lit. Jew], of aristocratic descent, a man of intelligence, of strong character, charitable, earned a tremendous income and likewise devotedly involved himself in the needs of the community. So important was he in town that no transaction however small would be undertaken without him. Besides all that, he was so widely trusted that all individual and communal monies were deposited with him. And because he was so wise, he was the chief spokesman at every meeting.

In a dense, reiterative style, replete with Hebraisms, the Dubner Maggid sets forth the protagonist in familiar, socioeconomic terms. (Women, we recall, were long accustomed to a learned Yiddish style.) A man's worth is his capital and communal involvement. Compare Reb Ephraim's sterling credentials with his antagonist's, the lowly town watchman, who lives on the outskirts of town, with a wife, daughter, and two dogs; "a guter khitrets, a gezunter yung, a guter shnapser, a groyser prostak un iz dertsu geven a knaper yid oykh" (a sly bird, strong and hearty, a hard drinker, a first-class boor, and not much of a Jew to boot). In a rational society, there can never be a contest between such disparate types. But two things upset the balance: Reb Ephraim's Jewish hubris and Boruske's sudden change of fortune.

Marriage and money. No girl is good enough for Reb Ephraim, who wants the legendary *telerl fun himl* (pie in the sky) for his son. Reb Ephraim is deaf to his wife Tshortke's warnings that if he holds out too long, he'll have to settle for the likes of Boruske. The latter, meanwhile, has just come into a fortune and the money apparently goes to his head, because he decides that his only daughter, "a gezunte shtik skhoyre," (a healthy piece of merchandise), must marry into the best family in town. Delivering the bait is the brilliant matchmaker Hertsl "Kreyne's" who knows just what to say and when to arrive for his impossible mission.

> Saturday night. From time immemorial, the night when matchmakers have the upper hand, because that's when they catch people still in the spirit of Sabbath, when they're well rested, and at home. There are also plenty of Sabbath remnants: schnapps, cake, cookies, a piece of herring, a cold piece of fish. And that's when hot coffee is brewed as well. In short, there's plenty with which to while away the time. (24)

All the characters are tainted, as their names indicate (Reb Ephraim and Hertsl are named after their wives, and Boruske—with the accent on the first syllable—is a Slavic corruption of Boruch). But since Reb Ephraim is of noble birth, his public humiliation at becoming watchman for a night, and his private grief at discovering that he hasn't a friend in the world, make his downfall a sad lesson indeed.

Having orchestrated Reb Ephraim's total humiliation, Boruske is then the one to renege on the match. This proves that a person who is blessed with proper standing in society should never consider a match with someone who is cursed, since in the end the former will be snubbed by the latter. The Maggid then sends his congregant home with a few biblical quotations thrown in for good measure, and the author wraps it all up with a rhymed finale.

This cautionary tale, worthy of a maggid both old and new, strikes just the right balance between homily and entertainment. However sad the fate of Reb Ephraim, we don't mourn his demise, any more than we shed a tear for Zaddok Pikante, Notte the Thief, Reb Traytl the Small-Town Rothschild,

Elinke Bulke, young Khaytsikl Himself, Shmaye the Happy Holiday Greeter, Kalmen the Country Bumpkin, or any other of the terribly flawed characters who people Dik's chapbooks. They have only themselves to blame, each of them bearing out the truth of some scriptural or otherwise eternal verity. Dik's medium is comedy, not tragedy; the old *must* die to make way for the new.

By imagining the Maggid, moreover, as an idealized version of himself— matrimonial strife and all—Dik gave form and substance to the anonymous, pseudonymous, and otherwise camouflaged author of the modern Yiddish mayse-bikhl. A professional writer working under contract could still play the role of preacher and teacher so long as he drew or pretended to draw from normative sources, from local memory, and from actual experience. The storyteller was a learned man from a well-known Jewish place who never compromised the truth, even when it cut close to home. The storyteller was a man whom women especially would turn to, because he spoke to them in the lowly vernacular in the hope that someday they would speak something else. In the meantime he expanded their narrow horizons by telling them timeless romances in which heroes measured their success by the distance they traveled from their benighted homes, and timely satires in which villains and schnorrers who refused to swim with the tide were ceremoniously swept away.[101]

Here today, gone tomorrow, the dirt-cheap mayse-bikhl was the perfect medium for those changing times. What remained was Dik's legacy. He put Vilna on the map by spawning a school of imitators who flourished well into the twentieth century.[102] That earned him the gratitude of Vilna printers from the famous Roms to my maternal grandmother, Fradl Matz, who published Hebrew prayerbooks and Yiddish mayse-bikhlekh until her death in 1921. Storytellers as far afield as Warsaw, Kiev, and New York could be grateful to Isaac Meir Dik for discovering how a writer could turn the most humble of media in the most vulgar of tongues into an open repository of Jewish wisdom and wit.

4

The Conjuror

I. L. PERETZ

Ayer yidishkayt iz efsher mayselekh? (Maybe your
religiosity is stories?)

—I. L. Peretz, 1904

The traveler, looking for all the world like a Polish Pan, has been plying
these back roads in the Tomaszow region for weeks. The locals feed
him the information he wants—on living conditions in the villages and
towns; on relations between Christians and Jews, rich and poor, husbands
and wives—but what really intrigues him is the local lore. His cape might
give him away as a writer; his Polish doesn't reveal that he is a Jew. On
this melancholy night the gentile coachman has already given him an earful
about Moshke, the Jewish tavernkeeper reduced to being a peddler, when
suddenly Moshke himself appears on the horizon. Offered a lift across the
shallow pond, Moshke recognizes at once that "the nobleman is not quite
a nobleman." So the two Jews start talking in Yiddish.

The traveler presses him for the story about the pond they are crossing,
but Moshke, now addressed more formally as Reb Moses, is reluctant to
tell it. He suspects his interlocutor of Zionist sympathies. "What has Zionism got to do with anything?" asks the traveler. Reb Moses replies that
these days, when "all of a sudden everything is topsy-turvy," Zionism turns
young men in the yeshiva into freethinkers and assimilated Jews back to
their Jewishness. The sum total of their newfound religion is eating kugel
in a Jewish restaurant, so who knows if he, the fancy traveler, isn't a bird
of the same feather. "Kugel is his piety. Maybe your religiosity is stories?
Is this the anniversary of a death for you?"[1]

The big-city intellectual finally gets his story of "The Pond," which he dutifully writes up in a Zionist Yiddish paper, just as Reb Moses suspected. Such stylized folktales and monologues have by now become the traveler's most celebrated trademark. Yet fourteen years have passed since I. L. Peretz actually set foot in the Tomaszow region. Why did he choose to relive his "Impressions of a Journey" taken in 1890, when he was just starting out as a writer? Was it merely to critique the Zionist revival—hardly discernible back then, but very much in vogue in these days of penitent return? And why does Reb Moses, a typical folk Jew, sound as if he's imbibed Heinrich Heine's wicked spoof on gastronomical Judaism, his ode to the Sabbath stew, *cholent,* "given / By the Lord himself to Moses / One fine day upon Mount Sinai"?[2]

Renowned for the restless, open-ended quality of his style, Peretz introduced a fictional informant in order to turn the most searching questions on himself. A moral question: What right have you, Mr. High-Class Writer, to exploit what others believe? Let the traditional Jew nurse his wounds with wonder tales about a hidden saint without your exploiting it for your own ends. An existential question: What makes you think that using my stories will compensate your estrangement from the real sources of *yidish-kayt* any more than eating kugel in a restaurant on the anniversary of your mother's death? An aesthetic question: Do you honestly think you can make this naive folk vehicle speak to your modern concerns? Can you camouflage your highbrow sensibilities behind this crude literary device? It is a tribute to Peretz that he could expose his doubts and critical self-awareness even as his efforts at folk stylization were being crowned with success. It is a measure of his estrangement from the folk and its traditions that he was still haunted by what he had heard as a citified traveler in the backwoods of Poland.

It had been a long day's journey into night. The thirty-nine-year-old native son returned to his home province armed with questionnaires and financed by a wealthy apostate from Warsaw, Jan Bloch. The upbeat positivist program of practical education, science, and hygiene, the integration of social classes and ethnic minorities, had been badly shaken by the recent upsurge of antisemitism. Believing that empirical evidence on the Jews' economic function and proof of their military service would stem the tide of reaction, Bloch financed a statistical survey. Among others, he hired I. L. Peretz, a disbarred lawyer who was struggling to make a life in Warsaw, to draw up the relevant questions and to take them to the provinces. Though the local police finally put a stop to the expedition, and its results were never published, Peretz returned to Warsaw with a mindscape so dense in social, cultural, and linguistic detail that no writer could wish for more.[3]

At the first stop on his fictional itinerary—the town of Tishevits (in Polish, Tyszowce), 17 kilometers from his native Zamoshtsh (Zamość)—the *shrayber* (recorder) confronts three ruined pillars of Polish Jewry: the

Ben-Zion Zukerman, in Peretz, *Zibn gute yor* (Seven Good Years; c. 1916)

rabbi, the maskil, and the hasid. The first is an ineffectual coward, summed up best by his threadbare dressing gown. The second is an insufferable boor, and the third is a true believer crushed by poverty.[4] At this early stage, the narrator still holds to his rational belief that poverty is the root of all evil. "If someone injected a couple of thousand rubles into Tishevits," he counsels the assembled men after evening prayers, all internal dissension would cease. The men were just discussing the community's and the hasidic leadership's failure to stand together. The voice of Reb Elye the hasid—"skinny, sallow, hunched, mournful, and in a coat for which the only match was the rabbi's dressing gown"—then emerges from the debate.

The shtetl is a culture of poverty whose very squalor produces its unique expressions of individuality. Here as elsewhere in Peretz's shtetl fiction, a string of epithets—no matter how bleak—are the mark of an exceptional person.[5] The compressed intimacy of the dialogue reveals both the insularity and the total cultural recall of even the average shtetl Jew: the men use biblical and rabbinic phrases, aphorisms, an elliptical style, and the rhetorical questioning of Talmud study.[6] Everyone speaks in the Polish-Yiddish dialect, including the narrator himself, whose journey through the provinces must make him feel linguistically at home.[7] But now the day is done. Before returning to their wives and children, the shtetl backbenchers initiate the visiting shrayber into the male bonding ritual of hasidic storytelling.

Reb Elye bears personal testimony to some miracles that nearly befell him. To be sure, there are skeptics in every crowd, but the Zaddik of Vorke (Warka) could take on any of them, even the Almighty Himself. Such were the rebbe's intercessionary powers that, when holding a baby during circumcision, he could exploit that singular honor of the Jewish life cycle to force the hand of God. "He said that when going to preside over a circumcision, when merely bethinking himself of the circumcisor's knife, he was transported to a state of awe" (Y 141, E 37). Closely guarding this secret of the rebbe's powers, Reb Elye waits until he can wait no longer: his own eldest daughter is about to die in childbirth. It happens that at this very moment the Zaddik is attending a circumcision at the other end of town, and Reb Elye rushes there with the cries of his dying daughter ringing in his ears. Seeing the Zaddik through a window, Reb Elye tries to leap for it but slips on a pile of manure just outside. By the time he is admitted, the ceremony is over and the moment of grace has passed; when he returns home, bleeding from the fall, his daughter is dead.

The maskil breaks the somber mood by poking fun at Reb Elye's credulity and by touting his own role in supporting the penniless hasid. "And what do you think he does now?" asks the maskil. "He's *my* children's teacher. If I were to fire him, goodbye livelihood! Goodbye his last crust of bread!" Visibly hurt by this added blow to his ego, Reb Elye appeals for greater tolerance, citing Maimonides, who was no less revered for *not* believing in magic. Prodded by the assembled men to continue, Reb Elye comes to the promised tale of how he missed becoming rich by a hairbreadth.

The death of his wife and a bad second marriage reduce Reb Elye to absolute poverty. This time he comes before the Zaddik at the precise moment of grace to plead: "I want to be rich!" The exchange between cowering hasid and towering rebbe works no miracle, for awe of the Zaddik reduces Reb Elye to pleading only not to starve to death and for his son to become a scholar. But the Zaddik dies a week later, dashing Reb Elye's hope of a reprieve.

> Here the Maskil breaks in: "Don't make things so complicated. Your story has a simple moral: first, nobody should pile manure under a window; second, take a rebbe's honorarium with you if you're going to ask him for anything; and above all, don't let any rebbe scare you!"
>
> Instantly, Reb Elye's sallow face crimsoned, his eyes burnt, his form straightened, and the room echoed to the pair of slaps delivered to the Maskil.
>
> I fear that neither will Reb Elye's second request be granted, and that he will yet starve to death.

So ends the performance, the first storytellers' session that Peretz dramatized. In the light of his later career as the great rehabilitator of Hasidism, it might seem that Reb Elye's moral victory is what this episode is all about. Surely the maskil dredging up the old canards about hasidic filth and exploitation deserves the slaps, even if it will cost the hasid his tutoring job. Yet the great hasidic legacy of religious fervor and charismatic leadership is now reduced to "twice-told tales," and in the story as retold, the hoped-for miracles do not occur. Listening between the lines, we cannot fail to catch the dark echoes of Reb Elye's stubborn faith. On her deathbed, the daughter confesses the sordid details of an unhappy marriage to a scholar who was foisted on her by her parents. No miracle could alleviate her suffering. Having martyred his daughter on the altar of his dreams, Reb Elye goes on to experience his own private hell. Dependent on a wife to win bread, he remarries solely out of economic need and is then saddled with yet more children to feed. He squanders what little he has and can make a go at nothing. Inside the circle of male listeners, the poor storyteller can still enjoy a brief moment of self-transcendence. The shrayber needs only to step outside to weigh the consequences of blind faith in an unredeemed world.

Peretz returned to the seat of Jewish law, prayer, and lore in order to write an epitaph. He captured the linguistic and emotional density of hasidic storytelling in order to play the maskil off the hasid off the rabbi. Telling miracle tales, the story-within-the-story made clear, was an opiate for ineffectual males whose passivity left death and ruination in its wake. By the time the statistical survey was over, the shrayber was almost driven mad by the data of destruction and was forced to abandon his own faith in statistics and social engineering.[8] But the impressions of this journey into the Jewish heart of darkness lived on. The first installment appeared in an ambitious new journal of literature, criticism, and popular science edited by Peretz himself and financed by the same group of Jewish positivists who had hired him in the first place. Peretz launched *Di yidishe bibliotek* (The Jewish Library) in 1891 to educate Yiddish readers in his own image. Using parody and realistic prose, satiric and lyrical verse, manifestos and reviews, he exploited his mastery of east European *yidishkayt* and the Polish dialect of Yiddish to promote an urbane, self-critical culture in the spirit of a fighting Poland.

Peretz revisited the scene of his travels to drive the message home. Even a short, uncomfortable trip, "In the Mail Coach" (1891), yields a wealth of data on the strained relations between husbands and wives, Christians and Jews, the old culture and the new.[9] Seated next to a smug and obsessive young man from Konskivole, the discussion turns to the Yiddish storybooks that a bookpeddler recently brought to town. The books provided welcome relief in the battle between husband and wife, who inhabit separate realms: her world of *lezn* (leisure reading) and his world of *lernen* (serious Talmud study). "To this day, I can't understand what there is in these stories," says the young husband. "Men surely won't find anything in them! Tell me, do you write only for women?" (Y 73, E 109).

What begins in the traveler's mind as possible material for a good romantic novel has evolved into a feminist critique of small-town society and a cultural critique of the literary fare then available for the distraction of smart Jewish women (the wife hails from Warsaw) and the derision of smugly orthodox Jewish men. When Janek Polniewski replaces Chaim Konskivoler as the writer's traveling companion, a new perspective is added to the plight of women. A Christian and former friend of the writer's, Janek confides his growing attraction to a shtetl housewife ignored by her husband. Just as Janek seems about to reveal his romantic liaison with a woman who matches the description of Chaim's wife—thus confirming that the stuff of Yiddish potboilers can actually occur in Konskivole, under the nose of the boorish husband—the bubble bursts on these sentimental expectations. "What a fool I was," admits the writer in the story's denouement. "Was there only one Jewish housewife who fit this description?"

Adultery was no way to bridge the growing animosity between Gentiles and Jews. But realistic fiction that exposed the hypocrisy of traditional Jewish values could close the gap between *lezn* and *lernen*. The storybooks of Isaac Meir Dik and his imitators were serious obstacles to the rational restructuring of society. Only a new literature in Yiddish and Hebrew, which appealed to both men and women and underlined their struggle, could rise above the level of mere diversion. The writer of such progressive fictions, alas, was constrained to do all his traveling by mail coach.

Peretz's travels—both real and fictional—took him on a route of regression: to a pond that covered the site of a ruined shtetl; to scenes from a marriage that were everywhere the same; to a culture that sustained itself on fantasy and pedantry. What these Jews read and prayed and sang was a measure of their flight from bitter reality. It was as if Peretz took Dik's encyclopedic impulse—of reappropriating classical tradition for the sake of enlightenment—and turned it on its head. What old pious women read—hell-fire sermons drawn from medieval works—they used to tyrannize their daughters and ruined their marital bliss ("The Marred Sabbath," 1891). What pious husbands studied—Talmud and still more Talmud—they used to dominate their wives and avoid confronting economic issues ("A Woman's Anger," 1893). What Jewish men prayed—on the holiest day of the year—was a cloak for their hapless schemes and fierce rivalries ("Neilah," 1894). What lovesick girls from good Jewish homes sang was rendered grotesque by the crass economic motives of their parents ("Married," 1896). No wonder the traveler felt alienated from his fellow Jews and from nature, and that only his *krekhts,* or heavy sighing, gave his identity away.

Indeed, Peretz was the Polish Pan, in literature as in life. From the day he announced to Sholem Aleichem that he wrote for his own pleasure and that if Yiddish readers couldn't understand him he would gloss the difficult words at the end of the poem, from that day in June 1888 until his death in April 1915, Peretz's fictional profile as a gentrified traveler was twinned with his push to innovate, to liberate Yiddish from the lifeless repertory of the study house and from the narrow concerns of the maskilic salon. While he agreed on the need to educate Jewish women in the history of their people, Peretz was equally keen to provide educated male readers with highbrow and especially scientific material in Yiddish, lest the men defect to reading only Polish, Russian, or German.[10] Later he carried out this ambitious literary and scientific program in the pages of his own almanacs, writing under various pen-names. Yet Peretz never adopted a folk persona in his writings, not a bookpeddler named Mendele from Kabstansk, or a maggid named AMaD from Vilna, or a disembodied presence named Sholem Aleichem from Kasrilevke. Peretz appeared in his writings as what he was: a modern secular Jew, urban and urbane, straddling several cultures and critical of them all.[11]

Meanwhile, throughout the 1890s, Peretz's critical eye remained fixed on the collapse of the shtetl. For all the folk wisdom and learning embedded in the speech of shtetl Jews, the rites, rituals, and content of formal Judaism invariably failed them. For all the time-honored means of achieving transcendence within the study house, the hasidic shtibl, and the yeshiva, the scholars and mystics whose task it was to achieve it were a sorry lot. Reb Yekl, the head of the Lashtshev (Laszczów) yeshiva, and Lemech, his last remaining pupil, were two such members of the shtetl intelligentsia.[12]

> The impoverished town gradually sent less food to the students, provided them with fewer "eating days," and the poor boys went off, each his own way. But Reb Yekl decided that here he would die, and his remaining pupil would place the potsherds on his eyes.
>
> They frequently suffered hunger. Hunger leads to sleeplessness, and night-long insomnia arouses a desire to delve into the mysteries of Kabbalah.
>
> For it can be considered in this wise: as long as one has to be up all night and suffer hunger all day, let these at least be put to some use, let the hunger be transformed into fasts and self-flagellation, let the gates of the world reveal their mysteries, spirits, and angels. (Y 20, E 152–153)

Their sole purpose in staying there is to die there. Making a virtue of necessity, the two heroes try to achieve some practical use as well by re-

Jakob Steinhardt, for Peretz, "In the Times of the Messiah" (1920)

vealing the secrets of the Kabbalah. In the first, Hebrew telling of the tale, the whole town waits with bated breath, not for the messiah, who will come of his own accord, but for the two novices to quit the contemplative stage and begin working with practical Kabbalah: "and then there would be great and wondrous miracles as in the generation of Reb Leyb Sore's."[13] Meanwhile, Reb Yekl uses the melody that "sings without voice . . . in the heart and bowels . . . the melody with which God created the world," to describe the highest rung of mystical contemplation. In the end, it is Lemech who achieves the top rung, leaving his envious master behind. "Only a few fasts more," says Reb Yekl, sighing, "and he would have died with the Divine Kiss."[14]

Primed to expect mock-miracles from earlier generations, the male Hebrew sophisticates to whom the story was initially told delighted in the satiric punchline, which owed more to De Maupassant than to the Ba'al Shem Tov. Three years later in 1894, Peretz prepared for a more subversive battle and launched his radical *Yontef-bletlekh*—Yiddish "holiday folios" that appeared each month in pious garb to cheat the censor. It was midsummer, and Peretz needed copy for the 17th of Tammuz issue. Those who expected to find something about the fast, commemorating the breaching of the walls of Jerusalem by Nebuchadnezzar's army, found instead a story about two pathetic characters, Yekl and Lemech, who turned their fasting to more ambitious ends. Young urban readers, who had already abandoned such arcane commemorative rites, were justifiably repelled by a society that allowed its mystics to achieve transcendence only by starving to death.

But there came a time when Peretz wanted to subvert his own subversion, to tell stories about Jewish mystics that did not try to score anticlerical or socialist points and took Lemech's idealistic striving seriously. When Peretz discovered the romance of Hasidism, he ranked Lemech alongside the other hasidic hopefuls: Reb Yoykhenen the Teacher, Reb Shmaye of "Between Two Mountains."[15] Even so, "Kabbalists" revealed a writer who was drawn much less to mysticism than to a romantic ideal of music as a source of transcendence.[16]

Though he would later blame Heine for infecting him with the virus of "brilliant mockery," the parodic strain ran deep in Peretz.[17] Wit and parody were the legacy of Zamość, his birthplace, where Sheyndele was the local rhymster, where the famed Singers of Brody paid occasional visits, and where, before that, Shloyme Ettinger (1801–1856) had laid the foundations for the modern Yiddish melodrama and Ephraim Fishlsohn had dug a theatrical grave for hasidic charlatans.[18] Peretz himself began his Yiddish apprenticeship composing rhymed pasquinades on local institutions and prejudices.[19] The other, lyrical side of his personality found expression in Polish or in Hebrew, rarely in Yiddish. "Yiddish has but quips and flashes," he proclaimed in his own defense,

> Words that fall on us like lashes,
> Words that stab like poisoned spears,
> And laughter that is full of fears,

> And there is a touch of gall,
> Of bitterness about it all.[20]

Insofar as Yiddish was associated in his mind with Jews and jesting, the more Jewish the subject, the more it became an object of ridicule. Where there was no music to be found, no informal outlet for one's individual strivings; where the tradition sold ready-made solace in the world to come or in a legendary past, Peretz was roused to heights of righteous anger. Until he discovered a positive use for this material, Peretz distilled his parodic venom into Yiddish miracle tales.

Verging on blasphemy, he turned the first-century miracle worker Hanina ben Dosa—a beloved figure of talmudic legend—into a heartless exploiter of his wife. Hanina studied while his family starved.[21] More subtly, Peretz retold the Golem of Prague legend to expose how the heirs of the great Maharal, Rabbi Judah Loew ben Bezalel, reduced the legacy of Jewish heroism to mere sophistry:

> To this very day the golem lies concealed in the uppermost part of the synagogue of Prague, covered with cobwebs that have been spun from wall to wall to encase the whole arcade so that it should be hidden from all human eyes, especially from pregnant wives in the women's section. No one is permitted to touch the cobwebs, for anyone who does so dies. Even the oldest congregants no longer remember the golem. However, Zvi the Sage, the grandson of the Maharal, still deliberates whether it is proper to include such a golem in a minyan or in a company for the saying of grace.[22]

Dead to Jewish collective memory, the golem lived on to delight the Jewish intelligentsia. Since cobwebs were the golem's only physical remains, they too were enshrouded in sanctity. If the Tishevits maskil knew how to tell stories, this is how he would tell them.

For parody to work, an audience has to recognize both the source and its subversion. Nothing could be more obvious than the set piece of Jewish sacred legend: the righteous rewarded for their suffering in the world to come. Nothing could be more accessible than a legendary hero who was neither scholar nor saint but a kind of *lamed-vovnik*, one of the thirty-six righteous men whose humility and anonymity secured the world from destruction. Such a down-and-out man was *Bontshe Shvayg* (Bontshe the Silent, 1894).[23] How then to alert the audience—thanks to Peretz's contacts in New York—that Bontshe's story was a parable for modern times? He invented a narrator who belonged more in the pages of the New York *Arbayter tsaytung* (Workers' Paper) than among the men swapping stories behind the study-house stove:

> Here on earth the death of Bontshe Shvayg made no impression. Try asking who Bontshe was, how he lived, what he died of (Did his heart give out? Did he drop from exhaustion? Did he break his back beneath too heavy a load?), and no one can give you an answer. For all you know, he might have starved to death.

The narrator's nervous tempo and complicated syntax; his string of rhetorical questions aimed at getting the facts straight—these suggested a formidable advocate in a court of law. Yet his sarcastic pronouncements on the human condition seemed to presage that the case would never be heard:

> The death of a tram horse would have caused more excitement. It would have been written up in the papers, hundreds of people would have flocked to see the carcass, or even the place where it lay. But that's only because horses are scarcer than people. Billions of people!

No man was better nicknamed than Bontshe, further evidence that he would make no waves: "He was born in silence. He lived in silence. He died in silence. And he was buried in a silence greater yet." So much for the facts. Erased from memory "here on earth," there was nothing more to say about this flattest of all flat characters. Happily, miraculously, the meaning of these facts was appreciated in the world to come. The heavenly hosts stood awaiting his arrival. Were it not for the mere technicality of a trial, the story of his becoming a celestial celebrity would be over.

Helping Peretz to narrate the trial were his ten years of practicing law in Zamość. Like similar trials held on earth, this one too was rigged. For one thing, the story was a melodrama complete with evil stepmother, sexual impotence, and a benefactor who sired the defendant's cruel son. Second, the presumption of innocence was so great that the presiding judge could undercut the defense at each rhetorical flourish. Third, the defendant was so terrified of the proceedings and so broken in spirit, that his wall of silence cracked when the grotesque story of his life was laid bare. Faced with such odds, the prosecuting attorney himself was cowed into silence.

Yet the heavens could not mend what the earth had destroyed. By trial's end, the folksy facade was just as surely obliterated as any pretense of heavenly justice. The divine judge—voicing the story's political message—counseled Bontshe if he had broken his silence, he might have brought down the walls of Jericho. Bontshe, no more prepared for heaven than he was for protest down below, responded with his long-awaited speech, asking simply, to be awarded a buttered roll each morning. The prosecutor burst out laughing at the very idea that a man so crushed could ever be recompensed, in heaven or on earth.

The folktale burlesque is what packed the final punch. The silent, suffering Bontshes could never make their protest heard until they renounced the heavenly claptrap about passive acceptance of their fate. Unlike Vladimir Korolenko's peasant hero Makar, who dreamt up a compensatory heaven out of his own religious imagination, Bontshe possessed no imagination at all, religious or otherwise.[24] Except for a near-fatal circumcision, Bontshe shared the lot of the lumpenproletariat. The whole folktale premise was foisted on him by a narrator who, from the outset, was skeptical of all rewards. Just as Bontshe stood by and watched the proceedings in terror, so the teller of his tale observed how the naive conventions, the supernatural trappings, and the grotesque characters all self-destructed in a gale of cynical laughter.

"Bontshe Shvayg" was an instant hit and helped Peretz to sell copies of the literary Yiddish miscellany in which it made its European debut. Elsewhere in *Literature and Life* (coedited by Peretz, David Pinsky, and Mordecai Spector), Peretz launched a spirited attack on the "Lovers of Zion" (*Hoveve Zion*) for making bedfellows of the reactionary rabbinate and for adulterating literary realism with a dangerous dose of romance and myth. "Sheydim af di beydim," began his brilliant polemic. "Demons in the attics" were believable once, in preindustrial times. Now, when Europe had already rejected realism, materialism, symbolism, and was caught up in occultism, of all things, the Jewish world was still mired in *komizm*, the comical mishmash of romantic Zionism.[25]

Peretz fought on all fronts. After alienating the old maskilic wing and new Zionists of the Hebrew literary establishment, he cast around for a new constituency. The wealthy Jewish positivists were only strategic allies, willing to support Peretz so long as he used Yiddish solely as a means of modernization. They dropped him after funding two volumes of *Di yidishe bibliotek*. Just then Peretz was discovered by the fledgling Jewish socialist movement; by the young radical David Pinsky in particular, on his way to

Vienna to study medicine. This collaboration resulted in the epoch-making *Yontef-bletlekh* (1894–1896).

"Passover is coming," announced the inaugural issue in Peretz's inimitable style, "and I'm inviting myself to your seder. Take me in!"

> I won't cost you much; *kneydlekh* I don't eat!
> Don't offer me the *khreyn*; I've had enough bitter herbs from birth!
> And don't make me pay with "plagues"; I've long ago forgiven the Egyptians. It's lost labor in any event since no one's ever gotten sick from written or printed plagues.
> And let's get rid of "Pour Out Thy Wrath!" . . . I'm much too young for that

Yosl Bergner, for Peretz, "It's No Good" (1950)

litany of curses. Don't poison my blood with revenge . . . I, for one, hope that better days will follow. . . .

I don't even want to recite "Next Year in Jerusalem!" Because "talkin' a lot won't make your belly hot."

So just let me wish you that come next year you'll forget the whole "How is this night different . . .?" and the "We were slaves in Egypt . . ."

And that when you open the door and call out—not in Laban's Aramaic formula "Let all who are hungry come and eat"—but as if you really meant it, that no one will enter; because there won't be anyone who *needs* to enter!

Stripped of all religious and national content, with all the hallowed phrases of the Passover rite subjected to ridicule, Peretz's socialist seder whetted young appetites for more. The elders—in Warsaw and St. Petersburg—were outraged. Wasting no time, Pinsky was off to Russia in the summer of 1894, where he organized the first of many "Jargon Committees," underground cells that distributed radical works in Yiddish. The innocent-looking, hard-hitting issues of *Yontef-bletlekh* were the hottest item.[26] Also, far from the reaches of the Russian censor and the Zionist opposition, Peretz enjoyed direct access to the socialist readers of the New York *Arbayter-tsaytung*.[27]

For all that, the radical honeymoon ended. With the police on his trail, Pinsky left Russia in 1896. All the highbrow and popular publications folded. Peretz's only son Lucian was suicidal. "Everything is lost, broken," Peretz confided to Pinsky, now in Berlin. "I have reached the conclusion that I lack the powers to attract people to myself; neither can I go serve others, so I wander about among different galaxies around a lone star with an ironic-silly tail and there is no place for me anywhere."[28] As part of a massive roundup by the tsarist police, Peretz was arrested in August 1899 for appearing at an illegal meeting called in support of striking workers.[29]

Where would a middle-aged, agnostic Jew doing time in a Warsaw prison at century's end find solace from his record of failure and his dread of the future? Like others around the world, in less dire straits than himself, he turned to myth and the irrational. He resolved the inherent contradiction of the fin de siècle (end or beginning? millennium or apocalypse?) by choosing flight, as others chose to fight for the brave new world. Although the direction of Peretz's flight—to the Bible, medieval romance, Yiddish lovesong, and hasidic legend—made him the standard bearer of Jewish neoromanticism, the force of his turnabout placed him in the company of

Freud, Einstein, and Lenin.[30] What Peretz rescued from the ruins of his personal and cultural past was to determine, if not the future course of humanity, then the future course of Jewish storytelling.

A loyal son of the Haskalah, Peretz valued the Bible as the arbiter of classical style and the prophets as the voice of Jewish conscience. Under the spell of romanticism, he conjured up the prophets as the font of poetic vision as well, the wellspring of modern literary movements.[31] For Peretz the positivist, the Bible was also the record of a nation's history. For Peretz the ideologue of cultural renewal, the Bible was the Jewish perspective on the world.[32] His first mandate to the Yiddishist movement in 1908 was to retranslate the Bible into a modern idiom.[33]

Peretz continued writing in Hebrew, or paid to have his works translated, but he never warmed to the idea of rescuing the legends of the Talmud for modern times. Excessive talmudic study, like excessive doses of modernist angst, produced nothing but madness, "zigzags and dilemmas and hair-splittings."[34] Peretz the neoromantic wanted to wipe the slate clean. He wanted a new oral Torah without its old content. He wanted a Jewish humanism and piety without Jewish law. He wanted folk narrators who raided the Talmud only for a legendary motif, a turn of phrase.

Instead of studying Talmud, a male prerogative in any event, Peretz re-imagined his Jews, male and especially female, singing Yiddish folksongs about love and death. Sitting in prison, he could recall with fondness the songs he himself had collected over the past four years among Jewish artisans and seamstresses in Warsaw. These anonymous lyrics were a mirror of the people's life.[35] They expressed the ethos and moral sensibility of the folk far better than any rabbinic dictum. The folksong recitals at his home with that indefatigable young fieldworker, Judah Leib Cahan (b. 1881), had the intensity of a revivalist meeting.[36] Peretz and the young intellectuals (aspiring folklorists and aspiring writers) spent their Saturday afternoons sharing a mystical experience of self-discovery.[37]

If rabbinic lore seemed stale, folklore offered a new and seemingly inexaustible source of poetic inspiration. If rabbinic lore seemed reactionary and remote, folklore was a secular alternative of the people, for the people. If Peretz had once thought that Yiddish, and Jews in general, were "without feeling for nature, for simplicity, for love, beauty and poetry," these folksongs proved otherwise.[38] And if the Poles, bereft of a political base and state support, could use folklore to affirm their national identity, then so could Jewish intellectuals. While his Polish compatriots, however, predicated the study of *Jewish* folklore on rapid assimilation, if not actual conversion, of the Jews, Peretz was among the first of the positivists to turn that study into a tool of Jewish national revival.[39]

The same ideal—self-knowledge as the basis of a new secular identity—inspired others to rehabilitate Hasidism as a Jewish folk phenomenon. Simon Dubnow, the dean of east European Jewish historians, began his explorations of the hasidic movement in the pages of the Russian-Jewish periodical *Voskhod* (1888–1893). There, or in the Polish translations of the Warsaw *Izraelita,* Peretz had surely seen the Ba'al Shem Tov described as a radical reformer and the tales *In Praise of the Besht* defended as latter-day Gospels. Perhaps Peretz also knew the work that had inspired Dubnow to begin with: Ernst Renan's *History of Christianity*. Like Renan, Dubnow separated the nature-loving spiritualist from the earth-bound institutions he spawned; the teacher from his disciples; the man from the miracles.[40] If the Besht could be Jesus, he could be anything at all.

Equally bold was Micah Joseph Berdyczewski's manifesto "The Soul of Hasidim" (1899), which identified the "new hasidic man" (the first generation of hasidim) with the Nietzschean transvaluation of values. "Standing upright, with the spirit of life in him, a spirit which penetrates the world open before him in all its breadth and depth . . . he will be like a king among troops, like a man with the wreath of God on his head among those who sit in darkness."[41] Virile antinomian, pantheist, king among troops, the Besht and his early followers were revolutionaries for all seasons. The fact that Peretz met a hasidic rebbe only once in his life, in the offices of the Warsaw Jewish community council, gave him freer rein than Dubnow, who had to mediate historical documents, and Berdyczewski, who had to reconcile his personal experience.[42] Peretz's hasidim were free to dance and sing to their hearts' content.

Peretz, much like his contemporaries, salvaged from the ruins only those aspects of Jewish culture that could stand for secular humanistic values: the Bible as prophecy and history; folksong as lyric poetry; sacred legend as collective saga; Yiddish as the surrogate for nationhood; Hasidism as the route to transcendence. He discovered these equations not by delving into his own soul or by "drawing from the well" of his personal past. He found them because his life had become a record of loss, and the road of return had been marked by "zigzags and dilemmas and hairsplittings." Had Peretz remained a provincial lawyer and never moved to Warsaw; had he not been hired to chronicle the impoverishment of Polish Jewry; had he not been exposed to various utopian alternatives; and had he not been imprisoned for endorsing one of them, he would never have become the master architect of Jewish modernism.

By the time he was released from the infamous Tenth Pavilion in November 1899, the blueprint was complete. The same shtetl whose epitaph he had just written was rehabilitated as an ideal setting for fantasy and heroism. The same hasidim whose quest for miracles and melodies condemned their loved ones to death now became narrators in their own right. The same folktales and legends that taught the repression of women, the sanctification of cobwebs, and the justification of suffering were now reenlisted as exempla of secular faith. Even that old well in Zamość became a significant landmark in his fictional landscape.[43] Peretz's self-transformation on the eve of the twentieth century effectively initiated the art of creative betrayal.

Now began the ordeal of simplicity. For mystical access to the poetry of the folk, he resumed the seances on Saturday afternoons. For physical access to the new Yiddish reader, he (along with other neoromantic writers) began publishing in *Der yid,* the first highbrow Yiddish newspaper, launched by the Zionist movement in 1899.[44] But having moved his career one way, how could he, at the age of forty-seven, veer in the opposite direction? As the first writer to explore the psychopathology of the shtetl talmudist, how could he turn the same student into a romantic hero? Past master at pitting one traditional voice against another, how could he rein in that satiric talent and adopt a folk persona? How could he make the miracles he disparaged come alive? Not easily.

Hasidism was so alien that the only way to write about it, at first, was in Hebrew, the language of learning, and intended for male readers from the house of study. As if to signal his profound discomfort with all that, Peretz built in a foil for each of his early hasidic monologues: a Lithuanian son-in-law who refused to dance at his own, hasidic, wedding; a teacher who constantly debated the freethinkers in his mind. "You must place yourself in the vantage point of the *believers,*" Peretz advised a young Hebrew writer from Kovno, "and speak and narrate just the way they do." Yet as one who did not believe in the miracles himself, Peretz could scarcely invent a credible narrator who did.[45]

Arthur Kolnik, for Peretz, "The Scholar from Radzivil" (1948)

Yoykhenen the Teacher is Peretz's first sustained folk narrator (1897), and a belligerent one at that.[46] Cognizant of the skeptical reader to the point of obsession, Yoykhenen defends the open-ended quality of his tale. Unlike "certain scribblers . . . who make up books for the common folk—for cooks and chambermaids—fellows who think up fairy tales about cutthroats and robbers, about forged promissory notes and counterfeiters: anything to frighten people, anything to make their blood run cold," he, Reb Yoykhenen, is constrained to tell nothing but the truth. He can impose no artificial beginnings or endings on what he himself has experienced. "Each thing hangs on something that came before," and each in turn can take us back to the mysteries of Creation (Y 49). Reality for Yoykhenen is grounded in faith, in subjectivity. The body, plagued by doubt, can be redeemed only through the spirit. So far, so good. The hasid's literary-theological credo should now segue into a believable, if meandering, faith tale—were it not that Peretz has already portrayed Reb Yoykhenen as an enlightened rela-tivist. "It's just that each person has *his own* rebbe, *his own* faith, his own little god, you might say" (Y 46, E 298). It's hard to believe in a hapless hasid who can reconcile secularism and faith by claiming them to be iden-tical; harder still to credit his own spiritual quest and discovery, at story's end. Yoykhenen's resounding moral, that "He Who Bestows Life Bestows the Wherewithal to Live Also," has a hollow ring if every belief is as good as any other.[47]

Old Chaim of *Mishnas khsidim* (The Teaching of Hasidim, 1894) is scarcely more reliable.[48] He is meant to be the ideal simple hasid, unable to follow the Lithuanian son-in-law's learned discourse. Contrariwise, whatever the rebbe spoonfed him is holy: learning is but the outer shell and Hasidism is the soul; all of life is a song and dance before the Lord. The hasidic doctrine of emanation is here transformed into a romantic quest for harmony in nature, music, dance, and the life of the collective. The hasid's faith in the zaddik becomes for Peretz a Nietzschean search for a leader who can bear the world's suffering. Most concretely, Hasidism be-comes a way of telling stories.

By 1900 Peretz finally succeeded in making these romantic, fin-de-siècle concerns speak through a credible hasidic storyteller. He packaged it as "a tale for Simhath Torah, told by an old *melamed,*" only this time Peretz came to celebrate the holiday, not to bury it. Perhaps "Between Two Mountains" succeeded where the others had failed because Peretz (reportedly) wrote it while in prison.[49] Or perhaps, on this third try, he had figured out how a domestic tragedy might be turned into a miracle tale. Besides, it happened long ago, not in the squalor of Reb Elye's own shtetl of Tishevits and not in Reb Yoykhenen's Warsaw tenement, but to members of the shtetl aris-tocracy. When *their* daughters went into labor, a miracle was assured. Most of the credit for "Between Two Mountains," however, went to its narrator, Reb Shmaye the Bialer Hasid, who found himself at a fateful moment teaching in the home of a wealthy misnagid. Here he could stand between the two mountains of misnagdic scholarship and hasidic fervor and live to tell the tale.

Reb Shmaye is a storyteller in Peretz's own image: he combines the language of learning with unusual descriptive powers. Though himself a man of faith, he can also envision other people's doubts. Shmaye understands why Talmud study without a social base and without aggadic flights of fancy can drive a young man like Noah (a future rebbe) out of the yeshiva at Brisk. The teacher's own spiritual yearnings are pure enough that he does not expect the young hasidic master to spend his time giving out amulets and performing miracles. Yet Shmaye is true believer enough to explain the labor pains of the Brisker rabbi's daughter as divine punishment. "It was known that because the Brisker rov had once ordered a hasid to be shaved—that is, to have his beard and sidecurls shorn by gentiles— the rabbi's good name had been tarnished in the eyes of the saintly men of his generation." How to turn the shtetl talmudist into a romantic hero? By charting his journey from the cold and empty precincts of the Lithuanian yeshiva to the warm embrace of the Polish-hasidic court. How to make the miraculous come alive in a skeptical age? By fashioning a narrator who perceives the hand of heaven at work the moment he sets out to fetch the Brisker rov.

Will the daughter merit a miracle for the sake of her learned father, or will the rabbi's sin be visited upon his child? Will the "two mountains" be reconciled? Meanwhile, "the wind increased, piercing the cloud as if it were tearing apart a sheet of paper. The wind began to chase one piece of cloud into and over another, as if herding ice floes on a river" (Y 109, E 189). Folk narrators, for Peretz, routinely yoked the concrete to the abstract.[50] With so versatile a storyteller as Reb Shmaye, Peretz can eat his cake and have it too.

The "cake" is the story's climactic vision, an apotheosis of romanticism called by another name.

> "And your Torah, Noah?"
> "Would you like to see it, Rabbi?"
> "See the Torah?" The Brisker was astonished.
> "Come, I will show you. I will show you the glory and the joy that radiate from it and touch all of Israel." (Y 115–116, E 194)

Accompanied by Reb Shmaye, the two spiritual giants look down from the rebbe's balcony at hasidim dancing in honor of Simhath Torah, but what they see is nature in perfect harmony with man, religion in harmony with life, and disparate individuals united in song. "Everything sang—the sky, the constellations above, and the earth below. The soul of the world sang. Everything sang!" Yet never was a miracle so filtered through the eyes of its beholders. The Brisker rov has only to remind his former pupil that it is time for afternoon prayers, and the spell is broken.

> Silence fell. The curtain closed again before my eyes. Above me, an ordinary sky, and below, an ordinary pasture; ordinary Hasidim in torn caftans murmuring old tattered fragments of song. The flames were extinguished. I looked at the rebbe. His face too was somber.

In Peretz's own day, the Brisker rov's disenchantment was shared by very few readers. Alone among contemporary critics, Hirsh Dovid Nomberg maintained that the rov, of plain speech and direct action, was far more memorable than the rebbe, who didn't even perform the deeds expected of a zaddik and was merely a mouthpiece for universal values.[51] But readers aspired to the rebbe's vision of things. Since they had no intention of becoming hasidim themselves, or for that matter of returning to the study of Talmud, they were content to read a story about Simhath Torah that celebrated the universal appeal of Judaism: music, joy, nature, unity.

Less obvious than the romantic betrayal of Hasidism was the aesthetic betrayal of folklore. Reb Shmaye's tale was perfectly structured, his descriptions clipped and vivid, his language learned. Dreams were rendered as transparent allegories; hasidic revelry was turned into a fleeting poetic vision. No trace remained in this or in any of the stories and monologues to follow of Reb Nahman's scatalogical flourish in "Master of Prayer." Never would Peretz's folk heroes be caught boozing and puking like Elinke Bulke of the Ayalon burial society, or even butchering the Passover Haggadah, like Kalmen the boor. Never would they speak the street Yiddish that Berdyczewski was just then introducing into his own neohasidic and stylized folktales. The appearance of Berdyczewski's chapbook, *A mayse fun eynem a koval vos hot farsamt zayn vayb* (A Tale of a Blacksmith Who Poisoned His Wife, 1902), outraged Peretz.[52] Not because it told of a Jew who would do such a thing, but because both the convict and the story's narrator employed coarse language. Folk characters were free to use regional expressions, Peretz argued, but the narrator had to rise above the crowd.[53] Yiddish stories and storytellers, in Peretz's scheme of things, had to conform to a modern poetic sensibility—even if it meant reinventing the folk.

What little Peretz knew about the folk in 1900 he knew from the Yiddish lovesongs he collected and rewrote, a few popular anthologies of hasidic tales, and his own ambivalent memories of Zamość.[54] Folk speech was for him the language of the Zamość study house, which is why his preferred folk narrators were still mostly *rebes* (teachers of boys) or *rebeim* (hasidic leaders). Peretz would never entrust a monologue to a semiliterate blacksmith who lusted after his brother's wife and poisoned his own. In retelling a tale of passion, Peretz ensured that the narrator was removed from the event in time, place, and temperament. Yoykhenen the Teacher spun a batch of tales of bygone days when rich ladies were too sophisticated to read the *Tsene-rene* or other medieval works, but could not yet wile away their time playing the piano or reading Yiddish potboilers ("The Curse"). Or he told of two brothers, one a famous rabbi, the other a good-for-nothing, who lived before the partitions of Poland ("The Punishment"). Or he counseled Itsikl his student, who believed in progress and technology, with a "true story" in praise of Reb Zishele, of blessed memory, that proved the decline of the generations.[55] In an advanced industrial age, when ghosts no longer "gallivanted in the attics," Peretz looked for storytellers who straddled the two mountains of faith and skepticism. Better yet, he found one who was a poet-visionary-and-author in his own right.

If Reb Nahman hadn't lived, Peretz would have invented him. For the narrator was central to the story's meaning and believability. The narrator alone grounded the supernatural in a real human experience. But this aesthetic justification for using such a mediating voice was not enough. For Peretz there had to be an ideological justification as well. A folk narrator was needed in order to allow for a range of concerns that could not be expressed any other way. And what Peretz was struggling with in the first decade of the twentieth century was a course of redemption after all sacred and secular schemes had collapsed. Nahman was the ideal mouthpiece for Peretz's hopes and fears.[56]

Surrounded by disciples to whom he could confide in moments of despair and to whom he could tell stories to ward off despair, Reb Nahman was also a wanderer—not, like Peretz, "among different galaxies around a lone star with an ironic-silly tail"—but in the metaphorical desert, far from human habitation. Though Nahman's body was engaged in restorative acts, even in artistic creation, his disembodied soul was lost in the sands of doubt and confusion. The misnagid, who followed the dictates of the Law, wandered according to a plan, but the hasid was ready to go wherever his search led him. This is what the rebbe confided near the conclusion of the Sabbath, in that between-time so beloved of hasidic storytellers, and this is what his loyal scribe recorded by way of introduction to "Reb Nakhmenke's Stories."[57]

During his desert wanderings, Reb Nakhmenke sees a *makhne foygl,* a flock of birds, hopping along in formation. Scrawny, almost wingless, these birds are organized behind a leader, but when Nakhmenke asks the bird king their destination, he replies that "he was in doubt whether he was

Jakob Steinhardt, for Peretz, "The Wandering in the Desert—From Reb Nakhmenke's Stories" (1920)

dragging the flock behind himself, or whether they were pushing him forward" (Y 195). In any event, they are about to attack the Old House, whose inhabitants have denuded the forests and caged the birds, leaving them with nothing to feed on but dried leaves. This is why they have no good wings to fly with. Reaching the Old House first, Reb Nakhmenke finds a dilapidated castle with rotting portraits, neglected treasures, and half-dead owners. These last are descendants of the old aristocracy, who know that there is no escape from the approaching birds and that the castle walls will not protect them. The only hope—a wild plan advanced by the youngest one, a kabbalist—is to burn the parchments scattered over the floor, a time-honored method of turning oneself into a bird. But just as the auto-da-fé is about to begin, an old man bellows "Forgerers, murderers, arsonists!" and blows out the only lamp, thrusting the Old House into darkness.

> "How does the story end?" we pleaded with him when Reb Nakhmenke fell silent.
> "There is no end," he replied. "Birds with wings like fins, with marks instead of wings, and thin sticks in lieu of legs, don't reach the Old House all that soon . . ."

The same birds once appeared to the real Reb Nahman in a dream dense with Lurianic symbolism. That dream ended on a resounding note of tikkun.[58] Peretz's revisitation of the dream is open-ended, its symbolism transparent. The birds represent the starving, dehumanized masses now politicized behind a feckless leader. The Old House, symbol of the ancien régime, is blamed for robbing society of its riches and natural resources. By destroying the parchments—the cultural remains of its civilization— the surviving elite hope to buy time from the cultureless mob. Only the old guardian prevents the last great leveling of society. That leaves the wanderer, the perpetual seeker, caught between an elite—too demoralized to defend its values—and the approaching mob, thirsting for revenge.

That a hasidic dream-tale could be used to address such concerns was precisely what Peretz valued in Reb Nahman's literary legacy. It is pointless to fault Peretz for reducing Nahman's multivalent texts to a single level of meaning.[59] Reb Nahman was another of Peretz's masks and Hasidism was another way of defending his doubts against the revolutionary slogans of the left and of staking his position against the intellectual sellout of the Right. Through the parable of the birds, Peretz warned those who mobilized the masses against being led by the masses. He exposed the writers, so frantic to save their own skins that they would destroy all the parchments entrusted to their care. Only the poet-seeker retained his independence, his clarity of vision. Never more secular than when posing as an imaginary hasid, and never more hungry for transcendence than when searching for raw data, Peretz was always the artist pushing for new expressive possibilities.

Reb Nakhmenke was a vastly more congenial stand-in than any of the others, first, because the historical Reb Nahman had intended his *Tales* to explore the crisis of leadership and faith in a world at war with itself. Secondly, Reb Nakhmenke presupposed a narrator modeled on Nathan of Nemirov, who bore witness to the zaddik's greatness. The narrator's mood-setting preamble, with the wind "reciting Dirges" outside the window (Y 188) and with every nuance of the Rebbe's voice inspiring awe, conjured up a community of faithful disciples (a Gemeinschaft) that justified the whole storytelling enterprise. Storytelling was a modern guide for the perplexed.

And not all is so somber. To break the despondency that descends upon them one Saturday evening, the rebbe's hasidim begin to swap miracle tales, some going back to the beginning of the movement, others concerning Reb Nakhmenke himself.[60] The narrator's special favorite is the miracle that occurred only weeks before, when quite by chance the zaddik's hidden powers were revealed. It happened through a nanny goat that had stopped giving milk, and it shows, so claims the hasid, the zaddik's humility and kindness. Just then the rebbe himself returns and begins to tell his own story, about a billy goat, not a nanny goat, which has something to do with the meaning of "revealing." By the end of this thricetold tale, told with verve and good humor, the hidden link becomes clear. The zaddik just told them about a billy goat whose magical horns could pierce the heavens and force the coming of the messiah. Once these cosmic powers were discovered, however, the billy goat sacrificed his horns in order to supply Jews with pieces of horn for their snuff boxes. Isn't this analogous to Reb Nakhmenke himself who, for the sake of an old lady whose nanny goat stopped giving milk, squandered his spiritual energy on the day-to-day needs of his people? And isn't this analogous to the writer I. L. Peretz, who knows that his reputation as a cultural figure and a secular rebbe has grown at the expense of his artistic aspirations?[61] Telling tales is a powerful way to cement a community, but it might also mean the end of his career.

Peretz overcame the otherness of Hasidism by imagining himself as a hasidic storyteller surrounded by faithful followers. It was a remarkable feat for someone raised on the stern rationalism of Maimonides and the acerbic irony of Heine. Along with mastering the forms—monologue, dialogue, exemplum, dream tale, miracle tale—Peretz recovered the context of hasidic storytelling as well. From Reb Elye's defiant slap in defense of foiled miracles, Peretz had come a long way to imagining the exaltation of Reb Nakhmenke's presence. It was a longer way still from playing the statistician to entering the character of the zaddik himself, merging with his dreams and speaking through his fears. Once the lawyer from Zamość became a zaddik in disguise, he was ready for other feats of storytelling magic. He was ready to invent Yiddish folktales and romances more perfect than any told before.

The secret to making fantasy and folklore come alive lay, paradoxically, in the very practice of law that Peretz had to abandon. Was it any wonder that his hasidic monologues and tales rested on the presence of an eyewitness who could vouchsafe the miracle, cut through the tangled web that separated the predictable from the supernatural, and testify to a miracle-working nonaverage man? During his storytelling clerkship, when Peretz made reason and faith adversaries, the jury was left to decide whether to follow the laws of nature and a regime of scientific self-study, on the one hand, or to keep faith in divine law on the other. In the trial between Elye the hasid and Shmerl the maskil, it was the shrayber who cast the deciding vote, just as in the world to come, it was the prosecuting attorney who had the last laugh. Lemech of yeshiva fame could either achieve transcendence or remain alive. Even Reb Shmaye the hasid could perceive the miracle of Simhath Torah only so long as he looked down on the proceedings with the rebbe's eyes. The hardnosed lawyer, more often than not, got a better hearing than the fabulist.[62]

Now, as Peretz set about fashioning *folkstimlekhe geshikhtn*—not folktales per se but "stories in the folk vein"—he discovered a new set of rules.[63] How much modern meaning a traditional narrative could plausibly sustain depended, for starters, on stricter adherence to the formal conventions of epic narrative. It wasn't always possible or desirable to let a stand-in folk Jew do the talking, even if he was really a yeshiva student in disguise. By obeying the historical (folklorical) laws that governed the telling of a romance or exemplum, the storyteller could produce a new set of meanings.

By playing with *variant* meanings of law, the storyteller could re-create the folktale and betray it at one and the same time. Peretz came into his own as a modern Yiddish storyteller when he took the narrative one step beyond the witness stand. There he found characters worthy of recollection because their lives were ruled by conscience alone. The freedom they enacted within the tale invariably clashed with the hierarchical universe presupposed by the orderliness of the tale itself. The drama of faith against reason had played itself out in the nineteenth-century courtroom. Free will versus determinism was the oldest—and most insoluble—case in the book and as such released the art of storytelling from its temporal boundaries.

So the world of romance beckoned, as it had to Reb Nahman long ago and to Isaac Meir Dik only yesterday. Peretz began by trying to adapt the unwieldy storybook conventions and the artificially cultivated Germanicized Yiddish of the Dik variety. The mixed result was "The Three Wedding Canopies: Two Red and One Black. A Tale from Beyond the Mountains of Darkness" (*Dray khupes: Tsvey royte—eyne a shvartse,* 1901).[64] Set on the other side of the legendary Sambatyon River, in a country known as Wonderland, in the reign of King Solomon XXVII, the story combines a few too many layers of Jewish and European fantasy. Ill at ease with so much blatant

Yosl Bergner, for Peretz, "The Three Wedding Canopies" (1950)

supernaturalism, Peretz has his bookish narrator deflate the story with humorous asides. The royal hunt only shoots at beasts of prey and poisonous snakes, he assures his readers, and the royal banquet is strictly kosher. The thieves sent by the usurper of the throne to murder King Solomon and his daughter "naturally did not talk about religious commandments and good deeds *(mitsves un maysim-toyvim)*" when plotting their next move. All very clever, but inappropriate for the burden that this elaborate tale was designed to bear.

"Three Canopies" was Peretz's design for the social revolution. That explains why the first two canopies are red, and not white, as should have been the case in the clear-cut world of the romance. There are also two canopies instead of one, because Peretz wanted the true and natural revolution to be carried out according to a visionary plan (the role of the dreamer-messiah) that is equally sensitive to man's artistic strivings (the role of the artist, with alabaster hands and glowing eyes, who worked "with the joy of God creating the world").[65] To assure the moral value of each individual come the End of Days, Deborah, one of the two heroines, awakens the sleeping messiah. Though raised as the villain's daughter, Deborah is beautiful and pure. Nature would prevail over nurture in the new age of individual freedom. Such pipedreams were still the stuff of romance in 1901. All the greater, therefore, was Peretz's sense of betrayal upon hearing of the violent Moscow uprising in December 1905. He shot back with "Hope and Fear" (1906), an anguished response to the fate of individual freedom with the coming of a classless society. Recognizing, too, that "Three Canopies" had been a flop, Peretz pushed it aside.[66]

Since the style of "Three Canopies" was too cute, the setting too remote, and the scope too ambitious, Peretz returned to what he knew best: the learned style of rabbinic storytelling; the Safed and Prague of the medieval Yiddish story; and the schematic *shtetlekh* of hasidic legend. Besides, Dik had already discovered that miracles were possible even in eastern Europe, so long as they happened "long ago," before the partitions of Poland. "There once dwelt in Safed a Jew of great wealth and good fortune," began Peretz's most accomplished romance, *Mesires-nefesh* (Devotion Without End, 1904), "who traded in jewels, diamonds, and other precious stones. He was truly a man of great wealth, not like the upstarts of our day." *Mesires-nefesh*, by one linguist's count, has the highest density of Hebrew-Aramaic words in all of Peretz's oeuvre, which was quite in keeping with its Palestinian setting and its miraculous occurrences.[67] As for its theme—why squeeze social revolution out of a love story when love carries its own transcendent message?

As in romance, where all the characters belong to a kind of aristocracy, so all the heroes and heroines of "Devotion Without End" are heightened human beings, each one a model of devotion. The nameless patriarch "of great wealth and good fortune," whom we first meet in his magnificent garden overlooking the sea of Galilee (Peretz later wondered whether the Sea was indeed visible from as far away as Safed), is especially devoted to his youngest and favorite daughter, Sarah. He marries her off to a brilliant young Talmud scholar named Chiya, the lone survivor of a grand lineage. Like King Solomon, Chiya knows the language of the birds and beasts. Like the hero of east European legend, his deeds of charity are numberless and he becomes "a spokesman for his people." Thus Chiya is a man equally devoted to the study of Torah and the Seven Wisdoms, to his people, and to his one and only daughter Miriam. Miriam's moral education is entrusted to his good wife Sarah. Lying on her deathbed, Sarah in old age promises to intercede from heaven should there be "any perplexity with regard to the child."

After Sarah's death, Chiya disposes of his wealth, turns his palace into a yeshiva, and throws himself heart and soul into training a generation of scholars. Among them Chiya secretly hopes to find his daughter a bridegroom whose devotion to Torah is utterly selfless. For even Torah study is open to corruption, Chiya confides to the head of the Babylonian yeshiva in a flowery Hebrew letter (which "must lose much of its sweetness" when transposed into "profane Yiddish" [Y 212, E 122]). There are five gradations of Torah study, all but the last corrupted by such ulterior motives as competitiveness, desire for fame, intellectual vanity, material greed. "But Reb Chiya desires for his Miriam only one that is pure within and pure without," and that someone he will recognize through his eyes and by his voice. No room for deception here. The route to transcendence, for men at least, is through the rigors of a mental curriculum that will master selfish desire.

While Chiya spends his days eavesdropping on his students, waiting for that voice of purity, Miriam is busy visiting her mother's grave. At the graveside she prays not for herself but for her father's well-being, to learn how to gladden his heart. Then one day the longed-for sign: a student arrives whose voice is pure. But he is ignorant of the Torah, illiterate even in prayers, and when the youth lifts his downcast eyes, Chiya sees before him "a soul that has been cursed." Chananiah is his name, and his extraordinary odyssey is a double tale of false devotion and divine anger.

Chananiah's mother, in her obsessive devotion to her son, neglected her daughter. What's more, she failed three times to discipline her son when a teacher of false Torah perverted his mind with "the art of negating all things," planting "the bitter herbs of pride and presumption" in the boy's heart (Y 220, E 127). Finally confronted with the crippling effect of nihilism, his inability to say anything that carried the power of "yes," Chananiah decided to repent. But then something happened to break his resolve.

There lived in Jerusalem a corrupt and wealthy butcher who was insanely devoted to his daughter. No one but a poor carpenter would agree to marry her. So the butcher hired two scholars to find an unsuspecting groom from afar. After two years of futile search, the candidate appeared of his own accord at the gates of Jerusalem: "a poor youth dressed in sackcloth, with a hempen rope around his loins and a staff cut from an almond tree in his hand." Despite appearances, this wandering beggar possessed purity of Torah, having been taught in the desert by Elijah the Prophet himself. Delighted, the miserly butcher rushed ahead with the wedding at which the bridegroom, according to custom, delivered a learned discourse on the Torah.

That was Chananiah's undoing, for as he sat among the wedding guests and overheard the others praise the young man's learning, Chananiah felt "as if a serpent had stung him"; he rose to demolish with his Torah of negation everything the bridegroom had said. The repercussions were swift: the butcher threw out the groom and dragged in the poor carpenter to marry the girl instead; Chananiah was punished and forgot all the Torah he had ever learned; Chananiah's mother was punished and forced to accept the humiliated bridegroom as a husband for her neglected daughter; and Chananiah exchanged clothes with his future brother-in-law whose forgiveness he had just secured. The sinner was cast into the wilderness dressed in sackcloth, instructed to pray that his staff might someday blossom to signal the restoration of his soul.

This double marriage effected an act of tikkun. The poor carpenter was revealed as a *lamed-vovnik,* one of the hidden saints, and the butcher's daughter was good and pious, her father notwithstanding. Yet unlike Reb Nahman's vision of things, the world of appearances did not yield to a higher reality. In Peretz's retelling, the supernatural is benign, and its primary function is to underscore free will and individual worth. With all the secondary characters happily married off, Chananiah is free to actualize his full human potential.

One day "he poured a handful of sand upon his head and then, in self-castigation, he stood on one leg, crying out toward heaven, 'Torah, Torah!' He cried with earnest devotion, *mit mesires-nefesh*" (Y 231, E 135). He then saw in a dream that his redemption was at hand if he went to Safed, entered the yeshiva there, was married, and through that marriage his staff would blossom and sprout almonds.

That is how the student of the pure voice and cursed eyes comes to study Torah, only for its own sake, without hope of reward; as Reb Chiya explains, even if the curse is lifted from the boy's head he will still have no share of paradise. He proves to be a most diligent student, single-minded in his dedication to the relearning of Torah.

Two very learned snakes, meanwhile, speak to Reb Chiya in the garden. Through their heavily Hebraicized debate, he discovers that Chananiah's fate has been sealed in heaven: "Half of his sin would be atoned for by the blessings of marriage, and the other half by his death."

> For Reb Chiya now found himself in a terrible dilemma. If he did nothing to further the marriage of Chananiah, he would be contesting the will of Paradise and Chananiah would never recover the Torah. If he helped Chananiah to marry, he would be destroying the youth with his own hands and would, furthermore, be helping to condemn a Jewish daughter [Miriam] to early widowhood. (Y 239, E 140)

Even before Reb Chiya receives instruction from his dead wife, the reader knows what the decision will be: the male route to transcendence is through intellectual pursuits. Faced with the terrible choice between sacrificing his daughter and betraying the Torah, Reb Chiya, like Abraham before him, chooses to heed the will of paradise and go ahead with the wedding.

But what of Miriam herself, whose marriageability set the whole plot in motion? Like every character, she follows her own conscience, and so, quite independently of her father, she has fallen in love with Chananiah. "I would surrender my life in his behalf," she announces to Reb Chiya. From a dream she learns that "true devotion, devotion without end, can be shown only by a wife," while from her mother's example she knows that a woman can show devotion even from the grave (Y 243–244, E 142–143). This is the female principle: a woman's route to transcendence is through sacrificing herself for others.[68]

Miriam finally has her chance at the end of the seven-day wedding celebration, when the white staff turns green, tiny blossoms begin to appear, and Chananiah begins to reveal to Reb Chiya the secrets and mysteries of the Torah. With the men happily engaged in what brings them greatest fulfillment, Miriam steals Chananiah's sackcloth, sneaks into the garden,

Arthur Kolnik, for Peretz, "Reb Khayiml at the Wedding" (1948)

and is fatally bitten by the snake Achnai, the messenger of the Angel of Death, thinking she's her husband. Realizing that they have been duped by Miriam's extraordinary act of self-sacrifice, the heavenly host order her soul restored at once. Miriam refuses unless they agree to a permanent substitution: her death for his. Husband and wife are reunited, and Achnai is promptly dismissed, never to be heard from again.

The ending is worthy of Reb Nahman: the Torah is restored and the Shechinah-Lover resurrected. The use of traditional motifs is equally worthy of the hasidic master: Elijah teaches Torah in the desert, a staff of knowledge miraculously blooms, and the rabbi's daughter triumphs over death on her wedding day, as it is written (Babylonian Talmud, Shabbat 156b):

> For R. Akiba had a daughter. Now astrologers [lit. Chaldeans] told him, On the day she enters the bridal chamber a snake will bite her and she will die. He was very worried about this. On that day [of her marriage] she took a brooch and stuck it into the wall and by chance it sank into the eye of a serpent. The following morning, when she took it out, the snake came trailing after it. "What did you do?" her father asked her. "A poor man came to our door in the evening," she replied, "and everybody was busy at the banquet, and there was none to attend to him. So I took the portion which was given to me and gave it to him." "And you have done a good deed," said he to her. Thereupon R. Abiba went out and lectured: "*But charity delivereth from death* [Prov. 10:2]: and not merely from an an unnatural death, but from death itself."

As in the rabbinic tale, the daughter's act of charity on her wedding day (when a poor man's cry would go unheeded) is a celebration of free will and female initiative.[69] But instead of pitting the daughter against astrological fate and a father's doubts, Peretz borrows the legend to complete the three stages of devotion he has so carefully laid out. First, there is Chiya's devotion to his daughter: he is ready to sacrifice her, but not himself. Then there is Chananiah's devotion to the Torah for whose sake he undergoes extraordinary self-sacrifice. Miriam's devotion to Chananiah, finally, is the highest level of all because she alone is willing to die for someone she loves.

The story ends where it began, in the garden, because this is nothing less than a reversal of Eden. There the serpent seduced Eve and led to the painful acquisition of knowledge. Here Eve outsmarts the serpent and reveals a woman's love that passes even the transcendence that men acquire through their pursuit of knowledge.

Without the cloying manner of Hans Christian Andersen in "The Snow Queen," and with a minimum of fantastical trappings, Peretz develops the identical theme of man's redemption by woman.[70] But Safed reimagined has more to offer than a castle in the snow. An apotheosis of love and spiritual discipline takes place in Peretz's garden. Body and soul are reunited. *Here on earth* the highest level of devotion is attained both by women and by men. Once more back in Eden, with rabbinic figures peeking through the branches and witty snakes quoting learned passages, Peretz has brought the Jewish romance to fulfillment.

Stories in the Folk Vein advanced the art of Yiddish storytelling by pitting, whether frontally or obliquely, the medium against the message. Reb Nahman had "betrayed" the medieval romance and folktale plot in the name of a kabbalistic world order. More modestly inclined, Reb Isaac Meir, the Vilna maggid, had invented a gallery of lovers, rabbis, and rogues to herald the new socioeconomic order, at least in tsarist Russia. Peretz, who began with a parochial agenda, had abused his folk materials to strip away the aura of sanctity from the silent Bontshes and starving kabbalists. But as Peretz discovered Reb Nahman, the romance of Hasidism, and the beauty of Yiddish folklore, he found a language of stories to advance his transcendent vision of life. If music, according to the romantics, was the purest expression of human feeling, then Peretz's "mute souls"—a water carrier, a fisherman, a bass violist—would triumph through their prayers and liturgical melodies. If sinning, according to Nietzsche (whom he read), was the way to test the limits of human freedom, then Peretz's heroes and heroines with downcast eyes would prove the purity of the soul. If doubt, according to the humanists, was the sine qua non of modern man, then Peretz would reward his God-fearing Jews for not believing in miracles. And if in the end he failed to redeem the world through his traditional, antitraditional tales, then he would at least allow himself the last laugh.

While Peretz's earlier stories were marked by adversarial relations, forcing the reader to choose between husband and wife, hasid and maskil, sinner and saint, here the storyteller conjures up a world of wholeness where women bring out the best in their men ("Devotion Without End"), where the zaddik is both charismatic leader and salt of the earth ("If Not Higher"), and where the ignorant join forces with the learned to combat the forces of evil ("A Chapter of the Psalms"). Left standing is the opposition between gentiles and Jews, which is now intensified to strengthen group solidarity.[71] The world of tradition is put back together, as the story

Arthur Kolnik, for Peretz, "Reb Khayiml Sets Out in Search of a New
Memorial Prayer" (1948)

is now refashioned out of a single mold—the better to replace the old
pietistic foundations with a secular humanistic base.

The bearers of redemption, proclaims the born-again storyteller with a
flourish, are the downtrodden and ignorant; not the scholars who can only
think, but the Thirty-Six Hidden Saints who can feel the pain of the world.[72]
Performing the deed and obeying the letter of the law are less important
than the intention behind the deed, especially if it flies in the face of the
law. Since this radical doctrine cannot be found in traditional sources, other

than the Gospels, Rabbi Isaiah Horowitz (c. 1565–1630) has recourse to parable in Peretz's "Mute Souls." Two parables of a king of flesh and blood grant a quasi-theological sanction. No less than three saintly lives—of Yokhanan the water carrier, Satia the Dutch-Jewish fisherman, and Abraham the bass violist of Tomaszow—then exemplify the new Torah of individualism and the cult of experience.[73]

Peretz adopts a shorthand for society's outcasts. Like Chananiah before them, they can be identified by their "downcast eyes."[74] This is not a new theme for him. He was struck, as early as his first visit to Warsaw in 1875, with the plight of fallen women.[75] Peretz now returns, through the symbolic language of stories, to distinguish between the inner and the outer eye, between two kinds of sin. He tells of two sisters both of whom "kept their eyes cast down and walked about estranged and dreamy." But whereas Malke (the "Queen") leads an exemplary married life, though continuing to lust in her heart, Nekhama (the "Consoler") lives in sin but emerges with her soul unscathed. So completely divorced is the body from the soul in Peretz's scheme of things that Malke's body miraculously remains fresh in the grave, while Nekhama's decomposes and leaves no remnant whatsoever. People are of course duped by this amazing proof of Malke's virtue. "Their eyes see only what lies on the surface," concludes the storyteller. "They never comprehend what goes on in the heart, nor grasp the true state of a human soul" (Y 131, E 242). The rest of humanity will rest its case if the laws of social convention are obeyed and a cheap miracle is thrown in for good measure. The teller and his antitraditional tale champion the other sister, the one who is totally emancipated from her body, as from the dictates of Jewish law. Nekhama stands for freedom of will and the triumph of libertarianism.

Even when they submit to martyrdom, Peretz's folk heroes follow their conscience rather than the laws of Moses. The Talmud rules that a Jew shall submit to being killed only if forced in public to commit murder, adultery, or idolatry (B. Sanhedrin 64). But in *Dray matones* (Three Gifts), the most famous of Peretz's reinvented folktales, one Jew dies to safeguard a sack of holy soil from the land of Israel, a Jewish woman protects her modesty as she is being dragged to death, and a third Jew runs a gauntlet twice rather than dishonor God. While the bloodied sack of earth, the needle, and the skullcap have been chosen to represent the "national, moral, and religious foundations of Jewish life," in that order, and each episode may be traced back to earlier sources, they share a total disregard of halachic guidelines. Peretz's heroes, whether acting in private or in public, will gladly forfeit their lives to preserve the purity of their individual souls.[76]

Peretz retells this tale of triple martyrdom with such precision and dramatic flair as to make it sound absolutely normative, and more compelling than any tale of old. What makes his version unique is that this seemingly unexceptional code of individual behavior is then offset by a code of metaphysical disorder. Surrounding the sacred tale is another tale of a poor Jewish soul consigned to purgatory because "down below, in the world it had come from," it often couldn't tell the difference between good and evil. Not that the heavens are exactly a seat of blind justice. As corrupt as any comparable body down below, the heavenly tribunal can be bribed with three extraordinary gifts. So the soul of mediocrity is sent off in search of acts of supreme human sacrifice in order to redeem itself in the eyes of a corrupt heaven.

The whole story, in other words, is a trompe l'oeil. The frame, which is supposed to establish a proper hierarchy (heaven and hell, sinner and saint), instead creates a moral and existential twilight zone. If the heavens are equivocal, how can the wandering soul ever be redeemed? And if the world's very redemption depends on the aggregate of individual self-sacrifice (as the storyteller reveals halfway through the story), how can the parts affect the ambiguous whole?

Injecting a note of urgency to the interpretive dilemma is the political crisis that gave rise to Peretz's story: the Kishinev pogrom of 1903 in which forty-nine Jews were murdered and hundreds more injured. The "martyrs of Kishinev" became the touchstone of Jewish political action—and reaction—at home and abroad, in literature as in life. If there is no heaven and the only measure of transcendence is the one that exists "down below," where it's always business as usual, then individual heroism has no cumulative effect on the global scope of human mediocrity. But if the modern soul, no matter how corrupt the moral universe it inhabits, and no matter how decayed the religious foundations on which it stands, can periodically be blessed by examples of true moral courage, then perhaps there is hope after all. The finely ambiguous ending may tip the scales, but does not constitute a final verdict. "Ah, what beautiful gifts!" exclaim the saints in paradise at the story's end. "Of course they're totally useless—but to look at, why, they're perfection itself!"[77]

Most readers misread the story's irony and took it as a paean to martyrdom—as they would consistently misread "Kabbalists" and "Bontshe the Silent." The problem with "Kabbalists" seems to lie with the author himself, who was drawn to mysticism as a possible means of achieving transcendence and was repelled by a society that let its mystics die. As for "Bontshe," perhaps the pacifist ideal that made him a hero had already become too weak or the counternorm of revolution was still too new. But in the case of "Three Gifts," it seems clear that the archetype of martyrdom was simply too strong to burlesque—if indeed that is what Peretz was trying to do. Following the Kishinev pogrom, the readers of Yiddish were to face ever-greater tests of their collective will, and they needed modern texts to help them cope with unwarranted suffering. And so Peretz's story was pressed into action, and never more forcefully than during the Holocaust. Dina Abramowicz, the chief librarian at the YIVO Institute, recalls that in the Vilna ghetto the story was read as a call to arms.

Irony requires a community that is sufficiently secure in its own self-identity to poke fun at itself. Such a community were the readers of the secular Yiddish and Hebrew press. And the best time of year to tickle their fancy was right before a major Jewish holiday. These readers may not have celebrated the holidays themselves, but they did love to read about such celebration once upon a time, in that prelapsarian shtetl where every beggar was Elijah in disguise.

As the holidays are familiar, so too are the plots: exempla in which the hero(ine) is tested and accordingly rewarded or punished. Some plots are so familiar that even the characters know beforehand what will happen. In "A Pinch of Snuff" (1906) the tempter is none other than Satan, the Evil One, surrounded by his devilish paraphernalia and "mephitic assembly."[78] Decadent, phlegmatic, and skeptical, the devil is startled to discover someone who is about to die utterly blameless. Communicating with the Almighty in scriptural stenography, he receives this guideline: "See Book Job, Chapter 1," meaning that he can do whatever he wants with his chosen victim "save that against the man's life he cannot put forth his hand." As it turns out, the legendary rabbi of Chelm cuts a pitiful Jobian figure indeed. No matter; the job must be done, and the army of demons even fight over the assignment.

As well grounded in Jewish law and lore as his opponent, the rabbi of Chelm is an easy match for the first temptation on a clear summer's day when a rich man pulls into town; for the second temptation of money that arrives in autumn in the guise of a beggar; and for the timeless temptation of sex. When Lilith appears disguised as a young Jewish woman with a ritual question, the rabbi is so absorbed in his prayers that he pays no heed to her seductive voice. "So the young woman, seemingly bored, sits down and begins to rock herself in the chair. The rocking and the humming fill the room. What of it? If a snake were to enter the room and bite the rabbi of Chelm, do you think that his attention would be deflected from his prayers?" (Y 260, E 256)

This is legendary ground so well traveled that the rabbi of Chelm will most assuredly follow the example of Hanina ben Dosa (see this book, Chapter 2). But what about that pinch of snuff announced in the title? We may remember the story of Joseph della Reina who caught the devil by a chain and was tricked into giving him a pinch of snuff. We may also know that Reina's defeat spelled the further delay of the messiah. Is the rabbi of Chelm a latter-day redeemer?

In fact, his strength derives from the utter routine of his life. His only weakness—taking a strong taste of snuff late on Friday afternoons—is strictly governed as to time, place, duration, and halachic permissibility. All you need, then, for this assignment is a *daytshl*—"a spindly-legged little fellow, dressed like a German in a derby hat and green-striped trousers"— who will alter the rabbi's routine just a bit. The last grotesque sight is of the saintly rabbi crawling after his rolling snuffbox with the holy Sabbath long since begun.

Trapped in a storybook world where all the epic struggles have already been won (by Job) and lost (by Joseph della Reina), the rabbi's problem is not the problem of evil. For such a rigid and morally incorruptible man, the arena of meaningful struggle remains the uncharted realm of the imagination. Here, in the vast gallery of human desire, his passion for a mere pinch of snuff (like Bontshe's dream of a buttered roll each morning) is what trips him up. The rabbi of Chelm deserves to be the jack-of-all-jokes not because he can't choose between right and wrong, but because he can't dream even an implausible dream.

When holidays come around, heroes and readers alike are most inclined to let their imaginations soar. Passover, the festival of freedom, is an obvious choice—though not, as we have seen, for the radical Peretz of the *Holiday Folios*. Passover stories are de rigueur, however, for a storyteller-journalist, preferably ones about Elijah the Prophet, the hands-down favorite of the Yiddish folktale, who appears at every seder to drink from his special cup, usually travels in disguise, and comes to the aid of simple, nameless Jews. Obeying all of these formula, Peretz writes "The Conjuror" for the Passover supplement of *Der fraynd* (1904).[79]

> A conjuror once came to a town in Volhynia.
>
> Although he arrived in the hectic days before Passover, when a Jew has more worries than hairs on his head, the newcomer made a great impression. Indeed, he was a walking mystery: he was dressed in rags but wore a creased yet still serviceable top hat, and while God had given him a clearly Jewish nose, his face was as clean-shaven as a Christian's. He had no travel papers either, and was never observed to touch food, whether kosher or treyf. It was anyone's guess who he was. If you asked him where he was coming from, his answer was "Paris," and if you inquired where he was going, it was "London." What was he doing in Volhynia? "I lost my way." And from the looks of it, he had come on foot! Nor did he ever go to the synagogue, not even on the Sabbath before the holiday. If a crowd gathered around him, he would suddenly vanish as if swallowed by the earth and reappear on the far side of the marketplace. (Y 147, E 218)

Jew or gentile? Local charlatan or cosmopolitan performer? In clipped, syncopated sentences, the storyteller introduces the main element of suspense. The problem of the conjuror's identity is the problem of Jewish identity as well, for if he is real, so too is his magic, and Jews have a tradition of skepticism on that subject. "Didn't the Bible say that Pharaoh's sorcerers worked even greater wonders in Egypt?" Then "why was such a talent such a pauper? The man scraped rubles off his shoes and couldn't afford to pay for his hotel room! He whistled up more rolls and khallahs than a baker could bake, pulled turkeys out of his boots, and had a face so pinched that a corpse's was better-looking! Hunger burned in his eyes like two bonfires. Instead of the Four Questions, the townspeople said, this year at the seder there would be five." Part of the audience is inclined to believe that what he conjures up is real. You can eat it and spend it. The other part suspects that if it isn't, then all he has to offer is cheap entertainment at a most inopportune time of the year. And if he should happen to be Elijah, why did he show up so early?[80]

The conjuror is a transitional figure living in a transnational time. The appearance within this ambiguous setting of Chaim-Yona, a man of perfect faith, must also arouse suspicion. No *lamed-vovnik*, no secret saint, Chaim-Yona is a ruined lumber merchant who now lives solely by his faith that God will provide. No one else seems to believe it: not his wife Rivke-Beyle, not the neighbors, not even the rabbi. "Faith in God was faith in God," the rabbi lamely declares when the neighbors come to protest Chaim-Yona's refusal to accept any assistance or food on the very eve of the festival. This stubborn man is clearly out of place in an age of practicality.

Then comes his reward, dramatized more subtly than in the average folktale. "That evening Chaim-Yona came home from the holiday prayer at the synagogue. In every house the windows were festively lit except in his own, which was like a mourner at a wedding, or like a blind man among those who can see" (Y 149, E 220). He tries to sustain a festive mood and concedes that he and his wife will have to join in someone else's seder. At that point the conjuror appears and turns darkness into light. "Abraca-dabra"—two silver candlesticks appear in midair. In short order the rest of the seder is miraculously provided: tablecloth, armchairs, white cushions, a platter of matzas, a bottle of wine, a festive meal. Even Passover haggadahs trimmed in gold.

Husband and wife, who until this moment were at loggerheads, are suddenly united in amazement and doubt. (This is the famous folktale convention that limits two to a scene: where three are present, two must act in concert.) After all, the conjuror did not invoke God's name. He merely went on with his show. Underscoring their doubt is their tactical indecision: Chaim-Yona is afraid to leave his wife alone with the conjuror, but Rivke-Beyle argues that the rabbi will never believe a "foolish old woman," should she be the one to go. So they leave together and are instructed that magic is only an illusion. "If the matza can be broken," says the rabbi, "if the wine can be poured, and the cushions are solid, you can consider it all a gift from Heaven that you're allowed to enjoy." Only upon returning home to a real seder do they realize that the guest, since vanished, was the Prophet Elijah.

How odd that the man of perfect faith, primed all the while for a miracle, did not recognize the miracle when it stared him in the face. How comical that he feared to leave his wife alone with the Prophet Elijah. In the traditional folktale, he who is skeptical of Elijah's appearance at the seder is immediately punished.[81] Here, at the critical moment, Chaim-Yona is rewarded despite his doubts. Born, as the storyteller makes clear from the

Marc Chagall, for Peretz, "The Conjuror" (1915)

outset, into an age of skepticism, Chaim-Yona may not have become fully human until that critical moment of doubt. Perhaps Chaim-Yona is rewarded *because of* his doubts.

Obeying all the formal conventions, miraculous reward and all, Peretz reinvented the Elijah tale. By making the supernatural benign, he reanimated a story of faith for a generation of readers who had lost their faith. By also introducing and celebrating the element of doubt, he undercut the Yiddish folktale in the name of secular humanism. Casting Elijah, moreover, in the ambiguous role of a conjuror, with a tophat and a Jewish nose, with a cleanshaven face pinched with hunger, he created a perfect stand-in for himself. Not a *kishef-makher* was he, the alternative Yiddish word that denoted "magician," but a *kuntsn-makher,* a conjuror, a maker of tricks and perhaps of *kunst* (art) as well.[82] The turkeys he could pull out of his boot you couldn't eat. But creating a faith tale for moderns was as good as any magic show in this age of disengagement.

Peretz had no sooner mastered the art of storytelling than he turned it on itself. He had no sooner begun writing holiday tales with an upbeat, though secular message than he used the form to reveal the extent of his own ambivalence. First in the Passover supplement to the Hebrew *Hatsofe* and later in Yiddish, he wrote the confession of a storyteller, which he titled simply "Stories" (1903).[83] It told of a starving Jewish artist in Warsaw intent on seducing a Polish seamstress with his fairy tales.

In fact, they are both of them "lost, desolate souls," longing for happiness, "willing to be deluded for a few minutes": she by the happy ending that will conjure her misery away; he by a stolen kiss at story's end. He has until evening to come up with a new one. Some of his narrative he takes from whole cloth: "there *had* to be a story of a king's son and a queen's daughter. She would have to be asleep somewhere on a mountain peak. A magician or a witch would have to be guarding her." Some of the story is inspired by "the banal and commonplace": the prince will start feeling hungry as he makes his way up the mountain to free the princess; the prince's followers will be seduced by the trivial things that children love. But beneath the fanciful plot and the scattered details from everyday life is the pitiful self-portrait of an intellectual in search of a princess who must settle for an ugly peasant woman instead.

The young man's reverie is interrupted when he discovers another reason for his malaise: tonight is the first seder. That explains the bustle on the streets all day and perhaps even the unruly waters of the Vistula. He is suddenly awash in painful memories of his last visit home for the seder when, "for the sake of truth," he irrevocably broke with his pious father. Returning to his empty apartment, the artist ruefully muses that "at least no scrap of the forbidden leavened bread" remains. Otherwise he shares nothing with the neighbors next door who are just sitting down to the seder and whose physical ugliness fills him with revulsion. Beauty is his religion, and despite his torn spats and dark complexion, he can still delight in his eyes that women always find so irresistible. But as he awaits the

Polish shiksa on this fifth year away from home, his Jewish guilt becomes too much to bear.

In a gory projection of his inner turmoil, he calls to mind a Passover legend of a blood libel that is averted when the assembled Jews devour a Christian corpse planted under the seder table. " 'Not for me,' he thinks. 'That needs a stronger pen than mine.' " Another, more benign version of the plot is dredged up, from the hasidic storytelling repertory this time, in which the Baal Shem Tov resuscitates the corpse planted under the table and even provides it with a Jewish burial.

A light tap on the door.
"Come in."
"Got any stories?"
"All kinds."

We never know, not in the Yiddish version at least, which of the stories the hero will tell: the fairy tale he has labored on all day or the fiercely tribal "Passover tales" that pop into his head the moment his Jewish guilt is aroused. (In the Hebrew version, the fairy-tale princess is eclipsed by the seder. The Polish seamstress is offered a choice only between one blood-libel story or another.) To compound the exquisite ambiguity of the Yiddish ending, Peretz was just then writing neohasidic tales of the kind he interpolated, and this whole story about how impossible it is to write a straight Passover tale was written for Jews to read on Passover.

The Jewish writer as conartist: his alternating discomforts and treacheries are what give the game away. In the very midst of retelling and reshaping Jewish folktales and legends, Peretz no doubt caught himself and asked: "Who am I kidding? I don't believe in this world of myth. What right do I have to exploit it?" But these stories, contrived and counterfeit, were his link to the people. And since the people craved not art but entertainment or Jewish propaganda, he was ready to oblige them. He had just the story for readers craving an escape to some magic mountain, just the story for young Zionists in search of a refurbished past, just the story for Yiddish-speaking workers who preferred reading about other people's seders to rereading the Passover haggadah on their own.

By 1906 Peretz had grown tired of storytelling. With his boundless energy he was already breaking new ground in the fledgling Yiddish art theater, for which he wrote naturalistic plays about the fate of fallen women and visionary plays about sin, redemption, and death.[84] Later visits by Ansky, who brought new folktales straight from the field, rekindled an occasional spark.[85] As a filler, in between performances of his one-act plays, Peretz himself would appear on stage to declaim "Between Two Mountains," which had become a classic.[86]

Peretz perfected the lost art of Yiddish storytelling in order to redeem

Moyshe Faygenblum, for Peretz, "The Chelemer Melamed" (1949)

his comic muse. Stories were neither the end-all of his *yidishkayt* nor the be-all of his career. They were a necessary bridge between "the ruins of the brain and corpses of the heart"—the anguished legacy of his childhood and youth—and the untrammeled world of self-expression he hoped someday to inhabit.[87] Through the hasidic monologue Peretz was able to affirm speech, song, and dance as acts of communal tikkun. Through the romance he celebrated love as universal tikkun. And through the exemplary tale he mandated acts of individual conscience into a code of personal tikkun. Drama was reserved for the tragic vision of life, and the life of the Jews in particular.

When the cup of tragedy, both personal and national, ran over, during the first total war in Europe's history, the comic muse did not fail him. With the bombs falling on Warsaw from German dirigibles and thousands of Jewish refugees flocking to the city, Peretz threw himself into philanthropic work that barely left him any time to write. Yet Ansky did find him at work, on another humoresque, "Yom Kippur in Hell" (1915), which proved to be the master's swansong.[88]

Its hero, like the nameless soul of "Three Gifts," is a figure of mediocrity: a small-town *baal-tfile* (prayer leader), "a no-account, a lightweight" (Y 336, E 260). His single asset is his voice, "pure music," thanks to which the Jews of Lahadam (Neverwasville) "repented of their sins with such fervor that all was forgiven and forgotten in heaven above." No one from Lahadam, as a result, was ever consigned to hell. The devil intervenes, predictably enough, to destroy this special power at its root. "Begone, O voice, until he dies!" declares the archfiend with devilish delight. Even the saintly rabbi of Apt is helpless to intervene. The prayer leader, after all, is no above-average human being.

So the latter rebels against his cruel fate the only way he can: by committing suicide and refusing to voice his confession before death. Not until he stands in hell itself does the prayer leader break his silence, with the liturgical high point from the holiest day of the year—the Kaddish of the Neilah service on Yom Kippur. No folktale hero of Peretz's ever waged so mythic a struggle, and none was so triumphant. All of hell's inmates repent upon hearing the Kaddish and are converted into saints. It is a selfless act as well, for "as in his lifetime, all repented through him but he himself could not repent."

Any other artist who had labored so hard at perfecting folk idioms would have been proud to present his last invented folktale, written in failing health, as the awesome Kaddish that is chanted just as heaven's gates are about to close. Anyone but Peretz would have let the redemption stand. Only this time, music did not work. This time, the netherworld was a more felicitous stand-in for the world at war than heaven had been in the past. A simple *baal-tfile* who tried to redeem this netherworld in a last defiant act was no master of prayer following the footsteps of Reb Nahman. The bid for immortality of a nameless cantor from Neverwasville was nothing compared to Miriam's selfless act of love beyond the grave, or even of the three martyrs whose gifts were regarded as useless in heaven. In the eyes of the world, the prayer leader died a sinner and was buried "behind the graveyard fence, as is the custom with suicides." As for the netherworld: "After a while hell filled up again. New quarters were added, but still the crowding was great."

Peretz was too much the maskil, the modern, the maverick, to credit the writing of mayselekh with ultimate redemptive value. Still, in the hell to which his artist's soul would be consigned, a heart-rending Kaddish counted for more than any other song.

5

Mythologist of the Mundane
SHOLEM ALEICHEM

Ale yidishe mayses, ale umglikn bay undz heybn zikh
on fun a kleynikayt. (All Jewish tales, all disasters that
befall us, begin with something trivial.)
—Sholem Aleichem, 1903

That a Jewish lawyer from the walled city of Zamość, a city renowned
for its freethinkers and diehard rationalists (the numerical value of the
Hebrew letters Z-A-M-O-Š-Z is 336, the same as the word A-P-I-K-O-R-S,
apostate), that such a person would become a latter-day rebbe and teller of
tales is remarkable enough. That a stockbroker from Kiev, a city off limits
to most Jews in tsarist Russia, would turn the fact sheet of Jewish life—an
unrelieved record of communal, familial, and psychological breakdown—
into the best loved of all Yiddish folklore is nothing short of miraculous.
Storytellers, we have learned, delight in the fictions handed down orally
from generation to generation, whereas hard facts are the stuff of daily
newspapers, the alienated world of the modern metropolis. Yet Solomon
Rabinovitsh became Mr. How-Do-You-Do and first displayed his great
mimic talents while writing satiric sketches for Russia's only Yiddish paper.
And when, in the first decades of the twentieth century, the Yiddish press
became the spiritual anchor for millions of east European Jews flocking to
the shores of the Vistula, the Thames, and the Hudson, it was reading
Sholem Aleichem's topical tales aloud from the local paper that brought
laughter to their homes. His comedy of dissolution became, in turn, the
source of a new Jewish folklore that transcended cities, seas, and severed
lives.

His own life as a writer had started out very well. Heir to his father-in-
law's fortune, the twenty-eight-year-old Solomon wasted no time estab-

lishing an urban foothold and diversifying his assets. His numbered, numerous, and effervescent letters from Kiev, where he, his wife Olga, and two infant daughters settled in the fall of 1887, told of a double life, and then some. "Four hours out of every day Solomon Rabinovitsh, praise God, is a doer, a *dreyer,* a sometime crackerjack, at the stock exchange. But from 5 PM until 3 to 4 AM I am 'Sholem Aleichem.'" By day he lived among the "exalted aristocracy," as he called them with tongue in cheek, "the merchant class, men of capital, who value my finances much higher than my literary talent." Thanks to Olga, who opened a dental practice in their home, the Rabinovitsh family enjoyed the coveted "right of residence" in this city of a thousand churches. Thanks to "Sholem Aleichem," the man who hardly slept hoped soon to enter the Temple of Art. "The pen is our wealth," he wrote to an impecunious writer in faraway Warsaw. "And here no one knows about [merchants of] the First or Second Guild; *for we are kinsmen* [Gen. 13:8]! Every littérateur has the right to make such a claim."[1]

At home there were Gobelin tapestries, Chinese porcelain, Irish linen, Viennese livingroom pieces, and a large black concert grand on which Solomon loved to improvise sad melodies.[2] Here a man of his formidable energies and financial means could raise the standard of Jewish literature almost single-handedly. "Right now I'm writing two novels, one short story, one feuilleton, one comedy, one editorial, and one review. Anything else? Should't one make time for reading? Don't you know that we're just a bunch of boorish upstarts? Don't you know that every littérateur must peruse Russian, German, and other literatures on a yearly basis? Even a poet, you know, must also study Adam Smith and John Stuart Mill."[3]

Above the desk where the young upstart wrote and read and wrote some more, there hung the portrait of S. Y. Abramovitsh. If, at this point, Rabinovitsh was concerned with fostering a highbrow literary culture in the lowly "exploited zhargon"; if he launched a vigorous campaign against the sensational potboilers flooding the Yiddish market; and if he rallied responsible "folk writers" to the cause of social realism, stylistic discipline, and high moral purpose, it was due in large measure to the example of Abramovitsh-Mendele. The older man had initially rebuffed the younger's claims to discipleship, never answering a first, obsequious letter, written in Russian. But Rabinovitsh's flair for self-dramatization finally won the day. Through a brilliant campaign, with the fifty-seven-year-old "Mendele" hailed as the grandfather of Yiddish literature, "Sholem Aleichem" successfully installed himself as its first legitimate heir.[4]

An invented tradition was just what the third world of Yiddish letters needed in the early 1880s, when the young Sholem Aleichem came onto the literary scene. Things were changing in tsarist Russia as never before. People were moving en masse from the villages and towns to the cities, or away from Russia altogether to the Golden Land. There was mob violence, political reaction, and universal unrest. Gone were the Jewish enlighteners' hopes for gradual, liberal reform. The revolutionary alternative that captured the minds of these despairing intellectuals was Jewish self-emancipation, first proclaimed by Leo Pinsker in 1882. It was a call for national self-determination on one's own land.

Against this backdrop, Sholem Aleichem embraced the cause of Yiddish literature, and of the novel in particular. The choice of genre was predictable, for if the stakes were Jewish national revival, then emulating the best of modern Russia—its great novelists—would earn one's own people a place among the nations. At age twenty-nine, Sholem Aleichem came out with what he touted as his first authentically Jewish novel.

Perhaps even more notable than the novel itself, a tragicomic love story about a Jewish musician named Stempenyu, was the venue in which it appeared: a large and handsomely produced Yiddish literary almanac modeled on the great Russian miscellanies of the nineteenth century.[5] The publisher-editor was none other than Sholem Aleichem himself, who paid his authors the unheard-of sum of 20 kopeks per word. (It was actually a sliding scale that did much to alienate the lesser-paid writers.) Among the most prominent contributors to *Di yidishe folks-bibliotek* (The Jewish People's Library) were I. L. Peretz, making his debut in Yiddish, and the newly acclaimed eminence grise, Mendele Moykher-Sforim. Sholem Aleichem prefaced his novel with an open letter to "the lovable grandfather, Reb Mendele Moykher-Sforim," who had been corresponding with him of late on literary matters. "You've got to sweat bullets over a work, dearest grandson," he quoted Grampa as writing. "You've got to work, polish each and every word. Remember what I say to you: polish, polish!" The master went on to instruct his disciple what to write as well: "I would not advise you to write any novels, for your taste, your genre, is something else entirely; what's more, if the *life* of our people actually contains within it the stuff of *novels,* they perforce will be different from those of other nations."

While Sholem Aleichem looked to Russian and European models to legitimate the new secular forms and forums he sought to introduce, he agreed with Abramovitsh that the content of this national culture had to be drawn from Jewish life. That is why Stempenyu, the passionate folk fiddler, was an ideal protagonist. Here was a romantic hero who spoke in musician's argot (faithfully transcribed and annotated throughout the novel) and who was also free to pursue the passions of his heart. After all, the European *roman* required a love story, and where else but on the fringes of respectable society could one find a bona-fide Jewish lover? According to the dictates of social realism and high moral purpose, however, this hero would have to be eclipsed by the married heroine, a model of bourgeois respectability, who successfully thwarted his advances. Anna Karenina would simply not have made it in the shtetl.[6]

Romantic love was safe, as long as it was bracketed in song and legendary heroes. So too was the world of fantasy if safely distanced in time. Rather than return, as Dik was forced to do, to the almost-forgotten historical past or, as Peretz was about to do, to the beginnings of the hasidic movement, Sholem Aleichem exploited another possibility recently opened up in the pages of Hebrew literature. He returned to the experience of children, for whom, presumably, marvelous things were an everyday occurrence.[7] For Sholem Aleichem, the experiment proved that recreating the realm of myth from a child's point of view was as difficult as from a hasid's.

Dos meserl (The Penknife, subtitled "A Foolish but Sad Story from My Childhood") was Sholem Aleichem's first little masterpiece.[8] It told of a Jewish boy from a good home who had a passion for penknives that ulti- mately led him to an act of theft. First written in 1886, the story suffered from two conflicting agenda: an exposé of the heder, with its debilitating effect on the body and soul of Jewish boys, and a universal tale of initiation. To achieve the first, Sholem Aleichem addressed his adult male readers (*mayne lezer, mayne brider*) in a modern European diction, complete with Russian proverbs. At the same time, through dramatic vignettes, he did what all modern authors after Rousseau tried to do: he vivified the child's world from within. The story turns fantastical when, on a midsummer's night, the moon intrudes upon the young hero as he fondles his stolen treasure. Suddenly images of hellfire crowd his mind, destroying the idyllic mood. When in heder the next day he is forced to participate in the trial of a poverty-stricken boy caught stealing from a charity box, it is enough to unhinge our hero completely and he falls into a delirium. Later the hero's mother tells him what happened: "how they picked me up from the floor half-dead; how I lay in bed for two weeks on end croaking like a frog, and kept on babbling something about lashes and penknives . . . people thought that I was already dead, God forbid . . . and then, suddenly, I sneezed seven times, and came to, as if arisen from the dead" (16).

When a Jewish lad sneezes seven times and then comes to, "as if arisen from the dead," there can be no mistaking the miracle: it recalls Elisha rescucitating the Shunammite woman's only son in 2 Kings 4. Though Sholem Aleichem's story lacks a man of God to effectuate the son's birth and rebirth, the hero's mother is surely being cast as the courageous and God-fearing Shunammite woman. The presence of mother and reborn child is enough to superimpose two complementary layers of myth. As the boy consistently translates his naive conception of reward and punishment into mythic terms, life itself replays one of the most poignant scenes in the Bible. The child's myth of good and evil is reinforced by the adult myth of death and resurrection.

Were it not for the young Sholem Aleichem's overriding need to be useful, to press for educational reform, to tell rather than to show, he might have been able to exploit this mythic yet believable tale by allowing for catharsis, some reconciliation between parent and son. (This is just what he did in the second version of the story, rewritten in 1901–1903 for children.) In the 1880s, however, the time had not yet come for integrating the mythic component of childhood into a fictional world.[9]

Retrieving the child was but one tentative step on the road to self-discovery. *Stempenyu,* written two years after "The Penknife," was Sholem Aleichem's first attempt to explore the limits of artistic freedom within respectable Jewish society. He was justifiably proud to have promoted a real Ukrainian-Jewish folk artist, and even made a special trip to Berdyczow to meet with Stempenyu's descendants. But when the author found that his fiction contradicted the genealogical facts, he stayed with what he had written. Stempenyu and wife had to be childless for greed and narcissism to be duly punished. The dictates of the "serious" novel still hampered Rabinovitsh's imaginative leap beyond his own class.[10]

Not so, however, Russia's Yiddish newspaper, *Di yidishe folksblat* (The Jewish People's Paper), terribly edited since 1886 by one Yisroel Levi but very widely read.[11] This is where the twenty-four-year-old Solomon Rabinovitsh had made his Yiddish debut in 1883, and this is where the satiric Mr. How-Do-You-Do, ready to take on any subject at the drop of a hat, became a permanent feature of the Yiddish press, establishing Sholem Aleichem's reputation as a humorist. The preferred vehicle for this man of a hundred masks who was always on the road, always getting sidetracked, always listening in on other people's conversations, was the feuilleton, the satiric sketch, which was born out of the daily medium newspaper.[12] Here Solomon Rabinovitsh of Kiev found his persona, his calling, and that vital link to the "folk" which, once forged, he would never give up.

The satirist, as he lectured his Zionist colleagues in 1886, did not share the novelist's lofty literary aspirations. "Shpetn, oyslakhn, khoyzek makhn, aranykrikhn yenem in di gargeres," all those synonymns for ridicule described the satiric craft; yet the satirist could also please his readers with his tomfoolery. Who was the feuilletonist if not one of them, a person grounded in the here-and-now, henpecked, down on his luck, but ever eager for a good story? Three years later he could no longer live without that love. To preserve the intimate bond with "all those people who read Yiddish," he would remain on the staff of the *Folksblat*—which he nicknamed *Di folksblote* (The People's Mire)—come what may.[13]

Like Mark Twain, with whom he is often paired, Sholem Aleichem learned much of his storytelling craft writing copy for newspapers. While the news, printed "above the line," pushed toward greater accuracy, the feuilletons printed below the line, pushed toward extravagance and fabrication. Not since the days of Joseph Perl were Jewish readers treated to such elaborate parodies of various letter-writing styles as in Sholem Aleichem's "Intercepted Letters from the Post Office" (1883–84), "An Exchange Between Two Old Friends" (1884), "The Counting-Room: A Drama in 2 pastiche-style letters, 18 business notes and 20 telegrams" (1885), and the various letters to and from the Editor, to Sholem Aleichem from "Gamliel ben Pedatsur," "Baron Pipernoter," and the like. Sholem Aleichem's various stabs at the journalistic hoax also told of not-so-harmless hoaxes perpetrated by the loansharks and charlatans who preyed on Jewish merchants. And that was something far more relevant to his (male, middle-class) readers than the bitter Kulturkampf of old between the enlighteners and the purveyors of hasidic darkness. Through the standard ploy of always being "on the road," moreover, Sholem Aleichem (or one of his personae) could eavesdrop on conversations of less-cultured, more pompous, or otherwise grotesque types from all walks of Jewish life. "Style," for Sholem Aleichem as for Mark Twain, became increasingly associated with artificiality, ideological excess, and lies. The new literary Yiddish aborning would be cleaner, universally comprehensible, and very clever.[14]

How tragic, then, when the closing of the *Folksblat* in 1890 broke his lifeline to the folk, and his own bankruptcy on the Kiev stock exchange (because he lacked the shrewd mind of a businessman? fell victim to un-scrupulous partners? spent too much time and money rehabilitating the lowly zhargon?), derailed Sholem Aleichem's plans for a Yiddish cultural revolution. In the fall of 1890, he fled his creditors and got as far as Paris before his mother-in-law—the indignity of it all—paid back his debts and ensured a safe return, not to Kiev but to Odessa, by sea. Suddenly, "fun Sholem-Aleykhem iz gevorn olev hasholem," Mr. How-Do-You-Do became Mr. Has-Been. This was the turning point in his career, a fall that presaged a miraculous rebirth.[15]

Compensating the loss of livelihood, self-esteem, and a stable publishing outlet (no matter how crude) was the discovery, in 1895, of a new kind of folk hero who could channel Sholem Aleichem's verbal skills in new direc-tions. At first blush, Tevye the Dairyman was a kind of noble savage: "a healthy, broadly built Jew, dark and hairy, hard to tell his age, wearing large boots and a grimy cloak over a warm undershirt, even in the greatest heat."[16] Tevye, like Stempenyu before him, had his own language, a densely idiomatic style replete with quotations and pseudo-quotations from scrip-ture and liturgy, Ukrainian proverbs, and imitations of other people's speech. "Tevye is always eager to talk, loves a folk saying, a proverb, a snippet of Scripture; he's no scholar, but he's no ignoramus either when it comes to Hebrew print." If, in the first of the Tevye monologues, there was a note of condescension in the narrator's voice and a touch of the grotesque in Tevye's self-involvement, it was because Sholem Aleichem did not yet appreciate what he had discovered and was not yet comfortable allowing the folk to speak so freely. Later he removed the professional narrator com-pletely, retaining him only as an implied listener, and enlarged Tevye's repertory so that his voice might represent all traditional fathers trying to make sense of a changing world.

Why, though, after working so hard to modernize Jewish culture through the novel and literary periodicals, did Sholem Aleichem suddenly revert to the outmoded monologue? More important, what prompted him to move from condescension to identification with the folk? Here we return to the paradox of creative betrayal. Just as the impetus to modernize had come from the outside, so too did the model of reclaiming one's lost resources. Sholem Aleichem's direct influence, I believe, was Nikolai Gogol (1809–1852), whose portrait, along with Mendele's, graced Sholem Aleichem's study. In the 1890s, Gogol became a presence in Sholem Aleichem's life. He kept a box marked "Gogol" on his desk for work in progress, often quoted Gogol in private correspondence, and even wore his hair as Gogol did.[17] Indeed, what is most prized today in Sholem Aleichem's oeuvre owes its inspiration to Gogol. The laughter-through-tears formula, so often cited in discussing the essence of Sholem Aleichem's humor, came from the well-known seventh chapter of *Dead Souls*. He copied these lines in their Russian original and in his own Yiddish translation and kept them among his personal papers "like some kind of amulet."[18] When, in 1897, Sholem Aleichem paid a second visit to Berdichev, he rushed to record all its sights and sounds, exclaiming to his brother: "If Gogol could make a hamlet so famous, why shouldn't I be able to immortalize Berdichev!"[19] From this visit, the fictional town of Kasrilevke (pronounced *Kahs-ríh-lev-keh*) would be born. Just as Gogol badgered his friends for anecdotal material to put into stories, so too did Sholem Aleichem, especially after leaving Russia. And as the spoken language became the center of Gogol's reality—a source of the comic, the grotesque, and the fantastical—so did Sholem Aleichem reinvent spoken Yiddish through a fusion of myth and the mundane.

Like Gogol's, his was a genius that departed from the norm by *not* inventing, by returning to Old World types, hackneyed plots, rambling monologues. Going back one generation, to the discarded elements of Haskalah literature, Sholem Aleichem came upon the letter, the monologue, and the maskilic chapbook. In his first *Menakhem-Mendl* series (1892), he revived the whole *brivn-shteler* (letter writer) tradition, with its archaic formulas at beginning and end and its inflated diction throughout. In his first Tevye story (1895), he revived a particular type of monologue—the pseudo-maggidic sermon, complete with scriptural epigraphs, a homiletic structure, and a dazzling array of proverbs. For his one and only stylized chapbook, *A Tale Without an End* (1901), later retitled *The Haunted Tailor,* he copied a mayse-bikhl by Dik, complete with invented Hebrew captions, farcical plot, and grotesque characters.[20]

What these three forms have in common is that they are "closed": closed by virtue of their stylized language, their rigid formal conventions, and their personal mode of narration.[21] In all there is a fixed, predictable structure that allows only for repetition, not for significant change, and the human experience is conveyed through clichés voiced by a presumably unsophisticated narrator. In contrast, the novel genre he had spent a decade

S. Yudovin, for S. Y. Abramovitsh (Mendele Moyker-Sforim),
The Travels of Benjamin III (1935–1936)

trying to master is an "open" form in which an omniscient narrator is expected to use a modern, fluid diction to represent the linear course of life in all its social causality. Though Sholem Aleichem continued writing novels until his dying day, this retrieval of old-fashioned genres was finally to unlock the source of his genius. Old Mendele had been right after all: Sholem Aleichem's taste, his genre, was something else entirely.

These closed narrative forms would not serve merely as a naive folk vehicle that Sholem Aleichem could then subvert or allegorize to his heart's content, as Peretz and Berdyczewski did with the hasidic tale and monologue. Instead, like Gogol, Sholem Aleichem discovered an affinity between his own imagination and that of the folk. The patterns of experience he drew from an old joke, a popular entertainment, a local legend, a letter-writing manual, a folk book, he found to mesh with aspects of his own psyche.[22] By appropriating the literary genres most recently rendered obsolete, he could now explore for the first time the interplay of stasis and change, fate and free will, myth and reality. And that exploration would corroborate the experience of the folk from below and from within.

Like Gogol, in his *Evenings on a Farm near Dikanka* (the hamlet mentioned earlier), Sholem Aleichem created a character so real, a folk milieu so rich, that the audience mistook it for ethnography. Tevye's speech was so thoroughly and quickly absorbed into modern Yiddish that linguists can no longer determine where folklore ends and Sholem Aleichem begins.[23] Gogol's *Evenings* is enlivened by four fictive narrators. None, though, is as memorable as Tevye, who alone speaks all the lines, plays all the roles, and keeps on appearing for twenty years. Tevye's ability to deflect the shock waves of history while remaining absolutely fixed in one tiny place accords him legendary status. (Even a trip to the nearest shtetl is a rare treat for Tevye, not to speak of a visit to the city of Yehupetz-Kiev. Tevye's place is in the forest, and his sole means of conveyance is a wagon drawn by his long-suffering horse.) It is Tevye's ability to reshape personal griefs and collective tragedies into finely wrought tales that make him the greatest storyteller in Jewish fiction.

There's a vast difference between Tevye and Stempenyu. The young Sholem Aleichem discovered Stempenyu the folk fiddler as a simple vehicle of romantic rehabilitation. The mature artist found in Tevye, in the Bible-quoting dairyman, a way to explore life's ironies. And the main irony is this: in a closed and crumbling world with scant intellectual resources, offering the most paltry economic and social rewards, a philosophical giant can exist, and persist. What's more, this hero, who would never be comfortable in someone else's idea of a modern European novel, is allowed to weave his own philosophical tapestry out of the most conventional cloth: a story whose moral is spelled out from the start, whose plot is utterly predictable.

"If you're meant to strike it rich, Panie Sholem Aleichem, you may as well stay home with your slippers on, because good luck will find you there too." [24] On that note of upbeat fatalism Tevye begins his first story, narrated live to the celebrated writer Sholem Aleichem in 1894. In life there are but two possible plots: a miraculous stroke of good luck or an undeserved catastrophe. Tevye experiences the first only once. He is fated to experience the second again and again.

What sustains him through this fatal predictability are his own story-telling talents; or, to be more precise, his ability to alter the nature of experience by narrating it. The smallest units of his narrative are dialogues, which Tevye strings together to make a story.[25] The use of dialogue has several advantages. Since nobody could play with language nearly as well as he did, this gave him an edge over all the others who caused him grief: his daughters, their suitors, the Jewish gentry, the local gentiles. Second, the dialogues, many of them internal, record the full range of Tevye's responses, which are always more important than the events themselves. Finally, the dialogues not only demonstrate Tevye's skills, but are themselves proof of the saving power of language in a world bent on self-destruction.

What also sustains him is having somebody who would listen. Besides Sholem Aleichem, available only now and again, Tevye can always rely on God to lend a sympathetic ear. God's presence is palpable, especially in the forest, where Tevye is most eloquent. But Tevye is no pantheist or mystic; he is an ironist. Drawing on the limited repertory of sacred texts known to a man of simple learning, he "misquotes" them, or undercuts them with his own commentary.

Now Tevye stands in a long line of Bible-quoting, sententious narrators, from Dr. Moyshe Markuze from Slonim, author of the first handbook for popular medicine written in modern Yiddish (Poryck, 1790), to the unnamed Galician merchant who told the story of Alter-Leb, the Jewish Robinson Crusoe, to the scholarly I. M. Dik of Vilna fame, to the wickedly clever Mendele, peddler of subversive books. The selective use of Scripture was for these earlier authors a way of bridging the cultural abyss that lay between east and west, piety and progress. From Markuze to Mendele, reform-minded authors wore maggidic masks.[26] But alongside the use of Scripture and quotation as a force for good, there was a counter-tradition at work in nineteenth-century Yiddish literature, where the parasitic use of fixed phrases (biblical or otherwise) on the part of typical Yiddish-speaking characters marked them as backward, feudal, hopelessly retrograde. The more positive a character, the less talkative and the less he or she used clichés. The worse the character, the greater the prevalence in his or her speech of clever phrases and pietistic Hebraisms.

Dubbed "linguistic folklore" by the literary historian Meir Wiener, this satiric technique was perfected as early as the 1830s by the playwright Shloyme Ettinger (c. 1801–1856). Ettinger divided his characters between the Old World villains, whose speech was studded with useless idiomatic expressions, and New World heroes, who spoke "like out of a book" (in German). Wicked Serkele's *oy, mayne koykhes* and Reb Yoykhenen the Matchmaker's *vos taytsh?* were almost enough to hoist them on their own petards. Folk locutions, in this scheme, were never the source of enlightened wisdom or earthy realism, but dead weight, linguistic artifacts, proof positive of the stunted growth of the Yiddish vernacular. Instead of a language becoming more precise, refined, and universal, Yiddish—still in thrall of the feudal marketplace and medieval study house—became all the more obscure, self-referential, trite, a vehicle of empty verbiage.[27] Forty years after Ettinger, there came along the satirist Yitskhok Yoel Linetzky (1839–1915), whose grotesque characters routinely butchered Scripture and the liturgy, who lived on a steady diet of folk sayings, and who fed directly into Sholem Aleichem's own style.[28]

So to which of these two traditions does Tevye belong? Dan Miron, building on Wiener's insights, distinguishes between the "transitive" damage that erudite Mendele did to Scripture and the "intransitive" damage done by the far more unsophisticated Tevye. Bible-quoting Tevye, who spends most of his days outdoors talking to his poor old horse, can therefore be seen as a benign midrash on the figure of Mendele. But Benjamin Harshav reads the whole of Tevye's monologues as "a parody of a world based on talking and of a culture steeped in quotations and commentaries of texts rather than in facing realities."[29] If true, that would place Sholem Aleichem back at the beginning of maskilic time.

Sholem Aleichem was a true child of the Hebrew Haskalah, a debt most apparent in his early Hebrew satires, but the personal and ideological crisis of the 1890s forced him to reexamine his own artistic legacy and that of his illustrious forbears.[30] Tevye himself, as we have seen, is a layered character, first conceived as a noble savage, a cleaned-up version of Dik's Kalmen the Country Bumpkin. In Tevye's inaugural tale, the author even has him play the fool in front of the fancy folk from Yehupetz—such a grotesque scene that the story's first translator into Hebrew downplayed it as best he could. By episode 2, however, written in the liminal year of 1899, when so much else in modern Jewish culture was up for grabs, Tevye has achieved a degree of nobility denied any "folk Jew" before him. Tevye knew whereof he quoted. Through twenty years of incremental sorrows, he continued to challenge God with God's own words, turning Tevye, as Itzik Manger later recognized, into the figure of a comic Job.[31]

Tevye's growing awareness of himself as a Jobian figure make his complaint against God, and his utter dependence on God, more poignant. At the low point of his paternal career, after fleeing the home of the rich uncle who disavows his nephew's betrothal to the pregnant Shprintze, Tevye bursts into tears:

> I went over to my wagon, laid my head on it, and—but promise not to laugh at me!—I cried and cried until I had no tears left. Then I climbed aboard, whipped my poor devil of a horse to within an inch of his life, and asked God an old question about an old, old story: What did poor Job ever do to You, dear Lord, to make You hound him day and night? Couldn't you find any other Jews to pick on? (Y 160, E 95)

To be sure, there is something ennobling in being chosen by God, in being paired with the biblical Job. It is also revealing of Sholem Aleichem's own humanistic outlook that the man chosen as Job's twin is not a rabbi, a zaddik, or a young revolutionary, but a simple dairyman. Tevye-Job is a new kind of archetypal figure who stands for the Jewish people as a whole. He embodies the "folk" without access to power, politics, or the press, but with the ability to protest its innocence and to demand redress.

Tevye's fortitude inverts the old spiritual hierarchy—more radically than Peretz's neohasidim and youthful sinners of the downcast eyes. Tevye is a true democratic hero. On the other hand, his very traditionalism defies at least two secular pieties. In the battle of "fathers and sons," as it was waged in nineteenth-century Russian, Hebrew, and Yiddish novels, the author's sympathies were always on the side of the young. But Sholem Aleichem, by allowing Tevye to upstage everyone, makes the young progressives into foils to the tragicomic patriarch.[32] From their first encounter, Pertchik the freedom fighter can hold his own against the old man, and that sparkling dialogue establishes an immediate rapport between the starry-eyed universalist and the folk philosopher. ("Who am I?" says Pertchik in response to Tevye's query. "I'm a child of God's." When that fails to satisfy Tevye's curiosity, Pertchik traces his lineage not to Abraham, Isaac, and Jacob, but all the way back to Adam, to the whole human race.) Later, though, when we get to sample Pertchik's revolutionary rhetoric, such as his rhymed credo, *Gelt iz a shkhite far der velt* (Money is the root of all evil), these words are undercut by Tevye's ironic commentary. Moreover, Tevye's sense of déjà vu, of being an actor in an ancient drama, belies all the political ideologies designed to harness the forces of history. "It's written [in the High Holiday Prayer Book] that *odom yesoydoy mi'ofor vesoyfoy le'ofor* [man is but dust and dust is all that remains of him], that a man can be weaker than a fly and stronger than steel—I tell you, that's a description of me!" (Y 95, E 53). Weak in the face of historical upheaval, Tevye is strong in his ability to respond. That combination of faith and fatalism is the first of several bridges that Sholem Aleichem erects across the abyss of modern times.

A mythology of the mundane is the second.

"**A** Tale Without an End" (1901) is the twice-told tale of a frenetic tailor named Shimen-Elye Shma-Koleynu, who was sent by his wife Tsipe-Beyle-Reyze on a wild goat chase.[33] Sholem Aleichem's direct source was an obscure chapbook by Isaac Meir Dik, *Oyzer Tsinkes and the Goat* (1868).[34] Also published in chapbook form, Sholem Aleichem's long story was supposed to introduce a series of endless tales, only one of which, "Eternal Life" (1902), actually followed. The retold tale of the goat remained his sole attempt at stylized folk narrative. Here he let fantasy loose and watched it wreak havoc in the real world. It taught him everything he still needed to know.

(1) Dik, who had perfected the game of providing mock-Hebrew sources,

here becomes the butt of his own joke. Lifted, presumably, "fun an altn pinkes un baputst" (from an old communal register and dandied up), this bizarre tale gives credit elsewhere. "Ish hoyo beZlodievke" is a comic allusion to the Book of Job ("There was a man in the land of Uz"; 1:1). The opening pseudo-quotation also alerts the reader that the story has a foregone conclusion. Like Job of the subtext, the hapless hero cannot escape his fate.

(2) The mock Hebrew-Yiddish storyteller then proceeds to situate the hero within a charmed circle of like-sounding towns: "there was a man in Zlodievke, a shtetl near Mazepevke, not far from Khaplapovitsh and Kozodoyevke, between Yampoli and Strishtsh, just on the way from Pishi-Yabede to Petshi-Khvost to Tetrevits and from there to Yehupets." This is a fictional geography redolent with legends (of Mazepa, the Robin Hood of Russia), with she-goats (kozes) and scoundrels (zlodeyi), with Slavic sounds and Slavic humor. Unlike Peretz's Wonderland and Neverwasville, whose very indeterminacy invited the reader to fantasize, here the allegorical setting is fiercely parochial, rooted in the here-and-almost-now.

(3) So too the hero whose confidence that his voice will finally be heard earns him the nickname Shimen-Elye Shma Koleynu (Simon Elijah Hear-Our-Voice). Narrowing the prospects still more, Sholem Aleichem endows him and everyone around him with repetitive, parasitic speech patterns, the product of limited minds that cannot cope with the slightest change, let alone with the inscrutable forces conspiring against them. This is linguistic folklore with a vengeance.

(4) Then, at the center of this grotesque and decaying little world, our storybook narrator introduces a nanny goat, the symbol of desire, the mythical creature who was supposed to mediate the polarities between husband and wife, rich and poor, town and country, but who would, through its constant transformations, turn the hero into a scapegoat and drive him mad.

(5) Finally, the most difficult part of Sholem Aleichem's exercise was figuring out how it should end since, by definition, it was a story never destined to end. At first, as Uri Eisenzweig argues in a superb exposition of the story, Sholem Aleichem tried to resolve the plot on the plane of history: the workers of Zlodievke took up Shimen-Elye's cause and set out in protest for the neighboring town.[35] But in the final version of 1909–1911, Sholem Aleichem introduces the storyteller himself as a deus ex

machina who alone can rescue the narrative from its subversive open-end-edness and, by extension, save the world.

Laid bare, as the formalists would say, in this one-of-a-kind stylized chap-book were the main elements of Sholem Aleichem's storytelling art: the reuse of anecdotes or well-worn plots that allowed for few structural changes; a self-contained symbolic landscape that was both nurturing and claustrophobic; a gallery of characters whose sole means of escaping dis-aster was to talk their way out of it; a mythic presence or ideal derived from the realm of everyday life—and all this within a larger contest be-tween the destructive force of history and the redemptive power of the storyteller.

Shimen-Elye, the main protagonist, is no Tevye.[36] The patchwork tailor's speech is itself a pastiche of Scripture, liturgy, and life; the ossified products of a mind that couldn't generate anything new. "Shimen-Elye liked to sprinkle his speech with passages—sometimes whole chapters—of Ge-mara, of Midrash, which made no sense at all *(vos nisht geshtoygn, nisht gefloygn).*"[37] Like Major Kovaliov, Gogol's assessor who woke up one morning in Petersburg to find himself without a nose, Shimen-Elye is a man of limited psychological resources, trapped by the world of experi-ence.[38] It is really too bad because Shimen-Elye's favorite slogans—*Hayom haras oylem* (Today the world was created), and *Undzer folk sher un ayzn—amkho* (Steam-iron and shears, our people Israel!)—bespeak optimism and concern for the commonweal. Although among his own—the other la-borers and guildsmen in town—Shimen-Elye was considered something of a scholar and a tolerable prayer leader, his voice was "somewhat loud," "tending toward a treble," and his verbal skills carried little weight with Tsipe-Beyle-Reyze, his wife. All he could offer in defense on that score was the biblical prooftext *Hu yimshol bakh* (He shall rule over thee; Gen. 4:16). Would that it were so.

Now when myth functions properly, one of its purposes is to mediate the binary oppositions of life and death, heaven and earth, purity and pol-lution.[39] Precisely because Shimen-Elye's world is structured in this binary fashion—husbands against wives, rich against poor, town against country-side—his failure to see the discrepancy between the ideal and the real, sacred text and actual experience, has fatal repercussions. For Shimen-Elye is a man hemmed in on all sides: tyrannized by a superregimented, emas-culating, and impoverished society, trapped by metaphysical forces outside his control. Only on one occasion, when released into the great outdoors for the first time in his life (the beginning of chapter 2), does he use the liturgy to express the ironic distance between the biblical promise and the shtetl reality. Immediately, buoyed up by his newfound sense of autonomy, he locks horns with his great adversary, Dodi the Innkeeper. And that is Shimen-Elye's undoing.

Dodi is the very embodiment of myth. He is the lord of enchantment, "a hairy, thickset Jew with a big belly and a potato nose and the voice of a wild ox," that is, an ogre. Dodi is the perfect foil to our curly black-haired hero Shimen-Elye with his goatee and flattened nose and groove down his lower lip, all of which make him look like a goat even before his trials begin. And the setting for this battle between ogre and man-goat is equally fantastical: an enchanted inn situated midway between the poles of desire. This enchanted setting is what characterizes both of Sholem Aleichem's "Tales Without an End," and it later reappears in many different guises.[40]

Just as Dodi's Oak Tavern exerts an ambiguous pull on all travelers— whether for good or for evil is uncertain—the goal of Shimen-Elye's expedition is a town of mere dissimulation. How, for instance, can one expect to find a nanny goat in a town where peasant women in the market confuse a rooster with a hen and where people's nicknames mask what they really are: Khayim-Khone the Wise is anything but wise and his wife Teme-Gitl the Silent never shuts up. Indeed, what Shimen-Elye discovers in Khayim-Khone is his exact counterpart—another henpecked husband who operates with a fixed repertory of religious formulas.[41] No chance to redeem one's manhood here.

The selfsame Khayim-Khone, however, calls attention to the goat as a multidetermined mythic figure. Through his discussion of the Gemara, which Shimen-Elye happens to walk in on, the reader is warned that goats beget sorrow, because as symbols of human desire they are bound to incur double damages.

> When the tailor entered the house of Reb Khayim-Khone the Wise, he found him at work . . . bent over the Gemara, leading his pupils at the tops of their voices through the Talmud passage "On Damages": "*Hahu barkho,* Now that goat, when it saw that there was food on the top of the barrel, that same goat leaped toward that same food. . . . *Khiyvo Rovo,* Rabba said 'Guilty,' and set it down that she must pay for the fodder and for the barrel that was damaged." (Y 14–16, E 14, 15)

Anatoli Kaplan, for Sholem Aleichem, "Dodi the Innkeeper" (1959)

Hebrew-Aramaic, the language of Jewish learning and rational discourse, becomes instead the main repository of the myth, at least for the male members of shtetl society. These hapless, henpecked husbands are non-plussed by it all. Whereas Shimen-Elye uses ineffectual mantras lifted from the liturgy, Khayim-Khone the *melamed* drills his unfortunate charges in a seemingly irrelevant passage from the Talmud. But the tailor's mythic quest for the nurturing nanny goat seems to have disturbed the status quo and endows all the goat texts with a power of their own.

Now many voices try to interpret the role of the goat—as goblin, as *gilgul*, as the kid of the Khad Gadya—but none dares verbalize its true mythic function: having failed to reconcile the polarities of life, the goat should serve as biblical scapegoat and be cast into the wilderness, thus expiating the failings of a flawed society. Instead, in the story's ultimate transformation, Shimen-Elye himself becomes the sacrificial victim while the goat runs wild and disappears.

In this way Sholem Aleichem was introducing a Jewish mythic component as a tragic subtext to a comic folktale plot. In the parodic folktale, the hero's back-and-forth movement between two essentially identical towns could conceivably go on forever, gaining in comic momentum as more people were drawn into the act. But through the biblical-talmudic-haggadic goat, Sholem Aleichem injected the fatalistic themes of thwarted desire, victimization, and vicarious sacrifice. The goat that was to provide the milk for Shimen-Elye's starving family caused his blood to be spilled instead.[42]

On every score, Sholem Aleichem's mock storybook is a tale of failed mediation. It tells of a traditional society that cannot not even reconcile the competing claims of two neighboring and almost identical towns, let alone the more extreme oppositions of nature and society. It renders a traditional language that does more to obfuscate reality than to break it down into manageable parts. What begins with a tailor's innocent quest ends by destroying him, his family, and the equilibrium of his community. Never before had a stylized Jewish folktale been used to expose so much dissolution. Never would Sholem Aleichem use this genre to do so again. Nor would he have to.

By dividing life down the middle like that, into two mutually exclusive domains, "A Tale Without an End" provided Yiddish literature with its master design: either you could go on dreaming the implausible dream or

Ben Shahn, in Sholem Aleichem, *Inside Kasrilevke* (1945)

you could inherit the earth, but you couldn't do both. For the nanny goat to remain the symbol of male desire, she could never make it home, to wife and native soil. No wonder so much Yiddish fiction from here on would be the story of passionate women and passive men. The "dangling" superfluous men in the writings of Nomberg and Lamed Shapiro, for instance, are destroyed precisely because they are forced to choose between the spiritual and the carnal. Even the *ba'al-guf* of later fame (all brawn and no brains), such as I. M. Weissenberg's Shloime the Fathead, who tries to fight the domination of his wife, succumbs to domestic tyranny in the end. Conceived as mock myth, Sholem Aleichem's master plot could be resolved within the realm of pure myth. Enter the Yiddish fabulist, Der Nister by name, who would inaugurate his storytelling career with "A Tale of a Hermit and a Kid," in which the hero gets to keep both the dream and his faithful nanny goat—as long as he never gives up the quest. The political, aesthetic, and pathological implications of the tailor's fate were therefore anticipated, adumbrated, in this, the most demonic of Sholem Aleichem's stories.[43]

Within Sholem Aleichem's oeuvre itself, there now emerges a normative mythology that Jewish literature had not seen before, a humanistic myth both profoundly consoling and deeply ironic. On the simplest level, what made it normative was that Sholem Aleichem conjured up a world of mainstream, misnagdic, east European Judaism: Hasidism, Kabbalah, demonology, heaven and hell—the stock in trade of Jewish neoromanticism—figured hardly at all. Dodi the Innkeeper who keeps switching goats on poor Shimen-Elye is the most demonic character in Sholem Aleichem's storytelling corpus, just as the motif of the *gilgul* is about the closest Sholem Aleichem ever came to Kabbalah. Even the Sabbath, so central to Heine, Bialik, and Asch, played no role in Sholem Aleichem's search for Jewish myth. (According to his biographer, Sholem Aleichem probably remembered the Sabbath as a time of boredom and intolerable restriction.[44]) Rather it was material culture, in the main, that mediated the myth.[45]

Sholem Aleichem understood that the folk apprehended the great myths of creation, revelation, and redemption through ritual objects and local custom. In particular, it was the holiday cycle—building a sukkah, buying an ethrog, dancing with a flag on Simhath Torah, leading the children through the Torah processions, lighting candles and playing cards on the night of Hanukkah, delivering platters of food on Purim or putting on a play at the Purim afternoon feast, and above all preparing for and celebrating the seder—it was on these communal and familial occasions that the ordinary Jew could experience the transcendent power of Jewish myth. It was the time, to use Bakhtin's term, that the carnival aspect of life broke through the everyday routine. (To be sure, the Jewish carnival was a far cry from Bacchanalia, or even from Breughel; still, in the relative asceticism of the shtetl, a few good drinks could go a long way.) Through his emphasis on material culture and carnival, Sholem Aleichem expressed his egalitarian and humanist bias. This was a Judaism equally accessible to all.

The myth could also be mediated by a certain type of folk hero (like Tevye) who was situated outside the synagogue, the study house, and the yeshiva, and got his hands dirty in the mud and muddle of everyday life. To a greater or lesser degree these characters had their own ironic sense of the discrepancy between the real and the ideal. Through them, as through the celebration of the holidays, the myth was invoked as a foil to reality.

Nowhere is the gap between present reality and future promise drawn so precisely and so poignantly as in the holiday stories that Sholem Aleichem began writing in earnest after 1900. What makes them so poignant— and so true to a certain "folk conception" of life—is that they show how fleeting is the moment of transcendence, if achieved at all. For the plot of these stories, such as it is, presents one of two alternatives: either the king-for-a-day motif or the marred holiday (der farshterter yontef). Yuzik the Orphan's chance to be "The Youngest of the Kings" (1904) came only once a year, when he sat at the head of the table leading the Passover seder. "Yes," says Meylekh, the hero of "The King and the Queen" (1902), "it's great to be a king, as I am a Jew . . . if only once a year, if only for half an hour!" More often than not, however, Leybl bit off the tip of the coveted ethrog before it could be used. Either way, the celebrant would have to return to the grind, to a life that was unredeemed.[46]

"The Guest" (Der oyrekh, 1906) is an exquisite example of the second type of holiday tale.[47] As in "The Penknife," the experience of childhood is evoked by an adult, and here too Sholem Aleichem uses dialogue to vivify and dramatize the past:

> "Do I have a guest for you, Reb Yonah, a guest for the seder such as you've never had since you became a married man."
> "Whom do you have in mind?"
> "What I have in mind is an esrog, not a guest of flesh-and-blood."
> "And what do you mean exactly by an esrog?"
> "What I mean is a person of real refinement, handsome and aristocratic. He has only one failing, though. He doesn't understand our language."
> "What language does he understand?"
> "The Holy Tongue."
> "From Jerusalem?"
> "Where exactly he comes from I don't know, but when he talks, it's all ahs."

Only now are we informed that this playful dialogue is taking place between Azriel the shames and the narrator's father, Reb Yonah, a few days before Passover. None of the characters—neither the two respected gentlemen nor the curious young eavesdropper—suspects what trouble is in store when you bring an esrog home for the seder.[48]

The clever play on the word esrog, the ritual citron of the Feast of Tab-

ernacles that is here used in a colloquial sense to mean someone very special, and the matter of the guest's Jerusalem connection are Sholem Aleichem's way of jogging the reader's memory. Rarely did Sholem Aleichem
draw his folk material from books, and even then it was from storybooks
that were not too old. Here his direct source was a stand-by of the badkhn's
repertory at weddings. It went by the name of "The Jew from the Land of
Israel" or "The Jerusalemite" and involved the wedding jester, appearing in
a red blanket or shawl and a funny red cap.[49] In Sholem Aleichem's version,
the exotic guest wears the traditional fur-trimmed *shtrayml* on his head and
a Turkish robe of yellow, blue, and red stripes. Instead of a lengthy dialogue
between the "Jerusalemite," who speaks in Hebrew, and his interlocutor,
who questions him in Yiddish, Sholem Aleichem concocts this brilliant
repartee between Reb Yonah and the guest as they wait for the seder to
begin:

Father: "Nu?" (Meaning in Yiddish, "Be so good as to say the Kiddush prayer.")
Guest: "Nu, nu!" (Meaning, "Go right ahead, *you* say it.")
Father: "Nu, aw?" ("How about you?")
Guest: "Ee-aw!" ("Please, you first!")
Guest: "Aw, ee!" ("You first, please!")
Father: "Eh, aw, ee!" ("I beg of you, you say it first!")
Guest: "Ee, aw, eh!" ("You say it, I beg of you!")
Father: "Ee, eh, aw, nu?" ("Will it harm you to say it first?")
Guest: "Ee, aw, eh, nu, nu!" ("Well, since you insist, I'll say it!")

Following this dialogue in Jewish Esperanto—an exercise in preverbal
communication that leaves the men on very intimate terms indeed—the
guest exploits the Passover seder, when the Jewish religious imagination is
most alive, to conjure up a dream world of the Ten Lost Tribes. "He says
that the entire wealth belongs to the inhabitants of the kingdom who are
called Sepharadim," is how the child recapitulates the guest's report,

> and they have a king, he says, who is terribly pious and wears a fur-edged
> hat; and this king's name is Joseph ben Joseph. He serves as their high priest,
> he says, and rides in a golden carriage drawn by six fiery horses, and when
> he crosses the threshold of the synagogue, Levites come to greet him with
> song . . .
> Splendid, gleaming fantasies lift me up and transport me to that fortunate
> Jewish land where the houses are built of fragrant pinewood and covered with

silver, where the dishes are made of gold and precious stones lie scattered about on the streets.

The child thinks not in abstractions but in concrete terms. He doesn't relate to the myth in terms of exile and redemption. Instead, he thinks about scattered treasures that he'll bring home to his mother.

As it turns out, the marvelous Sephardic guest from the Jewish Kingdom has the same idea. In the midddle of night, the family awakens to discover that the guest has vanished with the family silver, jewelry, and maid. "My heart is shattered," says the child-narrator at the end,

> But not on account of the loss of our silver goblets and silverware or of my mother's scanty jewelry and the money. Not on account of Rickel the maid— the devil take her! But because now I will never see that happy, happy land where rubies, pearls, and diamonds lie scattered about in the streets, where there is a holy temple with High Priests, Levites, an organ, and an ancient altar with sacrifices. All these marvelous things cruelly, wantonly stolen from me, taken away, taken away, taken away.

So the end of both story types is essentially the same: Jews experience the tragic discrepancy between dream and reality. For even if a Jew is lucky enough to celebrate with an ethrog, a paper flag, a deck of cards, a Purim play, or a guest for the seder, the gray dawn brings back the sobering week. The king for a day returns to being a henpecked schlemiel or a penniless orphan. Precisely because the myth has been rendered palpable, turned into real priests and Levites in a seemingly real place, the loss is that much greater. Every Jew becomes a child again when the holidays roll around. And just as the child experiences life intensely and subjectively, so each holiday can become a mini-drama of shattered dreams and expectations.

"The Guest," and the seventy-odd holiday stories like it, was written under a deadline. With the rapid growth of the Yiddish press after 1900, writing holiday stories became part of every professional Yiddish and Hebrew writer's job description. In a pinch, Sholem Aleichem even ghost-wrote a story or two for his friend Mordecai Spector (1858–1925). To make ends meet, Sholem Aleichem wrote for several papers at a time; since none allowed for duplication, the holiday period between Rosh Hashannah and Hoshana Rabba (the early fall) could be frenetic.[50] And so Sholem Aleichem learned to write these stories fast and to make each one fit the holiday supplement.

He also learned that any narrative hook to a given holiday might do, however tenuous. "Dead people? In honor of Purim?" he asked rhetorically in the preamble to the first chapbook in a series called Sholem Aleichem's Holiday Library:

> On a holiday when a Jew is enjoined to get drunk and an author is enjoined to act foolishly, to play the jester? I know, reader, that today is Purim and that you have to get drunk and I have to act the fool—yet still I'm giving you a story about two dead people. Tough luck. All I can offer is the following advice: if you've got weak nerves, don't read the story after nightfall.[51]

The pressures of the media were only one reason that these stories were so playful and so divorced from the warp and woof of Jewish religious practice. Sholem Aleichem, like Peretz, was engaged in a last-minute rescue operation. The more overtly religious the setting of a story, the more secular were its concerns. But Peretz, through the learned style of his narrators, and the use of such folklore genres as the romance and sacred tale, returned the Yiddish story to its seat of honor within the study house and the hasidic prayer house. In so doing, Peretz effectively *de-emancipated* the Yiddish story, even as he subverted it in the name of radical individualism. Reversing the process, Sholem Aleichem began by totally liberating the act and art of storytelling from its learned settings. Try as he might, as late as 1903, to launch a series of Stories of the Study House, Sholem Aleichem could pull it off only in Hebrew, the language of study, and never wrote more than one such monologue.[52] Tevye, for all his piety, did his praying out doors, never in the assembly of other Jews, and never once had to match wits with anyone more learned than the local matchmaker. Sholem Aleichem, for all his profound debt to Gogol, had no truck with Gogol's devil. Compared to Leskov's encyclopedic knowledge of Russian icons and knowledge of the Old Believers, Sholem Aleichem's ethnographic mandate was very narrow indeed. What he finally salvaged from the culture of the shtetl was much less than meets the eye.

Reb Nahman, we may recall, who observed the letter of the Jewish law and then some, made no reference to the Sabbath or festivals in his tales. His drama of cosmic redemption was marked by weddings alone. Dik, the social reformer, warmed to the subject of Jewish rites and rituals—the midnight bacchanal on the 15th of Kislev, Tisha b'Av in the town of Heres, the ceremony of the Torah completion, Reb Shmaye Aliter's quick-change act on the night of Hoshana Rabba, Kalmen Sheleykesker's kaddish and seder—only when there was something to burlesque. Of these two approaches, Peretz, as storyteller, went along with Reb Nahman to celebrate the redemptive possibilities of a conjuror coming to town before Passover or a prayer leader holding out in hell until the kaddish of Neilah. So long as Sholem Aleichem went the maskilic route, writing topical satires "below the line," the holidays served as a cover for something else: a series of character sketches ("Four Cups," 1888), a veiled—and failed—response to the pogroms ("Lag b'Omer," 1887). Spector, who churned stories out just as fast as Sholem Aleichem, never succeeded in treating the holidays other than as matters of topical concern: male-female relations, life's inherent disappointments, social injustice, Judeophobia. Even old Abramovitsh tried to jump on the bandwagon with a paltry five stories on holiday themes. Two were vintage Mendele; the rest were sorry concessions to sentimental taste.[53]

With perhaps a bow to Dik—and to Dickens—and against the backdrop of Spector's utterly forgettable holiday mood pieces, Sholem Aleichem can take the credit for inventing the modern Yiddish holiday story. Certainly the rehearsal of childhood, with all its concomitant terrors and Pyrrhic victories, owes something to Dickens, just as the carnival and the ethnography owe something to Dik. But only Sholem Aleichem was able to strip away the multiple layers of theological belief, local custom, maskilic critique, and journalistic excess to arrive at the bare essentials: a still usable myth accessible to all Jews, inasmuch as every Jew was once a child, celebrated some festival or other in one way or another, and knew how to talk.[54]

Problem: If the author no longer cherished the belief system of Judaism, how could he find a narrator who did? Solution: He would return to the child's world and to the child within himself—not to distance the past through veils of satire and sentiment, the way the maskilim and their journalistic heirs were wont to do, but to recover the unadulterated experience, the primal language, the bold colors, the startling sights and raucous sounds; in short, the joy, fear, and transcendence that were the wellsprings of myth.[55]

Sukkos finally came, thank God, and I bought myself a large, yellow, two-sided flag. Painted on one side were two beasts with catlike faces—lions, really, with open mouths. Their long tongues were decorated with some sort of whistles—shofars, I guess—because *With trumpets and ram's horn* was printed next to the lions, and beneath them were the lines: *The flag of the Tribe of Judah* on the right and *The flag of the Tribe of Ephraim* on the left.

And that was only one side of the flag. The reverse side was even prettier, for it had true-to-life portraits of Moses and Aaron. Moses wore a large vizor on his forehead and Aaron had a golden hoop over his red shock of hair. Between Moses and Aaron stood a whole gang of little Jews, crammed in tight against one another and holding Torah Scrolls in their hands. They all looked alike, as though one mother had borne them. All wore the same long gaberdines belted below their hips, and the same socks and shoes. And they all seemed to step forward and sing: *Rejoice and be merry on Simhas Torah.*[56]

The child is old enough to read the classical Hebrew inscriptions, but what sets his imagination on fire is the primitive iconography, which tells of friendly mythic beasts, almost-living prophets and priests, and a motley of hasidic-looking Jews having a whale of a good time. However poor, tiny, and arcane the world of the child—the culture of the shtetl in miniature—there is always something to delight the eye and ear. Even the synagogue on a weekday, not to speak of a Sabbath, is a cacophony of voices, with young and old alike talking, singing, swaying, running, jumping.

Storytelling had become the politics of rescue. Once, during his apprenticeship, Solomon Rabinovitsh pushed to reform the traditional heder, not to abolish it by administrative fiat, as the more radical maskilim wanted to do. As an adult and responsible "folk writer," Sholem Aleichem joined with those who tried to rally the fragmented people of Israel around its ancient flag. He became a Lover of Zion and later, as of 1897, a card-carrying Zionist. His first tour of duty as a reader of zhargonic literature was under Zionist auspices, in 1890. By 1902 his appearance on the Zionist circuit was cause for mass rejoicing: much crowding, clapping, laughing, and talking. The audience clamored for enlightenment: what was the hidden meaning of "The Pot," and who exactly was this Yente? The rescue operation succeeded beyond the author's wildest dreams: Zionism brought the carnival back to town, with the storyteller as master of ceremonies, his repertory taken from the audience itself and designed to uncover the hidden pattern of their lives.[57]

One way, then, that the great myths operated in Sholem Aleichem's stories was through the actual behavior and speech of ordinary Jews. Myth, on the one hand, allowed them a momentary reprieve from the pain and drudgery of life; on the other it highlighted the unbridgeable gap between transcendence and life's inherent constraints. Myth meant two different but complementary things. (1) It tokened an heroic past, fragments of which could still be retrieved for the present. Priests and Levites, Moses and Aaron, the Israelites in the wilderness and the Ten Lost Tribes on the far side of the Sambatyon, the Song of Songs and the Book of Job—these were the proud relics of the people's biblical beginnings. (2) Myth also expressed the deep, and recurrent, structure of Jewish life in exile. Because Jewish history was so full of archetypal experiences, the myths used by Sholem Aleichem had to be apprehendable by all. Myth was fate and it was inescapable.

Especially for Jewish women. Though men and children *could* escape, making them that much more vulnerable to dreams of personal salvation and (as we shall see) to the terrors of historical reality, mothers and daughters stayed behind, to pick up the pieces. How tenaciously they held on, those women, to folkspeech (beginning with Sholem Aleichem's own stepmother and her curses), to the family (beginning with Sheyne-Sheyndl and her frenetic letters), to shtetl morality (beginning with beautiful Rachel and her brief flirtation with a fiddler); and none with greater tenacity than Yente the Dairy Vendor, the character who so intrigued Sholem Aleichem's audience on the Zionist lecture circuit. Despite the plainness of her name (*yente* is Yiddish for a vulgar/sentimental woman, a chatterbox), she was totally absorbed by questions of life and death.[58]

Like her mother, Basye the Candle Fitter, Yente has to deal with the hard aspects of life, and like her mother she is surrounded by fragile things: glass tops that burst, husbands who die young, an only son who suffers from the same accursed cough, and not least of all by a small and rapidly diminishing supply of cooking pots.

> That is, as for pots, I used to have three meat pots. But then Gnessi (may she sink into the earth) once borrowed a pot from me, a brand new pot, and then she goes and gives me back a crippled pot. So I said to her, "What kind of pot is this?" So she said, "It's your pot." So I said, "How come I get back a crippled pot when I gave you a brand new pot?" So she said, "Shut it. Don't yell like that, who needs your things? First of all, I gave you back a brand new pot. Second, the pot I took from you was a crippled pot. And third, I never even took a pot from you. I have my own pot, so get off my back!" There's a slut for you! (Y 24, E 80)

It has taken her almost this long (nine-tenths into her monologue) for Yente to mention the meat pot, Exhibit A of her rabbinical inquiry, because only now is she finally poised to ask the real question. Yet if communication breaks down between two women who share the same pot, all the more so between a marketwoman pleading her case before the rabbi. The comic repartee on the meat pot precisely captures the circularity of Yente's speech, which admits no interlocutor. Despite her rhetorical trick of introducing each new thought with "Now what were we saying? Yes, you said . . . ," the rabbi never utters a word. What's more, he faints just when she gets to the point: "If something's got to break, count on it, it'll be the good pot. That's the way it's been since the world began. What I'd like to know, see, is why that is." The analogy, almost spelled out, is to her only son Dovidl, the apple of her eye, the one crippled by a chronic cough, while her neighbor Gnessi has more pots than she knows what to do with—a brood of unruly children. Since the tragic iniquity of life is a question with no answer, the rabbi adjourns the hearing, dropping in a dead faint.[59]

Women, by virtue of their hysterical loyalties, reveal the deep structure of life at its most mundane. One old and well-known joke about a crippled pot, rendered much earthier and naive-sounding by the Slavic adjective *shtshe-re-ba-te,* gives the game away. It was the joke that inspired the monologue to begin with, as surely as Dik's satiric storybook inspired "The Haunted Tailor" and the wedding routine inspired the bittersweet "The Guest." Garrulous women like Yente, graduated from the school of hard knocks, don't sit around telling jokes, however; they are the very stuff of true "folklore." Folklore works by constant repetition: a henpecked husband caught between two almost identical towns; an exotic guest who communicates in staccato sounds; a mother who creates the impression of endlessness by talking in circles. Folklore is secular; the rabbi doesn't get a word in edgewise. Folklore is the people's Torah, the universe of human discourse compressed into a tiny, overused vessel. The pot stands for Yente: a flawed pot whose husband died young and whose son is chronically ill; someone so obsessed with her own plight, so hysterically loyal to her son, that she is incapable of empathy. The pot is life itself, that private, tragicomic realm you invade at your peril. Beware what happens when you look into another's life.

By 1900 Sholem Aleichem had put in place a fixed repertory of stories so artfully fashioned that no aspect of the contemporary Jewish experience would remain outside its purview. The dialogical monologues of Tevye; the exchange of letters between Menakhem-Mendl the *luftmentsh* and his harping, practical, wife; the writings of young Motl, son of Peyse the Cantor; the cycle of tales about the old Kasrilevke and the new; stories for the holidays and stories for children; various and sundry monologues—all this allowed the author to deconstruct the course of current events into its constituent parts: the dissolution of the community, the family, and the individual.[60]

The year 1905 was the best and worst of times for Sholem Aleichem. The best, because the granting of civil liberties within the tsarist empire meant that Yiddish newspapers of various persuasions could compete on the open market, that the twenty-three-year ban on the Yiddish theater was lifted, and that the most beloved of Yiddish storytellers could now take his show on the road under his own banner. The worst, because the counterrevolutionary pogroms hit Sholem Aleichem and his family directly, forcing them to flee the beloved city of Kiev and, for all intents and purposes, to quit Mother Russia.

Something also happened to the stories. Adapting his well-known tales for a live audience, Sholem Aleichem turned them into theatrical set pieces. The written-as-spoken monologue became a scripted performance; the naive *melamed* of Kasrilevke reappeared through the good graces of a European narrator who now stood before a cosmopolitan crowd. Words like *kultur, progres,* and *tsivilizatsye* started cropping up where they didn't belong. America was the new frontier where millions of readers could follow the stories and serialized novels of Sholem Aleichem in the pages of the popular press. His own arrival in October 1906 was heralded by the hastily written and almost hysterical "Pogrom Scenes," featured in the orthodox daily *Tageblat.* But what of the American scene itself? Like Kafka, Sholem Aleichem had the chutzpah to bring one of his fictional characters to these shores quite independently of the author. (Sholem Aleichem wisely expunged this episode from the final version of *Menakhem-Mendl.*[61]) Upon arrival, Sholem Aleichem found structural similarities between Russian parvenus and American alrightniks that gave him license to recycle the same story. By exchanging Russianisms for Americanisms and one card-playing salon for another, he could expose the same decline of holiday observance in both places. All these changes in the rhetoric of Sholem Aleichem's fiction allowed him to stay one step ahead of his upwardly and horizontally mobile audience.[62]

The extraordinary pace of change, however, had greatly exacerbated the problem of closure. If Kasrilevke itself was now on the move, lock, stock, and barrel, and the utopian solutions of a liberal Russia and a Zionist haven seemed ever more remote, then one could not count on the chronicle of current events to supply the endings. Whereas his novels and, more recently, plays, grappled with competing theories of history (was it exile or merely dispersion?), and so were notoriously weak when it came time for them to end, the stories began to play with history in novel ways. Sholem Aleichem invented a new kind of topical tale that was open and closed at one and the same time: framed within a narrative with an arbitrary ending was a story that was structurally complete. The only one who could move in and out of the two frames was the storyteller within the tale, which made him, by default and by design, the story's proper hero. To raise the stakes in the contest between history and story, Sholem Aleichem transplanted the art of storytelling to the most secular and unstable setting yet: the third-class compartment of a Russian train.[63]

Ever since Mendele the Bookpeddler first boarded a train, back in 1890, Jewish storytellers found that trains and technology had benefitted Russian Jews very little. There was still no place to go to make a living within the Pale of Settlement. In the eight-year span covered by Sholem Aleichem's *Railroad Stories* (1902–1910), the political situation dramatically worsened, the constitutional reforms giving way to pogroms and still more pogroms. Sholem Aleichem's personal odyssey was also bracketed by disaster. Driven from Russia by the Kiev pogrom, he did return for a triumphant tour in 1908, only to collapse in its midst from tuberculosis. This was followed by years of convalescence in European spas. Thus his own state of exile was perfectly matched by the crowded third-class cars rumbling across the Ukraine, where the only reprieve from the rain always falling outside was to play another game of cards and listen to a half-crazed fellow passenger narrate another tale of woe.[64]

What began in Sholem Aleichem's mind as a series of *peklekh*, or personal sob stories, became, after his own self-imposed exile and subsequent run-in with death, a vast panorama of dissolution. (Every plot, even the most ludicrous, has a basis in historical fact, backed up by newspaper clippings sent to him expressly for this purpose.[65]) Blackmail, suicide, bankruptcy, police raids, draft exemptions, and draft quotas were a staple of these travelers' tales. The third-class compartment was a welcome refuge from the bleak economic and political conditions prevailing in Russia, because it was a place where the act of storytelling could still flourish; where, in the words of the anonymous traveling salesman, "suddenly everyone is telling everybody everything, and everything is being told to everyone. The whole car is talking together at once in a splendid show of Jewish solidarity" (Y 302, E 283). Though solidarity often broke down, and encounters en route were notoriously fickle, Jews were more likely to let down their guard among their own. And once the barriers were down, they could share a "world of experience," in Walter Benjamin's well-worn phrase. For these uprooted men (it was still an all-male subculture), storytelling was never an escape from reality, a return to some preindustrial paradise. It was a communal release, a temporary means of turning chaos into comedy.

Storytelling on board a train became for Sholem Aleichem the last frontier of hope because this vehicle made a mockery of everything salvific. This chunk of moving metal was as far removed from Kasrilveke, from the community of the faithful, as a Jew could go. Nothing in the arsenal of horror stories prepares the traveling salesman, whose collection of true stories this presumably is, for the likes of "The Man from Buenos Aires," arguably the most venal of all Sholem Aleichem's fictional characters. A successful immigrant, who is going home to find himself a traditional Jewish bride, he uses speech so duplicitously and has manners so seductive that the salesman never suspects him of being a white-slave trader. Where community and communication suffer total breakdown, the moments of reprieve, let alone transcendence, will be few and far between.[66]

In order to wrest some ironic consolation from this bleak historical landscape, Sholem Aleichem divides the route into two. Yes, miracles can still happen on a train, but only on the *leydikgeyer*, the Straggler Special, or the Slowpoke Express, which the Jews have managed to domesticate. An entire folk repertory has already grown up around this train, such as "The Miracle of Hoshana Rabba" that took place in 1909 or the averted pogrom described in "The Wedding That Came Without Its Band."[67] These Jewish-gentile confrontations are greatly mitigated by the slowness of the Straggler Special, its highly irregular schedule, the density of Jewish habitation along its sleepy route, and the traditional methods still employed by those who hate Jews. Indeed, Jews regard the train's failure of efficiency and technology as its chief virtue.

Here Berl Vinegar can still engage a priest in a theological debate on the meaning of life and emerge the victor. And what could be better than "punkt um Heshayne-rabe nokhn kvitl," on the very day of Hoshana Rabba (the third-to-last day of the Succoth festival) after each individual's fate for the coming year has already been sealed in heaven? So the holiday has not lost its intercessionary power after all, even if it is Berl and the runaway train that effect the miracle and not the hand of God. Even more remarkable is that Berl wins his verbal victory over the priest before realizing that he possesses the technical knowledge to save the two of them from death.[68] The real miracle, then, still occurs on the moral plane of one on one, an old-fashioned story complete unto itself, not to be confused with the comic frame tale, of how a near-apocalyptic disaster (exponentially inflated with each telegraph that courses through the wires) is narrowly averted. The only thing holding the disparate parts together is the intricate web of narration, which gets denser the closer we get to the story's dramatic core. Berl Vineger recounted it to the businessman from Haissen who told it to the traveling salesman who passed it on to Sholem Aleichem who turns it over to us.

Aboard the Straggler, no one bombards the narrator with tales of private sorrow; with "all the time and space in the world," the businessman from Haissen, "sprawled out as comfortably as if he were in his own living room" (Y 113, E 187), regales him with semitraditional narratives instead.[69] This underscores the alienation of other peklekh—people who have become so immersed in private grief that, while mouthing phrases in praise of God, they have lost connection with Him and with humanity.[70] The repertory of stories aboard each train keeps pace with its schedule.

On the heavily traveled line that passes through "Baranovich Station" (1909), therefore, a storyteller can hold the attention of all the other men if he is a connoisseur of Jewish suffering, down to the last detail of how Jews were forced to run the gauntlet in the reign of Tsar Nicholas I. Perhaps more than any other story of Sholem Aleichem's, "Baranovich Station" draws its material directly from the Jewish historical experience. It begins at the most secular time of the day, right after morning prayers, with the men all in the mood to talk—very much so, in fact. About what? About anything and everything. Everyone tried to think of some fresh, juicy item that would make all the others sit up and listen, but no one was able to hold the stage for long. The subject changed every minute. No sooner did it light on the recent harvest—that is, the wheat and oats crop—than it shifted, don't ask me why, to the war with Japan, while after barely five minutes of fighting the Japanese, we moved on to the Revolution of 1905. From the Revolution we passed to the Constitution, and from the Constitution it was but a short step to the pogroms, the massacres of Jews, the new anti-Semitic legislation, the expulsion from the villages, the mass flight to America, and all the other trials and tribulations that you hear about these fine days: bankruptcies, expropriations, military emergencies, executions, starvation, cholera, Purishkevich, Azef. (Y 41–42, E 152)

Azef, the notorious double agent who infiltrated the ranks of the Socialist Revolutionary Party before being exposed in 1908, is the cue for the master storyteller to step forward. He is "a generously proportioned individual with a good silk cap on his head, twinkling eyes, a rosy, freckled face, and no front teeth." Despite this speech impediment, or perhaps because of it, this native of Kaminka takes center stage with "a story about a stool pigeon, and a hometown boy from Kaminka at that, who makes Azef look pale by comparison!"

Azef's perfidy can only be matched by another true story, since this story is most assuredly true, for it concerns the teller's own grandfather, Reb Nissl Shapiro, as rehearsed many times by his father. What's more, the storyteller from Kaminka is a master at manipulating the plot with strategic interruptions that keep the men in suspense.[71] Most enjoyable is the way he taunts his listeners' expectations of a miracle.[72] Only a miracle, it seems, can save Kivke, the hometown boy, from running the gauntlet, and this miracle is orchestrated by none other than Reb Nissl Shapiro himself, as president of the burial society, with the collusion of a few local officials. Kivke feigns death in prison, and his body is carted straight from the cemetery over the border into Austria.

This is just the thing to lift the spirits of uprooted men reeling from the litany of Jewish woes. A spoof on Kivke's death and resurrection is less worthy of being passed on through the generations than a feat of communal bravery that upholds the great moral principle of redeeming captives. "After all, *pidyen-shvuim* [ransoming a Jew] is nothing to sneeze at—and one saved from a flogging, yet!" (Y 49, E 157) Because true heroism in the secular world does not require miracles, the secular plot can be said to have reached its climax with Kivke's great escape.

But the act of betrayal that follows destroys these heroic pretensions. Letters soon began to arrive from the dead man. Eight letters and four payments of hush money later, Kivke's last blackmail missive to Nissl Shapiro delivers the punch: "I'll let them [the tsarist authories] know that we Jews have a great God who rescued Kivke from the grave" (Y 158, E 162). Thus does Kivke's cynical parody knock out whatever pride still remains in the holy community of Kaminka and its illustrious leader, Reb Nissl Shapiro.

Then at Baranovich Station the storyteller jumps off the train, to the accompaniment of shouts and curses from his fellow passengers. "I wouldn't mind if Baranovich Station burned to the ground!" is the narrator's parting shot. Here, as elsewhere in *The Railroad Stories,* the narrator's judgment is not to be trusted, for in fact the story is already over. What more can one say after all its mythic and moral pretensions have been shattered? Besides, the real miracle of the story is that stories can be told at all; that out of "bankruptcies, expropriations, military emergencies, executions, starvation, cholera," there can emerge a teller of antitraditional tales who has the audience eating out of the palm of his hand. True, he is only fully engaged when telling the story, and for all we know he is as much a con artist as everyone else who travels this route. But for a brief moment he is able to suspend time and to reshape historical experience, no matter how bleak, into a spellbinding story that eclipses anything you could read in the papers. He can defy death itself, as Sholem Aleichem himself did when he collapsed on tour—in Baranovich.[73]

Like history, like the train, the parable of Kivke the stool pigeon is dead-ended, a story heading for the brink. But the storyteller manages to jump off just in time, to save himself and the story from its terrible finality. By playing heroism against miracles and calculated betrayal against communal solidarity, the author leaves only one person standing, albeit on the platform as the train is speeding away, and that person is the storyteller as hero. *His* story defies the fragmented nature of modernity by turning some motley travelers into a congregation of listeners. His story defies the vagaries of historical exile by forcing travel time to obey the rules of story time. And his story subverts the absurdity of life by interposing its own parodic reading of redemption and resurrection.

Train time is linear time, historical time. Jewish time is cyclical, and mythic. For the final face-off between them, in 1913, Sholem Aleichem pitted a hapless Jew from Kasrilevke named Sholem Shachnah Rattlebrain against the vagaries of the train. To raise the stakes (and perhaps for the sake of a holiday hook), he had Sholem Shachnah try to get home in time for Passover, when every Jew heads in the same direction.[74] Narrating this story is "a respectable merchant and dignitary of Kasrilevke, who deals in stationery and is surely no *littérateur*" but who has read the works of his traveling companion, Sholem Aleichem. The merchant has this to say about technology and the Jews: "When the wise men of Kasrilevke quote the passage from the Holy Book, '*Tov shem mishemen tov*'[Eccl. 7:1], they know what they're doing. Now how would your Tevye explain it? '*Svami dobre, a bez vam lutshe,*' [which in Ukrainian means:] When I'm alone, I'm happy; without you—I'm even happier. In other words, we were better off without the train."[75]

Like Tevye, like the Jew from Kaminka, and like the whole gallery of stand-in storytellers, the merchant from Kasrilevke delights in the knowledge that he is playing with reality. Chances are that readers also recall an old joke about a Jew and gentile who accidentally exchange clothing. (In a raunchier version told to me by Yehuda Elberg, a Jew swaps his gaberdine with that of a Russian Orthodox priest.) Sholem Aleichem delights in bracketing this well-known anecdote within a Passover frame and introducing multiple narrators (Sholem Shachnah who told it to the merchant who told it to Sholem Aleichem who tells it to us) so as to underscore who's really in charge.

Consistent with the norms of the modern Yiddish story, Sholem Shachnah is none too heroic or learned, just a typical down-and-out, unsuccessful middleman. His Jewish profile is similarly standard: like every good Jew, he's going home for the seders and would never think of being seen without a hat (as we learn from the story's dream sequence). But he also knows enough Russian to send a telegram home ("Arriving home Passover without fail") and to argue with officials at the Zlodievke train station. Like other celebrated scatterbrains and henpecked husbands (poor Shimen-Elye Shma-Koleynu comes to mind), Sholem Shachnah must cover up his failures as a man and a breadwinner through verbal exuberance—hence the rashness of adding "without fail" to his telegram.[76] This telegram marks his only real achievement, and it foretells his ignominious fate.

As a typical shtetl Jew, Sholem Shachnah must negotiate between two classes of gentiles: the Russian bureaucrats who speak High Goyish and are personified by Buttons and the conductor; the speakers of Low Goyish (Ukrainian), Yeremei the porter (in reality) and Ivan Zlodi (in his dream).[77] On native ground, talking is never a problem for a Sholem Aleichem hero. The art of communication gets stretched to the limit only when the hero travels by train.[78]

Arriving at the Zlodievke train station in the dead of night, with the walls of the station covered with soot and the floor covered with spit, Sholem Shachnah prepares himself to suffer the proverbial tortures of *khibet-hakeyver* (Y 246). In lieu of being beaten in the grave after death, he has a long night's wait in the station, and the only spot to lie down is occupied

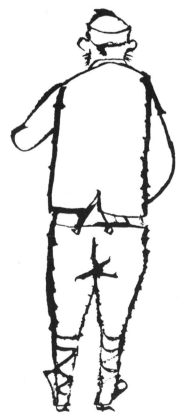

Ben Shahn, in Sholem Aleichem, *Inside Kasrilevke* (1945)

by a tsarist official decked out in sartorial splendor. "Who this Buttons was, whether he was coming or going, he hadn't the vaguest idea—Sholem Schachnah, that is. But he could tell that Buttons was no dime-a-dozen official. This was plain by his cap, a military cap with a red band and a visor. He could have been an officer or a police official" (Y 246, E 113). Since this high official with no identity save for his military cap (might he be a provincial commander, Sholem Shachnah wonders, "or even higher than that," the infamous Purishkevich himself?), our hero can engage his adversary only in the abstract, and only in his own mind. "But then he says to himself—now listen to this—Buttons, he says, who the hell is Buttons? And who gives a hang for Purishkevich? Don't I pay my fare the same as Purishkevich? So why should he have all the comforts of life and I none?" (Y 247, E 114).

After this pep talk, Sholem Shachnah faces the one remaining gentile on the scene, Yermei the porter, to whom he speaks rudely in Ukrainian, which does little to alleviate the hero's anxiety. In the nightmare that follows, Sholem Shachnah dreams that he's riding home for Passover in a wagon "driven by a thievish peasant, Ivan Zlodi." Though wagons are preindustrial and the language is Ukrainian, the wagon is soon out of control and Sholem Shachnah loses his hat.

As in the folktale, the hero is most lucid when he's dreaming. The dream not only foreshadows what will happen to a Jew when an antisemite holds the reins, but is also the point at which reality gives way to hallucination. Once Sholem Shachnah awakens, he never regains his bearing. It is all he can do to grab the first available hat under the bench and run off to buy a ticket. Thrust into a comedy of errors, with everyone staring only at the official's hat with the red band and visor, Sholem Shachnah is treated deferentially by the crowd, the ticket agent, and the conductor. Everyone addresses him in Russian as "Your Excellency" but the words fail to register; they make him angry. He vacillates between anger and confusion until the conductor ushers him into a first-class compartment, though he only paid for third class:

> Left alone in the carriage, Sholem Shachnah looks around to get his bearings—you hear what I say? He has no idea why all these honors have suddenly been heaped on him—first class, salutes, Your Excellency. Can it be on account of the real-estate deal he has just closed? That's it! But wait a minute. If his own people, Jews, that is, honored him for this, it would be understand-

able. But Gentiles! The conductor! The ticket agent! What's it to them? Maybe he's dreaming. Sholem Shachnah rubs his forehead and while passing down the corridor glances in the mirror on the wall. It nearly knocks him over! He sees not himself but the official with the red band. That's who it is! "All my bad dreams on Yeremei's head and on his hands and feet, that lug! Twenty times I tell him to wake me and I even give him a tip, and what does he do, that dumb ox, may he catch cholera in his face, but wake the official instead! And me he leaves asleep on the bench! Tough luck, Sholem Shachnah old boy, but this year you'll spend Passover in Zlodievke, not at home." (Y 252, E 116–117)

It is a brilliant shorthand for the modern crisis of identity. A Jew looks into a mirror and sees—the most unlikely image of himself he could ever imagine. So great is his shock that he jumps off the train to awaken his "real" self and the train leaves without him.

After spending Passover in Zlodievke, Sholem Shachnah makes it home to Kasrilevke where his wife heaps scorn upon him and the community treats him with mock respect. The Russian words "Your Excellency! Your Excellency!" ring in his ears as a bitter reproach. On native ground, where all languages are spoken, there is no escape from the wrath of the collective. From neutral, to alien, to native ground: the familiar tripartite structure of many Sholem Aleichem stories and of the European folktale in general. First the hero leaves home and makes good. In order to return he must pass through enemy turf (the Zlodievke train station) where he comes up against the ogre (Buttons). The hero then steals the ogre's weapon (his military cap with the red band and visor) and is magically transformed. He fails at the final test, however, and is duly punished (by missing the train and by the verbal abuse he suffers at home). And so what begins playfully enough in the realm of mock real-estate deals and impossible train schedules ends by turning into a parodic parable about lost identity.

The assumption of such a story, written in a semitraditional mold, is that Sholem Shachnah could never become Buttons. The hero grabs the first available hat because he can't go home hatless. At issue are not the barriers that prevent a Jew from becoming a gentile, but the vagaries of modern life (the train, the presence of antisemites) that make it so precarious to live as a Jew or to maintain any fixed identity whatever.[79]

As a late addition to the train stories, "On Account of Hat" shows what havoc historical time wreaks with mythic time. You can forget about Passover if you're going home by train. (Fishl the *melamed* could still make it, back in 1903, because he crossed the mighty River Bug by rowboat.) Yet just as in "Baranovich Station" it is the storyteller who has the last laugh. It is he (the stationery dealer from Kasrilevke, surely no littérateur) who puts everything back on track, safe in the knowledge that "plus ça change, plus c'est la même chose": schlemiel stays schlemiel, bruised but by no means crushed by his encounter, because save for his nightmare the evil is not internalized. Sholem Schachnah is no cousin of Kafka's Gregor Samsa. The Jew's misadventures have merely added to the fund of communal wisdom. Meanwhile, both the teller and his captive audience—the celebrated Sholem Aleichem himself—presumably make it home in time for their own seders, just as did the readers of this story who found it in the Passover supplement of their favorite Yiddish paper.

In the folklore of Slavic and Germanic nations, the operative myth was heroic, a tale of conquest and happy endings. Among Jews the best that could be hoped for was a tale of averted disaster. In contemporary Jewish folklore Sholem Aleichem found the one recurrent plot that confirmed his innermost sense of life: "all Jewish tales," he wrote in 1903, "all disasters among us begin with something trivial." (For Sholem Shachnah it is nothing more ominous than a telegram home.) And as for endings: "Jewish stories, for the most part, end sadly." (Sholem Shachnah at least does not go mad, like Shimen-Elye Shma-Koleynu, but neither does he make it home for Passover.[80])

As a writer of novels, as a so-called realist, Sholem Aleichem bowed to convention by trying to end his well-made plots on a more-or-less happy note. As a storyteller, Sholem Aleichem tried as best he could to mitigate the tragic ending common to all Jewish stories.[81] He did it most boldly in the final version of "A Tale Without an End," renamed "The Haunted Tailor." The new ending deserves to be quoted in full (and in Yiddish) even though it is well known:

Un der hayoytsey lonu mize? Un der may-ko-mashmo-lon fun der mayse?— vet fregn der lezer. Tsvingt mikh nisht, kinder! Der sof iz geven nisht keyn guter sof. Ongehoybn hot zikh di mayse zeyer freylekh, un oysgelozt hot zi zikh, vi dos rov freylekhe geshikhtes, oy-vey, zeyer troyerik. Un makhmes ir kent dem mekhaber fun der geshikhte, az er iz beteve nit keyn moyre-shkhoy-renik un hot faynt klogedike un hot lib beser lakhndike mayses, un makhmes ir kent im un veyst, az er hot faynt "moral" un zogn muser iz nit undzer derekh—lokheyn gezegnt zikh mit aykh metokh skhok der farfaser, lakhndik, un vintsht aykh, az yidn, un glat mentshn af der velt, zoln mer lakhn eyder veynen. Lakhn iz gezunt. Doktoyrim heysn lakhn.

"What is the moral of this tale?" the reader will ask. Don't press me, friends. It was not a good ending. The tale began cheerfully enough, and it ended as most such happy stories do—badly. And since you know the author of the story—that he is not naturally a gloomy fellow and hates to complain and prefers cheerful stories—and you know that he hates insisting on a story's "moral," and that moralizing is not his manner . . . Then let the maker of the tale take his leave of you smiling, and let him wish you, Jews—and all man- kind—more laughter than tears. Laughter is good for you. Doctors prescribe laughter.

This could not have been written in 1901, for then, at the beginning of his career as storyteller, Sholem Aleichem was still looking to history to pro- vide him with an ending. Now it was 1911, after the failed revolution of 1905; after his permanent departure from Russia; after his near-fatal attack of tuberculosis in the midst of a triumphal return visit; after years of re- cuperation in various European spas; and after he had composed most of his major story cycles, none of which had actually ended.[82]

As opposed to the comic Hebrew-Yiddish glosses with which the story began, this finale was written in a weighty, repetitive, super-Hebraic style, suggesting the importance the author himself attached to these thoughts. It was the closest he ever came to an explication of his storytelling art. The closed form of the story, he might have been saying, was addressed to Everyman ("Jews—and all mankind"), and therefore could yield as many meanings as there were readers. Unlike the novels serialized in the news- papers, stories did not require an Ideal Reader to respond in a prescribed way—and so "moral" be damned.

Now, too, the storyteller was the doctor of the soul. He alone knew the diagnosis, having laid bare the recurrent pattern underlying the vagaries of life. He alone could describe the myth as actually lived—truncated, ironic, tragic. He alone could piece it back together by playing the different forces against one another: language and life, stasis and historical change, fate and free will. If there was a cure, it lay in the recognition of how uncannily close the outline of myth was to the inner core of life itself. The very act of self-recognition would elicit nervous, cathartic laughter.

In the end, it was the story that kept hope alive or, more precisely, the ability of Jews anywhere to reconstitute themselves into a community of listeners—whether as third-class passengers on a Russian train or aboard ship bound for America or even as a one-time audience to hear the famous Sholem Aleichem himself read aloud from his works. And the story they heard, as told to them by a master raconteur, an expert in Jewish life and lore, was a story that could happen to anyone precisely because versions of it had happened countless times before: in the home of a Shunammite woman, in the land of Uz, in some enchanted forest.

Just as endings could be rigged to make the story better, so too could beginnings. By the winter of 1915, the Jews of eastern Europe who only months before enjoyed equal access to the great Sholem Aleichem were now divided into warring camps. The folk writer and his family had returned to America leaving their eldest son behind, to die of tuberculosis in a Danish sanatorium.[83] It was a good time for the father to write his will and to rewrite his autobiography—not the story of Yiddish literature, as originally planned, but the tale of a man born to be a storyteller whose very failures as a (step)son, student, lover, and provider were part of some mythic quest. Touting it as his Song of Songs, Sholem Aleichem serialized *From the Fair* for a New York Yiddish daily. Omitting all evidence of inner struggle, all serious reference to his intellectual origins, all dates and extraneous data, he reinvented himself as a traditional Yiddish storyteller.[84]

To begin with, there was his putative birthplace of Voronko, not so much a shtetl in the Ukraine as a cornucopia of legends. Whether in the marketplace, bursting with produce, the tumble-down study house, the dilapidated bathhouse, a spot at the bottom of the big hill, or inside the overgrown cemetery—everywhere the child turned there were local legends. His particular favorite was buried treasure, from the time of Chmielnicki. When it came to mining the past, however, the adult narrator drew the line at sad stories. "I have no desire to probe too deeply," Sholem Aleichem editorialized, "because I hate sad stories, no matter how venerable they may be" (Y 21). All in all, Voronko was as jovial and Jewish a place as its mythic counterpart, the storybook town of Kasrilevke.[85]

Then there was Reb Nokhem Vevik's home, also bursting with unnamed children of whom the hero was the middle child. Father was a kind of Renaissance man; mother, distant and preoccupied. The hero was loved only when he took ill or when he performed well, so long as his pranks and his mimic talents did not get out of hand. This is why his closest friends were deviants, orphans, or dogs. In their unsupervised company his creative—and aggressive—instincts found their natural outlet.

Like Isaac Luria and the Besht before him, our hero received the inspirational Torah outside the usual channels of transmission. Shmulik the orphan, with his red cheeks and dreamy eyes, inducted the author into the hidden reaches of the Jewish imagination and then disappeared from the scene. "To this day" the narrator could not account for the miracle. All he knew was that "the stories poured out of him as if from an everlasting spring. Smooth as oil, the stories flowed from him, drawn out like threads of silk. His voice and diction were as sweet as sugar. And his cheeks were red, his eyes dreamy and moist, as if covered with a slight film" (Y 29, E 9–10). The preferred storytelling hour was Friday afternoon, Sabbath after lunch, or on a holiday evening, at those in-between times of the Jewish calendar. The place: at Voronko's highest hill, "whose peak almost touched the clouds." The repertory: literary fairy tales, historical legends, tales of the supernatural. Shmulik's forte was the Kabbalah, first-hand knowledge of which he claimed to have from the saintly rabbi of Voronko, who had taken him on as a charity case. As opposed to the rabbi who, according to Shmulik, wanted to suffer in this world to be worthy of the next, the hungry orphan sought a more palpable form of compensation. He was after the treasure, whose secret burial place was known to the rabbi alone. Shmulik's talk about the treasure stirred the deepest emotions within his adoring playmate, Sholem.

Such was the essence of myth for the child as for the adult: it was knowable through simple legends about real things. Its main function was compensatory: to inject a sense of wonder into the drabness of everyday life. Even as it heightened the discrepancy between dream and reality, the myth kept miraculous possibilities alive. This fund of local legends was universally accessible. It was not the property of kabbalists, hasidim, or saints but of average men, women, and especially children.

Later in his fictional travels Sholem, the son of Nokhem Vevik, discovered a hasidic grandfather in Moshe Yossi, who embodied the world of religious mythology. This last encounter with the shtetl reawakened his memories of Shmulik.

> But the difference between Shmulik and Grandfather was that Shmulik spoke of treasures, wizards, princes and princesses—things that were part of the world of here and now; while Grandfather Moshe Yossi disdained this world and brought himself and his grandson, who listened with great suspense, to

the other world—to the righteous, the angels, seraphim and cherubim near the Seat of Glory, and very close to *Him* Himself, the King of the King of Kings, the Holy One Blessed Be He. (Y 240, E 121)

Though Sholem's grandparents got six chapters to Shmulik's two, and though old Moshe Yossi appeared at the high point of the Jewish calendar— from Rosh Hashannah and Yom Kippur through Sukkoth—the narrator viewed all the carryings on in the shtetl of Bohuslav from the outside, as a marvelous or grotesque spectacle, as a carnival. "The houses, the streets, the very cobblestones—*everything* sang and clapped, danced and made merry. Older Jews weren't the only ones to get drunk—youngsters too staggered on their feet" (Y 257, E 131). Sholem Aleichem worked hard on these chapters, adding ethnographic detail inspired by the recently published memoirs of an old Yiddish writer, Yekhezkl Kotik.[86] Just as Sholem Aleichem made Grandmother Sosye a more likable figure in the final, "ethnographic" version of the story, his portrait of Shmulik became altogether wondrous by the fourth and final draft.[87] The contest between religious and mundane myths became far more compelling.

There was no mistaking the author's bias, however. Shtetl grandparents inhabited a self-contained world that one could visit only briefly. They did not welcome an extended stay, nor did the children themselves warm to the moralizing that accompanied the legends and prayers. Shmulik, in marked contrast, was a projection of the hero himself—just as the hidden treasure became Sholem's most sustained and sustaining personal mythology.

Shmulik was the hero's deus ex machina, his Elijah in miniature. He was Sholem Aleichem's necessary invention to explain the late and miraculous rise of a Yiddish storyteller who, in actuality, had dreamed of very different treasures. As far as the audience was concerned, though, Sholem Aleichem need not have bothered, on the way back from the fair and so late in the day, to cover his tracks. That was because, from the moment he began turning fact into stylized fictions, Sholem Aleichem provided his readers, scattered over the far reaches of earth, with what they needed most: the holidays recloaked as carnivals; the grotesque reality as broken-down myths; the Russified reformer as beloved raconteur.

6

The Storyteller as High Priest
DER NISTER

Shteyt oyf, lerer un shiler mayne, vayl dos, vos s'iz mir
gekumen, dos iz mir gegebn, un ikh hob aykh tsu bezoyen gebrakht, un ir mikh tsu ash. (Stand up, my
teachers and students. I deserve what was done to me. I
brought you to shame, and you turned me to ash.)

—Der Nister, 1929

The great Sholem Aleichem died and was buried in New York. Any place, after that, could be home to a Yiddish storyteller. Berlin, so close linguistically and geographically to the Yiddish heartland, was another haven for expatriate Russian-Jewish artists. Indeed, the experience of exile united the entire Russian émigré colony, with the likes of Andrei Bely, Marina Tsvetaeva, Boris Pasternak, Alexei Remizov, Ossip Mandelstam, Maxim Gorky, Sergei Yessenin, Sergei Eisenstein, Vasili Kandinsky, and Igor Stravinsky. Graphic artists, free of linguistic constraints, fared best of all after 1922, when the first Russian art exhibition was held at Berlin's Galerie Vom Diemen, Unter den Linden.[1] Thus Berlin held out many possibilities for reconciling old cultural divisions and animosities: between the Russian modernists and their Yiddish and Hebrew counterparts, between German Jews and their benighted brethren from the east, between Yiddish and Hebrew writers. Some of the writers, such as the essayist and master anthologizer Micah Yosef Berdyczewski (1865–1921), the poet and critic David Frischmann (1860–1922), and the critic Ba'al Makhshoves (1873–1924), would die in Berlin. Others were en route to the promised land.

The Hebraists among them, led by Hayyim Nahman Bialik (b. 1873), left Russia forever. With eleven other Hebrew writers, Bialik managed to escape the Bolsheviks by boat to Constantinople thanks only to Gorky's intervention.[2] Despite this traumatic break, or perhaps because of it, members of the group spent their brief time in Berlin by fostering a neoclassical, monumental approach to the writing and collecting of Jewish stories. Berdy-czewski's project of using myths, legends, and tales to bridge east and west, Christian and Jew, psyche and symbol, had its direct analogue in Bialik and Ravnitsky's *Sefer ha'aggadah* (Book of Rabbinic Lore, 1909–1911.)[3] These Russian-Jewish intellectuals of the older generation made no distinction between the role of the storyteller as translator-anthologizer and his role as creative artist. Martin Buber, by the same token, conjured up so compelling a portrait of living mysticism with his *Tales of the Hasidim* as to turn even self-hating German Jews back to their "oriental" roots.[4] In 1921 he and the young Shmuel Yosef Agnon began collaborating on a major anthology of hasidic tales in Hebrew, the contract for which they had just signed with Bialik's new publishing house, Dvir. And Agnon's own love stories, *'Al kapot haman'ul* (Upon the Handles of the Lock, 1922), appeared from the Jüdischer Verlag of Berlin where Agnon had also worked as an editor.[5]

Jewish publishing flourished in Berlin as never before. Besides the trilingual works of Berdyczewski, which the Stiebel and Insel publishing houses were putting out in elegant editions, the Klal-farlag, recently acquired by the huge German publishing house of Ullstein, began marketing new and cheap editions of everything from the medieval *Mayse-bukh,* the *Tales* of Reb Nahman, and stories by Isaac Meir Dik to translations of Chamisso's *Peter Schlemiel, the Man without a Shadow* and the stories of Anatole France.[6] The marriage of Jewish avant-garde artists and writers, which had been consummated in Moscow and Kiev during the Revolution, also bore offspring in Berlin.[7] Mark and Rachel Wischnitzer were the husband-and-wife team responsible for the most lavishly illustrated journal of Jewish arts and letters ever produced, issued in parallel editions: *Rimon* in Hebrew, *Milgroym* in Yiddish (both meaning "pomegranate"). The full-color pages of the journal resembled a modern illuminated manuscript, with the secular stories and songs of the foremost Yiddish and Hebrew writers replacing the old sacred texts.[8] The Rimon publishing house also put out yet another Yiddish edition of Reb Nahman's *Tales.* From Shveln (Yiddish for "thresholds") came two works for children: Der Nister's *Tales in Verse* (4th ed.; illustrated by Chagall), and Leyb Kvitko's folio-sized *Birds,* illustrated by Issachar Ber Ryback (whose album of lithographs, *My Home in Ruins,* was Shveln's most ambitious production). Finally, from Wostok (Russian for "east") came a modern version of *The Selling of Joseph* by Max Weinreich (fresh from defending his dissertation on Yiddish linguistics at Marburg University), designed and illustrated by Joseph Tchaikov. Wostok's most expensive offering for 1923 was a deluxe, signed, and numbered edition in 100 copies of David Bergelson's *Mayse-bikhl,* illustrated and individually colored by the Vilna-born artist Lazar Segal.[9]

If Jewish storytelling—aided and abetted by publishers and illustrators—could offer some coherent vision in the wake of war, revolution, and pogroms, Berlin during the early years of Weimar was where it ought to have happened. Yet it was already too late. The storytellers themselves were split along a deep and unpassable divide.

The new crop of postwar Yiddish storytellers—as the names "Shveln" and "Wostok" suggested—had not burned their bridges behind them. Economic exigency more than anything else drove them from home; should they return, they would do so armed with the radical, cosmopolitan platform hammered out in German exile. Aside from the short-lived experiment of *Milgroym-Rimon,* the worlds of Yiddish and Hebrew seldom met. While the Hebraists and more well-to-do émigrés had their separate reserved tables at the Café Monopol, the Yiddishists returned after a day's work to the Scheunenviertel, Berlin's Jewish slum, there to drink tea and to argue politics at the Progress Cultural Club. Within a decade, most of the Wostok group were back in the Soviet Union. The Hebraists moved to Palestine.[10]

The founding fathers (Peretz, Sholem Aleichem, Abramovitsh, Ansky, Frischmann, and Berdyczewski), who had tried to be all things to all people and almost succeeded, disappeared from the scene in one fell swoop, between 1915 and 1921. For the succeeding generation of Jewish writers, who finally had to choose among languages and allegiances, it was hard enough remaining true just to one/self. Jewish storytelling had entered a period of high political stakes when the utopian path one took would be a matter of life and death.

Der Nister, born Pinkhes Kahanovitsh, was at the pinnacle of his career in 1922, and if anyone believed that stories would suture the wounds of the world, it was he. His fantastical tales were appearing simultaneously in Moscow, Berlin, and New York, and a two-volume collection with the enigmatic title *Gedakht* (Imagined) had just been published in Berlin.[11] Proclaiming that the world war and the Bolshevik revolution had given rise to a modern myth, a new apocalyptic vision, the literary critic S. Niger placed Der Nister at the center of the Yiddish pantheon.[12] The Wischnitzers, meanwhile, had recruited Der Nister and his good friend David Bergelson as the literary editors of *Milgroym*. Here in Berlin, the Mecca of Yiddish high culture, Der Nister might have found the only Gemeinschaft willing to support his elitist, uncompromising, and utopian art. In a sacred fellowship of Yiddish utopian dreamers, Der Nister would have officiated as high priest.

What happened in fact was a different story. The critical reception of Der Nister's fantastical tales was stillborn. Except for Marc Chagall, in 1917, Jewish artists ignored them altogether. None of Der Nister's verses for children was ever set to music. After 1929 it was impossible to find his fantasies for grownups anywhere but in a private or specialized library. Tales that brilliantly refashioned the Yiddish tale were never channeled back into the folk. They were either discarded as so much decadent trash or simply forgotten.

What happened to these dreams of a literary-cultural renaissance is that Bergelson and Der Nister left the editorial board of *Milgroym* after the first issue (1922) and threw in their lot with the Bolsheviks. Later that same year, the Moscow-based *Shtrom* carried this one-sentence letter to its editors, signed by the two men, which arrived just as the issue was going to press:[13]

> We wish to inform our colleagues, whom we had invited by word of mouth or in writing to collaborate in *Milgroym,* that we no longer have any connection to the Editorial Board of this journal and are no longer contributors thereto.

Der Nister made an even cleaner break with his bourgeois and nationalistic past in 1923. Under his joint editorship, an anthology titled *Geyendik* (Walking) was published by the Jewish Section at the Commissariat for Public Education in Berlin, with a dedication to *Shtrom* and featuring Der Nister's most programmatic tale, "Naygayst" (New Spirit). This story, dated "Moscow-Malakhovka, Summer 1920," ends with an ecstatic vision of the rising East, and there could be no doubt whatever that this Holy East was the site of Lenin's great experiment.[14] Der Nister and his fellow pilgrims were not quite ready to set out for the New Jerusalem on foot, as the title of their journal suggested, but their trajectory was set by the Red Star above.

Pinkhes Kahanovitsh came from priestly stock that did not abide any compromise. His father, Menakhem-Mendl, once lost himself so completely in a Talmudic tractate that he remained oblivious of the civil war raging in the streets outside. Aaron Kahanovitsh, an older brother, became a Bratslav hasid and cut himself off from the world. Max, the sculptor, was off and away in Paris. And Pinye, who sculpted each word, who was the harshest critic of his own work, discarding whatever struck him as inferior; who absorbed the style and structure of Reb Nahman Bratslaver's *Tales,* dreamed of redemption through art.[15]

Pinkhes Kahanovitsh means Phineas, Son of the Priest, or Cohen. It was unmistakably the name of a Russian Jew. But the writer who called himself Der Nister, a pen name so redolent with Kabbalah and Jewish esoteric traditions, served notice from the outset that he belonged to the world, to the cosmos. For all that this "Hidden One" probed the depths of purity and danger and wrote an almost liturgical prose, he had no intention of placing the Jewish perspective at the center of consciousness. Unlike previous Yiddish writers who tried to pass themselves off as preachers, pietists, or folk philosophers, Der Nister donned the cloak of Jewish mystic, high priest, or prophet, the better to explore the universal reaches of creation, revelation, and redemption. He delighted, moreover, in mixing poetry and prose, cosmology and folklore, and made religious syncretism into the gospel of a new idealistic religion. The name for Der Nister's faith was Symbolism, as practiced in Russia in the first decade of the twentieth century. Its credo was the ability of art to transform mankind.[16]

Just about everything in Der Nister's method—the attempt to go beyond the denotative limits of language and achieve musicality through repetition, connotative sound relationships, word inversions; his preference for myth, the occult, and the demonic; his view of the poet as prophet—was inspired by Vladimir Soloviev and Andrei Bely. Like them, Der Nister communed with the spirit of E. T. A. Hoffmann, master of the supernatural rendered in realistic manner. If fellow symbolist Aleksei Remizov was moved to write for children, so too was Der Nister. And if the Russian poets and storytellers mined the Eastern Orthodox Church for underground traditions and still potent Christian myths, Der Nister sought access to the Jewish mystical traditions.[17]

Reb Nahman's stock, as we have seen, had risen greatly by the 1920s, at least in Berlin. Buber (1908), Horodetzky (1922) and Kleinman (1923) all tried their hand at rewriting the *Tales* in modern idiom; back home in Berdichev, brother Aaron was trying to revive the tradition from within. Though Aaron's tales did not survive, it is safe to assume that they partook more of the eighteenth century than the twentieth. His was not an art of creative betrayal. But Pinye, in the now familiar pattern of rebellion, loss, and return, was able to reclaim the hasidic master thanks to the prophets and poets of Russian renewal. Had Der Nister not made a flamboyant break with his past, Nahman would never have become the patron saint of Yiddish symbolism.

From studying Nahman's numinous *Tales,* which he would soon put to his own artistic purposes, Der Nister learned the following: (1) every real plot involves a quest; (2) describing the process of tikkun or mending is more important than describing its product, and so it is better to have no ending than to have a forced one; (3) nameless, archetypal heroes are preferable to historical ones, and so the model to follow is the fairy tale and not the legend; (4) the storyteller should create his own symbolic landscape in which the forest, say, is the abode of demons, the desert a place of radical self-confrontation; (5) the way to plumb levels of being is through stories within stories, preferably narrated in a dream. Der Nister hoped to create a sense of arrested time, a reverence for the suggestive possibilities of each word, and to remake a sacred fellowship of readers with the storyteller as seer at its center.[18]

Titling his inaugural tale simply "A mayse" (1913), in much the same way as Reb Nahman had announced without fanfare that "the time has come for me to begin telling stories," Der Nister introduces his central cast of characters: a *nozir,* a hermit living far from human habitation, his animal companion (a kid), and a fairly ludicrous bunch of petty demons—*khoyzek, lets, nisht-guter* (mocker, imp, evil spirit)—who speak in rhymes and riddles.[19] It is winter, literally in the middle of no place, and the demons are bored. The best they can do is to kidnap a billy goat who belongs to a witch, keeping it hostage against her telling them a story: the tale of a hermit and his *vald-tsigele* or forest kid—herself a virginal double of the demonic billy goat. It may sound familiar, this technique of story-within-a-story. Only on the surface, because the hermit of the witch's tale acts in a peculiar manner. After years of isolation, each day spent praying on his knees (as Christians pray), the hermit accepts his mission without question; it does not arise from an inner struggle. The hermit's whole story, his very quest, is only the product of a witch's mind.

Todros Geller, in Mikhl Davidzon, *In veldl* (In the Woods, 1926)

One summer's day the hermit sets out into the forest and meets an un-identified person who gives him some vague directions until he meets a eunuch-faced, clownlike dwarf. This demonic figure gives the hermit his marching orders: to find a scroll hidden in a mountain cave, which in turn will reveal that truth lies in the ground, in the "seed." "But see," warns the Person, "Beware advice, guard against encounters . . . your desire is your foe, hurry—your betrayer, chance is your friend, and patience—the one who loves you" (139). The logic of this apparent happenstance points to the suspension of conflict, human will, and initiative. Passivity is the highest attribute of man, and the hermit must submit to this condition even if it is set by the devil.

If this is the mystic's *via passiva,* then something is not quite right. "Truth lies in the ground" is familiar enough as the Kotzker Rebbe's famous para-phrase of Psalm 85:12, the slogan of his lifelong struggle for absolute truth-fulness.[20] But the seed of ineffable truth that the hermit is after is at the farthest remove from the religious discipline that the Kotsker tried to instill in his elite corps of truth seekers. The essence of the hermit's quest is its extreme individualism. However many magical donors he meets along the way, including a wanderer much like himself, truth can only be appre-hended alone. "Az heylik di vegn, nor heyliker geyers," says the Wanderer to him in perfect amphibrachic meter. "Gebentsht iz der gang un ge-bentshter dos geyn, un geyn heyst . . . bazunder" (Holy are the ways, and even holier the wanderers; blessed is the march, and more blessed the marching, and to march is to be . . . separate; 149). The deeper he gets into the forest, the more the hermit must draw from within himself, "from the holy in the Holy of Holies" (139).

Within a quest so inward, the trials that the dwarf and the forest imps force the hermit to undergo—tempting him with riches, plaguing him with fear and skepticism, fright and lust—are nothing compared to the last: to do nothing at all, to remain with the kid in a state of perpetual longing. Nahman's viceroy once had to undergo a similar trial, in the "Tale of the Lost Princess," except that here the trial becomes an end in itself, just as the kid comes to symbolize the suspension of will, the ideal state of ironic wonder.[21] The very act of waiting, in Der Nister's scheme, is a form of self-purification.

Three-plus-one and the very long story is over. Three trials followed by a third and three donors (the Person, Birdie, and Man in the Moon), the last of whom informs the hermit about a witch who will be forced to tell the demons a tale in order to free her billy goat. The place where they will be sitting is where the seed lies buried. And so, at the bewitching hour, the billy goat arrives and calls for the hermit and his kid to set out again. In the time it takes to trudge through the snow, the witch is busy telling her demons the very ransom story we have been reading all along; the ending is interrupted by the arrival of the hermit, who scares the demons away, frees the witch, and liberates the spot where the kernel lies buried. The quest comes back to consume its literary frame.

Rivaling Reb Nahman's most optimistic plots, "A Tale of a Hermit and of a Kid" (as Der Nister later renamed it) is a tale of triple tikkun: a witch liberates her billy goat from captivity by telling a long and seductive tale about the very demons who hold her hostage; a hermit, accompanied by his forest kid, arrives at the kernel of truth by overcoming his individual desire; and the two-tales-in-one prove the ultimate victory of the human, creative realm over that of the demons. The key to the story's meaning lies, as it does for Reb Nahman, in the defamiliarization of the standard story-telling repertory, of the "tales as the world recounts them." The central action consists of inaction; the scene of greatest struggle is within an empty space—a clearing in the forest, an abandoned ruin. The presence of specifically Jewish markers serves only to camouflage the subversion of traditional Jewish values. For even if this were a modern rendering of the mystic's *via passiva,* the truth lies buried in the ground; it directs the seeker within himself and to the power of the imaginative realm. There is no Godhead, Ein-Sof, or messiah figure anywhere on the scene. There is only the virgin *tsigele,* utterly passive and awestruck, and the clever witch, who can wind her way out of captivity with a complicated tale.

To live is to wander. The circular structure of Der Nister's stories suggests that whatever life's ultimate goal, it can be found only within the closed circle of the human mind, within the purview of *Gedakht.* That is not what Reb Nahman meant when he refused to spell out how the viceroy rescued the princess. Each listener could understand the process and purpose of the viceroy's quest according to a fixed set of external referents. Der Nister's stories, in contrast, are self-consuming artifacts in which the sought-for destinations have no objective correlative either in heaven or on earth. The route to salvation lies somewhere in the meeting of the real and the fantastic.

That the twain do meet in the year of troubles for Russian Jewry, 1913, was Der Nister's way of calling for the redemption of history through art. For 1913 was also the year Sholem Aleichem came out with the revised ending of his own man-and-goat-saga—the reprieve of Shimen-Elye, his family, his town, and the twin town of Kozodoyevke by the storyteller himself. Der Nister was said to have admired the monologues of Sholem Aleichem, and insofar as the act of storytelling is central to the work of both writers, there is a deep affinity between these native sons of the Ukraine.[22] Yet "A Tale of a Hermit and a Kid" is "The Haunted Tailor" turned upside down and inside out.

Sholem Aleichem's shtetl landscape is immutable, sanctioned by centuries of stagnation. There is a tavern situated halfway between the poles of deprivation and desire wherein resides the devil. The quest is doomed from the start, and the milk-giving goat can never make it home. Der Nister begins by framing each story within a fantastic setting of his own invention. He weaves one story into another and yet another so as to keep the boundaries between the real and imaginary blurred and unstable. The stories take place "At the Border," "In the Desert," "In the Forest," "there, in the middle" of some indeterminate space, and are narrated by a motley crew of witches, wanderers, cuckoo birds, eagles, moles, camels, giants, and stargazers.

Crises that seek resolution are resolved within—and by—this self-consuming world of the storyteller's art. How do the hermit and his kid arrive at their goal? By becoming immutable themselves.

The claustrophobic familiarity of Sholem Aleichems's fictional world is here replaced by a "mythical atmosphere," as one reader put it, evocative of half-forgotten legends and folktale plots, in which the dimensions of time and place converge only at the beginning and the end. As for the rest, time and causality go their separate ways.[23] Instead of citing mock quotations to show what a learned and witty narrator he is, Der Nister uses almost no Hebraisms or Slavicisms, cites nothing directly from classical sources, and in general affects a tightly controlled, thoroughly artificial literary style that recalls the medieval world of romance and extreme asceticism. That *nozir,* for example, hasn't been heard from since the days of Abraham Ibn Ḥasdai's *The Prince and the Hermit* (Constantinople, 1518), a Hebrew adaptation of the life of Buddha.[24] Salvaged from the distant past, this medieval landscape is traversed by the life of the mind. A mind that does nothing but wait and narrate: *Gedakht.*

Only the elect, in vows of silence, quiescence, and celibacy, will inherit the seed of truth. The hermit's quest is emancipated from worldly constraints all the better to dedicate himself to the pursuit of perfection. The hermit is that tiny piece of the past that Der Nister has salvaged in order to embody his own artistic and ethical ideal. The hermit's ascetic regime is of a piece with Der Nister's exacting otherworldly style, and both stand at the furthest remove from Sholem Aleichem's linguistic abundance and the tragicomic attempts of his shtetl Jews to wrest some joy from the humdrum of life. As Sholem Aleichem rewrote shtetl satires and folktale plots to yield a new folkist faith, Der Nister will soon turn everything—even the granddaddy of all Yiddish romances, the swashbuckling tale of Bove and Princess Druziana—into a hermitage. The hermit stands as a bulwark against materialism, the accommodations of bourgeois life, the compromises of commercial art.

For better or worse, Der Nister was not Sholem Aleichem's disciple but Peretz's. It was to Peretz that the twenty-three-year-old Pinkhes Kahanovitsh made a pilgrimage. It was from Peretz that Der Nister learned to cultivate a visionary style. It was Peretz who taught him how to betray Jewish messianism, mysticism, and folklore in the name of artistic renewal and individual freedom. Peretz's aristocratic demeanor and idealistic rhetoric were the stuff that Der Nister's persona and poetic prose were made of. Yet when maintained in an environment more hostile than any Peretz could have imagined, this discipleship exacted a heavy price.[25]

World War I and the Bolshevik revolution strengthened Der Nister's faith in the marriage of high art and reality. From his perspective, the collapse of the old order in Russia presaged the rise of a new holy community composed of wandering writers, graphic artists, and teachers. When he moved to Kiev with his wife and three-year-old daughter in the winter of 1916, the thirty-two-year-old paterfamilias had little to show for himself except the coveted "white ticket" exempting him from active military service. He hated the thought of tutoring Hebrew and hoped to make his living as a translator.[26] The stories of Hans Christian Andersen were his first project.[27] A year later Der Nister published *Tales in Verse* for children, with striking illustrations by Chagall.[28] Active as well in the newly organized network of Yiddish secular schools, Der Nister by war's end had come to view education as the frontline in the aesthetic revolution.

Among the goals that the Kiev circle of artists, writers, critics, and educators set for itself was the creation of a suitable Yiddish children's literature. So they compiled an inventory of all the prewar Yiddish chapbooks by Peretz, Sholem Aleichem, Avrom Reisen, and so on, and evaluated their suitability for preschoolers and school-age children. The pedagogue Ch. S. Kazdan rendered this service in a new literary review, *Bikher-velt* (Kiev, 1919), where he demoted the classicists to the status of folklore and elevated folklore and folk art as vehicles of abstract modernism.[29]

Central to the new aesthetic was the word *lubok*, the Russian term for the folk art of primitive broadsides.[30] In the same issue of *Bikher-velt*, Kazdan and Yekhezkl Dobrushin commended the primitivism of the *lubok* as specially suited for a Jewish child. If one could reclaim Jewish folk iconography, they argued, one would have the key both to the mass psychology of the child and to the uniquely spiritual qualities of Jewish folk life. Chagall was the artist whom both authors held up for particular praise, and Chagall's illustrations to Der Nister's *Tales in Verse* were hailed as the ultimate synthesis of visual and verbal folk stylization.[31]

The belief that the abstract form of the *lubok* was the essence of art and that the national element was always expressed in its purest form was a belief shared by such young artists as Issachar Ber Ryback and Borukh

Marc Chagall, in Der Nister, *A mayse mit a hon, Dos tsigele*
(A Tale of a Rooster, The Little Kid; 1917)

Aronson, whose manifesto "The Paths of Jewish Art" also appeared in Kiev in 1919.[32] All these artists, critics, and pedagogues were calling for a new art form that would shift the emphasis of creative betrayal from seeming artlessness to the most artful stylization. The basis of the new art was to defamiliarize folk culture, to play with different perspectives, to call attention to the linguistic surface and frame, and above all to mix symbolic systems at will—in other words, to do what Der Nister had been doing since before the war.

Der Nister's translations and original verse for children were of a piece with his fantasies for grownups. True to the Haskalah ideal of expanding the cultural horizons of the Jews, Der Nister resisted the temptation of Judaizing Andersen's stories, which was standard procedure in the fledgling field of Yiddish children's literature, and gave the source as it was, New Year's Eve, Christmas tree, and all.[33] His own stories also encouraged a return to nature—to roosters, goats, bears, dogs, cats, farmers—no longer for the sake of ethical exhortation, as in the fable, but in order to cultivate a primitive, sometimes grotesque, and always marvelous setting. Like Andersen, Der Nister told how-so tales for children: how the rooster comes to crow for the dead (because of an old granny who once took care of a rooster). Like Peretz's goat in "Reb Nakhmenke's Stories," Der Nister's goat also sacrifices its horns, but for the sake of a queen's newborn thumb-size infant. This is both a child's world, full of wonder, and a poet's world, full of symbolic action.[34]

One salutary result of writing for children is that Der Nister's stories became more playful—and plot-full. The funniest of Der Nister's twenty symbolist tales is "Demons" (1918), a reworking of the famous "Story of the Jerusalemite," a favorite of Micah Yosef Berdyczewski.[35] The standard version tells of the accidental or involuntary marriage of a young man and a demon and describes the netherworld in startlingly human terms. Der Nister's version begins (and ends) with two demons in a cave, the older one goaded by the younger into telling a story. This is a spoof on the master-disciple relationship that Der Nister elsewhere takes so seriously. For the old demon, his horns and claws dulled with age, and his skin soon to be used for a drum, is tickled and prodded (in a faintly obscene manner) into confessing a none-too-heroic episode from his youth. It is the story of how he and a young imp (*lets*) waylaid a traveler in the forest by donning various disguises and by finally provoking him to spit into a well, thus putting him into their clutches.

Dragged inside the well, which turns into a tavern, the traveler is drugged into changing places with the imp, and to perform in front of a veritable Noah's ark of demonkind that behaves "*mit khoyzek un khalyastre*, with wildness and [like a] wild gang," "*breyt un badkhonish un fray un freylekh*, with largesse and jest with free and frolick" (97, 98). These jingles are worth remembering because they capture the difference between demonic and human freedom. Demons are a faceless bunch. Their freedom is ephemeral, selfish, and self-consuming. Only humans can behave selflessly and effect true liberation through the mind's eye. When humans don a disguise, moreover, they can discard it at will; demons when they strip leave nothing but their skins behind. The crux of the story is the demons' challenge for the captive to reveal his nakedness under the skin: "So let him show us something of his and his alone, of man and humanity, and what a man can do and of what he is capable" (99). Give me total autonomy, he demands, and swear to listen in silence. They in turn exact an oath by his horns.

This proves the demons' undoing, for a human cannot be bound by an oath to a set of fake horns, and the story he tells—about the love of a she-demon for a human wanderer (a *geyer*) and the child he sires—demonstrates the superiority of human love, creativity, and imagination. Demons are undifferentiated, until they fall in love. As the she-demon is redeemed by the wanderer's love in the story the captive conjures up, the faceless assembly of demons grows ever more hostile and frightened. When their panic is at its peak, the waylaid traveler escapes into the mirror of his own invention, finally proving just how free a human being can be. He leaves them all shouting: "He will tell of our shame!" (115)—as indeed he does, and as the doddering demon now retells it to his young charge.

Storytelling is the essence of "what a man can do and of what he is capable." The demons are but parodies of the human condition. What they create is insubstantial. They are governed by their false desires, whereas man can wander in and out of reality at will. He will cohabit and collaborate with demons if he must, but the freedom, the love, and the artfulness he displays reveal man at his most human, humanity at its most divine.

It is a breathtaking vision, beyond historical exigency. Not only does the traveler's dissemblance save himself and teach a she-demon to love, but it

Todros Geller, in Mikhl Davidzon, *In veldl* (1926)

exposes the whole cast of demons to ridicule. If the demons represent on some level the forces of evil in the world, then Der Nister's optimism at this point in time is truly fantastical.

History itself dissembles into story, romance, and adventure as Der Nister borrows next from the most famous of all Yiddish stories, the sixteenth-century *Bovo-bukh,* to offer his most spectacular scenario of redemption wrought by human hands. Of all the young wanderers, none has greater fortitude than Bove. Of all the trials that must be overcome, none requires more vision and precision than the restoration of the three kings. Of all the historical plots that Der Nister adapted, none served him better than this medieval romance.[36]

"A Bove-mayse, or A Tale of Kings" begins with a king who falls ill.[37] "He trembled for his crown and his throne, he no longer believed in his kingdom and his people." After all else fails, and when the king despairs of being healed, a beggar appears who offers to heal him with a story.

> In a certain country, under a certain king, in an enormous field, right in the middle, there lived an old man, eighty years old; in a shack that could barely stand with age, with crooked walls, and a tiny roof that was full of holes. The shack lay low, close to the earth, with a tiny window, only one, and a tiny door that was bent and bowed, leading in, right into the ruin. This was where the old man lived, this was his home and his alone, and day and night he talked to his walls, and never saw a living creature, ever, except for them, and he never *needed* anyone, ever, except for them. And time wore on, a good long time. (Y 138, E 462)

This is the story's proper beginning: a monastic setting in the middle of time and space, where a man's only companions are the living walls. Then "from the horizon, and from where the sun was drooping" there comes a youngster who administers to the old man. Whereas his namesake, the Bove of Yiddish romance, learns martial and magical arts, our young hero undergoes the Nisterian regime of waiting—and communing with the living past, embodied by the old man and the walls of his hovel. On his deathbed the old man prophesies that, as Bove brought comfort to an aged man, so shall he stand before kings and comfort them. Other prophecies soon make clear that only such a one as Bove can bring solace to the world.

The first of the three kings who requires solace has an only daughter who longs for a companion, someone to help her in her troubles, "and all the time, and be prepared to risk his life for her at any time" (E 467). Lowly Bove, who alone fits the stargazer's profile, is brought to court where he becomes the princess's companion—and her destined bridegroom. But before that can happen, the annual hunt takes place, which becomes an act of *shevirah*.

> And then, when the king with his daughter and Bove, had vanished deep inside the woods, and all around them, except for their tracking, no human could be sensed, nor a human sign, and not a dog and not a bark of other dogs, and only their own hounds and forerunners, from bush to bush, tore onward, seeking with long noses and sharp noses, and sniffed and pried and all in vain, and then dashed on, and, with the king and the king's children, reached the heart of the forest, and the woods grew denser, and overgrown with undergrowth, and interbranched and intertreed, and silent, unusually silent, and undisturbed by any noise—when all at once, from a bush, an animal, a terrified beast, aroused from its rest, from its lair and its wooded life, streaked past the king and past his escorts, bumping past them and startled and not counting on being saved, it suddenly halted in front of them, not knowing where to turn, not having anywhere to flee—and all at once, with a cunning animal-leap, it sprang upon the princess's breast, and with its hurling leap and its bewilderment, it flung the princess upon the ground. (Y 161, E 474)

There is contemplative space and dramatic space. To reach them, you must leave behind the commonplace world of the "human" and "human signs" and enter an alternative reality through a series of cognitive displacements: a royal hunt, all its senses primed, penetrates a living, palpably silent forest where it awakens a slumbering beast, who in turn wreaks havoc in this heart of primordial silence, directing his violence in the end at the virginal princess. The familiar is rendered strange by the teller's alliterative spell, the hypnotic rhythms, and the dense imagery that shift the reader's attention to an inanimate object—here, the forest—with a life of its own. The repetition of key words plays their sound quality against their denotative sense. The effect of all these poetic devices is to eliminate the actual players and concrete particulars so as to remain with an archetype. The goal of Der Nister's description is to create something that is noticeably an artifice, but so perfect that it reflects, in a way, all levels of reality and no level in particular. In a word, this is the storyteller's revision of cosmic *tsimtsum*, contraction, followed by the inevitable *shevirah*, chaos.

Though Bove is present, he does not risk his life, as one might expect. Instead, he and the king take aim and shoot the beast dead. But the damage is done. The princess remains in a coma from which she cannot be roused. The true test of Bove's courage comes with the next revelation: the princess will recover only when she is joined with her beloved in marriage. "But he must know, he who assumes this love, that the princess will not recover so soon, that she will lie on her bed for long, and he will have to wander through the world and endure much hardship and overcome many obstacles and impediments, and at last, and when he has overcome all, only then will he come to his beloved, only then to his desire" (Y 171–172, E 479).

Here at last is a trial worthy of Bove's special talent and training. Bove now comes forward, in his first fully self-conscious act, utters the word "I," and offers his hand in marriage. No longer the hermit's apprentice or the princess's adolescent companion, he must act as adult lover. And as always in the ascetic fantasy world of Der Nister, the real action involves waiting, wandering, deferral, sublimation, self-sacrifice. This story takes its place in a long line of spiritualized romances from Reb Nahman's "Tale of the Lost Princess" to Peretz's "Devotion Without End" to Ansky's *Dybbuk*.

Bove's curriculum is neither mystical nor ethical, though; it is rigorously psychological.[38] Following his successful apprenticeship (ministering to the old man) and initiation (ministering to the princess and growing to love her), he must now engage in solitary acts of self-confrontation. As the first old man gave him access to the past, the aged stargazer in the king's palace now gives him access to the future. Echoing the old man's prophecy, the stargazer says: "You shall stand before kings and comfort kings. And know: Each king for your comfort will give you something, and from every king you shall receive a present" (Y 175, E 481). The stargazer, meanwhile, gives Bove a magical whetstone, which will become an agent of prophecy and introspection all in one.

Bove's third and final role—as wandering visionary—is also divided into three. Standing back from the myriad details of this rich and symmetrical plot, it becomes clear that each of the kings represents an aspect of Bove that he must confront and vanquish. The watery spirits whom the first king's heir-apparent discovers in the royal garden, sending him into a state of shock, suggest the dark regions of the unconscious, the buried and anarchic memories of the past. Bove is shown in a dream that the prince's therapy is to stare into the whetstone "as though there were *nothing* before his eyes" (Y 192, E 490), curing darkness with darkness, as it were. Having conquered the darkness within himself, Bove is now self-assured, serious, and responsible (Y 194, E 491). He appears before the catatonic prince, and a glow comes from the whetstone, "starlike and unwonted, streaming and bluish white, and turning the darkness of the room even darker, and the stillness of the room even stiller" (Y 196, E 492–493).

The second king and queen are a childless couple to whom a stillborn child is finally born—by recourse to magic. (The queen's excruciating labor recapitulates the violent hunt in the forest and the ghoulish water spirits in the king's garden.) These are the forces of false creativity that Bove must combat. Again it is through dreams that Bove is shown how to administer the cure and how to speak with sufficient "clarity and simplicity" that the king would believe in him (Y 241, E 517). An old midwife at the festive banquet that follows gives Bove a wolf's tooth handed down through generations "to hearten all hearts, and to dishearten all fears and terrors" (Y 247, E 521); and a good thing too, since the last king to be comforted is terror-stricken in the wake of his defeat in a wrestling match.

The circus, for Der Nister, is the arena of deceit, falsehood, externals, inequality, nudity—and will later be the setting for his artistic auto-da-fé.[39] The third king stages wrestling matches for his courtiers to watch him vanquish the strongest athletes in the land. Of course the contest is a sham because the visiting athlete would look around at the crowd, "and he would see their refinement and their composure, their dress and their comport-

Yosl Kotler, in Herman Gold, *Mayselekh* (1928)

ment, their courtly background and their familiarity with the king and closeness to the king" (Y 257, E 527) and would be nonplussed. And while the athlete is invariably "dressed in something light, and flesh-colored and snug and skintight," his royal opponent appears in regal splendor:

> The moment the strong man caught sight of the king in his dress, his royal attire, in his wealthy attire aglow with golden tinsel; and the moment the king stood before him with his height and pride, with his body and bodily solidarity, with his assurance and certainty, and as the king approached the strong man with his bold tread, and with his confidence, and came before him—and the strong man lost his courage and strength, he felt like a common man before the king, and obedient subject of the king. (Y 257–258, E 527)

Then the king decides to stage one last wrestling match in full view of the public and faces off against a proud athlete, who "would fulfill his task with perfection, come what may, and be what will" (Y 262, E 529).

The moment of shevirah—when for the first time the king is felled—is here compounded by the sight of the spectators clearly favoring not him, the king, but his opponent. The king's fragile ego, propped up all this time by externals, is battered beyond repair, and he sinks into depression and delirium. The last hope is that somewhere at the border and frontier of his kingdom there is to be found a beggar, for only he can know of a cure. A wandering beggar, in other words, who lives in a world devoid of ego gratification, free of false pride and position, is ideally trained to heal shattered souls.

Just as we reach the cure for the third and final king, the storyteller pulls *his* most extraordinary sleight of hand: the vanquished king is the very one whose illness set the story in motion, and the beggar who has been narrating this very story in order to cure him is none other than Bove. Once again, and most brilliantly, the hero's quest has swallowed up the literary frame, though there is still a ways to go: Bove takes the wolf's tooth out of his pouch and hangs it around the king's neck. More than the magic tooth, it is Bove's "faithful and believing" smile that brings the king around to believing in a cure (Y 271, E 534). Then all else falls into place: the king is cured; he celebrates with a banquet, where Bove is offered a king's ransom, but all he wants is a single gift—the king's wolf-horse that is missing its front tooth. When reunited with the sight of its lost tooth, the wolf whisks Bove back to the palace where his bride is finally roused from her slumber by his triumphant return, the lovers embrace, and the story ends with their marriage.

The most "proactive" of Der Nister's stories is also the most cathartic, and so the teller signs off in the first person, albeit formulaically: "And I, too, was there at that wedding and ate gingerbread, and . . . whoever doesn't want to remember this tale, he can forget it."[40] Storytelling offers the ultimate cure. Only the artist can awaken the sleeping beauty. Only he who has communed with the past can see into the future, and only he who has struggled to achieve self-knowledge can cure those whose souls are divided. Of all Bove's roles, the role of storyteller is the most inclusive—and exclusive. He is the chosen, the healer of all humanity.

In his fictions, the boundary between dream and reality is fused and confused. In life, the frontier is mined. The hero of his stories, though guided by celestial powers above and instructed by helpers below, takes sole charge of his destiny. Real life—history—was never lived alone. What choices did Der Nister have, and why did he make the choices he did? *Milgroym-Rimon,* with its accent on the Jewish and artistic heritage, and its great admiration for Peretz, ought to have been a more congenial home for Der Nister's hermits, goats, and petty demons than any house organ of fellow travelers. Der Nister, who laid so much store by tradition, should have welcomed the chance to rub shoulders with Hayyim Nahman Bialik (to whom he had made a pilgrimage in 1912); to compare messianic visions with the poet and playwright Moyshe Kulbak; to reinvent Jewish folk narrative alongside Israel Wachser and S. Y. Agnon.[41]

The one story Der Nister published in *Milgroym,* "At the Border," certainly harmonized with the Jewish universalism of the journal's other contributors.[42] Once again, the story's redemptive theme is couched in romantic terms—the story of a giant, "the last of his kind," and his search for the emperor-giant's daughter, who lives in an ancient tower by the sea. In Der Nister's symbolic shorthand they clearly stand for the forces of Good, especially when faced with the leper who thrice diverts the giant from his quest. The people, provoked by the leper, repudiate the giant's vision of restoration. But the giant perseveres, reaches the ancient tower, and consummates his marriage, vouchsafing the continuation of his race. It remains only for a camel to return with two lit candles on his hump as the sign of *tikkun,* the very sign that the creature "at the border" so eagerly awaits.

Elitist and supremely optimistic—such were Der Nister's symbolic fairy tales in the period leading up to his sojourn in Berlin and his brief tenure as literary editor of the glorious journal of Yiddish arts and letters. Then suddenly things changed: Der Nister abandoned this aristocratic home of neotraditional art. He left Berlin—the city he hated for its pretense, its poverty, and its distance from the Yiddish-speaking people—and joined his friend Leyb Kvitko in Hamburg, where they both worked for the Soviet export agency.[43]

The stories changed too, growing even more allusive, using satire to conceal and reveal their critical perspective. Between 1922 and 1923, Der Nister bid farewell to the tale of tikkun and turned to variations on shevirah instead. Reb Nahman departed from his stories with a flourish, as did the open-ended forests, deserts, and oceans. The stories now featured taverns with walls of black enamel; porcelain puppies suffering from toothache; slimy bridges; towers filled with dust; clowns, comedians, and circus ladies. Increasingly, Der Nister's tales begin with a real and recognizable setting before moving off into the upper reaches of the imagination.

True to its title, "In the Wine Cellar" (1922) is set in an inn, The Blind Man, with its black walls that provide a night's shelter for drunks who think they can change the world, and from there ascends to the unrequited love of Aquarius for Virgo. Aquarius, smitten star, neglects to water the world as a result. And although the embedded tale ends with Virgo's imminent marriage to a higher and much younger star than Aquarius, a wedding to be attended by (Reb Nahman's) Seven Beggars, there is no escape from the story's frame. Back in the tavern, the drunks wake up, step outside and take a leak. Moral: when the wells of the world go dry, the human earthsavers pass dirty water.[44]

The faultline we are looking at marks more than just a shift from quest to inquest in Der Nister's storytelling art. When he left *Milgroym* to publish his own anthology, he also adopted the Soviet Yiddish orthography, whose most radical sign was the phonetic spelling of Hebrew-Aramaic words. Instead of making Yiddish culturally self-sufficient—by "emancipating" the most ancient stratum of the language from its clerical setting and naturalizing it on the printed page—the new orthography was exploited by Jewish communists to insulate Soviet Yiddish literature from the past and to isolate it from the West.[45] Now, Der Nister and his friends proclaimed a mini-revolution, through the very form that their Yiddish writings would assume, both here in the West and soon home in the Ukraine. When *Gedakht* was reissued in the Ukrainian Socialist Republic, however, Der Nister was forced to omit those "reactionary" tales that spelling alone could not rehabilitate.[46]

Among the tales that never made it home is an extraordinary story-within-a-story-within-a-story called "Beheaded" (1923).[47] At first blush, it is about a man named Adam finding a cure for his headache. The headache appears a little before midnight in the person of a dandified comedian, complete with a white perfumed handkerchief, who identifies himself within a caustic line or two as a close cousin of the demons and lepers who populated Der Nister's earlier tales. There is no mistaking the story's psychological, if not pathological, intent. What do they have in mind? To crown him? Who would have a head for such a thing? Certainly not *he*!

Rather than ease us into the fantasy realm with a cosy one-on-one story-telling round, the story thrusts a modern scene of self-confrontation upon us. With biting repartee, Adam's cynical double debunks the whole issue of crowning. "Crowns become thorns," Comedian instructs him. "Spare me," comes Adam's reply. "We've already exhausted that topic." Whatever religious or transcendent significance this crowning might have is immediately undermined.

Comedian then launches into a detailed accounting of Adam's "estates"—a richly ambiguous term that cuts in two directions: all that a person like Adam possesses is his internal landscape, but within it there is room enough for pride, materialism, megalomania. This is brought home to Adam by a vision of his "subjects" taking up a collection on market day to erect a monument to him. It is a scene of contention, class conflict, and hypocrisy. Adam furiously rejects this projection of himself as a power-hungry ruler, so Comedian distracts him with the news that his master is to arrive at midnight. But before he does, Comedian has more tricks up his sleeve: a new and very crowded vision full of Adams and servants, the former who acclaim the Master, the latter who ridicule him. At this point, Adam has had enough. He rebels against the negative conjurations, opens the lid of his head, and forces Comedian back inside.

Having regained a sense of self, Adam is ready for a vision of his own, a countervision to the mass rally in the market. He sees a midnight crowning—a ritual of induction into a monastic order of harmony and egalitarianism. Like Jesus at the last supper, the Master bids the disciples to "eat the bread and drink the wine and have our new disciple in your thoughts," for "today he will be crowned with our good and our fate" (177). Together they enter Adam's room, which abruptly dissolves into the Plaza of the Beheaded, scene of the story's most bizarre vision. If once Der Nister told of a dense forest and a predatory beast, he now describes a "wild plaza" dominated by a wall that reaches up to heaven and against which there stands a ladder with rungs made of human skulls:

> and the rungs are still very few, and there remains yet a very great distance to heaven and to the highest height of the wall . . . And the plaza is empty, and none comes on it, and on its borders an emptiness rules, and whoever approaches is overcome with fear, and whoever is weak keeps *quite* far from the borders, and whoever is stronger dares to approach, but they all soon become frightened and turn back . . . Especially when they see the wall, how high and far it is, and in addition—when they take a look at the ladder from afar—at what the rungs and steps are made of . . . but one person in a generation *does* step over the border once, and one person once in a while *does* take a risk . . . comes and approaches the wall. And there a place already awaits him, a court and a place of judgment, with a wooden block, and an executioner by the block with a large sword ready. And the one who takes a risk lays his head on the block, and the executioner cuts it off in the way he cuts . . . And when the head is cut off, the executioner places it in the hands of the beheaded, and the beheaded takes it and mounts the ladder with it, and the ladder then becomes one head higher, and the ladder receives another rung. (178)

All of Der Nister's heroes have stood at a border; none has had to give up his head in order to cross. None has faced a court of judgment that leads directly to the executioner's block. That this invitation to a beheading will ultimately prove redemptive does little to ease the sense of apocalypse that threatens to destroy Der Nister's estates.

The beheading itself is not the end of the ordeal, for no sooner will the "disciples and crowned ones" return home, the Master warns, than they will be ridiculed, each by his private comedian. The only thing that can possibly shut him up is (as usual) a story, of the Bridge and the All-Bridge.

At first there is little to connect the story of a dutiful bridge to the awesome spectacle of a midnight beheading. The bridge, however, is tormented by a clown, who urges it to give up its thankless task, and after a steady diet of such ridicule, the bridge sinks into melancholy—just as Adam did earlier when badgered by his sidekick Comedian. And just as the Master has ready a therapeutic story for his disciples, so a wanderer appears one night and offers to console the despondent bridge with a story of his own. The story of the All-Bridge, in fact, is but a mythic retelling of the story of the bridge. Though not essential to its understanding, the following mishnah from Ethics of the Fathers does provide a clue to its origin (5:8):

> Ten things were created on the eve of the Sabbath at twilight, namely: the mouth of the earth [which swallowed Korah]; the mouth of the well [which supplied the Israelites with water in the wilderness]; the mouth of the ass [which spoke to Balaam]; the rainbow [given as a sign after the flood]; the manna [dropped from heaven]; the rod [of Moses]; the *shamir* [used for splitting stones at the building of the temple]; the shape of the written characters [of the Hebrew alphabet]; the engraving instrument; and the tablets of stone. Some include also the demons.

Except for that throwaway line about the demons, everything on this neo-Platonic roster speaks of prophecy, deliverance, divine retribution, and the eternality of the Torah. What they have in common is that they are all miraculous in nature—they are exceptions to the ordinary workings of creation, were created as exceptions to serve particular divine purposes. Der Nister, who started his career rewriting the myth of creation, gives the mishnah a new twist by positing a miraculous All-Bridge, "which leads from the deepest abyss to the palace sublime." The heavenly palace (or temple) was the abode of the Lord God who had spent that first Friday night of creation with His Sabbath "after the week- and world-weariness." Now the All-Bridge

> was very happy with its head and not much so with its feet, since its feet made it cold and wet, and wetness and sliminess and the wild swarming things that swarmed in them made it not feel good with them. It did not think well of them, and such thinking led to dissatisfaction, and dissatisfaction led to complaints; complaints that it had been given no choice, complaints that the Lord God had hurried away from it soon after its creation, hurried away and spent no time with it at all—And when he received such complaints, Satan came to it with his first night visit to the world. (182)

Not merely the demons, then, but Satan himself is present at creation, waiting his chance. He finds his opening when the All-Bridge begins to think and complain and to imagine a state of pure light, grace, and closeness

Todros Geller, in Mikhl Davidzon,
In veldl (1926)

to God. Working the All-Bridge over, Satan convinces it of the divine injustice: imagine being created in order to serve others with their sliminess
and wetness. Once the All-Bridge grows disgusted with its role, Satan returns with a practical solution: "Collapse!" Then, instead of standing upright, joining heights and depths, it will unite length and breadth, "and
everyone will find it easy to walk on, and will arrive directly wherever they
wish; and the matter is justified, because the abyss too has rights, and why
should we serve *Him* when we *ourselves* can be lords."

Satan's plan—to exchange the vertical axis of the world for a horizontal
one because "the abyss too has rights"—carries an obvious political message, especially since the result will be catastrophic. But the primal sin of
creation for Der Nister is not Satan's leveling of humanity, his proletarian
agenda, but the pathology of doubt he has been hammering away at since
the story began: left alone to think it over, the All-Bridge "waited and
doubted, reflected and hesitated." Acting on that doubt, the All-Bridge does
not abandon the heavens completely, as Satan had wanted, but shakes off
the abyss.

In that moment the light of its palace, where its head had been, became dark, and the Lord God came out of the door of the second palace; rested and astonished He glanced at the All-Bridge, glanced and said nothing, glanced and turned back to His Sabbath rest . . . Satan did not turn back from his turning away from the All-Bridge; angry and dissatisfied and insulted by the meager success of his first visit, he disappeared from before the All-Bridge's eyes and returned to the place from whence he came. (183–184).

And so this most psychological of Der Nister's stories hinges on a primal act of shevirah in which the light of God's palace becomes dim and the bridge that held depths and heights in permanent suspension is leveled out. Satan now rules the expanse of bridges everywhere and has stationed his clowns to dissuade them from their mission; and "for the sin of the All-Bridge's head and for the diminution of its light many heads must be decapitated, in order to fill that palace-light with the light of their heads."

With all the elements of the midnight beheading accounted for (that crowning is beheading, that both the ladder and the All-Bridge must ascend to heaven, that the light in God's palace can only be restored when many heads have been put on the executioner's block), the embedded stories rapidly merge with the outer frame. The Master and disciples leave, Adam returns home, tolerates the expected wisecracks and ridicule, calms himself and Comedian, and begins to tell the stories the Master had told him. That is the cure for headaches.

Poised somewhere between Kafka's "Penal Colony" (1919) and Agnon's *Sefer hama'asim* (The Book of Exempla, 1932), Der Nister's Hamburg tales brought Jewish fantasy to a new level of formal and philosophical maturity. As analyses of "Beheaded" have shown, its symmetries are functional and faultless.[48] The story of Adam and his comedian provides the psychological frame for everything that follows. The Master's tale in turn is the "realistic" counterpart to the Wanderer's tale, which is the story's mythic core. Philosophically, as we have seen, Der Nister's All-Bridge likewise hovers between a mythic and a personal pole. In the beginning, according to Der Nister's version of the Lurianic creation myth, was the miracle of a bridge that stood between the slimy abyss and the sublime palace. With the primal act of shevirah, man was cut off from heaven. But if enough Adams become *gekept*, decapitated, the missing part of the All-Bridge will be restored and those below will once more attain the divine realm. Keeping that Promethean struggle alive, that unconsummated yearning, so much like the yearning of the spring for the heart of the world in Reb Nahman's "Tale of Seven Beggars," is the beggar-wanderer, already and forever engaged in the quest.[49]

Der Nister's story can also be read as a guide to spiritual healing. Each individual who lives in the modern world is plagued by headaches and cynical comedians. That is the doubting soul, rendered skeptical by technology, positivism, modernity. Only the artistic soul can bring the dead and divided soul back to life. That is the master storyteller, who sutures the wound and restores internal harmony. He teaches Adam how to put the lid back on his hyperactive head. Yet the parable doesn't end with the Master and his story. It ends, more ambiguously than any of Der Nister's tales so far, with the newest disciple having to face a headless future surrounded by skeptics and comedians.

One needn't look far to discover why this story was excised from the Soviet edition of Der Nister's writings. If the presence of a luminous God wasn't bad enough, casting Satan as a closet Bolshevik bordered on blasphemy. The quality of hiddenness that had served Der Nister so well became a distinct and ultimately fatal liability when he returned to the Soviet fold. Why, then, couldn't he see the writing on the wall? How could a writer of such notoriously difficult stories see a future for himself in a place where all bridges were uniformly horizontal?

I have no answer! After stringing the reader along, using all my rhetorical ability to place Der Nister's Weimar years at the critical juncture of his life and work, the pivotal event of his return to the Soviet Union still eludes me. I envy my colleagues who can retrieve every nuanced motive in the lives of Janet Flanner, Ernest Hemingway, or Gertrude Stein, that famous Lost Generation, which sowed its wild oats in Paris and reaped the harvest back in America.[50] But like a festering wound at the heart of modern Yiddish culture is the question of all those expatriate writers—the brightest and the best, without whom there would have been no Soviet Yiddish culture to speak of—who chose to return, and paid with their lives.

All the more puzzling in the case of a symbolist like Der Nister. As distinct from the Russian futurists, the symbolists saw nothing to celebrate in the ruination of the past and never looked "at their nothingness from the heights of skyscrapers." The symbolists feared the incursions of technology and stayed put within their tower of High Art, where they hoped to find a way to win over the masses.[51] The symbolists, moreover, unlike most Russian intellectuals, had less reason to complain about the bourgeoisie. The Blue Rose group of symbolist painters had once enjoyed the patronage of Old Believer families like the Riabushinskys. Der Nister, though never so blessed, neither in the heyday of the Kiev group nor in the boom years of Weimar, would much later recapitulate the fall of a Jewish merchant family, producing the most finely wrought portrait of a hasidic merchant in all of Yiddish literature.[52]

Others, to be sure, were drawn by the promise of a state-supported Yiddish culture and, like the Bundist pedagogue Esther Rosenthal-Shneiderman, were only too willing to believe that Soviet nationality policy would allow for a Jewish cultural renaissance.[53] But where, in that monastic order of hermits and stargazers, where on that All-Bridge stretching from the abyss to the heavenly heights, where in that mental curriculum of mysticism and Hasidism, of medieval romance and modern fairy tale, was there room for Marxism, let alone for Bolshevism? Until there is more biographical information to work from, the best evidence is the stories themselves. Here the inquest comes to dominate the plot, and the fictional hero comes to resemble the implied author more closely. So does "The Hidden One" serve notice that he is to be held responsible for his actions as well as his words—as one would expect from a high priest.

Never was Der Nister more explicit about his own utopian ambitions than in "New Spirit," his ecstatic manifesto of 1920.[54] Here alone does he reconcile his elitism and esoteric knowledge with the demands of the collective. "Your calling is to be below," Ishmael the High Priest prophesies to young Phineas the Priest as both are seated in heaven, "and with others, and with *your kind* to build a *new* tabernacle there . . . Because people there have long grown unaccustomed to a tabernacle, and because for long now and for quite some time God's word and the Spirit's voice have not been heard among the Priests" (13). Following through, young Phineas, son of Menahem the Priest (whose name, like everything else in this story, can be identified with the author), meets with other priests in a mountain cave below, where they join in sacred fellowship to redeem what's left of the world. While a mountain spirit prophesies the imminent redemption with imagery borrowed from the Gospels, the Revelation of John, and Reb Nahman's "Master of Prayer," the young hero addresses an impassioned plea to his brothers and friends who belong "to a single generation and a single

idea": that which existed in a disparate state before must be brought together and distributed among the folk, for we possess the spark and spirit
that everyone else has lost (23). Then all emerge from the cave and face
the east, the sun rising from its slumber.[55]

Though written in the heat of apocalyptic events, in the summer of 1920,
when he and other Yiddish writers from war-torn Kiev had fled to Moscow
and were seriously considering escape to America, Der Nister thought
highly enough of this messianic manifesto to publish it three times, under
Soviet auspices.[56] That he addressed his most public and propagandistic
story to the radical Soviet fellowship means that he did not choose to return
to Soviet Russia by default.

"New Spirit" gave voice to Der Nister's most personal and cherished
dreams as well. From Berlin he wrote repeatedly to S. Niger in New York
(whom he would never meet) of the need for a central forum that would
express "all our accumulated seriousness, our growth and awareness," and
would unite the best and greatest talents now dispersed throughout the
world.[57] Yet given the rootlessness of Yiddish cultural life in German exile,
he despaired of such a center. "A whole generation of ours will die without
a final confession," he wrote in a striking turn of religious phrase, "a gantser
dor undzerer vet shtarbn on vide."[58]

The ritual confession of sins is a pious Jew's last living act. It can be
performed without a rabbi present, but it presupposes both a God and a
holy community to which one is accountable. Here, in Weimar Germany,
"everyone took liberties," Der Nister went on to lament, "everyone went
along, everyone let the ropes get slack, and our cause fell apart." "Compromise, making peace with the middle," were the sins for which there was
no expiation, unless there appeared "a strong and mighty arm, the great
and necessary unification."

There could hardly be such a center since Der Nister himself had just
broken with both of his publishers, in Warsaw and Berlin, and had the
most disparaging things to say about the Yiddish press and periodicals in
New York. How did he expect Abraham Lyessin, editor of the literary
monthly *Di tsukunft* in New York, to continue publishing his stories when
the cover letter inveighed against "your American ignoramuses"? They
don't understand my stories? he raged. "So they'll learn to understand. In
any event, it's not my mistake but their disgrace. Bekhol-oyfn iz dos nisht
mayn feler, nor zeyer bezoyen."[59] Perhaps the Soviet Union beckoned be-

cause it possessed a strong and mighty arm and would spare no effort to recenter Jewish culture on Yiddish alone. Or as David Bergelson put it in his programmatic essay on the "Three Centers" of Yiddish culture—America, Poland, and the USSR—socioeconomic conditions in the Soviet Union had destroyed the rotten foundations of the Jewish bourgeoisie, leaving the field open for an organic bond to be forged between the Yiddish intellectuals and the Jewish laboring masses.[60] In 1926, the year of Bergelson's essay, Der Nister went back, as did Peretz Markish and David Hofstein—to rebuild the tabernacle of Yiddish culture "down below."

The figure of the priest is a distillation of all the values Der Nister held sacred: patience, stubborn attention to detail, the ability to work quietly, far from human habitation.[61] By casting the storyteller in the role of radical priest, Der Nister wanted to ensure that the Yiddish story would never become fully emancipated from its religious (though not exclusively Judaic) heritage. This had been his credo all along, the reason for his becoming a storyteller. Only now, with so few sites available for the building of a tabernacle, the priest in him must have lowered his sights. Once so close to the educational establishment in Kiev, Der Nister harbored no illusions about the Soviet Jewish working class returning to a fullblown spiritual curriculum. Besides, his own stories now required more formalism and Freud than Judaism to be properly understood. Perhaps he hoped that just as the artistic discipline required to write such stories had kept the high priest free from selling his soul, so the mental discipline required to decipher his stories would itself keep the altar glowing.

Even that diminished hope proved disastrously misguided. There was precious little time, now that the New Economic Policy was being phased out, for a fellow traveler like Der Nister to adapt his personal style to the demands of the collective. During that three-year period (1927–1929), the guardians of proletarian culture mounted ever fiercer attacks against him for decadence, aestheticism, indeed for *nisterizm*.[62] As a result, Der Nister's game of hide-and-seek took on a desperate urgency the likes of which had not been seen since Reb Nahman's race against death.

Nahman—the first Jewish intellectual to oppose official ideology by using Yiddish, stories, and the voice of the folk—made storytelling into the tool of choice of political subversives.[63] Beneath their surface simplicity, his stories carried hidden messages that, if acted upon, would threaten not only the hasidic establishment but the peace of the empire as well. Because they were lumped together with other pietistic writing, hasidic stories did indeed run afoul of the enlightened despots in Petersburg and Vienna, who hired local maskilim to scour the religious literature of the Jews for expressions that offended morality, rationality, and temporal authority.

The maskilim, in turn, became masters at subterfuge. When they weren't petitioning the seats of government with secret memoranda aimed at forcing their benighted brethren to reform, change, modernize, get with it, they were circulating learned parodies of the most revered texts among themselves. When neither tactic gained them access to the outback, they discovered Yiddish and began telling subversive tales and composing satiric songs. Infiltrating the most despised, plebeian, and ungovernable medium—the chapbook—Dik, among others, made it into a mouthpiece of official ideology. This gave the art of hiddenness a new twist, for the key or code of the Yiddish story now lay outside the system of *yidishkayt*. Sacred tales and exempla that had for centuries been used to support in-group norms, to fortify the Jewish minority against foreign domination, became under the maskilim a means of breaking this society open.

Peretz played both ends against the middle. So long as he believed that only a revolution could make the dead Jewish bones live again, he used pious tales and playful romances as a cloak for his radical agenda. But when, at century's end, east European Jewish culture turned inward, Peretz led the way, smartening up the traditional tales in order to seduce wayward Jews back to their discarded past.

The hidden strands in Sholem Aleichem's stories were more interwoven with the here-and-now. His direct forays into political allegory—a satiric chapbook on the Russo-Japanese war, *Uncle Pinye and Aunt Reyze,* and a pogrom parable about a "Little Bear" that destroyed the Jewish home where it had found shelter (a holiday story, no less)—were too deeply moored in his readers' immediate experience to weather the test of time.[64] When he achieved immortality, it was by domesticating the terror of current events with a strangely familiar plot and by playing the dissolution of Jewish life against the manic speech and comic taglines of the Jews who were living it.

The storyteller who laid claim to Hasidism and (parts of) the Haskalah, to Peretz and (parts of) Sholem Aleichem, and went by the pen name of "Mr. Hidden" himself, perfected an art that should have resisted all forms of domination. Every inverted sentence, every alliteration, repetition, and allusion advertised his hiddenness. It was an art for initiates. The tyranny of profit-hungry European publishers and an ignorant American public made Der Nister's stories that much tougher, temporal, and self-reliant. Forged in the crucible of Weimar, this hidden art might have seemed, if not impervious, then at least resilient enough to weather the brave new world of Soviet power. Yet Weimar Germany was mere child's play compared to the domination of body and soul under the proletariat's dictatorship. There was nowhere to escape the combined wrath of the party, the censors, the press, the publishers, and the public, when ideologically blinded Jews were to be found manning every sector and when art, in order to survive, could be national only in form, socialist in content.

In his priestly fictions, Der Nister maintained a hierarchy of values and a strict separation between good and evil, spirit and matter, fantastical story and everyday life. In his political fictions, written in the Soviet Ukraine, everything became the antithesis of everything else, victim turned tyrant, the hero's quest collapsed into a maze of self-betrayal, suicide, drunkenness, miscegeny, promiscuity, and greed, and the ravenous bears stood ready to tear his heart out. It was as if the guilt of Der Nister's betrayal weighed so heavily on him that he turned the vicious attacks inward; as if the possibilities of dialogue and true discipleship had now been reduced to one long monologue, soliloquy, and confession; as if the art he had fashioned with so much care and hope was abandoned by his fellow priests, leaving only *Der Nister aleyn*—Der Nister alone, by himself.

Abandoned though he was, he did not go down without a fight. Der Nister delivered a catalogue of blasphemies aimed at all he had held sacred. The vehemence and vulgarity of "A Tale of an Imp, of a Mouse, and of Der Nister Himself" (1929) can take your breath away, so great is the stench that emanates from all the copulating, pissing, farting, defecating, and fat-producing that goes on there.[65] Its menagerie of rodents, insects, and lascivious demons make this a sequel to Kafka's "Metamorphosis" and a precursor of Art Spiegelman's *Maus*, the first X-rated Yiddish fantasy. Like "Der Nister Himself," the story's Pied Piper and parodic autobiographer, the reader is torn between laughter and revulsion.

The story takes place in two different lands, one inhabited by people of glass whose only fleshy part is their navel, so they can't eat, sleep, or copulate; and a fleshy country where all they do is eat, sleep, and copulate.

Der Nister visits both and, great healer that he is, restores the first to passion by making their navels grow and grow, and inspires the second to abstinence, only to discover that one country is the mirror of the other.

A wanderer as always, this beggar-hero is likewise accompanied by a loyal animal companion, here a donkey. Donkey gives Der Nister a good laugh when it teaches the glass people how to piss and perform other important bodily functions. Donkey's manure, it turns out, carries seeds of plenty (from the species of wondrous seeds encountered before in "A Tale of a Hermit and a Kid") that the glass people carefully remove before planting. Der Nister's ministrations and the donkey's bountiful manure do not save them from the people's wrath. When the cure becomes a curse and glassiness turns to fleshiness, Donkey is stoned to death and Der Nister narrowly escapes the same fate.

What a pathetic figure "Der Nister" cuts, engaged in senseless repetition moving in a maze but somehow convinced he can still redeem the world. At first he is oblivious of the cries of the glass people, now turned hyper-fleshy, whose surplus fat is made into candles that attract armies of mice. Der Nister is too busy in his attic being served hand and foot by a personal imp. Later he and Mouse Catcher (whom he brings in to exterminate the rodents) go their separate ways, because the catcher has only one purpose in life, whereas Der Nister is welcome in many countries and has "various goals and various callings" (55). Yet the joke is on Der Nister because were it not for Mouse Catcher, whose name resonates with Rattenfänger, German for Pied Piper, and who decides to diversify into catching imps, the story would have to end "here, in the middle" (59). Then we would would never learn that among Der Nister's various callings is his talent for stargazing (like Bove of old), which proves a mixed blessing. All it earns Der Nister is a heavenly handout that he uses to buy a flea-ridden pelt made from a dead demon. In the end, the story is all about skins: skins of glass and skins of oozing fat; about Der Nister's attempt to save his own—which of course is not his own—skin, while his *real* skin is a body so emaciated that anyone who sets eyes on it loses all desire. No wonder that "he concluded from all this that in the end, after all his wanderings, when he probably arrives at one last and very distant land, where no one needs him and no one knows about him, and no one will miss him, and he'll remember the imps, maybe they need him, and he'll appear before the imps, and in their company and at the weddings of mice he'll hire himself out as a prankster and a rhymster"

(79). "Der Nister" has in fact been doing just that—entertaining a mouse bride and her demon groom—and he ends the horrific tale with a hearty *Mazl-tov!*

Remember the traveler who triumphed when forced by the demons to show his nakedness beyond the skin? Remember the hermit who found the seed of truth at story's end? Remember Bove who had to consummate his marriage offstage? None of them, apparently, ever had to eat. They could afford to spend their vigorous young lives exploring the mind's inner landscape. They didn't have to worry about "saving their skins." Not so the aging outcast with the highfalutin name of "Der Nister." He followed his Jewish and artistic destiny and found himself coming back into the cold, a place where he now kept company with venal mouse catchers, copulating imps and mice, a hybrid species of bedbug-fleas, and wandered about in countries filled with all-or-nothing.

This last was most subversive: Der Nister's revelation that the land of capitalist pigs, with the fat oozing from their bodies, was the same as the land of glass where there was nothing to eat and people were robbed of desire. In postwar Europe, west or east, capitalist or communist, there was no longer any difference, no choice to be made, between spirit and matter.

In "From My Estates" (1928), Der Nister shows how real goods are dematerialized while spiritual goods are turned into tradeable commodities.[66] Starring "Der Nister" in a return engagement as narrator and autobiographical hero, he first appears with a mudpatch on his forehead that promptly turns into gold that buys him a copy (at a reduced price) of Der Nister's *Writings of a Madman*.[67] In the course of the *Writings* that follow, mud and gold become the coin of the realm. In the Land of Mud he is punished for not adapting; in the Land of Gold he buys up all the estates and is punished for his pride. In the lunatic asylum to which he is consigned by Ursa Major (the Bear Star), he can't readapt and ends up selling off the light of his remaining estates to feed ten hungry bears, the last of which is about to tear out his heart. The transparent symbolism of the (Russian) bears swallowing the artist member by member can scarcely have escaped the Soviet reader, even if Sholem Aleichem's allegory about "Berele" biting the (Jewish) hand that fed him was a thing of the tsarist past. Der Nister is playing with fire, and his last stories show it with their drastic, hallucinatory plots and their debased symbolic landscapes.

Der Nister was forced to give up writing symbolist tales one year before the terror-famine began that was to claim the lives of some 10 million peasants in his native Ukraine, and seven years before the show trials of the Great Terror. But judging from what little he did write between 1927 and 1929, he could have produced a Yiddish storytelling corpus commensurate with the Stalinist horrors. His years of training and mastery did not fail him. Even more, the painful experience of trying to conform to party dictates suggested to him a higher, universal level of struggle, which he then recast into the language of Yiddish fantasy. To do this, the settings neccessarily became more crowded, urban, noisy, smelly, venal, and hazardous. No more leisurely strolls through the forest or desert; there were no more quests at all, only senseless trials and tribulations. In "Under a Fence: A Revue" (1929), the last will and confession of Der Nister as a storyteller, the main event was a trial within a trial, culminating in an auto-da-fé.[68] If Der Nister had warned Shmuel Niger back in 1923 that their generation would "die without confession," here was the writer's last chance to do penance for betraying his artistic mission. In so doing, Der Nister unwittingly wrote the forced confessions of the many writers—Jews and gentiles—who would soon perish without a trace.

Der Nister offers several clues that "Under a Fence" is to be read as his final and most personal statement—perhaps even as an answer to "New Spirit," his utopian manifesto of 1920. It is the most modern of all his stories, the most overtly psychological, and the most openly derivative of European literary sources. The subtitle, "A Revue," points to the contemporary world of the cabaret or, in this case, of the circus. The story's outer frame is similarly grounded in reality. A scholarly type, someone with proper bourgeois credentials, is rejected by a circus lady. He gets drunk, is awakened by a cop, goes home to sleep it off, and is awakened later by his daughter, to whom he tries to tell the whole story. "Under a Fence" is thus a variation on the theme of Heinrich Mann's *Professor Unrat,* better known in its unforgettable screen version with Marlene Dietrich, *The Blue Angel.*[69] Here the artiste is played by Lili, a distant relative of the arch-seductress of Jewish lore, Lilith. Otherwise the only identifiable character is the monk Medardus, hero of E. T. A. Hoffmann's *The Devil's Elixir,* a novel that also features a double trial.[70]

The "revue" is also a "re-view," or a transcript of what the groggy, guilt-ridden professor says to his daughter the morning after. As his opening line, "I am sick to death with grief," attests, the burden is great and there is much to work through—as much as for Jesus, who spoke those very words to his disciples at Gethsemane. Here is a man obssessed with his own guilt. So his confession follows a psychological rather than a logical sequence. After confessing his love for the circus performer, he imagines himself as a circus rider, dressed in flesh-colored tights and whip in his hand.[71]

> I was in the center ring of the circus. A beautiful horse was brought and I mounted him. And just ahead of me an even finer horse was in full gallop, and Lili rode it, balanced on one leg, her other leg stretched out behind her. The packed audience passed dizzyingly before my eyes. All around us the circle of seats and the crowd, all eyes and enthusiasm. Each pass of Lili's took their breath away. Each "hup-hup!" each shout excited and enchanted them. And I, too, was excited, and I stood on the back of my horse and rode, as Lili, weightless in her light costume, rode before me.
>
> And suddenly she turned as her horse galloped. Now her back was to his head and she stood facing me. And the crowd burst into applause as Lili stretched her hand out to me and I reached out to her. We couldn't touch because the horses were between us, but we felt just as though we had. Lili's success was mine too, and I had my share of the crowd's excitement and applause. (Y 189–190, E 577)

The circus: made for mobility, the circus tent goes anywhere, as befits a place of passing diversion. Whoever occupies the circle-within-the-triangle of the tent is always in the public eye, and the vitality, the thrill, is electric. The circus is brightly lit and is packed to the rafters, but backstage there is room for love—and it is free. Usually the circus is fiercely competitive, with those who create the best thrill or illusion rising to the top of the bill. Here it would seem the professor turned circus rider is feeling noncompetitive—"Lili's success was mine too"—but this will soon prove a fatal error. In theory, love should make all questions of value meaningless (as he had explained earlier to his student). In practice, the circus star will destroy all competition.

The professor's beloved daughter has somehow joined the circus, and at the climax of their three-person act, Lili lets her (quite by accident, it seems) crash headlong into the crowd. The circus vanishes and there, back in his room, lies his wounded daughter, compounding the guilt of his escapade with Lili. To make matters worse, the student reappears to report that the whole town is talking about his circus act and the accident. So much for the selflessness of love, when the professor is really in love with himself. So self-important and grandomaniacal is he that he imagines the whole world to be concerned with his actions. The fantasy of the student's second visit only corroborates the earlier fantasy. At this psychic juncture the vision turns surrealistic: the walls of his study crack open and begin pelting father and daughter with stones. He manages to protect her, but one stone hits him in the head and knocks him out cold.

Therein begins his trial and formal confession. So far the dreams and hallucinations developed a sense of guilt that was egotistical. From now on he is referred to as a *nozir,* a hermit, as he stands accused before his teacher and fellow monks of betraying the faith.[72] "I feel like a turtle without a shell," he confesses, "completely naked" (Y 194–195, E 580). Not the seductive nakedness of skin-tight leotards, the nakedness that casts its illusory spell on the crowd, but the nakedness of a monk who has spent his whole life within the stone tower of his monastery and has left it, and his habit, forever.

How could anyone move from one such home to another? The tower was built for permanence as a repository of eternal truth. It supported a monastic life that was run according to a strict and exclusive hierarchy. In his initial defense, the hermit blames the fallen state of things inside the tower: it is hollow, cold, and dark; the light has gone out. The world outside considers it a museum piece, while inside there is no love; straw children suckle from (male) breasts of straw. He even blames Medardus, his teacher: "You should have foreseen it, Medardus, my teacher, and told us to abandon the house." The hermit defected because he lost faith in his own convictions, because of public opinion, because of financial pressures, and because of—the Dustman. Dustman is to the tower what Lili was to the circus: the id, the seducer. Dustman convinces the hermit to burn the monastery down. Dustman makes his strawbaby come alive and then leads her and her father to a lucrative job in the circus. There, in the circus, Dustman stages a mock trial of the hermits, to the hysterical delight of the crowd, at which the nozir outdoes the rest in ridicule: "And I mocked more than any of them, and when I told the monks off, I was wittier than anyone. And finally the sentence was pronounced: dirt and garbage that had to be burned" (Y 211, E 591). Lili, meanwhile, is jealous of the hermit's daughter and plots her downfall. Because he could foresee what would happen and did nothing to stop it, the father accepts responsibility for her accident, and for everything else:

> And it is my fault, my judges. This is what happened to me after I left our house. I betrayed my teachers and made my only daughter a cripple. And it all came about in the course of time because the corners of our house were broken up, and dustmen and those who lived off our mold got control of us, and we were good for nothing and completely unprepared for the outside world, and they took over and led us where dustmen have to lead us, to the street and the marketplace, to tricks and the circus and to giving up the shirt off our backs, the eyes in our heads, and the daughter of our loins, for a piece of bread. Sentence me and do what you want with me. Deny me, just as I denied you, and just as I injured my daughter, do me injury too, and carry out your sentence on me. (Y 213–214, E 593)

That is not all he is ready to confess, for abruptly the circus act changes and it is he, once more, who stands at the docket, with Medardus and his students playing the judges. This final confession, a *vide* by any other name, is reserved for their ears alone. Since the crux of his defense is that Dustman made him do it, he must now confess that "dustmen and similar creatures are not persons or living creatures at all, but only illusions, born in the sick minds of hermits, and to allow oneself to be led by them and do as they do is a disgrace." He is therefore burned at the stake for believing in witchcraft and, rising from the ashes, says: "Stand up, my teachers and students. I deserved what was done to me. I brought you to shame, and you turned me to ash. *Un ikh hob aykh tsu bezoyen gebrakht, un ir mikh tsu ash.*" (Y 216, E 595). Then he wakes up with his head under a fence—the place, according to Jewish custom, where suicides are buried.

The worlds of the monastic tower and the circus tent are mutually exclusive. So he is torn apart. The first is a world of religious faith in which the artist serves God through traditional means. Medardus embodies that sacred trust, the old literary traditions that once had worth. But in the secular world, it is each man for himself. Here the dustman takes over: the artist ready to sell himself and the conartist who can make strawbabies come to life. Whoever betrays his artistic mission by allowing it to be identified with idolatry, with political witchcraft, can only end in guilt, condemnation, and self-annihilation.

"Under a Fence" is, of course, open to other ominous readings. It can be read as a statement on assimilation to European society. The hermit's conversion to the circus is real, but Lili's acceptance of him is not. Agnon developed this theme in his Nisterian parables written during the Holocaust. Yet Der Nister did not labor so long and hard in the forbidding stone tower of his utopian art in order to agonize over the fate of the Jews. However profoundly he grieved over betraying his messianic calling, allowing his art to be used by the communists to further their own utilitarian ends, he remained as surely a disciple of Hoffmann as of Nahman. Even at the point when the state apparatus was conspiring to rob the Jewish writer of his Judaism *and* his art, Der Nister produced a universal parable on the fate and function of art in the modern world.

"Under a Fence" marked the end of Jewish fantasy, and for all intents and purposes Jewish messianic dreams, in the vast Soviet empire. Yet despite the horrible strictures of that time and place, the high priest was able to bid farewell to Yiddish fantasy not in a programmed confession of error, but in an amazing symbolist tale in which he did penance for a wrong political choice six long years before.

7

The Last of the Purim Players
ITZIK MANGER

Suddenly, I saw the light: this is it! The figures of the
Brody Singers lighted up in my imagination. All the
wedding jesters and Purim players who had entertained generations of Jews suddenly came alive. I will
become one of them, one of "our brothers dear."

—Itzik Manger, 1961

After 1920 there was only one place left where Yiddish storytelling
could grow and prosper, and that was Poland. The pace and political
pressures of Jewish life in the Americas, the Soviet republics, and Palestine
had turned folklore, fantasy, and the stylized folktale either into pablum
for precocious children or into the lethal dregs of a bourgeois and reactionary past. In Poland, with poverty so great, the pace of change so gradual,
and the vestigial presence of the past so much a part of the living present,
ethnography was almost the only thing the Jews were producing in abundance.

In Poland between the two world wars, as in Rumania and the Baltic
countries, tradition and modernity could still compete on the open market.
Here the folk did not have to be rarefied and reinvented because it was
alive and kicking. Here folklore became the vehicle of Jewish self-determination, the basis for the Jewish claim to normality and nationhood, to
land and landscape. Here, when the intellectuals went slumming, they discovered folklore at both ends of the spectrum: in the urban Jewish underworld and in the hundreds of decaying shtetlekh where corporate behavior
was still governed by Jewish law and lore. While Jewish pimps, prostitutes,
and pickpockets made the case for Jewish "normality," the surviving culture
of the shtetl staked the Jewish claim to the "land."

The largest, liveliest, and lewdest collection of Yiddish folklore ever produced came out in Warsaw in 1923. Titled *Bay undz yidn,* it ought to have

been followed either by a question mark or an exclamation mark: how could such things be found "Among Us Jews?" With unintended irony, the book's publisher and contributing author, Pinkhes Graubard, dedicated this huge collection of underworld songs, sayings, stories, and "philology" to the memory of S. Ansky, including two full-page portraits and a facsimile of Ansky's last letter to him.[1] If the volume (six years in production) had appeared in Ansky's lifetime, he would have been appalled to see his oral Torah dragged through the mud. Could anyone still believe that Jews had cornered the market on monotheism and morality after reading through so many trickster tales and convicts' songs? Back in 1908, Ignaz Bernstein had shown good sense by publishing his Yiddish sayings, *Erotica und Rustica,* in a limited edition.[2] Now the dirty words were printed for all to see.

More shocking perhaps than the underworld materials (where one would expect some loose talk) was Shmuel Lehman's pioneering collection of children's folklore in the same volume: amoral at best, sacrilegious at worst. The parodic rhymes and games of Jewish children (including a rhyme to identify who in the group had just farted) showed how normative and idealized, by contrast, was Sholem Aleichem's vision of the child's world. If anything, children enjoyed mixing the sacred and profane, Slavic, Hebrew, and Yiddish even more than did the hasidim whom Ansky and Prylucki celebrated. In folklore, parody reined supreme, and those with the least to lose in Jewish society had the most to gain from spoofing all its relics.

What thieves and children were to the pious portrait of shtetl society, the Jews of Poland were to the self-image of the new Polish state, a blight and embarrassment. And so the point of *Bay undz yidn* was not to turn the Jews into a nation of parodists but to make a virtue of necessity. There were sound political reasons for the renewed interest in Jewish folklore. The more Jews were excluded from the warp and woof of Polish life, the more important became their claim to self-sufficiency. Behold the richness of Yiddish culture across the social spectrum. Bawdy, earthy, and irreverent, it was a folklore worthy of the Slavic soil. The discovery of aboveground and especially underground Jewish folk traditions in Poland was closely aligned to *landkentenish,* the study of national customs through hiking and tourism.

The Polish Society for Land Study excluded or severely limited Jewish membership and granted no status to Jewish historical landmarks. Jewish intellectuals saw their exclusion from the historical landscape as both an attempt to delegitimate the Jews as a people and to exclude them from the enjoyment of nature; this last was a piece of unfinished business from Enlightenment days. "It is a fact," began the inaugural issue of *Land un lebn* in December 1927, "that we Jews, especially from Warsaw and also from the other larger cities in Poland, are mostly far removed from nature. There will be many among us who have never in their lives seen a sunrise or sunset; or ever seen the sea or mountains; who cannot distinguish between the simplest species of trees; who have no idea what stalks of corn or wheat look like . . . who possess no sentiment whatsoever for nature and her wondrous creations." Emanuel Ringelblum took up the maskilic litany in a more sociological vein: "The centuries of urban life, the remoteness from nature, the living within narrow, stifling ghetto walls have caused the Jew to feel distant and estranged from the beauty and glory of nature." The return to nature was part and parcel of the Jewish call for "productivization."[3]

There was no felt contradiction between breaking out of the ghetto to enjoy nature's bounty and returning to the culture of the ghetto to commune with the folk. Following through on this double-barreled program, the Jewish Society for Knowledge of the Land in Poland established its own camps and resorts, sponsored lectures, published Yiddish travel guides, worked to train a cadre of amateur ethnographers, and argued for the power of folklore as a unifying force in an age of fragmentation. Since religion was no longer binding, the novelist Mikhoel Burshtin, a spokesman for the movement, urged his fellow urbanites to tour the countryside, bringing secular Yiddish culture to the folk and assuring that the folk culture would become theirs.[4]

This know-your-land movement contributed a profound sense of place to the stories told by Polish Yiddish writers. Moyshe Kulbak, for one, turned White Russia into the semilegendary meeting ground of Slavic paganism, popular Christianity, Jewish muscle, and Jewish messianic dreams. He did it in a long narrative poem about Jewish rafters on the Nieman River (1922); in an ode to Vilna, the Jerusalem of Lithuania (1926); and in a stylized folk narrative about a legless bird dealer called Munie (1928).[5] "Surely songs about Munie were sung in the swamps and in all the remote woods of Byelorussia!" rhapsodized the storyteller (342). And a strange song it is, seeing that Munie at story's end becomes a caged bird himself, choosing a life of utter passivity.

What better way for this revolutionary cadre of east European Jewish writers to decenter the universe than to invent a newly grounded landscape? Kulbak's ode to Vilna begins with an allusion to Isaiah 62:6 ("Upon your walls, O Jerusalem, I have set watchmen"), but it ends with the poet celebrating the more modern sights and sounds of redemption: "The red tunic of the steely bundist. / The blue student who listens to gray Bergelson—/ Yiddish is the homely crown of the oak leaf / Over the gates, sacred and profane, into the city." By the same token, Zalmen Szyk's *1000 Years of Vilna,* an exemplary Yiddish guidebook, recommends that a tourist with only one day to spend in the city begin at Ostra Brama Street and its famous Catholic shrine and end at the Ansky museum. The Jewish quarter, with its renowned synagogue and study houses, was sandwiched into fifth place. Not until after the Holocaust would former rebels like Vilna-born Chaim Grade reclaim the synagogue courtyard for Yiddish literature.[6]

Pour épater les orthodoxes, Yiddish writers had merely to take a place already hallowed by tradition and turn it to secular ends. Unlike, let us say, the American writer Washington Irving, who had to invent a legendary link to such uncharted regions as the Catskill Mountains, Yiddish writers had a surfeit of local legends from which to choose.[7] This is how the Carpathian Mountains, birthplace of Hasidism, reappeared on the literary map. And this is why places like Jassy, Rumania, birthplace of the Yiddish theater, figured so prominently on the same tour. As Yiddish storytellers and songsters took up the struggle for Jewish autonomy in the postwar landscape of Europe, they dusted off old myths of origin and found new ones. This was not a literature of exile. It was a literature of homecoming.

There was probably no Yiddish poet with a keener sense of adoptive place than Itzik Manger, and certainly none who had more fun inventing a personal myth of origins. What was wrong with being born Isidore Helfer, in Czernowitz, 1901? Having served as the site for the Czernowitz language conference of 1908, the city was to Yiddishism what Basel was to Zionism. In Czernowitz, after stormy debate, Yiddish was finally proclaimed "*a national Jewish language.*"[8] Manger remembered all too well that for the Jews (as for the entire bourgeoisie) of Czernowitz, real culture was German high culture, and so he probably dismissed the yidishkayt claim to the city as propaganda. Besides, German was his first love as well, despite being thrown out of the Kaiser-Königlicher Dritter Staats-Gymnasium for behavioral problems in his second year. Czernowitz was too ambiguous a birth-

place for someone who wanted to be both a modern secular poet and salt
of the earth. So Manger invented a biography for himself, almost out of
whole cloth.[9]

"Born in Berlin as the son of a tailor," we read in Zalmen Reisen's *Lexicon
of Yiddish Literature, Press, and Philology* (1927), "an immigrant from Rumania. Came to Jassy at age fourteen where he learned Yiddish and until
very recently, worked at his [tailor's] trade." Not bad to be both the prodigal
son adopting the language of his people, like some Moses figure, and the
card-carrying member ("until very recently") of the Jewish laboring masses.
Berlin was the poet's shorthand for his profound debt to modern German
culture, and especially to Rilke, whom he singled out for special mention
in his brief biographical sketch. Manger might also have mentioned that
German was the source of all his worldly knowledge. In his notebooks for
1918–19, he jotted down the titles of seventy-five books he had read in
German—Kant, Kleist, Mann, Hesse, Gogol, Turgenev, Dostoevsky,
Gorky.[10]

Luckily for young Isidore, however, the outbreak of world war forced
him and his family to move to Jassy. (That much, at least, was true.) Otherwise he might never have known his ancestral eastern Galician (later
Rumanian) landscape and, what's worse, might never have become a Yiddish troubadour. Jassy was a godsend for a young romantic poet in search
of inspiration. Here, in "the old city with secluded crooked streets," one
could hear a girl singing Yiddish lovesongs from her window, and one could
still commune with the spirit of those "nocturnal vagabonds," "hungry,
pale, and joyous," who raised their cups and voices in song. Most famous
among the latter was Velvl Zbarzher (1826–1883), easily recognized "By
his lively large eyes, / By his dusty, dark green cape, / His head rakishly
bent to one side." This inspiring figure was "Drunk from the stars, wine,
night, and wind."[11] Where the song and sorrow of troubadours once blos-
somed, where their living memory still glimmered from every window,
lulling the passer-by with longing, here was a place that a budding Yiddish
poet could call his own.

Manger spent his real adolescence not as a German-born refugee learning
Yiddish while he slaved away at the sewing machine, but as a self-conscious
poet-apprentice looking to place himself within Yiddish precedent. Besides
the old lovesongs and maskilic parodies, there was a new Yiddish lyric
aborning across the Atlantic, and Manger was an avid disciple.[12] The family

apparently gave Yiddish poetry pride of place as well. Breaking with tradition, Manger's younger brother Notte took over the trade, while the master tailor and amateur rhymster Hillel Manger punned the foreign-sounding *literatur* with the hallowed "Torah" to coin the felicitous term *literatoyre*. No wonder that Manger included his ode to Jassy under the chapter title "My Poem—My Portrait—My Home." Though he possessed but one handwritten copy of his poems, never issued by the fictitious Yiddish-Is-Ownerless Publishing House, Manger could boast what no other Yiddish poet before him could: a doting, loving audience in his own home. For the rest of his adult life, Manger would try to find surrogate homes for his poetry as intimate as the one he had known in Jassy.[13]

Confident that his poetic apprenticeship was over, nineteen-year-old Yitskhok headed back to Czernowitz soon after the war was over. He wanted a big-city venue for his lyric verse, one volume of which he called *Kveytn* (Blossoms, 1919–20), and the other, *Harbstike oygn* (Autumnal Eyes, 1918–1925).[14] The local Labor Zionist paper *Di frayhayt* accepted a few poems for publication, and the young Manger was invited to speak at the fourth anniversary of Sholem Aleichem's death. He spoke so quietly, however, about Topele Tuturitu and other of Sholem Aleichem's child-heroes that no one could hear a word he said.[15] Neither volume of his juvenilia was published and anniversary lectures paid no honorarium, yet Manger was insulted when an older writer offered to find him a job clerking in a store.[16] Yiddish literature was all Manger lived for and all he wished to live from. Even being drafted into the Eighth Fusilier Regiment of the newly established Rumanian army did not cramp his style. For one thing, he was stationed in Czernowitz. For another, he gave German lessons to the captain of his regiment. And for still another, there were pretty young things from orthodox homes who loved nothing better than a Yiddish poet in uniform.[17]

Manger was on his way toward resurrecting the song, the sweet sorrow, and the bohemian lifestyle of the hard-drinking Yiddish troubadours of old Galician glory. But he was by no means the only show in town. The Yiddish secular establishment, especially its pedagogic wing, the Czernowitz Union of Yiddish Schools, was dominated by Eliezer Steinbarg, the most exacting stylist and premier fable writer in Yiddish letters. Steinbarg bears out the paradox noted by Ruth Wisse, that "the neo-folk poets are the most refined of all modern Yiddish craftsmen."[18]

Manger could not have found a better model. Steinbarg demonstrated, first of all, that if highbrow culture obeyed the strict conventions of oral poetry, it could transcend the limitations of print. Even though Steinbarg delayed publication of his fables for decades, waiting until they were letter-perfect, they circulated throughout Rumania by word of mouth. A fair number of his children's lyrics were also set to music.[19] When a delegation of Yiddish cultural activists was invited to Czernowitz in 1928 by the Union of Yiddish Schools to mark the anniversary of the famous conference, Stein-barg found a wider audience still. The hit of the program was a *vortkontsert*, a dramatic recitation, by the young actor Hertz Grosbard, whose imitation of animal talk brought Steinbarg's fables alive, and whose training on the German stage did the same for Manger's ballads. Fables and ballads were henceforth to become an integral part of the modern Yiddish repertory.[20]

Steinbarg's example, furthermore, taught Manger the staying power of a single genre. Whether Manger's choice of the ballad was inspired by reading such German authors as Goethe, Schiller, or von Hofmannsthal, or by his reading of Mani Leyb, Zishe Landau, or Moyshe-Leyb Halpern, is an open question. But it was certainly Steinbarg, a name synonymous with the fable, who showed his Rumanian landsman how an outmoded form of didactic verse might be turned into a modern classic.

Late in 1928, when Yitskhok Manger made his first fateful trip to Warsaw, the twenty-seven-year-old poet knew exactly where he was coming from, where he was heading, and what he uniquely had to offer. On the one hand, he compared himself to Tantalus, son of Zeus, punished in the lower world to suffer eternal hunger and thirst. Manger-Tantalus, coming from the provincial backwater of Rumania, could only dream of drinking from the Yiddish waters that flowed from across the Soviet border or to eat of the fruit that grew on the Polish-Jewish vine.[21] Warsaw, then, was the cosmopolitan haven. On the other hand, in interviews and lectures he gave upon arrival, he spoke authoritatively about Yiddish poetry in Rumania (and his own central role), about the folksong traditions of Rumanians, gypsies, and Spaniards, about the fundamental link between folklore and modern lyric poetry, and above all about the ballad. To the critic Shloyme Bickel he pronounced: "My major work will yet be my ballads in the folk-vein *(di folkstimlekhe baladn),* which will encompass the balladistic accents [in Jewish culture] beginning with the Bible until the present day. It will be an attempt to create the second Yiddish folk epic after Peretz's *Folkstim-lekhe geshikhtn*."[22] Warsaw may have been Paris, but Rumania was the font of the modern Yiddish "fable, grotesque and ballad," the home of Goldfaden and Zbarzher, and possibly the site of Peretz's reincarnation.[23]

If the ballad was indeed Manger's conduit back to the Bible as early as Shloyme Bickel claims it was, the paper trail that Manger left behind shows something else. The ballad, for Manger, was a window to the world and the mystical source of all great poetry; the vision of blood and death; Goethe's "Erlkönig" and Poe's "Raven."[24] There was also a world of difference between choosing the fable—a time-honored form of Jewish self-expression—and the ballad, the least developed and least Jewish of Yiddish folk genres. Though clearly rooted in oral traditions, the ballad spoke to Manger because it was universal—and closely tied to nature. In the lyrical ballads he wrote during his apprenticeship, landscape was all, and the more suggestively vague the better: "The Wondrous Ballad of the Old Fisher Woman Who Went Off in Search of Her Dead on a Dark Autumn's Night," "The Ballad of the Ways," "The Ballad of the Smiles," "The Ballad of the Night-Figure with the Blue Lantern," "The Ballad of the Hussar and the Night-Figure," "The Ballad of the Wanderer with the Silver Star," "The Ballad of the Night." He did well not to publish them.[25]

Had Manger used the ballad merely as a vehicle for *geshpentster,* gothic midnight settings, the project would have been stillborn. Instead he discovered a form of lyric that operated through dialogue, character, symbolic landscape, strict rhythms and rhymes, refrains, and a diction close to that of the folksong. These he fully exploited in the fifteen formal ballads about love and death included in his first published volume of verse, *Shtern oyfn dakh* (Stars on the Roof, 1929). Manger was no less the *modern* balladeer, able to make his private vision a vehicle of communal experience, free to use sophisticated poetic techniques to arrive at a purity of tone that attested to the power of the folk and that of the individual poet. A dialogue between a Jewish mother and her mournful daughter, a meeting between a verminous man and Jesus on the cross, became symbolic tableaux of a new poetic order. Manger enlisted the compressed and conventional format of the ballad to combine the lyric sensibility of a German poet, the ethical sensibility of a modern secular Jew, and the dramatic sensibility of a born storyteller.

In telling the story of tragic loss and unrequited love, the typical ballad brings worlds into collision: children and parents, eros and death, this world and the next. Manger's are no exception: "The Ballad of the Bridal Veil," "The Ballad of the Three White Doves," "The Ballad of the Red Ring," and the exquisite "The Ballad of the White Glow" all elaborate the theme of a maiden whose longing for a mate ends in death or loss of home. The modern balladeer brings this well-worn plot back to life by animating colors—white (purity, virginity, death) played against red (love, passion, life)—and by rendering all that is outside—light, darkness, storm, snow— as states of inner consciousness.[26]

> "Genug geyomert, tekhterl,
> Un oysgeveynt dem payn!"
> "—Ze mame, oyfn fon fun nakht
> A vaysn kiln shayn."
>
> "You've grieved enough, my daughter dear,
> You've mourned enough, your woe."
> "Mother, see, in the depth of night—
> A cool white glow."

The three-beat lines (in the Yiddish) and traditional abcb rhyme scheme obscure the fact that we come in as mother and daughter are engrossed in a dialogue over the meaning of light. For them it is no abstraction. Try as the mother does to conjure away the white glow with the time-tested formula, "May it always wander the empty fields / And come here nevermore," the daughter has already internalized the light: "Because my heart, in that cool glow, / Is throbbing with desire." Seduced by that intangible white light, the daughter follows her destiny, turning into a dark and ominous projection of that same light. Later Manger will add the colors gray and especially blue to his palette.

While retaining the ballad's three-part structure and the arrangement of characters in groups of three (mother, daughter, white-glow), Manger also restored to the Yiddish ballad something it never had: a character-specific dialogue differentiated by gender and age (the mother uses folk speech while the daughter's diction is "poetic"); a landscape at once geographically specific and symbolically charged; and a musical quality both familiar and new. The ballad was a natural for someone like Manger, who composed his poetry out loud, not on paper, and memorized all his own verse.[27]

The ballad was also a programmatic choice for a Yiddish writer of the postwar generation who viewed folklore as a ticket to the League of Nations. By championing the ballad, Manger threw his weight behind the radical secularists who were trying to sever the umbilical cord that tied Yiddish culture to the synagogue and cast the newborn out, at the Slavic crossroads. In eastern Europe every such crossroad was marked by a crucified Jesus or a shrine to the Virgin Mary. The opening manifesto of Manger's fly-by-night journal *Getseylte verter* (Measured Words, 1929–1933) painted an apocalyptic landscape in which "the disheveled head of Hamlet hovers through our sleepless nights. The suffering of our generation left bloodstains and scattered crosses over all the byways of the world. The head of Christ weeps symbolically in our dream . . . The hand of Saint Francis of Assisi lies upon our heart . . . The golden figure of the Baal Shem Tov stands out clearly against the horizon." In a later issue, Manger castigated the Yiddish classicists for never noticing "the crucifix that stands in the very middle of the road, and the figure that hangs on said crucifix." By retrieving the man on the cross, the modern Yiddish balladeer could add a universal dimension to the theme of tragic suffering and cast an ecumenical net wider than even the fairy-tale marriage of a Jewish man and a gentile princess.[28]

Modern yet accessible ballads; an emaciated poetic figure offset by a ubiquitous hat perched at the back of a bushy head of hair; an effortless and melodious delivery (no problem hearing him now); progressive politics—all this and more won Manger the hearts of the Warsaw Yiddish audience. Manger-Tantalus had beaten the odds. To remove the last barrier, he changed his name from the formal "Yitskhok" to the folksy "Itzik." Here indeed was a poet for the people, of the people.

Though Manger moved around a lot and was probably heard by more Jews than any Yiddish writer since Sholem Aleichem, and though he was often at odds with the Warsaw literary establishment, he considered Warsaw his "great inspiration," and the decade he spent there on and off was the happiest in his life. One immediate effect it had on his ballads was to make the folk and Jewish elements more prominent, the better to play them off against a poetic sensibility that was distinctly secular and modern.[29]

> This song is old. Still, there's no harm
> Singing it from time to time,
> Specially when poor folks huddle by

> The oven at wintertime.
> And the willows tremble beside the cool river.[30]

A folksy narrator, a rustic setting, a free-standing refrain that breaks the rhyme scheme—all this points to a popular ballad. Yet what follows is the story of a simple musician's two daughters, who dream so fiercely of counts and kings who will carry them off that they dream their lives away. By the eleventh refrain—the ballad's main structuring device—the willows merge with sister Malke's consciousness and the possibility of her becoming a true "queen" evaporates. At that point the dream and the poetry it awakens within them eclipse the bleak reality of their lives. By ballad's end, the two Jewish sisters have themselves become the stuff of a lovely gypsy ballad sung to them in their old age.[31]

Manger makes the struggle between the mundane and the magical more explicit in "The Ballad of the Rabbi of Podeloy," a poem he himself struggled with for many years.[32] There is, to begin with, no such place as "Podeloy" and there was never, to end with, a rabbi who refused to recite the final confession for the reasons given. All day long he prays and worries, worries and prays, mourning, as a good Jew should, the exile of the Divine Presence. Then he sees that all this grieving has disgraced "the holy mid-week." Going blind, his perspective becomes ever sharper. Now he hears the river, the rustle of the trees at the roadside, and as he goes tapping along, his feet dance praises to the creator. When it comes time for him to die, the blind rabbi protests: "Confession is sorrow, and weeping stains the earth. / It desecrates the wonder of creation." The last word is given to the moon, Manger's stand-in for the magical and mysterious: "May all my loved ones be granted such a death."[33]

Were this the parodic storyteller of Peretz's "Kabbalists," the ballad would self-destruct. Modern Jewish storytellers, after all, were never more secular than when they sang the praises of God, rabbis, and hidden saints. Manger's subversion was far more subtle, however. He wanted everyone—rabbis, the Baal Shem Tov (whom he audaciously called "Saint Besht"), a musician's daughters, a poor Jew dressed all in gray—to join with him in celebrating God's universe. There was no "holy mid-week" until Manger came along; only the holy Sabbath, as with the Bible, or the festivals turned carnival, as with Sholem Aleichem. The master narrative of Manger's ballads is the story of how people caught in the grind of everyday life—and religious routine—are turned, despite themselves, into poets.

Manger included a fair number of self-consciously modern and urbane ballads in his second volume of verse, *Lantern in the Wind* (1933), and these perhaps reflect his response to life in the Polish metropolis even more directly than do his ballads in the folk vein. Never for a moment did Itzik Manger consider himself a poet merely of the Jewish underclass. But these dark and difficult ballads—about a marquis and marquise, two nurses and a naked man outside the hospital, about a lady in green and a lady with a red umbrella, about God revealing himself through a whore, a child, and a murderer—underscore how much effort it required for a poet of Manger's sensibility to rein himself in, how difficult was the striving for simplicity, how great the effort to "return the Golden Peacock from her exile."[34]

Manger's restorative impulse, his fervent desire to reconnect modern Yiddish literature with the wellspring of its own and the world's folklore, found stunning expression in "The Ballad of the Star Necklace."[35] It too begins with a folksy narrator who seduces the listener into expecting a traditional tale with a conventional moral:

> Raboysay, ikh vel aykh zingen a lid,
> Dos lid funem troyerikn glik,
> Vos flatert vi a foygl farbay
> Un kert zikh nisht um tsurik.
>
> In Yas, der shtiler un sheyner shtot,
> Mit alte shuln bakheynt
> (Azoy shteyt geshribn, ikh hob es a mol
> Mit di eygene oygn geleyent),
>
> Hot gelebt an alter un frumer yid
> Mitn nomen Reb Mikhele Blat,
> Un s'hot der alter un frumer yid
> Eyn-un-eyntsike tokhter gehat.

> Gentlemen! I will sing you a song,
> A song of the sorrowful joy,
> That flutters away like a bird
> And never more comes by.
>
> In Jassy, the quiet and beautiful town
> Graced with synagogues old
> (That's what is written, with mine own eyes
> I once read the way it was told),

> There lived an old and pious Jew
> Whose name was Reb Mikhele Blatt
> And this old and pious Jew,
> A one-and-only daughter he had.

It is a familiar patriarchal landscape (hence the opening address to the men, the same "Raboysay" who convene the grace after meals), in which "old" and "pious" are two sides of the same coin. To put us further at rest, the balladeer uses lulling alliterations: *flatert a foygl farbay; in Yas, der shtiler un sheyner shtot.* Word pairs (*shtiler un sheyner, alter un frumer, eyn-un-eyntsike*) add to the folksy effect. Working against the static and stable tableau is the opening stanza, which not only wrenches together two opposites (sorrow and joy) but insists upon the evanescence of life. So the idealized portrait one finds in old books is tempered at the outset by the more worldly perspective of the troubadour. How ironic (and brilliant) that Reb Mikhele Blatt should carry both nature and culture, future and past, within his very name: *Blat* means "leaf" and the "page" of a Gemara.

> A yor geyt farbay, dos tsveyte kumt,
> Kumt un geyt un farshvindt—
> Un s'iz di tokhter gevaksn shnel
> Un shlank, vi a sosne in vint.
>
> Un s'hot geshmeykhlt der alter yid,
> Ven s'hot geklapt in der tir
> Der friling mit a bintl bez,
> Vos er hot gebrakht far ir.
>
> Un s'hot geshmeykhlt der alter yid,
> Ven shpet in a bloer nakht
> Hot royte kalines tsu ir bet
> Der kenig zumer gebrakht.
>
> Nor az der harbst hot ongeklapt,
> Hot oyfgetsitert der yid,
> Ven s'hobn geklungen di regntrit:
> Di yugnt fargeyt un farflit.

> A year goes by, another arrives,
> Comes, goes, and is gone—

And the daughter grew slender
And true, like a pine tree in the breeze.

And the pious old man smiled
When Springtime knocked on the door
Bearing a bunch of lilacs
It had brought for her.

And the pious old man smiled yet again
When late on a bluish night
Summer came and placed
Red berries on her bed.

But a shudder seized the old man
When Autumn came knocking at the door;
At the sound of the rain on its beat:
Youth passes and is no more.

Linked to the earth and the seasonal cycle, the nameless daughter has time on her side—or so it seems to Mikhele Blatt as her suitors start coming by. A benign presence, the Springtime leaves its lilacs by the door, but Summertime, appearing on a "bluish night," brings its bright red berries directly to her bed. Hers is a sexual awakening that should come to fruition now, in the summer, and when the summer passes, the old man suddenly awakens to the dark and indifferent side of nature: oblivious of human desire, it marks the passage of youth and life itself. The father's piety and perennial smile cannot release him from the tyranny of time, as "a year goes by, another arrives." Then what of his daughter?

Nor eyn mol in a vayser nakht
Hot in ir kholem genent a shtafet
Un a zaydn hemd avekgeleygt
Oyf ir eynzamen bet.

Un az der yid hot zikh oyfgekhapt
Tsu shakhris in der fri,
Iz a shnirl shtern gehongen in shoyb,
Vi a zilberne melodi.

Un farn shpigl iz geshtanen shlank
Di tokhter in zaydenem hemd,
Di oygn ofn, di hent oyfn harts,
Vayt un troyerik un fremd.

Then once on a winter's night
A courier approached in her dream
And left behind a silken gown
On her solitary bed.

When the old Jew awoke
To his morning prayer
He saw on the pane a necklace of stars
Hanging like a silver melody there.

And before the mirror his daughter stood
Slender, in a silken gown,
With opened eyes, hands on her heart
Looking distant, sorrowful, foreign.

Come winter, and the boundary between her outer and inner world collapses. No longer can the white gown that Winter leaves on her lonely bed be explained away as an image of the snow, because her father will awaken to see her actually wearing that gown. To heighten the dramatic irony, the father has no premonition that this will be her combined wedding gown and shroud, but the listener knows, thanks to that "silver melody" left behind by the frost, a synesthetic fusion of color and sound. (To the Yiddish ear, the High German *melodie*, emphasized by its rhyme position, is the essence of lyric poetry.[36]) The daughter is already a stranger in her own home. Her slender figure no longer partakes of the forest in springtime and can no longer bring a smile to her father's face. It is a mirror image of her own solitary longing, as fleeting as the frost on the windowpane, as beautiful as a song.

The next night there comes another stranger; he leaves a golden crown on her bed. When Reb Mikhele awakens the next morning, he sees the star necklace in the window and his daughter in her silken gown before the mirror, wearing the crown of gold. Then the pious old man understands, and he tears his clothes and puts ashes on his head, intoning the prayer for the dead. His daughter, dressed in silken gown and crown of gold, goes away barefoot, walking slowly and softly across the snow.

What makes this a perfect ballad—better, I would argue, than any in the Yiddish oral tradition—is the extraordinary way it balances the lyric and dramatic perspectives. To portray as normative the father-daughter relationship (instead of the more common tale of mother and daughter, father and son), Manger stresses the patriarchal setting; after all, the balladeer is himself a man addressing other men. But even as Manger can empathize profoundly with Reb Mikhele Blatt, whose religious routine was so utterly transformed and shattered by the presence of his daughter, the most poignant—and poetic—passages are reserved for the dreamscape of his nameless daughter. When all is said and done, the ballad's temporal scheme is thoroughly subjective: the seasons come and go and a young woman succumbs to her longing. To render this real within "the quiet and beautiful town of Jassy," surrounded by the splendid Slavic landscape (*sosne*, "pine tree," *bez*, "lilac," and *kalines*, "berries of a water-elder," are words of Slavic origin), and to make it sound like the work of a traditional balladeer was something only Manger could achieve. The critic Abraham Tabachnik, whose measure of excellence was the poetry of the New York "Yunge," prized Manger's ballads for arriving at the "lyric subjectivism" of a Mani Leyb or Zishe Landau.[37] Without minimizing the achievement of the New York Yiddish symbolists, I would confer the highest honor upon the seemingly artless, seemingly ageless, and seemingly impersonal ballads in the folk vein of Itzik Manger.

Manger's self-transformation into a folk bard was not yet complete. For all that Czernowitz provided an address for the modern Yiddish fable and ballad, and for all that Jassy provided a convenient pseudo-traditional setting for his verse, there was something missing. Manger's ballad revival, as we have just seen, was more a statement of aesthetic than of Jewish ethnic purpose. His interest in the ballad was sparked by reading modern European poetry, not by direct contact with the folk. The opposite, in fact, is true: Manger came home to the folk only *after* reinventing himself as a born-again troubadour. It was in Bucharest, no later than 1929, that Manger found his personal link to a living past.

Late one night he was sitting in a tavern with the child psychologist Israel Rubin, visiting from Berlin.[38]

> Long past midnight an old man in his seventies dropped in. He was really soused. It was the last of the Brody Singers, Old Man Ludvig.
>   We invited him over to our table. He poured himself a large glass of wine,

recited some kind of Yiddishized Kiddush, and then began to sing from his Brody repertoire.

When he finished singing Velvl Zbarzher's song, "The Tombstone Engraver," he improvised a stanza of his own:

> Here lie Avrom Goldfaden and Velvele Zbarzher, our brothers dear,
> Who, to so many brought cheer
> With their songs so sweet.
> Today they lie without any heat
> Though once their heads, so refined, could do any feat.
> And my end will be the same as theirs.

Suddenly, I saw the light: This is it! The figures of the Brody Singers lighted up in my imagination. All the wedding jesters and Purim players who had entertained generations of Jews suddenly came alive. I will become one of them, one of "our brothers dear." What they created and sang was possibly quite primitive, not exalted poetry by any means, but they themselves were poetry.

I recalled the beautiful folksongs that I had heard in my father's workshop. What an orgy of color and sound! A legacy that lay abandoned, gold that lay strewn about at our feet.

And I took in their sound and their sight.

Reliving this epiphany in front of an American Yiddish audience, Manger added the following comparison: "In every shtetl there was one *rov* for every hundred Purim players. Here in America every city has a hundred rabbis and not even one Purim player."

There was never a modern Yiddish writer who came to storytelling or songwriting without a struggle. Manger's is the only honest record of how it happened. At the end of his career, at his sixtieth birthday celebration, he might have claimed always to have cherished the folksongs heard in his father's workshop, and who would be the wiser? Especially after the Holocaust, it would be comforting to believe that one Jewish survivor, at least, had sprung directly from the folk. Instead Manger wanted us to know that even a Yiddish poet predisposed to the ballad, someone who had actually come of age in a town where Avrom Goldfaden (1840–1908) and Velvl Zbarzher were still a living memory, would scarcely look for inspiration to mere rhymsters, wedding jesters, Brody Singers. A poet was someone who kept company with Goethe, Rilke, and Poe.[39]

So what exactly was it about old Ludvig's drunken doggerel that so in-

S. Yudovin, sketches of King Ahasuerus and Mordecai from a Purim-shpil in
Beshenkovichi, Byelorussia (1939)

spired Manger? That here was a usable, if somewhat disreputable, past on
his own doorstep? That he made Kiddush in Yiddish? Or was it that Ludvig
was the last of the Brody Singers, in which case whoever came after him
would be free to recloak—and betray—that legacy in his own image? No
other modern storyteller had the good fortune to grow up with a father
who delighted in his son's Yiddish writings. Not Ansky, not Peretz, not
Sholem Aleichem, not Der Nister, and most certainly not Isaac Bashevis
Singer. Yet only upon meeting this relic of Yiddish literary lore did Manger
really come home. Like every other first-generation Jewish rebel, he had
never considered the old songs as anything more than a quaint or romantic
subject. Suddenly what lay outside, an abandoned and ruined legacy, could
become part of what lay inside. His own father's workshop had been an
orgy of color and sound, and he, the poet-apprentice, had never even
known it. Rather than imagining the spectral figure of Velvl Zbarzher hov-
ering over the streets of Jassy, or inventing an elaborate scheme to sell

Rumanian-Yiddish literature on the Warsaw market, he could turn his own family into the source of myth. Forget about being born in Berlin. Now Manger could eat his kugel and have it too: both his poetry and parody grew directly from native soil. The Brody Singers were dead—Long live the Brody Singers![40]

Perhaps it was after meeting Ludvig that twenty-eight-year-old Manger resolved to "create the second Yiddish folk epic after Peretz's *Folkstimlekhe geshikhtn.*" To become a Yiddish *klasiker* required mastery of master texts, living and dead. It required a restorative program to bring people and culture together. It required that Manger drop his bad-boy image, his persona as a lonely drunk, and become a sober, almost scholastic, Purim player instead. And Manger succeeded, despite the Great Depression, the rise of Stalin and Hitler, and the ultimate Destruction, to produce a modern Yiddish classic based, like the *Purim-shpil* itself, on the Bible.

Much had happened since Peretz first challenged Yiddish writers to return to the Bible (in 1910). For one thing, there was now a bona-fide modern Yiddish translation of the Hebrew Bible, the life's work of an American Yiddish poet who went by the biblical pen name of Yehoash.[41] For another, Yiddish literary historians since the mid-twenties had been busy discovering a Yiddish renaissance, complete with freewheeling biblical epics, bawdy Purim plays, and true romances. What Isaac Schipper, Max Erik, Max Weinreich, and Nokhem Shtif found, or thought they had, was a lost secular heritage presumably written and performed by *shpilmener,* wandering Yiddish minstrels. This last was a godsend for someone like Manger, who already claimed Velvl Zbarzher, the Brody Singers, and Avrom Goldfaden as next of kin. Now, as biblical folk bard, Manger could trace his roots back to the sixteenth and seventeenth centuries.[42]

But the 1930s were not an auspicious time for Manger's rescue operation. Retrieving the Bible for secular Yiddish ends in the midst of the depression and the terrors of Stalin and Hitler was viewed as heresy by the right and the left. Upon the publication of Manger's first *Khumesh-lider* (Bible Poems) in the Polish Yiddish press, Horav Arn Kotler, the head of the Kletsker Yeshiva, issued an open letter (never mentioning Manger by name) in the Vilna-based organ of the Agudas Yisroel Party. What roused Horav Kotler from his silent disdain for the *hefkeyres,* the wantonness routinely preached by Yiddish writers, is that Manger had enlisted the hallowed patriarchs for his nefarious ends. "Sacrilege!" screamed the talmudic sage. So much for Manger's reputation in Vilna.[43]

On the other side of the Polish-Soviet border, Manger was so treyf that all mention of him was forbidden. The very idea of transplanting the matriarchs and patriarchs into a turn-of-the-century Galician shtetl was anathema to the architects of a deracinated and de-Hebraicized Yiddish culture. If anything, the Bible belonged to the Zionists, but in the spirit of fin-de-siècle orientalism and Else Lasker-Schüler's *Hebrew Ballads* (1913), they preferred to reimagine the Bible along Bedouin lines, and in pure Sephardic Hebrew. A biblical melodrama, *Jacob and Rachel,* performed in Warsaw by the Ohel Theater from Palestine, was presumably the foil for Manger's counter-midrash.[44] That left only the Bund, the party for which Manger evinced the greatest sympathy since it alone gave pride of place to Yiddish. This vanguard of Yiddish proletarian culture would perhaps accept the Bible—if properly packaged as folklore and parody.

To disarm potential critics, Manger claimed to be acting out of filial loyalty. "Against the backdrop of this [eastern Galician] landscape," he wrote in the preface to the *Khumesh-lider,*

> my father, as a wandering tailor's apprentice, composed his Purim plays and performed them along with his buddies.
>
> The roguish cap of the Jewish Purim player always hovered before my eyes as I wrote this book.
>
> And the lyric-pious silhouette of my mother bent over her Yiddish Bible.[45]

What was revolutionary could now pass as standard, as almost genetic in origin. No matter that Manger's interest in reviving Yiddish folk theater owed more to Hofmannsthal than to his father, the tailor's apprentice, or that Manger's technique of zany juxtapositions borrowed from German expressionism as much as it did from the *Purim-shpil.* No matter that on his way through eastern Galicia Manger stopped over in Bucharest where Old Man Ludvig—no friend of the family—held forth in a somewhat less laudable forum. The impetus for internal renewal always came from the culture at large, and the born-again bard always covered his tracks.

Purim was Manger's cloak and master metaphor for putting Jewish parody, drama, and the Bible back on the map. In "Folklore and Literature," his manifesto published in April 1939, Manger argued that the main sources for an authentic Jewish myth were the Bible, as mediated through Jewish

Yosl Kotler, in Herman Gold, *Mayselekh* (1928)

folklore, and drama, as mediated through the ballad. Yiddish literature could only bring solace in these tragic times if it was rooted in folklore. And there were two different strands of the tradition from which to choose: the lyrical strand of Peretz and the Jewish neoromantics, which drew in turn on religious and hasidic sources, and the grotesque-realistic strand that Sholem Aleichem perfected.[46] Manger was arguing for an art of creative retexturing, and not of betrayal. He wanted the lyric interwoven with the grotesque, his mother with his father, Peretz with Sholem Aleichem. Manger had already sewn the garment himself and, when finished, would call it *Medresh Itzik*.

Itzik's midrash drew more than formal inspiration from Peretz and Ansky. Peretz's betrayal of religious and hasidic folklore in the name of secular humanism reintroduced an ethical dimension into modern Yiddish writing. Manger took these ethical concerns one step further. Manger's midrash, as Wisse has written, used the mock-biblical epic to suggest that "the present, however puny, is an ethical improvement over the past."[47] Shifting the source of Jewish morality from above to below was a stunning reversal of traditional perspective, dating back to Ansky's pathbreaking essay of 1908. For Ansky, biblical monotheism was tainted with violence and tribalism, as compared to the principle of *spiritual* struggle characteristic of Jewish folk creation. Manger's Bible folk were the people of the Humanistic Book.[48]

There was no room in that book for the grand scheme of creation, revelation, and especially redemption. Moses the Lawgiver was nowhere to be
seen. There was neither Exodus nor Sinai. No messianic figures either, not
even Elijah. Matriarchs, patriarchs, kings, and courtiers were laughable
figures, full of self-importance, while Manger's midrash turned their shtetl
offspring into an ethnic and ethical aristocracy. Raiding the Bible for its
domestic dramas, Manger took the side of the underdog or otherwise decentered the hallowed source. Thus Abraham gave a tongue lashing to Lot
for his drinking, but in the end it was the status-conscious patriarch who
gave himself away. "Hagar's Last Night in Abraham's House" gave poignant
voice to the jilted lover who had to take her bastard son and go work "in
some alien kitchen." It was this implicit mockery of the biblical pantheon
that outraged the orthodox establishment.

The connection to Sholem Aleichem was equally deep. Sholem Aleichem
taught Manger how to distill the raw materials of a living folk into a dis-
ciplined art form; how to root his own work in the impersonal and highly
conventional folk tradition; how to find the magic in the mundane; and
how to give voice to the folk and not merely sing its praises from afar.

The voices heard in *Medresh Itzik* are not only the silenced voices of Esau
and Hagar; of Mother Sarah, still childless at age ninety; or of Leah crying
her eyes out over a *shundroman*, a potboiler. They are also the voices of
Goldfaden; of E. T. A. Hoffmann, who could describe a tear talking to a
shadow on the floor; and above all, the voice of the Golden Peacock, the
personification of the Yiddish folksong. *Medresh Itzik* bears eloquent testimony to the poetry and emotion that resonate from Yiddish lullabies and
lovesongs, not to speak of proverbs and maxims. In the best of the biblical
folk poems, voices are orchestrated within other voices: a stanza from a
lovesong ("How like the smoke of a chimney, / How like the smoke of a
train / Is the love of a man, dear mother, / The love of any man") becomes
part of Hagar's indirect monologue as she tries to justify Abraham's cruelty,
which in turn is controlled by the seemingly impersonal voice of the poet.

That voice is Manger's great achievement. It is quite unlike the voice of
Peretz's narrators, so bookish and ironic, and equally distinct from Sholem
Aleichem's surrogate storytellers, recorded "live." Manger's folk voice rarely
deviates from the four-beat, three-beat rhythm and the abcb rhyme, never
goes on for more than eleven stanzas, in the course of which a three-act
drama plays itself out.[49]

The scene opens with Hagar in the kitchen—her combined prison and refuge—with the shadows cast by a lamp playing a cat-and-mouse game on the walls. She is the mouse; Sarah, the high and mighty *pushke-gabete* (charity collector), is the cat. Only hours before, Abraham cast her out of his heart and home, with such callousness and venom that Hagar must spend whatever time she has left to recall the world she knew.[50]

> Di shifkhe Hogor zitst in kikh,
> A roykhik lempl brent
> Un shotnt same kets un mayz
> Oyf ale groe vent.
>
> Zi veynt. Se hot der balebos
> Ir haynt geheysn geyn.
> "Klipe, hot er ir gezogt,
> Du tretst mikh op, tsi neyn?"
>
> Surtshe di pushke-gabete
> Hot im shoyn vider ongeredt:
> "Oder du traybst di dinst aroys,
> Az nisht vil ikh a get."

> Hagar, the servant, sits in the kitchen,
> A smoking oil lamp spills
> The shapes of shadowy cats and dogs
> To flicker on the walls.
>
> She weeps because her master
> Fired her today.
> "Beat it, you bitch," he told her;
> "Can't you let me be?"
>
> It was Sarah who egged him on—
> That proper deaconess
> Saying, "Either get rid of the girl
> Or give me a divorce."

It is time (in act 2) to recapitulate the love affair itself. Hagar opens her hope chest to rummage through the gifts Abraham gave her, when he dolled her up for their trysts by the railroad right-of-way. The kitchen's oppressive smoke is transformed in this act into the smoke of a train, a ready-made and consoling image for the fleeting love of men.

Un Hogor nemt fun kufert aroys
A baytshl kreln vi blut,
A fartekhl fun grinem zayd
Un a shtroyenem zumerhut.

Di zakhn hot er ir geshenkt,
A mol ven zey zenen gegan
Shpatsirn iber der lonke,
Dort, vu es geyt di ban.

"Oy, azoy vi a roykh fun a koymen
Un azoy vi a roykh fun a ban,
Azoy iz, mame getraye,
Di libe fun a man.

Vu vel ikh mikh itst ahintun
Mitn pitsl kind oyf di hent?
Saydn nemen zayn benkart
Un geyn dinen in der fremd."

Hagar takes out her trunk
A summer hat of straw;
She takes her green silk apron
And her blood-red beads of coral.

These were the gifts he gave her
Once upon a day
When they strolled the meadow
By the railroad right-of-way.

"How like the smoke of a chimney,
How like the smoke of a train
Is the love of a man, dear mother,
The love of any man."

God knows where we shall run to,
Myself and his bastard child,
Unless in some alien kitchen
We are allowed to hide.

Though she is merely a servant—and a shiksa at that—Abraham's house
has been her home. In a few hours she will be driven into exile, perhaps
on that same train. As the folk wisdom about smoke and men's love console

her in her moment of greatest grief, she returns to it while scouring and cleaning. Fortified by her memories—and her righteous indignation—she uses the routine of physical labor to work through the trauma and to serve as a sign of her own abiding love.

> Zi nemt in der hant dem bezem
> Un kert tsum letstn mol di shtub
> Un epes unter der bluzke
> Filt, az s'hot im nokh lib.
>
> Zi vasht nokh eyn mol di teler
> Un shayert di kuperne fan—
> "Azoy vi a roykh fun a koymen
> Iz di libe fun a man."

> She takes the kitchen broom,
> She sweeps the kitchen floor.
> Under her blouse something still says
> She loves him—and sweeps some more.
>
> Again, she does the dishes,
> And scours the copper pan.
> "How like the smoke from a chimney
> Is the love of any man."

Manger's midrash (like the classical midrashim of old) thrives on anachronism, and this one plays it to the hilt: the whole premise of Abraham's extramarital affair with a servant girl producing a bastard child flies in the face of biblical and Middle Eastern polygamy—not to speak of the chimney, the train, the pots and pans, the straw hats, the bill of divorce, and the ideal of romantic love. In "Hagar's Last Night in Abraham's House" the modern is not only better than the ancient, but the gentile is better than the Jew and the woman better than the man. (In other poems, which focus on their personal sorrows, Abraham and Sarah are much more compassionate.) The language, too, abounds in zany anachronisms: Abraham calls Hagar a *klipe*, literally a shell or husk, a demonic term of kabbalistic provenance, and Hagar responds by throwing Abraham's *benkart* up to him. *Mamzer*, the standard Yiddish word for "bastard," would not work nearly as well because the word has lost its bite, if not its literal meaning, through overuse. *Benkart* is the Polish equivalent, which not only restores the sense of illegitimacy but also lends an obscene edge to Hagar's words. *Benkart,* Abraham's view of Ishmael as excess baggage, contrasts powerfully with Hagar's bitter fate, left as she is *mitn pitsl kind oyf di hent,* with the tiny tot in her arms.[51]

Most midrashic of all is Manger's use of alternative prooftexts, the scriptural passages used by the rabbis to legitimate new interpretations. Yiddish folk speech or the occasional quatrain of a Yiddish folksong are Manger's chief source of quotation. But as the maskilim knew long ago, this "linguistic folklore" bespeaks a People of the Book who could rattle off countless quotations without ever generating something new. Manger, the great rehabilitator of folklore in modern times, is much more the maskil than meets the ear. Just where one would expect a liberal dose of Yiddish folk speech, in his so-called Bible Poems, his use of such materials is actually quite sparing—and bold.

Abraham, for example, waxes philosophical in the opening stanzas of "Abraham and Sarah," articulating his creed with the homespun phrase "Bitokhn mayn vayb, az got vil shist a bezem oykh" (Faith, good wife, if God wills it, even a broom can shoot). Once this becomes the old patriarch's refrain, however, his patterned response to Sarah's ever more eloquent yearnings for a child of her own, the phrase takes on new meaning, perhaps unintended by Abraham. Isn't he (aged ninety-nine) the old broom that might, if God wills it, shoot again? And isn't this, the poet-midrashist insinuates, what the well-worn phrase meant all along?[52]

So too with Hagar's recollected lovesong. Yes, love is like the smoke of a train, but not until a poet can get inside that simile, unpack it into a three-act drama with the train joining past, present, and immediate future, does it live as experience or poetry. Only then can the hidden drama of Yiddish lullabies, lovesongs, women's prayers, proverbs, and maxims breathe new life into Bible stories learned by rote.

Like the fields where Rachel goes to fetch water, fields that smell of twilight and hay (*fun demerung un hey*), the poems in *Medresh Itzik* are a web of poetic yearning and everyday life. Thanks to this disparate quality— the bold and sometimes zany mixture of high and low, pathos and parody, Yiddish, German, Slavic—the pattern remains fresh and artful. Thanks to Peretz and Sholem Aleichem, whose designs Manger long since made his own, the poet-storyteller achieves a perfectly modulated voice, which makes the pattern seem timeless. Having the homespun yield its parody, plots, and poetry, what remains for Manger to master is its sense of place.

The gray light of the dawning
Touches the earth with dawn.
Eliezer, the loyal servant, puts
The black team's harness on.

Taking the child in his arms,
Old Abraham shuts the door.
Over his ancient roof, there gleams
A blue and pious star.

"Up, Eliezer"—the whip rings out,
The road has a silvery look.
"Sad and lovely," the poet says,
"Are the roads of the Holy Book."

The graying willows on the way
Run to the house again
To see if his mother weeps beside
The cradle of her son.[53]

The only real landscape, for Manger, is a poetic landscape. *Demerung,* a German loan word that Nietzsche, Wagner, and the expressionists used to conjure up the Apocalypse, signals the ideal state of transition, preferably one from darkness to light. The blue morning star shining above Abraham and Sarah's house adds another optimistic touch. At this point, the "sad and lovely" formula comes down in favor of lovely. But just then we see the willows rushing back to see who else is weeping. Once the trip has begun, the die is cast.

"Daddy, where are we going now?"
"To Lashkev—to the Fair."
"Daddy, what are you going to buy
At Lashkev—at the Fair?"

"A soldier made of porcelain,
A trumpet and a drum;
A piece of satin to make a dress
For mother who waits at home."

Abraham feels his eyes grow moist
And the steel knife pressing, where

It scalds the flesh beneath his shirt . . .
"It's going to be some Fair."

Everyone knows the lullaby "Daddy's Away at the Fair," just as everyone
has read the story of Abraham taking Isaac to the Akedah. The one adds
pathos and tension to the other because something has already gone wrong:
it is always the mother who stays home with the child, and here the cradle
is empty, the innocent child accompanying his father on the fateful journey.
"It's going to be some Fair," the father mumbles under his breath.

> "Eliezer, stop at the water mill.
> Stop for a while and wait.
> Isaac, my son, and I will go
> Alone from there on foot."
>
> Eliezer sits on the driver's seat
> And casts an anxious look.
> "Sad and lovely," the poet says,
> "Are the roads of the Holy Book."

Now the balance has measurably shifted to the sad side of the scale. Sad,
but by no means terrifying—either in comparison to the biblical account
of the sacrifice or in comparison to Goethe's "Erlking," the famous ballad
of a father driving his only son into the hands of death. Manger's midrash
domesticates God's terrible test of faith and Goethe's sexual and supernatural overtones. The modern midrash ends not with the angel staying the
executioner's hand or with the Erlking claiming his innocent victim, but
with two benign figures: the somewhat apprehensive Eliezer, whom
Abraham addresses in Ukrainian, and the poet, who knows that the story
will end well.

Eliezer and the Bible-quoting poet are emblematic of Manger's midrash
as a whole. The fusion of natural landscape and biblical past is captured in
the poem's untranslatable rhyme: *Tanakh* (the Hebrew acronym for the
three main divisions of the Holy Book) rhymes twice with the resoundingly
Slavic word for "road," *shlyakh*. Poets who operate in the realm of pure
lyric begin and end with *demerung*. Poets of a Jewish nationalist bent fill
their verse with biblical locutions and historical events. Yiddish poets who
wish to lend an earthy, spoken quality to their verse play up the Slavic
component in the language. The perfect poet, the sum of all poets who

preceeded him, the one who from the age of twenty-eight dreamed of becoming a *klasiker,* can make Hebraic past rhyme with Slavic present and transform them both into a lyrical dawning.

Is it any wonder that Manger reserved the most balanced and beautiful of the Bible poems for his namesake, Isaac? In this he joined a proud line of Jewish writers named Saul (Tchernichowsky), David (Pinsky, Frischmann), and (Yokheved Bat-) Miriam, who wrote of their biblical counterlives. But once Manger discovered, after meeting old Ludvig, that the parodists could inherit the past—better than any progeny or self-appointed prophets—he found the door open to a collective memory that was also his own. No need to tread lightly across the biblical story: he and his father and mother were the biblical story. No need to reimagine the ancient Near Eastern setting: eastern Galicia was the biblical setting. No need to study Scripture and midrashic commentary because Yiddish language and folklore were the sacred texts.

When the first slim volume of his *Khumesh-lider* appeared, in 1935, followed a year later by a second edition and a sequel, the *Megile-lider* (Songs of the [Purim] Megillah), Manger did not suspect that the Bible, rather than the ballad, would become his permanent—and portable—homeland. He had too much going for him. Along with Moyshe Broderzon (1890–1956), he was the most sought-after Yiddish songwriter in Poland, and probably the first to write expressly for the Yiddish screen. Through translations of Rumanian, Spanish, and gypsy ballads and essays on them, he championed the brotherhood of man and the revival of folklore, and through his own dramatizations he tried to breathe new life into the Yiddish stage. His literary essays, including a brilliant appreciation of Sholem Aleichem, appeared regularly in the *Literarishe bleter.* He was the darling of the Yiddish writers' club, Tłomackie 13. He was married to (or living with) the Polish-Yiddish journalist, Rokhl Auerbach, who made sure his shirts were ironed and his valise neatly packed. After his own *Getseylte verter* folded, he planned to launch a new highbrow journal called *Di svive* with the following editorial lineup: Jankel Adler (plastic arts), Itzik Manger (poetry), Y. M. Neyman (essays), Ephraim Kaganovski and Yitskhok Bashevis (prose). Manger also branched out into prose, with a gallery of *Noente geshtaltn* (1938), intimate portraits from Yiddish literary history, and his fantastical *Adventures of Shmuel-Aba Abervo,* or *The Book of Paradise* (1939).[54]

Allied to the Jewish Labor Bund, the largest Jewish political force in Poland, Manger remained well within the range of its left-of-center politics. That too boosted his reputation. Manger's *Megillah* was a proletarian midrash on the Purim story, whose unsung hero, the tailor's apprentice Fastrigosse, failed to assassinate King Ahasuerus and was executed.[55] Manger's ecumenicism (expressed in the early ballads about Jesus, the Bible poems in praise of Hagar and later of Ruth) were of a piece with the bundist outreach program to the Socialist International. And so long as one disregards how Manger actually treated women, his protofeminism put him far ahead of his time.

If anything, Manger was a Yiddishist. His portrait gallery of Yiddish literary figures situates each of its subjects within a clearly defined landscape (Worms, Berlin, Zamość, Odessa, Dubno, Vilna, Brody, Lodz, Przemysl, Kiev, Mezhibozh, New York, Chelm), each a dramatic vignette that focuses on the subject in old age or in a moment of intense introspection, and all of them united in their love of the mother tongue. Yiddish culture, in Manger's scheme, was a child of the Haskalah, emancipated from Hebrew and (interestingly enough) from Hasidism. Since the maskilim were progressive by definition, there was no need to doctor the evidence (as Soviet revisionists were doing) with class conflict. The only worker-poet Manger portrayed (Yoysef Bovshover) was mad. The longest chapter was on Velvl Zbarzher, portrayed as a purely lyric poet. Manger dedicated the book to the teachers and students of the Yiddish secular school system in Poland.[56]

As even the titles of his poetry collections reveal, however, it became difficult for the poet to preside over his kingdom in the face of historical events: *Stars on the Roof* (1929), *Lantern in the Wind* (1933), *Twilight in the Mirror* (1937), and *Clouds over the Roof* (1942). "Baym rand funem opgrunt vert dos gelekhter nokh farshayter," he wrote in the preface to *The Book of Paradise*. "At the edge of the abyss even laughter becomes desperate." And so Paradise was now divided into three—the Turkish, the Jewish, and the Christian—and you needed a passport to get from one to the other. Up there in Paradise Reb Zeydl the photographer had no takers for his latest Purim play about Noah in the ark, where, amid other shenanigans, a delegation of pigs did the Hitler salute as they marched across the stage singing:

> Heil, Reb Noah, heil!
> Hear us for a while.
> Indeed, we're flesh you musn't touch

> But your stingy missus
> Your old and stingy missus,
> Is a true-born witch.

While Purim parody was an obvious vehicle for political satire, Zeydl's bravado only masked the bitter reality: even in heaven the Jews are at the mercy of the goyim. When the two Jewish angel heroes, Shmuel-Aba and his sidekick Pisherl, enter the Christian paradise in their effort to rescue and redeem the runaway Messiah Ox (the *shor-habor*), they are met by Dmitri Angel, a traditional, Jew-hating Ukrainian angel, and only then by *der heyliker Petros,* kindly Saint Peter who speaks Russian and takes them under his wing. Luckily, folklore and love are still the great equalizers in heaven as on earth. Shmuel-Aba and Pisherl confuse Saint Nicholas with Elijah the Prophet, and Pisherl falls head over wings in love with Anyella, a girl angel with blond braids and blue eyes. (Pisherl, for all that, does not marry the shiksa angel; he returns to the Jewish paradise when his mission is over.) Thus Paradise is animated by the same mysteries as all of Manger's earlier verse—by unrequited love, birth, death, longing, melancholy. Not since Sholem Aleichem had the folk repertory and the Slavic landscape been used so effectively to argue for an egalitarian humanism.[57]

And not since Sholem Aleichem had a born-again storyteller invented a life history that matched his new calling with such panache. Paradise, like Kasrilevke, gave the writer a second chance: to live the ideal childhood, to be born with the storyteller's gift, and never to abandon the security of home. Manger's hero, who alone retained total recall of life in Paradise, could regale the shtetl elders on earth in much the same way as baby Jesus had inspired the magi in Bethlehem. By redeeming them with the lost collective memory of Paradise, the fallen angel Shmuel-Aba Abervo also redeems himself, as his odd name attests: *Aber-vo* is how the Jews of Czernowitz peppered their speech to show that they were really native German speakers and not Ostjuden from Galicia. "Not on your life!" "You couldn't possibly mean it!" are some of its colloquial equivalents. But this time Manger aimed the joke at himself. "Aber-vo, Manger," he seems to be saying, "once you start inventing a past, you might as well turn it all into myth." To complete the picture, the artist Mendl Reyf, a close friend of the author's, used Itzik and Notte Manger as the real-life models for "two infatuated angels" whom Shmuel-Aba and Pisherl spy walking late one night through the streets of Paradise.[58]

Mendl Reyf, "The guests seated themselves," in Itzik Manger,
Dos vunderlekhe lebns-bashraybung fun Shmuel Abe Abervo
(The Wondrous Biography of Shmuel Aba Abervo; 1939)

Then came the war. In the trials and torment that followed—Manger was stranded without a usable passport in Paris, then fled to Marseilles, escaped to Tunis, from there to a hospital in Liverpool, and finally found refuge with Margaret Waterhouse in London—he saw all his dreams for a Yiddish renaissance destroyed along with his audience. "Where now? What next?" sang the Jew who found a half-moon in a cornfield (written in London, 1941). "I've become a wanderer through space and time, a restlessness between God and man, a sad and wanton melody swinging from the horn of the moon."[59] Manger was left with an abiding hatred for the Germans, whose culture he had once so admired, and for the Yiddish literary establishment that treated its great poets so piteously. The worst blow came in March 1944 upon learning of the death of his beloved brother Notte. The news unhinged Manger to such a degree that he wrote an open letter to I. J. Segal and Melech Ravitch, resigning not only from Yiddish literature but from the Yiddish language itself.[60]

Notte became Manger's dead muse. Since the grotesque reality, as he explained in a saner moment to Melech Ravitch, had made writing ballads superfluous, Manger turned to the sonnet and wrote an exquisite sonnet

cycle in memory of his brother. He also went back to the Bible, this time
to the books of Ruth and Job and to the story of Cain and Abel.

> Dost thou sleep, my brother Abel,
> That thou art so wonderfully fair?
> Never have I seen thee
> As beautiful before.
>
> Does the beauty lie in my ax
> Or is it, perhaps, in thee?
> Before the day is done,
> Speak—answer me.

"The Tailor's Apprentice Notte Manger Studies the Bible" added fifteen *khu-mesh-lider* based on the book of Samuel. Thus the Bible became for Manger
a book of memorial, perpetual exile, expiation. It became a weighty tome
that one would rescue from the flames—to help its bereaved author cross
the great divide.[61]

His songs survived much better than his psyche. There is no evidence
whatever of Manger's personal pathology in his poems, or that the war and
its aftermath saw Manger at his worst, cruel and narcissistic. Then again,
if Rokhl Auerbach, who miraculously survived the Warsaw ghetto and rescued Manger's papers along with other buried treasures after the war, only
to be met with Manger's fit of rage upon their reunion in London—if Rokhl
Auerbach could pass over everything that happened between them in silence, who are we to pass judgment? Manger deserved far more than the
hagiographers who painted his saintly portrait for posterity. But he was
fortunate to belong to a literature that upheld a Victorian standard of propriety. Manger's archive (housed in Jerusalem) contains the vilest literary
letters in the language. When it came to the writing that really mattered—
to his poetry—Manger was and remained a prince.[62]

Manger sought refuge, for a while, in storytelling proper. Boccaccio was
always Manger's favorite, "firstly for his sheer mastery, then for his ability
to purify and raise to absolute beauty the instincts that the respectable
citizen trivializes."[63] Manger now planned to write a sequel to *The Decameron* in which ten symbolic survivors of the Holocaust gather in a bunker
to swap stories, but he published only two: "The Adventures of Hershel
Summerwind" and "The Squire's Moustaches."

The first is a fanciful evocation of childhood, worthy of Sholem Aleichem. As a child, visiting his beloved grandmother and aunts in the town of Stoptshet, Itzikl (in real life) had accidentally fed the geese—and the hated gander—a bottle of whiskey.[64] The adventure story splits the episode in half, turns kindly Babe Taube into an evil stepmother who lives in a world of grotesque memories, makes the hero into a primitive rhymster who reacts viscerally to anything that smacks of death, and ends with young Hershel Summerwind being carried through the air by flocks of inebriated birds. Dreams and nightmares abound, adding a gothic quality to the tale, but death is resolutely vanquished by childhood and good cheer. "From this story you can see what a great and good God we have. For if He helped such an idler as Hershel Summerwind, He will certainly help all faithful and God-fearing Jews, who follow His commandment and live by His word."[65] Thus did Manger repudiate the German children's literature he was raised on—the *Max and Moritz* stories by Wilhelm Busch that epitomized the cruelty and sadism of German culture. Max and Moritz show no remorse for killing the widow Bolte's hens, and no tears are shed when the pranksters are ground to death in a flour mill. Hershel, by contrast, captures the empathy and poetry of a lost Jewish childhood.[66]

Manger's animus toward the goyim—and their God—is nowhere more apparent than in the tale of "The Squire's Moustaches."[67] "Motl Parnass was a barber by trade. He earned his bread by cutting the hair of Gentiles and shaving their gentile mugs." Motl suffers abuse from both sides: he is a henpecked husband whose only salvation from grinding poverty is the squire, "a dog with Polish moustaches." The *porits,* in turn, suffers from a wife named Maria who "went on burning candles and keeping fast days and growing skinnier all the time—like a shadow with a cross between her breasts," until the day he meets the beautiful Magda Walczynska, owner of the adjoining estate, and summarily poisons or strangles his penitent spouse. On the morning of his engagement, the squire calls for his Jewish barber. All nerves, Motl snips off more of the nobleman's moustache than he meant to, and is sentenced to 150 lashes. Upon learning of her husband's death, Motl's wife utters a curse that has fatal repercussions. There is no room for subtlety in this terrifying parable about what happens when a local despot with a moustache can find no better way to still his raging passions than by murdering the Jew who serves him.

Ironically, it was Manger's categorical enmity toward Germans, Lithuanians, Poles, and other Nazi collaborators which bedeviled his first trip to

Israel in 1958. Manger, now fifty-seven, gave an interview in which he stressed the need for historical objectivity as a prerequisite of epic art. Because Jews felt such hatred toward their murderers, he argued, and because the catastrophe was too great and too recent, Jewish artists were incapable of fashioning an epic response to the Holocaust. The point was much too subtle for Israeli journalists, and for once Manger got embroiled in a controversy he had not intended.[68]

Manger returned on periodic visits to Israel, where he had come to "wallow in his own home." While he was recuperating from a near-fatal visit in 1965, his *Megile-lider* opened in the Tel Aviv equivalent of Off-Broadway. Thanks to Dov Seltzer's neo-folksy score that recontextualized this proletarian *Purim-shpil* within Israeli popular culture, the *Megile-lider* broke the taboo against Yiddish in the state of Israel. Manger's popularity peaked during the yearly benefit concerts organized by the indefatigable Sholem Rosenfeld on Manger's behalf (in 1967 and 1968). These concerts inspired a new generation of Israeli singers to interpret Manger's songs in Yiddish and eventually in Hebrew. Chava Alberstein, for one, in her cabaret-style renditions of Manger's ballads, captures a haunting and gritty quality in Manger that is lost in Dov Seltzer's sing-along score.[69]

Manger knew that his songs would survive. He was awed to learn that his playful and popular "Oyfn veg shteyt a boym" (There Is a Tree That Stands) was sung by a young woman fighter in the ruins of the Warsaw ghetto.[70] He also knew that his life as a poet was spent. What was left was the shaping of his canon. Two retrospective volumes produced on the occasion of his fiftieth birthday, one arranged by genre, the other by theme, determined his future status as a *klasiker*. *Lid un balade* (1952), the more inclusive volume, is as close to Manger's Complete Poems as we are likely to come. But the success enjoyed by *Medresh Itzik*, first published in 1951, finally vindicated his dream.

The title *Itzik's Midrash* can only belong to a modern classic, which rewrites the past in a way that no rabbi or traditional commentator would presume to do. When an augmented edition of these biblically inspired poems was chosen to inaugurate the Hebrew University series of Yiddish texts in 1969, reissued in 1984, the editor Khone Shmeruk rearranged the poems in order of their biblical sequence and combed through Manger's writings to locate everything of biblical import. Thus *Medresh Itzik*, unlike *Lid un balade*, blurred the poet's chronology and his generic distinctions in the service of literature's most canonical text. Through this editorial procedure, Manger's lifelong dream of producing a new Yiddish folk epic was finally realized. What began in the mid-thirties as a discrete series of *Khumesh-* and *Megile-lider*—a lyric-dramatic genre that Manger invented—became in the fifties and sixties a Yiddish *seyfer*, a *medresh*, a traditional tome that made the poet's inventiveness into yet another tribute to the immutable past.

The son of "a wandering tailor's apprentice" who "composed his Purim plays and performed them along with his buddies" was now a long way from home. In his travels, the son had become a master tailor himself who could fashion a splendid garment. As the master recloaker of the oldest and the newest literary traditions, Itzik Manger alone produced a Yiddish folk epic to outlast the living folk, the living language, and the living landscape at once lovely and sad. He died in Tel Aviv, in 1969.

8

The Demon as Storyteller
ISAAC BASHEVIS SINGER

If Hell exists, everything exists. If you are real,
He is real.

—I. B. Singer, 1943

Nothing is more Jewish than a Jewish demon. What the golden-haired Lorelei are to the Rhine, the dark-haired *sheydim* are to the Jewish home, creeping out from behind the stove on a Sabbath afternoon, when the household is away at prayers. From birth until death a Jew must contend with these sheydim, who eat and drink just like humans; with *ruhin,* disembodied spirits, and with *lilin,* who are possessed of human form but also have wings. Ketev Meriri is most harmful at noon and in the heat of summer, while Lilith, Samael's consort, attacks newborn infants and their mothers. (This goes back to a time before time when Adam and Lilith got into a marital squabble; together, nonetheless, they produced many demons.) Jewish men, warned by the mystics of demons that are sired from every nocturnal emission, had good reason to tremble at bedtime. Bratslav hasidim recite a prayer composed by Reb Nahman to guard against such acts of pollution. And when, at death's door, a Jew's soul literally is up for grabs, the living must enlist all their accumulated wisdom to ward off the demons who live for this very moment.[1]

It was a rich field for Jewish preachers, of the old school and the new. The maskilim were especially fond of exploiting Samael-Ashemdai, king of the demons, to articulate a program for religious reform, to expose his unholy alliances among the Jews, or, most radically, to personify evil both on earth and in heaven. Of the maskilic writers, only Abramovitsh-Mendele dared to cast Ashmedai as arch antisemite, reactionary, and root cause of

El Lissitzky, in Leyb Kvitko, *Vaysrusishe folkmayses* (1923)

universal strife. The devil's powerful presence and supernatural powers in Mendele's *The Mare* (1873) argued for the moral regression of humankind and marked a turning point in the political fortunes of the Jewish Enlightenment.[2]

Yet so long as he was clothed in allegorical garb, the devil of modern Jewish literature remained a cloak for something quite human. From first to last, Peretz portrayed a devil who was decadent, phlegmatic, skeptical—and subject to protocol. "One morning," we read in *Monish* (1888), Peretz's "tragicomic poem,"

> as Samael lay in bed smoking cigarettes,
> and Lilith saw to her toilette
> by the light of the *tsoyer*
> (the gem that lights the ark),
> the doorbell tinkled in the foyer:
> "Enter!"
> and there a trembly demon stood,
> teeth all a-clatter,
> who flung himself flat on his face and then flatter.

The scene is Ararat, where Noah's ark rested after the flood, but humanity has fallen so far since then that the legendary *tsoyer* (Gen. 6:16), which once illuminated the ark, is now but a light in Lilith's boudoir. In such decadent surroundings, the devil perforce speaks a Germanized Yiddish ("Herein!" is what he actually cries), and his surrogates down below appear in the guise of wealthy merchants from Danzig. The seduction of the virtuous—and very handsome—Talmud prodigy named Monish is as farcical as the demons who conspire against him.[3]

Following Peretz's lead, Yiddish storytellers turned out demonological tales that were ever more upbeat and celebratory. Sholem Aleichem rescued "The Haunted Tailor" (1901) from the clutches of the ogre-like innkeeper Dodi with a little sermon on the beneficent power of laughter. S. Ansky in 1912–1917 transformed the dybbuk from a sinner to a saint and made Khonon a victor beyond the grave. Exactly thirty years after *Monish*, Der Nister wrote "Demons" (1918), still believing that freedom and creativity could vanquish the forces of skepticism. Not until a decade later, in that horrific "Tale of an Imp, of a Mouse, and of Der Nister Himself," did Yiddish-speaking demons regain some of their venality, vulgarity, and malevolence. But it was too late to reverse the betrayal of Jewish demonology in the name of secular humanism.

It would take a writer thoroughly versed in modern and classical Jewish sources to rehabilitate the powers of darkness; a writer who could wage a fierce oedipal struggle with the very literature that spawned him and who, in the wake of a midlife crisis, discovered storytelling as the consummate demonic art. Some have claimed Isaac Bashevis Singer to be the very image of the demons he wrote about and professed to believe in. One artist even sketched him accordingly. Reading Singer in the original and from start to finish, however, allows us to see him for what he really was: never more Yiddish than when writing about demons; never more playful, youthful, or hopeful than when writing as a demon.

Singer's life, like that of other born-again Jewish storytellers, follows the pattern of rebellion, loss, and return. At a certain point in his career he found his way back to Jewish fantasy and folklore; to a simplified world where people still sat around for hours swapping a good yarn; and to a superidiomatic Yiddish that was no longer spoken. Having found a formula that worked, Singer did what other Yiddish rebels had done before him: he rewrote his own life to make it seem as if it had all been preordained. To be sure, he added spice to the story by throwing in some scenes of bedroom and boudoir, and made much of being a loner, a pariah, and a heretic. But for all that, Singer's autobiographical persona was as much a fiction as Monish, seduced and abandoned; as the happy-go-lucky Sholem Nokhem-Veviks, hero of *From the Fair*; and as Shmuel-Aba Abervo, the angelic visitor from paradise. Yiddish literature provided Yitskhok Singer, the rebellious son and grandson of Polish rabbis, first with an escape route from the crumbling edifice of orthodox Judaism, then with the means of reclaiming some part of the ruins, there to nurture and redirect his formidable talents.

The familiar facts, known to almost every reader of contemporary fiction, are these.[4]

(1) My name: Yitskhok Singer. My father's: Rabbi Pinkhes Menakhem. (2) Born in the small town of Leoncin near the Vistula, where my father was the rabbi. Born 1904. (3) My mother's name Bathsheba, daughter of the Bilgoraj Rabbi, in the Lublin Province. (4) Religious education. Studied for a short while in the Warsaw Rabbinical Seminary Tahkemoni. (5) Moved to Warsaw when I was three years old.

From here on in, the biographies of Y. Bashevis, pen name of Yitskhok Singer, a card-carrying member of the Polish-Yiddish literary establishment, and I. B. Singer, the magician of West 86th Street, diverge in so many ways that it would be too confusing to play one off against the other.

So let us begin with a Yiddish storyteller whose life is free of serious obstacles, since he learned everything he needs to know about art in his father's court and mother's kitchen on Krochmalna Street, and everything that will inspire him to become the chronicler of Polish Jewry he saw with his own eyes in a prelapsarian shtetl called Bilgoraj between the ages of thirteen and nineteen. The third of four children crowded into a Warsaw tenement, young Isaac is clearly meant to become a writer.

> I was still a little boy, so I was allowed to look at women. I observed all kinds of shenanigans in this [rabbinical court]room, and my head was full of thoughts and fantasies. It occurred to me that perhaps the bride and groom weren't human at all, but demons? . . . Maybe the young man is a sorcerer from Madagascar and he placed her under a spell? I had come upon quite a few such tales in the storybooks I read. I already felt then that the world is full of wonders.[5]

Doubtless he is destined to become the kind of writer who makes the fantastical real while reveling in the metaphysics of human love and passion. For when his mind is bursting with all the marvelous goings-on inside the apartment, young Isaac can always cool off on the balcony where he contemplates the larger scheme of things, and where no one else but he ever ventures.[6]

Everything he reads is grist for the mill: Yiddish storybooks, the Talmud (especially the tale about the man and the harlot), the Kabbalah, even Dostoevsky's *Crime and Punishment*. In the Darwinian struggle for survival that rages in the neighborhood heder to which he is consigned, the dreamy-eyed Isaac finally wins over "The Strong Ones" by retelling them stories out of "literature." Thankfully, he spends almost no time receiving formal instruction in heder, so rich is the informal instruction he receives at home. "Although later in life I read a great deal of philosophy," he tells us in an editorial aside, "I never found more compelling arguments than those that came up in my own kitchen. I even heard at home the strange facts that are in the province of psychic research."[7] But Isaac is often left painfully alone with his questions concerning God, creation, heaven, and hell because his older brother Israel Joshua is busy painting realistic landscapes and reading Copernicus, Newton, and Darwin.

The home, when you come down to it, is a study in solitudes and irreconcilable contrasts. Father sits in his room all day and hates to be distracted from the study of Torah. Mother is where she belongs, in the kitchen, because "at that time it was a woman's accepted lot to bear children, run the household, and earn a living" (Y 141, E 44). Whenever the litigants invade her kitchen, or something particularly egregious happens in the room next door, her wig will get disheveled, and the contest between her "cold logic" and father's unquestioning faith will invariably begin ("Why the Geese Shrieked"). And how could it be otherwise, seeing that Krochmalna Street itself is a study in contrasts: Jewish whores with hearts of gold ("A Wedding"); learned publishers who smuggle on the side ("My Father's Friend"); businessmen so corrupt they would forge a rabbi's signature ("They Forged My Father's I.O.U."); vulgarity and refinement in one and the same person ("The Purim Gift"). There are also any number of hidden saints, such as Reb Chayim Gorshkover, who loves nothing better than reciting Psalms and reminiscing about Gorzkow; Reb Asher the Dairyman, "whose whole life was one big Yes"; and the unnamed Polish washerwoman, who couldn't die until she returned the Singers' laundry.

From Krochmalna Street, the best school a budding writer could want, the thirteen-year-old Singer is whisked away by his mother to the Polish equivalent of Brigadoon. Leaving the harsh and hungry German-occupied city of Warsaw for his ancestral home within the Austrian war zone, Singer unwittingly reverses the trajectory of every other Yiddish writer. No one ever goes back to the shtetl, save on a statistical or ethnographic mission. Yet Bilgoraj is home to uncles, aunts, and attractive cousins; a preserve of a vanished Jewishness and an older, uncorrupted Polish-Yiddish speech. "In this world of old Jewishness I found a spiritual treasure trove," writes Singer wistfully. "I had a chance to see our past as it really was. Time seemed to flow backwards. I lived Jewish history" (E 290). For the benefit of his Yiddish readers he adds: "Everything inside of me said: This must someday be described" (Y 340).

Conversely, Bilgoraj is a place to make new friends and to eat from the tree of secular knowledge. Back in Warsaw, Boruch Dovid the orphan boy taught him the secrets of the Kabbalah and the facts of life ("Reb Yekl Saffir"). Here, in the shtetl, young people are openly reading forbidden books, writing and speaking in Hebrew. Constrained by his rabbinic lineage, Isaac does most of his reading in an attic. It is here that he falls under the spell of Spinoza.

Because *In My Father's Court* was Singer's first "experiment in joining memoir and fiction," and was written by the second of his literary personae, Yitskhok Warshawski, an official stenographer and occasional literary critic of the *Jewish Daily Forward* (D. Segal, his cover as a tabloid journalist, was the third), it lays bare the strengths and weaknesses of his storytelling art. Where the plot is too thin to fill up the weekly installment, Warshawski relies on contrivances, a mysterious knock on the door, a string of rhetorical questions to suggest a preternatural occurrence, an interlude on the balcony where the precocious narrator philosophizes. Yet the experiment also gives play to the multiplicity of voices and perspectives that make up a communal speech act. First there are the litigants themselves, divided over every issue. Then there are Pinkhes Menakhem and Bathsheba Singer, at odds with each other over the proper course of action. Finally there is the narrator, who stands both in the story and out. Warshawski does a sloppy job juggling his worldly perspective with that of the actors involved, whose very faith is on the line. To compensate, he prefaces the work with a mini-sermon on the universal import of the Beth Din. The ideal of human progress, Warshawski preaches, is a return to the model of the rabbinical court. "There can be no justice without godliness," he warns.[8]

Singer had many reasons to rehabilitate the moribund institutions of the Polish-Jewish past. One was to rewrite his own biography. Another was to expand his creative repertory. Still another was messianic. With this experiment, as with the distillations in story form, Singer found the best medium for conveying his conservative outlook on life. Whereas the fantastical and hypnotic tales of Der Nister held out a utopian vision of a future that had never existed in the past, and the deceptively simple Bible poems of Itzik Manger conjured up a restorative image fusing present and past, the learned and sometimes occult tales of Isaac Bashevis Singer aimed at subverting the present in the name of a more perfect, if intransigent, past. In the beginning there was little Itchele Singer, training to become a traditional storyteller. And in the end of days, there would again be storytelling, rooted in God and an absolute standard of morality.

The other, demythologized, life of Yitskhok Singer is antimessianic to a fault. When submitting his biography for a new edition of a Yiddish lexicon that would never appear, Singer made no mention of his sojourn in Bilgoraj. "(5) Moved to Warsaw when I was three years old. (6) Began writing in Hebrew . . . Soon went over to Yiddish." The rest was taken up with the Yiddish dailies he wrote for, the literary periodicals he contributed to and coedited (with his lifelong friend Aaron Zeitlin), the major European novels he translated, and the one book he published, *Satan in Goray,* before moving to New York. Altogether, this modest document bespoke a career within the mainstream of Polish-Yiddish letters.[9]

The real Yitskhok Singer was on the inside literary track not because of his orthodox upbringing, but through the efforts and example of his older brother. After a bruising experience in Kiev and Moscow, where he felt betrayed by the modernist mandarins Der Nister and Bergelson, Israel Joshua Singer moved back to Warsaw in 1921. Warsaw was rapidly becoming the political, pedagogical, and publishing center of secular Yiddish culture, and I. J. Singer wasted no time there. In 1922 he teamed up with Peretz Markish and Melekh Ravitch to found *Khalyastre,* the first expressionist journal in Yiddish, and with the same team (plus Nachman Meisel) founded the secular Yiddishist *Literarishe bleter* in 1924. Since Isaac had just moved back to Warsaw himself, Israel Joshua landed him his first real job as a proofreader (and occasional staff writer) for the new literary weekly. It took another year for Isaac to stand on his own feet as a writer of fiction, a year of crisis and profound self-doubt. His blind submission finally won that paper's short-story contest and was published, pseudonymously, in June 1925. Five months later "Yitskhok Bashevis" made his first appearance, the pen name Singer thereafter used for all his serious fiction.[10]

In those days, naturalism was the dominant school of serious Yiddish fiction, particularly in Poland, and twenty-one-year-old Bashevis was its ardent disciple. The very titles of the short stories and novellas he published from 1925 to 1932 (and refused to republish) were a dead giveaway: "In Old Age," "In the Cellar," "A Village Undertaker," "In the World of Chaos," "On the Way Back," "In an Old House," "Remnants," "Between Walls," "The Déclassé," "In the End of Days." This was textbook naturalism of the kind that I. M. Weissenberg, Joseph Opatoshu, Oyzer Warshawski, A. M. Fuks and even I. J. Singer had been writing in Yiddish for quite some time. All the characters were drawn from or consigned to the lower strata of society. Ruled by hereditary factors and instinctual drives, they usually acted in a self-destructive way. When Shamay Vayts (1929) got tough, as he had many occasions to do in Warsaw, his ears would get red, just like his late father's.

In lieu of individual heroes, there were "Women" (1925), "Sisters" (1926), "Two" (1930), and "The Déclassé" (1931). The dialogue read like a transcript of everyday speech.[11]

Most breathtaking in their bleakness and depravity were young Bashevis' slices of traditional Jewish life. The drunken recluse, Reb Sender Leyvi Karver, of hasidic lineage, who drove his wife to an early grave, who could not remember whether he had buried his daughter, and who was now left with a severely retarded son, finally took the only viable course of action: he hanged himself. The story's title says it all: Behold the "Eyniklekh," the hasidic "Grandchildren" or "Descendants" of our spiritual aristocracy. Or take Reb Beynish Bialodrevner, at the opposite end of the orthodox spectrum, once a leading rabbinic authority in Poland. He had long since stopped opening his mail and was refusing all human contact now that he was left without progeny. No one would ever learn of his rabbinic scholarship because his arduous trip to Warsaw failed to secure a publisher. "The Torah is not yet dead!" he shouted upon leaving the Jacobi Press with a last spark of fervor, but by the time Reb Beynush reached home, he himself was as good as dead. This was truly "The End of Days."[12]

Singer's landscape, in which all the sustaining structures—familial, communal, spiritual, political—had failed, was familiar to any reader of postwar Yiddish fiction, where all survivors face the end alone. The expressionists, moreover, recently upped the ante by perfecting an apocalyptic art, complete with mythic imagery of destruction and redemption. Singer branded this form of writing exhibitionistic on the grounds that it tore down barriers and tried to "penetrate directly to the very essence." Consistent realists, he countered, accepted the binding limitations of narrative as the first condition of success. "In graphic form it isn't possible to render everything," he concluded his manifesto of 1927, "but everything in a realistic narrative must be given graphic form."[13]

Even while defending the fiction writer who is sentenced to details, Singer was already testing the limits of realism. The problem was how to communicate the full complexity of the individual through objective description alone. Only in dialogue could one have a "tiny window" into the unseen inner life of the characters. The problem was more acute when the character was an intellectual. Was the consistent realist forced into favoring the folk types, those who didn't think too much? And in general were there no other direct sources, apart from the natural world apprehended through the senses?

One extreme answer came from Aaron Zeitlin (1899–1974), the most formative influence on Singer after his own brother. Zeitlin and Bashevis both came from rabbinic homes, were shy and standoffish, and read a lot. Soon after they met in the Warsaw Yiddish writers' club, they appeared next to each other in the pages of a massive literary miscellany, the first of its kind in postwar Poland. Here Bashevis' hypernaturalist story, "Descendants," rubbed shoulders with Zeitlin's zealous manifesto, "The Cult of Nothingness and Art as It Ought To Be." Zeitlin presented only two alternatives: either what he called a "cosmic art" or "the mirroring of nothing in one's own nothingness," as displayed, for example, in the writings of I. M. Weissenberg. Zeitlin's cosmic art was another name for Italian futurism, though nowhere did Zeitlin reveal the source. What Marinetti and others of his school had tried to achieve through pseudomathematical equations, spiraling geometric forms, musical terminology, and above all the glossolalia of machines, Zeitlin proposed achieving through the mystical sources of Jewish culture: "We, the people of Song of Songs poems and Zohar-plastic global visions, have become the most inartistic people of all, because we're stuck in a reflexive art and have lost the irrational and unrealistic artistic instinct."[14]

This was creative betrayal. Just as Hillel Zeitlin (Aaron's father), along with Peretz and Berdyczewski, betrayed Hasidism a generation earlier in the name of neoromanticism and Nietzsche's transvaluation of values, so was the Kabbalah being reclaimed in the name of revolutionary values. Aaron and Isaac did not turn to the wellsprings of Jewish mysticism because their fathers were kabbalists. That, if anything, would have guaranteed the opposite. Only the discarded past could safely be refashioned in one's own iconoclastic image. "From childhood I had been steeped in Chassidism, cabala, miracles, and all kinds of occult beliefs and fantasies," Singer would write in his fictional autobiography. "After lengthy stumbling and groping I rediscovered what I had been carrying within me the whole time."[15] But why, and how? That is something he never revealed, for that would make the story too secular, too predictable, and too Yiddish. Born-again kabbalists had to cover their tricks; otherwise who would believe in their magic?

The elitist, antipopulist thrust of Zeitlin's manifesto must have appealed to Bashevis, based as it was on a very esoteric body of knowledge. Yet so long as Bashevis remained true to his artistic credo, he could not render irrational powers using only the tools of mimetic realism. "In the World of Chaos" (1928), Bashevis' first sortie into "kabbalism," shows just how difficult the conversion to irrational art would be. "Certain that he had thoroughly mastered the practical Kabbalah, that he knew the magical names and had penetrated the most hidden reaches of the upper spheres, Shimen decided to correct that which Joseph della Reina had spoiled: to discover Satan and mercilously destroy him."[16] There followed a horribly grotesque story, another slice of decaying shtetl life. Shimen, it soon emerged, was not merely a study in extreme isolation and self-deprivation; the young kabbalist was stark raving mad.[17] The "mysteries of the Kabbalah" were as unassimilable for Shimen as for the tough realist who committed him to paper.

The other side of reality for a struggling Yiddish writer in interwar Poland was not Satan but *shund,* trashy novels. To stay alive you had to be on the payroll of a political party or write for one of the Warsaw Yiddish tabloids. Yiddish literature had by this time become thoroughly professionalized; there was something for everyone—even scintillating potboilers bordering on pornography. In the first round of flailing between the yellow press and the ideological purists, which took place in 1924, the purists won, thanks to a vigorous campaign launched by the bundist *Undzer folkstsaytung* and the new *Literarishe bleter.* The serialized trashy novels that ran an average of three to an issue in the *Varshever radio* and elsewhere were temporarily discontinued. Facing fierce competition from the Polish-language press, the Yiddish dailies tried again, in 1929, and this time even the combined efforts of the Bund and the Orthodox Agudas Yisroel couldn't deliver the final blow.[18]

Chief among the writers who churned out recycled trash (sometimes produced by committee and almost always published anonymously) were none other than Aaron Zeitlin and Yitskhok Bashevis. Threats (launched by Kadia Molodowsky) to blackball pornographers and exclude them from the Yiddish writers' club were to no avail. The communists even published their names for all to see. The sensationalist tabloids like *Undzer ekspres* were simply putting on too good a show, with their screaming headlines, personal advice columns, sports pages, beauty contests, matchmaking services, public opinion polls, and even signed and serious fiction.[19] Among the latter were a number of sketches, some of them extremely witty, by Y. Bashevis: "Berl Formalist," a farce about a one-man political party; a farcical biography of Dr. Feinschmeker, "The Aesthete"; a brief note on beards, blushing, and bad writing; the veiled autobiographical story of a student teaching "In a Dump" who manages to find love. There was light and laughter here, such as Bashevis would not rediscover for many years to come.[20]

The next joint venture by Aaron Zeitlin and Yitskhok Bashevis was a Yiddish monthly with the unfrivolous and pretentious title *Globus* (The Globe). This became the forum for Bashevis to launch an all-out attack on engagé literature of any stripe. "The real poet, so long as he lives, will never serve the hangman," he proclaimed in his manifesto "To the Question of Poetry and Politics."[21] "The poet embodies the categorical imperative." In defense of pure art, Bashevis dared in the pages of *Globus* to topple the giant of modern Yiddish prose, David Bergelson, for selling his soul to the communist hangman, and expended almost as much effort demolishing the first novel of a Polish-Yiddish writer on strictly artistic grounds.[22] Bashevis was flexing his critical muscles in advance of the serial publication in *Globus* of his first major work, *Satan in Goray*.[23]

The medieval Polish shtetl of Goraj, torn apart by the messianic heresy of Shabbetai Zvi, becomes Bashevis' fictional laboratory within which to explore the moral and political crisis of contemporary Jewry. The illusion of historicity is brilliantly sustained by several layers of stylization; by short syncopated sentences; by a heavily Hebraicized and archaic diction; by embedded rhymes, a richness of descriptive detail, a grotesque landscape redolent with demons, golems, messianic signs, and portents. The characters, drawn from the rabbinic or monied aristocracy, are larger than life and arranged in binary oppositions: Rabbi Benish Ashkenazi, his body and soul intact in the wake of the Ukrainian massacres, versus the broken and impoverished Eliezer Babad; Itche Mates, who abnegates his body and views sex in theological terms, as opposed to the charismatic and sexually active Reb Gedalye.[24]

Standing in the eye of the storm is Rechele, her weird behavior psychologically grounded by virtue of her total isolation as a child, her special education, her suppressed sexuality. She is the first character Bashevis turns successfully into a metaphysical portrait. Instead of embodying the Shekhinah, the feminine aspect of the divinity, as she herself imagines, she becomes the *kelippah*, the shell into which evil finds its way. Itche Mates is attracted to her because of her wildness; he sees in her the unclean vessel that must be purified. Manipulated by all, she is finally left to Satan.

The ending is a tour de force. Inspired by a seventeenth-century mayse-bikhl about an exorcism in the town of Korec, the storybook finale show-cases Bashevis' virtuosity. More to the point, its pious formulas deliver the story's antimodernist message. Primed by all the data and detail to expect a resolution on the plane of history, the reader is left baffled. Whatever happens to the town proper? To the rabbi's sons? Does Reb Mordecai Joseph, the penitent sinner, become the community's new spiritual leader, as this marvelous and patriarchal narrative suggests? Why does the arch-villain Reb Gedalye get off scot-free? For all the revealing facts about Rechele's psychological makeup, how is it that her dybbuk has a biography of his own, totally separate from the Sabbatean heresy that presumably gained him entry to her body in the first place? By collapsing history and psychology into a moral parable, as the characters themselves might have done, the storyteller frustrates any secular, twentieth-century reading of the story, which in turn delivers the ideological punch. The only thing that can save society from being destroyed by its self-appointed prophets is the artificial imposition of a moral order from above. Lest there be any doubt that even normative society is corrupt to its core, the dybbuk blasphemes openly against the entire religious and social order.[25]

Above all, *Satan in Goray* is a terrific story. The only other place one could find such plots (MARRIED TO TWO MEN, POSSESSED BY A DYBBUK) was in the pages of the yellow press. By returning to premodern times Bashevis could transcend the poverty of Jewish life in Poland. He could discard the modernist tradition he had been trying so hard to emulate, the "lyrical prose à la Hamsun, à la Bergelson, where you take a single piece of action and make endless variations on it, like a leitmotif in a symphony." It had taken him years, he later admitted (in Yiddish but not in English), before he realized that this kind of writing was not for him because to survive as a writer he needed a good plot.[26] By returning to a time when Satan was real, moreover, he could heed Zeitlin's call for a cosmic art and find metaphysical experiences that arose out of a concrete historical moment.

Once again in the history of Yiddish letters the experience of writing for a newspaper, of being wedded to the world of facts and forced to produce copy under deadline, proved beneficial to the career of a self-styled modernist. In the 1880s, the novelist and stockbroker Solomon Rabinovitsh delighted Yiddish newspaper readers as the all-knowing, ever-present, and slightly naughty Sholem Aleichem, just as writing for the press later taught him how to turn even the grimmest news into the stuff of everyday miracles. Newspapers did not penetrate the Singer home, apparently, until the very eve of World War I, and young Itchele had a hard time assimilating their diction and zany mix of piety and sensational romance.[27] Writing for that same press two decades later allowed the uncompromising young realist to let his hair down on occasion, as he experienced the freedom of an outlandish plot, a satisfying ending, a good laugh. *Satan in Goray* was Bashevis's synthesis of romance and novel, past and present, metaphysics and life. But could it appeal to popular taste?

Abraham Cahan, the tsar of American Yiddish letters, believed it could. The talent scout for many of Yiddish literature's brightest and best (including I. J. Singer), Cahan hired Bashevis to write for the *Jewish Daily Forward,* which, at the height of the Depression, was a plum of a job. Bashevis promptly began the serial publication there of *The Sinful Messiah* (Jacob Frank, 1726–1791), so dismal an artistic failure in the eyes of its author (though not of the editor) that Bashevis stopped writing fiction for the next seven years (1936–1942).[28] The thirty-two-year-old novelist was now lost in America.

The midlife crises that run like a faultline through the biographies of the great Yiddish writers seemed to grow in severity. Sholem Aleichem, Peretz, and Ansky each picked himself up with relative speed, perhaps because all three were in great demand. Der Nister, casting about for a new home, found a temporary haven in Weimar and a utopian solution in the Soviet Ukraine, never suspecting that storytellers would be the first targets of the new Inquisition. In the midst of the Holocaust, Itzik Manger suffered a complete breakdown, for what was the point of being the troubadour to a dead people? Singer's crisis of faith was curiously egocentric, if no less profound: he stopped believing both in his own artistic abilities and in Yiddish itself.

"The seed of redemption," wrote Ansky in *The Dybbuk,* "is contained within the fall." When I. B. Singer recouped his losses in 1943, the annus mirabilis of his career, he did so in both theory and practice, after "subjecting the literary traditions to ruthless scrutiny." The substance of what Bashevis had to say was not new, but the timing was stunning. In August the leading Yiddish literary monthly *Di tsukunft* (The Future) published a Holocaust issue to honor the memory of Polish Jewry. Marc Chagall's "The Martyr" (1940), the most Jewish of his crucifixion series to date, had pride of place, in lieu of an editorial. Amid a chorus of laments and jeremiads, Bashevis produced a sober, unsentimental, and devastating critique of Yiddish literature in Poland.[29]

His was a two-pronged attack, exposing the formal limitations of the Jewish intelligentsia in interwar Poland and the inherent limitations of Yiddish language and culture. Like Peretz before him, Bashevis disparaged the worldly pretensions of Yiddish writers. The sum total of their European culture was borrowed forms and imported ideologies. Futurism, all the rage, was but an escapade in literary Sabbateanism. These experiments not only underscored their provincialism, their narrow intellectual horizons, but also revealed how utterly unsuited was the Yiddish language itself to negotiate in the modern world. And so when all the false messiahs failed them, the writers had to start using the expressive vocabulary of a *yidish-kayt* in which they no longer believed. Yiddish writing in Poland, he concluded, had been godly without a God and worldly without a world. "Zi iz geven getlekh on a got, veltlekh on a velt" (471).

Yet all along, in their own backyard, was the shtetl, the perfect laboratory of modernity and its discontents. To conjure up that microcosm of tradition and revolution, Yiddish writers need not have relied on personal memory. They could have gone out and worked the shtetl field. Each shtetl had its own unique character and local legends. Much like Peretz, then, whose name he invoked as the standard bearer of renewal, Bashevis concluded his manifesto by reminding the wayward modernists of their own neglected treasures. No matter that he falsified the historical record and issued aesthetic judgments that were as myopic as they were self-serving (only I. J. Singer and Zeitlin come out looking good). As an ideological critique, "Concerning Yiddish Literature in Poland" was far-reaching and profound. The know-your-land movement in Poland, which had indeed made an effort to reclaim the shtetl for modern Jews, had done so in the name of *doikayt,* the struggle for cultural autonomy and national rights. For Yitskhok Bashevis, writing in America, the rediscovered folk life of shtetl Jews was an aesthetic and intellectual resource predicated on the collapse of all temporal hopes. The best Polish-Yiddish writers, he said, could already foresee the disaster.

Bashevis was not only unshaken by the Holocaust; he felt vindicated by it. Now liberated from the petty politics and illusory dreams of the entire Yiddish writers' club, he was ready to strike out on his own. The seed of redemption was contingent on the fall.

Harsher still was Bashevis' verdict on American Yiddish culture. Published in a little magazine, "Problems of Yiddish Prose in America" was so controversial in its cultural pessimism that it carried a disclaimer from the editors.[30] What Singer argued is that Yiddish as a modern secular language was dead. More precisely, since Yiddish in America had become an obsolescent language, spoken by a marginal sector of American Jews, it was impossible for Yiddish prose writers to render the totality of the American Jewish experience in the language they had from home. The writers were faced with two equally unacceptable choices: either to use the vulgar Yiddish actually spoken in America or to invent a pseudo-language to cover the full range of American Jewish life and thought. "It sounds almost laughable," he claimed, "when someone writes: *Dvoyre-Leye iz avek tsu Vanemeykern un gekoyft a koftl* (Devorah-Leah went to Wanamakers and bought a jacket)." Or try writing this sentence in a Yiddish story: "When Benny returned on the ferry from Staten Island, Pessy served him a supper of lamb chops with mashed potatoes and string beans, smothered in gravy." Rendered in pure idiomatic Yiddish, it would sound like this: "Ven Bunem hot zikh umgekert af der prom fun Stetn Ayland, hot im Pese-Brayne derlangt a vetshere fun shepsene kotletl mit tseribene kartofl, mit arbes-shoytn, bashmoltsn mit brotyoykh." But in real life, an American Jew would put it this way: "Ven *Benny* hot zikh umgekert af der *Stetn Ayland ferry* hot im *Pessy* derlangt a *supper* fun *lem tshops* mit *meshed potatoes* mit *string beans* bashmoltn mit *gravy*." Singer couldn't imagine a writer using such "potato Yiddish."

To cut the Gordian knot, Singer proposed a radical solution: renounce the present in favor of the past; renounce America in favor of an Old World setting where at least the characters used Yiddish as an integral part of their lives. Books of history, theology, folklore—the world of sforim—would provide the Yiddish writer with materials where contemporary life had buried all hope.

Even with so bleak a prognosis, however, Singer did not advocate a return to the past for its own sake. He responded to the revolutionary impulse in the art of creative betrayal as well as to its restorative program. The past was to be retrieved in the name of values and sensibilities gleaned in the contemporary world. The catchword for this modern agenda was psychoanalysis. Just because the characters, settings, and themes would be drawn from the past, he wrote, was no reason not to apply the best tools that western civilization had to offer. Even though, in other words, the return to storytelling would exact a huge price from the Yiddish prose writers, requiring them to renounce all claims to the present, it would still revitalize the literature: from within, by forcing it to draw on its religious and historical heritage; from without, by introducing a spirit of modernist inquiry and pessimism into a literature that was too idealistic for its own good.

"We believe that the Jewish attachment to the past can accommodate an extremely progresssive outlook," Bashevis wrote in conclusion, "for the history of the Jewish people is the history of an ongoing revolution against the powers of darkness." These were fighting words, and the way to turn them into the craft of fiction was through the *yeyster-hore,* the power of darkness lodged in the soul of every Jew, male or female, rich or poor, young or old, learned or simple. It was through a demonic narrator who knew everything about this world and the next, and who read everything, from the *Mayse-bukh* and the *Tales* of Reb Nahman to Gogol, Dostoevsky, Peretz, and Sholem Asch. It was through monologues reverberating with Jewish learning, wit, and anger. It was through Yiddish storytelling, turned into a demonic art.

> S'vert gezogt, dos ikh der yeytser-hore, nider arop oyf der erd un red on tsu zind; dernokh gey ikh oyf in himl un bin mekatreg. Der emes iz, az ikh bin oykh der yeniker, vos gib dem zindikn di ershte shmits, ober ikh tu dos ale mol mit a shpitsl, s'zol kloymersht oyszen vi a derekh-hateve, azoy az di andere poyshim zoln zikh nisht aropnemen keyn muser, nor vayter zinken in sheol-takhtis.[31]

> They say that I, the Evil Spirit, after descending to earth in order to induce people to sin, will then ascend to Heaven to accuse them. As a matter of fact, I am also the one to give the sinner the first push, but I do this so cleverly that the sin appears to be an act of virtue; thus, other infidels, unable to learn from the example, continue to sink into the abyss.[32]

Judging by his style, this evil spirit must be Jewish. His syncopated rhythm, archaic diction (*dos* for "that" instead of *az*), and especially the learned Hebraic vocabulary (*mekatreg, derekh-hateve, poyshim, shoel-takhtis*) betray a good few years spent in the Celestial Yeshiva. All this book learning and pious moralizing is, of course, itself betrayed in the name of values quite at variance with rabbinic Judaism. But which values?

Perhaps the evil spirit can claim Goethe's Mephistopheles—master thinker and talker—as a distant relative. The evil spirit, whose diary we

Yitskhok Broyner (Wincenty Brauner), "The Devil Dances,"
in the journal *Yung-yidish* (1919)

are supposedly reading, might very well be a closet romantic representing articulation, detached intelligence.[33] By dominating the story, he forces us to identify with the criminal and his experience, and each of Bashevis' protagonists does enter into a Faustian bargain with the devil. Reb Nathan Juzefover succumbs first to the pleasures of the flesh, in the person of his venal servant Shifra Zirel, then to the mercy of his divorced wife Roise Temerl, with whom he lives in sin ("The Unseen"). Zeidel Cohen agrees to convert to Christianity in order to achieve a position of power in the church hierarchy ("Zeidlus the Pope"). At the moment of death, each man experiences an epiphany, much as one would expect from satanic heroes who achieve an extraordinary visual perspective for the price of their moral rebellion. But if these stories were written to celebrate human choice and individual experience, the Nathans and Zeidels would hardly be described, from the opening lines, as mere pawns in the devil's game. The romantics would scarcely have recognized the *yeytser-hore* or his victims as their own.

Because the evil spirit performs his labors "so cleverly that the sin appears to be an act of virtue," victims are made to believe that they are acting out of free will. But where the devil reigns, moral choice and self-development are illusory; compassion, beauty, intellect—like every human trait—can be made to serve evil as well as good. Especially the intellect, for the ability to rationalize one's behavior is the beginning of sin. The evil spirit works patiently behind the scenes until a person confronts an object of desire. Then, as the human intellect works overtime, concocting elaborate schemes of self-justification (with each side marshaling precedents from the Holy Book), the devil has the victim in his net.

The evil spirit's godfather is sooner Freud than Faust. True to classical Freudian theory, the devil plays both the id, which "induce[s] people to sin," and the superego, which "will then ascend to Heaven to accuse them." Like the seasoned psychoanalyst who prefers the serious cases, the evil spirit saves the truly extravagant sinners for his *gedenkbukh* (diary). A corpulent husband and wife completely devoted to pleasures of the bathhouse are obvious favorites ("The Unseen"). But so too is a bald recluse, with pointed skull, reddish eyelids and a pair of yellow, melancholy eyes, a crooked nose, the hands and feet of a woman, though such a one would surely seem immune from the satanic virus ("Zeidlus the Pope"). Either way the ego sinks into the abyss and "other infidels [are] unable to learn from the example" because each individual will succumb to his own particular passion. For the intrepid scientist whose diary this is, the uncharted depths of human pathology have much more to offer than the heady, well-traveled reaches of the soul.

The evil spirit reigns supreme because he alone knows the difference between good and evil, health and perversion. And the way we know that he knows is through his superidiomatic and extremely witty speech. "Der yid hot ale yorn oysek geven in der mitsve fun USHMARTEM ES NAFSHOYSEY-KHEM," he writes of Nathan Juzefover, "dehayne: er hot gegesn, getrunken un zikh gelozt voylgeyn" (This Jew dedicated his whole life to the commandment AND YOU SHALL KEEP YOUR SOULS, i.e, he ate, drank, and made merry; Y 206). As for Roise Temerl, "di ishe aleyn hot oykh nisht geleygt hintern oyer . . . man-un-vayb hobn, a ponim, gehaltn az kayen iz nisht hevel" (The good woman herself did not merely make airs about her appetites . . . husband and wife were apparently of one mind, that self-indulgence was nothing to sneeze at; Y 207). That last is particularly pithy, irreverent, and untranslatable. "Cain is not Abel" is a bilingual pun which understands Kayin/Cain as *kayen,* to chew, and Hevel/Abel as "vanity" (as in *hevel havolim,* vanity of vanities). So even before the story begins, Nathan and Roise Temerl are undercut by a parodic style that plays Scripture, idiom, and proverb against a pair of none-too-learned hedonists. "Mit loshn-koydesh iz er nisht geven shove-beshove" (he [Nathan] was frankly at odds with the holy tongue) the devil adds with a showy display of Hebraic style. While the two lovebirds may waver between hedonism and strict adherence to Judaic law, the devil telling the story is as firmly rooted in *yidishkayt* as is the Yiddish he so cleverly speaks.

Nathan and Roise are fairly easy prey, and the sin of adultery is all in a day's work. The devil's finest hour comes when he faces off against Reb Zeidel Cohen, "the greatest scholar in the whole province of Lublin," because here is room for lengthy intellectual debate and the stakes are nothing less than faith and apostasy.[34] To best so formidable an opponent, the devil dons the mask of a maskil, and to undermine Zeidel's faith he unleashes a litany heard many times before: Jewish law is nothing but hairsplitting, its language deliberately corrupted to keep the people ignorant; Jewish majesty has been stripped of its glory by sniveling rabbis who accept the inferior status foisted on them by the Christian world. Only temporal power is real, and only the gentiles possess it. Waxing more philosophical still, the devil portrays a supremely indifferent God, who has no special claim on His people Israel and could care less about the punctilious observance of His laws. "Is there no reward or punishment?" Zeidel finally asks in amazement. "No," comes the devil's reply.

Where the deity is supremely indifferent, man can be omnipotent, says the devil, provided the divine pretender abandons Judaism for Christianity. "Since their God is a man, a man can be a god to them . . . They don't care what else a man is: if he is great, they idolize him" (Y 277–278, E 345). Without moral accountability, without a personal God, and in a world where God and *gets* (idol) are one and the same, religious faith itself is a logical absurdity. The only thing left is to take what you can get. Christianity is idolatry, but it can get you a ticket to power.

Master cynic and polemicist, the devil is having a field day. With an eye to the future, he can see that the church of today is the Enlightenment dream of tomorrow. Trading God for man is the same as aping the gentiles for access to power and privilege. How better to expose these goals as illusory and self-destructive, how better to launch an attack on the heresy of secular humanism, than through the mouth of a devil? This walking encyclopedia of Jewish self-deception, however, is also a talking thesaurus of Jewish hostility toward the values of a secular world. The Yiddish he speaks, which insists on dissociating itself from everything Christian, cuts to the heart of Bashevis' argument that Yiddish will either be an expression of Jewishness or nothing at all.[35]

Within Yiddish itself there had come into being what Max Weinreich termed *lehavdl-loshn,* a built-in, double vocabulary to distinguish or differentiate the Jewish from the Christian realm. Since, from the Jewish point of view, what is "ours" is automatically better than what is "theirs," the words that signify their world are loaded with pejorative meaning. More than a motley of ethnic slurs, of the kind that Philip Roth and other American satirists later came to exploit, this is a linguistic structure that serves to insulate the Jews even as they live and work among Christians. Bashevis' storytellers all employ this denigrative language, none more fully than the devil and nowhere with greater relish than in "Zeidlus the Pope."[36]

Zeidel succumbs to the devil's argument and is accepted into the church as Benedictus Janovsky. Reaching for the top, he decides to write the definitive anti-Talmudic tract. The devil-narrator waxes eloquent over Zeidel's scholarly endeavors (the key phrases are given in italics):

Far eyn vegs hot Zeydl zikh farnumen tsu gefinen naye rayes fun tanakh, az di neviim hobn kloymersht foroysgezen Yeyshus kumen un zayn *mise-me-shune* un zayn tkhies-hameysim. Er hot oykh gevolt aroysdringen dem kristlekhn das al-pi khokhmes-halogik, astronomye, un khokhmes-hateve. Zeydl's khiber hot gezolt vern, *lehavdl,* a *goyisher* yad-khazoke, a shrift, vos zol Zeydlen avektrogn fun Yonev glaykh in Vatikan. (Y 281)

At the same time, Zeidel undertook to find fresh proofs in the Bible that the prophets had foreseen Jesus' birth, martyrdom, and resurrection; and to discover corroborative evidence for the Christian religion in logic, astronomy, and natural science. Zeidel's treatise would be for the Christians what Maimonides' *The Strong Hand* was for Judaism—and it would carry its author from Janov directly to the Vatican. (E 349)

But just now Zeidel undergoes a crisis of faith:

Zeydl hot ongehoybn aynzen, az bay di *areylim* iz gornisht azoy voyl. Di galokhim hobn mer in zinen dos gold vi dem *opgot.* Di prediker in di *botey-tume* zenen ful mit ameratses. Psukim fun tanakh in dem bris-khadoshe vern gefelsht un farkriplt. Fil galokhim konen nisht keyn vort latayn. Oykh zeyer poylish loshn iz ful mit grayzn. (Y 282)

Zeidel began to realize that even among the gentiles things were far from perfect. The clergy cared more for gold than for their God. Their sermons were full of errors. [They falsified and misquoted verses from the Bible and the New Testament.] Most of the priests did not know Latin, but even in Polish their quotations were incorrect. (E 349)

The storyteller is unmoved by Zeidel's fate. What is there to be tempted by if, as the devil knows but as Zeidel has presumably forgotten, all the gentiles are nothing but *areylim,* heathens, their houses of prayer are really *botey-tume,* or houses of filth, the crucifixion was a *mise-meshune,* a grotesque and violent death, and above all that their God is but an *opgot,* an idol? Careful not to mention the sacred and profane in the same breath without a verbal separation between them, the devil can only compare Zeidel's treatise, written in Latin, to a *goyisher* (goyish, gentile) version of Maimonides' *The Strong Hand,* and that only after inserting the word *lehavdl,* to differentiate. Elsewhere he refuses even to utter the name of Jesus and speaks instead of the *shikuts meshoymem,* the "appalling abomination" mentioned at the end of the book of Daniel (Y 282). From first to last, in form and substance, the devil's verbal aggression against what is "theirs" leaves no doubt that he will have no truck whatever with the falsehood and corruption to which he tempts the ascetic and scholarly Zeidel.

"Alienated from all traditions and conventions, the romantic hero is a suitable agent of experience."[37] By this well-worn critical standard, Zeidel should be in for something really big. In his fanatical pursuit of absolute knowledge, he ceases to believe in truth or falsehood of any persuasion. But once baptized, there is no going back. Cut off from both Judaism and Christianity, he goes blind and becomes a beggar. He comes to acknowledge the futility of his quest and discovers that the reward of intellectualism is illusion. Alienated from without and from within, Zeidel experiences an epiphany:

> Suddenly I, the Tempter, materialized. Although blind he saw me. "Zeidel," I said, "prepare yourself. The last hour has come."
>
> "Is it you, Satan, Angel of Death?" Zeidel exclaimed joyously.
>
> "Yes, Zeidel," I replied. "I have come for you. And it won't help you to repent or confess, so don't try."
>
> "Where are you taking me?" he asked.
>
> "Straight to Gehenna."
>
> "If there is a Gehenna, there is also a God," Zeidel said, his lips trembling.
>
> "That proves nothing," I retorted.
>
> "Yes it does," he said. "If Hell exists, everything exists. If you are real, He is real. Now take me to where I belong. I am ready." (Y 287, E 352–353)

As the hero of romantic fiction, Zeidel the blind beggar would be considered a reliable witness. But the truths revealed to him at the moment of death repudiate the credos of modernity—and of romanticism. Man is an effect, not a cause, of creation, and despite his efforts to rule the world through reason alone, there is after all a Judge and a Judgment. There was never any contest between ours (the worship of one God) and theirs (the adoration of idols). The man of true learning would never be seduced by Christianity, by the allure of Enlightenment, for both are the pursuit of vanity. Conversion is a victory for the forces of evil, denying the crucial separation between the nature of God and the nature of man. Zeidel's joyous acceptance of the torments of hell signify an ironic victory over the powers of darkness, for Israel will never be destroyed so long as Israel bows before its creator.

"If God does not exist," cries Kirilov in Dostoevsky's *Possessed*, "then I am God!" Bashevis became a storyteller so that he could address these metaphysical questions all over again—and answer them from the other side of reality. Not since Gogol brought the devil back to roost in a Ukrainian hamlet and Dostoevsky exposed man's demonic drive to depose the Almighty had modern literature seen as malevolent and powerful a force as the *yeytser-hore*. Not since Rabbi Nahman had the contest between faith and reason been waged for such high stakes. The return of Satan—as narrator and prime mover—signaled a return to a time just prior to the flood, when the fate of creation hung in the balance. It was the year of Our Lord, Nineteen Hundred and Forty-Three, when evil of metaphysical proportions was unleashed on the Jews by nations that professed to be Christian. Should life on earth continue, there would have to be a metaphysical counterweight to evil. "If you are real," cries Zeidel to the devil, "then He is real!" Over Kant and Nietzsche, Zeidel reaches back to reclaim the negative theology of Lurianic Kabbalah.

Storytelling also meant a return to a world of piety, densely Jewish in both style and substance. The storyteller's fierce polemic with Christianity covered an attack on other Jewish heresies, the most recent of which, just east of the Polish-Soviet border, saw a host of Jewish commissars trying desperately and disastrously to be *frimer farn poyps,* more Catholic than the pope. Bashevis had one response to these yeshiva students turned masters of dialectical materialism: he sent them all to hell.

But there was more. A good story seduced the reader by recalling other stories of the same kind. Had not the story of a Jewish pope, the kidnapped son of the rabbi of Mayence (some say of Frankfurt) been recounted by Isaac Meir Dik and before that still, in the medieval *Mayse-bukh?* Bashevis retold the story but with a radical twist. He did not preach passive resignation to a miserable lot of ghetto Jews, nor did he seek, conversely, a reconciliation of Jews to a secular, enlightened world. Instead, the setting of "Zeidlus the Pope" was moved from Germany to Janów, a "dump in the sticks among Jews," to clinch Bashevis' case against the grandiose fantasy of enlightenment and the destructive secular aspiration of Jews. In Janów there was no contest to begin with. In the cosmopolitan centers of Europe one might well be swayed by the Christian disdain for the Jews, and one might be seduced by the power and glory of the church. In Janów, the whole notion of converting or defecting was a bad joke, a mean trick played by the devil.[38]

Equally familiar is the story's farcical ending. Two mocking imps stand at the threshold of Gehenna, "half-fire and half-pitch, each with a three-cornered hat on his head, a whipping rod on his loins. They burst out laughing. 'Here comes Zeidlus the First,' one said to the other, 'the yeshiva boy who wanted to become pope.' *Der yeshive-boker, vos hot gevolt vern an apifyor*" (Y 286, E 353). It was a scene every modern Yiddish reader knew, for the same satanic entourage had once given Peretz's Monish the same darkly comic welcome.

When Zeidel is first introduced to the reader, the devil describes him as the greatest Talmud scholar in all of Poland, using the same hyperbolic phrases as Peretz's balladeer.[39] As surely as they were literary twins, however, Zeidel was just as surely a genetic mutation, for Monish was vital, handsome, and seductive, a hero worthy of romantic ballad, while Zeidel belonged in Madame Toussaud's. Peretz, the modernist, used the legend of Faust to mock the whole idea of virtue and sin in a nonheroic age. Yitskhok Bashevis returned to the scene of the crime—a small town in old Poland—and made Zeidel impossibly grotesque in order to parody the master.

Ever the secular humanist, Peretz staged the struggle between good and evil as a contest between equal adversaries. Even as he cut the devil down to human size, making him something of a skeptic, Peretz endowed his men and women with the intellectual and moral capacities to exercise free will. Bashevis launched his rebuttal in the same court of legendary justice, then raised the ante by putting knowledge and intellect themselves on the dock. Beginning with Rechele in *Satan in Goray,* all of Bashevis' protagonists came with a reading list. Nathan Juzefover may rarely have exercised his brain, but at least he knew about the River of Fire from reading the *Nakhlas tsvi* (Inheritance of the Deer), a Yiddish ethical tract. His wife, Roise Temerl, in a moment of indecision was reminded of a Yiddish storybook "where a [Christian] landowner, whose wife had eloped with a bear tamer, later forgave her and took her back to his manor." Zeidel's bibliography was prodigious, as befitted an intellectual hero. Yet Zeidel's learning (like Rechele's) did not strengthen his bond to society, community, or God. Nobody delighted in the sound of Zeidel's voice, as they did when Monish was hard at work on some tractate. Learning intensified isolation; it set a Jew apart from communal norms and ultimately became an instrument of the devil.[40]

That is because, in learning, there is none to match the devil. More steeped in the sacred texts than even the greatest sages in Poland, the devil could cite chapter and verse to buttress his satanic designs. "Why not?" he says to Nathan Juzefover whose lust for the servant girl seems to leave him no recourse but to divorce his wife.

> Did not Abraham drive his bondwoman, Hagar, into the wilderness, with nothing but a bottle of water, because he preferred Sarah? And later, did he not take Keturah and have six sons with her? Did not Moses, the teacher of all Jews, take, in addition to Zipporah, another wife from the land of Kush; and when Miriam, his sister, spoke against him, did she not become leprous? (Y 219, E 120–121)

The Devil is never at a loss to find the scriptural or rabbinic precedent to fit the crime, as when he works Zeidel over with this litany:

> You know the Jews have never honored their leaders: They grumbled about Moses; rebelled against Samuel; threw Jeremiah into a ditch; and murdered Zacharias. The Chosen People hate greatness. In a great man they sense a rival to the Holy One, blessed be He, so they love only the petty and mediocre. (Y 277, E 345)

A devil's-eye view of civilization sees a very thin line between the sacred and profane. Not only does learning *not* protect a person from sin; the hubris born of learning is the hardest sin to extirpate. How easily the acquisition of knowledge becomes an end in itself, a license to blaspheme, to fancy oneself a god. The learned devil deludes man into believing that evil is a problem of human proportions when the humanist fallacy (Bashevis intimates) is itself the root of all evil.

The use of perverted precedent is not merely part of a devilish design to provoke victims into crossing the line between sacred and profane. Nor is it a way of playing out the theme of seduction using only the materials of Jewish tradition. The devil's demonic prooftexts also give voice to Bashevis' own protest against heaven.

There is something unnerving about so much gratuitous evil in these stories of *The Devil's Diary*. "Two Corpses Go Dancing" (1943) and "From the Diary of One Not Born" (1943) are relentless catalogues of innocent folk destroyed by satanic powers.[41] There is something heretical, Manichean, about a devil invested with such boundless energy to do evil, who starts his story off by boasting: "It is well known that I love to arrange strange marriages, delighting in such mismatings as an old man with a young girl, an unattractive widow with a youth in his prime, a cripple with a great beauty, a cantor with a deaf woman, a mute with a braggart."[42] Accountable to nothing but his own perverse whims, and knowing the outcome beforehand, the devil is lord and master. The problem posed by *The Devil's Diary,* as Ruth Wisse so aptly puts it, is not the problem of man's free will but God's.[43]

The devil alone is free because he stands for the author. And that author is angry. As the devil is free to blaspheme against God, His Torah, and His People, so the devil, master storyteller that he is, blasphemes at will against all who preceded him, in particular those storytellers who misled the flock with false hopes and panaceas. A Yiddish devil writing in 1943 can easily identify the chief offender—at that moment the most popular Yiddish writer in the world, Sholem Asch (1880–1957).

The attack against Asch began with *Satan in Goray.* One compelling reason for choosing the period of the Cossack revolts of 1648–49 was that Sholem Asch had already trodden that path, in *Kiddush Hashem* (1919). Using the Chmielnitsky massacres as a fictional cloak for the civil war raging in the Ukraine, Asch ended his historical saga on a note of equivocal *bitokhn,* faith in the future. Bashevis took the notion of messianic faith within the same historical setting and turned it into a horrifying vision of apocalypse.[44]

Bashevis followed that a decade later with "The Destruction of Kreshev" (Kreszew; 1943). By now Asch had won the hearts of Yiddish readers for his paeans to the brotherhood of Christians and Jews in the natural Polish landscape. Thus "Kola Street" (1905–06) begins with a long and lush description of a triangular area on the western tip of Mazowsze, which includes Kutno, Zychlin, Gostynin, Gombin, "and a number of smaller towns." Possessing none of the mystery or music of the neighboring province, its fields are "flat and monotonous . . . and the peasant who cultivates them is as plain as the potatoes they yield." Similarly, "the Jew native to this region partakes more of the flavor of wheat and of apples than of the synagogue and the ritual bath."[45] Not to be outdone, the primeval snake, the Evil One, also begins by situating his story within the differentiated landscape of Mother Poland:

> Kreshev is about as large as one of the smallest letters in the smallest prayer books. On two sides of the town there is a thick pine forest and on the third the river San. The peasants in the neighboring villages are poorer and more

isolated than any others in the Lublin district and the fields are the most barren . . . And finally, so that the peasants shall never be rid of their wretchedness, I have instilled in them a burning faith. In that part of the country there is a church in every other village, a shrine at every tenth house. (Y 194, E 94)

There follow some nasty comments aimed at the Catholic faith. In response to Asch's ecumenical fantasies, moreover, the devil recounts more dramatic instances of Jewish-Christian rapprochement: young peasant women are routinely seduced by Jewish peddlers in the barn, "so it is not entirely surprising that here and there among the flaxen-haired children one comes across a curly-haired, blacked-eyed imp with a hooked nose." Even the plotlines turn in on one another. Kreshev's Leybl Shmayser (inexplicably translated by Gottlieb and Flaum as "Mendel the Coachman"), is a carbon copy of Notte Zychliner: both strapping young men chase pigeons and shiksas. Notte, with his noble-savage passions, provokes a pogrom in Kola Street, which only subsides when his pigeons are sacrificed on the communal altar. In Kreshev, however, anarchic passions burst out not from the deviant sidelines of shtetl society but from its spiritual center: from Shloimele, the Talmud scholar and kabbalist. Because these passions are hidden behind the false messianism of Shabbetai Zvi, they lead to the heroine's death and the destruction of Kreshev.

Many parodic strands run through the demonic fictions of Yitskhok Bashevis. They reveal an author deeply enmeshed in the fabric of modern Yiddish writing, who manages to extricate himself by beating the Yiddish masters at their own game: the work of creative betrayal. Manifestoes alone—which in any event he stopped writing after 1943—would not suffice to shake the ideological foundations of Yiddish secularism. In the guise of a demonic storyteller, and by parodying stories heard many times before, Bashevis succeeded in subverting the subversion. Where Peretz and Asch had raided the shtetl past for parables of individual action and self-transcendence, Bashevis revisited the same sites to strike a final blow at the redemptive schemes that gave rise to modern Yiddish literature in the first place.

Waging holy war was Bashevis' way of internalizing the war raging elsewhere. Yet demonic storytelling, the secular equivalent of the hellfire sermon, was only the Other Side, the *Sitra aḥra,* of Bashevis' restorative program in the wake of the Holocaust. Laying his demons to rest, if only for a while and only in his role as storyteller, Bashevis produced three works in rapid succession that were breathtaking in their humanity: "The Spinoza of Market Street" (1944), "Gimpel the Fool" (1945), and "The Little Shoe-makers" (1945). Here, instead of using his genius to parody the work of others, Bashevis reused his own plots, characters, and descriptive methods for good instead of evil.[46]

Gimpel the Fool and Zeidlus the Pope: both are loners whose mental curriculum isolates them morally, then physically, then metaphysically. Gimpel's mental faculties are protected by his status as an orphan, by his foolishness, by being the butt of Frampol's laughter, and by the repetition of the ordeal. His desire for love, albeit for Elke, the town whore, and his compassion for the children, albeit not his own, protect him from doing wrong and from succumbing to the temptation of the devil. To complete his isolation, after the death of Elke, Gimpel goes into exile, becomes a wandering sage and storyteller, and finally arrives at a statement of other-worldly faith. These ascending levels of isolation are the price one pays for achieving goodness in so cruel a world as Gimpel's. Yet his appelation leaves no doubt that Bashevis meant the story not to parody but to reha-bilitate the life of simple faith as a moral possibility. For the genealogy of the *tam*, Gimpel's Yiddish nickname, connects him with the biblical Jacob and Job, with the third of the four sons of the Passover Haggadah, and especially with Nahman of Bratslav's "Tale of the Hakham and the Tam." The last is the closest to Bashevis' hero, for Gimpel achieves goodness in his personal life by ignoring, then willfully rejecting, the evil and skepticism around him. But unlike Reb Nahman, Bashevis does not hold out hope for global redemption. The most one can hope for is love between a man and a woman, which in turn is the conduit for one's love of God. Both I/Thou relationships require a leap of faith—and the renunciation of worldly pur-suits. So too for "The Spinoza of Market Street."[47]

Jewish storytelling in the midst of the Holocaust was a form of triage in which the storyteller's most valuable resource became the Hebrew Bible. It restored for the Jews the elemental vocabulary of good and evil, redemption and destruction. It was also the greatest family saga of them all. Writing in the European tradition, Bashevis chronicled the rise and fall of *The Family Moskat* (1945–50), doomed along with the great city of Warsaw and the multitudinous Jews of Poland. As a storyteller Bashevis could only rescue

"The Little Shoemakers," a modest and industrious shtetl family, and bring them to the haven of America.[48] Both novel and story were concerned with the covenantal meaning of Jewish history. In one, the patriarch, his sons, his private secretary, and most of all his son-in-law succumb to their anarchic passions. Not so the shoemakers, who behave more like a tribe than a family, guided by Abba, their fecund and faithful patriarch. Nothing can break his spirit: not the gradual collapse of his ancestral home or the defection of Gimpel, the educated son, and the emigration of the others; not even the Nazi apocalypse. For Abba is an archetype, his life a replay of the biblical past. He is Moses and Jonah, crossing the perilous sea. He is Jacob, finally reunited with his sons in Egypt. Defying the rules of realism, and working against the centrifugal forces of history, Abba is not supplanted by his sons. It is Abba, in New Jersey of all places, who brings the generations back together, cobbling the old-fashioned way and singing the family hymn.

Playing the wandering sage, Bashevis threw his wit, his knowledge, his ear for the music of Yiddish into restoring however many fictional contexts he could wherein to cultivate the lost art of Yiddish storytelling. Like Peretz and Sholem Aleichem before him, he created the illusion of live speech by turning to the monologue, and like them he decentered the world of tradition by favoring outcasts, deviants, children, and women—all within a linguistic setting that could not have been more Yiddish. Gimpel, the saintly fool, narrates his life's story in a flophouse to a melange of old men. Here he feels quite at ease recalling how he was cuckolded by his wife, ridiculed by all, and how the most heroic act of his life was not to urinate into the dough for the next day's bread. His statement of faith in the world to come over cynicism in this world was certainly not lost on his immediate audience. A year later, in "The Wife Killer" (1945), Bashevis restored the concept of a *bobe-mayse,* an old wife's tale, to its literal meaning: he created Matl, surrounded by a group of old women, whom she held in the palm of her hand with a wealth of local traditions, superstitions, and pious formulas designed to titillate even as they displayed the storyteller's impeccable modesty.[49]

"Did I hear you say a husband killer? *Bahit un bashiremt zol men vern,* May one be spared and protected. *Nisht do gedakht, nisht kegn nakht gedakht, nisht far keyn yidisher tokhter gedakht,* May it never happen here,

Uri Shulevitz, in Isaac Bashevis Singer, *The Fools of Chelm and Their History* (1973)

never toward nightfall, and never happen to a daughter in Israel; *s'zol oysgeyn tsu sonims kep un tsu zeyer layb un lebn,* may such things happen to our enemies, to their lives and livers." A woman's world, more earthbound than a man's, centered on such things as the fatal attraction of one sex for the other. Why would any woman want to marry the likes of Pelte, that ugly misanthrope from the town of Turbyn, who kept his hoarded wealth in a formidable oak chest built to outlast all disasters; a man who became more isolated with each wife he buried? Perhaps because the whole story bore out the truth of what the rabbi had said at the eulogy for wife number three: " '*Zimen shkhoyrim umotso levonim,* He ordered black and got white.' In the Gemara [Beitza 10b] this is about a man ordering pigeons, but the rabbi—peace be upon him—made it mean wedding garments and burial shrouds" (Y 60, E 43). This is another way of saying that these horrible reversals of fate were all from above. "When God wants to punish someone," Matl reminds her listeners, "He deprives him of reason." In God's inscrutable universe, it is Zlateh the Bitch, the husband killer, the *katlonis* mentioned in the story's opening, who finally gives Pelte a run for his money—or is it she who gets her just desserts by trying to defeat the infamous wife killer? Either way the battle of the sexes turned logic on its head and left the oaken chests broken and abandoned. "The Wife Killer had outlived everything," says Matl at the end of her long and artful tale, "his wives, his enemies, his money, his property, his generation. All that was left of him—may God forgive me for saying so—was a heap of dust."

Once again, as in the days of Sholem Aleichem, Yiddish storytelling became a communal speech act (reserved for the Yiddish reader alone, as it happens, because Matl's rhetorical asides to her listening audience are elided in English translation). As Sholem Aleichem played *what* was being narrated—a tale of utter dissolution—against the frenetic *manner* in which it was narrated, so too did Bashevis. Lascivious tales about outsiders and deviants were an obvious way to confer sanction upon the group ("May such things happen to our enemies"), which seemingly made a perfect fit between the what and the how. Yet what kind of survival tactic were the Matls and Gimpels preaching if every tale is a tale of extreme isolation and if all the proverbs and maxims add up to the same relentless message: fate and inscrutable forces rule all of human destiny.

In the mid-1960s Bashevis' "Aunt Yentl" picked up where Matl left off, with her own richly idiomatic style and a repertory even more geared for female consumption. Bashevis opened the monologue into a storytelling round by returning to the normative realm of the study house. Each of the men in "Three Tales" (1964) comes from a different stratum of shtetl society: Zalmen the Glazier from the artisan class, Levi-Yitskhok Amshinover from the merchant class, and Meyer Tumtum ("Eunuch") from the mystically bent intellectual class. As one ascends the social ladder, each storyteller draws from his particular world to produce an even taller tale than the one just heard. Finally, in the mid-seventies, Bashevis pulled Bendet Daddy out of retirement, the man from Bilgoraj whose daughters ran a whore house on the outskirts of town. Though he and his buddies also frequented the study house, it was for want of a tavern and after the learned regulars had left. Bendet recounted the racy exploits of the old Polish nobility with a style as aggressively anti-Christian as the *yeytser-hore*'s.[50]

Whether it is a recluse quoting from the Talmud and Zohar or Aunt Yentl and Bendet Daddy peppering their speech with Polish proverbs—

regardless of a person's background, he or she will cite chapter and verse to deny the exercise of free will. The communal medium of storytelling *is* the message insofar as the community insists on a single standard of morality, maintains an absolute distinction between ours and theirs, and sees humans as passive victims of their fate. Yet the stories play with fire. They tell of fools, messianists, and deviants of every stripe and social class, most of whom are crushed in their attempt to break free and a few of whom manage to save their souls by finding love or by going into permanent exile. The proverb-quoting folk extol passivity even as they vivify the anarchy and temptation that threaten to turn everything upside down.[51]

In this, as in other respects, the devil is the model storyteller, for he has read more, seen more, and remembers more than any other person living or dead, and he harbors no illusions about the perfectibility of man. His sententiousness hearkens back to the beginnings of modern Yiddish storytelling—to a time when Yiddish was being used for satiric ends and when the arch-satirist was the Bible-quoting, all-knowing, and peripatetic Mendele the Bookpeddler. In much the same way as Mendele progressed, in the course of the late nineteenth century, from bystander and editor to author and protagonist, so Bashevis' devil assumes ever greater narrative responsibilities during the late 1950s. His monologues become theatrical performances, in which a familiar plot provides the backdrop for his verbal pyrotechnics, delivered in the style of Jewish culture's original satirist, the ever-popular badkhn at the wedding.

The plots are a foregone conclusion: "For everything hidden must be revealed, every secret longs to be disclosed, each love yearns to be betrayed, everything sacred must be desecrated. Heaven and earth conspire that all good beginnings should come to a bad end."[52] So says the devil in his artful and rhythmic monologue about "The Mirror" (1956), lifted straight out of Peretz's *Stories in the Folk Vein*. Zirel, like the heroine of Peretz's "A Passion for Clothes" (1904), is wealthy and well educated. They both succumb to earthly pleasures, as the name Zirel, "ornament," suggests. But there is no contest at all in the devil's version of things, for Zirel is doomed the moment she looks into the mirror—symbol of her vanity—and no one can resist so likeable a character as the devil. His will is their command. To rouse a woman's pity, he makes up a sad story, casting himself in the role of outcast. To excite her, he recites a litany of licentiousness: "Like the mule I am the last of a line. But this does not blunt my desire. I lie only with married women, for good actions are my sins; my prayers are blasphemies; spite is my bread; arrogance, my wine; pride, the marrow of my bones. There is only one other thing I can do besides chatter" (Y 4, E 60). To while away his own time, between one appearance and the next, he recapitulates this credo in rhyme:

> Ober vos iz Khave on a shlang? Vos iz bsomim on geshtank? Vos iz zun on a shotn? Un vos iz got on a sotn? (Y 5)

> But what is Eve without a serpent? What are spices without a stench? What is the sun without a shadow? And what is God without a devil?

Zirel's whole seduction, in fact, is just a brief distraction from the devil's stream of consciousness, as he flits back and forth between prophecy and profanity. Once he has her in his net, poor Zirel doesn't get a word in edgewise. Only then does the curtain go up on the devil as he recites bawdier rhymes than any badkhn dared to mouth, and poses theological questions so densely allusive that they are reserved for the Yiddish audience alone:

> Tut di kdushe mit der tume fekhtn? Vet got dem sotn shekhtn? Oder iz Samoel gerekht, az cr iz der hekht fun ale hekht? Vos veyst a shedl ver s'firt s'redl? (Y 10)

> Do the sacred and profane fight it out? Will God deliver the devil a rout? Or is Samael right after all, that he's the belle of the ball? What does a petty demon know about who's running the show?

Can it be that the world is only matter, the devil probes on, created without rhyme or reason? Or is there a prime mover at one end of creation and a messiah at the other? "*Efsher vet der ish-tamim fort kumen tsu a takhlis be'akhris hayomim? Lesate zenen mir balebatim.* Perhaps the man of faith will be vindicated in the End of Days? Meanwhile, at any rate, we are still the ones at the gate." The devil loves speaking in rhymes; he's never feistier than when sparring on the creator's own turf.[53]

Zeidel's answer to the devil is Bashevis' answer to himself: there can be no demonic art without a God. Once the parameters of good and evil fall away, there is no use for tales of seduction. Once Yiddish is divorced from *yidishkayt,* there is no longer a way to sustain the creative tension between the what and the how. There has to be someone, somewhere, still rooted in the law and lore of the past, struggling with meaning and blasphemy. And that someone is the Yiddish writer in American exile, disguised as a demon-storyteller, and most poignantly portrayed in *Mayse Tishevits* (1959).[54]

Why Tishevits (the same place Peretz visited on his statistical mission)? Because back in 1943 Bashevis argued that "each Polish shtetl, each Jewish street, had its specific character," but that his colleagues had woefully neglected this rich imaginative realm. In Tishevits, for example, there had lived and died Messiah ben Joseph.[55] (This local tradition is borne out by the memoirs and memories of former inhabitants.[56]) Bashevis filed the data away for a quarter century, until he was ready to exploit Tishevits for its messianic potential.

Why "*Mayse* Tishevits"? Because *mayse* followed by a place name is the storyteller's code word for a martyrological tale, as in *Mayse Uman* of the eighteenth century. What better way to respond to the latest Jewish catastrophe, the Holocaust, than through the example of martyrologies past? Why a demonic monologue, when the issues at hand were redemption and destruction? Precisely for that reason, the demonic monologue having become the storyteller's forum for the questions that really matter.

> I, a demon, bear witness that there are no more demons left. Why demons, when man himself is a demon? Why persuade to evil someone who is already convinced? I am the last of the persuaders. I board in an attic in Tishevitz and draw my sustenance from a Yiddish storybook, a leftover from the days before the great catastrophe. (Y 12, E 300)

Instead of allowing the demon to to roam free, as in the previous tales, he is stuck in this domestic setting because once upon a time, in Bilgoraj, Itchele Singer had sat in his grandfather's attic reading forbidden books, and now, as the aging writer looks back on his career, he wonders how much longer and to what end he might continue drawing sustenance from the severed past. Especially since these "Yiddish storybooks" (the Yiddish secular heritage) were "pablum and duck milk," products of a bankrupt Enlightenment ideology.

Tales of temptation are the stuff of these newfangled books, like Peretz's story of how a skeptical devil targets the aging rabbi of Chelm to prove the miracle of the righteous man. Because the legendary victim was endowed with free will and grounded in Jewish law, the contest was fair enough, but the rabbi of Chelm failed the ultimate test, failing to aspire beyond a pre-Sabbath pinch of snuff. That was long ago, before the great catastrophe. Since then, and once again, evil has become a metaphysical problem, a force so pervasive that even the demons cannot understand or control it. "It has reached a point where people want to sin beyond their capacities," says the demon-narrator to a fellow imp. "They martyr themselves for the most trivial of sins" (Y 14, E 302). Thus the choice of the young rabbi of Tishevits is accidental, and the evil touches him gratuitously, lacking moral significance; and the critical third test, the climax of every sacred tale, never happens because the Germans come and murder the Jews of Tishevits and all the other Jews of Poland, leaving only one demon-survivor.[57]

Peretz's Chelm story is a spoof on the legend of Joseph della Reina, who tried to force the hand of God but was tricked by Samael into offering the devil a pinch of snuff. Bashevis' demonic monologue is an indictment of Peretz and all like-minded humanists who believed that redemption could be wrought by human hands. Of these writers the demon says: "They know all our tricks—mockery, piety. They have a hundred reasons why a rat must be kosher. All that they want to do is to redeem the world" (Y 14, E 302–303). And so Tishevits, birthplace of the false messiah, was a fitting place for the last temptation of the just man—and a fitting refuge for the last Yiddish storyteller, who ended his truncated tale with a children's ditty on the letters of the alphabet.[58]

For the demon, time stands still, allowing him to act the role of tempter in a Yiddish-speaking shtetl and to step outside time, there to question the very tale he has just told. In that attic he has everything a storyteller can want: a legendary landscape complete with local messiahs; a library of old storybooks; the solitude to test the limits of his own parodic art and stylized language. Of course no attic can constrain him, because the jester is just now warming up to the infinite possibilities of mixing this world and the next, past and present, demons and humans.

If the demon can pass as a badkhn, why not the reverse? Elkhonon, the amateur badkhn and lowly teacher's assistant, happens upon Taibele one moonless summer evening as she weaves a tale of demonic love for the benefit of her female friends, and he hatches a plan to bring her story to pass. Enlisting all his verbal skills, he appears in her bedroom and seduces her by whispering satanic nothings into her ear. Eventually, despite her initial dread, she comes to anticipate these biweekly trysts, the first real passion she has ever known, until one day Hurmizah-Elkhonon becomes deathly ill. "There are so many devils," Taibele cries out in anguish, "let there be one more."[59] Though it may be a devilish game, sex has its rewards, and "Taibele and Her Demon" (1962), a remarkably poignant love story, is one of them.

Life is stranger than fiction as demons pale in the face of true desire. The next step for Bashevis is to break down the fiction of fiction altogether. Enter Aaron Greidinger, famous Yiddish author, who speaks extemporaneously about unusual events that happened either to him or were related to him by his readers. Sometimes the result is parodic, as when the writer-narrator, vacationing out of season at Miami Beach, keeps getting his signals crossed with the hidden powers ("Alone," 1960).[60] At other times the result is chilling, as when Esther reveals that she has seen Adolf Hitler in "The Cafeteria" (1968).[61]

> The moment I sit down at a table, they come over. "Hello, Aaron!" they greet me, and we talk about Yiddish literature, the Holocaust, the state of Israel, and often about acquaintances who were eating rice pudding or stewed prunes the last time I was here and are already in their graves. Since I seldom read a paper, I learn this news only later. Each time, I am startled, but at my age one has to be ready for such tidings. The food sticks in the throat; we look at one another in confusion, and our eyes ask mutely, Whose turn is next? Soon we begin to chew again. I am often reminded of a scene in a film about Africa. A lion attacks a herd of zebras and kills one. The frightened zebras run for a while and then they stop and start to graze again. Do they have a choice? (Y 43–44, E 287)

How quickly the conversation among aging Yiddish speakers turns to the subject of death, a subject that preoccupies the writer himself, though he is a busy man, much in demand. "Almost every day on my walk after lunch, I pass the funeral parlor that waits for us and all our ambitions and illusions," he tells us. "Sometimes I imagine that the funeral parlor is also a kind of cafeteria where one gets a quick eulogy or Kaddish on the way to eternity." (Y 45, E 288). It is a most conducive setting for swapping life experiences. Like the study house of old, this cafeteria on the Upper West Side of Manhattan is frequented mostly by men: "old bachelors like myself, would-be writers, retired teachers, some with dubious doctorate titles, a rabbi without a congregation, a painter of Jewish themes, a few translators—all immigrants from Poland or Russia." This explains why Yiddish is still spoken here, albeit with a generous dose of modern words. Unlike the old study house, however, the clientele is transient. "One of them disappears and I think he is already in the next world; suddenly he reappears and tells me that he has tried to settle in Tel Aviv or Los Angeles." Sounds innocent enough, a here-today-gone-tomorrow motif, until the barrier between this world and the next begins to break down, revealing a terrifying hole in the fabric of reality.[62]

The cafeteria, like its clientele, is a survivor of the Holocaust. One day it burns down, and when eventually rebuilt it attracts new customers who drop all pretense to wordliness, revert to speaking "plain Galician Yiddish," and begin to bare their souls. Now the jungle analogy only alluded to earlier takes on a sinister meaning. These are all people who have experienced life in extremis: depraved sex in the labor camps; friends denouncing each other to the secret police. "To get a bowl of soup or a place to stay," they tell Aaron, "you had to sell your soul" (Y 55, E 293). Among the returnees is the lone woman in the pack, beautiful Esther, who had earlier confided her disenchantment with politics and the future. "How can we hope when everything ends in death?" she taunts Aaron. "For me, death is the only comfort. What do the dead do? They continue to drink coffee and eat egg cookies? They still read newspapers? A life after death would be nothing but a joke." Yet this hardened woman is the very one who gains a fleeting glimpse of a demonic realm, while Aaron who preaches that "hope itself is a proof that there is no death" comes to see reality as psychotic, his innermost life as barren—the accumulated papers in his apartment get drier and ever more parched, until one day they too will go up in flames.

The New World is an unstable place. Hotel Row on Miami Beach turns into the primordial staging ground for a contest of the gods, and the friendly neighborhood cafeteria burns down just after hosting a reunion of Hitler and his henchmen. Many times Bashevis uses sudden storms and extremes of nature to signal a correspondence between the human and the cosmic realms. But these new people and places are off the beaten track of Yiddish storytellers. Compared to America, heaven and hell are cosy and familiar.

These new settings for storytelling, which include the offices of the *Jewish Daily Forward* on the Lower East Side and darkened apartments all ready for a seance on Central Park West, are not exactly a cross-section of America, nor is Aaron Greidinger a died-in-the-wool rationalist. "I have played with the idea that all humanity suffers from schizophrenia," he muses aloud after hearing the sensational climax to Esther's story. "Along with the atom, the personality of *Homo sapiens* has been splitting" (Y 66, E 298). Aaron in his own way is as receptive to the hidden forces at work in the universe as Rabbi Pinkhes Menakhem Singer of Krochmalna Street. Both men swear by the prophets of another reality: the son, by Einstein, Freud, and Vaihinger; the father, by Simeon bar Yohai, Isaac Luria, and the Ba'al Shem Tov. Both go through the motions of their everyday lives as if they were answerable to hidden powers. But after each encounter the father is further dazzled by God's miracles while the son is left to improvise. The best the modern storyteller can do is to end on a note of ambiguity. Did Esther get a glimpse of another reality? Does she or does she not live on after death?[63]

Yiddish storytelling in the New World becomes an ever more isolated—and isolating—act. The author's dire predictions of 1943 are borne out by his own American tales in which the spoken language no longer reveals a densely layered world of folk belief and religious passion. As a result, Bashevis' American tales (which he begins to write around 1960) lose little in translation because there is nothing much to lose: no cadences; no plethora of idioms, proverbs, maxims; or no use of dialect; no speech patterns unique to women, demons, or underworld types; most significantly, no in-group code designed to separate the Jews from the gentiles. The syncopated and sententious folk speech of the Old World storytellers is absorbed by the rambling newspaper copy of Yitskhok Warshawski, and before too long—thanks to a stable of translators working overtime to simplify and even bowdlerize the stories and monologues set in eastern Europe—folk speech and news speech become the undifferentiated English of one "I. B. Singer."

Even the poor devil gets his wings clipped in the process. In his English persona, the devil who inveighed so relentlessly against the church not only has his mouth washed out, but he also becomes something of an expert in Christianity. English is, after all, a language steeped in Christian culture, and so a neutral "string of beads" (*shnur patsherkes*) easily suggests a rosary; "he lived at the priest's" (*baym galekh*) becomes "he lived in the priest's rectory"; and the toughly worded Zeidel "no longer wished to bow down before the little Jesus" [*zikh bukn tsum yoyizl*] is prettified into "nor was he inclined to kneel before an altar." Made to sound downright ecumenical, this devil is less of an embarrassment to American Jews in the late-fifties (when "Zeidlus the Pope" was first translated), and may in fact represent the mellowing of Bashevis in the face of America's more tolerant brand of Christianity. But it wrecks the story. Once there's no one left to draw the line between truth and falsehood, the devil also becomes a moral relativist and Zeidel's rise and fall become an exercise in absurdity. This makes the story more modernist, and much less Yiddish.[64]

The same devil who presides over the death of Yiddish storytelling also points to an escape from the creative impasse. At the end of *Mayse Tishevits,* the last demon finds solace by improvising rhymes for the letters of the alphabet, just as Yiddish-speaking children in Warsaw and Bilgoraj were wont to do. The speech of children, with its unselfconscious mix of high and low, exalted truth and satiric insight, could reopen a world of primordial and comical tales. Children, as Singer would later be fond of saying, had no use for psychology, sociology, Kafka, or *Finnegans Wake.* The aging author whose creative powers were clearly waning, who couldn't help plagiarizing himself, who now used memoir and autobiography to settle old scores, suddenly found his alter ego in the utterly benign figure of "Naftali the Storyteller and His Horse, Sus" (1975).[65]

Was it merely for the sake of young readers that Bashevis created in Naftali such a radically simplified version of Gimpel the Fool? Perhaps the storyteller had in mind the earliest purveyors of a truly modern Yiddish literary fare—Mendele and his long-suffering horse. If so, the layering effect of Bashevis' demonic tales is used here to cover up the multiple losses of faith and community, story and collective memory, that heralded the birth of secular Jewish culture. Naftali has it all. Though of humble origins, he procures an upper-class patron, a lifelong venue for his tales, a permanent home, and a mythical resting place for himself and his horse. The only recognizable trademark is this: the hero ends his career far from Jewish habitation, somewhere on the road between Lublin and Warsaw.

The success of Singer's stories for children, of which lavishly illustrated editions have appeared in every major language save Yiddish, suggests that the art of Yiddish storytelling must be viewed from the outside. Henceforth, the stories tell us, when a Yiddish writer reaches a certain advanced age, he becomes a saintly figure by default. Certainly Singer comes across this way in his English-language interviews in print and on film.[66] Then all of

Yiddish culture perforce becomes a take for children—not demonic stories that even grownups fear to read at night, but pleasant parables of a bygone age in a forgotten language. The demon, whose parodic anger had done so much to rescue its author from despair, was finally laid to rest. It is a soppy ending to a long and pugnacious career, for no culture can hope to go on without a *yeytser-hore*.

9

Estates of Memory
After the Holocaust

Now to whom shall I turn who can tell me the words
of the song? To the old cantor who knew all the hymns
of the holy poets?—I am all that is left of all their tears.

—S. Y. Agnon, 1962

For many years a large oil painting hung in my parents' livingroom. Here was a crowded Warsaw street full of Jewish figures large and small, going about their various trades. My mother's particular favorite was the *sharamanshtshik*, the organgrinder, who looked straight out at you from the center of the canvas: he reminded her of the street singers in the Vilna courtyards of her youth and of herself at that time, half smiling, half sad. As for me, I remember admiring the porter with a huge basket of coals on his back, because even as a child I realized that he was all out of proportion, much bigger than the others. How, I wondered, could such a grown-up artist as Yosl Bergner paint no better than a child?

As I now see it, the oversized porter was a key to Bergner's refiguration of the past. Although he intended this painting to evoke the actual Warsaw courtyard where he was raised by his father Melech Ravitch—"Wolinsky Street, Warsaw, 1927" is scribbled on the back of the canvas—and although the light emanating from the garret at the upper-left-hand corner of the painting may represent the garret on Nowolipki 46 described by Ravitch in his memoirs, Bergner's approach was not merely mimetic.[1] The porter was meant to be none other than Bontshe the Silent, and the scrawny little boy carrying a jug was Bergner's rendition of Motl the cantor's son selling soapy kvas in the streets of Kasrilevke.

Bergner reappropriated his Polish-Jewish past through a mixture of fact and fantasy because after 1940, and living in faraway Australia, there was no effective way back other than through creative betrayal. Commenting with a touch of disapproval on Bergner's later illustrations to Peretz, where several more versions of Bontshe appeared, the poet I. J. Segal put his finger on the nature of that betrayal: Bergner had rendered in a naturalistic and slightly grotesque style the idealized figures of the Yiddish literary canon.[2] Segal probably also took exception to Bergner's angels, who seemed the spitting image of mendicants and mystics hanging out in a nearby shtibl, and to the goats, dogs, and doves who looked almost human. Segal might have added that the drawings of Bontshe, whose grotesque tale never belonged in *Stories in the Folk Vein* to begin with, were a betrayal in the opposite direction: Bergner recast Peretz's most pathetic character in a tragic mold.

Peretz and Bergner define the outer limits of my discussion, the one standing at the gate of the east European Jewish cultural revival, which I call the art of creative betrayal, and the other at the finish line. Peretz, I have argued, invented this technique of selective retrieval as a way of over-

Yosl Bergner, for Peretz, "The Three Gifts" (1950)

coming the loss of religious and secular faith and of restoring a usable past to a fragmented society. He showed his generation that modernity was a two-way street, that one could reinvent the past in one's own image and still create a cultural artifact that others would mistake for the real thing. Because Bergner was himself a product of the Yiddish school movement that drew its original inspiration from Peretz, Bergner's urban landscapes combined the muscular Bontshes and the emaciated Motls of Yiddish fiction with the clutter of a remembered Jewish Warsaw. And in the middle stood the bearded, sadly smiling organgrinder, whose hurdy-gurdy churned out the *skarbove* (stock) melodies so beloved of every urban folk culture. He was the artist who held the pieces of the past together, balancing the coal-carrying giant to his left and the ice-carrying giant to his right; surrounded by barrels of fish, a basket of bagels, heder boys and beggars; by a mother and child, a market woman, a woman in the window. He and his tunes were the sum of what remained: canned melodies that resounded, under a threatening sky, in the presence of a folk half real and half imagined.

In Warsaw's Jewish quarter itself, sealed off from the "Aryan side" as of November 15, 1940, the robust organgrinder was replaced by the ghetto peddler, "with pale face and half-extinguished eyes," hawking Yiddish books at bargain prices.[3]

> "Hello, my friend," he accosts someone, "you must buy the book *Hunger* [by Nobel Prize laureate Knut Hamsun], for just 50 groschen."
>
> "And you there, without a home," he turns to someone else, "you must be from Lublin or Slomatycz, so why not buy [Hayyim Nahman Bialik's poem about the Kishinev pogrom] *The City of Slaughter!*"
>
> "Jews! Have I got bargains for you! A complete set of Mendele for next-to-nothing. Why waste a złoty to get through to [the Judenrat office on] Grzybowska or [the office of the Jewish Self-Help on] Tłomackie? For the same price you can have [Mendele's satires] *The Parasite* or *The Communal Tax* in your own home library. Buy, Jews! The very best books: [Leivick's] *Chains,* [Schiller's] *Robbers, Behind Bars,* [Hitler's] *Zayn krampf,* [Peretz's] 'At the Bedside of a Dying Man'—for 50 groschen apiece!"

By 1942 these "lost books"—the abandoned property of a murdered ghetto population—would be used for toilet paper. Yet notice how this street lore bespoke a culture that was or felt itself to be equally at home in European and secular Jewish culture. Notice that someone (who signed his name "Sh.") transcribed the verbal traffic on ghetto streets and that someone else (from the underground archive code-named "Oyneg-shabes") took equal care to bury this scrap of folklore for the future edification of readers in the free world. And notice, finally, how a cryptic lore that once made sense to the average Jew on the street now requires intrusive annotation, which undercuts its spunk and spontaneity.

The first thing to be betrayed in the wake of the Holocaust were the depths of relations inherent in the lost cultures that produced the lost books: relations between people and places, present and past, the purveyors of culture and the folk. Vicarious survivors were quick to perceive the radical break. In Palestine, veteran Hebrew novelist Shmuel Yosef Agnon returned to the stylized folk narrative as a way of compensating for all these losses. In 1943 he produced a horrific allegory on the demonic love of a gentile lady for a Jewish peddler. (They devour the Jews, these goyim, the moment you get into their beds.) When news reached him a year later that all the Jews in his native town of Buczacz had been killed, he sat down to write a dreamlike lament, which he later expanded into the moving auto-biographical tale, "The Sign" (1962). Agnon also added multiple layers of ethnographic and historical detail to his great comic novel, *The Bridal Canopy* (1931), turning the book into a veritable encyclopedia of nine-teenth-century Galician Jewry. After he was gone, who else would re-member? Because he wrote in Hebrew, for an ideal reader as learned as he was, Agnon shouldered the responsibility of a *sofer ivri,* a [modern] Hebrew writer, who was also a *sofer ivri,* a Hebrew scribe. Like another Polish Jew named Yitskhok Bashevis, living far from home, Agnon used the art of learned—and ironic—storytelling to rebuild a vanished world.[4]

East European Jewish writers and artists, whether they lived through the Holocaust or not, tempered their personal desire to innovate with the col-lective need to commemorate. This was especially true for Yiddish writers in America, where all the sustaining isms of Yiddish culture—the "JesusMarxes," as the poet Jacob Glatstein put it—were publicly repudi-ated; and the Yiddish secular schools, the Yiddish press, the Yiddish theater, the *landsmanshaftn* and fraternal societies, were all in marked decline during the 1940s. Poets who only a decade before had inveighed against the reigning schools of Yiddish letters in the name of modernism, became literary historians, champions of the Yiddish literary "canon." Glatstein, the preeminent and most polemical of Yiddish modernists, reimagined himself as Rabbi Nahman of Bratslav.[5] For these writers to sustain any notion of historical continuity, they had to betray the modernist credo that vehemently denied the continuity.

Yiddish writers in the Soviet Union—provided they survived the purges—faced a more limited set of choices. Der Nister emerged from a period of "reeducation" with *The Family Mashber* (1939–1941), his brilliantly wrought saga of fraternal and spiritual crisis. But only after the Nazi invasion of the USSR in the summer of 1941, and after the Jewish Anti-Fascist Committee was established in April 1942 to rally international support, could Der Nister and his fellow writers express their grief and solidarity. They could do so, moreover, only by drawing on eyewitness accounts of what had happened "over there," across the Soviet-Polish border, or once upon a time, in the days of the sixteenth-century adventurer and harbinger of the messiah, *Prince Reuveni*. The martyrdom of Soviet Jewry itself was strictly taboo. In addition, these chronicles of vicarious heroism and suffering, produced mostly for export, had to be cleared by the censor. As servants of Stalinism, Soviet-Yiddish writers, with their Orders of Lenin, coveted apartments in the writers' compound, and membership in the Union of Writers, enjoyed less freedom of expression than their fellow scribes and songwriters dying a sure death in the Nazi ghettos.[6]

What of the ultraorthodox and hasidic Jews who, between the two world wars, had become energetic followers of their own political parties, voracious readers of the Yiddish press, and talented writers, poets, and essayists in their own right?[7] There was an understandable desire among Yiddish secularists after the Holocaust to reach out to their bearded and sidelocked brethren in the face of Hitler's near victory. Writing against this backdrop, Chaim Grade produced a profound philosophical response to the Holocaust. "My Quarrel with Hersh Rasseyner" (1951) pits a militant pietist against a penitent secularist who chance to meet in the Paris Metro. Eventually a healing rain helps to suture the wounds left by the war against the Jews and their God. This moving philosophical "essay," however, was written in a form that orthodox Jews couldn't possibly recognize, unless they knew the Grand Inquisitor section of *The Brothers Karamazov*.[8]

Grade never returned to the extreme pietism of his youth, but he did turn to writing autobiographical fiction in order to recast the relations between the lost Jews of eastern Europe and their zealous God. In opposition to I. B. Singer's portrayal of the Beth-Din, the rabbinical court, where a mystically inclined and hopelessly impractical father presides over a melange of wives and widowers, prostitutes and conmen, Grade sought to restore the inner world of the Lithuanian yeshivas, the world of scholars and "their human temptations, their frame of mind and way of thinking, their social circumstances and family life, and the ones of great faith for whom the world to come was a tangible thing, often truer than the world of their daily lives." Whereas Singer had begun his novelistic career with the romance of Rechele, caught between two extremes of messianic heresy, Grade produced a realistic novel about *The Agunah*, caught between two exemplars of rationalist, mainstream "Litvak" piety.[9]

Because of the Holocaust, every teller of local traditions became a teller of exotic places. For what could be more exotic than slum-dwelling Jews of prewar Warsaw and Vilna playing out their passions and perversions inside a rabbinical courtroom; or members of the learned aristocracy swapping tales behind the stove on a late winter's afternoon; or chimneysweeps and leech breeders, chiromancers and pigeon fanciers, all of them speaking a poetically charged Yiddish? Storytelling, after the Holocaust, became a form of reminiscence, yet no less difficult to master, late in life and far from home.

The first Polish refugee to compose a folk epic culled from his own life was Chil Szaja (Yehiel Isaiah) Trunk (b. 1888). Almost from the moment he arrived in New York City, at the beginning of April 1941, via Warsaw, Vilna, Kovno, Central Asia, Japan, and San Francisco, Trunk began dictating his autobiography to his wife, Khane (Hannah). When the words began pouring out of him, he took up his own pen and didn't stop until all seven volumes of *Poland* were completed a decade later. This work, born of exile and catastrophe, ended by circling back to its own genesis: "We left on foot with packs on our backs. The windows in all the buildings were pasted up with black paper so that Warsaw would lie in darkness at night. We felt as if we were walking inside a black coffin. Up above Hitler's airplanes stormed the sky like terrible demons." The title was no mere act of bravado. If ever there was a Jew who could say of himself, "La Pologne, c'est moi!" it was Y. I. Trunk, scion of both rabbinic-hasidic and aristocratic ancestors. On his father's side, he hailed from the hasidic master, Reb Yitskhok Vurker, and the rabbinic sage, Horav Shiele Kutner. The Gzywacz family on his mother's side were among the wealthiest Jewish landowners in all of Poland. Making good on his blue blood, Trunk married into the Prywes family of textile magnates from Lodz. Whereas Yiddish writers long since settled in America would often pine for the "Polish woods," Trunk's family actually owned some. Whereas virtually every male writer could recall his first visit to Peretz's home, only Trunk had actually slept there, and befriended Peretz's deeply troubled son, Lucian. World traveler and man about town; proud owner of a pedigreed poodle; card-carrying bundist and ardent socialist; equally at home in Hebrew and Yiddish, Gilgamesh and the ancient Greeks, Freud and Jung, poetry and prose—Trunk was the Polish Jew for all seasons. Now, during the twenty-year-long winter of his life, while Hannah worked in a New Jersey sweatshop to make ends meet, Trunk drew from this great wealth of experience to erect a many-faceted monument to a vanished world with himself at its center.[10]

Nothing this readable had come out in Yiddish since Sholem Aleichem's *From the Fair*. Each self-contained chapter of *Poland* came with upbeat, amusing captions; none was longer than a single, or at most double, installment of a Friday literary supplement. Foremost among the large cast of characters were the elite Polish-Jewish families (the Bialers, Viners, Pryweses) whom the author knew well and whose rise and fall reflected the changing fortunes of Polish Jewry. Love was the great anarchic force that broke down barriers between city and shtetl, slums and uptown salons, the pious and the heretics—one harbinger among many of a new age of equality. Art, literature, and socialism were others. Trunk's focus on a single, usually grotesque character trait, whether of an Old or New World figure, also lent coherence to the whole. Many readers were shocked that Trunk could be so cavalier and even callous about the Polish-Jewish martyrs, but as Trunk later said in his own defense, he needed distance in order to write about them at all, in order not to go mad. Here and there a flash forward to the tragic end of these Jews was allowed to intrude upon their shenanigans; in general, Trunk tried to balance, to synthesize, as he loved to put it, the dialectical forces of *shikzal* and *kholem,* of Jewish historical fate and quixotic Jewish dreams.[11]

Above all, Trunk's dreamers and lovers belonged; they were as rooted in the Polish landscape as his beloved forests and mountains. Peretz, with his dressing gown and proud demeanor, his fluent Polish and tireless campaign for a modern Yiddish culture, was for Trunk the wellspring of Jewish ideals and idealism. It was in Peretz's kitchen that the adolescent Chil Szaja, still dressed in hasidic garb, had his first forbidden taste of nonkosher milk. It was Peretz who convinced him to switch from Hebrew to Yiddish. It was in Peretz's literary salon that Poland's great misfits (S. L. Kave, Hirsh-Dovid Nomberg, Lucian Peretz, and many others) seemed to find a home. Most important, it was Peretz who pointed young Trunk toward the one writer who would change his life and would unlock the secrets of the Yiddish-speaking folk—Sholem Aleichem.

Should further proof be needed, *Poland* is the ultimate prooftext of how alienated east European Jewish intellectuals were from the materials of their folk. In Peretz's salon, a snobbish disdain for the seemingly naive folk writers Avrom Reisen and Sholem Aleichem was enough to qualify you as a member of the inner circle. Trunk was especially adept at capturing what each new disciple contributed to the Yiddish cultural renaissance. There was Menakhem Boreisho, who brought a decadent's delight in irrational visions, but was also the first to sing authentic Yiddish folksongs; and there was Itshe Meyer Weissenberg, salt of the earth, who introduced an earthy naturalism. The artist Shimen Kratko returned from his training at the Bezalel School in Jerusalem to introduce his flamboyant young wife, Totshe, and the spirit of orientalism. Kratko's campaign to adapt ornamental Jewish art for the frontispieces of modern Yiddish journals and books was perfectly timed, since Peretz was busy with his stylized folk- and fairy tales (which he apparently rehearsed beforehand to his grandson, Janek, in Polish). According to Trunk, Kratko's was the first Jewish atelier in Warsaw—an institution that would later convert another hasidic youngster, Itshele Singer, from the strictures of Hebraism to the pleasures of Hellenism.[12]

Himself an early convert to Hellenism, Trunk introduced the Yiddish *peyzazh,* the lush description of nature in all its splendor. Since money was not an issue, Trunk hired two artists to accompany these sketches *Fun der natur* with ornate drawings. Inspired, moreover, by Kratko's exotic tales of Zion, Trunk and his bride set out on a lengthy cruise of the Mediterranean and Middle East. He arrived in Palestine carrying a Hebrew Bible in one hand, a translation of Josephus' *Jewish War* in the other. When the outbreak of World War I prevented the Trunks from going home, they found refuge in Switzerland where Chil Szaje had plenty of time to further his study of Jewish history, particularly the hellenistic period. There he discovered Ernst Renan's *Histoire du peuple d'Israël des origines à l'époque romaine* (1887–1893).

Trunk took strong exception to Renan's view that Jewish history was but a prelude to Christianity. Still, this great historian of religion revealed that

Shimen Kratko, cover for Peretz, *A mol iz geven a meylekh*
(Once There Was a King; 1909)

a guiding spirit, an archetypal plot, informed the Jewish people's historical experience. Suddenly Trunk saw the sequel to Renan's book laid out clearly before him: it was the great human comedy of the Jews, their feet planted firmly on earth, their heads in the clouds. And the expert witness to these internal dynamics of Jewish fate had been none other than Sholem Aleichem—the only writer (save Shakespeare) whom Peretz ever envied. So once again, as with Peretz himself, and in the peculiar dialectic of creative betrayal, a young Jewish rebel far from home discovered that his claim to the world lay not in mastering the wonders of nature, or ancient civilizations long since vanished, but sat right on his own doorstep, in the discarded culture of the folk.

The death of Peretz and Sholem Aleichem during the war added a sense of urgency to Trunk's conversion experience in the early twenties. If a choice had to be made between Peretz the hard-nosed materialist and Peretz the utopian visionary, that time was now. The Polish republic to which Trunk returned after war's end seemed radically transformed, and yet the condition of its three million Jews was as precarious as it had been before the war. Who would explain the destiny of the Jewish masses to themselves? To provide an alternative myth of origins, one that anchored the Jews within western civilization, Trunk began writing historical novellas set in ancient Greece and Rome. To provide a direction through present and future, he arranged all of modern Yiddish letters into rival philosophical camps—the naturalists versus the idealists—and came down firmly on the side of the latter. To complete his own identification with the folk, Trunk joined the Jewish Labor Bund, in 1923.[13]

Within this grand Hegelian scheme, Trunk reserved pride of place for Sholem Aleichem. But it wasn't easy, for Trunk's ambivalence ran deep. Perhaps that's why *Sholem Aleichem, His Essence and His Works* (Warsaw, 1937), a splendidly published 443-page book, opened with a portrait not of Sholem Aleichem but of Trunk. Like other critics before and after, Trunk maintained that Sholem Aleichem never transcended the petit-bourgeois mentality of his own fictional characters. Trunk denied Sholem Aleichem any intellectual sophistication. Yet at the same time Trunk brought enormous philosophical and historiographic weight to bear upon this "folk writer" and his "little Jews." Enlisting Freud and Jung (possibly for the first time in Yiddish criticism), Trunk saw Sholem Aleichem's literary creativity—his autobiography in particular—as a form of compensation for his shattered dreams. Projecting outward from his own felt contradiction between dream and reality, Sholem Aleichem captured the historical farce of a nation full of dreamers, thus unlocking, according to Trunk, the collective unconscious of the Jews. Of all the monomaniacal dreamers, none was more Jewish, in psyche and self-expression, than Sholem Aleichem's Menakhem-Mendl.[14]

Trunk struck gold with the discovery of Jewish historical archetypes in the wild terrain of Sholem Aleichem's sprawling oeuvre. Not a moment too soon. As chairman of the Yiddish writers' club, Trunk was warned to run for his life when the blitzkrieg on Poland began. He fled with only the shirt on his back—and the manuscript of his next book, a study of Menakhem-Mendl.[15] But for all that Trunk identified completely with this peripatetic schlemiel, the embodiment of Jewish historical fate, nothing that Trunk wrote before, during, or immediately following World War II in any way resembled the writings of Sholem Aleichem. In his essays, short stories, and novellas, Trunk cultivated an urbane, philosophical style, at the farthest remove from learned or colloquial Yiddish.[16] What finally released the old-fashioned storyteller pent up inside the critical theorist was the experience of writing *Poland*.[17]

Why look for a world of eccentrics in Sholem Aleichem when he had only to reach back into his own memory to find them? If all of modern Yiddish storytelling was born of the knowledge that the tradition was dead, what closure could be more complete than the one being wrought right then in Poland? And so it behooved this Polish-Jewish exile to write a *comédie humaine* at least as inclusive as the works of Sholem Aleichem. To aid the act of remembrance, each character became something of a caricature. His bevy of hasidic ancestors behaved like the mad eccentrics of I. J. Singer's *Yoshe Kalb*. Nomberg the hypochondriac, in his smoke-filled bachelor's apartment, looked every bit a character out of Nomberg's own stories. Hershl Yedvab, the resident mime and storyteller from the slums of Lodz, reincarnated the naughty folk jester, Shayke Fefer. And even that temple of art, the Yiddish writers' club at Tłomackie 13, was a latter-day house of study, reeking of cheap food. (The new house of study could also boast a female following, dubbed *di literarishe baylages,* the literary supplements, by budding young talents looking for sex.[18])

"O, you Yiddish storybooks!" Trunk rhapsodized at one point. Once upon a time the penny-dreadfuls starring Simkhe Plakhte or the Three Brothers had brought love, adventure, and mystery into poor Jewish homes. Whatever happened to these marvelous books? They were passed by, as Trunk recalled, during Peretz's campaign for the literary fairy tale and the folksong revival of the 1920s.[19] Thirty years later, with his magnum opus complete, Hannah dead, and rent to pay on his spartan widower's flat in Washington Heights, Trunk began churning out a library of Yiddish folk classics rewritten in superidiomatic Yiddish. His goal was not merely to revive a popular medium, but to turn the Yiddish language and European Jewish folklore into the dual repositories of Jewish myth and Jewish truth.[20]

But the major legacy that Trunk left during his last years in America was the autobiography repackaged as *The Storybook of My Life. Poland,* with its bouncy captions and piquant tales, was a kind of serialized chapbook, which other Yiddish autobiographers, such as I. B. Singer and Melech Ravitch, were soon to emulate. The past repackaged in weekly installments; the writer's complex personality externalized into memorable encounters; all of life's traumas glossed over for the sake of readers who no longer looked to Yiddish literature to teach them something new but rather to confirm what they already knew—these were the modest remains of a great cultural experiment that never recovered from its multiple disasters.

No Yiddish storyteller has lived a more dramatic life than Abraham Sutzkever (b. 1913), but none reveals so little. His categorical refusal to tell his life story "straight," when, at the age of fifty-seven he began setting forth "fragments of purported autobiography"—and his categorical refusal to bow before the demise of Yiddish culture—contributed to the revival of a modern Yiddish storytelling legacy that might otherwise have been lost: the metaphysical and grotesque fantasy world of Der Nister.[21]

"A young man and a Priest, and from the sons of Priests am I, and have been brought up here with the help of my time and of a new prophecy." This came from an exultant Der Nister at the peak of his messianic fervor. Only nine years later, appearing as "Der Nister Himself" in his scatological travesty, he was reduced to offering himself for hire as a flea-infested prankster and rhymster. For Der Nister, the jester's demonic nihilism marked the end of the road to self-transcendence. For I. B. Singer, once he concluded that Yiddishism was no more, it was a point of departure. The ability of a postwar Yiddish writer to reinvent himself as a spinner of yarns— whether as visionary prophet or venal bard—was predicated on the betrayal of history, thenceforth inseparable from his-story.

Sutzkever displaces his autobiographical narrative by means of a densely poetic idiosyncratic style, by using multiple time frames that defy the rules of causality, and by flirting with the fairy tale and romance tradition. Like Der Nister's enigmatically titled *Gedakht,* Sutzkever's collections of tales suggest by their very titles that they are calculated to stretch the art of

Yiddish storytelling to unsettling limits: *Messiah's Diary* (1975), *Where the Stars Spend the Night* (1979), and *The Prophecy of the Inner Eye* (1989). He does describe "The Coin from Heaven," which fell the day he began to study the Hebrew alphabet; and he does recount an idyllic tale about first love, and his grandmother's peculiar Yiddish speech merits a story of its own. But the unspeakable memories of what happened to the Jews during the years of "the locust" keep gnawing at the fabric of the tales, diverting the flow of time, upsetting the psychic balance of the storyteller.[22]

This troubled storyteller, as in the late stories of Singer, bears a striking resemblance to the actual author. Today the narrator-protagonist lives in Tel Aviv, on the top floor of an apartment building without attic or chimney, reluctantly using electricity in lieu of kerosene. He frequents the Aladdin Cafeteria in Jaffo by the sea, edits the Yiddish literary quarterly *Di goldene keyt,* sometimes travels abroad, but seems to spend most of his time dreaming and hallucinating. He gets many visitors from Over There, that other time and place, which for the survivor means prewar Vilna, the ghetto and death camps, the world to come, or all these places and times together. The visitors are largely projections of his own other self, the one that saw and heard and lived beyond the Destruction.

Just as two selves struggle for self-expression in Sutzkever's tales of this world and the next, there are two competing agendas. The one is to mythologize every nook and cranny of the past that lies across the Great Divide, or as he puts it in typically paradoxical fashion, "hinter di likhtike harey-khoyshekh," (beyond the luminous mountains of darkness; *Nevue,* 126). Sutzkever's mythopoetic narrative is enormously seductive, charged with striking sensual images, bizarre twists of plot, and the most exotic Yiddish names ever assembled. There is Grandma Tsvyokele, the inveterate teller of *bobe-mayses;* Fayvke the Pigeon Fancier, who takes a shine to Slaughterknife's Daughter; Little Isaac the Snowman ("He was about eighty, and I was minus the zero, but we were both the same height"); Zvulik Podval, son of Tsale the Chimneysweep; the lovers Dondele and Roytl; Yonte the Chiromancer, or "the *yeshiva-bokher* with the Three Eyes"; Hore the Leech Breeder; Madame Trulelu, a healer from the (mythic-sounding but geographically locatable) town of Baltermantz, and many more. They are remembered for their aphorisms, as well as for their unique—and obsolete—professions, altogether a treasure trove of Vilna language and lore.

What makes them the stuff of legend, as opposed to autobiography, is

the storyteller's penchant for the grotesque and the ephemeral. In his mini-
Bildungsroman, "Portrait in a Blue Sweater" (1985), Sutzkever makes a
point of telling us that he decided to keep his nighttime lodging in the
Warsaw flophouse opposite the Pawiak prison because there he could hear
the stories and learn the argot of the Jewish underworld (*Nevue*, 86). The
Vilna stories, by the same token, are peopled by characters drawn from the
fringes of Sutzkever's life: a chiromancer he consulted only once, a chimneysweep, a first love whose name he can barely remember. Missing are
Freydke, his true love from the age of fifteen on, the woman he married
and who later rescued him from death; Sutzkever's closest friend Miki
Tshernikhov-Astour, who introduced him to Russian poetry—and to the
writings of Edgar Allan Poe; his fellow writers in Vilna. There are no stories
about Max Weinreich, who took young Abrasha into the Yiddish scouting
movement he founded, taught Sutzkever Old Yiddish literature, and men-
tored him throughout. Unlike Sutzkever's ghetto poetry where they loom
so large, there is no mention of Zelig Kalmanovitsh, the Prophet of the
Ghetto, Mira Bernshteyn (*Di lererin Mire*), Itzik Vittenberg, commander of

Yonia Fain, in Abraham Sutzkever, *Dortn
vu es nekhtikn di shtern* (Where the Stars
Spend the Night; 1979)

the Vilna partisans, or of the other young resistance fighters. Poetry for Sutzkever is the exalted domain of parents and true prophets. Storytelling is the stuff of memory traces that exist on the faultline of time: a blue sweater, a name, a tattooed number. Personal reminscence is something else again: tall and sometimes comical tales retold in the home or at a gathering of former partisans and Vilna neighbors.[23]

Occupying a middle ground between sacred verse and profane anecdote is storytelling, the repository of a secular folklore devoid of Scripture, with God's name invoked only with heavy irony. "I don't know whether there's a God," Fayvke the Pigeon Fancier is wont to say, "but there sure is someone acting out of spite" (Akvarium, 63). Ayzikl the Snowman conjures up wondrous images of paradise for the benefit of his fiery wife, from whom he once received this rejoinder: "It would all be well and good, were it not for that gateway to Paradise, the black grave" (Akvarium, 102). "I don't care if the Messiah speaks Turkish," Aunt Malke's eldest son Bere says, "so long as I live to hear his voice" (Nevue, 128). Some stories, such as "The Beggar with Blue Eyeglasses," are hardly more than a list of zany aphorisms. Folk wisdom, in Sutzkever's approach, is born not out of ancient texts but out of actual experience. So whatever miracles and mishaps occur, whatever oracles are pronounced and messiah figures encountered, they confirm the existence of a God and otherworld contingent on this one for survival.[24]

Messiah's Diary begins with a tale replete with such lore, "The Slaughterknife's Daughter."[25] He placed it first because it tells of first love and establishes how myth, destiny, and a person's name determine the outcome of life. All is playful at the outset, as the storyteller waxes eloquent to retrieve, after so many years, the real name of a pubescent and passionate girl: Glikele. Mock heroics and parodic myths are strewn everywhere. The young cavalier defends the honor of his lady before the foul-mouthed herring vendor, Royze-Eydele, who repays the young couple by turning this encounter into a cause celèbre. Now Glikele's widowed father, Reb Elye the Ritual Slaughterer, conveniently absents himself from home, leaving only the paralyzed, bedridden Grandmother Tsvyokele (so old she can remember how the Viliye River came into being), who gladly indulges the young suitor with tall tales of her own romantic exploits.

Midway through the story things begin to go wrong, for no better reason than Fayvke's aphorism about a force out there up to mischief. The narrator breaks his arm trying to bring a slaughterknife down from the attic, then

experiences a terrible itch under his plaster cast. Quite independently, Glikele learns to her sorrow that her father is about to remarry. May his broken
arm wither if he allows Glikele to be dispossessed, the young hero swears;
he is even prepared to hock his watch to help support her. The Jewish
calendar is likewise primed to aid the young lovers, who first meet just
before the festival of Purim and now depart on their first real outing in
honor of L'ag b'Omer—he with the coveted slaughterknife in hand.

Freudian determinism has nothing to do with the sorrowful outcome of
this tale, for all the obvious symbolism of a young man wielding the forbidden knife of a ritual slaughterer. The scene is charged instead with
primal imagery, an edenic idyll suddenly invaded by a stalking lizard, the
snake of paradise, who somehow causes a primeval storm to erupt.

> A redness spurts from the slit bough as from a throat. The slaughterknife, too,
> is no longer blue. The blue streamlet is awash in sunset, in the same color as
> Glikele's flowing hair.
>   A storm in the forest . . . A crowing of roosters, a honking of geese, and a
> mooing and bleating of cows and calves drives the forest wild with fright and
> breaks its branches. (*Akvarium*, 70–71)

Not only is the love between them permanently lost because of "the lizard's
magic and the turmoil in the forest," but the young man also loses memory
of her name. And in the story's grotesque dénouement, the Slaughterknife's
Daughter also loses her granny, who is broiled alive in her bed.

Whenever Sutzkever invokes the conventional markers (first love, fairy
tale, sweet reminiscence), it is only to trip us up. The whole business of
retrieving the name Glikele, which means "little joy," can only end with
the smell of burning flesh because there is no escape from the epithet,
Slaughterknife's Daughter. Romance and apocalypse are one.

The same Glikele returns five years later in another story where, arm in
arm with her old flame, she walks back in time to find the son she had
given birth to after fleeing, naked, from the killing fields at Ponar. There
she had met Elijah in the figure of a ninety-year-old peasant woman named
Papusha; somewhat later, in a magical forest of firs, a wolf nursed Glikele
back to life. Are there still more miracles in store for her in one deathtime?
Apparently not, for the peasant woman's hut is now off limits, even to the
imagination, and the young man she imagines to be her son does not answer
to the call "Papusha, Papusha." Recurrent despair is the sum total of Gli-

kele's story: "Again somebody else . . . How long will he be somebody else?" (*Nevue,* 50; E 399).

The precise meaning of a name, as of any other Jewish memory trace, is only clarified in the specific crucible of time known in Sutzkever's tales as "*di khalofim-tsayt,* the time of the slaughterknife" (*Akvarium,* 134). Before the slaughterknife, during the slaughterknife, and after the slaughterknife: these are the temporal divisions in Sutzkever's tales.

Take, for example, the survivors Dondele and Roytl, who are the first couple to be married in that first summer after the "sunset," which in calendar time would be August 1944, that is, upon the liberation of Vilna. Here the division of time is fairly conventional. Sandwiched between the tale of liberation and preparations for "The First Wedding in Town" is a flashback to prewar Vilna and the Holocaust. Typically, the prewar memories are painfully sweet. Dondele was a chimneysweep apprenticed to his father, and while the prewar status of this trade was none too great, the passage of time has reversed the priorities:

> Der mekhaber fun der mayse lebt itster in a shtot vos ire dekher zenen on beydemer un zenen meynstns nit bakoymet. Un az nito keyn koymen iz nito in shtub keyn leymener oder kalkhner oyvn; iz nito keyn freylekher fayer; iz nito keyn bereze-holts vos baym flakern vert es a regn-boygn; iz nito keyn kotshere, pomele un keyn yushke, vos me nemt on mit an onitse tsu farmakhn dem koymen; un ibern dakh iz nito keyn roykh—der groyer leyter tsu di shtern.
>
> Un az nito keyn koymens un di oytsres vos loykhtn fun ineveynik, zenen oykh nito mer di heymishe koymen-kerers.

> The author of the story now lives in a city where roofs have no attics and are mostly not bechimneyed. And where there is no chimney, the house has no clay or lime oven; and no happy flame; and no birchwood to produce a rainbow as it burns; and there's no shovel, hearth broom or flue which you grasp with a leftover legging wrap to close up the chimney; and over the roof there is no smoke—that grey ladder up to the stars.
>
> And when there are neither chimneys nor the treasures that shine inside of them, there are no familiar chimneysweeps either. (*Akvarium,* 133)

By yoking the mundane and the visionary, the author of the story provides a genealogy of magic, poetic and egalitarian.

History bears that bias out because, once the ghetto is established, Dondele has the wherewithal to rescue his mother from one round-up after another (only her *tkhine,* her book of women's prayers, is lost in flight), and working as a chimneysweep for the German occupiers, he is able to scout out hiding places, to smuggle arms and gunpowder back into the ghetto for his buddy Zvulik Podval and the other "hotblooded boys and girls" of the resistance (135). (In Vilna, where everyone seems to speak only Yiddish, that language bridges all spheres of life and death.)

But again at the halfway mark, between chapters 5 and 6, the heroic-romantic narrative suddenly ends. Not only has Dondele's mother lost her book, but Dondele's "magical pail lost its magic powers. There's no longer any broom that [ritually] immerses itself in soot; there's no longer any rope that throws dreams across from one roof to another" (136). Dondele is rounded up for the corpse-burning brigade at Ponar, a place unlike any other. "Young man," someone informs him in Yiddish. "The place you are at is Hell." "Since when is Yiddish spoken in Hell?" And another voice, the color of ash, replies: "Since Frankenstein became King of the Pits" (137). Here, where life and death literally cohabit, a father discovers the corpse of his son, and shouting "I am the luckiest of all the dead!" jumps into the burning pit.

Just as suddenly Roytl, disguised as a man, miraculously appears among the corpse burners and urges them not to lose heart. "S'iz Roytl oder toytl," she says, playing on her name. "It's either red or dead." They continue digging their escape tunnel to the nearby woods. Dondele and Roytl are among the few who survive that escape, and in another bittersweet dé-nouement, Dondele returns to the brick factory where he had hidden his mother only to find that her last wish has been answered: she died in her own bed, which was smuggled in from the ghetto.

But what of the wedding, now that the last reef of time has been crossed? When Roytl rushes back to her "parental little stone house," to prepare for the wedding, she finds the Frankenstein monster sitting at her table, bent over a bowl of borscht. She runs out in hysterics into Dondele's waiting arms. The story ends with the wedding on a magic mountain, the stars scattering their wedding gifts on the luminous bride below. No mention of Frankenstein's fate, or of how it came about that the Big Bad Wolf did not finally devour Little Red Riding Hood.

Sutzkever's return, through Der Nister and other Yiddish fabulists, to fairy tale and romance, was a matter of timing. For time cleft in three was most easily achievable in the realm of fantasy and the miraculous. Time, for Reb Nahman, was cosmic and messianic. That ultimate progression from Ur-time to profane time to a time beyond time was but opaquely reflected by human actions. For Peretz, the disillusioned maskil, only the artificial infusion of legendary time could redeem the dreary chronology of the material present so at to yield an ethical dimension. Time, for Der Nister, was the all-inclusive drama of personal redemption, for it allowed the seeker introspection, self-confrontation, and purification. Time, for I. B. Singer, was a battleground between the seductions of modernity and the harsh certainties of tradition. Over such extreme polarities only the devil's nihilism could reign supreme. For Sutzkever, there is time before, when poets and chimneysweeps had access to the heavens; time during, when Frankensteins walked the face of the earth destroying time itself; and time after, when through a crack in the mirror one can glimpse the beauteous and barbarous past. Only by exerting total control, what Wisse calls his maximalist approach to storytelling, can Sutzkever prevent each of the disparate times from running off with the tale.[26]

Sutzkever's stories are "difficult" because he insists on sustaining the tension between each of these time frames. If *Green Aquarium* was the poet's earlier attempt to maintain a living dialogue with the dead, his latest stories aim at the reverse effect: to divert the flow of time present with the death-delivering current of Holocaust time and the life-giving current of time before the flood. While each time flow has its own potential for the macabre and the miraculous, any confluence is hazardous, to all save the master storyteller.[27]

"Janina and the Beast" (1971) is a Holocaust retelling of "Beauty and the Beast."[28] Beauty appears as the noblewoman, Janina, who once shared the narrator's love for Polish romantic poetry but now, in April 1943, receives from him a knapsack containing a newborn Jewish infant whose mother handed it through the barbed-wire fence at Ponar. The slaughter continues unabated, dragging its victims into the pit "with the power of a natural law" (*Akvarium*, 80); only a fairy tale can change the landscape of universal destruction. The Beast is Nazi officer Hans Obermann, always accompanied by his wolfhound, who stalks Janina's house in search of hidden Jews. Sutzkever first describes the prowling Nazi as if he were a beast; only then does the human beast enter Janina's house in immaculate dress. Neither Janina nor the reader is quite sure where nightmare ends and reality begins. But Janina never drops her guard or her alibi: the child is hers through a liaison with a Polish army officer. The story's turning point, when the narrator finally admits that "di realitet hot moyred geven in zikh gufe" (reality rebelled against its very self; *Akvarium,* 90), comes when the Nazi beast forces her to swear by the cross that the child is hers, and when she does so, he shoots his wolfhound, falls down and kisses Janina's feet, beats his head against the floor, tells the mother and child that they must flee at once, and thanks Janina for turning him back into a human being.

There are two endings to this story, the first of which takes place in the next spring in the Husaczer forest where the storyteller, now a partisan, is coopted to interrogate a German officer who deserted his regiment and fought on the partisan side to expiate his Nazi past. Though about to be executed, the officer, one Hans Obermann by name, refuses to divulge the reason for his desertion. The second ending is a postscript: Janina's adopted daughter has just been married; details on the wedding will follow, sometime.

True to the legacy of Peretz, Sutzkever has betrayed the famous fairy tale in the name of secular humanism. The truly fantastical moment comes not when a German turns into a beast—a commonplace in the time of the slaughterknife. The miracle occurs when he reasserts his humanity thanks to the deceitful but selfless devotion of a Christian mother for a Jewish child. "Janina and the Beast" is also a secular saint's tale, recapitulating the one act of Christian charity that Sutzkever was willing to allow after the Holocaust. In private conversation, Sutzkever sometimes (though very rarely) admits to other stories, of Jewish mothers abandoning their children in quivering knapsacks in order to save their own lives, or of Christians readily betraying their Jewish neighbors. Horror stories like these, however, do not document life's private victories over death, which are the humanistic underpinning of *Messiah's Diary* and the storybooks that follow. By taming the beast, Janina stops (war)time itself in its tracks, allowing (life)time to take its own course.

The storyteller's survival is no less a miracle, as he asserts in a cryptic tale called "The Vow" (1972). The recurrent perception of that miracle cries out for a metaphysical gloss far removed from anything that Peretz might have contemplated.[29] "The Vow," Sutzkever explained to me, is the most realistic story in *Messiah's Diary,* by which I presume he meant that it is the most overtly autobiographical. In it he reveals his sense of election and consecration following the "night of miracles" on a Thursday-going-on-

Friday during the winter of 1942. Never in the annals of Yiddish storytelling has there been a teller of exotic places who engaged death in a "cosmic duel" and emerged the temporary victor. In terse, poetically charged detail, the storyteller recounts how he was transformed from being a "cellarman" to a "forestman" thanks to a hidden hand that rescued him from his hiding place just moments before the hut was ambushed and then saved him twice more in rapid succession. In response to this triple miracle the forestman utters a triple vow: should he survive the war he will resist all temptation and go to live in his ancestral homeland; he will seek the Other Self who sent him the salvific sign and unite both selves into one; and a third vow that is too intimate to reveal. What happened that night, Sutzkever wishes us to know, is true: as true as the fact that he now resides in Israel, that the life-giving self and the self that should have died are finally united, and that as a result he has resolved to tell life-in-death and death-in-life stories as intimate as they are revealing.[30]

To carry so great a cultural burden, both the storyteller and his subjects are endowed with prophetic powers. They are inspired madmen—and women—the functional equivalents of Der Nister's priests, hermits, stargazers, and soothsayers. Perhaps this is why Sutzkever sidestepped the central people in his life as being somehow too constant and cerebral, in preference for the mad and marginal figures he encountered along the way. Among the most memorable is Grunye, the twin who has lost her other half. The storyteller meets Grunye in his favorite haunt, the Aladdin Cafeteria in Jaffo, the very spot, he reminds us, whence the prophet Jonah fled to Tarshish. Her veiled figure emerges after a portentous storm at sea, as if from the belly of the whale. He is drawn to her by the last two digits of her blue tattooed number, the same 13 that has mysteriously guided his own life. And so, even before Grunye's story begins, time present is charged with archetypal meanings.[31]

The older of the two, by thirteen minutes, Grunye wears the prophetic mantle as unwillingly as Jonah before her.[32] While her twin sister Hodesl was the virtuoso violinist who soared to the heavens, Grunye fought and suffered for the revolution down below. Their father cut a strange figure, indeed, having patented a serum he called Antikinin, designed to heal a person—and eventually all mankind—from pangs of jealousy. Once the ghetto is established, however, the mad scientist injects himself with a powerful enough dose of serum to be rid of all feelings, jealous or otherwise. In the unnamed death camp, the twins are more twinned than ever before—until commandant Siegfried Hoch sets up an orchestra of prisoners, Hodesl playing first violin. She alone, following the performance of Beethoven's Eroica, refuses to devour the orange peels the commandant scatters on the ground, and for this act of defiance, her number is selected. Grunye, whose number is different, fails to stand in for her divinely inspired sister.

There remains a thirst for revenge, something that no serum in the world can cure, and Grunye joins forces with Zvulik Podval, son of Tsale the Chimneysweep, in trying to track down the former camp commandant, now hiding out somewhere in South America. But when Grunye finally nets her prey, Siegfried Hoch has already been made into a *tsantsa,* a shrunken head, by Peruvian bushmen. Too little, too late. And when God, too, scatters His orange peels down from the clouds, as the story returns to the storm at sea, Grunye is just as adamant as her sister: "Hodesl will not bow down! Hodesl will not bow down!"

"A twin who takes upon herself the incompleted loves and hatreds of her murdered sister," in Wisse's words, "is Sutzkever's ideal symbol for the survivor who perpetuates 'the half' that is dead."[33] Grunye is the storyteller so driven by her tale that she will seek out anyone, anywhere, who can help her recollect the life of the deceased. (The narrator, we learned midway into the story, was once in love with Hodesl, which explains why Grunye sought him out in the cafeteria.) Grunye is also the angry prophet who throws God's paltry reparations back in His face. There is no easy way to tell a story after the Holocaust. For each tale to tell the truth, it must link prophecy with horror, merge messianic time with the journalistic precision of a diary, engage the still living with the never fully dead.

Prophecy and profanity meet only on the border of reality—exactly as charted by Der Nister but readjusted for an Israeli landscape—where Old Jaffo meets the ocean shore in a tremendous storm, or at the western wall of the temple at the very moment when Jerusalem is reunified. There, at the wall, the storyteller-survivor meets the owner of the messiah's diary, Yonte the Chiromancer, better known as the Yeshiva-bokher with the Three Eyes.[34] This story too, like "The Slaughterknife's Daughter," "Janina and the Beast," "The Twins," and "The First Wedding in Town," yokes a romantic and a horrific plot; romantic insofar as it describes the genesis

of the storyteller's poetic vision, and horrific insofar as Yonte, once dom-
iciled in the Vilna ghetto, now resides in the world to come, where censorship and oblivion are banished. "I remember" is Yonte's sixfold refrain
in a monologue perhaps unmatched in all of Sutzkever's published writings.

> I remember how they fought over a piece of horsemeat, dubbed *susine* by the
> ghetto people; I remember a mother whose child was torn away from her and
> her screams made the trees turn grey from shock; I remember a boy who
> called out to his friend: "Drink eau de Cologne and you'll turn into toilet
> soap"; I remember a passer-by being called for a *minyan* and he lifted up his
> fist against himself and cried: "Pray, I dare you, when Hitler has gone into
> partnership with God!" I remember how the *goyim* hung a sign above the
> municipal slaughterhouse that read: GHETTO. And I remember how the
> rulers of the Jerusalem of Lithuania played chess with pieces carved out of
> Jewbone. (*Akvarium,* 152)

The memory lives on, albeit only among the dead. Their words linger, albeit
only at chosen border crossings. Some of this becomes the stuff of stories,
recorded in some arcane Jewish script, and written in a convoluted archaic
style, preserved in some kind of diary, or scroll, that will probably lie
hidden and unread—until the Messiah comes.

The two Yosls—Bergner and Birstein—met in the port city of Gdynia. Both
seventeen-year-olds were leaving Poland for Australia, where members of
their family had already settled. But whereas Bergner carried a valise full
of papers belonging to his father, the eminent Yiddish poet Melech Ravitch,
and had spent the last eleven years of his life in the heart of Jewish Warsaw,
Birstein came from an impoverished home in the godforsaken town of Biala
Podlaska (population 6,874), where the only source of Yiddish novels were
installments cut out of the Warsaw papers, borrowed from the town's one
and only bookbinder. Even more, Bergner had a girlfriend in a stylish green
beret who came all the way from Warsaw to see him off, while Birstein was
celibate. Neither boy had enough money to bribe the Polish barber who
shaved the heads of these dirty *zhids* before they left the motherland for
good, in 1937. Shorn of their locks, the boys sailed to London and from
there to Le Havre across the English Channel. Next they traveled to Paris

(where a Jewish taxi driver took Birstein into his home over the protests of his non-Jewish wife), and on to Marseilles. From Marseilles they took another boat to North Africa (in Algiers both Yosls were fleeced by a street urchin wearing a Star of David) to Fiji, and from Fiji a third boat, the *Pierre Loti*, destined for Sidney, Australia. Jewish tailors aboard the *Pierre Loti*, meanwhile, protested the French cuisine of wine and bloody meat and addressed a petition to Melech Ravitch requesting a Jewish diet of chopped liver, chicken soup, and the like, which Bergner refused to endorse on the grounds that his father was a vegetarian.[35]

The hijinks of these two Polish lads, who went on to share a tent for four and a half years in the labor corps of the Australian army, and settled (with their respective wives) in Israel within two years of each other, have entered the annals of modern Jewish culture because both of them became storytellers in their respective media, with a penchant for the irreverent and the grotesque. The story of how Yosl Birstein became a storyteller is just as compelling as the stories he learned to tell.

Australia, off the beaten track, became an outpost of militantly secular Yiddish culture. Melbourne in particular, where both Yosls settled, was (and remains) a stronghold of the Jewish Labor Bund. The apolitical Ravitch, who wielded some influence there for a time, left Australia just before his son arrived, relinquishing the field to Pinkhes Goldhar (1901–1947), editor and typesetter of Australia's first Yiddish weekly, mentor of the antiestablishment Society for Contemporary Art. Also aspiring to high art, Birstein wrote verse, in between odd jobs in the *shmatte* business. These short lyrics about the life of a young Jew *Under Alien Skies* were well matched by Bergner's somber realistic drawings. Before leaving for Israel, in 1950, Birstein helped to edit a posthumous edition of Goldhar's stories and essays about Australian Jewish life.[36]

Similar dreams of transplanting the serious and secular traditions of Yiddish literature onto virgin soil inspired ten young poets and prose writers fresh off the boat from Europe, Australia, and Cypress to form a group called Yung-Yisroel (Young Israel). And a new mentor, in the person of Abraham Sutzkever, appeared on the scene to offer the Young Vilna of his own youth as a model and his new quarterly as their forum, until they could strike out on their own. Because most of them were survivors of one hell or another, and because they were committed Zionists of one stripe or another, they tried to use Yiddish as a bridge across time and place. The landscape of Zion fairly cried out for biblical-liturgical analogies, despite their secular upbringing. Rivka Bassman (b. 1925) heard God's voice from a pyre burning in the field. H. Binyomin (pen name of Benjamin Hrushovski-Harshav, b. 1928) discovered God's hand in the primeval rawness of the desert. Avrom Rinzler (b. 1923) refracted the reality of Israel through overlaying prisms. "Terra Sancta," he apostrophized, "rozhinkes mit Manger / iber ale dayne zamdn" (raisins and Manger / over all your sands.)[37]

Birstein belonged to the sober end of the spectrum. For one thing, he joined the left-wing Kibbutz Gevat and became a shepherd, which gave him time to think but little encouragement to develop as a writer. At the inaugural meeting of Yung-Yisroel, convened in Meshek Yagur, autumn 1951, Birstein confronted the anomaly of living as a *halutz*, a Hebrew pioneer, while still feeding off the Yiddish books of a diaspora existence. Rejecting all utilitarian or sentimental reasons for the perpetuation of Yiddish (a bulwark against assimilation, a repository of the past), he insisted that the justification he sought was "only here, within the life lived by the people."[38] For another, he switched abruptly from writing poetry to prose.[39]

The other prose writers in the group—Zvi Eisenman, Avrom Karpinovitsh, and Shloyme Vorzoger—favored the short story and a setting that could bridge the Old World and the New: a Warsaw courtyard miraculously visited by a Sephardic donkey driver (in a fine dreamlike story of Eisenman's), or a motley crew of Jewish laborers paving "The Road to Sodom" (Karpinovitsh).[40] Usually the dialogue betrays a preference for the Yiddish-speaking characters. Birstein almost at once set his sights on the novel, situated in a kibbutz, where even a casual perusal of the bulletin board reveals "different names entirely, which didn't mesh with the names of a prior generation and generations."[41] "Kibbutz Yallon," described in a leisurely manner by a narrator who luxuriates over routine events and offers up only snatches of meaningless dialogue, resembles nothing so much as the existential wilderness of David Bergelson's prerevolutionary shtetl. With its focus on ordinary people embroiled in mundane pursuits, Birstein's *On Narrow Paths* subverts the cultural agendas of both the Yiddish and the Hebrew literary establishment.[42] Not surprisingly, Birstein left the kibbutz in 1960, a year after the Hebrew translation of his novel appeared. He took a job as a bank clerk in the nearby town of Kiryat Tivon, surely the worst of all petty-bourgeois professions.[43]

Yung-Yisroel ceased its group activities at about this time, and it was now each writer for himself. Abandoning all pretense to render the new Israeli reality, Karpinovitsh, for one, carved out a comfortable niche with highly idealized tales of the Vilna Jewish underworld. A perennial favorite among Yiddish readers, they bespoke a time when every Yiddish-speaking whore had a heart of gold and kidnappers always took pity on their victims.[44]

For Birstein, the Yiddish past was neither exotic nor glorious. From the moment he arrived in Israel, he abdicated responsibility for the fate of the Jewish people and accepted the "normal" existence of a new nation on its own soil as his artistic and ideological baseline. Casting off the two pillars of postwar Yiddish literature—utopian faith and collective lamentation—he refused to prop up his "folk Jews" with great idealistic strivings, as did Trunk, or to endow his Holocaust victims and survivors with prophetic powers, as did Sutzkever. Birstein the hardnosed realist was thus faced with a new nation in the making, which could manage perfectly well without benefit of highbrow novels in Yiddish. So he stopped writing altogether, for almost ten years, in the familiar midlife crisis that marks the careers of so many modern Yiddish writers.

His rebirth as a teller of tales came about when under the topsoil of the New World he unearthed remnants of the Old. Once on the kibbutz, desperate for a better work assignment, he latched onto the goatherd by retelling Sholem Aleichem's story of "The Haunted Tailor" and his goat. A week into the story it emerged that the fellow didn't understand a word of Yiddish, though he laughed in all the right places.[45] Instead of merely invoking the world of Sholem Aleichem, however, Birstein could actually *relive* it, once he started clerking in a provincial bank. His tragicomic vision of the bank as the great Jewish dream machine, greased by a nation of Menakhem-Mendls, later inspired his second novel, *The Collector* (1981).[46] Yet customers in the bank were no more likely to speak Yiddish to "Adon Yosl" than they would on the kibbutz. To devote himself solely to writing, Birstein moved to the development town of Upper Nazereth where, for the first time since his youth he could hear Yiddish spoken in the streets by ordinary Jews from all walks of immigrant life. And so, while continuing to draw only from "within the life lived by the people," that life now reverberated with echoes from the past.

In the meantime Yosl Bergner had become an accomplished visual artist. Through his old friend, Birstein encountered the very un-Yiddish world of a former insurance-company executive named Kafka, where the spare, visual perspective was grotesquely out of joint. Bergner's new style of simplified line drawings, devoid of foreground and background, retained a strong narrative flow that was a perfect complement to stories by Kafka, and later by Birstein. Also through Bergner, Birstein began a close collaboration with his first Israeli translator, the Bulgarian-born playwright Nissim Aloni. Bergner, Birstein, and Aloni became something of a threesome in the Tel Aviv–Haifa artistic scene. Accompanied by his new literary contacts and sensibilities, Birstein was now free to revisit the lost worlds of Yiddish—as an outsider.[47]

To signal his new insider-outsider status, Birstein switched to writing in the first person. Henceforth, as an eyewitness, he was no longer privy to the thoughts of his characters and was limited instead to eavesdropping on a conversation through the wall or being otherwise drawn into what people were saying around him. Birstein's formal debut as a Yiddish storyteller came with "A Tale of a Coat of a Prince" (1967), which he dedicated to Audrey and Yosl Bergner.[48]

And a marvelous story it is, for the way it uses a grandfather's princely coat to embody the earthbound dreams of Polish Jews and to chart its fate across several continents.

> During his lifetime he would actually pick up and leave. Once he went out to close the shutters and took off for London. Another time—for America. He returned from London wearing the coat of an English prince. Riding on a bus he met the prince and as they were talking he took a good look at the other man's coat and later made an exact copy of it. And when he came back from America he told us how two gangsters had held him up in the street and demanded his life or his money. So he marched them off to the police station with their hands twisted behind their backs.

The short, action-filled sentences are retold after grandfather's "lifetime," thus allowing the grandson even greater latitude than the mock-legendary coat to roam across time and space. The copied coat that keeps being sent back and forth between Poland and Australia stands for the thread of personal memory that holds this and all of Birstein's subsequent stories together.[49]

But Birstein's time had not yet come: neither his freewheeling manipulation of time and space nor his matter-of-fact focus on street beggars and

Nurit Inbar-Shani, in Yosl Birstein, *Ketem shel sheket: ktsartsarim*
(A Drop of Silence; 1986)

old Jews made waves on the Israeli literary scene. But he did catch the eye
of a still obscure Israeli author named Yaakov Shabtai and of Israel's up-
and-coming cultural impressario, Menahem Perry. The publication of Shabtai's extraordinary first novel, *Past Continuous* (1977), one endless paragraph about memory, male neurosis, and old Tel Aviv, marked a new age
of formal experimentation and anti-ideological prose in Israel. Where the
antics of three ineffectual males could qualify as serious literature, the
ragtag world of Yiddish stories might not be far behind. If anyone could
move what was marginal into the cultural mainstream, Shabtai's publisher
Menahem Perry was the one to do it. With great flair, Perry introduced
Birstein to the readers of his avant-garde journal, *Siman kri'ah* (Exclamation
Point) as a latter-day maggid. Birstein, in turn, obliged his mentor and
future translator by coming across in the interview as a benign, Tevye-like
figure who learned to tell stories by talking to his donkey and embellished
each theoretical point with a string of anecdotes, some of them rather piquant. Later he perfected an image of himself as a schlemiel, a circus clown
who succeeded best when he fell.[50]

Armed with a new style and self-image, and with a new novel under his
belt, Birstein moved to Jerusalem in 1981. The storyteller within him came

to the fore when he discovered that his Hebrew was good enough to dispense with Yiddish. And it happened during the Lebanon war.[51] On the strength of some stories that had appeared in *Siman kri'ah,* Birstein was invited by Galei TSaHaL, the popular and very secular radio station of the Israel Defense Forces, to fill a three-minute slot once a week on Thursday evenings. Having never faced a "sound bite" before, Birstein was at a loss. When he tried to tell a story from notes, forgetting one line threw the whole thing off. When next he came to the studio with a written text, it sounded too wooden. Finally he hit upon a written style that *affected* orality, grabbed the listener within a sentence or two, and began with a chance encounter on the street. This "naked" colloquial style soon won him a national following, plus spot appearances on television, but roused the ire of purists who complained that his Hebrew smacked too much of Yiddish. The critics were right, and yet they were not.[52]

The storyteller was a presence like Sholem Aleichem who, though clearly born in Poland, transcended the barriers of language, age, and ideology. A writer by profession who sometimes threw in a serious comment or two on the craft of writing, Birstein now drew his repertory exclusively from his *landslayt* from Biala Podlaska, his Yiddish teachers from Australia, his old friends from Kibbutz Gevat, his customers from the bank in Tivon, his neighbors from Upper Nazareth, the street beggars of Jerusalem, and especially from strangers sitting on the Number 9 bus, whom he captured in a series of related vignettes. By rearranging these encounters analogically instead of chronologically, the storyteller broke open the cramped urban settings of present-day Israel to create his own Yiddish Jerusalem of strange and familiar sights. It was the narrative equivalent of Yosl Bergner in Melbourne conjuring up a Warsaw courtyard peopled by real and fictional Jews. More often than not, though, Birstein played one scene off another, the sublime against the ridiculous, in order to arrive at a moment of suspended animation, a fourth time zone, or what he called "a spell of silence." He credited that juxtaposition of surprise and the sublime, the grotesque and the tragic, to Sholem Aleichem.[53]

Yet nothing could be further from Sholem Aleichem's loquaciousness than stories so short that they required the author to invent a new term: *ktsartsarim,* very-very short stories.[54] No one but the author could get in more than a direct quotation or two. People in extremity, Birstein once explained to an interviewer, taught him the art of brevity. *He is getting off* the bus and *she* is getting on. The driver yells at everyone to move. So she spills out her heart to the narrator in a single line: "Er hot zikh ayngekoyft a shtik fleysh," she says of her husband. "He bought himself a piece of meat," which is to say a lover.[55] And unlike Sholem Aleichem, the stories are often vulgar. With almost maskilic venom, Birstein describes a Jewish matchmaker in Jerusalem sitting opposite "with his feet spread out and his hat pushed up, as if he were getting ready to put on his tefillin. The crotch of his pants was half ajar and his mouth, too. Both gave off a bit of darkness and emptiness" (Y 59, H 49). Small wonder that the pious matchmaker is later overheard to talk shop as if his crotch were in his mouth. Whatever the mini-tale's particular thrust—satiric or atmospheric—its driving force is the observant traveler moving effortlessly from present to past imperfect.

Birstein replaced Sholem Aleichem's multiple narrators with himself. Instead of Berl Vinegar who told it to the merchant from Haissin who retold it to the traveling salesman who records it for us—that old trick reemployed by Sholem Aleichem to restore a lost cultural dialogue—Birstein used his little tales to restore a temporal dialogue within himself. "How is a story made?" he asked outright. There was a lost uncle who once paid him a visit, accompanied by his petite aunt, and Uncle leaned his substantial arm on her head as they walked from the bus. And that arm reminded the nephew of another, once belonging to Yankev the Coachman, his one-time neighbor in Kiryat Tivon, who claimed that he could wrestle a bull to the ground with those arms, back in Poland, and were Yosl to "give him five" would gladly prove his vigor even now—but for ten years Yosl didn't take him up on it until Yankev lay dying, reduced to a small bundle of humanity. Then, thinking there was nothing more to fear, Yosl felt the hand of a dying man that had not lost its cunning. The same thing happened to a bull once on Kibbutz Gevat: in the morning he was all vigor; in the evening, all that remained was his flayed hide, lying in a heap. These disparate memory traces of arms, hands, and bundles came together at the end of Uncle's visit as they walked back to the bus stop and passed Uri the Rumanian examining a leather hide, saying that he wondered whether the hide would ever produce a good pair of shoes. That is also how a story is made.[56]

Birstein achieved the great dream of emancipating Yiddish from the dead weight of the past by emancipating his stories from most everything that modern Yiddish literature held sacred: folklore as Torah; Hasidism as guardian of the Jewish spirit; the shtetl as home of Jewish solitude and solidarity; Jerusalem as model city of God; poetry as prophecy; the Holocaust as source of revelation; history as collective memory. In Birstein's travels through Meah Shearim, he came upon a young hasid wrestling a skimpily clad female correspondent down to the ground ("The Girl and the Yeshiva Student"). His recollections of Biala Podlaska include a scene of his father going down the list of all the prominent Jews who might support his appeal before the local leather magnate; the father in the end erases all the names ("The List"). The son turns down an apartment in the orthodox neighborhood of Jerusalem because it reminds him too much of home: "I was raised in this kind of crowded, noisy environment. The shutters closed on summer nights so as to block even the tiniest bit of shouting from the outside are still etched into my memory" ("Still Life"). His parting shot of Jacob Weislitz is of the aging Yiddish actor declaiming the most famous of Leivick's poems in front of an antisemitic drunk on a Melbourne trolleycar ("A Yiddish Actor"). No genuflection to the past.

Traveling by bus—the most public, plebeian, and presentist mode of transport in Israel (the radio news is always on)—was Birstein's way of saluting and finally subverting the great Sholem Aleichem. Like the third-class compartment in tsarist Russia, the Egged bus was the locus of "the folk," the place where all its dreams and disappointments were played out. But Birstein's scheme allows for no heroes or histrionics, no mad monologuists who steal the show, if only between stops. When all the world's an Egged bus, "nothing is inherently strange or marginal" because

> Lots of things happen on the bus. One of the passengers wants a seat. He feels humiliated by the other passengers. He's a blue collar worker. You can see it from the color of his beard that's growing prickly, always in bitterness. The whole bus looks at him as if he were some misfit on the margins of society. Until the bus pulls up in front of a *ma'abara* [a transit camp for new immigrants during the fifties], and he goes out, and two or three kids are waiting for him, *Aba, Aba,* and they embrace him, and they rejoice in him, and he with them. Is he on the margins of life just because the bus looked at him that way?[57]

Rehabilitated, but given no lines of his own to speak, the blue-collar worker is remembered for his basic humanity.

This radical flattening of perspective is much more pronounced in the original, Hebrew version of his stories than in their Yiddish translation, done at Sutzkever's bidding. The Hebrew stories are numbered, 1 to 101, while the Yiddish stories each carry a separate, often interpretive, title. Birstein's daughter, Nurit Inbar-Shani, adorned each of the Hebrew stories with a semi-abstract (and occasionally bawdy) sketch to create the overall effect of a modern *Thousand and One Nights*. A few hyperrealistic line drawings accompany the Yiddish, making the stories seem almost journalistic by contrast. The Hebrew collection has the modernist title *Ketem shel sheket* (A Drop of Silence), while the Yiddish promises a reverential journey through *Your Alleys—Jerusalem*. The Hebrew style is clipped and very colloquial. The Yiddish is wordier, full of parenthetical clauses. "I picked up the two baskets and went to Mahane Yehuda," is the way Birstein began the first of his stories, in Hebrew. "I got there from the other end, not from Jaffo Street, and there the entrance to the market was blocked. Lots of people. I decided to wait it out. I found some shade next to an electric pole—it was really hot—and I waited. When they thin out, I'll go in." In Yiddish it sounds something like this:

> With two baskets I set out for Mahane Yehudah, the large market in Jerusalem, to buy something for the house. I arrived there from the other side, not from

Nurit Inbar-Shani, in Yosl Birstein, *Ketem shel sheket* (1986)

Jaffo Street, and there the entrance was packed with people. It was really hot, between two and three p.m., so I positioned myself to wait it out in the shadow of an electric pole. When they start thinning out, I'll make my way into the market.

The Hebrew was based on the live performance of these stories on the Israeli airwaves before an extremely diverse Hebrew-speaking audience. Later Birstein honed his craft by taking the show on the road to kibbutzim, adult education groups, hostels for new immigrants, where he told an average of fifty stories per program and was followed around by a graduate student from a university theater department who took copious notes.[58]

Here, at last, we can see in minute detail how a born-again Jewish storyteller tells his stories live; how he dresses ("Yosl . . . always wears the same shirt. A black polo shirt in the winter, a blue-and-white striped shirt with short sleeves in the summer"), and how his body language speaks a version of himself, never of his characters. We learn how he refines and recycles his stories over time in response to verbal cues from the audience, and how the slapdash nature of the event is of a piece with his stated goals: neither to inform nor to instruct but rather "to open hiddden rooms" of human experience. "Yosl," the student avers, is a "unique phenomenon" on the Israeli cultural scene.

This kind of attention is usually lavished on storytellers who perform a traditional repertory among their own, say, in a Hungarian peasant community transplanted lock, stock, and barrel across the Danube during World War II, or in a Yiddish-speaking immigrant community in present-day Toronto, Canada.[59] Yosl's repertory and audience, in contrast, are as changeable as the airwaves. The spoken versions of his tales (we learn from the Israeli graduate student) differ significantly from their written form. She may or may not know how radically the Hebrew differs from the Yiddish; the latter is a cleaned-up, drawn-out, literary version designed for diaspora consumption. When Birstein speaks and writes in Hebrew, his stories are suitably wacky and low-keyed. In Yiddish he aspires to eternity. Yes, Birstein found the lost art of storytelling and a living Jewish audience—but in so doing, he lost Yiddish.[60]

When they returned to storytelling, in the hope of harnessing the folk tradition, writers put their own lives on the storyline. Some, like Reb Nahman, Peretz, Der Nister, Singer, and Sutzkever, displaced their personal struggle and rebellion onto a metaphysical plane. Others, like Dik, Sholem Aleichem, Manger, Trunk, and Yosl Birstein, made themselves into the folk's repository, salvaging both its wisdom and its folly. As tellers of exotic places, those of the messianic-supernatural school preferred the fairy tale and romance. As tellers of local traditions, those grounded in the present preferred to adopt the legend and ballad. No one can argue that one approach is more "authentically Jewish" than the other, though readers are certainly free to make their own choice.

Storytelling, subject to the dictates of generations past, but open to new models of personal heroism and villainy, to new maps of home and exile—this universally accessible form of self-expression offers a unique perspective on how Jewish culture has changed in modern times. Whereas the tales of Reb Nahman reveal the earliest breakthrough in Jewish eastern Europe of a singular narrative style and an anguished sensibility, the storybooks of Isaac Meir Dik reveal the staying power of the homiletic tradition among the self-styled reformers. Hasidism at its most daring and the Haskalah at its most didactic meet in the selfsame medium. Nahman and Dik launched the first of four phases in the revival of Yiddish storytelling. They vastly expanded the existing repertory of plots and players. Through their seekers and saints, wise men and simpletons, rabbis and merchants, flunkies and fakes, they redrew the map of redemption, either *from* history or *through* history.

Before a new phase was ushered in, there came a thorough revision of the old. A class of Jewish revolutionaries arose whose first objective was to burn the bridges that linked them to the traditions of generations past. At the height of his rebellion, Peretz invited the readers of his *Holiday Folios* to a socialist seder—sans miracles, stripped of all national significance, even devoid of Passover prayers. The Jewish left, increasingly identified with the language of the laboring masses, proclaimed the Messiah and Judaism dead in its authorized hymn of 1902, written by S. Ansky. As late as the 1930s Jewish socialist scouts in Vilna and environs (among whose ranks was a young Sutzkever) were marching to the rhyme, "So never tire of hammering and stick to your last / For ours is to liberate the present from the past!"[61]

The same group of rebels who had so drastically contracted the universe of Jewish discourse (*tsimtsum* by any other name) then set out in search of a usable secular past. Storytelling became the vessel into which a new ideology of the folk was poured, whether amalgamated from a class of spiritual rebels (Peretz) or from a crew of schlemiels who could talk their way out of any corner (Sholem Aleichem). Purim, Passover, Hanukkah, and Hoshana Rabba were turned into folk fests by this second generation of Yiddish storytellers as a way of reestablishing the necessary engagement with the people—the folk—who might compensate for the loss of an ancient civilization by proving to be the truest resource for renewal.

With the apocalypse of World War I, the Bolshevik revolution, and the Ukrainian civil war, the rehabilitation of the lost folk was obsolete. The next generation of Yiddish writers resorted to storytelling both as an escape from the strictures of realism and as a response to the anarchic forces that history itself had unleashed. Whether reining those forces in through lyrical farce (Manger), or giving voice to them through idealistic and nihilistic fantasy (Der Nister, Singer), the third generation of Yiddish storytellers treated the received traditions—Jesus, Satan, and Elijah; Hans Christian Andersen, Reb Nahman, and Peretz—as if they were treasures of the ancien régime: a set of symbols waiting to be looted. As reward for this ecumenical piracy, Yiddish storytellers taught their folk, their hermits, beggars, stargazers, demons, and imps, their lovers and fornicators of all ages, how best to negotiate the new frontier of the storyteller's mindscape. Yiddish storytelling between the wars was betrayed in the name of positive eclecticism and through a decisive shift from objective to subjective reality.

With phase three, the story should have ended because 3 is the magic number of Indo-European folklore; 3 is the dialectical movement of rebellion, loss, and return we have been following throughout; and 3 is the triad of tale, teller, and audience. With the Yiddish tale and ballad redressed in modernist drag, with the dispersion of the Yiddish-speaking folk, and the death of the last of its big entertainers, Singer, the whole story should have drawn to a close. But it did not, for three reasons.

(1) The art of modern Yiddish storytelling cannot be understood merely as a layering process, as Walter Benjamin would have it, of local traditions and exotic lore recycled by a master craftsman living or pretending to live in preindustrial time. Our master metaphor is triage, not ecology. At every stage, beginning with Reb Nahman of Bratslav (who properly belongs in the Jewish Middle Ages), storytelling represented that which could be salvaged in the wake of spiritual, historical, or personal crisis. The ruptures of time and space—as opposed to the filial loyalty of prodigal sons or the

essential bond between Yiddish and *yidishkayt*—made it far more likely that the lost Yiddish folk art would be found again.

(2) One more generation of Polish-born storytellers remained. As Jewish rebels whom historical forces had cast into exile far from the land of their dreams, they perfected the autobiographical story in order to create a personal—and portable—memorial. Trunk recast his life as melodrama, with Peretz acting the proud patriarch and all of Polish Jewry playing the extras. Sutzkever staged a symbolic drama in which acts of miraculous rescue—including his own—testified to the survival of the dead. Using a minimalist set design, in the style of Israeli avant-garde, Birstein introduced a fourth, and very un-Yiddish, dimension of recollected time—the zone of silence.

(3) Lost and found, the art of Yiddish storytelling is being transmitted yet again, this time through but not in Yiddish. Birstein delivers his three-minute story segments on the radio in a Yiddishized Hebrew, while far, far away from Yiddishdom the following reenactment occurs.

Having returned home to Memphis, Tennessee, after a long and unproductive detour through New York and London, the writer Steve Stern lands a job at the Center for Southern Folklore. Weeks and months of transcribing archival tapes finally yields a legendary landscape literally on his own doorstep, at a time when "the bayous would back up and the basin of Beale Street itself would be transformed into a lagoon, across which its citizens would ferry themselves in lantern-hung wooden skiffs." "And wouldn't you know it," he adds in the next breath, "there were Jews in it too." And because Memphis isn't Minsk, and America isn't Poland, Stern is made director of the Ethnic Heritage Project, his mandate to resurrect "the old ghetto community of the Pinch from its current desolation along North Main Street." Second-generation Jewish Memphisites, though reluctant this late in life to revive the seamier side of their parents' past, are coopted into the cultural restoration of their ethnic heritage. What happens next? The inevitable last act in the melodrama of creative betrayal. This improbable cast of characters takes over Stern's fiction—now reshaped into stories and monologues, but informed by a thin layer of irony and a sustained reading of Malamud ånd Manger. One of Stern's most memorable characters, Shimmele Fly-by-Night, recapitulates "The Adventures of Hershel Summerwind," with Manger's plot adapted for a southern American clime.[62]

What survives even when the storyteller gets his material in translation (courtesy of the Howe and Greenberg *Treasury of Yiddish Stories*) is the paradigm of rebellion, loss, and negotiated return. "What an amazing home Jewish culture is," writes the filmmaker Michal Goldman, chronicler of the klezmer music revival in America, "that generation after generation ends up straggling back, our pockets stuffed with all the flotsam and jetsam of the world beyond."[63] Since their headlong embrace of modernity left them cut off from both past and future, the heroes of this story cast about for something they can make to serve as a buttress against assimilation, an affirmation of the human spirit, a personal confession, or a living memorial. Der Nister envisioned a mythic All-Bridge joining the abyss to the palace. After the Destruction, vicarious survivor Jacob Glatstein conjured up a two-way bridge of longing: a diminished God on the one end, His bereaved people on the other. Failing either venue, Yosl Birstein boarded the Number 9 bus in Jerusalem to take in snatches of Jewish conversation.

Once the world of traditional faith collapsed, abandoned from within and beleaguered from without, the voices of the living Jewish past were silenced: the Talmudists, pietists, kabbalists, and preachers; the prayer leaders, wedding bards, and Purim players; the *zogerkes* (women who prompt other women in the prayers), the *klogmuters* (who lament the dead), and the *opshprekherins* (who exorcise the demons)—even the voices of children learning the Hebrew alphabet by rote. New Jewish voices were heard, singing satiric songs and stirring hymns, hawking novels and political treatises, declaiming poems. Amid the cacophony, something old could be heard that somehow sounded new, composed by Yiddish writers who seemed to be flesh of the people's flesh, although in actuality they resided in the more elegant parts of Kiev and Warsaw or in faraway Berlin and Miami Beach. A story here, a song there, nothing too fancy. Sometimes, when the words appeared in print, a local artist would add a touch of color.

Then the cacophony too was silenced. And here is what is left, reverberating in an echo chamber outside time:

> The stargazer said: "Now!" And so they brought out the wedding canopy, and the court was overjoyed with a rare joy, and all caroused with a rare delight, and the two children loved one another and couldn't stop weeping, and— and I, too, was at that wedding and ate gingerbread, and . . . whoever doesn't want to remember this tale, he can forget it.
>
> And the author of this story, one among the honored guests, can bear witness: the first wedding in the city since time immemorial took place—up above, on the mountain, washed very clean beforehand by the rains. The stars

scattered golden wedding gifts and Roytl, more clean and more radiant than all the stars, fluttered beneath them.

They fingered the cushions, poured the wine, and broke the matza—and only then, realizing their guest had been the Prophet Elijah, did they sit down to have a merry seder.

Whatever may be there, it will be real, without complication, without ridicule, without deception. God be praised: there even Gimpel cannot be deceived.

Then let the maker of the tale take his leave of you smiling, and let him wish you, Jews—and all mankind—more laughter than tears. Laughter is good for you. Doctors prescribe laughter.

The storyteller's words stuck in my mind and when the bus pulled up, I couldn't control myself any longer, and on the way home I laid this out in my mind: Uncle placing his hand on his wife's head, the hand of the dying man, small bundles, the coachman and the bull. I asked myself, with Uri the Shoemaker's intonation, Will you ever make a story from all of this?

We left on foot with packs on our backs.

The windows in all the buildings were pasted up with black paper so that Warsaw would lie in darkness at night. We felt as if we were walking inside a black coffin.

Up above Hitler's airplanes stormed the sky like terrible demons.

"Here comes Zeidlus the First," one imp said to the other, "the yeshiva boy who wanted to become pope."

After a while Hell filled up again. New quarters were added, but still the crowding was great.

All those marvelous things cruelly, wantonly stolen from me, taken away, taken away, taken away.

Again somebody else . . . How long will he be somebody else?

"Sad and lovely," the poet says, / "Are the roads of the Holy Book."

And how he freed the princess, the Rebbe did not tell.

But finally he did free her.

Perhaps this is redemption enough for the People of the Lost Book.

Notes · Index

Notes

1. The People of the Lost Book

1. See Barbara Kirshenblatt-Gimblett, "The Concept and Variety of Narrative Performance in East European Jewish Culture," in *Explorations in the Ethnography of Speaking,* 2nd ed., ed. Richard Bauman and Joel Sherzer (London: Cambridge University Press, 1989), pp. 283–308. The quote is from Harris Pearlstone, "Memoirs of a Young Man in Search," unpublished manuscript, translated from the Hebrew by Eli Lederhendler. Pearlstone, born in Stavisk (Stawiski), near Bialystok, in 1870, wrote the first draft of his memoirs in 1889 and revised them in 1945. My thanks to Dr. Lederhendler for making the manuscript available. Similar passages can be found in the fiction and memoirs of Yitskhok Yoel Linetsky, Moshe Leib Lilienblum, Sholem Yankev Abramovitsh, and many others.

2. On the rise of orthodoxy as a studied response to modernity, see the essays by David Ellenson, Michael K. Silber, David E. Fishman, Harvey E. Goldberg, Lawrence Kaplan, and Menachem Friedman in *The Uses of Tradition: Jewish Continuity in the Modern Era,* ed. Jack Wertheimer (New York and Jerusalem: Jewish Theological Seminary, 1992), part 1.

3. David Lowenthal, *The Past Is a Foreign Country* (Cambridge: Cambridge University Press, 1985), chap. 7.

4. *After the Tradition,* a wonderfully ambiguous phrase, is the title of Robert Alter's first collection of *Essays on Modern Jewish Writing* (1969; New York: Dutton, 1971).

5. Robert Escarpit, " 'Creative Treason' as a Key to Literature," *Yearbook of Comparative and General Literature* 10 (1961): 16–21. It was first applied to the study of Jewish culture by Gershon Shaked to describe translations of European and Yiddish clas-

sics into modern Hebrew. See "Between Jewish Tradition and Western Culture," *Ariel* 42 (1976): 46–54.

6. The original Hebrew term for literature was *sifrah* (from Psalms 56:9), first used, it seems, by S. Y. Abramovitsh in *Limdu hetev* (Learn to Do Well; Warsaw, 1862), p. 28. Abramovitsh may also have coined *sifrut*, the term that stuck. See his article "Im kabbalah hi nekabel," *Hamelits* 5 (1865), nos. 34–38, 41–45; reprinted in *Ein mishpat* (The Font of Judgment; Zhitomir, 1867). Ben-Yehudah's first entries for *sifrut* both date from 1868.

7. I. L. Peretz, "What Our Literature Needs," tr. Nathan Halper, *Voices from the Yiddish: Essays, Memoirs, Diaries,* ed. Irving Howe and Eliezer Greenberg (Ann Arbor: University of Michigan Press, 1972), p. 25.

8. Max Weinreich, *History of the Yiddish Language,* trans. Shlomo Noble, with Joshua A. Fishman (Chicago: University of Chicago Press, 1980), pp. 206–210.

9. The folklorization of Jewish life, S. Y. Agnon maintained, was the surest sign of its disintegration. See Dan Ben-Amos, "Nationalism and Nihilism: The Attitudes of Two Hebrew Authors Towards Folklore," *International Folklore Review* 1 (1981): 5–16. "Fakelore" was coined by the American folklorist Richard Dorson in 1950 as a term of opprobrium, but has since become a value-free analytic term to describe the necessary evolution of oral literature in a technological world. See Dorson, *Folklore and Fakelore: Essays toward a Discipline of Folk Studies* (Cambridge, Mass.: Harvard University Press, 1976), esp. pp. 1–29, 67–73; Alan Dundes, "Metafolklore and Oral Literary Criticism," *Monist* 50 (1966): 505–516; Hermann Bausinger, "Toward a Critique of Folklorism Criticism," in *German* Volkskunde: *A Decade of Theoretical Confrontation, Debate, and Reorientation (1967–1977),* ed. James R. Dow and Hannjost Lixfeld (Bloomington: Indiana University Press, 1986), pp. 113–123; Regina Bendix, "Folklorism: The Challenge of a Concept," *International Folklore Review* 6 (1988): 5–15.

10. Upon meeting Sholem Aleichem for the first time in Kiev, Warshawski admitted "that although he once studied in the Rabbinical Seminary (in Zhitomir), he had learned so little *yidishkayt* and forgotten so much, that he could barely commit his own songs to writing." Sholem Aleichem, "Di geshikhte fun Varshavskis lider," in *Yidishe folks-lider fun M. M. Varshavski,* 2nd ed. (New York: Max Meisel, 1918), p. x. The preface was written in Nervi on 20 February 1914.

11. For *Afn pripetshik* and *Der rebe Elimeylekh,* see *Mir trogn a gezang: yidishe arbeter-un folks-lider,* ed. Eleanor Gordon Mlotek, 2nd rev. ed. (New York: Workmen's Circle, 1977), pp. 2, 168.

12. On the alienation of nineteenth-century Yiddish writers from Yiddish and the folk, see Dan Miron, *A Traveler Disguised: A Study in the Rise of Modern Yiddish Fiction in the Nineteenth Century* (New York: Schocken, 1973), esp. chaps. 1–2; and his "Folklore and Antifolklore in the Yiddish Fiction of the *Haskala,*" *Studies in Jewish Folklore,* ed. Frank Talmage (Cambridge, Mass,: Association for Jewish Studies, 1980), pp. 219–249. Yiddish literary scholarship is seriously divided over this issue. Each of the following chapters takes up the question in greater detail.

13. *"Bezalel" shel Schatz 1906–1929,* ed. Nurit Shilo-Cohen, 2nd ed. (Jerusalem: Israel

Museum, 1983); Albert Weisser, *The Modern Renaissance of Jewish Music: Events and Figures, Eastern Europe and America* (New York: Bloch, 1954), chap. 3.

14. The life and work of Rappoport-Ansky warrants a separate chapter. It appears as my Introduction to *The Dybbuk and Other Writings* by S. Ansky (New York: Schocken, 1992), and in a more specialized vein as "S. Ansky and the Paradigm of Return," in *Uses of Tradition,* pp. 243–260.

15. Dan Miron, *Bo'ah, laylah* (Come, O Night: Hebrew Literature Between the Rational and the Irrational at the Turn of the Twentieth Century; Tel Aviv: Dvir, 1987), p. 14.

16. New York and London: New York University Press, 1989.

17. Cambridge, Mass.: Harvard University Press, 1978.

18. *Hapreidah min ha'ani he'ani* (Taking Leave of the Impoverished Self: Ch. N. Bialik's Early Poetry, 1891–1901; Tel Aviv: Open University, 1986). Bialik's famous essay of 1917, "Halachah and Aggadah," was translated by Julius L. Siegel (New York: Bloch, 1923) and deserves greater currency. A complete English translation of his *Sefer ha'aggadah,* coedited with Y. H. Ravnitzky, has recently appeared. See *The Book of Legends (Sefer Ha-Aggadah): Legends from the Talmud and Midrash,* tr. William G. Braude (New York: Schocken, 1992).

19. See Mark W. Kiel, "Vox Populi, Vox Dei: The Centrality of Peretz in Jewish Folkloristics," *Polin* 7 (1992): 88–120; *Yiddish Folktales,* ed. Beatrice Silverman Weinreich, tr. Leonard Wolf (New York: Pantheon, 1988): Sonye di khakhome (nos. 50, 174); Peshe Rive Sher (nos. 22, 102); Khinye Lifshits (nos. 42, 59); Khave Rubin (no. 32), Brokhe di tsulotshnitse (nos. 64, 122, 154); Rokhl Cahan (no. 24). The distinctive styles of these and other women storytellers comes through even in translation.

20. Children's verse: Ida Massey, *Lider far kinder* (Warsaw: Brzoza, 1936); Kadia Molodowsky, *Mayselekh* (Warsaw: Yidishe shul-organizatsye in Poyln, 1931), and *Yidishe kinder* (New York: Tsentral-komitet fun di yidishe folks-shuln, 1945). A grandmother's piety through a narrative veil: Miriam Ulinover, *Der bobes oytser,* photo-offset ed. of Warsaw, 1922, with parallel Hebrew text, tr. Yehoshua Tan Pay (Jerusalem: Mossad Harav Kook, 1975). For a scholarly treatment of these issues, see Kathyrn Hellerstein, " 'A Word for My Blood': A Reading of Kadya Molodowsky's 'Froyen-lider' (Vilna, 1927)," *AJS Review* 13 (1988): 47–79; and her "Faith and Fear: The Subordination of Prayer to Narrative in Modern Yiddish Poems," in *Parable and Story as Sources of Jewish and Christian Theology,* ed. Clemens Thoma and Michael Wyschograd (New York: Paulist Press, 1989), pp. 205–236.

21. See Mark William Kiel, "Bialik and the Transformation of Aggadah into Folklore," chap. 2 of "A Twice Lost Legacy: Ideology, Culture and the Pursuit of Jewish Folklore in Russia until Stalinization (1930–1931)" (Ph.D. diss., Jewish Theological Seminary of America, 1991); and Uzi Shavit, "Shirey-'am belashon she'eynah meduberet," in *Lirikah velahit* (Lyric Poetry and the Lyrics of Pop: The Israeli Popular Song as a Cultural System and a Literary Genre), ed. Ziva Ben-Porat et al. (Tel Aviv: Porter Institute for Poetics and Semiotics, 1989), pp. 254–263.

22. See Jacob Kabakoff, *Naphtali Herz Imber 'Baal hatikvah'* (Lod: Haberman Institute

for Literary Research, 1991), chap 5. On the making of Ansky's *Shvue*, see *The Dybbuk*, p. xvii, and for its prehistory, Moshe Beregovski, "Jewish Folk Music (1934)," in *Old Jewish Folk Music: The Collections and Writings of Moshe Beregovski*, ed. Mark Slobin (Philadelphia: University of Pennsylvania Press, 1982), pp. 34–35.

23. The open letter was published concurrently in *Hamelits* 58 (March 23, 1898); *Hatsfirah* 71 and *Nedyelnaya Khronika Voskhoda* 11, 19 (1898). In his introduction to *Yiddish Folksongs in Russia* (Ramat Gan: Bar-Ilan University Press, 1991), Dov Noy claims that the Russian text was probably more influential. The letter inspired the first essay in Hebrew on the history of folksong research by Pinhas Minkovsky. Despite his erudition and mastery of several European languages, Minkovsky had only the scantiest knowledge of Yiddish songs, which he threw in at the very end. All the texts he cited were in fact songs of known authorship. See "Shirei 'am," *Hashiloah* 5 (1899): 10–20, 105–114, 205–216.

24. All further references are to the photo-offset edition reissued by Dov Noy, which also supplies a Yiddish translation of the Russian-language introduction and notes. Of the 376 songs published (in Yiddish with romanized text), 38 were variants.

25. Judah Leib Cahan, "Dos yidishe folkslid" (1910), in *Shtudyes vegn yidisher folksshafung* (Studies in Jewish Folklore), ed. Max Weinreich (New York: YIVO, 1952), pp. 9–42; quote on p. 41. A shorter version of this introduction appeared in *Literatur* 2 (1910): 122–141, thus forging a link to the Yiddish aestheticists of the Lower East Side. On the latter group, see Ruth R. Wisse, *A Little Love in Big Manhattan: Two Yiddish Poets* (Cambridge, Mass.: Harvard University Press, 1988).

26. See M. Kipnis, *Hundert folks-lider* (Buenos Aires: Tsentral-farband fun poylishe yidn, 1949), pp. 239–240.

27. "A por verter tsu Varshavskis lider fun Sholem-Aleykhem," rpt. in *Yidishe folkslider fun M. M. Varshavski,* 2nd ed., pp. v–xvii.

28. For a brief biography of Engel and a discussion of his role in the Jewish music revival, see Weisser, *Modern Renaissance of Jewish Music,* pp. 31–31, 71–80. See also Beregovski's introduction to "Jewish Folk Songs (1962)" in *Old Jewish Folk Music,* pp. 287–288. All the relevant documents in the Sholem Aleichem–Engel debate have been collected and translated by Menashe Ravina in *Mikhtavim 'al hamusika hayehudit* (Letters on Jewish Music; Tel Aviv: Davar, 1941). For the text of Engel's feuilleton from *Voskhod* 18, see pp. 16–21. The debate has also been summarized by Menashe Geffen in *Mitahat la'arisah 'omedet gdiyah* (Under the Cradle Stands a Kid [In the Footsteps of Jewish Song]: Essays and Studies; Tel Aviv: Sifriat Po'alim, 1986), p. 226.

29. Sholem Aleichem, "A briv tsum h' Engel fun'm 'Voskhod,' " *Der yid* 24 (June 13, 1901): 14–16, or Ravina, pp. 31–38.

30. Ginzburg-Marek, no. 82. The photo-offset edition of 1991 was made from the marked-up copy once owned by Sholem Aleichem. See pp. 113*–114*.

31. Paul Mendes-Flohr, "Fin-de-Siècle Orientalism, the *Ostjuden* and the Aesthetics of Jewish Self-Affirmation," in his *Divided Passions: Jewish Intellectuals and the Experience of Modernity* (Detroit: Wayne State University Press, 1991), pp. 77–132; "Bezalel" shel Schatz, 1906–1929.

32. See "Yidishe folks-mayses" serialized in *Der yid* 1 (1899), nos. 7:13–14, 17:11–12. Two of the three stories were apparently taken from the German-Jewish folklore journal *Urquell*. The impetus to include them, an editorial note explained, was Ginzburg's and Marek's open letter on collecting Yiddish folksongs.

33. *Yidishe folkslider*, ed. Noyakh Prylucki, vol. 1 (Warsaw: Bikher-far-ale, 1910). The name is pronounced "Prilutski," with the accent on the second syllable.

34. This song is beautifully recorded in *Songs of the Bobover Chassidim*, sung by Rabbi Laizer Halberstam, Collector's Guild 627 (also distributed on cassette by House of Menorah). For a succinct summary of the whole subject, see Uriel Weinreich, "Di forshung fun 'mishshprakhike' yidishe folkslider," *YIVO-bleter* 34 (1950): 282–288.

35. The best available guide to Yiddish pop songs in America is *Pearls of Yiddish Song: Favorite Folk, Art and Theatre Songs* ed. Eleanor Gordon Mlotek and Joseph Mlotek (New York: Workmen's Circle, 1988) and the two accompanying cassettes, *Pearls of Yiddish Song* (1990) and *On Wings of Song* WC 21 (1993). Both in turn draw on the pioneering effort of Eleanor Gordon Mlotek and Joseph Mlotek to collect and identify the scattered remains of Yiddish lyrics among first- and second-generation Jews in America. See their *Perl fun der yidisher poezye* (Pearls of Yiddish Poetry; Tel Aviv: Y. L. Perets, 1974), and their weekly column under the same title in the Yiddish-language *Forverts*.

36. For Zeitlin's two theater songs, "Dona, Dona" (1940) and "Reb Motenyu," see *Pearls of Yiddish Song*, pp. 142, 175. For a spirited defense of Lebedeff's songs, see my "Ideologies of the Yiddish Folksong in the Old Country and the New," *Jewish Book Annual* 50 (1992–93): 161–166.

37. As they do in Don Bluth's animated feature film *An American Tail* (1986) and in Barbara Lebow's play *A Shayna Maidel* (New American Library, 1988), to name a few American examples.

38. Jack Wertheimer, "The German-Jewish Experience: Toward a Usable Past," *The German-Jewish Legacy in America, 1938–1988: A Symposium*, ed. Abraham J. Peck, special issue of *American Jewish Archives* 40 (1988). See also Gerson D. Cohen, "German Jewry as Mirror of Modernity," *Leo Baeck Institute Year Book* 20 (1975): xi; Steven E. Aschheim, *Brothers and Strangers: The East European Jew in German and German Jewish Consciousness, 1800–1923* (Madison: University of Wisconsin Press, 1982), p. 213.

39. On Havurat Shalom and its ideology, see *The New Jews*, ed. James A. Sleeper and Alan L. Mintz (New York: Vintage, 1971), and Riv-Ellen Prell, *Prayer and Community: The Havurah in American Judaism* (Detroit: Wayne State University Press, 1989).

40. Mark Zborowski and Elizabeth Herzog, *Life Is with People: The Culture of the Shtetl* (1952), foreword by Margaret Mead (New York: Schocken, 1962).

2. The Master of Prayer: Nahman of Bratslav

1. See Manger's Afterword to *Noente geshtaltn un andere shriftn* (Intimate Portraits and Other Writings; New York: Itsik Manger yoyvl-komitet, 1961), p. 516.

2. Walter Benjamin, "The Storyteller: Reflections on the Works of Nikolai Leskov" (1936), in *Illuminations*, tr. Harry Zohn, ed. Susan Sontag (New York: Schocken, 1968), pp. 83–109.

3. For the Jewish presence at the Jonesborough festival, see Peninnah Schram, "Telling Stories at NAPPS," *Jewish Storytelling Newsletter*, 1:2 (Winter 1986): 7.

4. Haim Schwarzbaum provides all the relevant variants in *The Mishle Shu'alim (Fox Fables of Rabbi Berechiah Ha-Nakdan): A Study in Comparative Folklore and Fable Lore* (Kiron: Institute for Jewish and Arab Folklore Research, 1979), pp. 394–408.

5. Baruch M. Bokser, "Wonder-Working and the Rabbinic Tradition: The Case of Hanina ben Dosa," *Journal for the Study of Judaism* 16 (1985): 77.

6. See Dan Ben-Amos, "Generic Distinctions in the Aggadah," *Studies in Jewish Folklore*, ed. Frank Talmage (Cambridge, Mass.: Association for Jewish Studies, 1980), pp. 66–67, and M[enahem] E[llon], "Ma'aseh," *Encyclopedia Judaica* 11:641–49.

7. Bokser, pp. 42–51.

8. Eliezer ben Hyrcanus, *The Fathers According to Rabbi Nathan*, chap. 6; and *Midrash Pirkei de Rabbi Eliezer*, trans. Gerald Friedlander (New York: Sepher-Hermon, 1981; rpt. London, 1916), chap. 2. This last is a sustained (and relatively late) cluster of biographical tales and traditions, which do not, however, build up to a climax. The account of Eliezer ben Hyrcanus' excommunication is absent. On Rabbi Akiva, see my *Against the Apocalypse: Responses to Catastrophe in Modern Jewish Culture* (Cambridge, Mass.: Harvard University Press, 1984), pp. 27–30.

9. The major exponent of the emancipation theory of Hebrew narrative prose is Joseph Dan, in *Hasippur ha'ivri bimei habeinayim* (The Hebrew Story in the Middle Ages; Jerusalem: Keter, 1974); précis in "Fiction, Hebrew," *Encyclopedia Judaica* 6:1261–1271. For a followup, see his "Letoldoteha shel sifrut hashvahim," *Jerusalem Studies in Jewish Folklore* 1 (1981): 82–100. In contrast, folklorists Heda Jason, Sara Zfatman, Tamar Alexander, and Eli Yassif stress the interplay of oral and written sources, learned and folk traditions, Hebrew and vernacular languages. Once they account for the strict conventions of folk literature and the conservative nature of any textual tradition, the desire or ability of medieval Jewish editors and compilers to achieve a free-flowing, "original" narrative appears greatly diminished. A third approach, exemplified by Jacob Elbaum, is to trace the subtle reworking of discrete motifs within their dense and immediate textual setting. See e.g. "From Sermon to Story: The Transformation of the Akedah," *Prooftexts* 6 (1986): 97–116.

10. Sara Zfatman-Biller, "Hasipporet beyidish mireshitah 'ad 'Shivhei haBesht' (1504–1814)" (Ph.D. diss., Hebrew University, 1983), vol. 1, pp. 9, 116–121.

11. Ibid., p. 97.

12. For the full text, see Sarah Zfatman, *Yiddish Narrative Prose from Its Beginnings to "Shivhei ha-Besht" (1504–1814): An Annotated Bibliography* (Jerusalem: Hebrew University, 1985), no. 17.

13. Though neither a scholarly nor a complete edition, Jacob Meitlis' annotated translation of the *Mayse-bukh* into modern Yiddish conveniently groups the stories into literary-historical clusters and refers the reader to alternative sources. See vol. 38

of the *Musterverk fun der yidisher literatur* (Buenos Aires: Literatur-gezelshaft baym YIVO, 1969). For a bowdlerized English ed., see *Maaseh Book,* 2 vols., ed. Moses Gaster (Philadelphia: Jewish Publication Society, 1934).

14. See Eli Yassif, "What Is a Folk Book?" *International Folklore Review* 5 (1987): 20–27. For one example of the refolklorization process, cf. "Eliyohu Hanovi un di dray zin" (Meitlis, no. 37; Gaster, no. 157) with "Der vortzoger," *Yidishe folks-mayses,* ed. J. L. Cahan (Vilna: YIVO, 1940), no. 23. Both are variants of "The Lazy Boy," AT 675. On the integration of Yiddish within the culture of medieval Ashkenaz, see Max Weinreich, *History of the Yiddish Language,* tr. Shlomo Noble and Joshua A. Fishman (Chicago: University of Chicago Press, 1980), chap. 3.

15. The quotation is from *Sefer ḥayyei MOHaRaN hamenukad* (Jerusalem, 1985), sec. 25. On the place of the tale in Beshtian Hasidism, see Joseph Dan, *Hasippur hahasidi* (The Hasidic Tale; Jerusalem: Keter, 1975), pp. 40–46; Mendl Piekarz, *Ḥasidut Braslav* [Bratslav Hasidism] (Jerusalem: Bialik Institute, 1972), pp. 104–105; and esp. Khone Shmeruk, *Prokim fun der yidisher literatur-geshikhte* (Yiddish Literature: Aspects of its History; Tel Aviv: I. L. Peretz, 1988), p. 253. Much has been written about the sanctity of the hasidic tale. Arguing for the absolute sanctity of the tale within all of hasidic tradition is Gedalia Nigal in *Hasipporet hahasidit: toldoteha venos'eha* (The Hasidic Tale: Its History and Topics; Jerusalem: Marcus, 1981), pp. 57–80. Piekarz (pp. 85–101) and Shmeruk (chap. 6) take a more casual view, one more recently corroborated by Yehoshua Mondshein in his facsimile and variorum ed. of *Sefer shivḥei haBesht* (Jerusalem, 1982), pp. 52–57. The debate is well summarized by Ada Rapoport-Albert in "Hagiography with Footnotes: Edifying Tales and the Writing of History in Hasidism," *History and Theory Beiheft* 27 (1988): 153–155. A new critical ed. of *Shivḥei haBesht* was published (posthumously) by Avraham Rubinstein (Jerusalem: Rubin Mass, 1991).

16. These words are quoted in Yiddish in Nathan of Nemirov's first Hebrew preface to the *Tales.* All Yiddish quotations (abbreviated Y) are from *Seyfer sipurey mayses* (Jerusalem: Keren hadpasah shel ḥasidei Braslav, 1979), a bilingual edition of the *Tales* based on the 1st ed. of 1815. This beautiful volume is the closest thing to a scholarly edition of the *Tales* now available and is the first in 164 years to restore the Yiddish to its original southeastern dialect. Professional Yiddishists and Bratslav hasidim refer to the town as "Breslov" or "Broslev." See e.g. the note "On Breslov" appended to Aryeh Kaplan's *Gems of Rabbi Nachman* (Jerusalem: Yeshivat Chasidei Breslov, 1980). I adopt the more common spelling.

17. Arthur Green, *Tormented Master: A Life of Rabbi Nahman of Bratslav* (University: University of Alabama Press, 1979), chap. 5; Yehuda Liebes, "*Ha-Tikkun Ha-Kelali* of R. Nahman of Bratslav and Its Sabbatean Links," in his *Studies in Jewish Myth and Jewish Messianism,* tr. Batya Stein (Albany: SUNY Press, 1993), pp. 115–150; Yoav Elstein, *Ma'aseh ḥoshev* (Studies in Hasidic Tales; Tel Aviv: Eked, 1983), chap. 6.

18. Green, chap. 5.

19. E stands for Arnold Band's translation, *Nahman of Bratslav: The Tales* (New York:

Paulist Press, 1978). To simplify matters, all page references are to this translation, even when I deviate from it.

20. *Sefer siḥot haRaN,* ed. Nathan Sternherz (Jerusalem: Keren ḥasidei Braslav, 1978), sec. 52. For discussion, see Piekarz, p. 111.

21. The analogy between Nahman and the Grimms was first drawn by Arnold Band. See his ed. of *Tales,* p. 29–30. See also *The Brothers Grimm and Folktale,* ed. James M. McGlathery (Urbana: University of Illinois Press, 1991).

22. I owe this insight to an unpublished paper by Seth Brody on the kabbalistic symbolism of Nahman's tales.

23. On the basic distinction between *Sage* (legend) and *Märchen* (fairy tale, folktale), introduced by the Grimms and now universally recognized, see Max Lüthi, *Once Upon a Time: On the Nature of Fairy Tales,* tr. Lee Chadeayne and Paul Gottwald, ed. Francis Lee Utley (Bloomington: Indiana University Press, 1976); William Bascom, "The Forms of Folklore: Prose Narratives," *Sacred Narratives,* ed. Alan Dundes (Berkeley: University of California Press, 1984), pp. 5–29.

24. See David G. Roskies, "The Genres of Yiddish Popular Literature, 1790–1860," *Working Papers in Yiddish and East European Jewish Studies* (February 1975), pp. 1–15. *Alerley mayse-bikhlekh,* an anthology of Yiddish chapbooks (Sudilkov, 1834), offers the best sampling of the kind of stories, popular chronicles, and ethical wills that circulated in the Ukraine in the decades right after Nahman's death. See also Zalmen Reisen, "Tsu der geshikhte fun der yidisher folks-literatur," *YIVO-bleter* 3 (1932): 240–259. An exotic *historye*—originally the term that denoted a non-Jewish narrative source—did not carry the same belief status as the more familiar *mayse.* See Zfatman-Biller, "Hasipporet beyidish mireshitah 'ad 'Shivḥei haBesht'," 1:27. The first to recognize that Nahman drew not from folklore but from literary sources was Meir Weiner. See his *Tsu der geshikhte fun der yidisher literatur in 19tn yorhundert* (To the History of Yiddish Literature in the Nineteenth Century), 2 vols. (New York: YIKUF, 1945), 1:34–35. Yoav Elstein identifies a thirteenth-century Spanish kabbalistic work as the possible Hebrew source for some of Nahman's motifs. See *Pa'amei bat melekh* (In the Footsteps of a Lost Princess; Ramat-Gan: Bar-Ilan University, 1984), pp. 161–188, 235–237.

25. Dan Ben-Amos, "Introduction" to *Folklore Genres* (Austin: University of Texas Press, 1981), p. xxii; Jack Zipes, "Once There Were Two Brothers Named Grimm," intro. to *The Complete Fairy Tales of the Brothers Grimm* (New York: Bantam Books, 1988), vol. 1, pp. xx–xxii.

26. Green, p. 347.

27. Band, Introduction to *Tales,* pp. 34–35; Piekarz, p. 121; Liebes, "*Ha-Tikkun Ha-Kelali,*" p. 188, n. 11.

28. This rare 1st ed. is described by Piekarz on pp. 184–185.

29. See Piekarz, chap. 5, and Elstein, *Pa'amei bat melekh,* chap. 1.

30. "The Yiddish original." There is much debate on whether Nathan recorded the stories in Yiddish first and then translated them into Hebrew, or the reverse. The question was first raised by Samuel H. Setzer in his Yiddish edition of the tales, *Sipurey mayses (vunder mayses) fun Rabi Nakhmen Braslaver* (New York: Feirberg,

1929), pp. xxxiv–xlii. It was picked up again years later by Piekarz and Shmeruk. The unfortunate effect of this scholarly debate has been to obscure the narrative power of the Yiddish and to promote the Hebrew as the primary source.

31. All this is stated explicitly in Nathan of Nemirov's "Hakdome af taytsh" (Yiddish preface) to the *Seyfer sipurey mayses,* pp. 15–16.

32. See Jacob Elbaum, "HaBesht uvno shel R. Adam—'Iyyun besippur mi*Shivḥei ha-Besht,*" *Jerusalem Studies in Jewish Folklore* 2 (1982): 66–75.

33. The newest edition of *Seyfer sipurey mayses* (Jerusalem, 1990), in which for the first time the entire Hebrew text is vocalized, contains a one-page apologia (p. 27), partially attributed to Nathan of Nemirov, for occasional lapses into ungrammatical, colloquial style. (The examples given—*vena'asah brogez aleha, velakaḥ et 'atsmo el hashtiyah*—are tame.) As the apologia makes clear, however, such "lapses" underscore the unique qualities of Nahman's teaching.

34. See David G. Roskies, "Yidishe shraybshpraklın in 19ın yorhundert," *Yidishe shprakh* 33 (1974): 1–11. Returning to Reb Nahman's Yiddish original after many years, I hear it as far more idiomatic than I did then.

35. Green, p. 4.

36. See Gershom Scholem, *On the Kabbalah and Its Symbolism,* tr. Ralph Manheim (New York: Schocken, 1965), pp. 57–62; Moshe Idel, *Kabbalah: New Perpsectives* (New Haven: Yale University Press, 1988), chap. 9.

37. See Shmeruk, *Prokim,* pp. 251–252; Liebes, "*Ha-Tikkun Ha-Kelali,*" p. 137.

38. Since Gershom Scholem's *Major Trends in Jewish Mysticism,* 3rd ed. (New York: Schocken, 1954), the sefirotic system has become common knowledge. For a lucid explanation in English, based on a kabbalistic source known to Nahman, see Louis Jacobs' introduction to *The Palm Tree of Deborah* by Moses Cordovero (1960; New York: Sepher-Hermon, 1974), pp. 20–37.

39. See Elstein, *Pa'amei bat melekh,* pp. 199–222, for an extended analysis. He was the first to note the precise sequence of events in this story.

40. Ibid., pp. 205–211; Jacob Elbaum, "Tavniot mishtarsherot venishberot be'Ma'aseh miberger ve'ani' leR. Naḥman miBraslav," *Jerusalem Studies in Hebrew Literature* 4 (1983): 76.

41. A huge topic, which will resurface in later chapters. The standard source is still Joshua Trachtenberg's *Jewish Magic and Superstition: A Study in Folk Religion* (1939; rpt. Cleveland: Meridian and Jewish Publication Society, 1961). See, more recently, Sara Zfatman, *Nisu'ei adam veshedah* (The Marriage of a Mortal Man and a She-Demon: The Transformation of a Motif in the Folk Narrative of Ashkenazi Jewry in the Sixteenth–Nineteenth Centuries; Jerusalem: Akademon, 1987); Tamar Alexander-Frizer, *The Pious Sinner: Ethics and Aesthetics in the Medieval Hasidic Narrative* (Tübingen: Mohr, 1991); Gedalyah Nigal, *Magic, Mysticism, and Hasidism: The Supernatural in Jewish Thought,* tr. Edward Levin (Northvale, N.J.: Jason Aronson, 1994).

42. For a brilliant analysis of this tale in its relation to the first, see Green, pp. 350–355.

43. Ibid., pp. 69, 186. Cf. the hasidic folklore brought by Samuel Zanvel Pipe in "Na-

poleon in Jewish Folklore," *YIVO Annual of Jewish Social Science* 1 (1946): 297–302.

44. For a convenient English sampling of this popular chronicle, see my *The Literature of Destruction: Jewish Responses to Catastrophe* (Philadelphia: Jewish Publication Society, 1989), nos. 30–33.

45. Green, p. 28.

46. On primordial man, see Scholem, *On the Kabbalah,* pp. 104–117.

47. Green, p. 74.

48. See Max Lüthi, *The Fairytale as Art Form and Portrait of Man,* tr. Jon Erickson (Bloomington: Indiana University Press, 1984), chap. 5.

49. Green, p. 44.

50. See *Sefer toldot haAri,* ed. Meir Benayahu (Jerusalem: Ben-Zvi Institute, 1967), esp. tales 5–8. Tales of how the Ba'al Shem Tov "drew close" new disciples play a central role in the *Shivḥei haBesht* (1815). See Joseph Weiss, "A Circle of Pneumatics in Pre-Hasidism ," in his *Studies in Eastern European Jewish Mysticism,* ed. David Goldstein (New York: Littman Library of Jewish Civilization and Oxford University Press, 1985), pp. 27–42; Avraham Rubinstein, "Sippurei hahitgalut besefer 'Shivḥei haBesht,' " *'Alei sefer* 6/7 (1979): 157–186.

51. On the historical and messianic dimensions of the story, see Shmeruk, *Prokim,* pp. 256–258. For the failed meeting between the Besht and Hayyim ibn Atar, see *Sefer shivḥei haBesht,* ed. S. A. Horodetzky (Tel Aviv: Dvir, 1960), pp. 188–189.

52. The incompatibility of biblical monotheism and tragedy in the classical Greek sense is something that obviously requires systematic study. I draw my conclusions from discussions on the subject with my friend and colleague, Raymond P. Scheindlin.

53. The first to make this identification was Joseph Weiss, the pioneer of modern research on Nahman of Bratslav. See his *Meḥkarim baḥasidut Braslav* (Studies in Bratslav Hasidism), ed. Mendl Piekarz (Jerusalem: Bialik Institute, 1974), pp. 22–23.

54. Louis Ginzberg, *The Legends of the Jews* (Philadelphia: Jewish Publication Society, 1968), 1: 276–278.

55. On the prevalence of this motif in "The Burgher and the Pauper," see Yaakov Elbaum's fine analysis in *Jerusalem Studies in Hebrew Literature* 4 (1983): 59–85.

56. See Green, chap. 6.

57. See *Beggars and Prayers: Adin Steinzaltz Retells the Tales of Rabbi Nachman of Bratslav,* tr. Yehuda Hanegbi, et al., ed. Jonathan Omer-Man (New York: Basic Books, 1985), p. 135. Steinsaltz provides a sustained and nuanced allegorical reading of the tale on pp. 133–147 of his retelling.

58. This was Moyshe Markuze's *Seyfer refues hanikro eyzer yisroel* (Poryck, 1790). For a full description of this work, the first written in Eastern Yiddish, see Khone Shmeruk, *Sifrut yidish beFolin* (Yiddish Literature in Poland; Jerusalem: Magnes Press, 1981), pp. 184–203. On Nahman's rebuttal, see pp. 201–202.

59. Steinzaltz (p. 134) finds the depiction of the simple man "rather flat" and "stereotypical," while the clever man "is treated with greater depth and understanding."

60. *Likutey MOHaRaN tanina*, p. 22.

61. Steinzaltz, *Beggars and Prayers*, pp. 109–110, with minor changes to conform to Band's translation.

62. See Cynthia Ozick's delightful rumination on this subject in "Prayer Leader," *Prooftexts* 3 (1983): 1–8.

63. The most intelligent guide to the multiple interpretations of this tale and to the many works of modern literature it inspired is a two-volume high-school curriculum edited by Zecharia Goren at the Center for Development of Jewish Study Programs at Kibbutz Oranim. See *Be'ikvot shiv'at hakabtsanim lerabi Nahman mi-Braslav* (In the Footsteps of Rabbi Nahman of Bratslav's Seven Beggars; Oranim: Afik, 1986).

64. Too many songs attributed to Nahman have been issued of late by hasidim in Israel to constitute the authentic core. Cassettes titled *The Songs of Rabbi Nachman of Breslav,* sung by Rabbi David Raphael Ben-Ami, are available in Judaica bookstores. Many of them were probably composed by his hasidim. For a more reliable source, see *Old Jewish Folk Music: The Collections and Writings of Moshe Beregovski,* ed. Mark Slobin (Phila.: University of Pennsylvania Press, 1982), p. 300, and nos. 130, 134, 146, and 150 of the "Textless Songs" published on pp. 449–490.

65. Green, pp. 301–304; Steinzaltz, pp. 180–181.

3. The Master of Lore: Isaac Meir Dik

1. Mendele Mocher Sforim, *Of Bygone Days,* tr. from Hebrew and Yiddish by Raymond P. Scheindlin in *A Shtetl and Other Yiddish Novellas,* ed. Ruth R. Wisse, 2nd rev. ed. (Detroit: Wayne State University Press, 1986), pp. 282, 300. See also Khone Shmeruk, "Di mizrekh-eyropeishe nuskhoes fun der 'Tsene-Rene,' 1786–1850," *For Max Weinreich on his Seventieth Birthday* (The Hague: Mouton, 1964), pp. 336–320.

2. *Ale ksovim fun Mendele Moykher-Sforim* (Odessa, 1888), 1:7; originally preface to *Dos kleyne mentshele* (The Little Man; Vilna, 1879).

3. Isaac Rivkind, "Verter mit yikhes," *Yidishe shprakh,* 14 (1954): 21–24.

4. Formulaic warnings: Khone Shmeruk, *Prokim fun der yidisher literatur-geshikhte* (Yiddish Literature: Aspects of its History; Jerusalem: I. L. Perets, 1988), pp. 40–46. For a complete bibliography, see Sarah Zfatman, *Yiddish Narrative Prose from Its Beginnings to 'Shivhei ha-Besht' (1504–1814): An Annotated Bibliography* (Jerusalem: Hebrew University, 1985).

5. *Der shivim moltsayt* (The Seventieth Anniversary Feast, pseud. AMaD; Vilna: Rom, 1877), p. 10. For a descriptive overview of what was available in his day, see my "The Genres of Yiddish Popular Literature, 1790–1860," *Working Papers in Yiddish and East European Jewish Studies* 8 (February 1975): 9–14.

6. For a sample price list, see Isaac Rivkind, "A. M. Diks bibliografishe reshimes," *YIVO-bleter* 36 (1952): 203, n. 30. *Nitsgelt* means user's or borrower's fee. See Rivkind's *Yidishe gelt in lebnsshteyger kultur-geshikhte un folklor* (Jewish Money in

Folkways, Cultural History and Folklore; New York: American Academy for Jewish Research, 1959), s.v. *nutsgelt, nitsgelt.*

7. On Yiddish chapbooks initially being exempt from the rabbinic index, see Avrom Papyerna, *Zikhroynes* (Memoirs, tr. P[uah] Ra[kov]ski; Warsaw, 1923), p. 23, describing the situation in Kapulie in the 1840s and 1850s.

8. *Treyf-posl,* according to Max Weinreich, was a nineteenth-century coinage. Before the Enlightenment, "an unfit book" meant a non-Hebrew (i.e., Christian) work. See Max Weinreich, *Geshikhte fun der yidisher shprakh: bagrifn, faktn, metodn* (History of the Yiddish Language: Concepts, Facts, Methods, 4 vols.; New York: YIVO, 1973), 3:313.

9. The main source on maskilic typography is an anonymous parody, but coauthored by Isaac Baer Levinsohn and Joseph Perl, *Divrei tsaddikim im 'emek-refa'im* (Words of the Righteous and The Valley of Ghosts, 2nd ed.; Odessa, 1867), p. 29. See also Zalmen Reisen, "Tsu der geshikhte fun der haskole-literatur," *YIVO-bleter* 2 (1931): 376. Glike, the female villain in Dik's *Di shtifmuter* (The Stepmother, 1859), divorces her first husband after he is caught reading poetry: "kleyne sforimlekh vos zayn gedrukt a shure arayn un a shure aroys" (little booklets printed with one line sticking out and the other line in). Quoted from Warsaw 1876 ed., pp. 8–9.

10. See *Seyfer haprenumerantn* (Hebrew Subscription Lists), ed. Berl Kagan (New York: Library of the Jewish Theological Seminary of America and Ktav Publishing House, 1975).

11. Joseph Perl, *Ma'asiyot ve'iggrot mitsaddikim amitiim umi'anshe shlomenu* (Hasidic Tales and Letters), ed. Khone Shmeruk and Shmuel Werses (Jerusalem: Israel Academy of Sciences and Humanities, 1969), and his *Uiber das Wesen der Sekte Chasidim,* ed. Avraham Rubinstein (Jerusalem: Israel Academy of Sciences and Humanities, 1977), esp. pp. 20–21.

12. *Divrei tsaddikim 'im 'emek-refa'im,* originally written by Isaac Baer Levinsohn around 1821 and published in 1830 by Perl, who prefaced three parodies of his own.

13. On the fate of *Megalleh temirin,* see Shmeruk, introduction to Perl's *Ma'asiyot ve'iggrot,* p. 34. The anonymous *Di genarte velt oder shver men nemt zikh fir, gringer helft got,* written in Lemberg between 1815 and 1830, was republished by Meir Wiener (Moscow: Emes, 1940) from the only copy he could find, a terrible reprint from 1863. Khone Shmeruk discovered a much better edition (Lemberg: Madfes, 1865), described in "Nusaḥ bilti yadu'a shel hakomediah ha'anononimit 'Di genarte velt,' " *Kiryat sefer* 44 (1979): 802–816.

14. See Judah A. Joffe, "Hundert un fuftsik yor yidish," *YIVO-bleter* 14 (1939): 87–88; David G. Roskies, "Yidishe shraybshprakhn in 19tn yorhundert," *Yidishe shprakh* 33 (1974): 1–11; Dov-Ber Kerler, "Di haskholes fun der moderner literatur-shprakh (1771–1798)," *Oksforder yidish* 1 (1990): 271–316. On the name *ivre-taytsh,* see Rivkind, "Verter mit yikhes," *Yidishe shprakh* 14 (1954): 50.

15. See Avraham Yaari, "Hotsa'ot hamaḥazeh 'Gedulat David umelukhat Sha'ul'," *Kiryat sefer* 12 (1936): 385.

16. For a modern critical edition of the play, see Yosef Ha'efrati, *Melukhat Sha'ul,* ed. Gershon Shaked (Jerusalem: Bialik Institute, 1968).

17. According to Jacob A. Benjacob, *Otsar hasfarim* (Thesaurus Librorum Hebraicorum; Vilna, 1880), p. 93, no. 62. The adapter's name does not appear in any of the editions cited by Yaari.

18. See Zippora Kagan, "Mekorot umekoriyut bamahazeh 'Milhama beshalom' le-Hayyim-Avraham KaTS," *Bamah* 43[96] (1969): 62–77; 44 (1970): 70–78.

19. Khaÿim Lieberman, "Tsu der frage vegn der batsiung fun khsides tsu yidish," *YIVO-bleter* 22 (1943): 207. See Kagan, 44 (1970): 70–78, for a partial listing of nineteenth-century editions.

20. Quoted from *Robinzon di geshikhte fun Alter-Leb*, 2 vols. (Vilna, 1894), 2:12. The first edition appeared in Galicia ca. 1820 and was reprinted many times. Ber Shlosberg identified the author as Yoysef Vitlin in "Khaykl Hurvitses *Seyfer tsofnas paneyakh*," *YIVO-bleter* 12 (1937): 558. This was corroborated by Simkha Katz and Mendl Neugroschel, who reported seeing Vitlin's name on the copy of *Alter Leb* in the Perl Library in Tarnopol. Dov Sadan, personal communication, 18 December 1973. The source of all the Yiddish and Hebrew adaptations of *Robinson Crusoe* was Joachim Heinrich Campe (1746–1818). For more on this subject, see my "The Medium and Message of the Maskilic Chapbook," *Jewish Social Studies* 41 (1979): 275–290.

21. See Joseph Dan, *Sifrut hamusar vehaderush* [Hebrew Ethical and Homiletical Literature] (Jerusalem: Keter, 1975); idem, *Jewish Mysticism & Jewish Ethics* (Seattle & London: University of Washington Press, 1986); Mendl Piekarz, *Bimei tsemihat hahasidut* (The Beginning of Hasidism; Jerusalem: Bialik Institute, 1978).

22. On the printing monopoly, see Pinkhes Kon, "Di proyektirte yidishe drukeray in Kiev, 1836–1846," *Bikher-velt* 1 (Warsaw, 1929), no. 3, pp. 31–37, no. 4, pp. 35–41; Saul M. Ginsburg (Ginzburg), "Tsu der geshikhte fun yidishn drukvezn," in his *Historishe verk*, 3 vols. (New York, 1937), 1:48–62; most recently, Eli Lederhendler, *The Road to Modern Jewish Politics: Political Tradition and Political Reconstruction in the Jewish Community of Tsarist Russia* (New York: Oxford University Press, 1989), pp. 95–97.

23. HaDaS, *Mahazeh mul mahazeh* (Vision Against Vision; Warsaw: Bomberg, 1861), pp. 4–5.

24. See Lederhendler, p. 93, for a list of government-appointed censors in 1827–1904. There is rich documentation on tsarist censorship during this period. For some of the early studies, see Majer Balaban, "Zur Geschichte der hebräischen Drukkereien in Polen," *Soncino Blätter* 3:1 (1929): 26–31; N. Prylucki, "Vi azoy di rusishe tsenzur hot gebalebatevet in der 'Bobe-mayse,'" *YIVO-bleter* 3 (1932): 354–370; Israel Zinberg, "Di rusishe tsenzur un di *Bove-mayse*," *YIVO-bleter* 4 (1932): 187–188; Pinkhes Kon, "Di rusishe makht un yidishe muser-sforim," *YIVO-bleter* 1 (1931): 187–88, and "Di tsarishe makht un der Rambam," *YIVO-bleter* 13 (1938): 577–582.

25. Michael Stanislawski, *Tsar Nicholas I and the Jews: The Transformation of Jewish Society in Russia, 1825–1855* (Philadelphia: Jewish Publication Society, 1983), pp. 97–109, 187–188.

26. Dan Miron, "Folklore and Anti-Folklore in the Yiddish Fiction of the *Haskalah*,"

Studies in Jewish Folklore, ed. Frank Talmage (Cambridge, Mass.: Association for Jewish Studies, 1980), pp. 219–223.

27. On Perl: Raphael Mahler, *Hasidism and the Jewish Enlightenment: Their Confrontation in Galicia and Poland in the First Half of the Nineteenth Century,* tr. Eugene Orenstein, Aaron Klein, and Jenny Machlowitz Klein (Philadelphia: Jewish Publication Society, 1985), p. 42. On Dik: Zalmen Reisen, "Ayzik-Meyer Dik," *Leksikon fun der yidisher literatur, prese un filologye,* 2nd ed. (Vilna: Kletskin, 1929), vol. 1. col. 714. On Abramovitsh: *Perek shira,* issued under his real name (Zhitomir: Baksht, 1875); Khone Shmeruk, "Mendeles tilim-iberzetsungen," *Di goldene keyt* 62/63 (1968): 290–312. On the religious conservatism of the Haskalah, see Meir Wiener, *Tsu der geshikhte fun der yidisher literatur in 19tn yorhundert,* 2 vols. (New York: YIKUF, 1945), 1:271–272.

28. On almanacs: Mahler, "Joseph Perl's Hebrew Almanacs," *Hasidism and the Jewish Enlightenment,* chap 6; Moyshe Shalit, *Lukhes in undzer literatur fun Mendele Moykher-Sforim biz der hayntiker tsayt* (Vilna: Altnay, 1929). On letter writers: Yehude Elzet [Judah Leib Zlotnik], *Mit hundert yor tsurik: shtudyen in dem amolign inerlekhn yidishn lebn* (Montreal, 1927); Max Weinreich, "Lewin Liondors brivn-shtelers," *YIVO-bleter* 18 (1941): 109–112; S. Niger, *Dertseylers un romanistn* (New York: CYCO, 1946), pp. 64–67; Isaac Rivkind, "Hebreisher yikhes in yidishe brivn-shtelers," *Yidishe shprakh* 25 (1965): 18–26; Judith Halevi Zwick, *Toldot sifrut ha'igronim* (The Hebrew Briefsteller, 16th–20th Century; Tel Aviv: Papyrus, 1990). On Bible translations: Khone Shmeruk, "Vegn etlekhe printsipn fun Mendl Lefins mishley-iberzetsung," *Yidishe shprakh* 24 (1964): 33–52; Chava Turniansky, "Nusah maskili shel 'Tsene-rene'," *Hasifrut* 2 (1971): 835–841.

29. On the maggidic self-image of the maskilim, see Lederhendler, pp. 120–123.

30. See Dan Miron, *A Traveler Disguised: A Study in the Rise of Yiddish Fiction in the Nineteenth Century* (New York: Schocken, 1973), and "Folklore and Anti-Folklore," pp. 237–245.

31. See Khone Shmeruk, *Sifrut yidish: perakim letoldoteha* (Yiddish Literature: Aspects of its History; Tel Aviv: Porter Institute for Poetics and Semiotics, 1978), chap. 7.

32. These are the main sources on Dik's biography: Zalmen Reisen, "Ayzik-Meyer Dik," *Leksikon fun der yidisher literatur,* vol. 1, cols. 711–726; Pinkhes Kon, "Ven iz Ayzik-Meyer Dik geborn gevorn?" *Filologishe shriftn fun YIVO* 2 (1928): 329–344 and 3 (1929): 616–617, and his "A. M. Dik a lerer in der kroynisher shul far yidishe kinder in Vilne," *YIVO-bleter* 3 (1932): 84–87. On parental failings, see *Zibn dinst meydkhn bay dem vaser rer mit zibn krig um tsu nemen vaser oyf tey* (Seven Servant Girls at the Pump with Seven Jugs Taking Water for Tea, pseud. AMaD; Vilna: Rom, 1873), p. 68; on parental discipline, see *Der purim shpigl* (The Purim Mirror, anon.; Vilna: Rom, 1870), pp. 7–15. Life with his first set of inlaws is wonderfully described in his satiric memoir *Zifronah,* pseud. I.A.M.D. yelid Vilna (Vilna: Dvorzhets, 1868).

33. Reisen, pp. 712–713.

34. The Russian text of the petition was published in *Perezhitoe* 1 (1908): 2:12–14,

translated into Yiddish in *Di geshikhte fun yidn in Rusland,* ed. O. Margolis (Moscow: Emes, 1930), doc. 140. See also Israel Klausner, "Hagzeirah shel tilboshet hayehudim, 1844–1850," *Gal-Ed* 6 (1982): 11–26.

35. "Matsav 'ir Vilna ba'itim ha'eleh," rpt. Ginsburg, *Historishe verk,* 2:293–298.

36. *Masekhet 'aniyut,* anon. in *Kanfei Yonah,* ed. Shneyer Sachs (Berlin, 1848), pp. 3–20; *Masekhet ein kesef . . . im perushim vetosafot uMaHaRSHA,* pseud. Had min talmidei hevraya (Zhitomir, 1850). "Zhitomir" is undoubtedly a fake. The Shapira brothers would never have published a sacrilegious work that was virulently antihasidic as well. For a sampling of this parody, see my "Ayzik-Meyer Dik and the Rise of Yiddish Popular Literature" (Ph.D. diss., Brandeis University, 1974), pp. 172–176. On Jewish parody in general, see Israel Davidson's still unsurpassed *Parody in Jewish Literature* (New York: Columbia University Press, 1907).

37. *Mahazeh mul mahazeh,* p. 4.

38. For the full text of the one-year contract (1864–65), see *Fun noentn over* 1:2 (Warsaw, 1937): 172–174. See also Sh. L. Cytron, "Vegn honorar-badingungen in der yidisher literatur," *Bikher-velt* 2 (1923): 330–336.

39. Reuven Brainin, *Fun mayn lebns-bukh,* ed. Nachman Meisel (New York: YIKUF, 1946), p. 221–222. For a comic self-portrait of Dik's life as a money broker, see "A Maskil's Utopia," a manuscript published in *YIVO-bleter* 36 (1952): 151–154.

40. Dik published *Zifronah* (1868) in a thousand copies at his own expense and was unable to make back even half the cost. See his letter to Hayyim-Jonah Gurland of 19 Iyyar 1869, *Reshumot* 2 (1927): 409. In 1861 he published *Mahazeh mul mahazeh.* For a recent study of Dik as a Hebrew satirist, see Ben Ami Feingold, "Satirah maskilit nishkahat—'Zifronah' me'et A. M. Dik," *Jerusalem Studies in Hebrew Literature* 9 (1986): 239–258.

41. Sh. L. Cytron, *Dray literarishe doyres* (Three Literary Generations; Vilna: Shreberk, 1922), 1:7. The visit took place in 1879. Samples of Dik's midrashic commentaries appeared in *Mahazeh mul mahazeh, Hanesher* 1 (Lemberg, 1863): 4, and *Hamelits* 10:20 (Odessa, 1870): 150. A manuscript of his exegesis on the Midrash Rabba and Tanhuma is kept in the Jewish National and University Library, Heb. 709 8.° On Dik's retaining traditional Jewish garb, see Y. L. Smolenskin, "Mas'a beRusia," *Hashahar* 5 (1874): 350.

42. See Smolenskin, p. 349, for a portrait of Dik in the Tohoras Hakoydesh. In addition to the two letters to Gurland published in *Reshumot* 2 (1927): 408–410, Isaac Rivkind published another four letters in Hebrew from the years 1843–1852 in *YIVO-bleter* 35 (1951): 222–228. Rivkind's annotations are especially important.

43. See Marc Saperstein, *Jewish Preaching, 1200–1800: An Anthology* (New Haven: Yale University Press, 1989), pp. 21, 39–44. Even the hasidim, supposed champions of Yiddish, published their sermon material only in Hebrew. All of Reb Nahman's sermons initially appeared only in Hebrew translation. The one work of hasidic mussar—not sermon material per se—to be published in Yiddish prior to Dik's time was Dov Ber Schneurson's *Poykeyakh ivrim* (He Openeth the Eyes of the Blind; Shklov: Yitskhok Yoysef Menin, 1832).

44. See my "Annotated Bibliography of Ayzik-Meyer Dik," *The Field of Yiddish: Studies in Language, Folklore, and Literature,* 4th collection, ed. Marvin I. Herzog et al. (Philadelphia: ISHI, 1980), pp. 117–184.

45. Brainin, p. 226.

46. Dan Miron, *Bein ḥazzon le'emet* (From Romance to the Novel: Studies in the Emergence of the Hebrew and Yiddish Novel in the Nineteenth Century; Jerusalem: Bialik Institute, 1979), pp. 60–71, 148–151. This Hebrew treyf-posl was also transformed into a pious Yiddish mayse-bikhl. See Shmuel Werses, *Hatirgumim leyidish shel Ahavat Zion leAvraham Mapu* (Jerusalem: Akademon, 1989).

47. *Di geduld,* pseud. Y. Shapiro (Warsaw: Lebensohn, 1855).

48. *Der shivim moltsayt* (1877), p. 10

49. *Di tsavoe* (The Will), pseud. Z.B.A.M. (Vilna: Fin-Rozenkrantz, 1873), stanzas 29–30. Dik invented new pseudonymns for those chapbooks he published with printers other than Rom.

50. On the obligation to recall the destruction of the temple whenever a Jew celebrates, see *Seyfer koyres Yerusholaim* (The Annals of Jerusalem), pseud. Avrom Aba KaB (Vilna: Rom, 1862), p. 5. The size (188 pp.) and religious subject matter of this Yiddish chapbook earned it the designation of *seyfer.*

51. Walter Scott, *Miscellaneous Prose Works,* 3:376, as quoted in Alexander Welsh, *The Hero of the Waverly Novels* (New York: Atheneum, 1968), pp. 21–22.

52. *Seyfer khokhmes hayad,* 1st bilingual ed. anon. (Vilna: Rom, 1869); Yiddish part only rpt. anon. (Warsaw: Shriftgiser, 1882). I compared this edition with one edited by Yehoshua Shterner for a hasidic audience (Lemberg: Balaban, n.d.) and noted that Dik omitted all mention of the Zohar, even when he supplied the quote.

53. The preface is quoted in Rivkind's "Annotated Bibliography," p. 201.

54. For other examples of this procedure, see Miron, "Folklore and Anti-Folklore," pp. 244–246.

55. *Hamisalef oder der shayntoyte* (The Fainter or the Man Who Appeared to Be Dead), pseud. Y. Shapiro (Warsaw: Lebensohn, 1855); *Pakhed balaylo, di shrekn fun di nakht heshayne rabe* (Terror in the Night: The Fears of the Night of Hoshana Rabba), pseud. Z. H. Shapiro (Warsaw: Kleyf, 1856).

56. *Der yoyred* (Warsaw: Lebensohn). Rpt. in modern orthography in *Chulyot: Journal of Yiddish Research* 1 (Winter 1993): 43–49; a Hebrew tr. by Shalom Luria, pp. 50–55. In 1872, Dik and Yekusiel Shapiro collaborated on a new Hebrew ed. of Nathan Nata Hanover's *Sefer yeven hametsulah* (Warsaw: Goldman, 1872).

57. See Mordecai Ben Yehezkel, *Sefer hama'asiyot* (Tel Aviv: Dvir, 1965), 2:501–503.

58. Dov Sadan, personal communication, 9 March 1973. A third version, from Ben Yehezkel on pp. 503–504, is an adaptation of Dik's story which also finds no way to resolve the bastard dilemma.

59. In a later version of the story, *Der shnorer,* anon. (Vilna: Dvorzhets, 1866), Dik offered an elaborate halachic explanation of the boy's bastard status.

60. See Dik's letter of 1852 to Jacob Katzenelson and Zalmen Risser in *YIVO-bleter* 35 (1951): 228.

61. See Joseph Dan, "Letoldoteha shel sifrut hashvaḥim," *Jerusalem Studies in Jewish Folklore* 1 (1981): 82–100; Sara Zfatman-Biller, " 'Ma'aseh shel ruaḥ beKaK Korets'—shalav ḥadash behitpatḥuto shel z'aner 'amami," *Jerusalem Studies in Jewish Folklore* 2 (1982): 17–65.

62. Anon., *Der siem hatoyre* (Vilna: Rom, 1868).

63. Dik used the same plot in *Der toyter kop* (The Dead Man's Head), pseud. M. M-na (Warsaw: Lebensohn, 1859).

64. *Sipurey mihagoen bal hamekhaber toysfes yontef zal,* anon. (Vilna: Dvorzhets, 1864), p. 48.

65. *Der shivim moltsayt,* p. 46. The story includes a lengthy excursus on the economic and cultural woes of Polish Jewry in the pre-partition period. For another expression of Dik's pro-tsarist, anti-Polish sentiment, see *Der soldatske sin* (The Conscript's Son), pseud. AMaD (Vilna: Rom, 1876).

66. See Dik's "Mayse ger tsedek—di geshikhte fun vilner ger tsedek Graf Pototski" (The Story of the Righteous Convert of Vilna Count Potocki), published from MS in *Di yidishe velt* 6 (Vilna, June 1913): 43–58. German tr. in *Das Buch von der polnischen Juden,* ed. S. J. Agnon and Ahron Eliasberg (Berlin, 1916), pp. 61–79.

67. *Shabse tsvi* (Sabbetai Zvi), pseud. Reb Yehezkl MaS (Vilna: Tipograf, 1864); *Sefer yeven hametsulah* (1872).

68. The only acknowledgment to a Polish source that I could find was in *Alte yidishe zagen oder sipurim* (Old Jewish Tales), pseud. AMaD (Vilna: Rom, 1876). He attributes the sixth tale to Ignacy Chodzko's *Przechadzki Przez Miasto Wilno* (Walks Through the City of Vilna). Dik's version of the Ger Tsedek legend is ostensibly drawn from J. I. Kraszewski's (1841).

69. *Di yidishe kleyder umvekslung (umbaytung) vos iz geshen in dem yor 1844* (The Change in Jewish Clothing That Occurred in 1844), pseud. AMaD (Vilna: Rom, 1870), was adapted from Lev Levanda's *Ocherki proshlogo* (Sketches from the Past, 1870).

70. See Shmeruk, *Sifrut yidish,* p. 292, n. 41.

71. *Gdules Rotshild,* anon. (Vilna: Fin-Rozenkrants, 1865); *Der goel,* anon. (Vilna: Dvorzhets, 1866); *Reb Shimen Barbun,* pseud. AMaD (Vilna: Rom, 1874). Joseph Sherman of Witwatersrand University, Johannesburg, has prepared a full translation and penetrating analysis of *Reb Shimen Barbun* in "The Jewish Pope: Interpellating Jewish Identity," MS.

72. AMaD, *Der plet oyf shabes* (Vilna: Rom, 1872). *Feygele der magid* (Feygele the Preacher), pseud. AMaD (Vilna: Rom, 1868), was adapted from Bernstein's "Vögele der Maggid," in Wertheim, *Kalendar und Jahrbuch* (Berlin, 1858), 2:5–108. A good example of Dik's embellishments is his rendering of "die Taglichter fur das Beshamidrasch und die schul zu ziehen" (p. 23) as "di veksene likht far di shul un di kheylevne likht far dem besmedresh" (p. 13). In adapting the story for an audience that still lived in the thick of Jewish folklife, Dik also added Hebrew captions—even though the original was in German.

73. All three were published by Rom, under the AMaD trademark.

74. On haunted houses see *Der yidisher poslanik* (The Jewish Ambassador), pseud. AMaD (Vilna: Rom, 1880), pp. 28–29; on werewolves, *Der yishuvnik* (The Country Bumpkin), pseud. ARSHaK (Vilna: Dvorzhets, 1867), p. 29; on ghosts, Lilith, and the ba'al-shem, *Alte yidishe zagen oder sipurim* (1876); on dreams, *Reb Shimen Barbun der rabiner fun Maynts* (1874).

75. AMaD, *Sipurey muser oder moralishe ertseylungen* (Vilna: Rom, 1875).

76. *Di nakht fun tes vov kislev*, anon. (Vilna: Fin-Rozenkrants, 1867), many rpts. Dik was justifiably proud of this work and even insisted it was the first he ever wrote. See S. Niger, "A. M. Diks ershte verk," *Pinkes fun Amopteyl fun YIVO* 2 (1929): 1–9.

77. *Der yidisher poslanik*, p. 21.

78. *Der erster nabor* (The First Recruitment), pseud. AMaD (Vilna: Rom, 1871), p. 13. On the drafting of Jewish minors, see Stanislawski, *Tsar Nicholas I and the Jews,* and my *Against the Apocalypse: Responses to Catastrophe in Modern Jewish Culture* (Cambridge, Mass.: 1984), pp. 57–62.

79. First published in Hebrew as *Habehalah* (The Panic), pseud. Ish AMID, *Hamelits* nos. 41–43 (1867), reissued a year later in Yiddish as *Di shtot Heres* (The Town of Heres; Vilna: Rozenkrants). A fuller version of the Hebrew was published in *He'avar* 2 (St. Petersburg, 1918): 37–44, intro. Saul Ginsburg (both rpt. in *Chulyot* 1 [1993]: 56–69); an edited version of the Yiddish was included in S. Niger's edition of Dik's *Geklibene verk* (New York: CYCO, 1954). Niger's copy, the only one extant, was stolen from the YIVO Library, making all comparisons between the Hebrew and Yiddish a matter of conjecture. The other marked-up copies from the Niger collection in the YIVO Library reveal the great liberties he took with the original.

80. On the archetypal significance of the Ninth of Av, see my *Against the Apocalypse,* chap. 2.

81. This off-color passage appears only in the Hebrew, but that could be from Niger's prudishness and not Dik's.

82. *Der shadkhn* (The Matchmaker), pseud. AMaD (Vilna: Rom, 1874), p. 4.

83. *Reb Traytl der kleynshtetldiker nogid* (Reb Traytl the Small-Town Croesus), pseud. AMaD (Vilna: Rom, 1872); an earlier version, written for men, appeared in *Warschauer Jüdische Zeitung* 1, nos. 34–40 (1867).

84. Anon., *Reb Shmaye der gut yontef biter* (Warsaw: Bomberg, 1860).

85. Ibid., pp. 19–24. For an earlier version of this list, see the Hebrew satire *Zifronah,* pp. 12–13, which is also discussed by Feingold, pp. 252–254.

86. *Yekele Goldshleger oder Yekele Mazltov* (Yekele Goldmine or Yekele Good-Fortune), pseud. M. M-n (Warsaw, 1859). I worked from the Lemberg 1873 ed.

87. For a fine stylistic anaylysis of *Reb Shmaye,* see Miron, "Folklore and Anti-Folklore," pp. 224–228.

88. *Der khazn* (1874), p. 36. A similar sentiment is expressed in the epigraph to this chapter, taken from *Der badkhn,* anon. (Vilna: Dvorzhets, 1864), p. 5.

89. *Der yishuvnik in tsvey teyl,* "copied by ARSHaK" (Vilna: Dvorzhets, 1867).

90. For a linguistic analysis of Dik's style in the 1870s and 1880s, see Uriel Weinreich,

"Vegn der shprakh fun Ayzik-Meyer Diks a manuskript," *Yidishe shprakh* 3 (1943): 43–47, and see the MS in question, "A Maskil's Utopia," *YIVO-bleter* 36 (1952): 168–169, for his readers' reactions.

91. See *Royze Finkl di bal akhsanyete oder di unatirlekhe tokhter* (Rosa Finkel the Woman Innkeeper or The Unnatural Daughter), pseud. AMaD (Vilna: Rom, 1874). The title says it all.

92. See *Di froyen oder der toydes engel (malekhamoves) in shpan der ehe (heyzlekhn lebn)* (The Women or The Angel of Death in the Harness of Matrimony), pseud. I. Kopelevitsh (Warsaw: Goldman, 1872), and preface to *Der shivim moltsayt* (1877).

93. *Der yidisher poslanik* (1880), p. 41.

94. *Der plet oyf shabes,* pseud. AMaD (Vilna: Rom, 1872), p. 6.

95. *Di tsvey unglaykhe brider Motke un Hershke* (The Two Unequal Brothers Motke and Hershke), pseud. AMaD (Vilna: Rom, 1873); *Reb Shimen Barbun der rabiner fun Maynts* (1874) and *Der aroys getribener und bald tsurik gerufener Yozef* (The Banished and Soon Recalled Joseph), pseud. AMaD (Vilna: Matz, 1877). For Joseph as a girl, see *Di dinst meydl oder eyn shpil dem shikzals* (The Servant Girl or A Trick of Fate), anon. (Vilna: Rom, 1868).

96. From title to chap. 1 of *Boruske der shoymer,* pseud. AMaD (Vilna: Rom, 1871).

97. For a semicritical biography, see Herman A. Glatt, *He Spoke in Parables: The Life and Works of the Dubno Maggid* (New York: Bithmar, 1957), and for an English sampling of his work, Benno Heinemann, *The Maggid of Dubno and his Parables* (New York: Feldheim, 1967).

98. The prototype for the shrewish wife was Xanthippe, described at some length in Dik's parallel-text edition of *Sipurey khokhmey Yovn o divrey khakhomim* (Stories of the Greek Sages), pseud. Avrom Aba KaB (Vilna: Dvorzhets, 1864).

99. For the midrashic source in its entirety, see Genesis Rabba 59:9.

100. The printed sources have the Maggid expounding on this verse, but with another parable altogether. See Jacob Kranz, *Sefer mishley Ya'akov hamenukad,* ed. Moshe Nisboym (Jerusalem, 1989), pp. 46–48, or Heinemann, *The Maggid of Dubno,* pp. 52–54.

101. For the next generation of women readers, see Iris Parush, "Readers in Cameo: Women Readers in Jewish Society of Nineteenth-Century Eastern Europe," *Prooftexts* 14 (1994): 1–23.

102. Here are the most prolific writers, all from Lithuania and most operating out of Vilna proper: Yisroel-Meyer Vohlman (1821–1913), Gavriel Ravitsh (1826–1892), Yehoshua Meyzakh (1834–1917), Benzion Alfas (1850–1940), Zvi-Nisn Golomb (1853–1934), and the ever-popular SHoMeR (Nokhem-Meyer Shaykevitsh, 1849–1905). For the other regional center of Yiddish popular literature, Warsaw, see Nokhem Oyslender, "Varshever mekhabrim in di 1850er–1860er," *Di yidishe literatur in nayntsetn yorhundert,* ed. Chava Turniansky (Jerusalem: Magnes, 1993), pp. 241–288. See also my "Medium and Message of the Yiddish Chapbook," pp. 285–286.

4. The Conjuror: I. L. Peretz

1. I. L. Peretz, "Dos vaserl (fun mayne rayze-bilder)," *Der fraynd* (1904), nos. 225, 228; later appended as chap. 23 to *Bilder fun a provints-rayze, Ale verk fun Y. L. Perets*, 11 vols. (New York: CYCO, 1947–1948), ed. S. Niger, 2:192–203. Tr. "The Pond" by Milton Himmelfarb in *The I. L. Peretz Reader*, ed. Ruth R. Wisse (New York: Schocken, 1990), pp. 74–84; quote on pp. 197 and 78. "Y" will henceforth denote the CYCO edition of Peretz's (far from) *Complete Works*; "E" will denote the Wisse anthology, except where otherwise indicated.

   Himmelfarb translates the word *yidishkayt* as "Judaism," which is a nineteenth-century, western European construct. In the folk speech Peretz is here trying to simulate, *yidishkayt* means "piety" or "religiosity," since Reb Moses and his ilk cannot contemplate a sphere of meaningful human existence outside the Jewish realm. See Peretz's important letter in Hebrew to Y. H. Ravnitzky of March or April 1899 in Nachman Meisel, "Tsen nisht-farefntlekhe briv fun Y. L. Perets," *Yidishe kultur* (April 1950): 26.

2. From "Princess Sabbath," *Romancero* (1851), book 3: Hebrew Melodies. See *The Complete Poems of Heinrich Heine: A Modern English Version by Hal Draper* (Boston: Surkamp/Insel, 1982), pp. 653–654.

3. On the expedition, see Yeshaye Margulis' memoirs in *YIVO-bleter*, 12 (1937): 308–309; Jacob Shatzky, "Perets-shtudyes," *YIVO-bleter* 28 (1946): 66–77, and review of Nachman Meisel, *Y. L. Perets: zayn lebn un shafn*, *YIVO-bleter* 28 (1946): 173, and "Oyf di shpurn fun materyaln fun Yan Blokhs statistish-ekonomisher ekspeditsye," *YIVO-bleter* 34 (1950): 296–298; Ruth R. Wisse, *I. L. Peretz and the Making of Modern Jewish Culture* (Seattle: University of Washington Press, 1990), pp. 3–25. Wisse is the first of Peretz's biographers to stress the lifelong impact of his being disbarred—for reasons never revealed and therefore never subject to appeal.

4. The maskil's true-life model, one Reuven Potolitsher, later bragged about appearing in Peretz's "Impressions"—despite Peretz's caricature and being renamed Shmerl. This was told to me by the late Jacob Zipper, a native of Tishevits.

5. Nokhem Oyslender, "Vegn tsvey shtromen in Peretses kinstlerisher shprakh fun di 90-er yorn," *Afn shprakhfront* 5:1/2 (1931): 55–68.

6. See Wisse, *Peretz*, pp. 21–22.

7. Yudel Mark, "Y. L. Peretses loshn," *YIVO-bleter* 28 (1946): 111–145; excerpted in "The Language of Y. L. Peretz," *YIVO Annual of Jewish Social Science* 4 (1949): 64–79. Mark's thesis is that the spoken language and Peretz's local dialect in particular formed the basis for his entire literary style. See esp. pp. 127 and 138–145 for a discussion of the scholarly style; or in English, pp. 65–75.

8. See Richard J. Fein, "Peretz Among the Jews," *Judaism* 29 (1980): 146–152, and my *Against the Apocalypse: Responses to Catastrophe in Modern Jewish Culture* (Cambridge, Mass.: Harvard University Press, 1984), pp. 110–111.

9. "In postvogn," originally pub. in *Di yidishe bibliotek*, 1 (1891); rpt. *Ale verk*, 2:67–85. Tr. "In the Mail Coach" by Golda Werman in *Peretz Reader*, pp. 104–118.

10. Letters to Sholem Aleichem of 17 June 1888, 4 July 1888, and 18 July 1888, in

Mikhtavim, Kol kitvei Y. L. Perets, ed. Shimshon Meltzer, 10 vols. (Tel Aviv: Dvir, 1966), 10B:212–221. For a Yiddish translation of these important letters, see *Briv un redes fun Y. L. Perets,* ed. Nachman Meisel (New York: YIKUF, 1944), nos. 74–76.

11. On Peretz and the persona school of nineteenth-century Yiddish fiction, see Dan Miron, *A Traveler Disguised: A Study in the Rise of Modern Yiddish Fiction in the Nineteenth Century* (New York: Schocken, 1971), esp. pp. 71–73, and his *Sholem Aleykhem: Person, Persona, Presence* (New York: YIVO, 1972).

12. "Mekubolim," *Der tones—shive oser betamuz bletl* (1894); rpt. *Ale verk,* 4:20–25; tr. "Kabbalists" by Shlomo Katz in *Peretz Reader,* pp. 152–156.

13. "Hamekubalim," *Gan perahim* 3 (1891): 83–85; rpt. *Kol kitvei Y. L. Peretz,* 2A:167–171. There are many other differences in this early version, including the choice of the satiric place name Ishekhanovka (as in "The Dead Town," ca. 1895) and the identity of Reb Yekl and Reb Lemech as Habad hasidim.

14. To die "with the [Divine] Kiss," as Jewish tradition ascribes to Moses, is the symbol of transfigured death. For the most exalted reading of this story, see Maurice Samuel, "The Kiss of Moses," in *Prince of the Ghetto* (Philadelphia: Jewish Publication Society, 1948), pp. 256–263. For the most nuanced reading, see Wisse, *Peretz,* pp. 30–34.

15. Peretz first collected them under the *Khasidish* (hasidic) rubric in *Shriftn; yubileum oysgabe* (Warsaw, 1901). The original order was: "Kabbalists," "If Not Higher," "A Conversation," "Joyful Rejoicing," "Between Two Mountains," "The Migration of a Melody," and three "Reb Yoykhenen's Tales."

16. On the varied reader response to "Mekubolim," see A. Rozentsvayg, *Der radikaler peryod fun Peretses shafn (di "yontev-bletlekh")* (The Radical Period in Peretz's Career [The 'Holiday Folios']) (Kharkov-Kiev: Melukhe-farlag fun di natsyonale minder-haytn, 1934), p. 82 n1.

17. See his letters to Pinsky and Yehoash, ca. 1907, in *Briv un redes,* nos. 139–140.

18. Shatzky, "Perets-shtudyes," p. 44. Fishlzon, about whom there is little biographical data, was the author of *Teyater fun khasidim,* pub. in *Historishe shriftn fun YIVO* 1 (1929): 623 693.

19. Peretz, *Lider un poemen* in *Ale verk,* 1:322–343. In his synoptic overview of Peretz's main genres, Gershon Shaked wisely put the comic genres—realistic and fantastic farce, feuilleton, grotesque—at the top of the list. See *Hasipporet ha'ivirit, 1880–1970* (Hebrew Narrative Fiction), vol. 1, *In Exile* (Israel: Hakibbutz Hameuchad and Keter, 1977), pp. 146–150.

20. From "Monish" (1888), as tr. in *The Penguin Book of Modern Yiddish Verse,* ed. Irving Howe, Ruth R. Wisse, and Khone Shmeruk (New York: Viking, 1987), p. 14.

21. "Reb Khanine ben Dosa (a talmudishe zage)" (1891), *Lider un poemen,* pp. 38–42. Only the Marxist critic D. Kurlyand seems to have recognized the parodic intent of this poem, as of "The Golem," discussed below. See "Tsu der frage vegn legendare syuzhetn in Peretses verk," *Sovetishe literatur* (October 1940): 126–128.

22. "Der goylem" (1894), first pub. in *Literatur un lebn; in Ale verk,* 2:310–311. Quoted here in Wisse's tr. from *Peretz Reader,* pp. 130–131.

23. "Bontshe shvayg," *Arbayter tsaytung* (9, 16 March 1894); *Ale verk,* 2:412–430. Tr. Hillel Halkin in *Peretz Reader,* pp. 146–152.

24. Peretz was accused of plagiarizing "Makar's Dream" (1885), the fantasy that made the social-activist writer Vladimir Korolenko famous. Though Peretz rebutted that particular charge, his colleague David Pinsky championed Korolenko's artistry and downgraded Peretz's achievement. "But Bontshe is dead," Pinsky wrote in an otherwise glowing reminiscence of Peretz, "and the heaven with its whole hullabaloo arise not from Bontshe's imagination but from the writer's feuilleton, which one cannot treat as a serious work of art." Pinsky, "Dray yor mit Y. L. Perets," *Di goldene keyt* 10 (1951): 26. See also Dov Sadan, "Bontshe shvayg un zayne gilgulim," *Folk un tsiyon* 27:24 (August-September 1978): 15–18.

25. "Literatur un lebn," *Ale verk,* 7:72–97.

26. Pinsky, "Dray yor mit Y. L. Perets," pp. 15–17, 21–29. For an earlier, more schematic version, see "Geshikhte fun di 'Yontef-bletlekh,' " *Di tsukunft* (May 1945): 321–324; (June 1945): 384–387. The opposition to the *Yontef-bletlekh* was led by the Hebrew-Yiddish writer and critic David Frischmann (1859–1922).

27. For a list of what Peretz published in the *Arbayter-tsaytung* in the years 1893–1895, see Rozentsvayg, *Der radikaler peryod,* pp. 183–184.

28. Undated letter to Pinsky in Russian, presumably from 1899, tr. in *YIVO-bleter* 28 (1946): 196–197. The syntactical ambiguities are Peretz's.

29. For all the conflicting versions of this episode, see G. Eisner, "Y. L. Peretses arest in 1899," *YIVO-bleter* 5 (1933): 353–361.

30. See Hillel Schwartz, *Century's End: A Cultural History of the Fin de Siècle from the 990s through the 1990s* (New York: Doubleday, 1990), esp. pp. 187–190; Dan Miron, *Bo'ah, laylah* (Come, Night: Hebrew Literature Between the Rational and the Irrational at the Turn of the Twentieth Century; Tel Aviv: Dvir, 1987).

31. See "Meh hayah Gordon, balshan o meshorer?" (1896), rpt. *Kol kitvei Y. L. Peretz,* 10:161–200, esp. 175. For a discussion of this essay, see Khone Shmeruk, *Peretses yiesh-vizye* (Peretz's Vision of Despair: New York: YIVO, 1971), pp. 101–106. For his later identification of poetry as prophecy, see also Khone Shmeruk, "Harkri'ah lenavi: Schneour, Bialik, Peretz veNadson," *Hasifrut* 2 (1969): 241–244.

32. See "What Our Literature Needs" (1910), tr. Nathan Halper, *Voices from the Yiddish,* ed. Irving Howe and Eliezer Greenberg (Ann Arbor: University of Michigan Press, 1976), pp. 25–31.

33. "Oyf der tshernovitser shprakh-konferents," *Ale verk,* 11:295.

34. The quote is from Hirsh Dovid Nomberg's superb memoir, "Isaac Leibush Peretz As We Knew Him," tr. Lucy S. Dawidowicz in her *The Golden Tradition: Jewish Life and Thought in Eastern Europe* (Boston: Beacon Press, 1968), p. 295.

35. I. L. Peretz, "Dos yidishe lebn loyt di yidishe folkslider" (1901), *Ale verk,* 7:129–157. On the provenance of this essay, see Samuel Zanvel Pipe, "Di zamlungen yidishe folkslider fun Y. L. Perets," *YIVO-bleter* 12 (1937): 286–290; for an ethnographic critique, see Y. L. Cahan, *Shtudyes vegn der yidisher folksshafung,* ed. Max Weinreich (New York: YIVO, 1952), pp. 104–120.

36. See Jacob Shatzky, "Yehude Leyb Cahan (1881–1937): materyaln far a biografye," *Yorbukh fun Amopteyl fun YIVO* 1 (1938): 9–38.

37. Nomberg's memoir, *Golden Tradition*, pp. 295–296. See also Mark W. Kiel, "Vox Populi, Vox Dei: The Centrality of Peretz in Jewish Folkloristics," *Polin* 7 (1992): 88–120.

38. Nomberg, p. 296; and recall the verse from "Monish" cited earlier. Leah, Peretz's tragic heroine of 1896, had fallen in love with a medical assistant when she heard him singing *lidlekh*, secular Yiddish songs, instead of *zmires*, the Hebrew Sabbath hymns. See "Khasene gehat," *Leshone toyve*, vol. 2 of *Yontef-bletlekh* (1895–98); *Ale verk*, 2:470–493. The relevant passage is on p. 480.

39. Kiel, "Vox Populi."

40. Rober M. Seltzer, "The Secular Appropriation of Hasidism by an East European Jewish Intellectual: Dubnow, Renan, and the Besht," *Polin* 1 (1986): 151–162. On Dubnow in Polish, see Shatzky, "Perets-shtudyes," p. 52.

41. Micah Joseph Berdyczewski, "Nishmat ḥasidim," first published in *Mimizraḥ umimimaʻarav* 4 (1899): 55–64. Quoted here from David C. Jacobson, *Modern Midrash: The Retelling of Traditional Jewish Narratives by Twentieth-Century Hebrew Writers* (Albany: SUNY Press, 1987), p. 23. For Berdyczewski's impact on Peretz's circle, see Nomberg's memoir, *Golden Tradition*, pp. 294–295. For a convenient summary of their mutual influence, see Nachman Meisel, *Yitskhok Leybush Perets un zayn dor shrayber* (New York: YIKUF, 1951), pp. 338–347.

42. See Peretz's autobiographical letter to Israel Zinberg, 3 December 1911, *Briv un redes*, no. 259. For Peretz's reaction to real-life hasidim, see Nokhem Oyslender, "Peretses 'Shtet un shtetlekh' [1902]," *Tsaytshrift* 1 (Minsk, 1926): 69–70.

43. "Di farsholtene brune" (The Accursed Well), published as the second in a series of "Scenes from Small-Town Jewish-Polish Life" in *Der yid* 1 (1899), nos. 9, 11; *Ale verk*, 2:539–549. Despite their ethnographic slant, the satiric element in these scenes predominated.

44. See Ruth R. Wisse, "Not the 'Pintele Yid' but the Full-fledged Jew," *Prooftexts* 15 (1995): 33–61. The 1899 volume of *Der yid* reads like a Who's Who of Jewish neoromanticism: Sholem Aleichem, Hayyim Nahman Bialik, M. M. Dolitzky, Sh. Frug, Hirsh-Dovid Nomberg, I. L. Peretz, Avrom Reisen, Yehudah Steinberg, Avrom Valt (Lyessin), Mark Warshawski, Leyb Yofe. Even Abramovitsh, that crusty old satirist, tried to join the club with his ethnographic memoir, *Shloyme reb Khayims*. The first volume also featured Yiddish folktales edited by "Sh."

45. Letter to Y. Y. Propus, ca. 1896, *Mikhtavim, Kol kitvei Y. L. Peretz*, 10B:296; tr. by Meisel in *Briv un redes*, no. 106.

46. Tr. "A Teacher's Tales" by Moshe Spiegel in *In This World and the Next: Selected Writings of I. L. Peretz* (New York: Yoseloff, 1958), pp. 297–314.

47. My critical judgments are supported by Shmuel Werses in " 'Al omanut hasippur shel Y. L. Peretz," *Sippur veshorsho* (Story and Source: Studies in the Development of Hebrew Prose; Givataim-Ramat Gan: Massada, 1971), pp. 128–129.

48. First published in the Hebrew *Haḥets; yalkut sifruti*, ed. I. L. Peretz (Warsaw: Halter

and Eisenstadt, 1894), then in *Der yid,* no. 19 (1902); *Ale verk,* 4:179–186 and tr. as "The Missing Melody" by David Aberbach in *Peretz Reader,* pp. 196–200.

49. "Tsvishn tsvey berg," *Der yid,* no. 40/41 (1900); *Ale verk,* 4:103–117; tr. by Goldie Morgentaler in *Peretz Reader,* pp. 184–195. It was cellmate Mordecai Spector who reported on Peretz's literary activities in prison. See Eisner, "Y. L. Peretses arest in 1899," p. 354.

50. See Yudel Mark, "An analiz fun Y. L. Peretses shprakh," *YIVO-bleter* 28 (1946): 342; "Language of Y. L. Peretz," pp. 76–77.

51. H. D. Nomberg, "Di revizye fun Peretses shafn," *Gezamlte verk,* 8 (Warsaw, 1930), pp. 104–107. This revisionist essay by one of Peretz's closest associates was a point of departure for my own view of Peretz.

52. Rpt. as "Der koval" in Mikha Yoysef Bin Gorion, *Yidishe ksovim fun a vaytn korev* (Yiddish Writings of a Distant Relative), 2nd rev. ed., 6 vols. (Berlin: Stybel, 1924), 1:144–157. Reviewed by Peretz in "In folk arayn" (1902), *Literatur un lebn, Ale verk,* 7:158–161. In the chapbook version, Berdyczewski provided glosses for the "difficult" words. See Shmuel Werses, "M. J. Beryczewski as a Yiddish Writer," introduction to M. J. Bin-Gorion, *Yidishe ksovim fun a vaytn korev* (Jerusalem: Magnes Press, 1981), pp. liii–liv.

53. This he stated explicitly in a Hebrew letter to Ravnitzky, ca. March 1899, tr. Nachman Meisel, *Yidishe kultur* (April 1950):25.

54. See Peretz, "My Memoirs," tr. Seymour Levitan, *Peretz Reader,* chaps. 2–3 (esp. description of his Polish nanny), and David G. Roskies, "A shlisl tsu Peretses zikhroynes," *Di goldene keyt* 99 (1979): 132–159.

55. "Vos a mol veyniker" (The Decline of the Generations), "Di klole" (The Curse), and "Der oynesh" (The Punishment), all form part of Reb Yoykhenen's *Tales.* See *Khsidish, Ale verk,* 4:66–90. The sequence of stories is somewhat different in Hebrew. Cf. Ḥassidut, *Kol kitvei Y. L. Peretz,* 1A:116–145; 2B:38–53.

56. See Shmeruk, *Peretses yiesh-vizye.*

57. Like "Yoykhenen melameds mayselekh," these were also published in Hebrew (*Hashiloaḥ* 13 [1903]: 289–297) before they were rewritten and augmented in Yiddish. While the Hebrew narrator—clearly modeled on Nosn Nemirover—is a professional writer aware of his skeptical audience, the Yiddish version begins by conjuring up the mystical Saturday-night setting. Cf. "Ha'ofot vehagevilim" (The Birds and the Parchment Scrolls), Ḥassidut, *Kol kitvei Y. L. Peretz,* 1A:83–97, and "Reb Nakhmenkes mayses," *Khsidish, Ale verk,* 4:187–201. For a discussion of the Hebrew version, see Jacobson, *Modern Midrash,* pp. 31–43. Peretz's use of the diminutive *-ke* in Nahman's name adds a note of endearment.

58. From Ḥayyey MoHaRaN (The Life of Rabbi Nahman, 1874), tr. Arthur Green, *Rabbinic Fantasies: Imaginative Narratives from Classical Hebrew Literature,* ed. David Stern and Mark Jay Mirsky (Philadelphia: Jewish Publication Society, 1990), pp. 335–336.

59. In fact, the story has been read very differently, by David C. Jacobson, for one (*Modern Midrash*).

60. "Hisgales, oder di mayse fun tsignbok" (Revelation, or the Tale of the Billy Goat, 1904), *Khsidish, Ale verk,* 4:202–208; tr. Maurice Samuel, *The Prince of the Ghetto,* rpt. *Peretz Reader.* This too is a betrayal of Bratslav Hasidism, which assiduously avoided ascribing any miracles to the rebbe.

61. Wisse, *Peretz,* p. 67.

62. These observations are inspired by Wisse, ibid., p. 33, and by Hillel Schwartz, *Striking Likenesses: The Culture of the Copy in the Modern World,* chap. 1, in manuscript.

63. On the origins and precise meaning of *folkstimlekhe geshikhtn,* see Sh[oshke] E[rlich], "Vos iz taytsh *folkstimlekh?*" *Yidishe shprakh* 33 (1974): 51–52, and Mordkhe Schaechter's rejoinder, "*Folkish* un *poshet-folkish,*" ibid., 52–55.

64. "Dray khupes," first serialized in *Der yid,* nos. 17–39 (1901), rpt. *Folkstimlekhe geshikhtn, Ale verk,* 5:14–72. Tr. Joachim Neugroschel in *Yenne Velt: Great Works of Jewish Fantasy and Occult* (New York: Stonehill, 1976), 1:60–104.

65. This interpretation is taken from Dan Miron's lectures on "Novel and Romance in Modern Yiddish Fiction" (Spring 1973), transcribed by Janet Hadda and Susan Slotnick.

66. In the 1908 ed. of his collected works, Peretz placed it at the end of the *Folkstimlekhe geshikhtn.* He omitted it altogether from his plan for the Russian edition. See M. Erik, "Sholem-Aleykhem un zayn iberzetser," *Tsaytshrift* 5 (Minsk, 1931), 2nd pagination, p 81. Responding to S. Niger's negative review in *Lebn un visnshaft* (February–March 1910), Peretz admitted the failure of "The Three Canopies." See *Briv un redes,* no. 260.

67. Mark, "Y. L. Peretses shprakh," p. 145.

68. Wisse identifies Miriam with the hallowed figure of Peretz's own mother. "In placing her at the heroic center of his Jewish myth," she writes, "he is ascribing to her the ultimate value from which all others flow." *Peretz,* p. 90.

69. This interpretation follows Jonah Fraenkel, *'Iyyunim be'olaman haruhani shel sippurei Ḥazal* (Studies in the Spiritual World of the Aggadic Story; Ramat Aviv: Hakibbutz Hameuchad, 1981), pp. 13–16. On the motif of the blossoming staff, see Dov Sadan, "Mateh Aharon vetse'etsa'av," *Bein she'ilah lekinyan* (Hebrew Literature Borrows and Absorbs; Tel Aviv University, 1968), chap. 9; Rella Kushelevsky, " 'Hamateh haporeaḥ'—'iyyun be'ikkaron hamkhonen shel hasidrah hatematit," *Jerusalem Studies in Jewish Folklore* 13/14 (1991–92): 205–228.

70. "The Snow Queen (An Adventure in Seven Tales)," in *Andersen's Fairy Tales,* tr. Pat Shaw Iversen (New York: New American Library, 1966); Wolfgang Lederer, *The Kiss of the Snow Queen: Hans Christian Andersen and Man's Redemption by Woman* (Berkeley: University of California Press, 1986). For other possible links between "Mesires nefesh" and European culture, see Sol Liptzin, *Peretz* (New York: YIVO, 1947), pp. 23–29.

71. See Israel Bartal, "Halo-yehudim vehevratam besifrut 'ivrit veyidish bemizrah eiropah bein hashanim 1856–1914" (Ph.D. diss., Hebrew University, 1980), pp. 147–167.

72. "Shtume neshomes" (Mute Souls, ca. 1904), *Ale verk,* 5:63.
73. "A kapitl tilim oder Yoykhenen vaser-treger un der Oyrekh-Khayim," "Shma Yisroel oder der bas," and "Nisim afn yam," *Ale verk,* 5:169–197, 139–146. In the Hebrew *Mipi ha'am, Kol kitvei Y. L. Peretz,* 1A:86–128, slightly different versions of the three stories appear in the same sequence.
74. "Aropgelozte oygn," *Ale verk,* 5:118–131; tr. Goldie Morgentaler in *Peretz Reader,* pp. 230–242.
75. See Yehudah Aryeh Klausner, " 'Henekama'—sippuro harishon shel Y. L. Peretz," *Kiryat sefer* 40 (1965): 413–420.
76. The quotation is from Wisse's introduction to *Peretz Reader,* p. xxiii; Hillel Halkin's tr. of "The Three Gifts" is on pp. 222–230. On the anti-halachic bias of the story, see Reuven Kritz, "Leha'arakhat sippurei ha'am shel Peretz uleha'arakhat haz'aner hadidakti," *Karmelit* 17/18 (1973–74): 205–206. For probable sources, see Menashe Unger, "Mekoyrim fun Peretses 'Folkstimlekhe geshikhtn'," *Yidishe kultur* 7 (March-April 1945): 57–58; Isaiah Berger, "Der moker fun der ershter matone in Peretses *Dray matones,*" *Di goldene keyt* 56 (1956): 238–241, and Kritz, p. 197.
77. On the Kishinev pogrom, see my *Against the Apocalypse,* pp. 83–92; and Wisse, *Peretz,* pp. 60–62, 91–92. "Three Gifts" was written sometime between 1904 and 1908. In "The Language of Y. L. Peretz," Yudel Mark dismisses this and a few similar lines as "several half-ironic interpositions" in what is otherwise a tale "narrated by a naive believer" (p. 66). I read the irony as central to the narrative voice, hence to the story as a whole. Based on the last line, Kritz takes the story's message to be "a bitter satire on those who seek in art only beauty while ignoring human suffering" (p. 198).
78. "Iber a shmek-tabek," *Der yid* 13 (1906); *Ale verk,* 5:254–263; tr. Maurice Samuel, *Peretz Reader,* pp. 251–258.
79. See Beatrice Silverman Weinreich, "Genres and Types of Yiddish Folk Tales About the Prophet Elijah," *The Field of Yiddish, Second Collection,* ed. Uriel Weinreich (The Hague, 1965), pp. 208–217; "Der kuntsn-makher," *Ale verk,* 5:147–151; and "The Magician," tr. Halkin, *Peretz Reader,* pp. 218–222 (I replace "magician" with "conjuror").
80. I am indebted to Alan Rosen for some of these insights.
81. Silverman Weinreich (p. 220) calls this type of Elijah tale "Sceptics Are Punished."
82. This reading was suggested to me by Alan Rosen. Peretz captures the same ambiguity in the authorized Hebrew translation that speaks of an *ose-nifla'ot* (doer of miracles) and not of an unambiguous *kosem, mekhashef* (sorcerer, magician).
83. "Ma'asiyot," Passover supplement, *Hatsofe* 75 (1903); rpt. *Kol kitvei Y. L. Peretz,* 5A:83–95. Maurice Samuel's English tr. (rpt. *Peretz Reader,* pp. 200–212) is based on the later Yiddish version in *Ale verk,* 3:462–477. Here, as elsewhere, the Yiddish Peretz is far more sophisticated—in his manipulation of time, his portrayal of character, and particularly his open-ended message—than the Hebrew Peretz.
84. On fallen women: "The Sisters" (1904–1906), tr. Etta Block, *One-Act Plays from the Yiddish, Second Series* (New York: Bloch, 1929), pp. 93–123. On sin: *In polish af*

der keyt (Chained to the Synagogue Anteroom, 1908), *Ale verk,* 6:335–372. On redemption: *Di goldene keyt* (The Golden Chain, 1903–1913), ibid., pp. 101–179. On death: *A Night in the Old Marketplace* (1906–1915), tr. Hillel Halkin, *Prooftexts* 12 (1992): 1–70, and the accompanying essay by Abraham Novershtern, "Between Dust and Dance: Peretz's Drama and the Rise of Yiddish Modernism," 71–90. For a cultural critique of the secular messianism inspired by Peretz's dramas, see Ruth R. Wisse, "A Monument to Messianism," *Commentary* (March 1991): 37–42.

85. See A. Mukdoni, "How I. L. Peretz Wrote his Folk Tales" (1945), tr. Moshe Spiegel, *In This World and the Next,* pp. 352–359; and S. Ansky, "Y. L. Perets," *Gezamlte shriftn,* 15 vols. (Vilna, Warsaw, and New York, 1920–1925), 10:151–167.

86. See Arn Gurshteyn, "Peretses biografye," *Tsaytshrift* 1 (Minsk, 1926): 84.

87. Peretz, "Mayne zikhroynes," *Ale verk,* 11:113; tr. Seymour Levitan as "My Memoirs," *Peretz Reader,* p. 346. For a close reading of this heart-and-mind drama, see my "A shlisl tsu Peretses zikhroynes."

88. "Nile in genem (humoreske)," *Ale verk,* 5:333–338; tr. Halkin, *Peretz Reader,* pp. 258–262. Pace Halkin, Peretz describes the hero as a *baal-tfile,* or leader of prayer, which is usually an unpaid position and implies a much lower status than a "cantor." On the echo effect with Reb Nahman, see below. Ansky's moving portrait of Peretz in 1915 appeared in the special Peretz issue of *Di yidishe velt* (April-May 1915): 16–30, and was partially reprinted in Ansky's *Khurbm Galitsye, Gezamlte shriftn,* 4:20–24.

5. Mythologist of the Mundane: Sholem Aleichem

1. Yiddish-Russian letters to Y. Kh. Ravnitsky, 30 November–1 December 1887 and 5 June 1887, in "Fun Sholem-Aleykhems arkhiv: zayne briv tsu shrayber un tsu fraynd," serialized in *Der tog* (1923–24), nos. 5, 3; Yiddish letter to Yankev Dinezon, 20 October 1888, *YIVO-bleter* 2 (1931): 25, letter 20. According to Nachman Meisel in his introduction to "Sholem-Aleykhems briv tsu Yankev Dinezon," Sholem Aleichem wrote more than a thousand numbered letters in 1888–89. See *YIVO-bleter* 1 (1931): 387. The letter to Dinezon is rpt. in Sholem Aleichem, *Oysgeveylte briv, 1883–1916,* ed. Y. Mitlman and Kh. Nadel, vol. 15 of *Oysgeveylte verk* (Moscow: Ogiz, 1941), no. 28; henceforth abbreviated *Briv.*

2. See Marie Waife-Goldberg, *My Father, Sholom Aleichem* (New York: Simon and Schuster, 1968), pp. 92–111.

3. Yiddish-Russian letter to Ravnitsky, 30 November–1 December 1887, *Der tog,* no. 5.

4. Sholem Aleichem, "Der yidisher dales in di beste verke fun undzere folks-shrift-shteler," supplement to *Yudishes folksblat* (St. Petersburg, 1888): 1075–90, 1101–10, 1149–57, 1183–89, 1205–16, and *Shomers mishpet, oder der sud prisyazhnik af ale romanen fun Shomer* (Berdichev, 1888); H. Reminik, "Sholem-Aleykhem in kamf far realizm in di 80er yorn," *Shtern* 5–6 (Minsk, 1938): 122–148. "Exploited Zhargon" is from Sholem Aleichem's first, self-promoting letter to Abramovitsh of

23 December 1884. Original Russian text and Yiddish tr. in *Dos Sholem-Aleykhem-bukh*, ed. I. D. Berkowitz (New York: Sholem-Aleykhem bukh-komitet, 1926), pp. 190–191; henceforth abbreviated *SAB*. For the later correspondence between them, as of July 1888, see *Tsum ondenk fun Sholem-Aleykhem: zamlbukh*, ed. I. Zinberg and S. Niger (Petrograd: Y. L. Perets-fond, 1917). For the making of the Mendele legend, see Dan Miron, *A Traveler Disguised: A Study in the Rise of Modern Yiddish Fiction in the Nineteenth Century* (New York: Schocken, 1971), pp. 30–33.

5. *Stempenyu* first pub. in *Di yidishe folks-bibliotek* 1 (1888). The best available ed. is in *Ale verk* (Moscow, 1948), 3:7–113, 315–321. For an idiosyncratic tr. see *The Shtetl: A Creative Anthology of Jewish Life in Eastern Europe*, tr. Joachim Neugroschel (New York: Richard Marek, 1979), pp. 287–375.

6. On *Stempenyu* against the backdrop of nineteenth-century romantic realism, see Nokhem Oyslender, "Der yunger Sholem-Aleykhem un zayn roman *Stempenyu*," *Shriftn fun der katedre far yidisher kultur bay der alukrainisher visnshaftlekher akademye* 1 (1928): 5–72; Anita Norich, "Portraits of the Artist in Three Novels by Sholem Aleichem," *Prooftexts* 4 (1984): 237–251.

7. See Dan Miron, *Bo'ah, laylah: hasifrut ha'ivrit bein higayyon le'e-gayyon bemifneh hame'ah ha'esrim* (Come, Night: Hebrew Literature Between the Rational and Irrational at the Turn of the Twentieth Century; Tel Aviv: Dvir, 1987), pp. 91–92.

8. All references are to the critical ed. of *Dos meserl* prepared by Khone Shmeruk (Jerusalem and Cincinnati, 1983). For English tr. see Curt Leviant, *Some Laughter, Some Tears* (New York: Putnam, 1968), pp. 113–128.

9. On the several false starts of Yiddish children's literature in 1867–1900, see Khone Shmeruk, "Sholem-Aleykhem un di onheybn fun der yidisher literatur far kinder," *Di goldene keyt* 112 (1984): 39–53.

10. On the fact-finding trip to Berdichev, see Russian letter to Simon Dubnow, 2 September 1888. Tr. into Yiddish in Sh. Dubnow, *Fun "zhargon" tsu yidish* (Vilna: Kletskin, 1929), pp. 72–73; rpt. *Briv*, no. 25. Sholem Aleichem "draws his subjects from a class of society with which the masses are not particularly well acquainted," wrote Leo Wiener in 1899. See *The History of Yiddish Literature in the Nineteenth Century* (New York: Scribner, 1899), p. 196. As late as 1904, Abraham Cahan of the *Jewish Daily Forward* still viewed Sholem Aleichem as a bourgeois writer.

11. On the decline of the paper under Levi's stuartship, see Sh. L. Cytron, *Di geshikhte fun der yidisher prese*, vol. 1 (Vilna: Fareyn fun yidishe literatn un zhurnalistn, 1923), pp. 150–170. The subscription base of the paper fell from 5,300 under Alexander Zederboym, its founding editor, to 1,650 under Levi. See Y. Serebriani and L. Dushman, "Eynike materyaln tsu der kharakteristik funem yungn Sholem-Aleykhem," *Shtern* 3/4 (Minsk, 1939): 90. Sholem Aleichem's correpondence with Ravnitsky during these years is filled with vitriolic comment about Levi.

12. See Dan Miron, *Sholem Aleykhem: Person, Persona, Presence* (New York: YIVO, 1972), esp. pp. 34–42; I. Nusinov, "Sholem-Aleykhem un Yudishes folks-blat," *Di royte velt* 5/6 (Kharkov, 1925): 104–125. Though woefully inadequate, Zvi Karniel's *Hafeliton ha'ivri* (The Development of the Feuilleton in Hebrew Literature; Tel Aviv: Alef, 1981) is still the only attempt to evaluate the Jewish uses of this enormously

influential genre. For a more detailed study, see Shmuel Werses, " 'Tsloḥit shel feliton' usamemaneha—omanut hafeliton shel Yudah Leib Gordon (Yalag)," *Jerusalem Studies in Hebrew Literature* 2 (1983): 105–125.

13. *Shpetn, oyslakhn, khoyzek makhn:* Yiddish letter of 5 January 1886 (from Belaya Tserkov) to Y. H. Ravnitsky and Ts. Z. Frankfeld, *Der tog* (1923–24), no. 1. On the intimate bond: Yiddish letter from Kiev, 24 January 1889, to Ravnitsky, ibid., no. 30.

14. See Shelly Fisher Fishkin's chapter on Mark Twain in *From Fact to Fiction: Journalism and Imaginative Writing in America* (New York: Oxford University Press, 1985), pp. 55–84. See also Miron, *Sholem Aleykhem,* pp. 9–11, 29–30. None of the satiric writings referred to here was republished either by Sholem Aleichem or by the executors of his estate. They appear only in the Soviet ed. of his *Ale verk,* 3 vols. (Moscow: Emes, 1948). For "on the road," see "Funem veg" (From the Road, 1888–89), ibid., 2:208–233.

15. Khone Shmeruk, *Shalom Aleichem: madrikh leḥayyav uleyitsirato* (Sholem Aleichem: His Life and Literary Work; Tel Aviv: Porter Institute for Poetics and Semiotics, 1980), pp. 17–18, or *Leksikon fun der nayer yidisher literatur* (New York: Congress for Jewish Culture, 1981), 8:680. For "Mr. How-Do-You-Do became Mr. Has-Been," see letter to editor, *Di toyb* (Pittsburgh), written from Kiev, June 1894. Reprinted in Sholem Aleichem, *Felitonen* (Tel Aviv: Beit Shalom Aleichem, 1976), pp. 27–33; quote on 31.

16. "Tevye der milkhiker," *Hoyzfraynd* 4 (Warsaw, 1895): 67. See also Khone Shmeruk, " 'Tevye der milkhiker'—letoldoteha shel yetsirah," *Hasifrut* 26 (1978): 29–30.

17. Asher Beilin, "Shalom Aleichem," in *Ketavim nivḥarim* (Tel Aviv: Association of Hebrew Writers and Dvir, 1956), p. 37; I. D. Berkowitz, *Undzere rishoynim: zikhroynes-dertseylungen vegn Sholem-Aleykhem un zayn dor* (Our Pioneers: Memoiristic Stories about Sholem Aleichem and His Generation), 5 vols. (Tel Aviv: Hamnoyre, 1966), 1:252. This semifictional memoir is the major biographical source on Sholem Aleichem, written by his adoring son-in-law. It was first published in Hebrew as *Harishonim kivnei adam* (1938). The following letters to Ravnitsky contain references to Gogol: 30 March 1887, 5 March 1888, 8 June 1888, all pub. in *Der tog.*

18. *SAB,* p. 189.

19. As reported by Volf (Vevik) Rabinovitsh in his memoirs, *Mayn bruder Sholem-Aleykhem: zikhroynes* (Kiev: Melukhe-farlag fun di natsyonale minderhaytn in USSR, 1939), p. 120.

20. The triple legacy of Haskalah literature is based on Dov Sadan's groundbreaking essay of 1959, "Three Foundations [Sholem Aleichem and the Yiddish Literary Tradition]," tr. David G. Roskies, *Prooftexts* 6 (1986): 55–63.

21. On the concepts of closed and open forms, see Umberto Eco, *The Role of the Reader: Explorations in the Semiotics of Texts* (Bloomington: Indiana University Press, 1984).

22. Donald Fanger, *The Creation of Nikolai Gogol* (Cambridge, Mass.: Harvard University Press, 1979), p. 100. For more on the Gogol connection, see I. J. Trunk, *Sholem-Aleykhem: zayn vezn un zayne verk* (Warsaw: Kultur-lige, 1937), pp. 41–47.

23. See Yudel Mark, "Sholem-Aleykhems vertlekh—geshafn oder geyarshnt?" *Di tsu-*

kunft (May 1946): 379–382. The major study of Sholem Aleichem's style is still E. Spivak, *Sholem-Aleykhems shprakh un stil* (Kiev, 1940). See also Khayim Rayze, "Sholem-Aleykhems aforistik," *Sovetish heymland* (January 1966): 133–140.

24. *Tevye the Dairyman and The Railroad Stories,* tr. Hillel Halkin (New York: Schocken, 1987), p. 3; henceforeth abbreviated F. *Tevye der milkhiker,* vol. 5 of *Ale verk,* Folksfond ed., p. 15; henceforeth, Y.

25. See Benjamin Harshav, *The Meaning of Yiddish* (Berkeley: University of California Press, 1990), pp. 102–107.

26. The precise genealogy of Sholem Aleichem's monologues has never been established. In "Three Foundations," Sadan argues for a direct link with the naive and satiric monologues of the Galician Haskalah. Victor Erlich implies a connection to the Russian *skaz* (hence to Gogol) in "A Note on the Monologue as a Literary Form: Sholem Aleichem's 'Monologn'—A Test Case," *For Max Weinreich on His Seventieth Birthday: Studies in Jewish Languages, Literature, and Society,* ed. Lucy Dawidowicz (The Hague, 1964), pp. 44–50. Nusinov (*Di royte velt,* p. 125) identifies "Arbe koyses," pub. in *Yudishes folkblat* (1888), as Sholem Aleichem's first monologue. On Markuze, see chap. 2 n. 58 of this book.

27. Wiener's pioneering essays on this subject are reprinted in *Di yidishe literatur in nayntsetn yorhundert* (Yiddish Literature in the Nineteenth Century: An Anthology of Yiddish Literary Research and Criticism in the Soviet Union), ed. Chava Turniansky (Jerusalem: Magnes, 1993). See "Di rol fun shablonisher frazeologye in der literatur fun der haskole (tsu der monografye vegn Sh. Etinger)" and "Dialekt un literatur-shprakh," ibid., pp. 71–116. For a critical ed. of *Serkele, oder di yortsayt nokh a bruder,* see Sh. Ettinger, *Geklibene verk,* ed. Max Erik (Kiev: Ukrainishe visnshaft-akademye, 1935). For the view of folklore and folk speech as healthy realism, see Nokhem Oyslender, *Gruntshtrikhn fun yidishn realizm,* 2nd ed. (Vilna: Kletskin, 1928), pp. 24–25.

28. See Y. Riminik, "Linetski un Sholem-Aleykhem," *Shtern* 9 (Minsk, 1939): 80–90. As Wiener notes, the most negative character in *Stempenyu* is Zipporah, the mother of tight-fisted Freydl. Zipporah's speech is replete with *shprakhfolklor.*

29. On transitive-intrasitive see Miron, *A Traveler Disguised,* pp. 169–179. On parody: Harshav, *Meaning of Yiddish,* p. 104. See also H. Binyamin [Benjamin Harshav-Hrushovski], "Dekonstruktsiah shel dibbur: Shalom Aleichem vehasemyotika shel hafolklor hayehudi," afterword to his tr. of *Tevye hahalban vemonologim* (Tel Aviv: Siman kri'ah and Hakibbutz Hameuchad, 1983), pp. 195–212.

30. On child of the Hebrew Haskalah, see esp. Sholem Aleichem, "Tmunot utslalim mihayyei hayehudim biMazepevke" (Sights and Shadows of Jewish Life in Mazepevke, 1889–90), in *Ktavim ivriim,* ed. Khone Shmeruk (Jerusalem: Bialik Institute, 1967), pp. 87–156. On ideological crisis: Oyslender, "Der yunger Sholem-Aleykhem," pp. 25–32; I. Klausner, "Sholem-Aleykhem der tsionist," *Di goldene keyt* 34 (1959): 82–87.

31. On the story's first translator into Hebrew, see Yitshak Bakon, "Beshulei tirgumo shel Brenner leferek mitokh 'Tuvia hahalban'," *Siman kri'ah* 1 (1972): 221–222. On

Tevye as a comic Job, see Itzik Manger, "Nor eyn mol Sholem-Aleykhem" (1933), *Shriftn in proze,* ed. Shloyme Shvaytser (Tel Aviv: Y. L. Perets, 1980), pp. 163–169; partially tr. as "Only One Sholom Aleichem," in *Melech Grafstein's Sholom Aleichem Panorama* (London, Ont.: Jewish Observer, 1948), p. 16. That Tevye willfully misquotes his sacred sources has, to my mind, been definitively proven by Michael Stern in "Tevye's Art of Quotation," *Prooftexts* 6 (1986): 79–96.

32. Ruth R. Wisse, *The Schlemiel as Modern Hero* (Chicago: University of Chicago Press, 1971), pp. 42–43. For Sholem Aleichem's critical stance on the problem of fathers and sons, see *Sender Blank un zayn gezindl: a roman on a "roman"* (1888), Soviet ed. of *Ale verk,* 2:111–201, esp. original version of chap. 4, ibid., pp. 313–316, where a confrontation takes place between Blank Senior and Blank Junior. In *Tevye* Sholem Aleichem brilliantly sidesteps the issue by making Tevye a patriarch without sons.

33. Sholem Aleichem, *A mayse on an ek* (Warsaw: Farlag Bildung, 1901). References to the Yiddish text (abbreviated Y) are to "Der farkishefter shnayder" in *Mayses un monologn,* vol. 13, Progres ed. (Warsaw, 1913): 3–51. English tr. (E) by Leonard Wolf in *The Best of Sholom Aleichem,* ed. Irving Howe and Ruth R. Wisse (New York: New Republic Books, 1982), pp. 3–46.

34. *Oyzer Tsinkes un di tsig* (Vilna, 1868), described by Khayim Lieberman in "Labibliografia shel A. M. Dik," *Ohel RaheL* (Brooklyn, 1980), pp. 498–499. The only extant copy of this chapbook is in the private library of the Lubavitcher Rebbe.

35. Uri Eisenzweig, "Le Chtettl, retroactivement" (*le Tailleur ensorcelé* de Cholem Aleichem), *Territoires occupés de l'imaginaire juif* (Paris: Christian Bourgois, 1980), pp. 196–198. See also Y. Serebriani, "Tsu Sholem-Aleykhems arbet ibern 'Farkisheftn shnayder'," *Sovetish* 12 (1941): 394–408.

36. See Dov Sadan, "Kmo shekosuv: araynfir-bamerkn tsu Tevye dem milkhikers toyres," *Tsvishn vayt un noent: eseyen, shtudyes, briv* (Tel Aviv: Yisroel-bukh, 1982), pp. 9–23. For a reading that contrasts Shimen-Elye's illiteracy with his nobility, see Zoya Prizel, "The Narrator in Sholem Aleichem's 'The Enchanted Tailor'," *Yiddish* 2:4 (1977): 55–60.

37. Literally, "which neither rose nor flew," originally a veiled reference to the resurrection of Jesus. But I doubt that Sholem Aleichem meant to invoke this anti-Christian polemic.

38. Cf. Fanger, *Gogol,* p. 236.

39. Claude Lévi-Strauss, "The Structural Study of Myth," in *Myth: A Symposium,* ed. Thomas A. Sebeok (Bloomington: Indiana University Press, 1970), pp. 81–106.

40. See Ruth R. Wisse on "Eternal Life" in *Sholem Aleichem and the Art of Communication* (Syracuse: B. G. Rudolph Lectures in Judaic Studies, 1979), pp. 19–21. The train station in Zlodievke functions as an enchanted setting in "On Account of a Hat."

41. Eisenzweig, "Le Chtettl," p. 149.

42. See the following in Stith Thompson's *Motif-Index of Folk Literature,* rev. ed., 6 vols. (Bloomington: Indiana University Press, 1966): man transformed into a goat (D 134), goat's milk is inexhaustible (D 1652.3.2), revenant as goat (E 423.1.9), the

devil in the form of a goat (G 303.3.3.1.6), and esp. tailor associated with a goat (X 222).

43. I owe the idea of the master plot to my students Michael Krutikov and Tina Lunson. For the literary evidence, see Janet Hadda, *Passionate Women, Passive Men: Suicide in Yiddish Literature* (Albany: SUNY Press, 1988); David G. Roskies, *Against the Apocalypse: Responses to Catastrophe in Modern Jewish Culture* (Cambridge, Mass.: Harvard University Press, 1984), chap. 6; I. M. Weissenberg, "Father and the Boys" (1908), in *A Treasury of Yiddish Stories,* ed. Irving Howe and Eliezer Greenberg, 2nd rev. ed. (New York: Penguin, 1989), pp. 297–307.

44. Berkowitz, *Undzere rishoynim,* 2:273.

45. I arrived at this understanding of Sholem Aleichem's "normative mythology" after reading and rereading him for many years—only to discover that I. J. Trunk had beaten me to it. See his *Sholem-Aleykhem—zayn vezn un zayne verk* p. 114.

46. These are collected in the following volumes of *Ale verk,* Folksfond ed.: *Fun peysekh biz peysekh* (vol. 2); *Lekoved yontef* (vols. 22–23), as well as in many of the *Mayses far yidishe kinder* (vols. 8–9), which also double as holiday tales. Others are scattered throughout *Fun Kasrilevke* (vol. 1) and *Alt-nay Kasrileveke* (vol. 13). See, in this case, "Der yingster fun di mlokhim," *Mayses far yidishe kinder,* 1:227–245; "Der meylekh mit der malke," *Fun peysekh biz peysekh,* pp. 77–88; and "Der esreg," *Lekoved yontef,* 2:21–38. There is tiny collection of *Holiday Tales of Sholom Aleichem* for young readers, tr. Aliza Shevrin (New York: Atheneum, 1979).

47. Sholem Aleichem, "Der oyrekh" (1906), in vol. 2 of *Lekoved yontef* and vol. 23 of *Ale verk,* Folksfond ed., pp. 103–115. I have used, but emended, Etta Blum's translation, from *The Best of Sholom Aleichem,* ed. Irving Howe and Ruth R. Wisse (Washington, D.C.: New Republic Books, 1979), pp. 281–288.

48. "Talking all in *ahs*" means that the guest used the so-called Sephardic pronunciation of Hebrew.

49. Khayim Lieberman, "Fun badkhonishn repertuar," *Judah A. Joffe Book,* ed. Yudel Mark (New York: YIVO, 1958), pp. 280–283.

50. On ghost writing a holiday story for Spector in spring 1902, see *SAB,* p. 351. *Undzere rishoynim* is also a mine of information on how Sholem Aleichem churned out these stories under deadline. See e.g. 1:118–120; 2:47–48, 62, 65; 3:127, 201; 4:63, 199.

51. Sholem Aleichem, *Tsvey toyte: a bild lekoved Purim* (Two Dead People: A Scene in Honor of Purim; Warsaw: Farlag mayselekh, 1909); rpt. *Alt-nay Kasrilevke,* p. 181.

52. Sholem Aleichem, " 'Olim veyordim," *Hatsofeh* (24 July 1903), rpt. *Ktavim ivriim,* pp. 236–240, Yiddish tr. in Sholem Aleichem, *Fargesene bletlekh,* ed. Y. Mitlman and Kh. Nadel (Kiev, 1939), pp. 191–197.

53. Mordecai Spector, *Purim un peysekh: bilder un ertseylungen* (Berdichev, 1893), and *Yontef-shtimungen* (Holiday Moods; Warsaw, 1906). For vintage Mendele, see "Khag ho'osif" (1904, 1909), "Der khilef" (1904). On concessions to sentimental taste: "A groye hor" (1905), "Shabes" (1911), and "Vos heyst khanike?" (1912). In *Shabes un yontef,* vol. 16, *Ale verk fun Mendele Moykher-Sforim* (Warsaw: Farlag Mendele, 1928). Sholem Aleichem's first (unpublished) holiday story was "Frier un atsind"

(1884), a sentimental love story on the decline of the generations; *SAB,* pp. 328–330. See *Lag boymer* (St. Petersburg: Levi, 1887), supplement to *Yudishes folks-blat* (never republished in its original form). For "Arbe koyses," see Soviet ed. of *Ale verk,* 2:202–207. On holiday stories as children's literature, see Shmeruk, "Sholem-Aleykhem un di onheybn fun der yidisher literatur far kinder," pp. 42–47.

54. See Rivke Rubin, "Der kleyner kasrilik," *Shrayber un verk* (Warsaw-Moscow: Yidish-bukh, 1968), pp. 222–244. For a preliminary sketch of Yiddish holiday stories in the modern era, see Khone Shmeruk, "Yitskhok Bashevises dertseylung 'An erev-khanike in Varshe,' " *Di goldene keyt* 132 (1991): 38–39. Also Uriel Ofek, *Sifrut hayeladim ha'ivrit, 1900–1948* (Hebrew Children's Literature), 2 vols. (Tel Aviv: Dvir, 1988), 1: part 1.

55. See Naomi B. Sokoloff's detailed reading of *Motl Peyse dem khazns* in her *Imagining the Child in Modern Jewish Fiction* (Baltimore: Johns Hopkins University Press, 1992), chap. 3.

56. Sholem Aleichem, "Di fon" (1900), *Mayses far yidishe kinder,* vol. 2 (vol. 9 of *Ale verk*); tr. Curt Leviant as "The Flag," in Sholom Aleichem, *Old Country Tales* (New York: Putnam, 1966), p. 79, with slight changes.

57. E. R. Malachi, "Shalom Aleichem hasofer ha'ivri," in his *Masot ureshimot* (New York: 'Ogen, 1937), pp. 25–33; I. Klausner, "Sholem-Aleykhem der tsionist," *Di goldene keyt* 34 (1959): 83, 89–90.

58. The famous "ABC of [his stepmother's] Curses," tr. Curt Leviant, *From the Fair: The Autobiography of Sholom Aleichem* (New York: Viking, 1985), chap. 45. Yente's monologue tr. as "The Pot" by Sacvan Bercovitch, *The Best of Sholom Aleichem,* pp. 71–81. Even this accurate translation, however, subdivides the fourteen paragraphs of Yente's carefully crafted monologue, each of which begins with a statement of her backtracking. Cf. "Dos tepl" (1901) in *Monologn, Ale verk,* 21:9–25. I owe some of the insights on the structure and meaning of this monologue to Dan Miron.

59. See Hana Wirth-Nesher, "Voices of Ambivalence in Sholem Aleichem's Monologues," *Prooftexts* 1 (1981): 161–164.

60. On the story cycles as situational-thematic clusters, see Shmeruk, *Shalom Aleykhem,* p. 60.

61. For the most thorough and provocative discussion of the text variants of *Menakhem-Mendl,* see Abraham Novershtern, " 'Menakhem-Mendl' leShalom Aleichem: bein toldot hatekst lemivneh hayitsirah," *Tarbiz* 54 (1985): 105–146.

62. On the subtle influence of his speaking tours on the shtetl stories, see Y. Dobrushin, "Tsvey grunt-oysgabes fun Sholem-Aleykhems 'Kleyne mentshelekh mit kleyne has-oges'," *Visnshaftlekhe yorbikher* 1 (1929): 152–159. On structural similarities between Russia and America, see Khone Shmeruk, "Sholem Aleichem and America," *YIVO Annual* 20 (1991): 228, and Berkowitz's editorial note at the beginning of *Fun Kasrilevke.* For more on Sholem Aleichem in America, see Nina Warnke, "Of Plays and Politics: Sholem Aleichem's First Visit to America," *YIVO Annual* 20 (1991): 239–276. On "Pogrom Scenes," see my *Against the Apocalypse,* pp. 172–173.

63. On the problem of endings, see Shmeruk, " 'Tevye der milkhiker'," pp. 34–37, and

his afterword to Sholem Aleichem, *Kokhavim to'im,* tr. K. A. Bertini (Tel Aviv: Dvir, 1992), pp. 600–601, 606–611.

64. See S. Y. Abramovitsh, "Shem and Japheth on the Train" (1890), in *The Literature of Destruction: Jewish Responses to Catastrophe,* ed. David G. Roskies (Philadelphia: Jewish Publication Society, 1989), no. 40. The *Ayznban-geshikhtes* (henceforth abbreviated Y) are in vol. 28 of *Ale verk* or newly translated by Hillel Halkin in *Tevye the Dairyman and The Railroad Stories* (E).

65. Halkin provides some of this background information in his introduction to *Tevye the Dairyman,* pp. xxxiii–xxxvi. On the historicity of Sholem Aleichem's fiction, see my *Against the Apocalypse,* pp. 163–183, and Anna Halberstam-Rubin, *Sholom Aleichem: The Writer as Social Historian* (New York: Peter Lang, 1989).

66. See Dan Miron, "Mas'a be'eizor hadimdumim," afterword to his Hebrew tr. of *Sippurei rakevet* (Tel Aviv: Dvir, 1989), pp. 227–300, esp. 246–247. This is the most sustained analysis of *The Railroad Stories* attempted so far that refines and refutes earlier criticism. Because Miron sees the breakdown of communication and community as the thematic core of this collection, he does not credit the salvaging of stories and "miracles."

67. See my *Against the Apocalypse,* pp. 173–176.

68. I owe this insight to my student Stephanie Greenblatt.

69. Though idiomatic, "as if . . . in his own living room" does not carry the same mock-mythic connotations as the Yiddish *vi baym tatn in vayngortn* (as if in his father's vineyard), a reference to the Garden of Eden.

70. I owe this insight to my student Edith Post.

71. For a structural analysis of the story, marred by the confusion of "Sholem Aleichem" with the narrator and by lack of access to the Yiddish original, see Victoria Aarons, *Author as Character in the Works of Sholom Aleichem* (New York: Edwin Mellen Press, 1985), chap. 5.

72. See Jonathan Boyarin, "Sholem-Aleykhem's 'Stantsye Baranovitsh,' " *Identity and Ethos: A Festschrift for Sol Liptzin on the Occasion of His 85th Birthday,* ed. Mark H. Gelber (New York: Peter Lang, 1986), p. 97.

73. See Wisse, *The Best of Sholom Aleichem,* pp. xiii–xiv.

74. Cf. the trials of Fishl the *melamed* in the mock-mythic story "Home for Passover" (1903), *The Best of Sholom Aleichem,* pp. 112–128.

75. Ever since its first appearance in Isaac Rosenfeld's brilliant rendering in *Treasury of Yiddish Stories,* pp. 111–118, this story has been a favorite of English-language anthologists. As I have discovered on the lecture circuit, however, the story is far less well-known among native Yiddish speakers. In this one instance I have emended Rosenfeld's translation to capture the trilingual wordplay. For the Yiddish original, see "Iber a hitl," *Fun peysekh biz peysekh, Ale verk,* 2:243–254.

76. See Rahel-Ruth Adler, "Mabat sotsio-psiḥologi 'al sippuro shel Shalom Aleichem 'Beshel kova'," *Hado'ar* (7 February 1986).

77. On the interplay of languages, see my *Against the Apocalypse,* pp. 163–172.

78. See Wisse, *Sholem Aleichem and the Art of Communication,* and Miron, afterword to *Sippurei rakevet,* pp. 249–299.

79. For more on this story as a parable of identity, see Delphine Bechtel, "Le Chapeau fait-il le juif? Aspects de la poétique de Sholem Aleykhem," *Yod* 31–32 (1990): 71–79.

80. The first quote is from "Konkurentn" (1903), *Fun peysekh biz peysekh, Ale verk,* 2:140, p. 140. The second is from "Di fon" (1900), *Felitonen,* p. 25.

81. Here I take issue with David Neal Miller, who argues that: "the logic of fiction insists upon unhappy endings, the vocation of the storyteller upon happy ones." See " 'Don't Force Me to Tell You the Ending': Closure in the Short Fiction of Sh. Rabinovitsh (Sholem-Aleykhem)," *Neophilologus* 66 (Amsterdam, 1982): 106.

82. In a letter of 1 May 1909 to his Yiddish publisher Y. Lidsky, Sholem Aleichem wrote: "Neither you nor I should publicize the 'Tale Without an End,' because what you have is the revised copy ('The Haunted Tailor')." Two years later he instructed his son-in-law Berkowitz to publish the story with its new ending (unpublished letters of 10 and 21 March 1911, in Russian). I am indebted to Abraham Novershtern for this information. As mentioned earlier, this new ending did not appear in print until 1913.

83. See Berkowitz, *Undzere rishoynim,* vol. 5, chap. 24.

84. See David G. Roskies, "Unfinished Business: Sholem Aleichem's *From the Fair,*" *Prooftexts* 6 (1986): 65–78. *Funem yarid* appears in vols. 26–27 of the standard Folksfond ed. of Sholem Aleichem's *Ale verk,* along with two earlier autobiographical sketches. E refers to Curt Leviant's English tr. *From the Fair: The Autobiography of Sholom Aleichem.*

85. On the mythic status of Kasrilevke and its relation to the real shtetl of Voronko, see Dan Miron, "Batrakhtungen vegn klasishn imazh fun shtetl in der yidisher beletristik," *Der imazh fun shtetl: dray literarishe shtudyes* (Tel Aviv: Y. L. Perets, 1981), pp. 21–26, 86–101.

86. See Sholem Aleichem's two effusive letters of 10 and 11 January 1913 that appear in the 2nd ed. of Yekhezkl Kotik, *Mayne zikhroynes* (My Memoirs), 2 vols. (Berlin, 1922), 1:9–12; rpt. *Briv,* nos. 183–184.

87. Roskies, *"From the Fair,"* pp. 73–74.

6. The Storyteller as High Priest: Der Nister

1. See John Willet, *Arts and Politics in the Weimar Period* (New York: Pantheon, 1978).

2. The other eleven were Benzion Dinur, Alter Druyanov, Avigdor Hameiri, Moshe Kleinman, Aharon Litai, Yehoshua Hana Ravnitzky, Aryeh Semyatitzky, Saul Tchernichowsky, Zvi Vislavsky, Mikhael Wilenski, and Ephraim Yerusalimski. See Yehoshua Gilboa, *Lashon 'omedet 'al nafshah* (Tel Aviv: Sifriat Poalim, 1977), pp. 108–109.

3. The best analysis in English of Berdyczewski's folklore-related work is by Dan Ben-Amos. See his introduction to *Mimekor Yisrael: Classical Jewish Folktales,* collected by Micha Joseph Bin Gorion, abridged ed., tr. I. M. Lask (Bloomington: Indianapolis: Indiana Universty Press, 1990), pp. xxiii–xlvi. On Bialik's colossal achievement, see Michael Fishbane, "The Aggadah—Fragments of Delight," *Prooftexts* 13

(1993): 181–190, and David Stern, Introduction, *The Book of Legends (Sefer Ha-Aggadah)*, ed. Hayim Nahman Bialik and Yehoshua Hana Ravnitzky, tr. William G. Braude (New York: Schocken, 1992).

4. See Paul Mendes-Flohr, "Fin de Siècle Orientalism, the *Ostjuden*, and the Aesthetics of Jewish Self-Affirmation," *Divided Passions: Jewish Intellectuals and the Experience of Modernity* (Detroit: Wayne State University Press, 1991), pp. 77–132.

5. Arnold J. Band, *Nostalgia and Nightmare: A Study in the Fiction of S. Y. Agnon* (Berkeley: University of California Press, 1968), chap. 4; Dan Laor, "Agnon in Germany, 1912–1924: A Chapter of a Biography," *AJS Review* 18:1 (1993): 75–93.

6. See Leo and Renate Fuks, "Yiddish Publishing Activities in the Weimar Republic, 1920–1933," *Leo Baeck Institute Yearbook* 33 (1988): 417–434.

7. See *Tradition and Revolution: The Jewish Renaissance in Russian Avant-Garde Art 1912–1928*, ed. Ruth Apter-Gabriel (Jerusalem: Israel Museum, 1987); Arthur Tilo Alt, "A Survey of Literary Contributions to the Post-World War I Yiddish Journals of Berlin," *Yiddish* 7 (1987): 42–52.

8. See Franceso Melfi, "The Rhetoric of Image and Word: The Magazines *Milgroym* and *Rimon* (1922–1924) and the Jewish Search for Neutral Loci" (Ph.D. diss., Jewish Theological Seminary of America, 1995).

9. A numbered facsimile edition of some of these rare and beautiful books was put out by the Yiddish Department at the Hebrew University, in collaboration with the National and University Library, on the thirtieth anniversary of the execution of Soviet Yiddish writers on August 12, 1952. The boxed set, *Sofrei yidish bevrit-hama'atsot* and *Yidishe shraybers in ratn-farband* (Jerusalem, 1983), contains 11 titles. See also the *Tradition and Revolution* catalogue for a more exhaustive treatment.

10. On the Yiddishists, see Arthur Tilo Alt, "Yiddish and Berlin's *Scheunenviertel*," *Shofar* 9:2 (Winter 1991): 29–43. On the Hebraists, see Stanley Nash, *In Search of Hebraism: Shai Hurwitz and his Polemics in the Hebrew Press* (Leiden: Brill, 1980), pp. 174, 181, 346ff.

11. Der Nister, *Gedakht*, 2 vols. (Berlin: Literarisher farlag, 1922–23).

12. Sh. Niger, "Moderner mitos," *Dos naye lebn* 1 (New York, 1923): 22–31. The essay begins with a quotation from the Russian symbolist Alexei Remizov.

13. *Shtrom* 3 (Moscow, 1922): appended to p. 83.

14. See Dov Sadan, "Der shtern fun derleyzung," *Toyern un tirn* (Tel Aviv: Yisroel-bukh, 1979), pp. 56–57.

15. For a portrait of his father, see Yankev Lvovski, "Der Nister in zayne yugnt-yorn," *Sovetish heymland* (March 1963): 106; on brother Aaron, see Khone Shmeruk, "Der Nister, ḥayyav veyetsirotav," introduction to Der Nister, *Hanazir vehagdiyah: sippurim, shirim, ma'amarim*, tr. Dov Sadan (Jerusalem: Bialik Institute, 1963), pp. 9–10; on brother Max, see Khone Shmeruk, "Der Nister's 'Under a Fence': Tribulations of a Soviet Yiddish Symbolist," *The Field of Yiddish, Second Collection* (The Hague: Mouton, 1965), pp. 285–286. The major source on Der Nister's personal life are his letters to Shmuel Niger from 1907 to 1923, now published and annotated by

Abraham Novershtern. See "Igrotav shel Der Nister el Shmuel Niger," *Chulyot* 1 (Winter 1992): 169–206. In his introduction (pp. 159–168), Novershtern points out the fact—unique in the annals of Yiddish literature—that Der Nister never republished any of his work that first appeared in the Yiddish press before 1913.

16. For the beginnings of Der Nister's career, see Delphine Bechtel, *Der Nister's Work, 1907–1929: A Study of a Yiddish Symbolist* (Berne: Peter Lang, 1990), chap. 3. Editions of Der Nister's early works are extremely rare. The only accessible selection is in *A shpigl oyf a shteyn: antologye* (A Mirror on a Stone: Anthology of Poetry and Prose by Twelve Soviet Yiddish Writers), ed. Khone Shmeruk, 2nd ed. (Jerusalem: Magnes Press, 1987), pp. 123–133.

17. The symbolist influence on Der Nister's writing has been dealt with by Shmeruk, "Der Nister's 'Under a Fence' "; Bechtel, *Der Nister's Work*, pp. 35–44; Daniella Mantovan, "Der Nister and His Symbolist Short Stories (1913–1929): Patterns of Imagination" (Ph.D. diss., Columbia University, 1993).

18. On Nahman's influence see Shmeruk (1963), p. 24; Bechtel, pp. 123–127; Mantovan, chap. 3.

19. "A mayse mit a nozir un mit a tsigele," first pub. as "A mayse" in *Di yidishe velt* 10 (1913), and later rpt. in *Gedakht*. Here cited from *A shpigl oyf a shteyn*, pp. 134–158.

20. See Abraham Joshua Heschel, *Kotsk in gerangl far emesdikayt* (Kotsk in Its Struggle for Truth), 2 vols. (Tel Aviv: Hamnoyre, 1973), esp. 1:71–73.

21. The importance of passivity in "A Tale of a Hermit and a Kid" was discussed by Dan Miron in his course, "Yiddish Fiction in the Twentieth Century: Continuity and Revolt after the Classicists (1900–1918)," Max Weinreich Center, New York, Fall 1976.

22. Lvovski, "Der Nister in zayne yugnt-yorn," p. 107.

23. Daniela Mantovan, "Der Nister's 'In vayn-keler': A Study in Metaphor," *The Field of Yiddish: Studies in Language, Folklore, and Literature. Fifth Collection*, ed. David Goldberg (Evanston: Northwestern University Press and YIVO, 1993), p. 206.

24. On *Ben hamelekh vehanazir*, see Israel Zinberg, *A History of Jewish Literature*, ed. Bernard Martin (Cleveland: Case Western Reserve University, 1972), 1:189–193.

25. Peretz's legacy is summed up by Bechtel, pp. 27–34. Thirty years later, Der Nister still vividly recalled the visit of 1910, though the passage of time made the disciple more forgiving. See "Perets hot geredt un ikh hob gehert" (1940), rpt. in Der Nister, *Dertseylungen un eseyen*, ed. Nachman Meisel (New York: YIKUF, 1957), pp. 279–289. Der Nister's letter of 9 January 1909 (no. 9) to Niger reveals a profound disappointment with Peretz, a view Der Nister shared with Bergelson. See Novershtern's introduction, pp. 162–164.

26. This new information on Der Nister's activities during World War I is gleaned from letter 26 to Shmuel Niger, November-December 1916.

27. *Andersons mayselekh*, tr. Der Nister (Kiev, 1919).

28. Der Nister, *Mayselekh: A mayse mit a hon, Dos tsigele*, illus. Mark Chagall (Petrograd: Kletskin, 1917); facsimile ed. (Jerusalem, 1983); 2nd ed. (Kiev: Kiever farlag,

1919); 3rd ed. (Warsaw: Kultur-lige, 1921). The Warsaw ed. has only two (anemic) drawings by Chagall. The 4th ed. pub. by Shveln (Berlin, 1923) has none.

29. Chaim S. Kazdan, "Undzer literatur far kinder," *Bikher-velt* 1 (August 1919): 23–31.

30. See e.g. *Loubok—Russian Popular Prints from the Late 18th–Early 20th Centuries from the Collection of the State Historical Museum Moscow* (Moscow: Russkaya kniga, 1992).

31. Kazdan, review of Der Nister, *Mayselekh in ferzn* (Kiev, 1919), *Bikher-velt* 1 (August 1919), pp. 90–93, and Y. Dobrushin, "Yidisher kunst-primitiv un dos kunstbukh far kinder," ibid., pp. 16–23. Dobrushin's essay is a self-contained artistic manifesto. For David Bergelson, writing a manifesto of his own in the same issue of *Bikher-velt*, the term *lubok* is pejorative, signifying the bare outline and surface universalism of literary art that satisfy the vast majority of readers. See "Dikhtung un gezelshaftlekhkayt," ibid., pp. 5–16.

32. Y. B. Ryback and G. Aronson, "Di vegn fun der yidisher moleray," originally pub. in *Oyfgang* (Kiev, 1919); rpt. *Yisokher-Ber Rybak: zayn lebn un shafn* (Paris, 1937), pp. 87–94. Excerpted tr. Reuben Szklowin as "Paths of Jewish Painting" in *Tradition and Revolution*, p. 229.

33. See Khone Shmeruk, "Yiddish Adaptations of Children's Stories from World Literature," in *Art and Its Uses: The Visual Image and Modern Jewish Society*, ed. Richard I. Cohen, vol. 6 of *Studies in Contemporary Jewry* (1990): 186–200; for Der Nister, see esp. p. 188. But as Mantovan points out in her dissertation, Der Nister omitted Andersen's "The Jewish Girl" because of its missionary bias.

34. Besides Kazdan's review, cited earlier, see Shalom Luria, "Kismo shel mini-mitos: 'iyyun be*Mayselekh in ferzn* shel Der Nister," *Chulyot: Journal of Yiddish Research* 2 (1994):151–168.

35. "Sheydim," first pub. in *Eygns* 1 (Kiev, 1918): 41–64; here quoted from *Gedakht* (Kiev: Kultur-lige, 1929), pp. 89–116. Cf. Micha Joseph Bin Gorion, *Mimekor Yisrael*, no. 200; Sara Zfatman, *Nisu'ei adam veshedah* (The Marriage of a Mortal Man and a She-Demon: The Transformations of a Motif in the Folk Narrative of Ashkenazic Jewry from the 16th to the 19th Century; Jerusalem: Akademon Press, 1987); Tamar Alexander, "Leshe'elat ha'itsuv haz'aneri shel sippur shedim," *Dappim lemehkar basifrut* 8 (1991–92): 203–219.

36. It is very doubtful that Der Nister ever read Elia Levita's original epic in ottava rima, *Bovo d'Antona* (Isny, 1541). Last published in Prague, 1767, it was not rediscovered until 1931. For a facsimile, see *Elia Bachur's Poetical Works*, ed. Judah A. Joffe, vol. 1 (New York, 1949). The title of Der Nister's story points to a far more probable source: any of the prose renditions that circulated in chapbook form and were reprinted under various titles. I worked from *Ayn sheyne historye vos vert gerufn Bove mayse* (Vilna: Rom, 1857). There are only 60 rhymed sections that survive in this adaptation, 40 of them in the dialogue. Most of the characters' names undergo folklorization as well: princess Druziana, for example, becomes Drenze, and Pelukan, half man, half dog, becomes Flekhunt ("spotted dog"). For a radically folklorized version of the *Bovo-bukh*, see Y. I. Trunk, "Bove-mayse loyt dem roman

fun Elye Bokher" (1955), *Kvaln un beymer: historishe noveln un eseys* (New York: Undzer tsayt, 1958), pp. 222–320.

37. "A Bove-mayse oder di mayse mit di mlokhim," originally pub. as "A bove-mayse" in *Eygns* 2 (1920): 1–33, in *Gedakht* (Berlin ed.), 2.135–286; abbreviated Y. "A Tale of Kings," tr. Joachim Neugroschel, *Yenne Velt: The Great Works of Jewish Fantasy and Occult,* 2nd ed. (New York: Wallaby, 1978), pp. 460–542; abbreviated E.

38. Bechtel, pp. 201–207, provides a Jungian interpretation of Der Nister's symbolism. My approach, in the wake of Miron's, is classical Freudian.

39. See Shmeruk, "Der Nister's 'Under a Fence,' " pp. 282–284; Bechtel, pp. 238–240. For a wrestling match in Yiddish oral lore, see *Yiddish Folktales,* ed. Beatrice Silverman Weinreich, tr. Leonard Wolf (New York: Pantheon Books, 1988), p. 71.

40. For similar formulaic endings, see *Yiddish Folktales,* pp. 66, 129. They are also common in Slavic folktales.

41. Fellow travelers is the standard English equivalent of *poputchiki,* non-Communist writers who accepted the revolution. They were officially tolerated until 1929. Essays in *Milgroym* that speak admiringly of Peretz include R. Seligman, "In Peretses drokhim," 2 (1922): 40–43, and Max Bienenstock, "Tsvey tkufes in der yidisher literatur," 6 (1924): 31–35. Israel Wachser (1892–1919) was a Yiddish-Hebrew writer of fantastical tales for young and old. He died fighting Ukrainian pogromists during the civil war. Two of his fairy tales were published posthumously in *Milgroym* 3 (1923): 35–39, and *Rimon* 3 (1923): 35–38, with a long, emotional preface by Bialik. Wachser's archive is at the Jewish Theological Seminary of America. Moyshe Kulbak wrote *Meshiekh ben Efrayim,* his most messianic, expressionist, and obscure work, while living in Berlin, where it first appeared in 1924. English tr., "The Messiah of the House of Ephraim," *Yenne velt,* pp. 268–345. For a detailed analysis, see Abraham Novershtern, "Moyshe Kulbaks 'Meshiekh ben-Efrayim': A yidish-modernistish verk in zayn literarishn gerem," *Di goldene keyt* 126 (1989): 181–203; 127 (1989): 151–170.

42. Der Nister, "Afn grenets," *Milgroym* 1 (1922): 29–36, cited here from *Gedakht* (Kiev ed.), pp. 226–246; tr. Joachim Neugroschel, "At the Border," *Yenne Velt,* pp. 44–59. On the English contents page in *Milgroym,* the title is "On the Frontier."

43. On Der Nister's alienation from the Yiddish cultural scene in Berlin, see Bechtel, pp. 14–15, and letter 34 to Shmuel Niger.

44. Der Nister, "In vaynkeler," pub. concurrently in *Shtrom* (Moscow) and *Di tsukunft* (New York), 1922. Rpt. in Berlin and Kiev eds. of *Gedakht;* tr. "In the Wine Cellar," *Yenne velt,* pp. 246–264. For an in-depth analysis, see Bechtel, pp. 178–187, who characterizes this as the first of Der Nister's complex narratives, and Mantovan, "Der Nister's 'In vayn-keler.' "

45. See Rakhmiel Peltz, "The Dehebraization Controversy in Soviet Yiddish Language Planning: Standard or Symbol?" in *Readings in the Sociology of Jewish Languages,* ed. Joshua A. Fishman (Leiden: Brill, 1985), pp. 125–150.

46. See Bechtel, p. 107, for a useful chart comparing the Berlin and Kiev eds. of *Gedakht.* Among the stories omitted from the latter are "Bove-mayse," "Muser," and "Gekept."

The last two were anthologized in *A shpigl oyf a shteyn* as part of Khone Shmeruk's effort to rehabilitate Der Nister as a Jewish writer.

47. Der Nister, "Gekept," published only in Berlin ed. of *Gedakht* (1923); cited here from *A shpigl oyf a shteyn,* pp. 171–185. The unpublished translation is by Michael Stern whom I thank for making it available, along with his diagram of the plot structure.

48. See Bechtel, pp. 134–143.

49. This interpretation was suggested to me by Michael Stern. For an alternative reading, see Shmeruk, "Der Nister's 'Under a Fence'," pp. 278–279.

50. See e.g. Brenda Wineapple, *Genêt: A Biography of Janet Flanner* (1989; Lincoln: University of Nebraska Press, 1992). Gertrude Stein, of course, elected to stay in Europe when the war broke out.

51. "From the heights of skyscrapers" is from *A Slap in the Face of Public Taste* (1912), the most famous of the Russian futurist manifestos. See Vladimir Markov, *Russian Futurism: A History* (Berkeley: University of California Press, 1968), p. 46. On the symbolist tower, see Vladimir E. Alexandrov, *Andrei Bely: The Major Symbolist Fiction* (Cambridge, Mass.: Harvard University Press, 1985), p. 17.

52. On patronage, see James L. West, "The Riabushinsky Circle: *Burzhuaziia* and *Obshchestvennost'* in Late Imperial Russia," and John E. Bowlt, "The Moscow Art Market," both in *Between Tsar and People: Educated Society and the Quest for a Public Identity in Late Imperial Russia,* ed. Edith W. Clowes, Samuel D. Kassow, and James L. West (Princeton: Princeton University Press, 1991), chaps. 4, 8. On the fall of a Jewish merchant family, see Der Nister, *The Family Mashber,* tr. Leonard Wolf (New York: Summit Books, 1987).

53. Her trilogy, *Oyf vegn un umvegn* (On Ways and Byways), is the autobiographical odyssey of a true believer who lived to chronicle both the dream and the nightmare of Soviet Yiddish culture. Vol. 1 (Tel Aviv: Hamnoyre, 1974); vol. 2 (Tel Aviv: n.p., 1978), and vol. 3 (Tel Aviv: Y. L. Perets, 1982).

54. Der Nister, "Naygayst," *Geyendik,* ed. Der Nister, L. Kvitko, M. Lifshits (Berlin: Jewish Section at the Commissariat for Public Education, 1923), pp. 5–30 (pp. refs. are to this ed.). Published simultaneously in *Shtrom* (Moscow) 4 (1923): 8–30; rpt. in *Fun mayne giter* (Kharkov: Melukhe-farlag fun der FSSR, 1928), pp. 7–40.

55. Some of these New Testament allusions have been identified by Sadan, "Der shtern fun derleyzung," and Mantovan, chap. 4.

56. See Khone Shmeruk, " 'Azivat sofrei yidish et Brit-hamo'atsot veshuvam eleha le'or iggeret bilti-yadu'a shel Der Nister," *Bein Yisrael le'umot* (Festschrift for Shmuel Ettinger; Jerusalem: Zalman Shazar Center, 1987), pp. 297–305.

57. Letter 31, summer 1922.

58. Letter 34, mid-1923.

59. Undated letter to Lyessin, YIVO Archive, quoted in Novershtern, n. 100. On Der Nister's break with the Kultur-lige (relocated in Warsaw), which published his translations of Hans Christian Andersen, see letter 32 of November 1922. Letter 34 of mid-1923 blames the Literarisher Farlag of Berlin for making excessive changes

in his text; he decided to break with them before issuing the third volume of *Gedakht.*

60. D[avid] B[ergelson], "Dray tsentern," *In shpan* (Vilna) 1 (April 1926): 84–96.

61. In letter 32, November 1922, to Niger, Der Nister uses the same terms to describe himself.

62. Shmeruk, "Der Nister's 'Unter a ployt' "; Bechtel, pp. 17–21.

63. The discussion that follows is inspired by James C. Scott's *Domination and the Arts of Resistance: Hidden Transcripts* (New Haven: Yale University Press, 1990). Scott's book has much to say about how Jews have used language(s) as a means of resistance, though they are nowhere actually mentioned, except for one (politically correct) reference to the Israeli domination of Palestinians.

64. On the former, which was never collected, see I. D. Berkowitz, *Undzere rishoynim,* 5 vols. (Tel Aviv: Hamnoyre, 1966), 1.141–142. On "Berele," see Sholem Aleichem, *Ktavim ivriim,* pp. 341–355, and *Fun peysekh biz peysekh, Ale verk,* 2:91–105.

65. Der Nister, "A mayse mit a lets, mit a moyz un mit dem Nister aleyn," *Fun mayne giter,* pp. 43–80.

66. Bechtel, p. 252. See Der Nister, "Fun mayne giter," *Fun mayne giter,* pp. 7–40; tr. Joseph Leftwich, "From My Estates," in *Anthology of Modern Yiddish Literature* (The Hague: Mouton, 1974), pp. 65–84.

67. Der Nister probably meant this as a double allusion to Gogol's *Diary of a Madman* and to his own piece of juvenilia, "A tog-bikhl fun a farfirer" (Diary of a Seducer, 1910). On Gogol's influence, see Bechtel, p. 251.

68. Der Nister, "Unter a ployt (revyu)," in *A shpigl oyf a shteyn,* pp. 186–217 (henceforth cited Y). After first appearing in *Di royte velt* (Kharkov), 7 (1929), the story was reprinted at the end of the Kiev edition of *Gedakht,* replacing "A Bove-mayse." The English translation cited here (E) is by Seymour Levitan, *A Treasury of Yiddish Stories,* ed. Irving Howe and Eliezer Greenberg, 2nd rev. ed. (New York: Penguin Books, 1989), pp. 574–596.

69. For a comparison between the two, see Mantovan, chap. 6.

70. See Shmeruk, "Der Nister's 'Under a Fence'," p. 281, and Bechtel, pp. 223–226.

71. Jesus at Gethsemane (Matt. 26:38), as noted by Mantovan, "Der Nister's 'In vaynkeler'," p. 206. I owe the psychological reading of the story to lecture notes of Dan Miron's course, "Yiddish Fiction in the Twentieth Century." Shmeruk allows for a Freudian interpretation but does not spell it out. See "Der Nister's 'Under a Fence'," n. 23.

72. Levitan, in an otherwise admirable translation, consistently renders *nozir* as "scholar," thus eliminating the religious dimension of the story.

7. The Last of the Purim Players: Itzik Manger

1. *Bay undz yidn: zamlung far folklor un filologye,* ed. M. Vanvild (Warsaw: Pinkhes Graubard, 1923).

2. Ignaz Bernstein, *Jüdische Sprichwörter und Redensarten im Anhang Erotica und Rus-*

tica, rpt. ed. Hans Peter Althaus (Hildesheim: Georg Olms, 1969); for the less scholarly inclined, *Yiddish Sayings Mama Never Taught You,* ed. G. Weltman and M. S. Zuckerman (Van Nuys: Perivale Press, 1975).

3. [Dr. I. Lejpuner], "Tsu undzere lezer," *Land un lebn* (Warsaw) 1:1 (December 1927): 1; [Emanuel Ringelblum], "Fun der redaktsye," *Landkentenish* (Warsaw) 1 (1933): 7. On the exclusion of Jews from the Polish society, see Ringelblum's comments on p. 4 of the editorial.

4. M. Burshtin, "A nayer faktor in yidishn lebn," *Landkentenish,* n.s., 1 (1937): 9–13. The journal carried periodic reports of the society's growth and activities, such as Burshtin's "Landkenerishe arbet oyf di kolonyes un vanderlagern," *Landkentenish* 2:20 (June 1935): 3–5. By far the most impressive document I have found, however, was written by my uncle, Hirsh Mac (Matz), *Kurerter un turistik in Poyln* (Health Resorts and Tourism in Poland; Warsaw: TOZ, 1935).

5. See Moyshe Kulbak, "From *Byelorussia,*" tr. Leonard Wolf, *The Penguin Book of Modern Yiddish Verse,* ed. Irving Howe, Ruth R. Wisse, and Khone Shmeruk (New York, 1987), pp. 388–401; "Vilna," tr. Nathan Halper, ibid., pp. 406–411; "Munie the Bird Dealer," tr. Norbert Guterman, *A Treasury of Yiddish Stories,* ed. Irving Howe and Eliezer Greenberg 2nd rev. ed. (New York, 1989), pp. 342–350. Because the first chapter of Kulbak's story was accidentally omitted from the translation, even the "revised" edition has Munie "walking" about. For the Yiddish original, see *A shpigl oyf a shteyn: antologye,* ed. Khone Shmeruk, 2nd rev. ed. (Jerusalem: Magnes Press, 1987), pp. 556–566.

6. Zalmen Szyk, *1000 yor Vilne,* part 1 (Vilna, 1939), richly illus. Part 2 never appeared. Szyk conjured up a city in which the Jewish traveler could move effortlessly from one ethnic enclave to another and across religious boundaries. This of course was a fictional construct. For a much more sobering tour of the same city, see Lucy S. Dawidowicz, *From That Place and Time: A Memoir, 1938–1947* (New York: Norton, 1989). My father, for one, was beaten up by his fellow Poles for not taking his hat off while passing the Catholic shrine on Ostra Brama.

7. See e.g. Michael Davitt Bell's discussion of associationism in his *The Development of American Romance: The Sacrifice of Relation* (Chicago: University of Chicago Press, 1980), pp. 16–18, 74.

8. See Joshua A. Fishman, "Status Planning: The Tshernovits Conference of 1908," in his *Yiddish: Turning to Life* (Amsterdam and Philadelphia: John Benjamins, 1991), part 4.

9. See Yitskhok Paner, *Shtrikhn tsum portret fun Itsik Manger* (Tel Aviv: Hamnoyre, 1976), pp. 62–63. Though poorly written and not altogether reliable, this is the only unglorified account of Manger's early years I have been able to find.

10. The Manger Archive at the Jewish National and University Library, Jerusalem, has his Notebook for 1918–19; 4°–1357, file 2:22. I assume that the reference to Rilke came from Manger because Reisen drew his biographical material from questionnaires filled out by the authors.

11. Manger, "Yas," in MS of *Harbstike oygn (1919–1925),* ibid., file 2:7. On Velvl Zbarzher-Ehrenkrantz, see Zalmen Reisen, *Leksikon fun der yidisher literatur, prese un*

filologye, 2nd rev. ed. (Vilna: Kletzkin, 1927), 2:832a-840; Chana Gordon Mlotek, "Velvl Zbarzher Ehrenkrants—tsu zayn 100stn yortsayt," *Di tsukunft* 90 (January 1984): 7–12, and (February 1984): 47–54.

12. On Manger's great admiration for Mani Leyb, see Ruth R. Wisse, *A Little Love in Big Manhattan: Two Yiddish Poets* (Cambridge, Mass.: Harvard University Press, 1988), pp. 229–230.

13. For an absurdly idealized portrait of Manger and his family in Jassy, see Yankl Yakir, "Itsik Manger un zayn yikhes-briv," *Sovetish heymland,* 11 (November 1969): 131–142. On *literatoyre,* see p. 140.

14. *Kveytn, Poesie von J. Manger;* his original title, now faded, was *Folks-lider.* Part 2 of the MS is dated 1919–20. Manger Archive 4°–1357, file 2:22.

15. Shloyme Bickel, "Di onheyb-yorn mit Itsik Manger," *Shrayber fun mayn dor* (Writers of My Generation), vol. 3 (Tel Aviv: Y. L. Perets, 1970), pp. 391–392. In an earlier version of this memoir, published in the *Tog morgn zhurnal* (30 March 1969), Bickel has this lecture occurring in 1919. That is also my source for the audience's not hearing a thing.

16. Bickel, "An intsident mit Mangern," *Shrayber fun mayn dor,* pp. 395–396.

17. See Paner, *Shtrikhn tsum portret,* pp. 16–19, 30–32.

18. Ruth R. Wisse, Introduction to Book II in *Voices Within the Ark: The Modern Jewish Poets,* ed. Howard Schwartz and Anthony Rudolf (New York: Avon, 1980), p. 241. For a small sample of Steinberg's fables, see *Penguin Book of Modern Yiddish Verse,* pp. 114–122.

19. *Eliezer Shteynbargs gezungene lider,* ed. Hersh Segal (Rehovot, 1977), illus.

20. See Paner, *Shtrikhn tsum portret fun Itsik Manger,* p. 76. Elsewhere (pp. 37–42) Paner claims that Steinberg snubbed Manger for his bohemian ways. Yet Manger, who was never one to forgive or forget any slight, made constant reference to Steinberg in the lectures and interviews he gave upon arriving in Warsaw. He even named Steinberg his favorite Yiddish author, after Sholem Aleichem and David Bergelson. See "Mayn balibster shrayber," *Literarishe bleter* 17 (April 25, 1930); rpt. Itzik Manger, *Shriftn in proze* (henceforth cited *Shriftn*), ed. Shloyme Shvaytser (Tel Aviv: Y. L. Perets, 1980), p. 326.

21. "A shmues mit Yitskhok Manger," *Literarishe bleter* (January 1929); *Shriftn,* p. 281.

22. Shloyme Bickel, "Itsik Manger," *Tog morgn zhurnal* (11 June 1961).

23. See the following essays by Manger originally published in *Literarishe bleter,* rpt. in *Shriftn:* "Di yidishe dikhtung in Rumenye" (1929); "Dos rumenishe folkslid" (1929), and "Di balade—di vizye fun blut" (1929).

24. Manger, "Di balade—di vizye fun blut," *Shriftn,* pp. 306–309.

25. All these are to be found in the MS of *Harbstike oygn.* In *Kveytn* he also identified the poem "Der kloyznik" as a ballad. On the ballad see Eleanor Gordon Mlotek, "Traces of Ballad Motifs in Yiddish Folk Song," *The Field of Yiddish,* Second Collection, ed. Uriel Weinreich (The Hague: Mouton, 1965), pp. 232–252; Yekhiel Hoffer, *Itsik Manger: eseyen* (Yiddish-Hebrew ed., Tel Aviv: I. L. Perets, 1979), p. 35.

26. "The Ballad of the White Glow," tr. Leonard Wolf, *Penguin Book of Modern Yiddish*

Verse, pp. 574–577. Eight ballads by Manger were translated by Sacvan Bercovitch with five illustrations by his sister, Sylvia Ary, in *Versus* (Montreal) 4 (Winter 1978): 19–26; a bilingual mimeographed edition of nineteen ballads, also translated by Bercovitch, was put out by the Jewish Public Library of Montreal in 1977. Wherever possible, I have made use of Bercovitch's unrhymed versions.

27. "You hack!" Manger shouted at Melech Ravitch in Warsaw, around 1929. "You need to write your silly verse with a pen. I write mine in my memory. *Ikh bin in gantsn lid,* my whole essence is a poem." See Melech Ravitch, *Dos mayse-bukh fun mayn lebn 1921–1934* (The Storybook of My Life), vol. 3 (Tel Aviv: Y. L. Perets, 1975), p. 286. For a structural analysis of a typical Yiddish ballad, see Dov Noy, "Dos meydl un der royber: farglaykhik-strukturele shtudye in yidisher folks-baladistik," *Khayfa-yorbukh* 5 (1969): 177–224.

28. Manger, "Ershter briv to X. Y.," *Getseylte verter* (Czernowitz) 1 (August 1929), *Shriftn,* p. 479; and "Driter briv tsu X. Y.," *Getseylte verter* 4 (September 1929), *Shriftn,* p. 487. See also Janet Hadda, "Christian Imagery and Dramatic Impulse in the Poetry of Itsik Manger," *Michigan Germanic Studies* 3:2 (1977): 1–12.

29. For the good news about Warsaw, see Chaim S. Kazdan, "Itsik Manger in Varshe," *Itsik Manger* (New York: CYCO, 1968), pp. 24–30. For the bad news, see Manger's editorials, "Eyns, tsvey, dray—forhang!!!" *Getseylte verter* 2:2 (23 May 1930): 1–2; "O—mit zeks!!!" ibid., 2:3 (30 May 1930): 1–2; and esp. his "Open Letter to Melech Ravitch," ibid., 2:7 (4 July 1930): 2–3.

30. Manger, "Altmodishe balade," *Lid un balade* (New York: Itsik-Manger-komitet, 1952), p. 114. While the abcbd stanzaic form may indeed be old-fashioned, it does not, to the best of my knowledge, correspond to anything in Yiddish oral tradition.

31. This reading of the poem was first suggested by Ruth Wisse in "Itsik Manger: Poet of the Jewish Folk," *Jewish Heritage* (Spring 1970): 35–36.

32. "Di balade fun podoloyer rov," *Lid un balade,* pp. 155–156. On the prolonged creative process, see Kazdan, *Itsik Manger,* p. 58 (misnamed "Balade fun dem podolyer rov").

33. In a letter from Warsaw to brother Notte (9 March 1934), Manger wrote of having heard from Avrom Lyessin, editor of *Di tsukunft,* the major Yiddish literary monthly in New York, that the "Ballad of the Podoloyer Rabbi" was the most impressive single work in modern Yiddish poetry. Manger Archive, 4°–1357, file 4:109.1.

34. Itzik Manger, "Tsveyter briv tsu X. Y.," *Getseylte verter* 3 (August 1929); *Shriftn,* p. 485.

35. "Di balade fun dem shnirl shtern," *Lid un balade,* pp. 178–180; translation mine. I first discovered the power of this ballad when hearing it declaimed by Hertz Grosbard.

36. Cf. Manger's line *Mari, melodi, melodi* (Mary, melody melody) in his translation of Rainer Maria Rilke's poem "Madness," *Getseylte verter* 2 (1929): 2. The standard Yiddish word is *melodye,* with the accent on the second syllable.

37. A. Tabachnik, "Itsik Manger un di naye yidishe balade," *Di goldene keyt* 64 (1968): 13–40, esp. 22.

38. Manger, "Mayn veg in der yidisher literatur," speech delivered at the Statler Hilton Hotel in New York City, June 1961, honoring his sixtieth birthday; *Shriftn*, pp. 364–365. According to the *Leksikon fun der nayer yidisher literatur*, Israel Rubin emigrated to Palestine in 1929.

39. The Brody Singers were named after their founder, Berl Broder-Margulies (ca. 1817–1868). These are the major sources on his life and work: N[okhem] Shtif, *Di eltere yidishe literatur: literarishe khrestomatye* (Older Yiddish Literature: A Literary Sourcebook; Kiev: Kultur-lige, 1929), pp. 195–199; Berl Margulies, *Dray doyres* (Three Generations: The Songs of Berl Broder, the Feuilletons of Yam Hatsiyoni; Narrative and Lyric Poetry of Ber Margulies; New York, 1957), pp. 7–32; Dov Sadan, "Zamarei Brod veyerushatam," *Avnei miftan: masot 'al sofrei yidish,* 3 vols. (Tel Aviv: I. L. Perets, 1962), 1:9–17.

40. Two examples of Manger's turning his father into a direct source for his art are "Nor eyn mol Sholem-Aleykhem" (1933), which begins with Manger reminiscing about his youth in Jassy, seeing the death notice of the great writer in a bookstore window, and hearing his father read and extol Sholem Aleichem's writings; and his introduction to *Hotsmakh-shpil* (London-Johannesburg: Farlag aleynenyu, 1947), a reworking of Godfaden's *The Witch* (1879), where Manger credits his father's workshop and his rhymed discourses with instilling a passion for theater in the son. For a lyrical memoir of his father, see "Mayn tate pravet a geburts-tog," in *Noente geshtaltn un andere shriftn* (New York: Itsik Manger yoyvl-komitet, 1961), pp. 480–487. Later his dead brother Notte would serve a similar function.

41. Yehoash [Shloyme Blumgartn, 1871–1927] began translating the Bible into Yiddish in 1910. It appeared in book form in 8 vols.: The Pentateuch (vols. 1–2; 1926), Prophets (vols. 3–6; 1927–29), and The Writings (vols. 7–8; 1936), all in Farlag tanakh, New York.

42. See Khone Shmeruk's important essay, "*Medresh Itsik* and the Problem of Its Literary Traditions," introduction to Itzik Manger, *Medresh Itsik*, 3rd rev. ed. (Jerusalem: Magnes Press, 1984), pp. v–xxix. Further refs. to *Medresh Itsik* are to this scholarly ed., which supersedes all others. In a letter from Warsaw to his brother Notte (15 April 1934), Manger asked that a copy of Nokhem Shtif's anthology *Di eltere yidishe literatur* (Kiev, 1929) be sent to Dvora Fogel for review purposes. Manger Archive, 4°-1357, file 4:109.1. This anthology would later serve as the inspiration for Manger's *Noente geshtaltn*, a fictionalized history of eighteenth- and nineteenth-century Yiddish literature.

43. "Ofener briv fun kletsker rosh yeshive hagoen rabi Arn Kotler," *Di vokh* (May 1935); a copy in the Manger Archive from Dov Sadan's collection, 8:85. For a summary of the controversy engendered by Manger's Bible poems, see Dov Sadan, "A makhloyke un ir videranand," introduction to *Medresh Itsik*, Hebrew pagination. For a hysterical reaction to these poems from out of the Holocaust, see Yitshak Katzenelson, "Pinkas Vittel," entry for 24–25 July 1943 in *Ktavim aharonim begeto Varshah uvemahaneh Vittel*, ed. Shlomo Even-Shoshan et al. (Israel: Ghetto Fighters' House and Hakibbutz Hameuchad, 1988), p. 40.

44. The impact of the Ohel Theater production was first suggested by Yekhiel Hofer in 1951. See "Itsik Mangers poetishe eygnartikayt," rpt. in *Itsik Manger*, p. 37. Dov Sadan later endorsed this hypothesis.

45. *Medresh Itsik*, p. 3.

46. Manger, "Folklor un literatur," *Oyfn sheydveg* (Paris) 1 (April 1939); *Shriftn*, pp. 327–334. For a partial translation, see "Folklore and Literature," *The Way We Think: A Collection of Essays from the Yiddish*, ed. Joseph Leftwich, 2 vols. (New York, 1969), 2:678–682.

47. Wisse, "Itsik Manger," p. 29.

48. See S. Ansky, "Di yidishe folks-shafung," tr. from Russian by Zalmen Reisen in *Folklor un etnografye*, vol. 15 of Ansky's *Gezamlte shriftn* (Vilna-Warsaw-New York: Farlag "An-Ski," 1925), pp. 27–95; orig. in inaugural issue of *Perezhitoe* (St. Petersburg, 1908). A somewhat different version appeared in Chaim Zhitlovsky's *Dos naye lebn* 1 (New York, 1909): 224–240. For a discussion, see my Introduction to *The Dybbuk and Other Writings* by S. Ansky (New York: Schocken, 1992), pp. xix–xx, xxii–xxiv, and "S. Ansky and the Paradigm of Return," in *The Uses of Tradition: Jewish Continuity in the Modern Era*, ed. Jack Wertheimer (New York: Jewish Theological Seminary of America, 1992), pp. 255–257.

49. On the rhythmic schemes used in *Medresh Itsik*, see B. Hrushovski, "On Free Rhythms in Modern Yiddish Poetry," *The Field of Yiddish: Studies in Language, Folklore, and Literature*, ed. Uriel Weinreich (New York: Linguistic Circle of New York, 1954), pp. 238–239, and Shmeruk, "*Medresh Itzik* and the Problem of Its Literary Traditions," pp. xix–xxi.

50. Manger, "Hogors letste nakht bay Avromen," *Medresh Itsik*, pp. 29–30, tr. Leonard Wolf, *A Treasury of Yiddish Poetry*, ed. Irving Howe and Eliezer Greenberg (New York: Holt Rinehart and Winston, 1969), pp. 277–278.

51. For a preliminary study of Manger's "Poetic-Linguistic Extended Digressions from the Biblical Narrative," see Joseph Gamzu, "Poetic and Linguistic Symbiotic Phenomena in Itzik Manger's Biblical Poetry," (Ph.D. diss., University of Texas, Austin, 1976), chap. 15. A far more rigorous and fruitful approach to Manger's deviations and anachronisms is Chana Kronfeld's "Deviant Uses of Collocation in the Poetry of Itzik Manger," paper read at International Conference on Research in Yiddish Langauge and Literature, Oxford (6–9 August 1979).

52. Manger, "Avrom un Sore," *Medresh Itsik*, pp. 21–22. This use of a standard folk phrase is discussed by Chana Kronfeld. Rella Kushelevsky believes that the expression derives from a tale in the medieval *Mayse-bukh* and before that from rabbinic lore about the staff of Aaron. See " 'Hamateh haporeah'—'iyyun be'ikkaron hamekhonen shel hasidrah hatematit," *Jerusalem Studies in Jewish Folklore* 13–14 (1991–92): 207.

53. Manger, "Abraham Takes Isaac to the Sacrifice," tr. Leonard Wolf, *Treasury of Yiddish Poetry*, pp. 275–276; Yiddish original, *Medresh Itsik*, pp. 39–40.

54. See Manger, *Felker zingen* (Nations Sing; Warsaw: Ch. Brzoza, 1936), and *Hotsmakh-shpil: a Goldfadn-motiv in 3 aktn* (Hotsmakh Play: Comedy in Three Acts and

Fourteen Tableaux; London-Johannesburg, 1947); Joseph Green, *Yidl mitn fidl* (Poland, 1936), starring Molly Picon, with lyrics by Manger. On the planned journal, see Rokhl Auerbach's letter of 26 June 1935 to Melech Ravitch, Manger Archive. The plans fell apart because Bashevis Singer left for America and Neyman immigrated to Palestine. Paner is our only source on Manger's prior marriage to a beautiful (unnamed) woman from Galicia. On this sordid episode, see *Shtrikhn*, pp. 44–47. In her own brief but poignant chapter on her years with Manger, Auerbach does not refer to herself as his wife. See her *Baym letstn veg: in geto Varshe un oyf der arisher zayt* (On the Last Road: In the Warsaw Ghetto and on the Aryan Side; Tel Aviv: Yisroel-bukh, 1977), pp. 164–174.

55. For an interpretation of this work against the political backdrop of the late thirties, see Ruth R. Wisse, "1935/6—A Year in the Life of Yiddish Literature," *Studies in Jewish Culture in Honour of Chone Shmeruk*, ed. Israel Bartal, Ezra Mendelsohn, and Chava Turniansky (Jerusalem, 1993), pp. 98*–99*.

56. Manger, *Noente geshtaltn* (Warsaw: Ch. Brzoza, 1938); *Shriftn*, pp. 11–134.

57. Manger, *Di vunderlekhe lebns-bashraybung fun Shmuel-Abe Abervo (Dos bukh fun gan-eydn)*, rpt. *Noente geshtaltn un andere shriftn*, pp. 131–348; tr. Leonard Wolf as *The Book of Paradise: The Wonderful Adventures of Shmuel-Aba Abervo* (New York: Hill and Wang, 1965). The *Purim-shpil* quote is on p. 215 of the English ed., except that Wolf missed the reference to the Nazis.

58. The adventure of the stolen goat described in chap. 4 of *The Book of Paradise* is loosely based on an episode from Manger's childhood. See his "Kinder-yorn in Kolomey (fun mayn togbukh)," *Shriftn*, pp. 442–443.

59. "Di balade fun dem yid vos hot gefunen di halbe levone in a kornfeld," *Lid un balade*, p. 424, tr. Sacvan Bercovitch.

60. For a cleaned-up version of Manger's life and letters during the war, see Chaim S. Kazdan, *Di letste tkufe in Itsik Mangers lebn un shafn, 1939–1969* (The Last Period in Itzik Manger's Life and Creativity; Mexico City, 1973), pp. 9–50. These letters caused quite a stir in the American-Yiddish press. Manger's "Open Letter to I. J. Segal and Melech Ravitch" disavowing Yiddish is dated London, 11 July 1944, Manger Archive, 4°-1540, box 95, file 3.

61. Manger to Ravitch "in a saner moment": letter from London, 4 October 1940, Manger Archive, 4°-1540; "Cain and Abel," Leonard Wolf, *Treasury of Yiddish Poetry*, pp. 278–279.

62. On the rescue of Manger's papers (which she gives as one reason for her remaining in Warsaw when the war broke out), see Rokhl Auerbach's two extraordinary memoirs: *Varshever tsavoes: bagegenishn, aktivitetn, goyroles 1933–1943* (Warsaw Testaments: Encounters, Activities, Fates; Tel Aviv: Yisroel-bukh, 1974), pp. 193–194; *Baym letstn veg*, p. 169. The historian Chimen Abramsky is my source for the reunion in London.

63. Manger, "Mayn balibster shrayber," *Literarishe bleter* (25 April 1930); *Shriftn*, p. 326.

64. Manger, "Bay der Babe Taube in Stoptshet" (1961); *Shriftn*, pp. 452–460. The story

as Manger tells it here is hilarious. What a shame that he stopped writing his memoirs of childhood after three chapters.

65. Manger, "The Adventures of Hershel Summerwind" (1947), tr. Irving Howe, *Treasury of Yiddish Stories,* p. 446.

66. See Manger's bitter comments in "Mayn veg in der yidisher literatur," *Shriftn,* p. 363.

67. Manger, "The Squire's Moustaches" (1949), tr. Joseph Leftwich, *Yisröel: The First Jewish Omnibus,* rev. ed. (New York: Yoseloff, 1963), pp. 650–655. I have slightly revised Leftwich's translation. Cf. "Di mayse mitn poritses vontses," *Shriftn,* pp. 149–159. The story bears a strong resemblance to "Di klole" (The Curse), one of Peretz's neo-folk tales.

68. On this episode, see Kazdan, *Di letste tkufe in Itsik Mangers lebn un shafn,* pp. 145–158. See also Rivka Rus, *Bemehitsato shel Itsik Manger* (In the Company of Itzik Manger: Encounters with and Letters from the Greatest Yiddish Poet), tr. Moshe Yungman (Tel Aviv, 1983). Manger himself published a rebuttal, "Khurbm un literatur," in *Der veker* (1 October 1958); *Shriftn,* pp. 387–389.

69. Manger, "With Closed Eyes" and "Sunset," in Chava Alberstein, *Hitbaharut. The Skies Are Clearing,* CBS record 81906 (1978).

70. Manger, "Der goyrl fun a lid" (1960), *Shriftn,* pp. 390–396, tr. "The Destiny of a Poem" by Joseph Leftwich, *The Way We Think,* pp. 506–510. For the lyrics, see *Penguin Book of Modern Yiddish Verse,* pp. 588–591; for the music, *Mir trogn a gezang: The New Book of Yiddish Songs,* ed. Eleanor Gordon Mlotek, 2nd rev. ed. (New York: Workmen's Circle, 1977), pp. 166–167.

8. The Demon as Storyteller: Isaac Bashevis Singer

1. Yehoash, "Undzere shyedim," *Fun der velt un yener* (New York: Oyfgang, 1913), pp. 253–257; Joshua Trachtenberg, *Jewish Magic and Superstition: A Study in Folk Religion* (Cleveland: Meridian Books and Jewish Publication Society, 1961), pp. 31–36; Yehuda Liebes, "*Hatikkun Ha-Kelali* of Reb Nahman of Brastlav and Its Sabbatean Links," in his *Studies in Jewish Myth and Jewish Messianism,* tr. Batya Stein (Albany: SUNY Press, 1993), pp. 115–160.

2. Shmuel Werses, "Motivim dimonologiim be'Susati' shel Mendele umekoroteihem," in *MiMendele 'ad Hazaz* (From Mendele to Hazaz: Studies in the Development of Hebrew Prose; Jerusalem: Magnes Press, 1987), pp. 70–86; Ruth R. Wisse, "The Jewish Intellectual and the Jews: The Case of *Di Kliatshe* (The Mare) by Mendele Mocher Sforim," *The Daniel E. Korshland Memorial Lecture* (San Francisco: Congregation Emanu-El, 1992).

3. I. L. Peretz, "Monish," tr. Seymour Levitan, *The Penguin Book of Modern Yiddish Verse,* ed. Irving Howe, Ruth R. Wisse, and Khone Shmeruk (New York: Penguin, 1988), pp. 52–81; quote on p. 62. For discussion see Ruth R. Wisse, *I. L. Peretz and the Making of Modern Jewish Culture* (Seattle: University of Washington Press, 1991), pp. 12–16.

4. "A biografisher notits fun Yitskhok Bashevis far Zalmen Reyzen," *Di goldene keyt*

98 (1979): 17. This was written when Bashevis was about thirty-five years old and living in New York City.

5. Yitskhok Bashevis, *Mayn tatns bezdn-shtub* (New York: Der kval, 1956), p. 34 (henceforth cited Y). This episode, titled "The Lame Bride," does not appear in the English ed. of *In My Father's Court* (henceforth E), tr. Channah Kleinerman-Goldstein, Elaine Gottlieb, and Joseph Singer (Philadelphia: Jewish Publication Society, 1966). Four additional chapters appear in *An Isaac Bashevis Singer Reader* (New York: Farrar, Straus and Giroux, 1971), pp. 285–313. No detailed comparison has been done of the two editions, but see "Dray 'farshpetikte' epizodn fun 'Mayn tatns bezdn-shtub'," introduction by Khone Shmeruk, *Di goldene keyt* 135 (1993): 173–188.

6. In chap. 31, "Mayn tate vert an anarkhist," the narrator's father pays a rare visit to the balcony (p. 186; only in Yiddish). For an excellent (and much more appreciative) reading of this memoir, see Steven David Lavine, "Rhetoric for the Spirit: Repetition and Renovation in 'In My Father's Court'," in *Recovering the Canon: Essays on Isaac Bashevis Singer,* ed. David Neal Miller (Leiden: Brill, 1986), pp. 116–132. Lavine discusses the importance of the balcony on p. 123.

7. Y 259, E 211. The Yiddish version, originally intended for readers of the *Jewish Daily Forward,* equates his kitchen curriculum with the history of western thought from Socrates to Bergson.

8. On the differences between "Warshawski" and "Bashevis," see David Neal Miller, *Fear of Fiction: Narrative Strategies in the Works of Isaac Bashevis Singer* (Albany: SUNY Press, 1985), chap. 2.

9. For the early career of Yitskhok Bashevis—before he became I. B. Singer—see Khone Shmeruk, "Bashevis-Zinger, Yitskhok," *Leksikon fun yidish-shraybers,* ed. Berl Kagan (New York: Rayah Iman-Kagan, 1986), cols. 60–68; Moshe Yungman, "Singer's Polish Period: 1924 to 1935," tr. Nili Wachtel (without notes) from *Hasifrut* 27 (1978): 118–133, in *Yiddish* 6:2–3 (1985): 25–38; Ruth R. Wisse, "Singer's Paradoxical Progress," *Commentary* (February 1979), pp. 33–38, rpt. in *Studies in American Jewish Literature* 1 (1981): 148–159. At least three full-scale biographies of Singer, by Janet Hadda, Khone Shmeruk, and Leonard Wolf, are now in progress. They will doubtless add much to our understanding of Singer's formative years.

10. On 1924 as a year of crisis, see Yungman, pp. 28–29. On I. J. Singer, see Anita Norich, *The Homeless Imagination in the Fiction of Israel Joshua Singer* (Bloomington: Indiana University Press, 1991); Melekh Ravitch, *Dos mayse-bukh fun mayn lebn, 1921–1934* (The Storybook of My Life; Tel Aviv: Y. L. Perets, 1975), pp. 87–114. On I. J. Singer's bitter experience in Kiev and Moscow, see his "Letter from America" in *Forverts,* 7 June 1941, tr. as "Appendix A" to Sholem Groesberg, "I. J. Singer's Novellas: The Vicissitudes of a Belletrist's Career," (unpublished M.A. thesis, Jewish Theological Seminary of America, 1991). In "A Boy Philosopher" Bashevis Singer suggests that the sexual deviance of the biblical Bathsheba was one reason for adopting the name as his own. *In My Father's Court,* pp. 208–209.

11. David Neal Miller, *Bibliography of Isaac Bashevis Singer, 1924–1949* (New York:

Peter Lang, 1983), does not include Bashevis' contributions to the Warsaw Yiddish press, but it's the best we have so far. For a critical discussion of these naturalist sketches, see Yungman, "Singer's Polish Period," and Miller, *Fear of Fiction,* chap. 1. For a popular overview of Yiddish naturalism, see Y. I. Trunk, *Idealizm un naturalizm in der yidisher literatur* (Warsaw, 1927), and *Di yidishe proze in Poyln in der tkufe tsvishn beyde velt-milkhomes* (Buenos Aires: Tsentral-farband fun poylishe yidn in Argentine, 1949).

12. Yitskhok Bashevis, "Eyniklekh," *Varshever shriftn* (Warsaw: Literatn-klub baym fareyn fun yidishe literatn un zhurnalistn in Varshe, 1926–27), 4th sequence, pp. 2–11; "In letste teg," *A mol in a yoyvl: zamlbukh* 2 (Warsaw-Vilna: Farlag B. Kletskin, 1931): 139–151.

13. Yitskhok Bashevis, "Verter oder bilder," *Literarishe bleter* 34 (1927): 663–665. For discussion see Wisse, *Studies in American Jewish Literature,* p. 152, and Yungman, pp. 31–33.

14. Aaron Zeitlin, "Der kult fun gornisht un di kunst vi zi darf zayn," *Varshever shriftn* (Warsaw, 1926–27), separate pagination. For the hidden connection to Italian futurism, see Yekhiel Szeintuch, "Ben sifrut leḥazon: tekufat Varsha beyetsirato haduleshonit shel Aharon Tseitlin," *Kovets meḥkarim 'al yahadut Polin: Sefer lezikhro shel Paul Glikson* (Jerusalem, 1987), pp. 117–139. Also, *Marinetti: Selected Writings,* ed. R. W. Flint (New York: Farrar, Straus and Giroux, 1972).

15. Isaac Bashevis Singer, *Love and Exile: An Autobiographical Trilogy* (New York: Farrar, Straus and Giroux, 1986), p. 97.

16. Yitskhok Bashevis, "Oyfn oylem-hatoyhu," *Di yidishe velt* (Warsaw) 1 (1928): 54; rpt. *Di goldene keyt* 124 (1988): 87–95, quote on p. 88.

17. Singer claims this story as veiled autobiography. *Love and Exile,* pp. 150–151.

18. See the fascinating article by Nathan Cohen, "Ha'itonut hasensatsyonit beVarsha bein shtei milḥamot ha'olam," *Qesher* 11 (May 1992), Eng. abstract, pp. 28e-29e; in Hebrew, pp. 81–94. On Yiddish *shund* in general, see Khone Shmeruk, "Letoldot sifrut ha 'shund' beyidish," *Tarbiz* 52 (1983): 325–354.

19. Cohen, pp. 84–87, 90–91.

20. These stories and sketches, published in *Undzer ekspres* from 1925 to 1931, do not appear in any published bibliography of Singer's writings. They were discovered by Khone Shmeruk. My sincere thanks to Devora Menashe for making available to me copies of the xeroxes Professor Shmeruk sent to her. The stories referred to here are, in chronological order: "In a hek" (27 January 1928); "Berl formalist" (18 April 1930); "Der estet" (9 May 1930), and "Stam azoy" (16 May 1930).

21. Yitskhok Bashevis, "Tsu der frage fun dikhtung un politik," *Globus* 3 (1932): 39–49.

22. Yitskhok Bashevis, "Vegn Dovid Bergelsons *Baym dnieper*," *Globus* 5 (1932): 56–65; "Eyn loshn," *Globus* 15 (1933): 67–78.

23. Yitskhok Bashevis, *Der sotn in Goray,* serialized in *Globus,* January-September 1933; pub. with foreword by Aaron Zeitlin (Warsaw: Bibliotek fun yidishn P.E.N.-klub, 1935); 2nd ed., *Der sotn in Goray a mayse fun fartsaytns un andere dertseylungen* (New York: Farlag matones, 1943), reissued in a photo-offset ed. (Jerusalem: Aka-

demon, 1972). English tr., Jacob Sloan, *Satan in Goray* (New York: Noonday Press, 1955).

24. On the stylistic features of the novel, see Khone Shmeruk, "Monologue as Narrative Strategy in the Short Stories of Isaac Bashevis Singer," in Miller, *Recovering the Canon,* pp. 99–101; Dan Miron, "Passivity and Narration: The Spell of Bashevis Singer," *Judaism* 41:1 (1992): 14–16. On the grotesque, see Maximillian E. Novak, "Moral Grotesque and Decorative Grotesque in Singer's Fiction," *The Achievement of Isaac Bashevis Singer,* ed. Marcia Allentuk (Carbondale: Southern Illinois University Press, 1969), pp. 44–63. For an early appreciation of the novel, see Avrom Ayzen, "Yitskhok Bashevis, 'Der sotn in Goray'," *YIVO-bleter* 12 (1937): 386–395. For an interpretation against the backdrop of contemporary events in Poland, see Seth L. Wolitz, "*Satan in Goray* as Parable," *Prooftexts* 9 (1989): 13–25.

25. For the *Mayse fun a ruakh in Korets* that served as Bashevis' source, see Max Weinreich, *Bilder fun der yidisher literaturgeshikhte* (Studies in the History of Yiddish Literature from its Beginnings to Mendele Moykher-Sforim; Vilna: Tomor, 1926), pp. 254–261. The characterization of Rechele owes much to Weinreich's analysis of the original dybbuk tale. See also Weinreich's chapter on Shabbetai Zvi in *Shturemvint* (Storm Wind: Scenes from Jewish History in the 17th Century; Vilna: Tomor, 1927), pp. 79–161, and Avraham Rubinstein, "Goray and Bilgoraj: The Literary World of Isaac Bashevis Singer and the Historical-Social World of Polish Jewry," *Ex Cathedra* (Ramat Gan: Bar Ilan University, 1982), pp. 49–82. Abraham Novershtern reads this pietistic ending as Bashevis' way of repudiating Yiddish modernism. See "Tsvishn morgnzun un akhris-hayomim: tsu der apokaliptisher tematik in der yidisher literatur," *Di goldene keyt* 135 (1993) 111–135.

26. Yitskhok Varshavski, *Fun der alter un nayer heym* (sequel to *In My Father's Court*), *Forverts* (15 February 1964). Singer here claims to have engaged in modernist experiments on a par with those of Joyce and Kafka, "although at that time I had not yet heard of them." For a scholarly treatment of Singer's autobiographical writings, see Khone Shmeruk, "Bashevis Singer—In Search of His Autobiography," *Jewish Quarterly* 29:4 (1981–82): 28–36.

27. I. B. Singer, "The Recruit," *In My Father's Court.*

28. Shmeruk, "Bashevis-Zinger, Yitskhok," col. 62.

29. Yitskhok Bashevis, "Arum der yidisher literatur in Poyln," *Di tsukunft* (August 1943): 468–475. For the cultural significance of Chagall's painting, see my *Against the Apocalypse: Responses to Catastrophe in Modern Jewish Culture* (Cambridge, Mass.: Harvard University Press, 1984), pp. 284–289.

30. Yitskhok Bashevis, "Problemen fun der yidisher proze in Amerike," *Svive* 2 (March-April 1943): 2–13; tr. "Problems of Yiddish Prose in America," Robert H. Wolf, *Prooftexts* 9 (1989): 5–12. All citations are from the English translation, except for the word "obsolescent." Bashevis speaks of Yiddish as "obsolete." See also Itamar Even-Zohar and Khone Shmeruk, "Authentic Language and Authentic Reported Speech: Hebrew vs. Yiddish," in Itamar Even-Zohar, *Polysystem Studies,* special issue of *Poetics Today* 11 (1990): 159–163.

31. Yitskhok Bashevis, "Der roye veeyne-nire (fun der serye dertseylungen 'Dos ged-

enkbukh fun yeyster-hore')," *Svive* 3 (1943): 16–31; 4 (1943): 24–43; rpt. *Gimpl tam un andere dertseylungen* (New York: CYCO, 1963), pp. 206–236. All page references are to the latter ed. The first to discuss *The Devil's Diary* as a discrete unit was Shmeruk, "Monologue as Narrative Strategy," in Miller, *Recovering the Canon,* pp. 102–107.

32. Isaac Bashevis Singer, "The Unseen," tr. Norbert Guterman and Elaine Gottlieb, *Selected Short Stories of Isaac Bashevis Singer,* ed. Irving Howe (New York: Modern Library, 1966), p. 108. Unless otherwise indicated, all further refs. are to this ed., which I consider to be the best volume of Singer's stories in English.

33. See Robert Langbaum, *The Poetry of Experience: The Dramatic Monologue in Modern Literary Tradition* (New York: Norton, 1957), pp. 57–61.

34. Yitskhok Bashevis, "Zaydlus der ershter (fun a serye dersteylungen u.n. 'Dos gedenkbukh fun yeyster-hore')," *Svive* 1 (1943): 11–24; *Der sotn in Goray* (1943), pp. 273–280; "Zeidlus the Pope," tr. Joel Blocker and Elizabeth Pollet, *Selected Short Stories,* pp. 341–353.

35. My reading of "Zeidlus the Pope" owes much to an unpublished essay by Joseph Sherman, "The Jewish Pope: Interpellating Jewish Identity."

36. Max Weinreich, *History of the Yiddish Language,* tr. Shlomo Noble (Chicago: University of Chicago Press, 1980), pp. 193–195, and "The Reality of Jewishness versus the Ghetto Myth: The Sociolinguistic Roots of Yiddish," in *Never Say Die! A Thousand Years of Yiddish in Jewish Life and Letters,* ed. Joshua A. Fishman (The Hague: Mouton, 1981), pp. 103–117.

37. Langbaum, p. 59.

38. The comparison with Dik is drawn from Joseph Sherman's "The Jewish Pope." See also David Levine Lerner, "The Enduring Legend of the Jewish Pope," *Judaism* 40 (Spring 1991): 148–170.

39. Cf. "tsu a yor finf, zeks un draysik, iz er [Zeydl] geven azoy a kener, az s'iz nisht geven zayns glaykhn in gants medines Poyln" (By the time he was thirty-five no one in all Poland could equal him in learning; Y 275, E 343) with "S'iz geven a mol an ile, / nisht gekent di velt afile, / nor in Poyln, un, a ponem / in der guter alter tsayt" (There was a prodigy, / precisely when or where is hard to say, / but in Poland, / in olden days). The balladeer, like the storyteller, then goes on to list the weighty tomes this prodigy has mastered.

40. The same is true of the learned characters in Bashevis' novels, especially *The Family Moskat.*

41. "Tsvey meysim geyen tantsn," in 1943 ed. of *Der sotn in Goray,* pp. 289–305; tr. Joseph Singer and Elizabeth Pollet, "Two Corpses Go Dancing," *The Séance and Other Stories* (New York: Farrar, Straus and Giroux, 1968), pp. 187–201; "A togbukh fun a nisht-geboyrenem," *Der sotn in Goray,* pp. 253–270; tr. Nancy E. Gross, "From the Diary of One Not Born," *Gimpel the Fool and Other Stories* (New York: Noonday Press, 1957), pp. 135–145.

42. "Der khurbm fun Kreshev" (henceforth cited Y), *Der sotn in Goray* (1943), p. 193; tr. Elaine Gottlieb and June Ruth Flaum, "The Destruction of Kreshev," *The Col-*

lected Stories of I. B. Singer (New York: Farrar, Straus and Giroux, 1982), p. 94; henceforth abbreviated E.

43. Ruth R. Wisse, unpub. essay, "Singer in the Yiddish Tradition."

44. See Sholem Asch, *Kiddush Hashem*, tr. Rufus Learsi (Philadelphia: Jewish Publication Society, 1946). See also Chava Rosenfarb, "Yitskhok Bashevis un Sholem Ash (a pruv fun a farglaykh)," *Di goldene keyt* 133 (1992): 75–104. Rosenfarb perceives striking similarities between the two writers, whereas I see fierce oedipal struggle.

45. Sholem Asch, "Kola Street," tr. Norbert Guterman, *A Treasury of Yiddish Stories,* ed. Irving Howe and Eliezer Greenberg (New York, 1989), pp. 260–261.

46. These are the dates of the original Yiddish versions. In English, the stories appeared in diverse and disparate settings, having no direct bearing on the Holocaust, or on anything else for that matter.

47. "Gimpl tam," orig. in Passover ed. of *Yidisher kemfer;* rpt. *Der shpigl un andere dertseylungen,* ed. Khone Shmeruk (Jerusalem: Yiddish Department, Hebrew University, 1974), pp. 33–47; tr. Saul Bellow, *Selected Short Stories,* pp. 3–19. My interpretation is based on Ruth R. Wisse, *The Schlemiel as Modern Hero* (Chicago: University of Chicago Press, 1971), chap. 4, and Janet Hadda, "Gimpel the Full," *Prooftexts* 10 (1990): 283–295. On the significance of *tam,* see Shmeruk, "Monologue as Narrative Strategy," p. 99.

48. "Di kleyne shusterlekh," orig. in *Di tsukunft* (April 1945); *Gimpl tam un andere dertseylungen,* pp. 18–43; tr. Isaac Rosenfeld, "The Little Shoemakers," *Selected Short Stories,* pp. 68–95.

49. Yitskhok Bashevis, "Der katlen (a bobe-mayse)," rpt. *Der shpigl un andere dertseylungen,* pp. 57–74; tr. Shlomo Katz, "The Wife Killer: A Folk Tale," *Selected Short Stories,* pp. 40–56. For a discussion of the female narrators in Bashevis' monologues—provenance, unique style, and subject matter—see Miller, *Fear of Fiction,* chap. 3.

50. Thanks to Khone Shmeruk's edition of *Der shpigl un andere dertseylungen,* the Yiddish reader can enjoy the best of Bashevis' monologues and study each subgroup in chronological order. For the English versions, see "Three Tales," *Selected Short Stories,* pp. 325–340; "The Blizzard," *A Crown of Feathers and Other Stories* (Greenwich: Fawcett, 1974), pp. 65–80. Of the later collections, *The Image and Other Stories* (New York: Farrar, Straus and Giroux, 1985) is especially rich in monologues of the Aunt Yentl variety. Bendet Daddy, whose narrative style depends on vulgarisms and *lehavdl-loshn* for its machismo, fares poorly in English.

51. See Miron, "Passivity and Narration." The quote is from "Tseytl un Rikl" (1966), *Der shpigl,* p. 93; "Zeitel and Rickel," tr. Mirra Ginsburg, *The Séance and Other Stories,* p. 117.

52. Bashevis, "Der shpigl" (1956), *Der shpigl,* p. 2; "The Mirror," tr. Norbert Guterman, *Selected Short Stories,* p. 58. See Ken Frieden, "I. B. Singer's Monologues of Demons," *Prooftexts* 5 (1985): 263–268.

53. Since it was Peretz who introduced satanic doggerel into Yiddish literature, it is appropriate for the devil to echo lines and rhymes from "Monish." Thus, "iz Samoel

gerekht, az er iz hekht fun ale hekht" echoes the famous opening stanzas of Peretz's mock-epic poem.

54. "Mayse Tishevits," orig. in *Forverts* (29 March 1959); *Der shpigl,* pp. 12–22; tr. Martha Glicklich and Cecil Hemley, *Selected Short Stories,* pp. 300–311.

55. "Arum der yidisher literatur in Poyln," p. 472. Reb Abraham Zalman, the local messiah of Tishevits, is also mentioned in chap. 3 of *Satan in Goray.*

56. See R. Avrom Shtern, "Der Tishevitser meshiekh ben Yoysef," in *Pinkes Tishevits,* ed. Jacob Zipper (Tel Aviv: Irgun yots'ei Tishevits, 1970), pp. 50–57. For more on the town, see Diane K. Roskies and David G. Roskies, *The Shtetl Book: An Introduction to East European Jewish Life and Lore,* 2nd rev. ed. (New York: Ktav, 1979), pp. 137–139.

57. The comparison to Peretz is drawn from Ruth Wisse's unpublished essay, "Singer in the Yiddish Tradition."

58. See my *Against the Apocalypse* for an analysis of this rhymed ending and its parallels in Yiddish folklore.

59. Yitskhok Bashevis, "Taybele un Humizah" (1962), *Mayses fun hintern oyvn* (Tel Aviv: Y. L. Perets, 1971), p. 86; tr. Mirra Ginsburg, "Taibele and Her Demon," *Selected Short Stories,* pp. 235–248.

60. "Aleyn," orig. in *Svive* (1960); *Gimpl tam un andere dertseylungen,* pp. 168–179; tr. Joel Blocker, "Alone," *Selected Short Stories,* pp. 312–324.

61. "Di kafeterye," orig. in *Di tsukunft* (March-April, 1968); *Mayses fun hintern oyvn,* pp. 43–71; tr. by the author and Dorothea Straus in *Collected Stories,* pp. 287–300.

62. "The whole in the fabric of reality" is Tzvetan Todorov's definition of the fantastic. See *The Fantastic: A Structural Approach to a Literary Genre,* tr. Richard Howard (Ithaca: Cornell University Press, 1975), chap. 2. I owe some insights on this story to Dan Miron.

63. For a comparison of the Old and New World settings in Singer's fiction, see Janet Hadda, "The Double Life of Isaac Bashevis Singer," *Prooftexts* 5 (1985): 165–181.

64. Other changes are more innocent, though more puzzling too. In Saul Bellow's otherwise exemplary translation of "Gimpel the Fool" only one sentence was omitted (by whom?), concerning the immaculate conception of Jesus. "Ot zogt men dokh," says Gimpel to himself, trying to rationalize the birth of his firstbon son a mere seventeen weeks after the wedding, "az s'yoyizl hot in gantsn keyn tatn nisht gehat" (Why, I've heard it said the Little Jesus didn't have a father at all! Y 38). For a spirited defense of the Yiddish originals, both of Bashevis' short and long fiction, see Khone Shmeruk, "A briv in redaktsye," *Di goldene keyt* 134 (1992): 64–66. There Shmeruk says he plans in subsequent work to expose the "unbelievable awkwardness and ignorance" that characterize the translations of Singer's work. In an unpublished paper, Monika Adamczyk-Garbowska of Maria Curie-Sklodowska University in Lublin has analyzed other ways in which Singer adapted his Yiddish works for the English reader, as when he turned "Joseph and Koza" from a Yiddish legend into an English fairy tale.

65. "Naftali the Storyteller and His Horse, Sus," tr. Joseph Singer, in Isaac Bashevis

Singer, *Stories for Children* (New York: Farrar, Straus and Giroux, 1984), pp. 167–183, and "Are Children the Ultimate Literary Critics?" ibid., pp. 332–338. For an appreciation of Singer's stories for children, see Thomas P. Riggio, "The Symbols of Faith: Isaac Bashevis Singer's Children's Books," in Miller, *Recovering the Canon*, pp. 133–144; Khone Shmeruk, "Arum Y. Bashevises dertseylung far kinder 'Yoysef un Koza'," *Di goldene keyt* 131 (1991): 131–133, idem, "Yitskhok Bashevises dertseylung 'An erev-khanike in Varshe'," ibid. 132 (1991): 38–40, and "Yitskhok Bashevis: der mayse-dertseyler far kinder," *Oksforder yidish* 3 (1995): 233–280. Most of Singer's stories for children, as Shmeruk points out, were written for adult readers of the *Jewish Daily Forward* and were signed by the middlebrow "Yitskhok Warshawski."

66. These interviews have now been collected by Grace Farrell in *Isaac Bashevis Singer: Conversations* (Jackson: University Press of Mississippi, 1992). In my review of that book, I try to show how Singer manipulated his interviewers. See "The Fibs of I. B. Singer," *Forward* (18 December 1992).

9. Estates of Memory: After the Holocaust

1. Melech Ravitch, *Dos mayse-bukh fun mayn lebn: yorn in Varshe, 1921–1934* (The Storybook of My Life: Warsaw Years), illus. Audrey Bergner (Tel Aviv: Y. L. Perets, 1975), pp. 60–67.

2. J. I. Segal, "The Theme in the Brush," tr. Shivke Segal, in Yossel Bergner, *59 Illustrations to All the Folk Tales of Itzhok Leibush Peretz* (Montreal: Hertz and Edelstein, 1950), introduction (unpaginated).

3. Sh. [Sheynkinder], "Oyf di gasn," *Tsvishn lebn un toyt*, ed. Ber Mark (Warsaw: Yidish-bukh, 1955), p. 99; written in the Warsaw ghetto, 1941. A different tr. is in *To Live with Honor and Die with Honor: Selected Documents from the Warsaw Ghetto Underground Archives "O.S." (Oneg Shabbath)*, ed. Joseph Kermish (Jerusalem: Yad Vashem, 1988), p. 679. *Zayn krampf* (His Cramp) is of course a parody of *Mein Kampf*.

4. S. Y. Agnon, "The Lady and the Peddler," tr. Robert Alter, *Modern Hebrew Literature*, ed. Alter (New York: Behrman House, 1975), pp. 201–212; Agnon, "The Sign," tr. Arthur Green, in my *The Literature of Destruction*, sec. 97. (The epigraph to this chapter is from chap. 42 of "The Sign.") See Dan Laor, "Did Agnon Write about the Holocaust?" *Yad Vashem Studies* 20 (1992): 17–63; Avraham Holtz, *Mar'ot umekorot: mahadurah me'ueret um'uyeret shel 'Hakhnasat kalah'* (Jerusalem: Shocken, 1995).

5. On Glatstein, see Janet Hadda, *Yankev Glatshteyn* (Boston: Twayne, 1980), chap. 4; *American Yiddish Poetry: A Bilingual Anthology*, ed. Benjamin Harshav and Barbara Harshav (Berkeley: University of California Press, 1986), pp. 204–206, 278–359, 803–804; *Selected Poems of Yankev Glatshteyn*, tr. Richard J. Fein (Philadelphia: Jewish Publication Society, 1987), pp. 68–125. On the retraditionalization of secular Yiddish culture in America in the wake of the Holocaust, see David G. Roskies, "The Emancipation of Yiddish," *Prooftexts* 1 (1981): 28–42.

6. See Khone Shmeruk, "Yiddish Literature in the U.S.S.R.," *The Jews in Soviet Russia since 1917,* ed. Lionel Kochan (London: Oxford University Press, 1970), pp. 261–264, and J. B. Schechtman, "The U.S.S.R., Zionism, and Israel," ibid., pp. 114–116. Der Nister's semifictional tales of Polish-Jewish martyrdom are collected in his *Dertseylungen un eseyen,* ed. Nachman Meisel (New York: YIKUF, 1957), pp. 31–256. See also David Bergelson, *Prints Reuveyni* (New York: YIKUF, 1946).

7. See *Antologye fun religyeze lider un dertseylungen* (Anthology of Religious Poems and Stories: The Literary Works of Writers Who Perished during the Years of the Jewish Catastrophe in Europe), ed. Moyshe Prager (New York: Research Institute of Religious Jewry, 1955). This 640-page anthology is merely a drop in the bucket. Now that orthodoxy has come into its own as a subject of scholarly research, others should pick up where Prager left off.

8. Chaim Grade, *Mayn krig mit Hersh Raseyner (esey),* photo-offset ed. (Jerusalem: Hebrew University, 1969). Cf. the famous abridged tr. by Milton Himmelfarb in *A Treasury of Yiddish Stories,* ed. Irving Howe and Eliezer Greenberg (New York: Viking, 1989), pp. 624–651. The connection to Dostoevsky's *Brothers Karamazov* has been extensively documented in an unpublished seminar paper (1987) by Shoshana Brown-Gutoff, then a graduate student in midrash at the Jewish Theological Seminary. Grade's story has been made into a full-length feature film, *The Quarrel* (Canada-United States, 1992).

9. Chaim Grade, *Di agune: roman* (Los Angeles: Yidish-natsyonaler arbeter-farband, 1961), p. 6, tr. Michael Stern. Cf. *The Agunah,* tr. Curt Leviant (New York: Menorah, 1978), where the author's preface is left out. On Grade, see Ruth R. Wisse, "In Praise of Chaim Grade," *Commentary* (April 1977), and Abraham Novershtern, "Yung Vilne: The Political Dimension of Literature," *The Jews of Poland Between the Two World Wars,* ed. Yisrael Gutman et al. (Hanover: University Press of New England, 1989), pp. 383–398.

10. Y. I. Trunk, *Poyln,* 7 vols. (New York: Undzer tsayt, 1944–1953). Only a fragment of vol. 6 has so far appeared in English. See Yehiel Yeshaia Trunk, "Lodz Memories," *Polin: A Journal of Polish-Jewish Studies* 6 (1991): 262–287. "Chil Szaja" is the spelling of his name on all of Trunk's official documents, whether Polish or American, now housed in the Bund Archive at the YIVO Institute. There he gives his birthdate as 15 March 1888. On Hannah Trunk working in a sweatshop, see A. Glantz-Leyeles, "Yekhiel Yeshaye Trunk," *Velt un vort: literarishe un andere eseyen* (World and Word: Literary Essays; New York: CYCO, 1958), p. 102. She died in 1944. Trunk interpolated a brief but moving eulogy to her in vol. 4 of *Poyln* (New York: Undzer tsayt, 1949), pp. 90–91.

11. See *Poyln,* 7:9–14, for Trunk's apologia to his critics, and A. Glantz-Leyeles, "Yekhiel Yeshaye Trunk," p. 104.

12. Trunk, *Perets,* vol. 5 of *Poyln* (1949). On Menakhem (pp. 23–24); Weissenberg (chap. 4); Kratko and his wife (chaps. 5–6); rehearsing the tales to his grandson in Polish (p. 76); the snobbish disdain for Reisen and Sholem Aleichem (chap. 9).

Judah Leib Cahan was actually the first to sing Yiddish folksongs in Peretz's salon, but Cahan left for London before Trunk appeared on the scene.

13. The most accessible edition of Trunk's prewar historical novellas and postwar philosophical essays is *Kvaln un beymer: Historishe noveln un eseys* (Springs and Trees: Historical Novellas and Essays; New York: Undzer tsayt, 1958).

14. Y. I. Trunk, *Sholem-Aleykhem, zayn vezn un zayne verk* (Warsaw: Kultur-lige, 1937); Shmuel Werses, "Shalom Aleichem: hamishim shnot bikkoret," in *Bikkoret habikkoret: ha'arakhot vegilgulehen* (Criticism of Criticism: Evaluations in Development; Tel Aviv: Yahdav, 1982), pp. 184–186.

15. Y. I. Trunk, *Tevye un Menakhem-Mendl in yidishn velt-goyrl* (Tevye and Menakhem-Mendl in the Jewish Historical Fate; New York: CYCO, 1944), pp. 231–249. This autobiographical (and rather self-indulgent) piece appeared earlier as "A mayse mit a manuskript," *Di tsukunft* (November 1942): 673–677.

16. For a glowing appreciation, see M. Vanvild (S.L. Kave), "Novatorisher gayst (Y. Y. Trunk in profil un *en face*)," in Trunk's *Idealizm un naturalizm in der yidisher literatur: tendentsn un vegn fun undzere moderne shriftshteler* (Warsaw: Kultur-lige, 1927), pp. iii–xxxi.

17. Couched in philosophical terms, Trunk says as much in his "Perzenlekhe kheshboynes," the preface to his last published work, *Meshiekh-geviter: historisher roman fun di tsaytn fun Shabse Tsvi* (New York: CYCO and Farlag "Yidbukh," 1961), p. 11.

18. Comparing the first volume of *Poland* to I. J. Singer's *Yoshe Kalb*, S. Niger wrote: "Y. I. Trunk raised anti-Hasidism to something of a romantic ecstasy." *Der tog*, 18 June 1944. On Nomberg: *Poyln*, 7, chap. 26; on Hershl Yedvab as a latter-day Shayke Fefer, 5, chap. 25; on Tłomackie 13, 7, chap. 6.

19. *Poyln*, 6:178–179; 7:52.

20. Not even Dik, writing under contract for the Widow Rom, produced as much in one decade as Chil Szaje Trunk (my tr. from Yiddish): *The Wise Men of Chelm or Jews from the Wisest Town in the World* (1951), *Simkhe Plakhte of Narkove or the Jewish Don Quixote* (1951), *The Jolliest Jew in the World or Hershele's Apprenticeship*, bound together with four medieval wonder tales set in Poland of yore (1953), *The World Is Full of Miracles or the Tale of Three Brothers* (1954), *The Bove-mayse* (1955), *The Jewish Pope* and *Joseph della Reina* (c. 1958), *Messiah Storms: Historical Novel about the Times of Shabbetai Zvi*, bound together with *Jews Look Out the Window* (*Eleven Tales of the Baal Shem Tov*) (1960). Each of these modernized "folk books" averages 130 chapters. Trunk's most coherent statements on Jewish myth, informed by Jungian psychology, are "Yidisher mitos," preface to *Di velt iz ful mit nisim oder mayse migiml akhim* (Buenos Aires: Tsentral-farband fun poylishe yidn in Argentine, 1955), pp. 13–20, and "Dialogn tsvishn leyener un mekhaber," part 9 of *Meshiekh-geviter*, pp. 234–265. On Trunk's last years, see Jacob Pat, *Shmuesn mit yidishe shrayber* (Conversations with Yiddish Writers; New York: Marstin Press, 1954), pp. 114, 126.

21. The quotation is from Ruth Wisse's indispensable essay, "The Prose of Abraham

Sutzkever," introduction to *Griner akvarium: dertseylungen* (Jerusalem: Hebrew University, 1975), p. xxiii. For Sutzkever's life and poetic career, see my *Against the Apocalypse,* chap. 9; Benjamin Harshav, "Sutzkever: Life and Poetry," introduction to A. Sutzkever, *Selected Poetry and Prose,* tr. Barbara Harshav and Benjamin Harshav (Berkeley: University of California Press, 1991), pp. 3–25.

22. Abraham Sutzkever, *Meshiekhs togbukh* (Messiah's Diary), in *Griner akvarium,* pp. 55–155; *Dortn vu es nekhtikn di shtern* (Where the Stars Spend the Night; Tel Aviv: Yisroel-bukh, 1979), illus. Yonia Fain; *Di nevue fun shvartsaplen: dertseylungen* (The Prophecy of the Inner Eye; Jerusalem: Hebrew University, 1989). The latter vol. also includes all the stories from *Dortn vu es nekhtikn di shtern,* without the illustrations. All quotations are from the 1975 and 1989 eds., henceforth abbreviated in text as *Akvarium* and *Nevue.* Thirteen stories, mostly drawn from *Where the Stars Spend the Night,* are included in the Harshav volume, abbreviated E.

23. After many failed attempts, I was able to capture Sutzkever on film speaking extemporaneously at the YIVO Institute in New York City, 9 May 1991. He brought the house down with his imitation of Leyzer Volf (1910–1943) doing a poetry reading in Vilna, around 1935.

24. Wisse, "Prose of Abraham Sutzkever," p. xxviii.

25. Sutzkever, "Dem khalefs tokhter," *Griner akvarium,* pp. 55–72.

26. Wisse, "Abraham Sutzkever the Storyteller," *Nevue,* p. viii. Elsewhere Wisse argues that by respecting the boundaries between the living and the dead, Sutzkever remains true to classical Jewish faith, as opposed to I. B. Singer, who succumbs to nihilist urges. See her "Di literarishe perzenlekhkayt fun Avrom Sutskever," *Di goldene keyt* 136 (1993): 52–53.

27. Fourteen of the fifteen prose poems that make up *Green Aquarium* (1953–54) were translated by Ruth Wisse in *Prooftexts* 2 (1982): 98–121. "Lady Job," the missing poem, appears in the Harshavs' *Selected Poetry and Prose,* pp. 364–366.

28. Sutzkever, "Yanina un di khaye," *Griner akvarium,* pp. 79–93.

29. Sutzkever, "Der neyder," ibid., pp. 73–78.

30. In private, the Sutzkevers often recount similar miraculous rescues and other instances of the poet's psychic powers. A good example, as retold by journalist Khayim Liberman, is "A misterye," *Di goldene keyt* 136 (1993): 145–153.

31. Sutzkever, "Der tsviling" (1973), *Griner akvarium,* pp. 118–130.

32. The interpretation that follows draws from Wisse, "Prose of Abraham Sutzkever," pp. xxviii–xxix.

33. Ibid., p. xxviii.

34. Sutzkever, "Meshiekhs togbukh" (1973), *Griner akvarium,* pp. 144–155.

35. See Nissim Aloni, "The Longing and the Grotesque," in Yosl Bergner, *Paintings, 1938–1980,* tr. Valerie Arnon (Jerusalem: Keter, 1981), pp. 210–203; Yosl Birstein, *Dayne geslekh—Yerusholayim, kleyne mayses* (Your Alleys—Jerusalem, Little Tales; English title on verso: A Spell of Silence; Jerusalem: Siman kri'ah and Hakibbutz Hameuchad, 1989), for "Frantseyzishe literatur," "Der Amsterdamer filozof," and all of section 12 titled "Mayn khaver Yosl Bergner."

36. Yosl Birstein, *Unter fremde himlen* (Melbourne: York Press, 1949), frontis. and illus. Yosl Bergner; Pinkhes Goldhar, *Gezamlte shriftn* (Melbourne: Fraynd fun der yidisher literatur, 1949). On the Society for Contemporary Art, see Aloni, p. 207.

37. Itzik Manger wrote a very positive review of the first issue of their journal. See his *Shriftn in proze* (Tel Aviv: Y. L. Perets, 1980), pp. 268–274. The only critical overview of *Yung-Yisroel* is an unfinished essay of mine published in *Yugntruf* 28–29 (September 1973), 33 (July 1975), and 34 (February 1976). See also Mikhal Gay, "'Vi der aker fun vor': Avrom Rintslers poetishe shprakh," *Di goldene keyt* 134 (1992): 26–34.

38. Yosl Birstein, "A yidisher shrayber in kibuts," *Di goldene keyt* 11 (1952): 162–167, quote on p. 164.

39. In their first anthology, published in *Di goldene keyt* 7 (1951): 150–179, Birstein still appears as a poet. But the first issue of *Yung-Yisroel* (Haifa: December 1954) features him as a prose writer and his byline reads: "during the past two years has published only prose."

40. Zvi Eisenman, "A mayse vegn Nisim fun Har-Tov, vegn a varshever hoyf un vegn a shpilfoygl," in *Di ban* (Yagur, 1956), pp. 119–122; Avrom Karpinovitsh, "Der veg keyn Sdom" in *Der veg keyn Sdom* (Tel Aviv: Y. L. Perets, 1959), pp. 63–101.

41. Yosl Birstein, *Oyf shmole trotuarn* (On Narrow Paths; Tel Aviv: Y. L. Perets, 1958), p 13. A slightly different version of this opening chapter appeared in *Yung-Yisroel* (Haifa, 1957): 3–22.

42. For a fine analysis of the novel against this dual cultural backdrop, see Abraham Novershtern, "The Multi-Colored Patchwork on the Coat of a Prince: On Yossl Birstein's Work," *Modern Hebrew Literature*, n.s. 8–9 (Spring-Fall 1992): 56–59.

43. Birstein now describes his leaving the kibbutz in a comic vein. See his interview with Wendy Zierler, "A Multifaceted Tale," *Jerusalem Post Magazine* (3 July 1992): 21.

44. Avrom Karpinovitsh, *Baym vilner durkhhoyf*, illus. Yosl Bergner; (Tel Aviv: Y. L. Perets, 1967), and *Oyf vilner gasn* (Tel Aviv: Farlag di goldene keyt, 1981).

45. See Menahem Perry's superb interview with Yosl Birstein, "Kavim yeḥefim utslil: Siḥah bein Yosl Birstein leMenaḥem Perry," *Siman kri'ah* 6 (May 1976): 299.

46. Yosl Birstein, *Der zamler* (Tel Aviv: Hakibbutz Hemeuchad, 1985); the novel was first serialized in *Di goldene keyt* in 1979–1981. The Hebrew tr., first titled *Hamutavim* [The Beneficiaries, 1982], then reissued as *Habursah* (The Stock Market; Israel: Siman kri'ah and Hakibbutz Hameuchad, 1984), is by Menahem Perry.

47. Birstein first mentions Kafka in a review of Avrom Rinzler's poetry. See "Aspektn," *Yung-Yisroel* (Haifa, 1956): 54. Bergner's sketches to Kafka, which represent a new, antirealistic trend in his art, are featured in the inaugural issue of *Yung-Yisroel* (1954). On Birstein's collaboration with Nissim Aloni, see Alex Zehavi, "Hasaharurim shel Yosl Birshtein," *Ma'ariv*, 23 June 1989.

48. Yosl Birstein, "A mayse mit a mantl fun a prints," *Di goldene keyt* 58 (1967): 143–159. Birstein later disowned "Kh'hob farloyrn di muzik in mayne oygn" (I've lost the music in my eyes), *Di goldene keyt* 55 (1966): 125–134, precisely because it

tried to touch up a simple street scene with a surrealistic trompe l'oeil. See his interview with Perry, p. 310. Both stories were reprinted in *A mantl fun a prints* (A Coat of a Prince; Tel Aviv: Y. L. Perets, 1969), pp. 9–34, 45–61.

49. See Novershtern, pp. 57–58.

50. "Kavim yeheifim utslil," *Siman kri'ah* 6 (May 1976): 297–310, 394–396. The later interview, with Leah Shnir, appeared in *Davar*, 12 June 1987, under the title "I Am a Clown. I Succeed When I Fall."

51. See his comments quoted by Rochelle Furstenberg, "His tongue set free," *Jerusalem Report* (18 July 1991): 44. In *Di goldene keyt* 106 (1981): 8–16, Birstein published seven "arabesques," which laid out his future repertory both in form and content. Had the Israeli novelist Anton Shammas not beaten Birstein to it, *Arabesques* would have made a fine title for the collected stories.

52. From an interview I conducted with Birstein on 23 August 1990. See also his comments to Rochelle Furstenberg, *Jerusalem Report* (18 July 1991): 44.

53. See "A Multifaceted Tale," Birstein's interview with Wendy Zierler, *Jerusalem Post Magazine*. In his interview with Leah Shnir, he expressed the same idea more graphically: "The combination of tallow [a nonkosher substance] and wick produces light." For his imbedded comments on the craft of writing, see the stories "A briv keyn Rumenye," pp. 91–92, and "Fentster," pp. 223–224.

54. Yosl Birstein, *Ketem shel sheket: ktsartsarim* (Israel: Hakibbutz Hameuchad and Siman kri'ah, 1986), illus. Nurit Inbar-Shani; henceforth cited H[ebrew]. In Yiddish he identifies them as "kleyne mayses."

55. From his interview with Shnir in *Davar*.

56. Birstein, "Vi azoy vert a mayse?" *Dayne geslekh—Yerusholayim*, pp. 25–27; not in the Hebrew version.

57. From the interview with Perry, p. 394.

58. See Dorina Bendor, " 'Siman vekolot'—mehkar mashveh ben hasipur hekatuv lasipur hamesupar beyetsirato shel Yosl Birstein" (M.A. thesis, Tel Aviv University, 1992).

59. See Linda Dégh, *Folktales and Society: Story-telling in a Hungarian Peasant Community*, tr. Emily M. Schossberger (Bloomington: Indiana University Press, 1989); Barabara Kirshenblatt-Gimblett, "Traditional Storytelliing in the Toronto Jewish Community" (Ph.D. diss. Indiana University, 1972).

60. There are 109 stories in the Yiddish, arranged under 13 headings, as opposed to 101 in Hebrew, arranged under 14. The most significant difference is this: the middle section is called "Visits" in Hebrew, "Your Streets, Jerusalem," in Yiddish. The last section in Hebrew is called "Gevat," for the kibbutz that serves as its setting, while the comparable section in Yiddish is "Your Fields, Israel."

61. On Ansky's anthem "To the Bund," see my Introduction to *The Dybbuk and Other Writings* (New York: Schocken, 1992), p. xvii. "Mir torn nit zamen nor shmidn un flekhtn / Mir muzn bafrayen dem haynt funem nekhtn." From "Undzer himn," by Sh. Volman, music by M. Gelbort, in *Binishe lider* (Vilna: Bin, 1932), pp. 25–26. On Jewish youth movements in general, see Moses Kligsberg, "Di yidishe yugnt-

bavegungen in Poyln tshvishn beyde velt-milkhomes (a sotsyologishe shtudye)," *Studies in Polish Jewry, 1919–1939*, ed. Joshua A. Fishman (New York: YIVO, 1974), pp. 137–228.

62. Steve Stern, "A Brief Account of a Long Way Home," *YIVO Annual* 19 (1990): 81–91; idem, "Shimmele Fly-by-Night," in *Lazar Malkin Enters Heaven* (1986; rpt. Penguin, 1988), pp. 89–112. See also Janet Hadda's "Ashkenaz on the Mississippi" in the same issue of *YIVO Annual*, pp. 93–103. Max Apple is a born-again American-Jewish storyteller who comes by his Yiddish past more directly: Apple's grandmother spoke to him in Yiddish. Hence the autobiographical slant of his *The Oranging of America and Other Stories* (1976; rpt. Penguin, 1981) and *Free Agents* (New York: Harper and Row, 1984). Of all contemporary American-Jewish writers, novelist Cynthia Ozick has the strongest literary and genealogical tie to Yiddish. Though she makes the occasional leap to storytelling in her tales of Puttermesser (Yiddish for "butterknife"), Ozick is best known for her translations and treatment of Yiddish high culture. Cf. "Puttermesser and Xanthippe," in *Levitations: Five Fictions* (New York: Dutton, 1983), pp. 74–158, with "Envy; or, Yiddish in America" (where a thinly veiled Jacob Glatstein takes on I. B. Singer), *The Pagan Rabbi and Other Stories* (1971; rpt. New York: Dutton,), pp. 39–100.

63. Personal communication, 6 August 1989. See Goldman's superb documentary film, *A Jumpin' Night in the Garden of Eden* (1988).

Index